Wine
Report
2008
Tom Stevenson

LONDON NEW YORK MUNICH
MELBOURNE DELHI

FOR DORLING KINDERSLEY
Senior Editor Dawn Henderson
Senior Art Editor Susan Downing
Art Editor Kathryn Wilding
Editorial Assistant Ariane Durkin
Production Controller Sarah Sherlock
Production Editor Jenny Woodcock

PRODUCED FOR DORLING KINDERSLEY BY
Sands Publishing Solutions
4 Jenner Way, Eccles, Aylesford, Kent ME20 7SQ
Project Editors David & Sylvia Tombesi-Walton
Project Art Editor Simon Murrell

FOR TOM STEVENSON
Editor Pat Carroll
Tasting Logistics Jeff Porter, Evenlode Press

This edition published 2007
by Dorling Kindersley Limited

THE PENGUIN GROUP
Registered offices: 80 Strand,
London WC2R 0RL, England

2 4 6 8 10 9 7 5 3 1

A CIP catalogue record of this book is available
from the British Library.

ISBN: 9-7814-0532-233-1

WD152

Printed and bound in China by
Leo Paper Group

Discover more at

www.dk.com

CONTENTS

Introduction
Changing faces

A belated welcome to three contributors who were new to *Wine Report* last year.

Ronald de Groot replaced Gert Crum as co-contributor (with Fiona Morrison) on Belgium, Netherlands, and Scandinavia. As editor of *Perswijn*, Ronald is in the ideal position to report on the fledgling Dutch wine industry, although, like his Le Pin owning co-contributor, he obviously spends most of his time tasting the great classics. With Christopher Fielden's retirement following *Wine Report 2006*, it made sense to split Chile and Argentina. For Chile I was lucky to grab Peter Richards, who has lived and worked in the country, won the first ever Young Wine Writer of the Year award in 2001, and has since blossomed into one of the UK's brightest wine writers. And, of course, for Argentina, who else could I choose but Tim Atkin MW, even though he is in such demand that I will be pulling out my hair every time he misses his deadline? An even more belated welcome to Pat Carroll, my personal editor since the second edition. Thank goodness Pat is so hawk-eyed, meticulous, and persistent; not only does she handle all the initial editing, she sometimes gets much more dumped on her when commitments to my Sotheby's wine encyclopedia take precedence. And the contributors adore her.

New this year

Charles Metcalfe takes over from Richard Mayson as the contributor for Portugal, although Richard continues to contribute on port and madeira. I am personally very sorry to lose Richard's sharp eye on all things non-fortified in Portugal, but he owns a vineyard in the Alto Alentejo region, and with his first wine, Pedra Basta, launched in 2007, he felt it would be easier to avoid any conflicts of interest. Charles Metcalfe is, however, as big a gain as Richard is a loss. One of the most genuine and immensely likeable guys in the wine-writing business, Charles has carved a reputation as an Iberian wine specialist since at least 1987, when *The Wines of Spain and Portugal*, coauthored with his wife Kathryn McWhirter, pipped my Sotheby's wine encyclopedia at the post for the Glenfiddich award that year. I couldn't have been robbed by two nicer people!

Tom Stevenson

About This Guide

This is not so much a "How to Use" section as an explanation of the brief that I gave to contributors and the parameters they applied (or did not!).

Contributors

Every contributor to *Wine Report* was my personal choice. For the most part, they are the expert's experts in their various specialist areas. For some regions there are no experts, and I had to twist the arm of the most strategically placed professionals to tackle such reports. There have been small changes in contributors since the first edition, and I imagine there will be more in the future. *Wine Report* has very specific needs, so if some contributors come and go, the going has nothing to do with their expertise on the subject and everything to do with how I expect it to be applied. Ideally, I would like to see no more than one report per contributor, since this would project the desired specialist ambience, but it will take time to achieve.

Opinions expressed by contributors

These are, of course, their own. I am not referring specifically to the Opinion section of each report (which is dealt with separately below), but rather the more general way in which they report a story. For example, the way that François Lefort (Grape Varieties) writes about GMOs could not be further from the way that Monty Waldin (Organic & Biodynamic Wines) covers the subject. I respect both of these contributors' opinions, although I do not completely agree with either of them. (Anyone interested in my view should look at www.wine-pages.com/guests/tom/gm.htm.)

Reader's knowledge level

Unlike most other wine books, *Wine Report* assumes a certain level of knowledge. Therefore, there are rarely any explanations of technical terms or even references to historical incidents. Readers are expected to know what these terms mean and what the references refer to, or at least have the intelligence and curiosity to look them up.

News and Grapevine items

Regional reports include news affecting the region and its producers, wines, and consumers. This may incorporate gossip and rumour but not marketing or sales stories unless they are of an exceptional or very hot nature. Non-regional reports have their own structure. It should be noted that, for Wine & Health, Beverley Blanning has been specifically commissioned to report the bad news as well as the good and, if anything, to err on the side of the former rather than the latter. I want to give readers as much good health news as possible, but *Wine Report* is for wine enthusiasts and cannot afford to be vulnerable to accusations of selective reporting of this sensitive issue.

Opinion

Contributors have quite a free hand to spout off about anything they feel strongly about, but there are certain categories of opinion that are obligatory. These are, essentially, anything that is currently practised, legally or not, that the contributor believes should not be, and anything that the contributor believes should be happening, but is not. Contributors should always attempt to balance their criticisms with practical solutions. Readers should expect to see the same opinions repeated or refined in each edition, unless the situation changes, which would be news in itself.

Vintage Reports

Each regional contributor provides an advance report on the very latest harvest (the year before date of publication for the northern hemisphere, the actual year of publication for the southern hemisphere), plus brief updates on the previous five vintages. In the first edition, it was difficult enough to get some contributors to rate vintages on a 100-point scale, but most toed the line. However, everyone was using a different yardstick, so, from the second edition, all vintage ratings conform to the following definitions.

100	No vintage can be accurately described as perfect, but those achieving a maximum score must be truly great vintages.
90–99	Excellent to superb.
80–89	Good to very good.
70–79	Average to good.
60–69	Disappointing.
40–59	Very bad.
0–39	Disastrous.

Vintage ratings should merely be seen as "betting odds". They express the likelihood of what might be reasonably expected from a wine of a given year. The higher the rating, the fewer the exceptions; quality and consistency do, to some extent, go hand in hand.

Top 10s

If percentile ratings for vintages did not set the cat among the pigeons, then these Top 10s of producers and wines certainly did. Very few contributors were worried about listing the 10 best of anything, but several were extremely reluctant to put that list in order of preference. Eventually most agreed to do this, but readers might come across the odd list that looks suspiciously as if it is in alphabetical order....

There was no requirement for each Top 10 to be fully utilized. If a contributor truly believes that, for example, only five or six producers or wines deserve a place in a particular Top 10, then that is perfectly acceptable. Furthermore, it was permitted to place the same producer or wine in more than one list. Such coexistence could even apply to the Greatest and Best-Value Producers or Best Bargain Top 10s.

Prices

All prices in this guide are average retail prices, including tax, per bottle, expressed in the local currency of the country of origin. This is not a buyer's guide; the wines listed are supposed to be the greatest, best-bargain or most exciting or unusual, without restricting the choice to those that happen to be available on any specific market.

Greatest Wine Producers

My guidelines to the contributors made it clear that their choice should be "regardless of status". In other words, even if there is some sort of acknowledged hierarchy, such as Bordeaux's *cru classé* system, the contributor should not feel restrained by it. On the other hand, if a contributor agrees entirely with a perceived hierarchy, there was nothing preventing him or her following it slavishly. Some contributors set themselves their own criteria. Dan Berger, for example, told me that for his greatest producers he had decided: (a) the winery had to be in business for at least 10 years, and production over that period had to have remained substantially the same; (b) the winery had to use substantially the same fruit sources, mainly from owned or leased vineyards, for the last 10 years, and not deviate from a house style; (c) the ownership and winemaking had to be consistent over the last 10 years; and (d) the winery must make at least two wines that have achieved the highest levels of quality without ever deviating from that level, even in a mediocre vintage.

Dan's criteria represent a very professional way of ascertaining greatness, but they are not ones that I would impose on all contributors. Furthermore, the term "greatest" is relative: it does not necessarily mean that the producer is intrinsically great. The best producer in California should be intrinsically great, but although the greatest producer in Belgium must, by definition, be its greatest, in practice it will be no more than "interesting". Readers should expect the Greatest Producers list to change the least of all the Top 10s from year to year.

Fastest-Improving Producers

Whether good or bad, reputations tend to stick well beyond their shelf life, which is why this particular Top 10 is probably the most useful. While the rest of the market lags behind, you can benefit from the insider knowledge of *Wine Report*, buying up top-performing wines long before others cotton on and prices increase.

New Up-and-Coming Producers

While Fastest-Improving Producers will probably be well-established wineries that have perked up, this Top 10 focuses on the newer producers that are the ones to watch. In some of the more conservative traditional areas, "new" will be relative and should perhaps be taken to mean newer or a producer whose wines used to be sold only from the cellar door but have recently become more widely available.

Best-Value Producers

This is self-explanatory.

Greatest-Quality Wines

Each contributor has his or her own method for determining their greatest wines. I am sure that many do as I tend to do, and that is to list the greatest I have tasted within the last 12 months, rather than the greatest wines per se. True experts in classic areas will probably have notes on thousands of wines tasted in the last 12 months, and of these there could be 50-odd wines that would justifiably achieve a top score. Most contributors could probably fill their Top 10 Greatest Wines several times over. (Most years I could fill the Top 10 Greatest Alsace Wines twice over with just Zind Humbrecht's wines.) Thus realistically this should be viewed as merely "10 of the greatest". Then, of course, we have to put them in order of preference, which can be a real pain. How, for example, is it possible to say whether the greatest red bordeaux is better than the greatest Sauternes, or the greatest Alsace Gewurztraminer better than the greatest Alsace Pinot Gris? If David Peppercorn and I find this difficult, what about Nick Belfrage and Franco Ziliani? The range of wines in Italy is far more complex. So, what most contributors end up with is "10 of the greatest in a less-than-logical order of preference". This would worry me in any other book, but readers of *Wine Report* are supposed to be sophisticated enough to understand that this is fascinating enough in its own right.

Best Bargains

Although most will be relatively inexpensive, bargains do not necessarily have to be cheap. It is easier to find bargains at lower prices, just as it is easier to find great wines at higher prices, but it is possible to find relative bargains at any price point. In theory, the greatest, most expensive bordeaux could be the number-one Best Bargain.

Most Exciting or Unusual Finds

This could be an unusually fine wine from what is normally a below-standard region, winery, or grape. It might be an atypical wine, or the first of a certain variety or style. Each wine listed will carry a brief explanation of why it is so exciting and/or unusual.

The 100 Most Exciting Wine Finds

Each contributor was asked to submit four wines for consideration for this section of the book, which meant approximately 160 wines. Only contributors for the emerging or more obscure wine regions were allowed to proffer wines from their Greatest Wines. The rest had to select wines from either their Best Bargains or Most Exciting or Unusual Finds, otherwise this section would be stacked with Pétrus, Krug, Romanée-Conti, the quality of which most readers will be aware of, but few can afford. I then tasted the wines blind, grouped by variety or style, culling almost 40 per cent (which is why I limited myself to just one wine from Champagne and one wine from Alsace). Contributors also provided a tasting note, which is followed by my own comment.

Bordeaux

David Peppercorn MW

In Bordeaux, 2006 was a year of "changing the guard". Two of the Médoc's iconic châteaux changed hands.

DAVID PEPPERCORN MW

Jean-Louis Charmolüe has sold Montrose to retire to the south of France. It has been bought by the Bouygues brothers – owners of a giant construction company – on their own account, with critical participation by the Moueix family. Later it was announced that Jean-Bernard Delmas, the retired director of Domaines Dillon (Haut-Brion and La Mission) was to be consultant.

Then, at the end of the year, after much speculation that Pichon-Longueville Comtesse de Lalande was to be sold to the Hermès family, it emerged that these protracted negotiations had broken down and a deal had been concluded with the Rouzauds of Roederer. May-Eliane de Lencquesaing had become concerned about the future of Pichon, since she is now 82 and none of her children was capable of taking over. As she said: "I spent a year talking to Hermès without a result, but the deal was done with the Rouzauds in a week!" There could hardly be a better result, with their professionalism and existing knowledge of Bordeaux. The exact terms of the deal are not yet clear, but May-Eliane de Lencquesaing is expected to remain in charge, at least for the time being.

DAVID PEPPERCORN MW When David Peppercorn went to Bordeaux as a Cambridge undergraduate in September 1953, it was the beginning of a lifelong love affair. He became a Master of Wine in 1962 and was chairman of the Institute of Masters of Wine from 1968 to 1970. It was while David was a buyer for IDV (International Distillers & Vintners) in the 1970s that he started writing about wine, making his debut as an author with the award-winning *Bordeaux* (Faber & Faber, 1982). His *Wines of Bordeaux* (Mitchell Beazley) has been updated regularly since 1986 (2004 being the latest edition). David now spends his time travelling, writing, and lecturing. He is married to Serena Sutcliffe MW.

Other changes

Château Guiraud 1er Cru Classé Sauternes: A consortium – headed by members of the Peugeot family, along with the Bernard family of Domaine de Chevalier, Stephan von Neipperg's Invest company (Canon-la-Gaffelière, La Mondotte, etc, and Bulgaria), and Xavier Planty (the manager of Guiraud since 1983) – finally bought this prime vineyard from its Canadian owners.

Château Cantenac-Brown Cru Classé Margaux was sold by AXA to Simon Halabi, a Syrian-born UK-based property investor who had an ambition to own a Bordeaux château. Christian Seely probably felt he had done all he could here to upgrade quality, and the price was tempting.

Château Marquis d'Alesme-Becker, another 3ème Cru Classé of Margaux and a long-time underachiever, has been sold to Hubert Perrodo, owner of Labégorce and Labégorce-Zédé. He will clearly expect to make a difference here.

Château Soutard Grand Cru Classé St-Emilion: The sale to the insurance group Mondiale, which owns nearby Château Larmande, was perhaps the biggest surprise in St-Emilion. It had been in the same ownership since 1811. The eccentricities of the former owner – not encouraging the malolactic fermentation till the spring and not assembling the wine till just before bottling – had effectively discouraged *en primeur* sales. One looks forward to seeing what the Larmande team can do to restore the reputation of this lovely property.

Château Belair 1er Cru Classé St-Emilion: At the end of the year came the news from Christian Moueix that his company had been collaborating with Pascal Delbeck and had now taken a minority holding and exclusive distribution.

Château Fourcas-Hosten Cru Bourgeois Supérieur Listrac has been sold by its largely American owners to two brothers from the Hermès family; long-time manager Patrice Pagès remains in place. This is an excellent *cru* but not easy to distribute in current market conditions, in spite of temptingly low prices.

Château Morin Cru Bourgeois St-Estèphe: This 10-ha vineyard in St-Corbian has been bought by the Rouzauds of Château de Pez. In general, they report that the property is not in good condition, but there are some old vines and the terroir is good.

Château Lynch-Bages Cru Classé Pauillac: Jean-Michel Cazes is handing over to his son, Jean-Charles, aged 32, who has been working with the Lynch-Bages team for four years. Jean-Michel's familiar face will still be around: he stays as chairman, as well as looking after Château Cordeillan-Bages and the Chapon Fin restaurant in Bordeaux.

Why are so many vineyards changing hands? It emphasizes the fragility of family-owned properties, given the French fiscal system, and is likely to continue unless some radical reforms are undertaken to reverse the extremely anti-business stance of successive French governments.

NEW CLASSIFICATION IN ST-EMILION

The first official classification of St-Emilion was promulgated in 1958. In theory, it should be revised every 10 years, and the practice has not strayed far from the intention, revisions having been published in 1969, 1986, 1996, and 2006. The Graves classification, promulgated at about the same time, has yet to be revised, although the intention to do so has recently been stated. With 61 *crus* classified in 2006, this is the smallest list to date. In 1958, there were 75 *crus*, growing to 84 in 1969. Then the tightening up began. The figure fell to 74 in 1986, then 68 in 1996, before falling again to 61 now. The changes/promotions from Grand Cru Classé to Premier Grand Cru Classé B are: Château Pavie-Macquin and Château Troplong-Mondot. So there are now 15 Premiers in all. Grand Cru Classé: These are now reduced to 46, down from 55 in 1996.

Promotions (new to the classification)

- **Château Bellefort-Belcier in St-Laurent des Combes:** Adjoins Larcis-Ducasse on an extension of the Côte de Pavie. Dominique Hébrard is involved.
- **Château Destieux:** The first *cru* in St-Hippolyte to be classified. For 20 years the life work of Christian Dauriac.
- **Château Fleur-Cardinale:** A first for St-Etienne de Lisse. The result of dedicated work by Claude and Alain Assès from 1983 to 2001, when it was sold to Dominique and Florence Decoster, who made the final push.
- **Château Monbousquet:** Gérard and Chantal Perse have shown what can be done by management on rather modest terroir – so a *vin de technique* rather than a *vin de terroir*. But the prices suggest that many consumers like what is offered and are prepared to pay what Perse asks.

Previously demoted *crus* now reinstated

- **Grand Corbin**
- **Grand Corbin-Despagne**

Demotions

- **Château Bellevue:** In spite of Nicolas Thienpont's improvements since 2000. But the vintages 1993–2002 were the basis of the judgments.
- **Cadet-Bon:** Classified in 1958, demoted in 1986, restored in 1996, now again demoted. A real roller coaster here! Again, a new regime came too late.
- **Faurie de Souchard:** I wrote in my 2004 *Wines of Bordeaux* that "there seems to be a lack of consistency and charm about these wines". The commission seems to agree.
- **Guadet St-Julien:** A long-time underachiever.
- **La Marzelle:** New owners have made recent improvements, but not in time.

• **La Tour du Pin Figeac (Giraud-Bélivier):** The only surprise here is that it was not demoted before!

• **La Tour du Pin Figeac (Moueix):** The good wines of the 1980s are now a memory. Things have slipped since the break-up of the old A Moueix firm.

• **Petit Faurie de Soutard:** The owner, Jacques Capdemourlin, from one of St-Emilion's oldest families, has devoted much of his energy to Balestard and Cap-de-Mourlin, but he began upgrading here in 2000. Clearly there were too many disappointments between 1993 and 1997 for the commission.

• **Tertre Daugay:** There will be lamentations at La Gaffelière and perhaps some apprehension!

• **Villemaurine:** To make fine wines on the limestone plateau needs a combination of richness and concentration, and the track record here is disappointing.

• **Yon-Figeac:** Again, recent investment has come too late.

Missing *crus*

• **Château Curé-Bon-la-Madeleine:** Has been bought by its neighbour Canon and, with the INAO's permission, incorporated into Canon.

• **La Clusière:** This enclave in Pavie, under the same ownership, has similarly been incorporated.

• **Château Clos des Jacobins:** Has dropped the "Château" part of its name and is now Clos des Jacobins.

STOP PRESS: Everybody has been shocked that the court has suspended the classification following an appeal by several declassified châteaux. The case will now be argued.

Grapevine

• **Wine fraud:** The famous Thomas Jefferson Lafites of 1784 and 1787, together with Brane-Mouton of the same vintages, have been pronounced fakes. Originally sold by Christie's, having been "discovered" by German wine dealer Hardy Rodenstock, the wines had their authenticity questioned by their current owner – a rich American collector. Scientific tests showed that the names and initials on the bottles were of modern origin.

• **The Union des Grands Crus Classés de Graves** has elected Véronique Sanders, administrator of Château Haut-Bailly, as its next president. Having worked with her grandfather at the château, she was retained to run it when the family sold to an American of Belgian origin, Robert Wilmers. This is a great compliment to her – and perhaps to her diplomatic powers, since high on her agenda will be the first revision of the classification since 1958.

• **Following an appeal** by more than 70 châteaux that failed to be classified, the 2003 Cru Bourgeois classification has been annulled, and it's back to the drawing board. The solution to the classification mess is, in my opinion, a simple one. In future, all participants should have to sign an undertaking to abide by the jury's decision as final and unappealable. If you don't like it, don't go in for it!

Opinion:
The record prices of 2005

The worst fears of everyone (the trade and their customers, not the handful of top producers!) about soaring prices turned out to be correct. As usual, the campaign started off rather reasonably as the lesser *crus* took modest increases and sold their wines. The first real shock came with Palmer. I was with an importer and *primeur* specialist when the offer came out. He could not believe that many of his clients would buy at such a price and subscribed to only five of the 50 cases he was offered. As soon as his offer went out, he realized his mistake: everyone wanted it! Prices in 2005 were 30 per cent up on 2000, in spite of many châteaux increasing by only 10–15 per cent.

If you read the wine press, you might have the impression that high prices are caused by growers' greed. They are, in fact, the result of the operation of a free market, which in wine terms is also a very large market. The Bordeaux *place* far exceeds any other wine market in turnover. This makes for a degree of volatility not experienced in the very fragmented burgundy market. Other factors are the global nature of the market, with super-rich buyers in the USA, the Far East, and London, and the strong influence of Parker scores in the USA and Asia, which means that the spread of demand has become narrower. With everyone wanting the same wines, prices rise very strongly for the perceived top wines.

You cannot beat the market. Plenty of growers come out at reasonable or good-value prices, but if the market perceives them as worth more, the price will rise. This happened to Léoville-Barton 2000 and to Montrose 2003. The problem for the proprietors is to calculate the demand and pitch the price at a level where they have a fair share of a boom price, leaving something in hand for the investor. If this price is pitched too low, market demand will push it up. If the price is too high, it will stagnate and investors will have to wait some years to sell at a profit. Look at the performance of Cheval Blanc since its new ownership pushed up its opening price compared to the Médoc Firsts.

So, were some 2005 prices too high? Maybe, but we shall have to wait and see.

Vintage Report

Advance report on the latest harvest

2006

Prospects for 2006 looked excellent till mid-August. A good flowering had been followed by hot weather through June and July. But heavy rain fell in the last half of August, followed by 100–120 mm (4–5 in) in the Médoc and 150 mm (6 in) on the Right Bank and in Sauternes between 11 and 25 September. Bordeaux has overcome these problems before, but this time the rain was followed by warm, steamy conditions. It was very hot immediately after the rain – classic rot conditions. Then more rain in mid-September, followed by more heat and humidity. In practice, everyone had rot to some degree. It was the condition of the vineyard and the time of picking that counted. In the Médoc, the Cabernets did best, provided growers waited for full ripeness. In St-Emilion, success is claimed for the Merlots. The April tastings revealed a wide range of quality in the reds of all areas. The greatest successes were for the dry whites, which are deliciously fresh and aromatic. Some good wines have been made in Sauternes, but in very limited quantities.

Updates on the previous five vintages

2005

Vintage rating: *Left Bank – Red: 99, White: 90, Sweet: 95; Right Bank – Red: 98*

Yes, the wines live up to the hype! The weather cycle was as near perfection as can be imagined, with drought the key factor. One general rule is that the greatest wines come from the greatest vineyards. If you want to know what any First Growth is capable of, you will find it in 2005. The only caveat is that there are, as usual, some overextracted wines, mostly in St-Emilion, at properties that harvested overripe Merlot. The other problem is that you are likely to have to wait a very long time – 20–30 years – to see these wines at their peak. But there are many wonderful lesser and middle-ranking wines, to say nothing of second wines, that will give immense pleasure after 5–10 years – and at moderate prices. While prices overall were 30 per cent higher than in 2000, many wines showed only 10–15 per cent increases – so top wines have correspondingly much higher increases. Again, the marvellous Sauternes are great value and will be enjoyable, if not at their peak, in five to seven years. And don't forget the lovely fruity dry whites!

2004

Vintage rating: *Left Bank – Red: 92, White: 90, Sweet: 93; Right Bank – Red: 92*

After the very small crop of 2003, the vines were raring to go in 2004, and most vineyards had to work to keep production down. Across the region there was lovely harmony, beautiful fruit flavours, well-integrated tannins, and the promise of real complexity. The Sauternes have a lovely freshness that balances the fruity richness of wines that have real character and are classic after 2003's exceptional sugar levels. This is a vintage that, overall, will give much pleasure.

2003

Vintage rating: *Left Bank – Red: 93, White: 80, Sweet: 98; Right Bank – Red: 82*

The extreme heat of June, July, and August caused growers many problems. Those who delayed picking until September were rewarded by more moderate conditions. The more vulnerable Merlots on the Right Bank suffered most and were very uneven. But great wines with a markedly exotic character were made in St-Estèphe, Pauillac, and St-Julien. Margaux produced some wines of great breed and typicity. Pessac-Léognan is less good. The crop was half the normal size or less. Sauternes had an exceptional year – better than 2001.

2002

Vintage rating: *Left Bank – Red: 92, White: 90, Sweet: 88; Right Bank – Red: 86*

Very nearly a disaster, this year was saved by a classic high-pressure system in September. The Left Bank Cabernets took full advantage, and very fine wines resulted in Pauillac, St-Julien, and St-Estèphe. The first tastings in bottle showed Margaux doing better than expected, while the general level in the Médoc was high. Excellent botrytis in Sauternes meant another fine vintage there. But *coulure* accounted for much of the old-vine Merlot on the Right Bank, and the weather change was too late to help. Those with good levels of Cabernet Franc benefited. The dry whites have an attractive fresh fruitiness.

2001

Vintage rating: *Left Bank – Red: 90, White: 90, Sweet: 98; Right Bank – Red: 90*

These wines continue to develop well. They are not 2000s, but they do have balance, length, elegance, and breed – even lovely succulent fruit flavours in the best *crus*. They are variable but superior to the 1999s. The dry whites are fruity and elegant. Sauternes are outstanding, probably the best since 1990.

GREATEST WINE PRODUCERS

1. Château Lafite
2. Château d'Yquem
3. Château Ausone
4. Château Pétrus
5. Château Margaux
6. Château Léoville-Las-Cases
7. Château Lafleur
8. Château Latour
9. Château Haut-Brion/La Mission Haut-Brion
10. Château Pichon-Longueville Lalande

FASTEST-IMPROVING PRODUCERS

1. Château Lafite *Very good from 1982 to 1990 but has moved into another gear as of 1996.*
2. Château Ausone *Some of the greatest wines in Bordeaux since 1998; more sensual and just more of everything – look out for 2002!*
3. Château Pavie-Macquin *Since Nicolas Thienpont and Stéphane Derenoncourt took charge in 1995, progress has been continuous and consistent. This was recognized by promotion to Premier Grand Cru in 2006.*
4. Château Calon-Ségur *A new generation of wine lovers has forgotten that this used to be one of the most sought-after crus in the Médoc. The climb-back was at first steady (1995, 1996) and is now spectacular (2000, 2002, 2003, 2004).*
5. Château Brane-Cantenac *This classic Margaux was criticized for being weak, but Henri Lurton is quietly rebuilding its reputation. Take a look at the underrated 1999.*
6. Château Pontet-Canet *Outstanding since 1996.*
7. Château du Tertre *The real potential is now being realized, especially since the marvellous 2000.*
8. Château Dauzac *André Lurton's team has been building an entirely new reputation here since 1996. The 1998 shone through in a Decanter blind tasting in 2005.*
9. Château Malartic-Lagravière *The investment and commitment of the new owners here are now paying off. The 2002 is outstanding.*
10. Château Berliquet *Since Patrick Valette began his consulting here, the true class of this well-balanced cru has started to shine through.*

NEW UP-AND-COMING PRODUCERS

1. Château Messile Aubert (Montagne-St-Emilion)
2. Château Trianon (St-Emilion)
3. Château Clauzet (St-Estèphe)
4. Château Joanin-Bécot (Côtes de Castillon)
5. Château La Sergue (Lalande-de-Pomerol)
6. Château Belle-Vue (Haut-Médoc)
7. Clos Puy Arnaud (Côtes de Castillon)
8. Château Haut-Carles (Fronsac)
9. Château Mille-Roses (Haut-Médoc)

BEST-VALUE PRODUCERS

1. Château Langoa-Barton (St-Julien)
2. Château du Tertre (Margaux)
3. Château Haut-Chaigneau (Lalande-de-Pomerol)
4. Château Sociando-Mallet (Haut-Médoc)
5. Château Lafon-Rochet (St-Estèphe)
6. Château Dauzac (Margaux)
7. Château Haut-Batailley (Pauillac)
8. Château Beauregard (Pomerol)
9. Château Durfort-Vivens (Margaux)
10. Château Tour Haut-Cassan (Médoc)

GREATEST-QUALITY WINES

1. Château Mouton Rothschild 1986 (€660)
2. Château La Mission Haut-Brion 1985 (€164)
3. Château Léoville-Barton 1990 (€87)
4. Château Montrose 1990 (€300)
5. Château Lafite 1990 (€288)
6. Château Palmer 1990 (€138)
7. Château d'Yquem 1988 (€259)
8. Château Pichon-Longueville Lalande 1982 (€431)
9. Château Sociando-Mallet 1996 (€33)
10. Château Angélus 1995 (€119)

BEST BARGAINS

1. Château Thieuley Cuvée Francis Courselle Bordeaux Blanc 2004 (€8)
2. Château Tour de Mirambeau Bordeaux Blanc Cuvée Passion 2005 (€14)
3. Les Pélerins de Lafon-Rochet St-Estèphe 2001 (€8)
4. Blason d'Issan Margaux 2001 (€7.50)
5. Château Pibran Pauillac 2003 (€15.30)
6. Château Messile-Aubert Montagne St-Emilion 2003 (€15)
7. Château de Malle Sauternes 1999 (€19)
8. Château Aney Haut-Médoc 2003 (€10.80)
9. Baron de Brane Margaux 2001 (€12.35)
10. Château Moulin Riche St-Julien 2001 (€27)

MOST EXCITING OR UNUSUAL FINDS

1. **Château Belle-Vue Haut-Médoc 2003** (€18) *With global warming, Petit Verdot is coming into its own – and nowhere more so than here. It is 27 per cent in this vintage, and the exoticism of the year is powerfully expressed, along with opulence and a long, silky finish.*
2. **Château Poitevin Médoc 2003** (€6) *From the furthest backwoods of the northern Médoc, this wine shone out at a Decanter blind tasting with its lovely juicy fruit textures and rich, supple tannins; attractive and quite complex.*
3. **Château Mille-Roses Haut-Médoc 2005** (€9.50) *A new star in the firmament from near Cambon La Pelouse. David Faure has crafted a wine with complexity and the real stamp of individual character. There is richness and purity of fruit. Still very young but really special.*
4. **Château Clauzet St-Estèphe 2005** (€10.50) *Another star in the making. New ownership took over in 1998; 2001 is better than 2000, 2002 is better still; 2003 is special, and 2004 classic – but this wine hits the bull's-eye. A wine with real breed and appellation character. The Cabernet has fine aromatic fruit and the tannins are supple. Young but a real beauty.*
5. **Château Hostens-Picant Ste-Foy Bordeaux Blanc 2005** (€15) *One doesn't see many wines from this appellation. It is oak-fermented with intense fruit acidity and length, an impressive effort.*

Grapevine

- Vintex, the Bordeaux *négociant*, has been sold by Bill Blatch and his colleagues to Fronsac proprietor James Grégoire, owner of Château de la Rivière. The new company is called Vintex Vignobles Grégoire.

Burgundy

Clive Coates MW

Henri Jayer, the first, and so far the only, Burgundian *vigneron* to have achieved iconic status, died after a long illness at the age of 84 on 22 September 2006.

CLIVE COATES MW

Born in 1922, Henri was the third son of Eugène Jayer, who had pieced together a small domaine before and after World War I, largely from land that had been abandoned after the phylloxera epidemic. In the early years of World War II, Henri Jayer was entrusted with the majority of the Méo-Camuzet domaine on a sharecropping basis. Once hostilities were over, the two domaines jointly acquired the *premier cru* Vosne-Romanée Cros Parentoux, a 1-ha piece of land between Richebourg and Vosne-Romanée Les Brûlées. It had to be replanted.

For many years, Henri Jayer continued to produce his wines in the traditional manner: high temperatures, most of the stems, not much new oak. Most was sold off in bulk. But Henri Jayer had an enquiring mind. Cellar work fascinated him. He left the vineyard work to others, and gradually he began to experiment. The Jayer method changed. He began to bottle under his own account. By the mid-1970s, the Jayer style, as we know it today, had been fully developed.

Purity and concentration are the targets. This is achieved by three things: a restricted crop, the elimination of all the stems, and meticulous

CLIVE COATES MW is the author of *Côte d'Or* (Weidenfeld & Nicolson, 1997), which has won various awards, including Le Prix des Arts et des Lettres from the Confrérie de Tastevin, "the first time that a book on wine and a non-Burgundian have been so honoured for 30 years". A second revised and enlarged edition, *The Wines of Burgundy*, will be available in 2008. From 1985 to 2005 he was author-publisher of the award-winning fine-wine monthly magazine *The Vine*. His latest books are *The Wines of Bordeaux* (Weidenfeld & Nicolson, 2004) and *The Great Wines of France* (Mitchell Beazley, 2005).

attention to the *élevage*. Jayer's view, now followed by most of the winemakers in Burgundy, was that the stems added nothing and, if they were green, were a distinct minus. He was vehemently against sloppy cellar practices: unhygienic conditions, inattention to sulphur levels, and topping up. In 1985, he was quoted as saying that 80 per cent of burgundy is good at the outset, only 20 per cent once it is in bottle.

Jayer retired in 1988, at which time responsibility for Méo-Camuzet devolved to Jean-Nicolas Méo. Subsequently the Jayer family vines, none of the three brothers having had any children, were taken over by a nephew, Emmanuel Rouget. Today the Jayer disciples and their peers ensure that perhaps 80 per cent of the original 80 per cent survives to show well in bottle. Sadly, I fear Emmanuel Rouget does not have the flair of his uncle.

PLC abolished in the Côte d'Or

As foreshadowed in earlier editions of *Wine Report*, the Côte d'Or part of Burgundy has abolished the PLC (*plafond limite de classement*), usually a 20 per cent allowance above the basic authorized yield. From the 2005 vintage, the authorities will determine a maximum for each vineyard each year. Growers may exceed these figures occasionally, but over a running 10-year period, their averages should be below the limit.

Thus, in 2005, the average decennial yield, the RMD (*rendement moyen décennal*) for Vosne-Romanée was 44 hl/ha, and for Vosne-Romanée *premier cru* 42 hl/ha. It was 48 hl/ha hitherto, including PLC. Moreover, in some *climats* in Santenay, where there had been hail in July 2005, the maximum permitted yield was reduced to 35 hl/ha.

Progress! Other *vignobles* please note.

Grapevine

• **The 7-ha Domaine Engel** in Vosne-Romanée was sold in June 2006 to François Pinault of Château Latour. The estate is currently being run by Frédéric Engerer and Frédéric Audouin of Latour. The price of Engel has been widely rumoured to have been in excess of €14 million. Château Latour refuses to comment.

• **Les Artisans Vignerons** de Bourgogne du Sud groups 14 wine growers of the Mâconnais who share a common view over the importance of the role of the soil in wine quality, as well as the need to control crops within reasonable limits. At a time when there is pressure from some of the cooperatives and merchants in the region for an increase in permitted yields, so that Mâcon can meet supermarket price points, this association is to be welcomed.

• **Hospices de Beaune** are no longer 100 per cent new oak. In a welcome move, for the first time since 1976, the winemakers decided to age some of the lesser *cuvées* in old rather than new wood. Formerly many of the wines from lighter-producing vineyards were excessively overoaked.

Affordable burgundy

Despite exaggerated price increases in Bordeaux, 2005 burgundies have remained splendidly affordable. Not cheap. That would be both fanciful and an insult to the quality of the wine. But by Bordeaux standards, Burgundy wines are reasonable.

The short vintage of 2003 caused increases of as much as 50 per cent on 2002 levels. The 2004s remained stable, even declined in some instances. At the top end, the 2005s have sold at 25–50 per cent more than the 2004s. But this means only 5–15 per cent more than the 2003s.

This all sounds alarming, until one points out that there is hardly a single bottle of 2005 burgundy priced at more than €200 ex cellars (except perhaps for Romanée-Conti itself, which will not be on the market until February 2008). By comparison, the average of all the various *tranches* of the Médoc-Graves first growths was €480, with Ausone and Cheval Blanc yet higher. This is four times the price of the 2000s and eight times that of the 2002 (admittedly a less good vintage in Bordeaux than in Burgundy). And the super-seconds in Bordeaux have followed suit.

If you can buy two – if not three – bottles of a really top Richebourg for what it will cost you for one bottle of Château Lafite, I fail to see any contest. Burgundy wins all round.

Grapevine

• **The 2006 vintage** was the one in which Marsannay-based Domaine Bruno Clair took back various vines that had been leased to Maison Louis Jadot since 2005. He therefore has more (and Jadot less) of Bonnes-Mares, Chambertin Clos de Bèze, and Gevrey-Chambertin Clos St-Jacques to offer.

• **Recent acquisitions:** Maison Chanson: 5 ha in Chassagne-Montrachet; Château de Pommard: 5.5 ha, including 1.3 ha of Caillerets, also in Chassagne-Montrachet; Château de Chassagne-Montrachet, owned by merchants Michel Picard, has bought the 7.5-ha domaine of Bernard Colin, also of Chassagne-Montrachet.

• **Rosés have always been** a very minor part of the Burgundian picture. There are said (often rosé statistics are included in those for red wine) to be 280 ha of vines producing rosé, including Crémant de Bourgogne. They saw a rise in sales of 57 per cent in 2006. Attitudes have changed and the product has evolved. Pinot Noir rosé can be delicious – indeed, one of the best rosés you can find. But only in Marsannay, where 35 ha produced just under 2,000 hl in 2005, can rosé be anything other than generic wine.

• **Anne-Claude Leflaive** of Puligny's Domaine Leflaive has, like neighbour Dominique Lafon, expanded into the Mâconnais, with 9.5 ha in the Verzé commune. The wines are made there, but matured and bottled in Puligny. In 2005, she also acquired four *ouvrées* (0.16 ha) of Chassagne-Montrachet *premier cru* La Maltroye. This has been replanted with Chardonnay.

Opinion:
The infiltration of Burgundy

It would be foolish to rail against inevitability. Evolution and renewal occur all the time. It is natural that Burgundian estates should attract the attention of outsiders. After all, loving the wine is not just for those in the Côte d'Or.

I note some of the most important changes in the last 20 years. Maison Chanson now belongs to Bollinger Champagne; Maison Bouchard Père & Fils is owned by Henriot Champagne; AXA owns the Domaine de l'Arlot in Nuits-St-Georges; François Feuillet, a Parisian businessman, recently more than doubled his interests by acquiring Domaine Truchot-Martin in Morey-St-Denis; Château de Pommard belongs to a millionaire from the Savoie region; the Domaine des Lambray to the German Freund family; Maison Camille Giroud to a consortium of US partners of Goldman Sachs; and now Domaine Engel has been acquired by François Pinault of Château Latour.

The vast majority of the above are expertly run by local administrators and winemakers. I have no quarrel with the quality of what is produced. In many cases there has been a marked improvement since the changeover.

Nevertheless, I view this trend with some concern. Twenty-five years ago, viewing similar changes in Bordeaux, I wrote that I feared there would be hardly a handful of top estates in private hands, with the proprietor living "over the shop" and making the wine, still left at the end of my life. My predictions have been correct.

An owner-manager is different from an employee. One of the joys of Burgundy — the cornerstone of its individuality, its complexity, and its current perfectionism — is that when you knock on a door, he or she who opens it will be the owner (responsible to the rest of the family perhaps, but still the boss), and at the same time the winemaker, *chef de cave*, *chef de viticulture*, etc. And the wine will have equally the signature of this individual as well as its terroir. An employee is not as free as an owner when difficult decisions have to be faced.

There is an additional problem. Death duties. The value of prime vineyards is based on the price paid on the last transaction, not on the profitability of the estate owning the land: Clos de Vougeot is now valued on the basis of what François Pinault paid for the half a hectare previously owned by Engel. Prices are rising. It is already difficult enough for one, say, of four children to buy out his or her siblings when he or she takes over from Papa. Are we going to get to the stage where, as in Bordeaux, only outside millionaires will be able to afford the *grands crus*?

Vintage Report

Advance report on the latest harvest

2006

A cold though reasonably dry winter was followed by a cool spring, broken only by one sunny week after Easter. Not until June did Burgundy begin to warm up. June was fine; July hot and rainless, good for holidaymakers but not so good for the vines, some of which were beginning to show signs of hydric stress, especially in the Côte de Beaune. August reverted to the cool conditions of the spring. It was also rainy (100 mm of precipitation in Nuits-St-Georges, but even more in the Côte de Beaune). Rot was widespread. Luckily the weather conditions radically improved in September. The botrytis dried up and was easy to eliminate. There was the usual summer hailstorm. In 2006, it occurred on 27 August and covered Chambolle-Musigny, Morey-St-Denis, and Gevrey-Chambertin, causing most damage on the Brochon side of the latter village. Hail also affected Rully.

The south of Burgundy announced a *ban des vendanges* on 1 September. In the Côte de Beaune, the *ban* was 18 September; in the Côte de Nuits the 20th; in Chablis, 15 September.

The best of the weather conditions in September came at the beginning. On 15 September it rained in the Côte de Beaune. The Côte de Nuits had 60 mm of rain over the weekend of 23/24 September, and more rain on 3 October, by which time only the Hautes Côtes had not yet finished. And throughout the harvesting period, while it was warm in the afternoon, it was cool at night. This helped control fermentations at a gentle pace.

In general, the early "on dit" is that the whites in the Côte d'Or are better than the reds. The whites are quite rich in alcohol but low in acidity: more in the mould of 2005 than 2004, but with less definition than either. The 2006s are high in malic acid. As with 2004 and 2005, they are slow to develop and won't really be judgeable until the autumn of 2007.

The red-wine crop is rather more variable. Luckily, from the quality point of view, it was a small harvest, only a little over 2005, itself 30 per cent more deficient than normal. Some talk of the Côte de Nuits being more irregular than the Côte de Beaune; others say the reverse. Owing to the July hydric stress, the tannins in the Côte de Beaune are less sophisticated than in the Côte de Nuits. Growers cite 2000 and 2001, especially in the Côte de Nuits: but riper, more supple wines with better tannins. In the Côte de Beaune, where it rained and hailed in 2000 and 2001, 2006 is much superior. Overall a useful, easy-to-enjoy vintage for the medium term. Prices will remain static.

There seems to be more early enthusiasm for this vintage in the Côte Chalonnaise and the Mâconnais than in the Côte d'Or. The whites, especially, seem very good. The Beaujolais, too, seems successful, though not up to the standards of 2005. Perhaps 2006 will be at its best in Chablis. Here we have good natural degrees of alcohol, no excessive yields, and refreshing acidities. The vintaging weather was benign.

Updates on the previous five vintages

2005

Vintage rating: *Red: 92, White: 90*

This was a dry vintage, though never particularly hot, save for a heat wave in May. A hailstorm on 17 July devastated the vines between Santenay and Chassagne-Montrachet. After a mixed August and much-needed rain on 6 September, the skies cleared and it became sunny and warm. The Côte d'Or harvest commenced mid-month and was all but complete by 1 October.

Initial reports were enthusiastic, a lower-than-average-sized vintage of very healthy, ripe fruit in both colours. The wines were slow to evolve: though the malic acid content was low, they were late in finishing. But by the late autumn of 2006, one could see a red-wine vintage that was richer than 2002, and more concentrated than 1999. And that means very high quality indeed. In general, the Côte de Nuits wines, which had less hydric stress, are proportionally better than the Côte de Beaune, where some estates, in retrospect, harvested a little too early. The whites, which some suggested might be a little too rich and not quite crisp enough, have improved over the past 12 months and are fine, though not as fine as the 2002s. A vintage for laying down.

There is similar success in Chablis, the Côte Chalonnaise, and the Mâconnais. The 2005 Beaujolais are classic: concentrated and harmonious, and rather more elegant than the 2003s, yet they will keep. The whites of southern Burgundy are excellent, better here than in 2002. In short, one of the best Burgundy vintages in recent years.

2004

Vintage rating: *Red: 82, White: 85*

The summer of 2004 was inauspicious, with problems of oidium (downy mildew) added to concerns about preventing vines from compensating for producing only half a normal crop in 2003. The latter was resolved by an even more Draconian approach to debudding and deflowering than usual.

The quality of the vintage had been mightily improved by fine weather in September. This resulted in very fragrant wines of medium body, with high acidities but delicious perfumes. In October 2005, growers were happy to acknowledge successful, virile, medium-bodied whites but were still undecided about the reds: they had the fruit; would they have the texture?

The 2004s took a long time to evolve. Malos were late, and there was a great deal of malic acidity. It was September 2005 before they could be safely judged. The whites are fragrant, forward, and not a bit too lean, if certainly brisk and fresh. The reds will continue to fatten out to their advantage. Like the whites, they are pure and elegant: again for the medium term.

This is a very good year in Chablis and the Côte Chalonnaise, though not up to 2002 or 2005. It is a good if not inspired vintage in the Mâconnais and the Beaujolais. The reds are better in the Côte de Nuits than the Côte de Beaune. It will be a vintage for drinking in the short term while we wait for the 2002s and 2005s to develop.

2003

Vintage rating: *Red: 80, White: 60*

In bottle, the 2003s are in many respects rather more civilized than they appeared to be in cask. Yet this is neither a very classic nor a very sophisticated vintage. After a torrid summer, the fruit was picked unprecedentedly early, before the tannins were fully ripe or the flavours had reached full maturity, despite sugars being high (and acidities low). Those red-wine producers who dared to hang on found themselves with wines that are more elegant and have greater dimension than those who panicked. But in general the whites are lush, somewhat tarty, and without the essential minerality of true burgundy (this applies to the Côte Chalonnaise and Chablis, as well as the Côte d'Or), while the reds have flavours that suggest California or Côte Rôtie rather than the purity of the Côte d'Or. They have good colour, soft tannins, and low acidities. There is a parallel with 1997: juicy wines, without great finesse, for early drinking. The Beaujolais, however, are excellent, though as they age they are becoming increasingly rustic.

2002

Vintage rating: *Red: 88, White: 93*

The more the 2002s evolve, the more I like them. We have whites that are yet better than 2005, 2000, 1999, and 1995, the standouts of the decade, and reds that, if not quite having the flair of 1999 and 2005, are a close third.

The whites are excellent all the way from Chablis to the Côte Chalonnaise, though just a tad too rich in the Mâconnais, and the reds are equally successful, for once, in the Côte de Nuits, the Côte de Beaune, and the Côte Chalonnaise. The Beaujolais are good, but eclipsed by 2003.

2001

Vintage rating: *Red: 80, White: 70*

My four-year-on comprehensive tasting (July 2005) demonstrated clearly that, like 2000, this is a divided vintage, though at a higher level. There was, simply, more rain in the Côte de Beaune than in the Côte de Nuits in September, and the weather improved towards the end of the month, enabling the Côte de Nuits, which normally harvests a week later than the Côte de Beaune, to enjoy better harvesting conditions. There are even some in Burgundy who prefer the slightly more austere 2001s in the Côte de Nuits to their equivalents in 2002. I personally find them less succulent, so less appealing, but I do not deny their balance, depth, or terroir definition. There are some fine Côte de Nuits reds, which should not be missed.

The whites, across the board from Chablis to the Mâconnais, are good but not as fine as 2000 or 2002; drink soon. The Beaujolais are indifferent.

GREATEST WINE PRODUCERS

① Domaine Jean Grivot
② Domaine Anne Gros
③ Maison/Domaine Louis Jadot
④ Domaine Leflaive
⑤ Domaine Leroy
⑥ Domaine de la Romanée-Conti
⑦ Domaine Georges Roumier
⑧ Domaine des Comtes Lafon
⑨ Domaine Armand Rousseau
⑩ Domaine Comte Georges de Vogüé

FASTEST-IMPROVING PRODUCERS

① Maison Bichot (Beaune)
② Maison Chanson (Beaune)
③ Maison Camille Giroud (Beaune)
④ Drouhin-Larose (Gevrey-Chambertin)
⑤ Humbert Frères (Gevrey-Chambertin)
⑥ Lamarche (Vosne-Romanée)
⑦ Jean-Marc Millot (Nuits-St-Georges)
⑧ Domaine Nudant (Ladoix)
⑨ Louis Remy (Morey-St-Denis)
⑩ Rossignol-Jeanniard (Volnay)

NEW UP-AND-COMING PRODUCERS

① Jean-Marie Burgaud (Morgon)
② Raphaël Coche (Domaine JF Coche-Dury, Meursault)
③ David Croix (Maison Camille Giroud & Domaine Duchet, Beaune)
④ Olivier Lamy (St-Aubin)
⑤ Benjamin Leroux (Comte Armand, Pommard)
⑥ Louis-Michel Liger-Belair (Vosne-Romanée)
⑦ Virgile Lignier-Michelot (Morey-St-Denis)
⑧ Hughes Pavelot (Domaine Jean-Marc Pavelot, Savigny-Lès-Beaune)
⑨ Sylvain Pataille (Marsannay)
⑩ Carl Voorhuis (Domaine D'Ardhuy, Corgoloin)

BEST-VALUE PRODUCERS

1. Domaine Stéphane Aladame (Montagny)
2. Domaine Anita & Jean-Pierre Colinot (Irancy)
3. Domaine Christophe & Fils (Fyé) (for Chablis)
4. Domaine Ghislaine & Jean-Hughes Goisot (St-Brix-Le-Vineux)
5. Domaine Christophe Grangemoulin (Rully)
6. Domaine Henri & Paul Jacqueson (Rully)
7. Domaine Gilles Jourdan (Comblanchien) (for Côte de Nuits Villages)
8. Domaine Bruno Lorenzon (Mercurey)
9. Domaine Lucien Muzard & Fils (Santenay)
10. Domaine Jean-Marc Pavelot (Savigny-Lès-Beaune)

GREATEST-QUALITY WINES

All these wines were sampled in 2006.
For laying down:

1. **La Romanée 2002** Domaine Comte Liger-Belair (€250) *2012–30.*
2. **La Tâche 2002** Domaine de la Romanée-Conti (€350) *2015–40.*
3. **Le Chambertin 2002** Domaine Armand Rousseau (€200) *2012–40.*
4. **Charmes-Chambertin 2002** Domaine Denis Bachelet (€150) *2014–30.*
5. **Corton-Charlemagne 2002** Domaine Bonneau du Martray (€150) *2010–25.*

For drinking now:

1. **Corton-Charlemagne 1985** Domaine Bonneau du Martray (€200) *Now–2020.*
2. **Musigny 1949** Maison Camille Giroud (€400) *Still plenty of life.*
3. **Richebourg 1990** Domaine Jean Gros (€350) *Now–2040.*
4. **Clos de Vougeot 1957** Maison Roland Remoissenet Père & Fils (€900) *Remarkably fresh still.*
5. **Chambertin 1996** Domaine Armand Rousseau (€180) *2010–30.*

BEST BARGAINS

1. **Pouilly-Fuissé La Roche 2005** Jacques & Natalie Sumaize (€12) *From a southeast-facing stony slope in Vergisson. The best Pouilly-Fuissé I've tasted this year.*
2. **St-Véran La Côte Rôtie 2005** Bret Bros (€9) *Plump, rich, but very mineral. Quite delicious.*
3. **Chablis Vieilles Vignes 2005** Domaine Christophe & Fils (€10) *A rising Chablis star is Sébastien Christophe, who lives in a farm surrounded by maize above the grands crus outside Fyé. This is very pure and really quite concentrated.*
4. **Bourgogne Rouge 2002** Ghislaine Barthod (€10) *The land on the "wrong" side of the road opposite the vineyards of Chambolle produces very stylish, similar wine. Ghislaine Barthod's example is delicious, and ready now.*
5. **Marsannay Rosé 2005** Bruno Clair (€12) *Pinot Noir makes delicious rosé. Clair's is one of the best. Drink this while it is young and fresh and as soon as it is on the market (midsummer probably).*
6. **Rully Les Pucelles 2005** Domaine Henri & Paul Jacqueson (€13) *My favourite Côte Chalonnaise white wine. Consistently full of fruit, harmonious, fresh, and elegant.*

⑦ **Côte de Nuits Villages 2002**
Domaine Denis Bachelet (€15)
*Not as well known as Côte de
Beaune Villages but well worth
investigating, especially from
a master such as Bachelet.
Potentially sumptuous.*

⑧ **Givry Clos Jus 2005** François
Lumpp (€14) *Clean, classy, and
very concentrated. A very fine
example of Pinot Noir from the
Côte Chalonnaise.*

⑨ **St-Aubin Clos de la Chatenière
2005** Hubert Lamy & Fils (€17.50)
*Half the price of Puligny-
Montrachet, yet better than all but
the top offerings of a handful of
the senior Puligny growers; 2005 is
a splendid white-wine vintage.*

⑩ **Moulin-à-Vent Rochegrès
Château des Jacques 2005**
Domaine Louis Jadot (€12) *Rich, fat,
succulent, and oaky. The complete
Beaujolais. Needs time.*

MOST EXCITING OR UNUSUAL FINDS

① **Pouilly-Fuissé Pierrefolle
2005** Château de Roncets (€15)
*Unusually, this comes from granitic
soil in Chaintré. Tastes as if some
Viognier was mixed in with the
Chardonnay.*

② **Nuits-St-Georges Les Perrières
Blanc 2005** Domaine Henri
Gouges (€30) *A rare wine from
Pinot Noir vines that have mutated
to produce white fruit. Individual
and delicious.*

③ **Gevrey-Chambertin Clos St-
Jacques 2002** Domaine Armand
Rousseau (€70) *In the view of
all the five owners in this climat,
Clos St-Jacques produces wine
third only to Chambertin and
Chambertin Clos de Bèze in the
commune: grand cru quality at
premier cru prices.*

④ **Bourgogne Blanc Cuvée
Oligocène 2005** Domaine Patrick
Javillier (€12) *Generic wine from
soil exactly similar to Meursault:
tastes like it, too.*

⑤ **Mâcon Milly-Lamartine Clos du
Four 2005** Lafon (€9) *Dominique
Lafon's venture into the Mâconnais
has gingered up the natives. This
delicious example is his best
wine so far.*

⑥ **Pouilly-Fuissé Le Clos Reyssié
2005** Bret Bros (€18) *Crisp,
minerally, forward wine. From
partly granitic soil in Chaintré.*

⑦ **Givry Blanc Clos de la
Servoisine 2005** Joblot (€12)
*It is literally only since 2004 that
anyone has produced white Givry
that was not rather neutral and
rigid. This is a revelation.*

⑧ **Morey-St-Denis Blanc Les
Monts-Luisants 2002** Domaine
Ponsot (€30) *Largely from very old
Aligoté: no malolactic. Unique.*

⑨ **Bourgogne Aligoté de
Bouzeron 2005** Domaine Aubert
& Pamela de Villaine (€8.50) *When
Aligoté is as good as this – and
this is the best – you wonder
why it is not more widely planted
(but only until you sample a
standard version).*

⑩ **Côte de Nuits Villages La
Robignotte 2005** Domaine Gilles
Jourdan (€12) *From the doyen of
this appellation and historically
the best site just south of Nuits-St-
Georges. Better than most of the
twice-as-expensive village wines
made further north.*

Champagne

Tom Stevenson

For a test period of five years, the maximum yield per hectare in Champagne will rise from 13,000 kg to 15,500 kg, or 98.8 hl, which is 8.8 hl above the limit at which producers of the lowliest *vins de table* can push their production before their wrists are smacked.

TOM STEVENSON

Sounds scarily high, doesn't it? But it gets worse. Or better, if you're a *champenois*. Hidden in the small print under what can only be described as an ironic heading – "Double-safeguard to prevent excessive yields" – growers must ensure that no block of vines exceeds 18 bunches per square metre and, however low the average yield for their entire viticultural holdings might be, no individual parcel of vines may exceed an average yield of 21,700 kg/ha (138 hl/ha).

Of course they cannot make wines from the officially sanctioned but non-usable 6,200 kg between 15,500 kg and 21,700 kg. However, if a grower's crop hits 21,700 kg/ha, there is no qualitative difference between grapes harvested up to 15,500 kg and those grapes harvested

TOM STEVENSON has specialized in champagne for more than 25 years. *Champagne* (Sotheby's Publications, 1986) was the first wine book to win four awards, and it quickly established Tom's credentials as a leading expert in this field. In 1998, his *Christie's World Encyclopedia of Champagne & Sparkling Wine* (Absolute Press, revised 2003) made history by being the only wine book ever to warrant a leader in any national newspaper (*The Guardian*), when it published a 17th-century document proving beyond doubt that the English used a second fermentation to convert still wine into sparkling at least six years before Dom Pérignon even set foot in the Abbey of Hautvillers. Tom has judged in France, Germany, Greece, the United States, and Australia, and he is chairman of the champagne panel at the *Decanter* World Wine Awards. His annual Champagne Masterclass for Christie's is always a sellout.

above this imaginary limit. When will the French understand that juggling the numbers does not equate with restricting yields? It is merely rationing what percentage of the yield that may be used and then chucking the rest away. This has no qualitative effect whatsoever. With demand seemingly insatiable, they might as well come clean and use the lot. There is no logic to rationing the amount of the crop that may be used, especially in today's market, when demand outstrips supply and there is a call to expand the appellation. Rationing merely puts pressure on stocks, which unnecessarily drives up the cost of grapes, resulting in an artificial inflation of the price of a bottle of champagne. This is precisely the sort of scenario that could spell disaster for the current boom in sales.

Sales of champagne are notoriously cyclical, going from boom to bust and back to boom again. Champagne's next bust is overdue. In theory, it should have happened by now, having been triggered by a series of economic, social, and climatic catastrophes that have blighted the first few years of the 21st century. In terms of the magnitude, the factors affecting the 21st century are off the boom–bust Richter scale compared to the events that precipitated the busts of the 20th century – so much so, that the first two questions I am asked whenever I visit Champagne are how long I think the current boom will last, and what might trigger a slow-down in sales?

So, what has saved champagne from nose-diving into its biggest crash yet? The millennium effect, that's what. The millennium effect was built on a hope that never materialized following 9/11, which only adds to the mystery of why the boom has gone from strength to strength under such unstable global conditions. More hope, perhaps? Whatever the uncertain reasons for the continuing boom may be, we now have what appears on the surface to be a very buoyant champagne market, but underneath it must be very fragile indeed. What is certain, however, is that there is a price level at which sales will suddenly drop off for any product, and the current strategy of artificially rationing supply when demand is so high has set champagne on a collision course that will determine precisely what that price level will be. This threatens to end the boom with an almighty crash; and since the bust that will follow is likely to last as long as the boom that preceded it, it is going to be a very long time before the champagne producers have their next profitable year.

In the long term, Champagne must reduce yields, not increase them, but in the here and now, using what is grown (rather than just a fraction of it) is the only policy that makes sense. Especially in a growing market where the houses that drive the economy have difficulty obtaining sufficient grapes to keep pace with their sales. By law, the growers have to harvest the entire crop and deliver any excess to the distillery by 31 December of the year of harvest (although this has been enforced only since 2004), so why not renegotiate with the growers to use all the grapes but at a significantly lower price per kilo? The growers would receive less per kilo but would be much richer by selling up to 40 per cent more grapes; houses would be free to increase sales without depleting stocks or reducing quality; and champagne would not hit the price level at which sales would drop off. Seems like a win-win situation for everybody.

Distilling the truth?

In 2004, when the imaginary maximum was set at 13,000 kg/ha, Champagne averaged a whopping 23,000 kg/ha (146.5 hl/ha), and the wine was – believe me – very good. There are those in Champagne who point to 2004 and other high-quality bumper years as proof that the largest crops produce the best champagne, thereby dismissing critics' concerns over increasing yields. However, they got away with it in 2004 only because the weather just before and during the harvest was unseasonably good. Had they experienced average weather conditions, the quality would have been at least as bad as in 2001. Furthermore, had the weather been a repeat of that experienced in 2001 (when the yield was "only" 18,000 kg), 2004 would have been the worst vintage on record. That is why it was so irresponsible to increase the maximum yield to 15,500 kg. It's like telling the worst offenders that they should grow more, and you can bet they will.

What really makes a mockery of Champagne's new yield is its toothless declaration that any parcel of vines exceeding the 21,700 kg/ha "double-safeguard" will lose its right to the appellation. Really? I sincerely doubt it. When I voiced this opinion to one very influential member of the champagne industry, he told me, "Oh yes, it will. We are very serious about punishing those who are responsible for excessive yields." But when I asked, "If Champagne had another 2004 vintage – a year in which the whole region averaged well in excess of 21,700 kg/ha – would they really distil an entire crop of good-quality champagne?", the only response was an enigmatic smile. Why do the French persist in burdening their wine industry with rules they cannot police and threatening penalties they will not invoke?

Opinion:
Conflicting strategies

The cause of Champagne's cyclical boom–bust economy, and the root of most of Champagne's problems, is the imbalance in vineyard ownership (see *Wine Report 2005*, p.34). The industry leaders try to make out that the houses and growers enjoy the happiest of marriages, but their actions speak louder than words. They say they are genuinely concerned about growers and cooperatives holding back the grapes and *vins clairs* the houses need to fuel the organic growth in their sales, yet we see champagnes sold at prices as low as £7.49 a bottle at Christmas in the UK. That's not organic – that's buying market share. When suffering from a short supply of grapes and faced with an unprecedented level of demand, those houses that sell champagne so cheaply are foolish. When it is the cooperatives that are responsible for such dirt-cheap champagne under these conditions, they are cynically and unfairly buying market share. Both are hypocrites.

Grapevine

• **Krug has released** the stunning 1985 in bottles and (my personal idea of heaven) the even more stunning 1995 and 1981, and they're in magnums, too. These are part of the Krug Collection and are not held on their yeasts for later disgorgement. Or not necessarily. Sometimes they come across a forgotten pile still on its first cork, but they are supposed to be the quintessential expression of normally disgorged Krug entering its second life and full of wonderfully rich, mellow, and mature post-disgorgement complexity.

• **English-born MW Stephen Charters** has been appointed the first ever Professor of Champagne Management at the Reims Management School on a cool €250,000 per year.

• **The Taittinger family** has bought back 37 per cent of its "own" firm, following the takeover of the entire Groupe Taittinger by American investment-fund specialists Starwood Capital in 2005 and the subsequent repurchase by Crédit Agricole du Nord-Est in conjunction with the Taittinger family. The bank now holds just 20 per cent of the company, with the remaining 43 per cent taken up by "friendly parties".

• **Ghislain Montgolfier** has been appointed president of the Union des Maisons de Champagne and, therefore, one of the joint presidents of CIVC. Montgolfier, who has been *président directeur général* of Bollinger since 1994, replaces Yves Bénard, who has taken the top job at INAO.

• **Hervé Jestin,** former *chef de caves* at Duval-Leroy, has set up Jestin Oenology at 58 rue de Vignolles in Epernay. This consultancy firm already has customers in Champagne, Bordeaux, Italy, and even Russia. His current areas of research include working without sulphur and trying to decrease copper usage in vineyards.

Vintage Report

Advance report on the latest harvest

2006

Definitely a "Chardonnay vintage", with some excellent base wines produced on the Côte des Blancs, but the Pinot Noir suffered more rot than producers were inclined to admit, and the Meunier was even worse. With nearly 16 per cent affected, the normally hardy Meunier was exceptionally rot-prone for the second year running. This does not mean that some fine-quality champagnes won't be produced from black grapes, just that selection will very much be the key. The Aube produced the most interesting Pinot Noir, although some grapes were overripe.

Updates on the previous five vintages

2005

Vintage rating: *85*

With about 14 per cent grey rot in the black varieties, particularly Meunier, 2005 cannot be classified as a true or great vintage. Definitely not in the class of 2002; probably just below 2004, although some producers may make better 2005s. This is a winemaker's year. Jean-Baptiste Lecaillon, the *chef de caves* at Roederer, told me: "If you are a good blender, one plus one can often equal three, but in 2005 one plus one equals four!" From tasting the *vins clairs*, I found Chardonnay overwhelmingly the best variety, with Le Mesnil-sur-Oger its most successful *cru*. As far as black varieties are concerned, Pinot Noir has the edge, with Verzy and Verzenay standing out.

2004

Vintage rating: *85–88*

This is a vintage on steroids: huge and boosted by an injection of exceptional sunshine. The quality is good to very good, with excellent acids and purity.

Grapevine

- **Béatrice Cointreau** has been relieved of her position as head of Gosset (and Frapin cognac) to "pursue other interests". What other interests? Gosset and Frapin were her life, and she dramatically increased sales of both at the top end. For another view of why she left, go to www.cognac-world.com/article. php3?id_article=3135.

2003

Vintage rating: *50–90*

Frost destroyed 50 per cent of the potential crop, then a pan-European heat wave ripened the grapes at an extraordinarily fast rate, resulting in the earliest harvest since 1822 (when records began), with high, but not excessively high, natural alcohol levels (an average of 10.6 per cent ABV). The speed at which the grapes went through *véraison* produced the lowest acidity and highest pH on record. It is therefore not another 1976, 1959, or 1947, as some *champenois* would have us believe. Considering the small size of the crop and proportionately greater scarcity of Chardonnay, a number of houses might not release a standard vintage, but any producer who has not done his or her best to make a small volume of pure 2003, even if only for in-house use, will live to regret it as global warming continues and they have no library bottles to learn from. The best 2003s released so far have been 2003 by Bollinger (see No.1 Most Exciting or Unusual Finds, p.36) and JM Gobillard Cuvée de Prestige.

2002

Vintage rating: *85–90*

This is without doubt a vintage year, and a very special one, too, marked by the *passerillage* that reduced the crop in some vineyards by up to 40 per cent and endowed the wines with the highest natural alcohol level since 1990 (which itself was the highest since 1959). It is definitely a Pinot Noir year, with Aÿ-Champagne the most successful village. There are some fine Chardonnays, but in general they are less impressively structured and lack acidity. Not that the Pinot Noirs are overblessed with acidity. Low acidity is a key feature of this vintage, with *vins clairs* tasting much softer than their analyses would have us believe. Many of the earliest 2002s to appear on the shelf have been disappointing, but the best are years away from release. The best 2002s so far released have mostly been *blanc de blancs*: Champagne Legras & Haas Grand Cru, De Saint Gall 1er Cru, and Jacquart Mosaïque, with Taittinger the only blend to stand out.

2001

Vintage rating: *35*

Dilute, insipid, and unripe. Anyone who declares this vintage needs his head testing. The best of the exceptions is Clos des Goisses. Agrapart's Venus Blanc de Blancs Brut Nature is the next-best 2001 I have tasted so far, but unless a producer is trying to make a point about an exceptional *terroir*, such as Clos des Goisses does, why would anyone want to put this vintage on the label?

GREATEST WINE PRODUCERS

1. Krug
2. Pol Roger
3. Billecart-Salmon
4. Louis Roederer
5. Bollinger
6. Deutz
7. Jacquesson
8. Gosset
9. Pierre Gimonnet
10. Vilmart

FASTEST-IMPROVING PRODUCERS

1. Moët & Chandon
2. Vilmart
3. Mumm
4. Pommery
5. Mailly Grand Cru
6. Jean Moutardier
7. Comte Audoin de Dampierre
8. Pannier
9. Vve Devaux
10. J Dumangin

NEW UP-AND-COMING PRODUCERS

1. Serge Mathieu
2. Henri Mandois
3. Fluteau
4. Bruno Paillard
5. Chanoine's Tsarine range
6. Henri Giraud
7. Audoin de Dampierre
8. Jean Moutardier

BEST-VALUE PRODUCERS

1. Charles Heidsieck
2. Serge Mathieu
3. Henri Mandois
4. Jean Moutardier
5. Alfred Gratien
6. Bruno Paillard
7. Lanson
8. Louis Roederer
9. Drappier
10. Piper-Heidsieck

Grapevine

- **Dominique Demarville takes a lower post.** Recognized as the inspirational force that reversed the downward trend in Mumm's quality, Demarville was promoted to director of wines and vines for both Mumm and Perrier Jouët in 2003. In December 2006, however, he left this highly prestigious position to serve as number two to Jacques Peters in Veuve Clicquot's winemaking team. Why? Demarville told me several years ago that Peters was his winemaking idol, so when head-hunted by Veuve Clicquot to take over from Peters in three years, the opportunity to study under him was not only his personal dream come true, but also a once-in-a-lifetime, never-to-be-repeated offer he could not refuse. What a wise and humble head on such young shoulders.

- **The incidence** of TCA-affected champagne appears to be at an all-time low. I kept a tally at both my own annual champagne tasting and the DWWA, and the number of TCA-affected bottles averaged 2.8 per cent over 540 samples (with only two in the first 319 samples!).

- **Rémy Cointreau** has again denied rumours that it is selling off its champagne business, but one should never say never. With shares at an all-time high at the beginning of 2007, and having restructured its business to concentrate on its two famous brands, together with the notice it gave Maxxium to end its distribution contract in March 2009, Charles Heidsieck and Piper-Heidsieck will, at that juncture, be at their most attractive ever for potential buyers.

GREATEST-QUALITY WINES

1. **Cuvée Prestige Blanc de Blancs 1996** Comte Audoin de Dampierre (€85)
2. **Cuvée Orpale Grand Cru 1996** De Saint Gall (€70)
3. **Clos des Goisses 1997** Philipponnat (€80)
4. **Cuvée William Deutz 1998** Deutz (€90)
5. **Blanc de Millénaires 1995** Charles Heidsieck (€60)
6. **Cuvée R Lalou 1998** Mumm (€120)
7. **Vintage Rosé 2002** Deutz (€35)
8. **2003 by Bollinger** (€65)
9. **Dom Ruinart Rosé 1996** Ruinart (€145)
10. **Millésime Brut 1999** Boizel (€28.90)

BEST BARGAINS

1. **2003 by Bollinger** (€65)
2. **Cuvée Millésime 1998** Jean Moutardier (€23)
3. **Blanc de Blancs Fleuron 2002** Pierre Gimonnet (€26)
4. **Grand Vintage 2000** Moët & Chandon (€35)
5. **Brut Réserve Mise en Cave 2003 NV** Charles Heidsieck (€29.50)
6. **Cuvée des Ambassadeurs 1er Cru NV** Comte Audoin de Dampierre (€25)
7. **Brut Croix Rouge NV** Champagne de Castellane (€16)
8. **Blanc de Blancs Cuvée Prestige NV** André Jacquart (€25)
9. **Vintage 2000** Pannier (€25)
10. **Blanc de Blancs Grand Cru 2002** Legras & Haas (€20)

MOST EXCITING OR UNUSUAL FINDS

1. **2003 by Bollinger** (€65) A one-off, released three years before Bollinger is due to release its Grande Année 2000, let alone its Grande Année 2002. Just one-tenth the volume of their normal vintage production, from only three villages (Aÿ, Verzenay, and Cuis — the historical heart of Bollinger's vineyards), this is a sumptuous champagne (genuinely dry), with the softest, silkiest mousse.

2. **Grand Vintage 2000** Moët & Chandon (€35) The largest-selling champagne brand starts to get serious with its 2000 vintage. It has not simply turned over a new leaf in the way it makes vintage champagne, it has ripped out all the pages and thrown the book away. This is only the beginning.

3. **Celebris Blanc de Blancs Extra Brut NV** Gosset (€150) The first blanc de blancs Celebris would have been even better with a full brut dosage, but a wonderful nugget of rich, mature, walnutty Chardonnay fruit gives it instant class.

4. **RD 1996** Bollinger (€125) I usually recommend readers to buy the very first shipment of Grande Année and cellar it themselves, since the RD is usually much too raw and needs post-disgorgement ageing anyway. However, the 1996 is the stunning exception to the rule. It's so powerful, with heaps of dry extract and high acids, that the barrique character is almost subsumed.

5. **Cuvée Millésime 1998** Jean Moutardier (€23) The exceptional fruitiness in this vintage demonstrates the revolutionary pressing quality of Coquard's PAI super-press in its inaugural year.

⑥ **Quattor Blanc de Quatre Blancs NV** Drappier (€25)
A blend of equal parts Arbane, Petit Meslier, Pinot Blanc, and Chardonnay.

⑦ **Brut Nature Sans Souffre NV** Drappier (€25) *The first non-sulphured champagne to be commercialized, and it's as fresh as a daisy. Hollow mid-palate, and would obviously have been better with a dosage, but perhaps the sugar would be too risky without any sulphur?*

⑧ **Brut 1999** J Dumangin (€21) *The single most improved vintage from any producer.*

⑨ **Cuvée Orpale Grand Cru 1996** De Saint Gall (€70) *You can buy this top-quality champagne in so-called rip-off Britain for just two-thirds the price at M&S.*

⑩ **Dom Pérignon 1999** Moët & Chandon (€99) *I'm sticking this down here to get a message across because DP is being released with insufficient post-disgorgement age. It should have at least 12 months before shipping; I'm assured that it has 9 months, but it regularly tastes like under 4 months. As I demonstrated at my Christie's Champagne Masterclass in 2006, the difference between this cuvée disgorged at 7 months and 30 months is mind-blowing, particularly on the mousse, which goes from being aggressive to silky smooth.*

Grapevine

• **Tasting the 2003s** ahead of their release, I was predictably disappointed with most of them, but the two best examples, Moët and Bollinger (see No.1 Most Exciting or Unusual Finds, opposite), were truly great wines in their own right. With the lowest acidity and highest pH on record, the knee-jerk reaction of many producers was to add sulphur as early as possible to prevent oxidation, to up the dose of sulphur because of the extraordinarily high pH (up to 3.7!), and to acidify (which is permitted in Champagne). The two most adept at acidification gained their experience in Australia. They are Moët's Richard Geoffroy, who seldom acidifies, and Roederer's Jean-Baptiste Lecaillon, who usually does. There were obvious acidification faults in some of the 2003s, but the most common area of disappointment was the lack of freshness and finesse, which I attribute to heavy-handed sulphuring. When I asked Benoît Gouez, the *chef de caves* at Moët & Chandon, how his 2003 was made, I discovered that LVMH had been putting a new device through its paces, and this was the secret to their success in 2003. Yeasts consume all available oxygen during the fermentation process, and this particular device, made by Oenodev, measures the amount of oxygen that grape juice ideally requires, which has led them to micro-oxygenating juice, rather than wine, for a smooth fermentation, rather than softening tannins in red wines. When they got the results on the 2003 juice, the decision was made not to add any sulphur at juice stage and just to let it oxidize to an alarming brown colour. This was counterintuitive to those working at the press houses, and as the juice got browner and browner, they kept phoning Moët's oenologists requesting confirmation. They were almost pulling out their hair in despair, but the yeasts did their job during the fermentation, and the result in freshness, mouthfeel, and balance is quite astounding.

Alsace

Tom Stevenson

After last year's lead story welcomed the fact that "after more than 30 years, the saga of Kaefferkopf's *grand cru* classification finally came to a head, as it became this region's 51st *grand cru*", some readers may be surprised to hear that the saga continues.

TOM STEVENSON

According to the new *décret*, some 70 ha have been delimited as Grand Cru Kaefferkopf, and this would seem to compare favourably with the 67.81 ha delimited by the Colmar Tribunal in 1932. However, the new Kaefferkopf includes just over 12 ha of vineyards not previously classified as Kaefferkopf and excludes 15 ha that were delimited in 1932, leaving 32 growers very miffed indeed. So miffed, in fact, that in March 2007 they took the case to court in Colmar, demanding the annulment of the new *grand cru décret*. According to the regional newspaper *Dernières Nouvelles d'Alsace*, this was the first occasion that a *grand cru* designation had been legally contested, and although the case was kicked out, the growers are now pursuing it all the way to the national court.

TOM STEVENSON specializes in Champagne, but he is equally passionate about Alsace. In 1987, he was elected a *confrère oenophile* of the Confrérie Saint-Etienne, when he was the sole person to identify a 50-year-old wine made from Sylvaner. In 1994, his 600-page tome *The Wines of Alsace* (Faber & Faber, 1993) won the Veuve Clicquot Book of the Year award in the USA and attracted the mother of all reviews in the UK from Malcolm Gluck, who declared: "It is not simply the best book about Alsace wines ever written, or the most penetrating book about a French wine region ever written; it is the greatest wine book ever written, period." A revision is in the pipeline but more than a few years away. Tom is chairman of the Alsace panel at the *Decanter* World Wine Awards.

I feel like grabbing hold of the 32 growers by the scruff of their necks and banging their heads together with those who delimited the new *grand cru*. Both sides have got it wrong, and the only ones laughing are the lawyers. When you consider the travesties of delimitation that have been committed in other *grands crus* (Brand, for example, which was originally barely more than 3 ha, whereas Grand Cru Brand today is a whopping 57.95 ha), would it not have been simpler to include the entire area of Kaefferkopf as delimited in 1932? And if the growers were included in the Colmar Tribunal delimitation of 1932, would they not have stood a better chance of using the courts to force their inclusion in Grand Cru Kaefferkopf than they do of getting the law annulled?

What's in a name?

On 17 April 2007, the Association des Viticulteurs d'Alsace (AVA) voted to ban the sale of Pinot Gris as Pinot Grigio on the grounds that it is not on the list registered with the EU by France of all its accepted varietal synonyms. The Turckheim cooperative had been supplying Marks & Spencer, which had rebranded its Alsace Pinot Gris in the summer of

Grapevine

• **At Sainsbury's,** you really can taste the difference. Sainsbury's Taste the Difference 2005 Gewurztraminer (produced by the Cave Cooperative Turckheim) walked off with the Alsace Dry Aromatic White Under £10 Trophy at the *Decanter* World Wine Awards (DWWA).

• **Other DWWA trophy winners** were Riesling Cuvée Frédéric Emile 2001 FE Trimbach (Best Alsace Riesling Over £10), The Wine Society's Exhibition Gewurztraminer (Alsace Dry Aromatic White Over £10), and Riesling Eiswein Silberberg 1998 Domaine Pfister (Alsace Sweet Wine Over £10). This was Alsace's most successful year yet at the awards. As chairman of the Alsace panel, I'm biased, of course, but the fact that this is the only wine competition in the world that employs specialist panels to judge wines on a regional basis and allows the chairmen to select and fine-tune their own specialist panels, it really is a different wine competition and, I believe, the best in the world. We are not judging Alsace Riesling against German, Austrian, or Australian. Or at least not until all the regional trophies go head to head for the international trophies. Other regions have taken this on board, but despite 2007 being the best yet for Alsace, it does lag behind other regions (Greece submitted four times as many wines, for example). More Alsace producers should support the DWWA by entering the competition. E-mail worldwineawards@decanter.com in any language for details.

2006 and attracted a lot of publicity with its labelling of Alsace Pinot Grigio. Marks & Spencer had caught on to the marketing fact that "the sexy and magical words 'Pinot Grigio'" sold wine, whatever happened to be in the bottle. This was taken very seriously by some in Alsace, who saw it as an erosion of the tradition and heritage of their wines – and I suppose it might have led to that, had it gone on. Certainly it happened at the wrong time, having coincided with the phasing out of Tokay Pinot Gris in favour of Pinot Gris. The loss of a Hungarian-influenced name at the same time as the emergence of an Italian varietal name was confusing to say the least. Furthermore, Pinot Grigio infers an essentially light and fresh style of wine, with relatively bland fruit (bar well-known exceptions) and absolutely no spice, whereas Alsace Pinot Gris is more structured, with higher alcohol, and a distinctive spice character. So am I happy with the AVA for stopping Alsace Pinot Grigio? Yes. Do I mind it ever happening? No, and nor should anyone in Alsace, since it gave some of their wines some publicity and sales to some consumers who might not otherwise have purchased an Alsace wine. Indeed, I look forward to the next "Pinot Grigio"-type episode in the certain knowledge that the AVA will act to protect the reputation of Alsace after it has benefited from a good breath of positive publicity.

Grapevine

• **Wolfberger** offers an amazing cache of mature vintages on its website: Pinot Blanc Médaillé 1960 (€15.60); Pinot Gris Cuvée du Schlossherr 1961 (€20.20); Muscat Grande Médaillé 1962 (€17); Gewurztraminer Sigillé 1964 (€13.50); Muscat Médaillé 1965 (€20); Gewurztraminer Sigillé 1966 (€20.60); Riesling Médaillé 1967 (€20); Riesling Cuvée 1969 (€19); Muscat Cuvée de la Comtesse 1970 (€13.80); Pinot Gris Cuvée du Schlossherr 1971 (€20.20); Gewurztraminer Cuvée St-Léon 1973 (€18.60); Riesling Armorié 1985 (€20); Pinot Gris Cuvée du Schlossherr 1986 (€13.20); Gewurztraminer Cuvée St-Léon 1988 (€16.80); and Gewurztraminer Cuvée St-Léon 1989 (€17.90). I've not tasted many of these wines for a long time, but I intend doing so for the next edition of *Wine Report*, if any are left! Obviously Riesling is longest lived, and a 48-year-old Pinot Blanc will be more interesting than actually enjoyable, but there are some fabulous vintages here, the wines have not moved from their ideal storage conditions since they were made, and the prices are ridiculously cheap. Why not enjoy a weekend in Alsace, buy a mixed case direct from Wolfberger in Eguisheim, chill them down, try them with a picnic, and go back to Wolfberger the next day to buy your favourites?

Opinion:
Sugar can kill!

There is no room for sweet wine in Alsace other than *vendanges tardives*, *sélection de grains nobles*, and maybe the occasional *vin de glace*. These are speciality wines and, as such, are expected to be rarities, prized and expensive. The increasing sweetness of all other Alsace wines is doing irreparable harm to the hard-earned reputation of Alsace as a dry varietal-wine region. They are killing Alsace. In 2006, Etienne Hugel was reported in a trade publication as saying, "In a restaurant, people expect a dry wine, so why is it that some people produce sweet wines? It's not the upper level where there's a problem – the problem lies with entry-level wines that are made sweet, not grown sweet." He is wrong – there is a problem in the upper level. Far be it for me to suggest that Etienne might not want to offend his colleagues in the "upper level", but that is precisely where the biggest problem exists. If there is also a problem with entry-level wines that are chaptalized but end up with residual sugar, there is a simple answer: get off your butt and push for this practice to be made illegal. It might be within the letter of the law, but it is certainly not within the spirit. If a wine ends up sweet, why would there be any need to chaptalize it? The technology exists to identify wines that have been chaptalized, so collect some examples and make your case, Etienne.

You are absolutely correct, however, about the dilemma in restaurants, although the biggest culprits are upper level, especially the *grands crus* and producers who believe in the false god of physiological ripeness. I taste more than 350 Alsace wines every year, and I don't know if a particular *grand cru*, *lieu-dit*, or *cuvée* will be dry or sweet from one year to the next, so how can the producers of these wines expect Joe Public to know? These sweet wines are killing Alsace from the top down. They are deterring people from ordering Alsace in restaurants, which is a pity, because they are such natural food wines. With the exception of VTs and SGNs, which should be produced in the most limited quantities to preserve their value, sugar is the long-term enemy in Alsace. But in the short term, is it too much to ask for an obligatory dry designation to help consumers make a choice?

Vintage Report

Advance report on the latest harvest

2006

As with most of France, this was a very strange year, with a baking hot, very sunny July (the hottest on record for Alsace) that pushed the vine's growth cycle way ahead of the norm, only for the *véraison* to be stopped dead in its tracks by a cool August. Then there was rain in September that not even the Vosges could stop, and rot set in. But it was the downpour on 3 and 4 October that caused the biggest problems. However, the crop ripened, thanks to a beautiful Indian summer soon after. Strict selection in the vineyard was vital, but some excellent wines have been made, including VT and SGN.

Updates on the previous five vintages

2005

Vintage rating: *Red: 88, White: 90*
Overall, 2005 is better than 2004, with brighter fruit flavours, and vies with 2001 and 2002. But the wines need time to confirm their precise qualities. Gewurztraminer was the best all-round performer, while Riesling was the most variable (although some Rieslings were as good as the best Gewurztraminers), and the Pinot Gris was excellent. All other varieties were good to very good. Ideal conditions for botrytis suggest excellent botrytized (as opposed to *passerillé*) VT and SGN.

2004

Vintage rating: *Red: 86, White: 87*
Definitely a more classic vintage, with good fruit and excellent acidity levels. Not in the same class as 2002 or 2001, but it has a distinct edge over 2000 and is certainly fresher, fruitier, and more classic than 2003.

2003

Vintage rating: *Red: 93, White: 65*

There is no doubt that the oppressively hot year of 2003 provided an exceptional and extraordinary growing season, but apart from – potentially – Pinot Noir and a handful of anomalies, the quality is neither exceptional nor extraordinary. Ploughing through 350 wines from this vintage in March 2005 was one of the hardest, most unenjoyable, but academically most instructive tasting experiences of my life. Acidification was allowed by special dispensation, but not everyone took advantage; of those who did, very few got it right, whereas many of those who did not acidify failed to produce wines of any elegance. Most are ugly with a deadness of fruit. Pinot Noir should be the star, but I have yet to taste a great 2003 Pinot Noir. The optimist in me hopes that one has not been released and is slowly maturing somewhere, just waiting for me to taste. Putting to one side Pinot Noir, the most expressive 2003 grapes were Pinot Gris, which in fact looked as black as Pinot Noir on the vine and were made with a natural *vin gris* colour.

2002

Vintage rating: *Red: 85, White: 89*

Although there is some variability in quality, the best 2002s have the weight of the 2000s but with far more focus and finesse. Riesling definitely fared best and will benefit from several years' bottle-age, but Gewurztraminer and Muscat also performed well. The Gewurztraminers are very aromatic, with broad spice notes, whereas the Muscats are exceptionally fresh and floral. Pinot Gris was less successful. Some extraordinary SGNs have been produced.

2001

Vintage rating: *Red: 88, White: 90*

Most growers rate 2000 over 2001, but size is not everything, and this vintage has the finesse and freshness of fruit that is missing from most of the 2000 bruisers. The hallmark of the 2001 vintage is a spontaneous malolactic that endowed so many of the wines with a special balance. You hardly notice the malolactic in the wines. It's just a creaminess on the finish, more textural than taste, and certainly nothing that can be picked up on the nose. Although I'm an avid fan of non-malolactic Alsace wine, this particular phenomenon left the fruit crystal clear, with nice, crisp acidity.

GREATEST WINE PRODUCERS

1. Domaine Zind Humbrecht
2. Domaine Weinbach
3. Trimbach (Réserve and above)
4. JosMeyer
5. Schlumberger
6. René Muré
7. Hugel (Jubilée and above)
8. Ostertag
9. André Kientzler
10. Léon Beyer (Réserve and above)

FASTEST-IMPROVING PRODUCERS

1. Schlumberger
2. Becker
3. Hugel
4. Robert Faller
5. Lucien Albrecht
6. Paul Blanck
7. Albert Boxler
8. André Rieffel
9. Antoine Stoffel
10. Dirler-Cadé

NEW UP-AND-COMING PRODUCERS

1. Laurent Barth
2. André Kleinknecht
3. Leipp-Leininger
4. Gruss
5. Yves Amberg
6. Domaine Stirn
7. Jean & Daniel Klack
8. Schoenheitz
9. Clément Klur
10. Fernand Engel

BEST-VALUE PRODUCERS

1. JosMeyer
2. Becker
3. Lucien Albrecht
4. René Muré
5. Rolly Gassmann
6. Schoffit
7. Laurent Barth
8. Meyer-Fonné
9. Jean-Luc Mader
10. Paul Blanck

GREATEST-QUALITY WINES

1. ***Seigneurs de Ribeaupierre 2005** Trimbach (€21)
2. **Gewurztraminer Altenbourg Cuvée Laurence 2005** Domaine Weinbach (€35)
3. ***Riesling Grand Cru Schlossberg Cuvée Ste-Cathérine 2005** Domaine Weinbach (€32)
4. ***Riesling Grand Cru Froehn Bio 2005** Becker (€11.50)
5. ***Riesling Cuvée Ste-Cathérine 2005** Domaine Weinbach (€28)
6. **Gewurztraminer Grand Cru Kessler 2005** Schlumberger (€17.50)
7. **Riesling 2005** Meyer-Fonné (€24.50)
8. ****Pinot Gris Grand Cru Hengst 2005** JosMeyer (€24.90)
9. **Riesling Holder Vendanges Tardives Cuvée Adrien 1998** Schoenheitz (€25.50)
10. **Gewurztraminer Grand Cru Kitterlé 2005** Schlumberger (€17.50)

BEST BARGAINS

1. *Riesling Grand Cru Froehn 2005 Jean & Philippe Becker (€11.50)
2. **Muscat d'Alsace 2005 Bott Frères €9.70)
3. *Riesling Les Pierrets 2005 JosMeyer (€19.50)
4. *Muscat Cuvée de la Comtesse 2005 Wolfberger (€7.50)
5. Gewurztraminer Grand Cru Kessler 2005 Schlumberger (€17.50)
6. Gewurztraminer Grand Cru Kitterlé 2005 Schlumberger (€17.50)
7. *Riesling Grand Cru Muenchberg 2005 Ostertag (€19)
8. *Riesling Grand Cru Mandelberg 2005 Bott-Geyl (€16)
9. *Gewurztraminer Turckheim 2005 Domaine Zind Humbrecht (€14)
10. **Riesling Réserve Personnelle Sigillé de la Confrérie St-Etienne 2005 Bott Frères (€11.80)

MOST EXCITING OR UNUSUAL FINDS

1. *Seigneurs de Ribeaupierre 2005 Trimbach (€21) *This stunning wine demonstrates that totally dry Gewurztraminer is not only possible in Alsace but can be top class.*
2. *Pinot Noir "F" 2005 Paul Blanck (€23.20) *This silky, seductive 2005 has great finesse and is the crowning glory of Frédéric Blanck's long search to perfect the feminine side of truly serious Alsace Pinot Noir.*
3. Riesling Grand Cru Wineck-Schlossberg SGN 2004 Meyer-Fonné (€28 per 50-cl bottle) *Not one of the sweetest SGNs, but undeniably one of the purest and most elegant.*
4. *Riesling Clos St-Urbain Grand Cru Rangen 2004 Domaine Zind Humbrecht (€45) *A dry Rangen from Zind Humbrecht with none of the hot, sun-baked, peaty, brûlée, volcanic goût de terroir of some vintages.*

Grapevine

• **Hugel** has always had one of the better websites, and it has now launched a fascinating interactive map that can show the spread of its own 27 ha of vineyards and overlay this with maps broken down by grape varieties, *grands crus*, and different geological areas. Interactive mapping of the entire Alsace region is also provided (see http://blog.hugel.com/en/).

• **At the 10th World Riesling Competition** in Strasbourg on 5 February 2007, 534 wines were tasted from 300 producers in 12 countries. Alsace scooped all three of the generic trophies awarded

(Riesling Zellberg 2005 Pierre Koch et Fils, Riesling Cuvée Brigitte 2005 Denis Meyer, and Alsace Riesling 2005 Ruhlmann-Dirringer) and one of the two Grand Cru trophies (Riesling Grand Cru Rosacker 2005 François Schwach et Fils) but only one of the three Vendanges Tardives trophies (Riesling Vendanges Tardives 2004 Louis et Claude Hauller, Domaine du Tonnelier). Germany bagged the rest, plus the only Sélection de Grains Nobles trophy and the only Eiswein trophy. Alsace also picked up 43 of the 79 gold medals and 58 of the 79 silver medals.

⑤ ***Riesling Grand Cru Muenchberg 2005** Ostertag (€25) *André Ostertag's Muenchberg just gets better, and the 2005 is his most elegant vintage yet.*

⑥ ***Pinot Noir Clos St-Landelin 2005** René Muré (€31.95) *Deeply coloured, but not overextracted, this is probably René Muré's best Pinot Noir so far.*

⑦ ***Pinot Noir BIO 2005** Jean & Philippe Becker (€12) *The best guzzling, fruity style of (red) Alsace Pinot Noir I've tasted in a long time.*

⑧ **Tokay Pinot Gris Grand Cru Furstentum 2005** Paul Blanck (€23.40) *This medium-sweet Pinot Gris just beats Blanck's dry Riesling Furstentum to the punch.*

⑨ ***Muscat Cuvée de la Comtesse 2005** Wolfberger (€7.75) *The best of the cheapest Muscats I've ever tasted, Cuvée de la Comtesse is a huge step up from Wolfberger's basic Muscat Médaillé for just one more euro.*

⑩ ****Gewurztraminer 2005** Gruss (€6.50) *Just a tad sweeter than off-dry, this very fruity, delicately spicy Gewurztraminer is a perfect example of why Gruss is such a highly thought-of up-and-coming producer.*

Notes: * Dry, ** Off-dry

Grapevine

• **Last year I reported** that Tokay would not be allowed as part of the Pinot Gris appellation in Alsace as from 2006. Well, I was wrong. Readers must forgive me for thinking that an agreement means what it says. In 1993, the EU and Hungary (then not a member) formally agreed that the Tokay Pinot Gris appellation will not be permitted when referring to Pinot Gris from Alsace, allowing a transitional 13-year period for producers to adapt to the new rule. That period ended on 1 April 2007 (which is either 14 years or an April Fool's Day joke). Furthermore, vintages up to and including 2005 will be permitted to be sold with the former appellation name until stocks run out. So, now it's going to be even longer than 14 years. Also, for the newer vintages, those wines that were put into retail distribution before 31 March 2007 may also continue to be sold as Tokay Pinot Gris until stocks run out. So even vintages beyond the 13-year transitional period are allowed to use the banned Tokay name more than 14 years later. Anyone who thought the Alsace people to be more German than French should think again!

• **Planning a visit?** With 46 fêtes and *foires* every year, there is the opportunity to taste Alsace wines in one village or another almost every week. Make sure your trip coincides with one of these festivities in the area of Alsace you will be visiting by downloading the most up-to-date calendar of events from vinsalsace.com/en/pdf/calendrier_manifestation.pdf.

Loire Valley

Charles Sydney

Since most serious producers along the Loire work to the environment-friendly rules of *lutte raisonnée*, it's pretty galling that the "fact forms" from many major importers only ask if the wine is organic or biodynamic.

CHARLES SYDNEY

Laudable as both these methods are when the vineyards are run as meticulously as they should be, the climate in the Loire Valley is perfect for growing grapes only as long as no short cuts are taken in the vineyard. With the obvious exceptions of growers like Jo Pithon and Alphonse Mellot, all too many organic vineyards seem to be left to run wild, with weeds and grass growing up among the bunches to provide a bridge for insects to attack the grapes and open the way for rot.

So I quite understand the relief with which less *intégriste* growers received two reports released from outside the region that seem to indicate that organic viticulture is perhaps less environmentally friendly than *lutte raisonnée*. The two comparative tests – one in Switzerland, on a plot of Chasselas run half organic, half *lutte raisonnée*, and one in Champagne, run half *lutte raisonnée* and half biodynamically – have been running for more than seven years, and both show that the move away from traditional intensive viticulture has a positive effect on the soil. However, both also note a greater mass and diversity of life in the plots run with "reasoned viticulture" than with organic or biodynamic methods.

CHARLES SYDNEY has spent more than 15 years in Chinon as a *courtier en vins* – a wine broker – specializing in the Loire Valley. Based at the heart of the region, he works exclusively on the export market, creating a partnership between the leading producers and the more forward-looking importers. He has an almost evangelical desire to encourage growers to make wines that appeal to the public, at the same time leaning on the specialist press to understand the sometimes dramatic changes happening in one of the world's richest and most diverse wine regions.

It comes as no surprise that this is partly due to a higher use of copper on the organically run vines, but more intriguing is the finding that the more frequent treatments applied in organic farming tend to compact the soil more and cause greater pollution.

Those responsible for both tests emphasize that seven years isn't enough to see the long-term effects of any products being used. In the meantime, however, perhaps press and buyers alike should understand that, here in the Loire at least, growers are using the most effective and least damaging products, actively working to look after the soil, the vineyard workers, and the consumer by producing fine wines from healthy grapes.

Too much bleeding rosé

It's good to see the Loire producing cleaner, fresher, and more fruit-driven wines than ever before. This is particularly the case with the *négoces* who buy in grapes from growers under contract and vinify the wines themselves. However, too many are still making *rosé de saignée*, running off the finest, fresh-run juice in the belief that this will help give concentration to the reds, while in reality it simply tends to reinforce those dry tannins and that impression of astringency that still seem to be the hallmark of the Anjou and Sancerre reds.

Disappointment (or is it?) for St-Pourçain

Despite their best efforts, the growers at St-Pourçain have been denied AOC status and stay in the neverland of VDQS. This is much to the relief of Jacques Vigier, director of the excellent local cooperative cellar, since it means he no longer has to blend boring old Gamay with his rather classy Pinot Noir. Even Jacques admits to some disappointment, however, since he'd got the growers to agree to a self-imposed maximum yield of 45 hl/ha (the official limit is 55), and the vineyard management techniques he's imposed have led to a dramatic improvement in maturity and to a 10-day advance in harvest date. Now that's not global warming but an improvement that comes with better work in the vineyard.

Grapevine

• **Oops! Our friends** over in the Coteaux du Vendomois called in CQFDégustation to help analyse the typical peppery style of the appellation's reds. They found this *typicité* in wines coming from not-quite-ripe harvests of 11–12 per cent ABV. Worse still, they found it in vineyards with low yields as much as in plots with yields of 50–70 hl/ha. And they'd thought it was down to terroir and to the local Pineau d'Aunis grape!

Opinion:
New definitions are needed

The organizers of the Loire Valley's very own wine fair – Angers' excellent Salon des Vins de Loire, which unites some 500 producers with 9,000 visitors from around the world each February – tell us that there are 68 appellations in the region. On their comprehensive and informative website (www.vinsvaldeloire.fr), Interloire – the Loire's interprofessional organization – confidently announces 63. So far I've counted over 100.

Okay, I admit that these include a number of VDQS appellations such as the Fiefs Vendéens and St-Pourçain. I've also assumed that if whites, reds, or rosés are made with different grape varieties and/or different production rules, they should count as separate appellations. But whatever the rules, the number is huge.

And there lies a trap that strikes at the heart of the region's ability to communicate on a national – let alone international – level. Many of the smaller appellations are hardly known outside the locality (just ask a Chinonais what a rosé from Azay-le-Rideau is made from!), so the chance of someone in the big bad world actually seeking out these wines is less than minute.

A simple calculation would say that if a smart UK wine merchant has 1,000 lines and France has 20 per cent of market share, France should have about 200 slots on the list. That's rubbish, of course, with the diversity of the offer and the historic associations between the two countries, so let's say France gets 300 lines. How many does that leave the Loire? Let's be generous and say 30, which will include two or three Sancerres and a couple of Muscadets, which leaves something like 75 unsellable appellations across the region – and we're in the process of adding to the list.

It is increasingly obvious that something needs to be done to simplify this offer, while at the same time respecting growers' pride in the specificities of their terroir.

The solution is there, waiting for INAO, Interloire, and the individual *syndicats* to take it up: let's redefine our wines, retaining the world-famous appellations as effective brands (Sancerre, Pouilly Fumé, Vouvray, Chinon, Bourgueil, Saumur-Champigny, Savennières, Coteaux du Layon, and Muscadet) and wherever possible create "Villages" appellations to reunite *crus* of similar style.

Nothing should prevent current appellations adding their commune name to the "Village" appellation, and we could even add in a quality designation such as *premier cru* for individual vineyard sites such as Quarts de Chaume, the Chêne Marchand, Monts Damnés et al.

The obvious example for such a simplification is in the Anjou, where there are seven individual village *crus* in the Coteaux du Layon, not counting Bonnezeaux and Quarts de Chaume. Not only are these appellations already locally known as Coteaux du Layon Villages, but they are pretty well indistinguishable one from another and generally quite tiny, with some of these villages declaring harvests smaller than 50 hl in some vintages.

In the Touraine (where the local *syndicats* decided to reject the Villages idea because they didn't want to be seen "copying" another region), let's unite the new AOCs of Chambord, Chenonceaux, Oisly, and Seuilly with older *crus* such as Amboise, Azay-le-Rideau, Mesland, Cheverny, and Valençay under one simple banner: Touraine Villages. Two new appellations could replace 16.

Similar redrawing of the boundaries along the northern tributary of Le Loir (Jasnières, the Coteaux du Vendomois, and the Coteaux du Loir), to the west in Muscadet, and further east to unite the Sauvignon/Pinot Noir *crus* of Menetou-Salon, Quincy, Reuilly, St-Pourçain, and the Coteaux du Giennois would go a long way towards opening up doors for some truly original wines to reach the shelves of the more discerning importers.

This redefinition is needed if the growers of the Loire are to prosper on the export markets, where it can be easily understood by that product of the Anglo-Saxon free market, the consumer. All that is needed for local producers to take this leap is for them to understand that their wines are good enough to take the competition, and that their ideas of terroir and character are close to those of the market and won't be lost in a sea of technological *vins de cépage*.

Grapevine

• **"Raisins triés à la main"** on the back label of a Sancerre red that was picked by machine? Okay, the grapes are re-sorted as far as possible on a *table de tri*, but some established growers in Sancerre are genuinely *shocké*!

• **Recent shuffling** among the region's bigger players continues. Georges Duboeuf has pulled out of the much-improved Haut-Poitou cooperative, which has been brought into the Alliance Loire group. With their takeover of the Cave de St-Romain sur Cher in the Touraine, that gives them a good supply of Sauvignon Blanc to better target the export market.

Vintage Report

Advance report on the latest harvest
2006

From the Touraine all the way through to Sancerre and Pouilly, 2006 is truly great for Sauvignon Blancs and perhaps better even than 2005, with memories of that wonderful 1996. More difficult in the west, though, which suffered from the tail end of some summer hurricanes that brought rain and warmth through Muscadet and across to Vouvray – difficult conditions that showed clearly the value of hard work in the vineyard. Growers who'd grassed through the vines, debudded in the spring, and deleafed around the bunches have made some really pretty, fresh, and aromatic wines. Those who hadn't suffered rot and dilution, so stick to the good growers.

Muscadet – A lot of hard work has gone into making some lovely wines for early drinking, with the best wines coming from producers who'd kept yields down through summer thinning. The cheapest wines could be pretty nasty, so do everyone a favour and trade up!

Sauvignon Blanc – Brilliant! After suffering too much rain in one afternoon in Chinon, I was a little sceptical when I saw the local rag in Pouilly say the vintage was between 2005 and 1989 in quality, but actually I think it's better than that. The Touraines, Sancerres, and Pouilly Fumés are delicious. The wines are among the best ever, showing great fruit and freshness. Go for it!

Reds – Serious rain just before harvest led to nearly everyone picking at the same time, but because ripeness at the end of September was on a par with 2005 and more and more growers are now running their vineyards properly, the wines are lovely, showing great fruit and freshness. There are some really ripe, attractive wines in St-Nicolas de Bourgueil, and the later-picked Chinons have depth and soft, ripe tannins.

Chenins – Conditions were difficult for the stickies, though the best producers in the Layon have made some deliciously pure, immediate wines that'll knock your socks off. The best bets, however, are the new-wave dry Chenins that have been hand-picked in successive *tris* and barrel-fermented. It's a real growers' vintage for *moelleux* Chenins, so quality goes from non-existent to immediately attractive. Go with the best Layon producers.

Updates on the previous five vintages

2005

Vintage rating: *Red: 95, Muscadet: 95, Sauvignon: 95, Dry Chenin: 95, Moelleux Chenin: 95*

A great vintage – on a par with the wonderful 2003 for reds and sweet whites, but with more freshness and fruit aromas for the dry whites from Muscadet through to Sancerre. And the wines have structure, too – making for some finely balanced reds and wonderfully intense sweet Chenins that are great now but will improve nicely over the next 5–10 years. This is certainly the best vintage ever for the new-wave barrel-fermented dry Chenins.

2004

Vintage rating: *Red: 85, Muscadet: 95, Sauvignon: 80, Dry Chenin: 80, Moelleux Chenin: 80*

Unusually uneven. In the west, the Muscadets had great concentration and freshness, and the dry Chenins of the Anjou are still delightful. The reds are balanced and fresh, along the lines of 2002. Further east, things were more difficult, with high yields for the Sauvignons from the Touraine through to Sancerre and Pouilly, though the better *cuvées* are now showing well. Stick to the good growers.

2003

Vintage rating: *Red: 95, Muscadet: 95, Sauvignon: 85, Dry Chenin: 90, Moelleux Chenin: 95*

One of the greatest-ever Loire vintages. Despite worries from outside the region that wines may be lacking in acidity, Muscadets, dry and sweet Chenins, and reds have concentration, fruit, and balance that surpass 1990 and 1997. Okay, so the Sauvignons weren't as aromatic as we'd have liked, but the top *cuvées* are lovely. Prices are still more than reasonable.

2002

Vintage rating: *Red: 85, Muscadet: 95, Sauvignon: 90, Dry Chenin: 90, Moelleux Chenin: 85*

Sauvignons are quite ripe, the Muscadets are of rare exception, and there are great Chenins: this is a superb year for dry whites – better than 1996. These are excellent wines for ageing. The reds, which are healthy, solid, and lively, are equal to the 1996s or slightly lower in quality. Their limiting factor is, sometimes, reduced potential longevity, yet they are better than the average quality of the reds produced further south in France.

2001

Vintage rating: Red: 75, Muscadet: 85, Sauvignon: 85,
Dry Chenin: 80, Moelleux Chenin: 75

The dry whites, Chenin and Sauvignon, are better than in 2000, but not as
exceptional as the 2002s, and they should be drunk up. The Pinot Noirs of
Sancerre et al are extremely average, as indeed are the Cabernet Francs,
most of which should be consumed between now and 2009. Generally,
Bourgueil and Chinon will outlive Saumur-Champigny and St-Nicolas de
Bourgueil. Although it was, at the time, the best year for sweet wines since
1997, you should still stick to better producers of *moelleux* Chenins and
look among the top *crus* of the Layon rather than Vouvray for finely
balanced and intense stickies.

GREATEST WINE PRODUCERS

1. *Jacky Blot, Domaine de la Taille aux Loups (Montlouis & Vouvray) & Domaine de la Butte (Bourgueil)
2. Claude Papin, Château Pierre-Bise (Anjou, Savennières & Coteaux du Layon)*
3. *Didier Dagueneau (Pouilly Fumé)
4. *Jo Pithon (Anjou, Savennières & Coteaux du Layon)
5. *Vincent Pinard (Sancerre)
6. *Philippe Vatan, Château du Hureau (Saumur-Champigny)
7. Alphonse Mellot (Sancerre)
8. *Domaine Charles Joguet (Chinon)
9. Jean-Pierre Chevalier, Château de Villeneuve (Saumur-Champigny)
10. Domaine Vacheron (Sancerre)

FASTEST-IMPROVING PRODUCERS

1. Château de Passavant (Anjou)
2. Philippe Pichard (Chinon)
3. *Couly-Dutheil (Chinon)
4. *Domaine de la Paleine (Saumur)
5. *Denis Goizil, Domaine du Petit Val (Coteaux du Layon)
6. *Domaine Henri Bourgeois (Sancerre)
7. *Pascal & Nicolas Reverdy (Sancerre)
8. *Jean Douillard (Muscadet Sèvre & Maine)
9. Joël Mesnard, Domaine des Sablonettes (Anjou & Coteaux du Layon)
10. Les Frères Couillaud (Muscadet Sèvre & Maine)

NEW UP-AND-COMING PRODUCERS

1. *Katia Mauroy, Domaine de Bel Air (Pouilly Fumé)
2. Damien Delecheneau, Domaine la Grange Tiphaine (Touraine)
3. *Ampelidae (Haut-Poitou)
4. Arnaud Hérivault, Domaine d'Orfeuilles (Vouvray)
5. *François Crochet (Sancerre)
6. Vincent Ricard (Touraine)
7. *Stéphane Branchereau, Domaine des Forges (Anjou, Savennières & Coteaux du Layon)
8. Stéphane Sérol (Côtes Roannaises)
9. Stéphane Cossais (Montlouis)
10. *Gérald Vallée, Domaine de la Cotelleraie (St-Nicolas de Bourgueil)

BEST-VALUE PRODUCERS

1. *Union des Vignerons de St-Pourçain
2. *Rémi & Jean-Jacques Bonnet, Château la Tarcière (Muscadet Sèvre & Maine)
3. *Luc & Jérôme Choblet, Domaine des Herbauges (Muscadet Côtes de Grandlieu)
4. Les Frères Couillaud (Muscadet Sèvre & Maine)
5. *Quintin Frères (Coteaux du Giennois)
6. Cave du Haut-Poitou (Haut-Poitou)
7. *Château Marie du Fou (Fiefs Vendéens)
8. *Jacky Marteau, Domaine de la Bergerie (Touraine)
9. Cave des Vignerons de Saumur (Saumur)
10. *Claude Papin, Château Pierre-Bise (Anjou, Savennières & Coteaux du Layon)

GREATEST-QUALITY WINES

1. Saumur-Champigny Le Grand Clos 2003 Jean-Pierre Chevalier, Château de Villeneuve (€14.50)
2. *Pouilly Fumé Silex 2005 Didier Dagueneau (€50)
3. *Montlouis Romulus 2003 Jacky Blot, Domaine de la Taille aux Loups (€50)
4. *Bourgueil Mi-Pente 2005 Jacky Blot, Domaine de la Butte (€15)
5. *Coteaux du Layon Beaulieu Les Rouannières 2005 Claude Papin, Château Pierre-Bise (€15 per 50-cl bottle)
6. *Saumur-Champigny Lisagathe 2005 Philippe Vatan, Château du Hureau (€15)

7. Sancerre Rouge La Belle Dame 2005 Domaine Vacheron (€23)
8. *St-Nicolas de Bourgueil Les Malgagnes 2005 Yannick Amirault (€17)
9. *Coteaux du Layon St Lambert Les Bonnes Blanches 2003 Jo Pithon (€18 per half-bottle)
10. Saumur-Champigny Marginale 2005 Thierry Germain, Domaine des Roches Neuves (€17)

BEST BARGAINS

1. Saumur Rouge Réserve des Vignerons 2005 Cave des Vignerons de Saumur (€3.95)
2. Chinon 2005 Domaine de Beauséjour (€5.70)
3. Touraine Amboise Rouge 2005 Domaine de la Gabillière (€3.70)
4. Saumur Rouge 2005 Lycée Viticole de Montreuil-Bellay (€5.60)
5. VDQS Haut-Poitou Sauvignon 2006 Cave du Haut-Poitou (€3.55)
6. *Bourgueil La Coudraye 2005 Yannick Amirault (€7)
7. *Touraine Sauvignon 2006 Jacky Marteau, Domaine de la Bergerie (€4.20)
8. *Muscadet Sèvre & Maine Sur Lie La Levraudière 2006 Rémi & Jean-Jacques Bonnet, Château la Tarcière (€3.10)
9. *Coteaux du Layon Cuvée Simon 2005 Denis Goizil, Domaine du Petit Val (€9.50)
10. *Vouvray Sec Clos de la Bretonnière 2005 Jacky Blot, Domaine de la Taille aux Loups (€10)

MOST EXCITING OR UNUSUAL FINDS

1 Vin de Pays du Jardin de la France Abouriou 2003 Domaine du Grand Logis (€2.60) *Hidden behind one of those awful "new" labels lies one of those lovely old-fashioned grapes I thought had ceased to exist. The inky-black colour and deep, soft tannins of the wine show what can happen when, in the hands of a young producer and with low yields, this forgotten relic meets the ripeness of a great vintage.*

2 Vin de Table Viognier 2003 Les Frères Couillaud (€4.30) *After living in a wine region for all these years, one of the greatest joys is finding something that shouldn't be there at all, so stumbling across the Couillaud brothers' Viognier was a real treat. Planted on Muscadet's classic micaschist rock, it has loads of ripe fruit (mangoes, peaches) to show what happens to these "southern" varieties in a great, sunny vintage.*

3 Vin de Pays des Coteaux Charitois Pinot Noir Les Pénitents 2005 Alphonse Mellot (€11) *The old Cave des Hauts de Seyr was bought out by Alphonse "Junior" Mellot in 2005, and the estate's Pinot Noir and Chardonnay are starting to show what they're really capable of, with low yields and a touch of oak giving concentration to the wine's fresh fruit. Not bad now, this should get better still as he starts to get the vineyards under strict control.*

4 St-Nicolas de Bourgueil Cuvée Eclipse 2005 Frédéric Mabileau (€14) *Fermented in oak barriques to get all the fat, sweet tannins from the new oak. Still awfully young, the wine has structure rather than softness, but it should mellow nicely.*

5 *Montlouis Pétillant Triple Zero NV Jacky Blot, Domaine de la Taille aux Loups (€8) *Made from hand-picked fully ripe Chenin Blanc (minimum 12 per cent at harvest), this was fermented in oak barriques and transferred to bottle to finish its alcoholic fermentation – all of which would show up any faults. Jacky Blot takes understandable pride in the triple zeros: zero chaptalization, zero dosage, and zero liqueur de tirage, all of which make for a wonderfully pure, mineral, and almost austere wine.*

6 *Touraine Malbec Vinifera Vignes Française Non-greffées 2005 Henry Marionnet (€9) *At long last, the INAO has agreed that the local Cot grape is actually Malbec, and Henry Marionnet shows just how wonderful the grape can be in the Loire, though he perhaps took things to the extreme back in 2000 by planting 1 ha with ungrafted vines. The result is stunning – the wine reached full phenological maturity at a mere 13 per cent alcohol, giving lusciously soft, inky fruit with structure and fruit all nicely tied together.*

7 *Vin de Pays du Jardin de la France Pinot Noir Rosé 2006 Union des Vignerons de St-Pourçain (€3.90) *When a client asked Jacques Vigier whether he could produce a Pinot Noir rosé, he didn't just say yes – he promptly sat on the cellar's growers to make them reduce yields and raise ripeness and then cocked a snook at the INAO by "declassifying" the resulting wine into a Vin de Pays, since, according to the appellation system, there's no such thing as a Pinot Noir rosé in St-Pourçain! The* result happily stands up to most Sancerre rosés, but at a third of the price.

⑧ ***Vin de Pays de Vienne Sacré Blanc 2006** Jérémie Mourat (€6) *Normally an oak-fermented Chenin needs a year in barrel and a year in bottle to let the flavours "marry". Being young and headstrong, Jérémie can't wait, so he's fermented this great Chenin Blanc in Vendée oak barrels and bottled it in the spring to catch its primary fruit. The result is a vibrant, fruit-filled odyssey a mile away from the more serious cuvées of the Anjou.*

⑨ ***Anjou Blanc Le Haut de la Garde 2005** Claude Papin, Château Pierre-Bise (€7.50) *In the Anjou, a band of go-ahead growers is radically changing the way they grow and vinify dry white wines, and Claude's helping lead the way. Picked by hand in successive selective pickings, the grapes are picked fully ripe (but not botrytized) before being fermented and then matured in 400-litre oak barrels, giving wines with freshness, fruit, and great rolling depths of flavour. South Africa, watch out – the Loire is real Chenin heartland!*

⑩ ***Vin de Table Cuvée Pauline 2004** Philippe Trotignon (€7 per 50-cl bottle) *Once again we have an hors normes wine that's just too good to be AOC! Philippe picked this Sauvignon Blanc with a potential 18 per cent ABV at harvest – not bad for the notoriously difficult 2004. Cool-fermented in stainless steel, the finished wine has close to 100 g of natural residual sugar per litre (beating virtually every Vouvray of the vintage) and is already starting to show attractively mellow, honeyed overtones.*

* An asterisk indicates a producer with whom Charles Sydney works as a courtier.

Grapevine

• **Another one bites the dust.** After just three years under the ownership of Rhône giant Gabriel Meffre (and three years after Caves St-Florent went under), Muscadet's much-loved *négociant* Donatien-Bahuaud went to the wall during the 2006 harvest, leaving its 40-odd suppliers worried they were going to end up with neither wine nor money.

• **The powers-that-be** have finally accepted that the Touraine's undervalued Cot is in fact Malbec and have agreed to let growers use the name of the grape on the label. However, they've also decided to change the name of an old grape, the Arbois (still planted across the Loir et Cher) into Orbois so as not to annoy the good burgers of the town Arbois. No panic for the consumer, though – I've never seen this *cépage* on a label.

• **Miracles may actually happen!** The *syndicats* of the various appellations with "Loire" in the name have agreed to let the region create a Vin de Pays du Val de Loire; we may even see one with the 2007 vintage.

Rhône Valley

Olivier Poels

Major changes are on the way for Jaboulet Aîné, following its sale to Jean-Jacques Frey.

OLIVIER POELS

Monsieur Frey, owner of Château La Lagune in Bordeaux, and one of the shareholders of the Billecart-Salmon champagne house, bought Jaboulet Aîné, located in Tain l'Hermitage, in 2006. Over the coming years, the estate will be completely restructured.

First, the new owner has changed the management team. The Jaboulet family members who had been running the estate have been ousted and replaced by a younger team, headed by Caroline Frey. Bordeaux wine professor Denis Dubourdieu is now supervising the winemaking.

In the vineyard, the new management has taken measures to significantly reduce yields and improve the way the vines and the soil are cultivated. These changes were visible during the 2006 harvest, when traditional buckets were replaced by small boxes, which help prevent the grapes from being damaged during transport from the vineyard to the crusher. In the winery, all the barrels have been changed. Only new oak and once-used barrels (from prestigious Bordeaux estates) will be used in the cellars.

The most dramatic changes are to come. New cellars will be built for vinification and barrel storage in the well-known Domaine de Thalabert, where a derelict building will be renovated. The refurbished building will house the Jaboulet headquarters, a reception room, and new offices.

Finally, the new owner plans to acquire more vines. The first step was the acquisition of 1.8 ha of Côte Rôtie, a new appellation in the estate portfolio. Land purchases in Châteauneuf-du-Pape are also in the offing.

OLIVIER POELS is a journalist at *La Revue du Vin de France* and a member of the Comité de Dégustation. He also produces wine programmes for French TV channel LCI and is coauthor of the *Guide Malesan des Vins de France* and *Classement des Meilleurs Vins de France*.

Opinion:
Settle the quarrel

The seeds of disagreement sometimes stretch so far back that no one remembers exactly where they came from, but that doesn't prevent the discord continuing. Châteauneuf-du-Pape sadly illustrates that bitterness dies hard, to the point of absurdity. The village is divided by the two local wine syndicates – the "intercommunal" syndicate and the producers' federation. The two enemy organizations have reached such a level of rivalry that their members barely talk to anyone from the other side.

This typically "French" – that is, ludicrous – situation would be laughable if it didn't have serious consequences for the whole appellation. Being too busy fighting each other, the Châteauneuf-du-Pape wine producers have not only stopped the common promotion of their wines, but they don't even want to share the same tasting sessions. Neither are they represented at the Inter-Rhône regional syndicate. All attempts, including recent ones, to reconcile the parties have been short-lived. Shame on Châteauneuf-du-Pape for this unacceptable behaviour.

Investment opportunities

While Bordeaux, Languedoc, Provence, and (most recently) Burgundy attract French and foreign investors, the Rhône Valley has remained relatively free from investment. Apart from the acquisition of Jaboulet Aîné by French financier Jean-Jacques Frey, no significant transaction has been recorded in the Rhône Valley for years.

Under present circumstances, however, this situation might change, since the crisis hitting French wine production has reached the Rhône Valley. Prices of wine real estate have slumped, especially in southern regions. In early 2007, specialized estate agents received an increasing number of enquiries about wine domaines for sale. Some great opportunities are coming up in Châteauneuf-du-Pape, Gigondas, and Vacqueyras. It can sometimes be difficult for older growers to reach an inheritance agreement within their families, which can lead to properties being sold. We can expect to see a growth in the number of investors in the Rhône Valley. Considering the high quality of the soils, there is potential for shrewd investment here.

Vintage Report

Advance report on the latest harvest

2006

French vineyards had mixed experiences in 2006, but the Rhône Valley was rather privileged. August was, as everywhere else, very "moody", but it didn't affect the maturity of the vines. By contrast, September was superb. It gave the grapes optimal weather conditions to mature, and with no rainfall, there was no trace of rot. The grapes were very healthy in both northern and southern regions. The wines show nice fruit, density, and good balance. The overall quality level is expected to be high.

Updates on the previous five vintages

2005

Vintage rating: *Red: 96 (North: 92–98, South: 90–98), White: 93 (North: 90–95, South: 90–94)*

A rainy spring, a dry summer, and a bright, sunny September gave a winning ticket to the Rhône Valley in 2005. With a maturity that came early, this vintage has produced rich though extremely balanced wines. In the north (Hermitage, Côte Rôtie), the 2005s could match the excellent 1990s. In the south, the same conditions produced the same results: the Grenache is stunning, with a remarkable balance between alcohol, fruit, and acidity. Yields were generous, so wines will be widely available.

2004

Vintage rating: *Red: 91 (North: 82–90, South: 90–98), White: 88 (North: 80–90, South: 89–95)*

After the 2002 rains and the heat wave of 2003, 2004 marked a return to a classic vintage in the Rhône Valley. Very favourable weather conditions during September produced healthy, ripe grapes. The harvest schedule was normal: between 6 September and mid-October. Concentration is remarkable and alcohol levels are quite high, but the consequences of 2003 are still visible: yields are 20 per cent lower than normal. In the south, the 2004s seem better balanced than the 2003s.

2003

Vintage rating: *Red: 95 (North: 90–97, South: 88–93), White: 89 (North: 83–90, South: 85–90)*

The north had one of its earliest vintages. The south needed more patience, since drought delayed ripening. The grapes were perfectly healthy and quality was exceptional, despite a slight lack of acidity. The wines have high alcohol levels and very rich, mature tannins: the 2003s will keep for a very long time.

2002

Vintage rating: *Red: 70 (North: 70–75, South: 55–60), White: 73 (North: 70–75, South: 60–65)*

Dramatic rainfall destroyed a large part of the harvest, especially in the Vaucluse region. An average vintage in the north.

2001

Vintage rating: *Red: 90 (North: 88–92, South: 85–90), White: 90 (North: 88–92, South: 88–90)*

A solid vintage in the north. Some wines are too acid and coarse, but the best are powerful and long. Some dilution and tartness problems in the south.

GREATEST WINE PRODUCERS

1. Domaine Jean-Louis Chave (Hermitage)
2. Château d'Ampuis (Côte Rôtie, Hermitage)
3. M Chapoutier (Hermitage, Châteauneuf-du-Pape)
4. Tardieu-Laurent (Cuvées Vieilles Vignes)
5. Domaine Georges Vernay (northern Rhône)
6. Château de Beaucastel (Châteauneuf-du-Pape)
7. Domaine Jamet (Côte Rôtie)
8. Domaine de la Janasse (Châteauneuf-du-Pape)
9. Henri Bonneau (Châteauneuf-du-Pape)
10. Domaine du Vieux Télégraphe (Châteauneuf-du-Pape)

FASTEST-IMPROVING PRODUCERS

1. Domaine de la Mordorée (Châteauneuf-du-Pape)
2. Domaine de Marcoux (Châteauneuf-du-Pape)
3. Domaine P&C Bonnefond (northern Rhône)
4. Domaine Charvin (Châteauneuf-du-Pape)
5. Domaine Jean-Michel Gérin (Côte Rôtie)
6. Domaine de la Présidente (Châteauneuf-du-Pape)
7. Domaine de la Vieille Julienne (Châteauneuf-du-Pape)
8. Domaine Gourt de Mautens (Côtes du Rhône Villages)
9. Maison Delas Frères (Rhône Valley)
10. Domaine du Tunnel (St-Péray)

NEW UP-AND-COMING PRODUCERS

1. Domaine de la Côte Saint-Epine (St-Joseph)
2. Domaine Les Bruyères (Crozes-Hermitage)
3. Domaine La Lorentine (Lirac)
4. Domaine des Hauts-Chassis (Crozes-Hermitage)
5. Prieuré de Montézargues (Tavel)
6. Domaine de Piaugier (Côtes du Rhône Villages)
7. Domaine du Trignon (Gigondas)
8. Mas de Libian (Côtes du Rhône Villages)
9. Domaine Les Grimaudes (Costières de Nîmes)
10. Château de l'Amarine (Costières de Nîmes)

BEST-VALUE PRODUCERS

1. Domaine de la Tourade (Gigondas)
2. Domaine du Moulin (Côtes du Rhône Vinsobres)
3. Domaine Thierry Farjon (St-Joseph)
4. Perrin & Fils (Côtes du Rhône)
5. Domaine du Cros de la Mûre (Côtes du Rhône)
6. Marcel Richaud (Côtes du Rhône Villages)
7. Domaine des Amadieu (Côtes du Rhône Cairanne)
8. Domaine Les Gouberts (Gigondas)
9. Château Val Joanis (Côtes du Lubéron)
10. Château Mourgues du Grès (Costières de Nîmes)

GREATEST-QUALITY WINES

1. **Hermitage Cuvée Cathelin 2003** Domaine Jean-Louis Chave (€250)
2. **Ermitage L'Ermite 2004** M Chapoutier (€150)
3. **Côte Rôtie Les Grandes Places 2004** Domaine Jean-Michel Gérin (€60)
4. **Hermitage Les Bessards 2004** Maison Delas Frères (€60)
5. **Châteauneuf-du-Pape 2004** Domaine de Marcoux (€100)
6. **Châteauneuf-du-Pape Cuvée Spéciale 2004** Tardieu-Laurent
7. **Châteauneuf-du-Pape 2004** Château de Beaucastel (€48)
8. **Côte Rôtie 2004** Domaine Jamet (€50)
9. **Châteauneuf-du-Pape Vieilles Vignes 2004** Domaine de la Janasse (€50)
10. **Châteauneuf-du-Pape La Reine des Bois 2004** Domaine de la Mordorée (€40)

BEST BARGAINS

1. **Côtes du Rhône Garrigues 2005** Marcel Richaud (€7)
2. **St-Joseph 2005** Domaine de la Côte Sainte-Epine (€11)
3. **Vacqueyras Les Deux Monardes 2004** Domaine de la Monardière (€10)
4. **Lirac 2005** Domaine La Lorentine (€15)
5. **Côtes du Rhône Villages Cairanne Réserve des Seigneurs 2005** Domaine de l'Oratoire St-Martin (€8.50)
6. **Vin de Pays Syrah 2005** Domaine Georges Vernay (€6)
7. **Costières de Nîmes 2004** Domaine Les Grimaudes (€6.50)
8. **Crozes-Hermitage Esquisse 2005** Domaine des Hauts Chassis (€9)
9. **Côtes du Rhône Sierra du Sud 2005** Domaine Gramenon (€8.80)
10. **St-Joseph 2005** Domaine Thierry Farjon (€10)

MOST EXCITING OR UNUSUAL FINDS

❶ **Hermitage Cuvée Cathelin 2003** Domaine Jean-Louis Chave (€250) *Impossible to describe in a few words. Just magic.*

❷ **St-Joseph 2005** Domaine de la Côte Sainte-Epine (€11) *Made by a young, talented winemaker in the spirit of the great St-Josephs of Raymond Trollat.*

❸ **Lirac 2005** Domaine La Lorentine (€15) *La Lorentine is a joint venture between two famous Châteauneuf-du-Pape producers: the Armenier sisters and Jean-Louis Canto. The 2005 vintage is a superb example of the appellation.*

❹ **Tavel 2005** Prieuré de Montézargues (€10) *A great rosé and one of the most complex Tavels, made on a very interesting terroir.*

❺ **Châteauneuf-du-Pape Vieilles Vignes 2004** Domaine de la Janasse (€50) *Made from very old Grenache, this outstanding cuvée offers incredible aromas of fruits and spices. Complex and very long.*

❻ **Vin de Pays des Collines Rhodaniennes Sotanum 2004** Les Vins de Vienne (€30) *Produced in a historic place where the first vineyards of the Rhône Valley were planted 2,000 years ago. An intense and deep Syrah – as good as a Côte Rôtie.*

❼ **Côte Rôtie 2004** Domaine Jamet (€50) *Once again, Jamet has produced one of the most exciting Côte Rôties. A perfect combination of fruit, elegance, and finesse.*

Grapevine

• One of the most renowned names in the Rhône Valley, Jaboulet Aîné has in the past produced some of the most exciting wine in the world. An impressive collection of Hermitage La Chapelle will be remembered by those who had the chance to taste famous vintages such as 1961, 1978, or 1990. It is to be hoped that the Frey family will meet the challenge of bringing the domaine back to the pinnacle of Hermitage wines.

• **The Jean-Michel Cazes family group,** owner of Château Lynch-Bages (Pauillac), Château Cordeillan-Bages (Pauillac), Château Les Ormes de Pez (St-Estèphe), Villa Bel-Air (Graves) in Bordeaux, and L'Ostal Cazes in Languedoc, has now acquired the Domaine des Sénéchaux in Châteauneuf-du-Pape. This 27-ha property has been in the hands of the Roux family since 1993. The wines from the Domaine des Sénéchaux will now be distributed in France and abroad by JM Cazes Sélection.

• **Guigal is extending his empire.** The premier owner and wine merchant in the Rhône Valley has acquired Domaine de Bonserine, which has a vineyard covering 22 ha of Côte Rôtie and 2.4 ha of Condrieu. The domaine will not be broken up and the Bonserine brand will be kept. Winemaker Stéphane Carrel will stay in place.

• **Jean-Louis Chave** believes in St-Joseph. The celebrated wine grower from Mauves, known for his excellent Hermitage, which is one of the most sought-after wines in the world, has planted vines on a large parcel of land in St-Joseph. He is so convinced of the high potential of the best hillside soils of the appellation that he now owns an ideally situated 5 ha of vineyard.

• **The 2007 film** *A Good Year,* directed by Ridley Scott, was made at the Château de la Canorgue and inspired by Peter Mayle's book of the same name. The story is expected to attract visitors to the region.

Jura & Savoie

Wink Lorch

"The good *vignerons* are not suffering. We all need to adopt a positive attitude," commented wine producer Michel Quenard of Chignin in reaction to a rather negative speech from Michel Cartier.

WINK LORCH

Cartier, the president of the Syndicat des Vins de Savoie, was speaking at the annual St-Vincent wine celebration in January 2007, held not, as most years, in a wine village but in the centre of Savoie's main town, Chambéry. In citing the growing crisis in France's wine industry, he berated the town's wine lovers for not drinking enough Savoie wine and urged their support. Savoie accounts for less than 2 per cent of France's wine production and has a ready market in the local ski industry, so theoretically it suffers much less than other wine regions. Yet there are many moans to be heard, mostly from producers I do not feature in this guide. Michel Quenard grasped the point in one. Quality is all, yet it comes at a price, and there is a valid debate as to who is going to pay for it.

Among potential customers for Savoie wines, in particular the local restaurants, there is a growing divide between those who search for the lowest possible price and those who claim that Savoie does not have sufficient numbers of high-priced wines for them to take the region seriously. Both types of restaurant can be found in the ski resorts.

WINK LORCH is a wine writer and educator with a passion for the mountains and a chalet in the Haut-Savoie. In 2007, she launched www.winetravelguides.com – a website for independent wine travellers, initially covering France. She is a past chairman of the Association of Wine Educators and has contributed to several books, including Time-Life's *The Wine Guide* and Le Cordon Bleu's *Wine Essentials*. Wink particularly enjoys enthusing about wines from vineyards in sight of snowcapped mountains, whether the Andes, the Alps, or the Jura. She divides her time between London and the French Alps.

Those catering for package deals in the more downmarket or family resorts seek rock-bottom prices, whereas in France's most fashionable resort, Courchevel 1850, the sales focus on magnums of First Growth clarets to a growing mega-rich foreign clientele (including many Russians) seems to preclude even the best Savoie producers from obtaining multiple listings. Not one Courchevel restaurant lists a series of vintages of Michel Grisard's Domaine Saint-Christophe, although his wines are listed in the top restaurants in the valley towns of Annecy, Thonon, and Chambéry. He plans to launch an offensive to rectify the situation. In an effort to address the problem, *négociant* Jean Perrier (known mainly for its good-value restaurant wines) has invested in advertising in the upmarket *Pure Courchevel* magazine. The company has just launched a new, more expensive Roussette de Savoie, limited to 3,000 bottles, which is listed in one Courchevel restaurant at €95. The Savoie selection in most of the top restaurants is pitiful.

In the Jura, the quality divide is also apparent, with many *vignerons* crying about increased running costs and customers who won't accept price rises. The best *vignerons* once again are bucking the trend. In 2006, Stéphane Tissot launched a new Chardonnay *cuvée* – Clos de la Tour de Curon 2004 – which sold out quickly at a price of €55, almost double that of *vin jaune*. It is produced in small quantities from very low-yielding vines, and Tissot justifies the price because of the extensive work in recreating this steep vineyard. A handful of other Jura *vignerons* are expected to follow suit with their own high-priced selections.

Grapevine

• **British woman Lisa Gilmore** has purchased a majority interest in an 11-ha vineyard in the Chautagne area of Savoie, well known in particular for its Gamay and other red wines. Gilmore, the first British owner of a Savoie vineyard, is in negotiations along with two local *vignerons* to buy a further vineyard of the same size nearby, which will create what for Savoie is a sizable estate.

• **Building of the Savoie Maison du Vin** has started in the village of Apremont, the largest *cru* in Savoie. As well as it being home to the administrative offices, tasting room, and laboratory of the Syndicat des Vins de Savoie, there are plans to

open an *oenothèque* – a shop that will sell wines from all the producers in the region at cellar-door prices.

• **Synthetic corks** are being used for Château-Chalon by Jacques Durand-Perron, current president of the Syndicat des Vins de Château-Chalon. He has changed to plastic corks for his whole range, including Château-Chalon, a wine destined to age for decades. Having tested them on his Chardonnay, he was so convinced by the results and the positive reaction of his customers that he decided to switch all his production, saving him around €1,000 per year compared to cork. Durand-Perron is satisfied that quality will not suffer.

UNCERTAINTY OVER HENRI MAIRE

Rumours and questions surround the future of the Société Henri Maire, *négociant* and the largest owner of vineyard land in the Jura region, with around 300 ha. The company, which celebrated its 60th anniversary in 2006, has purchased fewer grapes over the past few harvests and is rumoured to have difficulties in the market. In April 2007, a new director-general was appointed to take over from Pierre Menez, long-term PDG (president director-general) who has retired. Thirty-seven-year-old Stéphane Zanella comes from a management background with Arthur Andersen and, since 2003, has been general director of the direct sales specialist Club Français du Vin. At the same time, Henri-Michel Maire has retired from active management and has been appointed president of the company. Madame Marie-Christine Tarby-Maire remains as associate director-general, assuring some continuity. However, she is a busy lady, since she is currently not only president of the Comité Interprofessionnel des Vins du Jura but also, since 31 January 2007, president of the French national industry lobby group Vin et Société. In April 2007, she was awarded the prestigious national award of Chevalier de Légion d'Honneur by the French Minister for Agriculture.

PERCÉE DU VIN JAUNE CELEBRATES 10 YEARS

On the first weekend of February 2007, the Jura wine festival was held in bright sunshine in the spa town of Salins-les-Bains, historically famous for its salt production. Celebrating 10 years of existence, the festival has become a fixture for the population of the region of Franche-Comté. One of France's largest wine festivals, with nearly 50,000 visitors, this has become an effective showcase, not just for *vins jaunes*, but for all the local wines and for tourism. Two neighbouring villages in the south of the region, Vincelles and Ste-Agnès, which together have a population of under 750, have agreed to host the next Percée festival on 2–3 February 2008.

SAVOIE *GARAGE* WINES LAUNCHED

Swiss-born wine enthusiast Georges Siegenthaler has created Savoie's first *garage* wines. Produced from vineyards on the almost-abandoned Vens-le-Haut slope in the Seyssel area of Haute-Savoie, they are made in his own garage. Siegenthaler aims to make only top-quality micro-*cuvées* of high-quality wines, primarily Mondeuse reds, some Gamay, and white Molette. By selecting grapes at optimum ripeness, using considerably lower yields than normal in Savoie, and longer extraction in the winery, Siegenthaler hopes to produce a Mondeuse that will appeal to international palates. He is assisted by Geneva-based international winemaker Jean-Michel Novelle. The 1,500 bottles of the 2005 vintage of Domaine Vens-le-Haut Mondeuse sold out before I had a chance to taste one.

Opinion:
Jura labelling continues to confuse

Opinions vary within this tiny wine region as to whether the large range of wine styles offered is a positive advantage or a hindrance. Personally, I applaud the variety if the quality levels are high, but only on condition that the style of wine is clearly shown on the label (back or front). Unfortunately, this condition is rarely fulfilled in the Jura.

The law requires only the appellation to be stated on the label in the case of most Jura wines. It is not even compulsory to state the grape variety; in fact, technically it is not allowed, although the authorities turn a blind eye. The only styles clearly stated are Crémant du Jura, an appellation in its own right, *vin de paille*, and *vin jaune* (and the latter is not stated on AOC Château-Chalon, where the whole world is supposed to understand implicitly that Château-Chalon is always *vin jaune*). Nothing needs to be written to describe the style of red, rosé, and white wines for the main appellations Arbois and Côtes du Jura, which make up the majority of the region's production. The three black grape varieties – Poulsard, Trousseau, and Pinot Noir – may be bottled singly or as a blend – most made as light, early-drinking reds that look more like rosés. An increasing (and positive) trend is to produce more concentrated, longer-lived reds aged in oak. Do they state this on the back label? In most cases, dream on.

For whites, it's worse. Even though there are just two varieties – Chardonnay and Savagnin, sometimes blended – they can be made in an oxidative style or in a so-called burgundian or floral style, or anywhere in between. Add to this an increasing trend to bottle single-terroir wines, or late-harvest wines, not to mention the occasional use of new barrels or *foudres*, and there is confusion. Without explanation from the *vigneron*, we have no idea what the wine will taste like. And here is the rub: for too long the Jura producers have relied on presenting their wines in person to the end user. Surely this can't continue for ever? With falling local sales, they need to expand their horizons. Currently they are targeting Paris, and in the future they might even launch an export initiative. But without clarity on the label, they haven't much chance of success, in my view.

Savoie still not selling itself

Each year the divide grows between the best Savoyard *vignerons*, whose wines impress more each year, and the deep lake of thin, underripe wines turned out by most of the local *négociants* and a large number of small producers, especially from the largest *crus* of Apremont and Abymes. The lack of promotion of the region as a whole, but in particular of its better wines, means that it's really only a sense of adventure that encourages a tourist to try a Savoie wine. If that drinker happens to be in a restaurant in a ski resort, more than likely the wine will be downright uninteresting or, worse, simply bad. It's enough to put them off Savoie wines for life, and they will be missing out. Improved controls are needed to raise the quality at the bottom and middle levels, and better promotion is required so that the good producers have the confidence to demand worthwhile prices. Otherwise, Savoie wines will continue to be categorized by most as, at best, "wines to drink on the ski slopes".

INAO restricts Jura, Savoie, and Bugey

The stalled discussions for changing and updating the national system of appellations has slowed progress for these three little regions. In *Wine Report 2007* I mentioned the request by the Bugey area for the INAO to restrict the use of the term *méthode ancestrale* to the sparkling rosés from Bugey Cerdon VDQS. It has not happened. Nor has the upgrading of Bugey from VDQS to AOC; nor the simplifying of *crus* in Savoie; nor the introduction of the tasting test, the *agrément* at the point of bottling, for *vins jaunes*. All these changes would serve to improve quality and reward the best producers with better prices. Meetings are held and papers written, but so far nothing has happened.

Grapevine

• Jura *négociant* CGVJ (Compagnie des Grands Vins du Jura) is expanding its domaine holdings, mainly to meet demand for sparkling wines. Sales of Crémant du Jura are growing faster than any other Jura wines, and CGVJ is the largest producer, making around 1 million bottles annually, of which 200,000 are exported. The company, which also makes a range of other Jura wines, currently owns 23 ha and buys in from around 230 ha, handling around 13 per cent of total Jura production. At the time of writing, negotiations to buy a nearby domaine had just fallen through, but general manager Paul Espitalié confirmed the intention to continue investing in the area.

• A collection of old Jura vine varieties is being preserved by Caves Jean Bourdy, a wine producer based in Arlay, in conjunction with the Société de Viticulture du Jura. Cuttings of rare varieties retrieved from vineyards all over the region were planted in May 2006. Bourdy is well known for its large collection of old Jura wines going back to the 18th century, and Jean-François Bourdy believes it is important to preserve varieties that were once widely planted but are no longer part of the officially recommended list of grape varieties.

Vintage Report

Advance report on the latest harvest

2006

Jura – "You had to be quick" was the most common refrain after the vintage. Deluges of rain were forecast in early October, and there was a rush to bring in the later varieties. The year had been topsy-turvy. A record-breaking, extremely hot July that at times blocked the grapes' development was followed by a very wet August cool enough to stop ripening. September was warm, with long periods of sunshine that saved what could have been a disastrous vintage. Rot was a problem for some and the harvest small overall, with little potential *vin de paille* made. In general, decent wines have been made by those producers who acted quickly and were selective.

Savoie – After localized hail in early summer, a very hot July, and a very cold, wet August, it was never going to be easy. September was a big improvement, but rain storms hit in late September and early October. Only those producers who really took care in the vineyards and made a rigorous selection at harvest have good wines in the making. Rot of various types was the biggest problem, and for reds there was a level of underripeness, too. Quality is uneven, though the best producers are confident of obtaining reasonable wines, but with quantities lower than average.

Updates on the previous five vintages

Ratings for vin jaune *and* vin de paille *are included in the scores for white wines.*

2005

Vintage rating: *Jura – Red: 90, White: 92; Savoie – Red: 88, White: 85*

Jura – The year gave a normal and healthy growing season, albeit fairly dry and hot. Weather remained good throughout the picking period, which extended into the latter half of October. Acidity was maintained, and this, combined with good concentration and modest yields, has produced successful wines from all varieties. The best wines show the magic combination of good flavours, structure, balance, and length, making them delightful to drink young and good for the long term, too. The vintage has a great future.

Savoie – Overall a good growing season with a few disease problems for the usual culprits, Gamay and Pinot Noir. September and October provided glorious, dry, warm, and sunny weather, good for early and late varieties alike. It was a year when there should be no excuse for bad wines. Most whites from Bergeron (Roussanne) and Altesse grapes did not need any chaptalization and the best show attractive flavours, balance, and length. Mondeuse reds are the real stars: lovely fruit flavours and ripe tannins resulting from better vineyard methods in combination with the weather.

2004

Vintage rating: *Jura – Red: 80, White: 82;*
Savoie – Red: 76, White: 78

Jura – After a wet summer, September was dry and warm. Crop levels were high and selection was essential. Much Crémant du Jura was made from Chardonnay. Savagnins were picked at good sugar and acidity levels, crucial for *vin jaune*. Trousseau was the most successful black variety.

Savoie – Excess quantity was the biggest problem in this year of variable weather, but the grapes were generally healthy. Late varieties did best, and those growers who were selective have produced reasonably concentrated wines. Some good Roussette de Savoie whites were made from Altesse, and the finest producers of Mondeuse did well.

2003

Vintage rating: *Jura – Red: 86, White: 76;*
Savoie – Red: 83, White: 81

Jura – The harvest was very early, and quantities were down 30 per cent. Dealing with low acidity was a big challenge, especially for wines destined for *vin jaune*. Some interesting Savagnin wines have been released, but most Chardonnays will be too soft by 2008. Reds, for once, are actually red in colour and taste of ripe fruit!

Savoie – The hot, dry conditions led to an early harvest of supremely healthy grapes that required careful cellar handling, especially of low acidity levels. Low quantities mean that few wines are still available. However, the best producers made deliciously fruity whites and some structured reds.

2002

Vintage rating: *Jura – Red: 86, White: 90;*
Savoie – Red: 79, White: 77

Jura – Overall, good quality after a fine autumn. Nearly all varieties show both good natural ripeness and high acidity levels, and this bodes well for *vin jaune*. Chardonnays and some Trousseau reds are proving excellent still, with good weight and balance.

Savoie – Good late September weather saved the harvest, following a difficult August. Mondeuse did well in places, with some good results. Whites are mainly drunk.

2001

Vintage rating: *Jura – Red: 65, White: 73;*
Savoie – Red: 60, White: 68

Jura – A difficult, fairly small, and variable vintage. AOC Château-Chalon was declassified, but some decent *vins jaunes* should be released in 2008.
Savoie – Medium-quality vintage, especially difficult for reds.

GREATEST WINE PRODUCERS

Jura
1. Domaine André & Mireille Tissot
2. Jacques Puffeney
3. Domaine Labet Père & Fils
4. Domaine Ganevat
5. Jean Rijckaert
6. Domaine Jacques Tissot

Savoie
1. Domaine Prieuré Saint-Christophe
2. Domaine Dupasquier
3. Domaine Louis Magnin
4. André & Michel Quenard

FASTEST-IMPROVING PRODUCERS

Jura
1. Domaine Pignier
2. Domaine de la Tournelle
3. Domaine de la Renardière
4. Domaine Ligier Père & Fils
5. Château d'Arlay

Savoie
1. Denis & Didier Berthollier
2. Cave du Prieuré
3. Jean-Pierre & Jean-François Quenard
4. Jean-Pierre & Philippe Grisard
5. Domaine Belluard

NEW UP-AND-COMING PRODUCERS

Jura
1. Jean-Marc Brignot
2. Rémi Treuvey
3. Julien Labet
4. Domaine Cybelline

Savoie
1. Gilles Berlioz
2. Domaine St-Germain
3. Bruno Lupin
4. EARL La Gerbelle

BEST-VALUE PRODUCERS

Jura
1. Daniel Dugois
2. Domaine Rolet Père & Fils
3. Domaine Baud Père & Fils
4. Frédéric Lornet

Savoie
1. Domaine de l'Idylle
2. Edmond Jacquin & Fils
3. Pascal & Annick Quenard
4. Domaine Jean Vullien & Fils
5. Jean Perrier (Gilbert Perrier range)
6. Cave de Chautagne

GREATEST-QUALITY WINES

Jura: *1999 is a wonderful, elegant vintage for vins jaunes. The wines will be at their best in 5–10 years. Chardonnays listed are non-oxidative in a style to drink or keep.*

1. **Arbois Vin Jaune 1999** Domaine André & Mireille Tissot (€30)
2. **Château-Chalon 1999** Domaine Berthet-Bondet (€29)
3. **Arbois Chardonnay Les Bruyères 2004** Domaine André & Mireille Tissot (€14.50)
4. **Côtes du Jura Chardonnay Les Chalasses Vieilles Vignes 2004** Domaine Ganevat (€12)
5. **Arbois Trousseau Cuvée Les Berangères 2004** Jacques Puffeney (€11)

Savoie
1. **Vin de Savoie Mondeuse Tradition 2004** Domaine Prieuré Saint-Christophe (€15)
2. **Vin de Savoie Chignin Bergeron Vieilles Vignes 2005** Jean-Pierre & Jean-François Quenard (€8.70)
3. **Vin de Savoie Chignin Bergeron Saint-Anthelme 2005** Denis & Didier Berthollier (€9.95)
4. **Roussette de Savoie 2005** Domaine Louis Magnin (€13)
5. **Vin de Savoie Chignin Bergeron Cuvée Noé Vieilles Vignes 2005** Pascal & Annick Quenard (€11)

BEST BARGAINS

Jura
1. **Crémant du Jura Brut Marcel Cabelier NV** Compagnie des Grands Vins du Jura (€5)
2. **Arbois-Pupillin Les Terrasses (Savagnin) 2005** Domaine de la Renardière (€11)
3. **Côtes du Jura Chardonnay A la Percenette 2005** Domaine Pignier (€11)
4. **Côtes du Jura Chardonnay La Bardette 2004** Domaine Labet Père & Fils (€11)

Savoie
1. **Roussette de Savoie Marestel 2004** Domaine Dupasquier (€8.50)
2. **Vin de Savoie Mondeuse d'Arbin 2005** Domaine Louis Magnin (€7.50)
3. **Roussette de Savoie 2005** Domaine de l'Idylle (€5.60)
4. **Roussette de Savoie Frangy Vieilles Vignes Cuvée du Pépé 2005** Bruno Lupin (€6.50)
5. **Vin de Savoie Mondeuse Le Pied de la Barme 2005** Domaine St-Germain (€7)
6. **Vin de Savoie Jongieux Gamay 2005** Cave du Prieuré (€5.50)

MOST EXCITING OR UNUSUAL FINDS

Jura
1. **Audace Passerillé Rouge 2005** Domaine André & Mireille Tissot (€28 per half-bottle) *At 8 per cent alcohol, this table wine is not allowed vin de paille status, even though the Poulsard grapes were dried on straw for more than six months. One of Stéphane Tissot's many follies, this sweetish red has*

structure behind and plenty of pure red fruit. A dream with vanilla ice cream.

② Côtes du Jura Savagnin Les Vignes de Mon Père 1998
Domaine Ganevat (€20) *From very old vines. The wine was kept in a barrel for eight years, topped up (unlike Savagnin for vin jaune). The result is a honeyed, rich, dry wine with stunning intensity of crystallized fruits and no hint of oxidation.*

③ Arbois L'Uva Arbosiana 2005
Domaine de la Tournelle (€5.50) *L'Uva Arbosiana is the old name for Poulsard. From low-yielding vines, this was made without SO_2, using carbonic maceration and retaining CO_2 to preserve freshness. It is a delicious, light, juicy red, with a touch of tannin.*

④ Château-Chalon 1986 Henri Maire (€35) *This huge négociant and domaine owner has splendid cellars for its vins jaunes and Châteaux-Chalons that stay in barrel for at least 10 years. Currently still available, this vintage Château-Chalon smells of dried figs and has a creamy, curry-spiced palate. Sip with mature Comté cheese and walnuts.*

⑤ Arbois Cuvée Marc 2005
Jean-Marc Brignot (€15) *This new producer bottles his wines without SO_2. He works hard in the vineyard to produce very concentrated wines, reflected in the dark colour of this red from 95 per cent of the pale Poulsard grape and 5 per cent Trousseau. It has great presence and intensity.*

⑥ Arbois Cuvée du 70ème Anniversaire Savagnin 2000
Domaine Rolet Père & Fils (€14) *To celebrate the 70th anniversary of Arbois becoming an AOC, Rolet released two superb cuvées in 2006: a good 2003 Trousseau and this traditional Savagnin. Aged as a vin jaune but for less time, it has a good balance of intense jaune character and acidity.*

Savoie

① Vin de Pays d'Allobrogie Schiste 2005 Domaine des Ardoisières (€13) *From the south-facing organic vineyard that Michel Grisard created near Albertville (see Wine Report 2005) comes this deliciously dry, herbal, and stony blend full of lemon and floral flavours. The basic Savoie white Jacquère grape is blended with 10 per cent Pinot Gris and 10 per cent Roussanne fermented and aged in oak.*

② Vin de Savoie Compostelle Mondeuse 2004 Cave du Prieuré (€12) *From vines situated on one of the pilgrims' routes from Geneva to Santiago de Compostelle, the Barlet brothers matured this Mondeuse in Côte Rôtie barrels. The result is a creamy and ripe Mondeuse that owes more to the New World than most Savoie reds.*

③ Vin de Savoie St-Jeoire Prieuré 2005 EARL La Gerbelle (€3.50) *Brothers André and Guy Quenard are converting their Chignin estate to organic viticulture. Quality is on the up, as proved by this deliciously fresh, dry white Jacquère from a tiny cru at a bargain price.*

④ Vin de Savoie Chautagne Autremont 2004 Jacques Maillet (€10) *Monsieur Maillet is a member of the Chautagne cooperative but chooses to market his wine himself. From old vines farmed biodynamically, this direct, fruity wine is a blend of 40 per cent Gamay, 40 per cent Pinot Noir, and 20 per cent Mondeuse.*

Southwest France

Paul Strang

The Comité Interprofessionnel des Vins du Sud-Ouest is enlarging itself to become the Interprofession of the Appellations d'Origine of the Bassin du Sud-Ouest.

PAUL STRANG

So what, you might ask? Hitherto, the Comité has acted under the handicap that it represented only some of the appellations in the region, not including important ones like Cahors and Irouléguy. Nor did it represent the all-important Gascony *vins de pays*. In the new process, the southwest has been redefined for official purposes as excluding Bergerac, Duras, Marmandais, and Buzet, all of which have been assigned to the *bassin* that includes Bordeaux. But all the AOCs, including the formerly excluded VDQSs, which are soon to disappear as a separate category, and the *vins de pays* of the rest of the southwest, spreading from the mountains of the Massif Central to the Spanish frontier, are now brought together under one organization for the first time. Constitutionally, the point to note is that the new Comité du Bassin will have legally enforceable powers and will not be just a loose voluntary association or talking shop.

The official handout is couched in terms of fuliginous gobbledygook, from which it is all too easy to deduce that this may be just another bit of French bureaucracy. But careful reading of some of the small print reveals some rather alarming ideas – for example, the suggestion that wines refused their *agrément* must be sent for distillation and cannot be

PAUL STRANG is recognized as one of the leading experts on the wines of southern France, where he has had a home for more than 40 years. He is the author of *Wines of Southwest France* (Kyle Cathie, 1994), which was short-listed for the Drink Book of the Year by the Glenfiddich awards. Another book, *Take 5000 Eggs* (Kyle Cathie, 1994), deals with the markets, fêtes, and fairs of southern France and was also short-listed for Glenfiddich in 1997. His latest book is *Languedoc-Roussillon: The Wines and Winemakers* (Mitchell Beazley, 2002).

marketed at all, even as *vins de table*. In recent years, this would have deprived wine lovers of some of the excellent wines of Plageoles, Issaly, and Lescarret in Gaillac (where the tasting committee has some strange ideas about typicity), Meakin in Coteaux du Quercy (where the tasters apparently deplore wines that are too fruity), and Michel Rieuspeyrous in Irouléguy. One wonders whether Michel Issaly, who is himself a member of the Comité, appreciates this?

Perhaps the good news is that the president of the Comité is André Dubosc, the president of Producteurs Plaimont, so we may well see some action and not just talk. The Comité awaits its formal legal recognition and statutory authority but is already working towards a "Southwest France" omnibus logo for all wines produced in the region and hopes that it will be able to use this on labels instead of "Produce of France".

Two steps forward, one back

Denis Dubourdieu dubs it "the Penelope Syndrome". The untimely death of René Renou, former head of the wine committee of INAO, seems to have brought the reform of the appellation system to a grinding halt. Once again, Gaillac's Michel Issaly, secretary-general of the Vignerons-Indépendants, has gone public. He cannot see who is going to take this project by the scruff of the neck, especially with the French elections happening in 2007.

Disagreeable practices

Désagrément is the name given by Michel Rieuspeyrous to his delicious 2004 white, which he cannot call Irouléguy because it was 0.002 g of residual sugar over the limit. Never mind that the margin of error for the analysis of residual sugar is itself give or take 0.5 g! Ludovic Bonnel and Magali Tissot may have to consider calling their excellent red wines from 2003 and 2004 (refused by the Buzet tasters) "Vignes du Pech" instead of selling them as Domaine du Pech AOC. They were told their wines were "insubstantial", but readers can be assured they were anything but that. Bernard Plageoles was denied his *agrément* in Gaillac because his Mauzac tasted too appley (apple being the defining characteristic of the grape variety). David and Sarah Meakin were similarly rejected in Coteaux du Quercy because their wine was "too fruity". Whatever reforms INAO or the new Comité du Bassin introduce, they must look at the way *agréments* are granted or withheld. The current practices are manifestly unjust and absurd.

Opinion:
Goodbye, Mr Chips?

INAO has definitively ruled out the use of oak chips in AOC wines, but maybe it will have to reconsider. While the idea of two levels of AOC is still on the table, perhaps chips will be allowed in the lower grade. The question is of special interest in the southwest of France, because their cause has been taken up by Patrick Ducournau, avant-garde Madiran producer. He was responsible for the invention of micro-oxygenation, among other things. Patrick now has a business, quite separate from his winemaking operation, called Boisé France, with 30 staff and a highly successful track record in making and selling oak chips to those who are legally allowed to use them, principally in the USA, Canada, Chile, Spain, Germany, and Italy. Production runs at the rate of 400 tons a year – enough, on average, to "dose" 800,000 hl of wine.

As a winemaker, Patrick uses the barrel in a masterly fashion. The debate is not about whether wine should be raised in wood, but whether the much more economical oak chip is an acceptable alternative to the cask. For those (and I tend to include myself among them) who are wary about new wood, or those who are totally opposed to it, resistance to the chip is to be expected. Patrick believes that the worst mistake a winemaker can make is to raise in barrel a wine to which it is not suited,

Grapevine

• **Domaine des Savarines,** the long-respected Cahors property, has been sold by Mme Biesbrouk to Rosie Kindersley and Eric Treuille. Kindersley is not only known as a member of the family that has given its name to the publishers of this guide, but to the excellent shop Books for Cooks, which she and Eric run in London's Notting Hill. The family has also opened an organic butcher's shop in northwest London, so, as you might expect, the new vineyard project became totally organic and biodynamic at the end of 2006. The Savarines wine was always good, but with a new *chais* and a general smartening up, great things can be expected.

• **All change** at the Buzet Coopérative. Pascal Lamothe, formerly with Cos d'Estournel in St-Estèphe, has been quietly changing the style of the wines here. There is now an easy, fruity, commercial Cuvée 44, a rather deeper Rocher d'Hillac with soft tannins and good legs that should age quite nicely, and another wine called Renaissance, all at supermarket prices, and none of them oaked. Good value. Let us hope that the Cave will relax its hostile stance to the few independents in the appellation to whom they have given a rough time over the years.

either because of the style of the wine or perhaps the vintage in which it was produced. He notes that less than 5 per cent of the world production of wine is in barrel; his interest is in the other 95 per cent. For these wines, the oak chip is eminently suitable because you can control its measurement and use.

Patrick believes that, if he wishes to sell his wine in the USA, he has to meet the taste of the American consumer, "trained on sugar and carbonic gas from the 150 litres of Coca-Cola he drinks every year; he does not like acidity, aggressiveness, tannins, and bitterness". Sadly, he believes, this will mean that the small independent growers and their wines will become the province of a sort of cultural elite, who will represent a relatively tiny part of the market.

It looks as if the authorities in Brussels and Paris will sanction the general use of oak chips, even in AOCs, quite soon. If this is to happen, the wine drinker must be unambiguously told on the label of the wine how the wine has been aged. *Elevé en fût* is already insufficiently informative (for how long, and in what kind of wood, and how old is it?). It would clearly be misleading to describe in this way a wine raised in steel with oak chips.

Perhaps the strongest objection to the use of chips is that, if a wine oaked with chips is no more expensive (or only marginally so) than a wine raised without any recourse to wood, the production of unoaked wines will gradually disappear. That would be a disaster – rather like being sentenced always to take milk in one's tea or, worse, chicory in one's coffee.

Grapevine

• **The cooperatives in Gascony** are showing some imagination. Plaimont has joined forces with its opposite number Crouseilles in Madiran and a number of independent growers there to prove to the public that Madiran is something they shouldn't be frightened of. The new 1907 Fruit et Passion represents a very substantial investment in a wine that, although based on Tannat and given just a touch of oak, is drinkable immediately on its fruit. There is virtually no acidity or tannin, so any resemblance to true Madiran is coincidental. Will it sell well?

• **Perhaps Alain Brumont** took his eye off the ball in 2002. His Montus Prestige of that year, which sells at about €30, didn't do nearly as well in an authoritative French tasting as his Bouscassé Vieilles Vignes, which, however, sells at nearly €40. Didier Barré's Charles de Batz from his Domaine Berthoumieu was well up there with them at a quarter of the price. Brumont really ought to be a bit more realistic, especially since his "cheapie", Torus, got a pasting from the same team (to my mind undeservedly).

Vintage Report

Advance report on the latest harvest
2006

The winter was long and cold with heavy rainfall and some snow in the east. Spring was wet, but the weather changed at the end of April. May was fine except for sporadic and sometimes violent storms, promoting some mildew. June and July were hot, and the threat of hydric stress was averted only by a sudden change in the weather in August, which was changeable, with rain at times. September started fine and warm, but the weather broke, especially in the west, just before the equinox. Some growers had already picked their early-maturing white grapes and the wines from these will be good. Others delayed, and the black grapes, particularly Merlot, will prove patchy. October was fine and warm, and Malbec and Tannat were picked in good conditions. In the east, Entraygues and Estaing had no rain after Easter, but in nearby Marcillac there was plenty and the harvest was late and difficult. In St-Mont there were bad hailstorms and a quarter of the crop was lost. Gros Manseng will have done well if picked in October, but the weather was changeable for Petit Manseng in Jurançon. Rot was a problem virtually everywhere, and rigorous selection at the sorting table will determine quality for many. Clearly there will be some good wines, but many growers will be cursing their timing. Production was roughly the same volume as 2005.

Updates on the previous five vintages
2005

Vintage rating: *Red: 93; Dry white: 90;*
Sweet white: Monbazillac, Saussignac, and Gaillac 90, otherwise 87
Drought between Easter and vintage time was sandwiched between a wet winter and a changeable autumn, but the vintage mostly took place in good conditions, once September storms and floods had receded. The continued drought, without the excessive heat suffered in 2003, gave excellent fruit, and most growers were more than pleased. Exceptionally, there were devastating hailstorms in microregions, especially in Bergerac, and rain in November prevented repetition of the fabulous success of Jurançon in the previous year. Production was down slightly on 2004.

2004

Vintage rating: *Red: 88, Dry white: 85,*
Sweet white: 86 (93 in Jurançon)
Warm and dry weather throughout the growing cycle persisted until August, when damp, humid weather made control of rot difficult. However, the crop turned out healthy and abundant. The whites show some acidity and lack of fruit and could be drunk up now; the reds were more satisfactory and could be at their best in 2008/09. Jurançon was the great success of the year; both the dry and sweet wines can be kept for a long time.

2003

Vintage rating: *Red and dry white east: 68, further west: 85,*
Sweet white: 92
This was the notorious heat-wave year, in which the southwest suffered worse than any other region. Drought was compounded by extraordinarily hot sun, which grilled the fruit on the vines. Early-picking reds were disappointing, lacking acidity and phenolic development but rich in ripe fruit, which will call for early drinking; some growers voluntarily declassified their wines. Later pickers, particularly in the hills of the east of the region and in Madiran and Irouléguy, did much better, profiting from mid-September rain. A splendid autumn yielded magnificent sweet wines throughout, although the acidity indispensable in Jurançon was often lacking.

2002

Vintage rating: *Red and white Cahors and westwards: 85,*
eastwards: 75, Sweet white: 89
The further west, the better the wines – a sudden burst of late sunshine in September producing a rise in sugar levels west of the A20, sometimes causing almost welcome problems. Fronton, Gaillac, and Marcillac never really recovered from a cool midsummer, though all areas made above-average sweet wines.

2001

Vintage rating: *Red: 90, Dry white: 85, Sweet white: 88*
An excellent year, now proving even better than expected, especially where growers were able to guard against low acidity and high sugar levels. The wines seem to be keeping better than at first thought, too. Still at their peak, though the sweet whites will continue to improve.

GREATEST WINE PRODUCERS

1. Domaine Robert & Bernard Plageoles (Gaillac)
2. Clos de Gamot (Gaillac)
3. La Tour des Gendres (Bergerac)
4. Château Tirecul La Gravière (Monbazillac)
5. Domaine Ametzia (Irouléguy)
6. Les Jardins de Babylone (Jurançon)
7. Elian da Ros (Marmandais)
8. Château du Cèdre (Cahors)
9. Domaine Capmartin (Madiran)
10. Domaine Cosse-Maisonneuve (Cahors)

FASTEST-IMPROVING PRODUCERS

1. Château Lestévenie (Bergerac/ Saussignac)
2. Domaine Vignau La Juscle (Jurançon)
3. Domaine du Grand Jaure (Pécharmant & Rosette)
4. Château Montdoyen (Monbazillac)
5. Domaine Jonc Blanc (Montravel)
6. Domaine du Mioula (Marcillac)
7. Château de Saurs (Gaillac)
8. Château d'Arlus (Gaillac)
9. Clos d'Yvigne (Saussignac)
10. Château Les Fontanelles (Bergerac)

NEW UP-AND-COMING PRODUCERS

1. Domaine du Vieux Noyer (Côtes de Millau VDQS)
2. Domaine Chator (Côtes de Duras)
3. Domaine de Cabarrouy (Jurançon & Jurançon Sec)
4. Clos Basté (Madiran)
5. Domaine Bordathio (Irouléguy)
6. Château Laurou (Fronton)
7. Château de Rhodes (Gaillac)
8. Clos d'un Jour (Cahors)
9. Château Famaey (Cahors)
10. Domaine des Savarines (Cahors)

BEST-VALUE PRODUCERS

1. Domaine d'Escausses (Gaillac)
2. Château Plaisance (Fronton)
3. Domaine de la Chanade (Gaillac)
4. Château Barréjat (Madiran)
5. Domaine Ametzia (Irouléguy)
6. Domaine Labranche-Laffont (Madiran)
7. Château Latuc (Cahors)
8. Domaine Bordenave (Jurançon)
9. Domaine San de Guilhem (Côtes de Gascogne)
10. Domaine de Lancement (Vin de Pays de Thézac-Perricard)

GREATEST-QUALITY WINES

1. **Monbazillac Cuvée Madame 1997** Château Tirecul La Gravière (€50)
2. **Madiran 1990** Château Montus (€25)
3. **Cahors 2001 Clos Saint Jean** Clos de Gamot (€20)
4. **Vin de Table Vin d'Autan 2005** Domaine Robert & Bernard Plageoles (€35)
5. **Cahors Cuvée Prestige 2000** Château du Cèdre (€12)
6. **Montravel Rouge 2003** Château Puy-Servain Songe (€18)
7. **Jurançon 2005** Les Jardins de Babylone (€45)
8. **Saussignac Cuvée Noble 2003** Château Richard (€15)
9. **Madiran 1995** Château d'Aydie (€18)
10. **Vin de Table Désagrément 2004** Domaine Arretxea (Rieuspeyrous's declassified white) (€12)

BEST BARGAINS

① **Fronton 2004** Domaine Caze Patrimoine (€6)

② **Bergerac 2004** Clos des Verdots (€5)

③ **Gaillac Blanc Mauzac 2005** Château d'Arlus (€4)

④ **VDQS Entraygues-et-le-Fel Rouge 2004** Domaine Laurent Mousset (€4)

⑤ **Irouléguy Blanc 2005** Vignerons d'Irouléguy Xuri Ansa (€8)

⑥ **Vin de Pays des Côtes de Gascogne Blanc 2006** Château Millet (€4)

⑦ **Bergerac Rouge Tradition 2005** Domaine de l'Ancienne Cure (€5)

⑧ **Marmandais 2002** Château de Beaulieu (€7)

⑨ **VDQS Entraygues-et-le-Fel 2005** Domaine Méjanasserre (€4)

⑩ **VDQS Côtes de St Mont Le Faîte Blanc 2005** Producteurs Plaimont (€8)

MOST EXCITING OR UNUSUAL FINDS

① **Vin de Table Verdanel 2005** Domaine Robert & Bernard Plageoles (€7) *Probably the only wine to be made from this grape in modern times.*

② **Rosette 2005** Château Romain (Colette Bourgès) (€5) *This tiny subappellation of Bergerac is declared by only six or so growers.*

③ **Cahors Pigmentum 2004** Georges Vigouroux (€6) *An all-Malbec Cahors for early drinking. One of the rare wines of this style to preserve the real Cahors character.*

④ **Irouléguy 2004** Domaine Bordathio (€9) *A newcomer to the appellation who is making eccentrically different wines from those of his colleagues but with a notably Basque accent.*

⑤ **VDQS Tursan Blanc 2004** Château de Perchade (€5) *Michel Guérard is the only other independent grower declaring in this appellation. This artisanal property can more than hold its own and is much more exciting than the cooperative. Mainly from the Baroque grape, peculiar to this appellation.*

⑥ **Jurançon Magendia 2003** Clos Lapeyre (Larrieu) (€12) *The grapes are left out in the sun for passerillage and brought indoors if there is a threat of rain. A hand-crafted, not in the least sticky wine of beautiful balance.*

⑦ **Montravel Blanc 2005** Château de la Mallavieille (Biau) (€6) *Notable for being aged in acacia barrels, which give the wine a characteristic flowery flavour on the palate.*

⑧ **Côtes de Bergerac Le Vin 2003** Clos des Verdots (€15) *A 100 per cent Muscadelle raised in barrel. From David Fourtout's top range.*

⑨ **VDQS Côtes de St Mont La Faîte 2004** Producteurs Plaimont (€8) *The Cave's flagship white from Gros Manseng, Petit Courbu, and Aruffiac, fermented and raised in barrel.*

⑩ **Gaillac Ondenc 2006** Domaine de Causse-Marines (€10) *Patrice Lescarret's latest eccentricity from this rare grape, of which Plageoles is the only other grower.*

Languedoc-Roussillon

Paul Strang

There is little doubt that one consequence of the "crisis" in the French wine industry will be the wholesale digging up of vast areas of vines in the Languedoc.

PAUL STRANG

Once the machinery starts to roll in Brussels, there will be no stopping it. But how many people have thought about what will happen to the swathes of countryside – 400,000 ha – affected? The worst scenario could mean that one-third of the Languedoc vineyard will disappear in the very near future, even though this may not by itself cure the problem of overproduction. What is certain is that the culture, the landscape, and the character of the area will be profoundly changed. Will this vast set-aside revert to scrub, as it already has in parts of the Hautes-Corbières, or will it perhaps be replaced by a concrete jungle of holiday flats?

Some have suggested that the vine could be replaced by the olive. They forget that the olive plantations in Languedoc can easily be wiped out by frosts, as they were in 1956: the olive tree will not survive temperatures below −6°C. Furthermore, the industrialization of olive production is likely to result in the same impoverishment of the soil caused by former massive overuse of fertilizers and insecticides. In any case, there are some areas where nothing but the vine will grow. If the production of wine is to be suspended there, how can the inhabitants make a living from the plant: verjuice, beauty products? You must be joking.

PAUL STRANG is recognized as one of the leading experts on the wines of southern France, where he has had a home for more than 40 years. He is the author of *Wines of Southwest France* (Kyle Cathie, 1994), which was short-listed for the Drink Book of the Year by the Glenfiddich awards. Another book, *Take 5000 Eggs* (Kyle Cathie, 1994), deals with the markets, fêtes, and fairs of southern France and was also short-listed for Glenfiddich in 1997. His latest book is *Languedoc-Roussillon: The Wines and Winemakers* (Mitchell Beazley, 2002).

The economists in Brussels and Paris seem to have given no thought to the consequences of their decisions. It is time that the prefectures of southern France did. Of the region's inhabitants, 80 per cent live in the big towns or along the coast. The *vignerons* are thus in a small minority. Perhaps an application to UNESCO for designation as a World Heritage site – as in St-Emilion, for example – might seem a bit over the top, but local activists must force their politicians to face up to the future. At present there is only a sense of resignation, a negative apathy about a problem that might just go away. It won't. We have already seen massive protests in the Midi. Unless sensible plans for redevelopment of the vineyards under threat are made, there is bound to be more and greater trouble.

The march of marketing

In 2008, the first wines of the 2006 vintage of the new AOC Languedoc label will come on-stream, provided French bureaucracy has processed the necessary paperwork during 2007. For Jean-Benoît Cavalier, president of the Syndicat des Crus des Coteaux du Languedoc and one of the most ardent promoters of this new regional appellation, "this will be an *appellation de référence*, with a style entirely characteristic of Languedoc, allowing the establishment of a true hierarchy, and to relaunch the inner appellations, which are on the way to being marginalized in Languedoc-Roussillon". The statutes of the new appellation will be based on the existing ones for the Coteaux, but problems remain. Will the wines of La Voulte-Gasparets, for example, call themselves "AOC Languedoc Corbières Cru Boutenac"? If so, is this any easier for the consumer than the old Corbières AOC? And if Cavalier is right in highlighting the marginalization of the inner appellations, is this not really due to the huge improvement in the quality and quantity of the *vins de pays* being produced alongside the AOC wines, rather than a need for complex hierarchies that cut right across the consumer demand for simplified marketing for French wines?

Grapevine

• **Philippe Maurel** (from the family that owns Domaine Maurel-Fonsalade in St-Chinian) leaves the dynamic Languedoc *négoce* business Maurel-Védeau, which deals in both varietals and top-of-the-range wines. Following "a divergence of view", he has made over his shares in the business, founded in 1992 by Stéphane Vedeau, to the powerful and little-known family Bonfils, the largest private grower in Languedoc-Roussillon, with 850 ha.

Return of the Black Death?

Bernard Mollot, a research scientist at the University of Nîmes, claims to have discovered the cause of a nasty disease called Black Dead Arm. First identified in 1999, this is a fungus disease that attacks the vine when it is pruned, not just in winter, but whenever the plant is pruned throughout the year – for example, when surplus young shoots are removed in the spring (*épamprage*). Mollot claims that it is this mid-cycle pruning, especially when done by tractor, that brings about the onset of Black Dead Arm.

Promotion for Côtes de Malepère

At the same time as approving the new AOC Languedoc, INAO has promoted Côtes de Malepère from VDQS to AOC status, with effect from the 2006 vintage. Reflecting the influence of Atlantic weather, the accent is on Bordeaux grape varieties. It seems that Grenache and Cinsault will be limited to the rosés; are they perhaps destined to disappear completely from the Côtes?

Grapevine

• **The ambitious Gérard Bertrand** has expanded his interests in the Languedoc and now has 270 ha of vines of his own, as well as a substantial business as a *négociant*. He has launched a range of wines from Tautavel, just over the border in Roussillon. Four cooperatives have been contracted for a minimum of 10 years, representing 85 per cent of their Tautavel production. With names like Tautavel Sang et Or, Tautavel Réserve, Tautavel Châteaux and Domaines, and Icône, prices range from €4.50 to €25. He is working on a commercialization of 4,000 hl, rising to 10,000 between 2010 and 2015. As well as being known for its terroir and as one of the villages in Côtes du Roussillon entitled to tack its name on to the end of the appellation, Tautavel is famous for the discovery in 1971 of *Homo erectus tautavelensis*, who lived 450,000 years ago, one of the first manifestations of European man.

• **Some quality growers** are getting their marketing act together. VIP des Vignes (mischievously de-acronymed as "Venez Immédiament Picoler"), which is headed by well-known figures such as Jean-François Izarn of Borie-la-Vitarèle, Jean Gardiès in Roussillon, and Luc Lapeyre in Minervois, is a new marketing grouping. Those involved aim to use communal presentation to increase their impact at trade shows such as Vinisud and the Paris salons, making direct contact with professionals and consumers alike. Not only is it cheaper for growers to show their wines together, but a stand with several exhibitors on it causes much more buzz than a solo performer at a diminutive table.

• **Drama at Château Cazeneuve** in Pic-St-Loup. Owner André Léenhardt reports that the whole of his stock of Sang de Calvaire 2003, worth about €75,000, was stolen from his cellars. Since the wine had scarcely been sold on the market, any bottles on sale would almost certainly be stolen. Members of the Wine Society need not worry. The wine the Society offers is from the 2004 vintage, and "clean".

Opinion:

Collaborating on a new brand

Watch the consequences of the launch at Vinisud 2006 of the new brand "Sud de France South of France", the direct result of the merger of the promoting authorities of Languedoc, the Vins de Pays, and Roussillon. This coming together of hitherto disparate forces, often at each other's throats, is much to be welcomed, but they will need to improve the quality of the basic wines of the region if the new system is not to be seen as a dumbing down of the whole of the Midi. Despite a budget of €15 million, the promoters will also have to overcome a great deal of typical French individualism to develop the necessary collaborative spirit to make the scheme work.

The launch of the new brand coincides with the implementation of the new system of Comités de Bassin Viticoles, under which France has been divided into areas, each of which will have considerable powers to govern the way the wine trade is carried on. Languedoc-Roussillon is one of the areas, and it has been given some autonomous powers to deal locally with the future of the region. However, in March 2006, a report commissioned by the French government was produced by one Bernard Pomel, who had been asked to prepare a plan for the coordination of these *comités* with a view to rebuilding the French wine industry. There will no doubt be a tendency among producers, especially the smaller ones, to say, "This won't apply to me," and to ignore it. That, however, will not be possible because, although it delegates specifics largely to the local *comités*, it contains statements of principle and central policy that are in some respects more worrying for Languedoc-Roussillon than some other areas of France.

Languedoc-Roussillon owes its recent renaissance, at least outside France, to its successful shedding of its reputation as a producer of plonk. This was initiated by a handful of far-sighted growers who demonstrated that the area was capable of producing wines of a quality that could compare with the best of wines from other parts of France. Today there are more than a thousand growers in the region producing, ageing, bottling, and marketing their own wines. In the wake of the pioneers came the brands and the expansion of sales to and by *négociants*. It would be an oversimplification to say that this has resulted in a polarization of quality, but it is broadly true that the independents represent the production of quality terroir-driven wines, whereas the brands are more often technique-led and bland but, because of their greater market pull, are capable of reaching the supermarket shelves denied to the artisan-growers. The reputation of Languedoc rests largely with the independents, though its commercial success lies with the business interests.

The problem with the Pomel report is that it will tend to increase the rate and extent of this polarization. The terroir producer believes the nature and style of the wine, provided there is technical competence in the *chais*, are pre-ordained in the vineyard. However, Pomel says, "The best product [sic] is not that which pleases the producer most. It is that which satisfies consumers the most." Of course, growers who cannot sell their wine will go out of business, but the implication is clear: demand, created by the marketing industry, is to be driven by Carrefour, Tesco, and Wal-Mart.

Pomel goes on to say: "There will always be those who love products of exceptional quality, whose personality, linked to a prestigious terroir, has been fixed for ever and in the wide recognition of a type of taste. But response is also imperative to the expectation of the consumers, most of whom want wines that are more fruity, supple, less acid, less alcoholized, and that will give them pleasure to drink."

This condescending sneer at quality, the implied preference for the bulk product, and the suggestion that what is good is elitist may prove the biggest headache for the Comité de Bassin de Languedoc-Roussillon if it is to avoid acquiring the "plonk" image again. It must support those who are producing good rather than globalized wine. The crisis in the French wine industry has arisen more because of the collapse of France's own internal wine consumption, and this market is not going to be recovered by flooding the market with international-style wines that the French, on the whole, don't like. To quote a Pomel statistic, wines from the New World represent less than 0.2 of 1 per cent of wines on French supermarket shelves.

Grapevine

• **Minervois Noble,** a movement making white Minervois in a different style, is still not officially recognized, but 20 or so growers are making it. Château Coupe Rose makes a wine in a dry *rancio* style after the Banyuls fashion; La Tour Boisée has a 100 per cent Marsanne version, combining notes of "dried flowers, quince butter, dried apricot, rhubarb, camomile, and saffron", according to one taster. Other versions come from Domaine Pique-Perlou (charred aromas with walnut husks) and Domaine Vordy-Mayranne, the quince and pear flavours going well with Cantal cheese.

• **Madame Soria,** considered by some to be the finest Languedoc producer of all, has suffered a serious blow. Her red wines demand three years' bottle-ageing before being marketed, but a sharp decline in the quality of her storage barrels has persuaded Marianne not to bottle her red 1999, 2000, and 2001. She is pursuing her *tonnelier*, whom she considers responsible. The good news is that her Syrah Leone and Clos des Cistes from 2002 onwards are once again back on the market.

Vintage Report

Advance report on the latest harvest

2006

The winter season 2005/06 was very wet to begin with and, from the new year onwards, cold until Easter. This allowed for good water levels, but budburst was delayed. The spring was dry and windy, with alternating bursts of warm and cool weather. Flowering was more or less on time, from the end of May through early June, with good fruit set. Midsummer saw a slowing down, particularly in the higher regions, because of drought and/or lower-than-usual heat. Mid-August onwards saw the return of showery weather, resulting in average volumes from smaller fruit. The vintage is characterized by high sugar levels, lower-than-usual acidity, and balanced pH. Likely to be an adequate rather than a great year.

Updates on the previous five vintages

2005

Vintage rating: Red: 88, White: 90

Almost a great year. A wet winter and late spring were followed by a good but not excessively hot summer, punctuated with convenient storms. Violent rain just before vintage time meant that this was yet another year when Grenache, Carignan, and Cinsault did rather better on the whole than the *améliorateurs*. An Indian summer ensured ripe fruit, especially from these varieties, with good balance and phenolic development. Excellent year for white wines. Quantities down everywhere.

2004

Vintage rating: Red: 90, White: 88

For most growers, a sigh of relief after the torrid heat of 2003. The wines are showing excellent balance, good but not too sugary fruit, and better acidity and riper tannins than the earlier year. The later-harvested Grenache and Mourvèdre were particularly successful. Some rot where the drying Tramontane wind failed to blow. Production levels were noticeably up. A vintage for drinking in 2008.

2003

Vintage rating: *Red: 78, White: 80*

The notorious hot year lives up to forecasts of wines rich in fruit and the best ready for early drinking. Acidity is weak except in some late-picked wines, and the tannins are sometimes stalky. This was a year that showed off the benefits of *assemblage* over varietals. High alcohol levels everywhere, sometimes too high, as in the Minervois. The whites were more successful than the reds, though Pic-St-Loup and Terrasses du Larzac did well because of the cooler nights. Production well down on 2002. Mostly for drinking now.

2002

Vintage rating: *Red: 83, White: 80 (60 for both in the flooded areas of eastern Languedoc)*

Much better than first expected. The style is generally more delicate than either surrounding year, with finesse and elegance even from producers noted for their macho tendencies. The best wines benefited from the Indian summer in Roussillon, Aniane, and Montpeyroux. The wines, bar the greats, need drinking.

2001

Vintage rating: *Red: 92, White: 92*

A heat-wave summer produced very ripe fruit, good sugar levels, and plenty of natural concentration. The quantity was down on 2000. The best year since the legendary 1998. Most whites will need drinking, but the reds will still keep a year or two – the best, longer.

GREATEST WINE PRODUCERS

1. Domaine Gauby (Calce, Roussillon)
2. Domaine Peyre-Rose (Pézenas)
3. Roc d'Anglade (Vin de Pays du Gard)
4. Domaine Alain Chabanon (Montpeyroux)
5. René Rostang (Sommières, Languedoc)
6. Domaine Ferrer-Ribière (Terrats, Roussillon)
7. Domaine Virgile Joly (Terrasses de Larzac)
8. Clos de Gravillas (St-Jean-de-Minervois)
9. Clot de l'Oum (Roussillon)
10. La Grange des Pères (Vin de Pays de l'Hérault)

FASTEST-IMPROVING PRODUCERS

1. Mas de l'Ecriture (Montpeyroux)
2. Domaine Padié (Calce, Roussillon)
3. Jean-Baptiste Sénat (Minervois)
4. Domaine Maria Fita (Fitou)
5. Terres Falmet (St-Chinian)
6. Mas Cal Demoura (Montpeyroux)
7. Château de Valflaunès (Pic-St-Loup)
8. Domaine des Grécaux (Montpeyroux)
9. Domaine de Montcalmès (Terrasses du Larzac)
10. Domaine Massamier-la-Mignarde (Minervois)

NEW UP-AND-COMING PRODUCERS

1. Cave Coopérative de Cascastel (Corbières/Fitou)
2. Domaine Boisantin (Montpeyroux)
3. Les Terrasses d'Elise (Terrasses du Larzac)
4. Mas Brunet (Terrasses du Larzac)
5. Domaine Arnal (Sommières, Languedoc)
6. Domaine La Balmière (Latour-de-France, Roussillon)
7. Domaine Mouscaillo (Limoux)
8. Mas de la Devèze (Tautavel, Roussillon)
9. Domaine d'Anglas (Montpeyroux)
10. Château Montel (Grès de Montpellier)

BEST-VALUE PRODUCERS

1. Pierre Clavel (Grès de Montpellier)
2. Domaine Ellul-Ferrières (Grès de Montpellier)
3. Domaine des Carmes (St-Chinian)
4. Domaine Matassa (Calce, Roussillon)
5. Mas d'Auzières (Grès de Montpellier)
6. Mas de Bressades (Costières de Nîmes)
7. Château de l'Euzière (Pic-St-Loup)
8. Domaine de Barroubio (St-Jean-de-Minervois)
9. Mas de la Seranne (Aniane, Terrasses du Larzac)
10. Domaine Coston (Terrasses du Larzac)

GREATEST-QUALITY WINES

1. **Côtes du Roussillon Muntada 2004** Domaine Gauby (€50)
2. **Vin de Pays du Gard 2004** Roc d'Anglade (€14)
3. **Coteaux du Languedoc Clos les Cistes 1994** Domaine Peyre-Rose (€30)
4. **Coteaux du Languedoc L'Esprit de Font-Caude 2001** Domaine Font-Caude (now Domaine Alain Chabanon) (€22)
5. **Vin de Pays des Côtes Catalanes Le Soula Blanc 2004** Domaine Gauby (€20)
6. **Vin de Pays de l'Hérault Blanc 2003** La Grange des Pères (€20)
7. **Côtes du Roussillon Villages Vieilles Vignes 2002** Domaine Le Roc des Anges (€15)
8. **Vin de Pays des Côtes de Thongue Cuvée Elie 1997** Domaine Les Chemins de Bassac (€12)
9. **Vin de Pays des Côtes Catalanes Blanc 2003** Domaine Padié Milousie (€25)
10. **Limoux Terroir Haute-Vallée Clocher de Conhilhac 1995** Les Sieurs d'Arques (€20)

BEST BARGAINS

Here, and in the "Most exciting" list, I am concentrating on attractive, relatively early-drinking wines, rather than blockbusting vins de dégustation.

1. **Coteaux du Languedoc Campredon 2005** Domaine Alain Chabanon (€8)
2. **Coteaux du Languedoc Terrasses du Larzac Clos du Prieur Rouge 2005** Domaine de l'Hortus (€8)
3. **Faugères Rouge Tradition 2004** Domaine du Météore (€4)
4. **Minervois Rouge Tradition 2004** Domaine Malys-Anne (€5)
5. **Costières de Nîmes Rouge Vieilles Vignes 2004** Domaine du Vieux Relais (€7)
6. **Coteaux du Languedoc Montpeyroux Rouge Tradition 2005** Domaine d'Anglas (€6)
7. **Corbières Blanc Vieilles Vignes 2005** Domaine Roque-Sestières (€7)
8. **Roussillon Rouge Tradition 2005** Domaine des Schistes (€6)

⑨ Coteaux du Languedoc Pic-St-Loup Rouge Tradition 2004 Domaine de Lavabre (€6)

⑩ Vin de Pays de Mont Baudile Le Carignan de Familongue 2004 Domaine de Familongue (€6)

MOST EXCITING OR UNUSUAL FINDS

① Vin de Pays de l'Hérault Les Pampres 2005 Clos Laval (€7.50) *A wine from a newly emerged Aniane grower for drinking young, but it has style and backbone.*

② Vin de Pays de l'Hérault Le Cas 2004 Mas Conscience (€10) *A broad and fleshy Carignan wine from the former owners of Mas d'Auzières.*

③ Vin de Pays du Torgan Le Méconnu Blanc 2005 Domaine Bertrand-Bergé (€7) *A first essay in white wine from this top Fitou grower. White Fitou does not exist as such.*

④ Vin de Pays d'Oc Viognier Elevé sous Voile 1998 Les Vignerons de St-Gély (€30 per 50-cl bottle) *An interesting essay in making a sherry-like vin de voile from this unlikely grape.*

⑤ Vin de Pays des Coteaux de Miramont Rouge 2005 Guido Jansegers (€8) *The owner of Château Mansenoble in Corbières is not above making a wine for drinking on its fruit.*

⑥ Minervois Cuvée Potère 2003 Domaine Entretan (€8) *Something of a cult property. This is aged for a year in wood and has an amazing cassis character.*

⑦ Vin de Pays d'Oc Les Oliviers 2005 Jean-Louis Denois (€6) *A Marsanne/Chardonnay blend from this master winemaker, with an intense floral and exotic character.*

⑧ Coteaux du Languedoc Emotion Occitane 2004 Mas de l'Ecriture (€12) *A lively, powerful wine, more than just a summer quaffer. A combination of raspberries and garrigue flavours on silky tannins is irresistible.*

⑨ Vin de Pays de l'Hérault L'Etincelle Blanc 2005 Mas Cal Demoura (€14) *The Gaumard family, which has taken over from Olivier Jullien's father, is making wines fully up to the standard of the property.*

⑩ Costières de Nîmes Compostelle Rosé 2006 Château Mas Neuf (€8) *Seductively aromatic, plenty of substance on the palate, and delicious hints of red summer fruits. Irresistible even for those who turn up their noses at pink wines.*

Grapevine

• The combative but brilliant Jean-Louis Denois has forged new links with the Grier family in South Africa. Denois took Old World know-how to Grier, which resulted in a bottle-fermented sparkling wine that has had great success south of the equator. Denois has identified an opportunity in Roussillon where Grier can return the favour. The project involves the purchase of a 22-ha vineyard planted with Syrah, Grenache, and Carignan in the Agly Valley, just 5 km (3 miles) from St-Paul de Fenouillet. An old cellar in the village has been purchased, and a period of experimentation and evaluation will determine the final direction of the project. Denois's track record suggests a bright future.

Vins de Pays
& Vins de Table

Rosemary George MW

At long last, after what seemed like endless discussion, two brand-new *vins de pays* were recognized for the 2006 vintage.

ROSEMARY GEORGE MW

The first is Vin de Pays de l'Atlantique, which covers the *départements* of Charente, Charente-Maritime, Dordogne, Gironde, and the northwestern part of Lot-et-Garonne. The Pyrénées-Atlantiques and Landes, which were originally considered to be part of this new *vin de pays*, have been excluded because they fit more comfortably into Vin de Pays du Comté Tolosan. The significant name in the list is the Gironde. *Départementale vins de pays* already exist for the others, but with the creation of Vin de Pays de l'Atlantique, the beleaguered producers of Bordeaux, who are having problems selling their wine as claret, will now be able to sell it as Cabernet Sauvignon and/or Merlot, and even add a third grape variety to the label. With the worldwide consumer recognition of grape varieties rather than regions, there is optimism that this may help many of the Bordelais producers who are facing possible bankruptcy. It is the *négociants* who are most likely to benefit initially, since they will have more freedom to blend grape varieties and areas and thus the capacity to create bigger-volume brands for the international market.

ROSEMARY GEORGE MW was lured into the wine trade by a glass of the Wine Society's champagne at a job interview. Realizing that secretarial work was not for her, she took the wine-trade exams, becoming one of the first women to qualify as a Master of Wine in 1979. She has been a freelance wine writer since 1981 and is the author of nine books, including *Chablis* (Sotheby Publications, 1984), *French Country Wines* (Faber & Faber, 1990), *The Wines of New Zealand* (Faber & Faber, 1996), and *The Wines of the South of France* (Faber & Faber, 2001). Her most recent book, *Walking Through the Vineyards of Tuscany* (Bantam Press), was published in 2004, and a new book on Chablis is in the pipeline.

The objective is an easier-to-drink, more accessible wine than the average claret, and the authorities are adamant that it will not be a dumping ground for undrinkable wine but a new wine with its own identity.

The permitted grape varieties are not uniform throughout the area, so there are many possible permutations of flavour. Pinot Noir is allowed in the Charente but nowhere else; Syrah features only in Lot-et-Garonne; Carmenère only in the Gironde; and Gamay is allowed everywhere except the Gironde. In line with modern winemaking techniques, oak chips are allowed, of a size no smaller than 2 mm.

The second is Vin de Pays des Gaules, which covers the 95 Beaujolais villages and not the larger area that was originally envisaged. The permitted grape varieties are those of Burgundy, namely Pinot Noir, Chardonnay, Gamay, and Aligoté, as well as the two varieties of the northern Rhône: Syrah and Viognier. You could well ask what will make it different from Beaujolais. First, given Beaujolais's attachment to *vin nouveau* or *vin de primeur*, no *primeur* wine can be sold as Vin de Pays de Gaules, for fear of perturbing the economics of Beaujolais Nouveau. Instead, a minimum *élevage* of three months in the cellar is mandatory. It will also allow a Beaujolais producer to experiment with Syrah – currently there is only about 1 ha within the confines of Beaujolais – and also with Viognier. Methods in both vineyard and cellar will be much less restrictive than for the appellation. Growers in southern Beaujolais, where the soil is more suited to white grapes, could be encouraged to plant Viognier, and Gamay could be vinified in a different manner from Beaujolais. Certainly Michel Deflache, director of Inter Beaujolais Union, is full of optimism that this new *vin de pays* will give the region a welcome flexibility.

Vin de Pays d'Oc continues to progress. It accounts for 16 per cent of all French exports and 79 per cent of all varietal *vins de pays*, with Cabernet Sauvignon, Cinsault for rosé wines, Sauvignon Blanc, and Chardonnay accounting for 87 per cent of the total production of Vins de Pays d'Oc, which leaves two dozen or so grape varieties somewhat standing in the shadows. The last council meeting of the Vin de Pays d'Oc put forward a proposal for what they called segmentation of the Vins de Pays d'Oc, to create three levels of quality: entry-level wines; a category of wines that would be labelled Style and would represent the heart of the range; and a superior Vin de Collection, which would be top of the range, with various constraints such as obligatory bottling in the region. All this is up for discussion and, at the time of writing, no more than a proposal. In a move to streamline marketing, the various organizations that run the vineyards of the south, the committees for Languedoc and Roussillon, as well as the Vin de Pays d'Oc, have joined forces to promote the whole region under the all-embracing banner "the South of France", with a budget of €15 million.

The issue of that old chestnut, a nationwide Vin de Pays des Vignobles de France, has finally been resolved. The council of Viniflhor, the organization responsible for these things, has voted in favour of the creation of the new *vin de pays*, with just one dissenting vote, that of Jacques Gravegeal, president of the Vins de Pays d'Oc. This means that there will no longer be any limitations on geographical blends, so that, for example, Sauvignon from the Loire Valley could be added to some from the Midi, providing freshness to balance weight. Concerns were voiced that the new category could become a dumping ground for wine that could not be sold elsewhere, but its supporters are adamant that this will not be the case. The technical details have to be finalized, but the new wines will have to pass two approval procedures, first as departmental *vins de pays*, or smaller areas, and then as Vignobles de France. With the all-important mention of France, there is an insistence that quality must be maintained, and the new wines will give the bigger players on the French wine market a better opportunity to meet the New World on its own terms, with a clear international message. If all goes according to plan, 2007 will be the first vintage of Vin de Pays des Vignobles de France.

Foreigners wanted

Despite the authorities' refusal to allow the more distinctive name of Côtes de Fenouillèdes in favour of the much larger and less individual Côtes Catalanes, progress in that particular corner of the Roussillon hills continues unabated, with an estimated creation of about 50 new estates in the past five years, each with an average of 20 ha, comprising a total of some 1,000 ha. These will by no means all be new vineyards. Some have old – often very old – vines, usually of Grenache Noir that once produced *vin doux naturel*. Its enormous potential for table wine is now being realized for both appellation wines and *vins de pays*. Often a producer's top wine will be a *vin de pays*, a *cuvée* of pure Grenache Noir, which does not conform to the appellation requirements of Côtes du Roussillon Villages, which demand a blend, with a minimum of 30 per cent Syrah. Newcomers include a joint venture between Jeff and Simon Grier from Villiera in South Africa with Jean-Louis Denois, who is concentrating on cooler sites, since he is anxious to avoid the traditional high alcohol levels of Roussillon. Chapoutier has bought vines around Latour de France, and another promising new estate is Domaine des Vents. The appeal of the region is such as to attract investors not only from other parts of France but also from other countries and continents.

Opinion:
Diversity and quality

The charm of the *vins de pays* is their diversity. The quality can encompass the greatest and the most dire, but their appeal is above all their variety, and particularly the inclusion of grape varieties that do not conform to the parallel appellation. There are numerous examples of these. Take Carignan, a once-decried grape variety that responded badly to attempts to produce it in vast quantities with ill-judged vinification methods. Nowadays, with old vines, careful work in the vineyard, small yields, and maybe carbonic maceration to enhance the fruit rather than the tannins, it is enjoying a considerable revival in interest from wine growers, as well as popularity with the consumer, and the choice of Carignan is growing apace, with numerous examples of satisfying wines. The most ardent proponents of Carignan are John and Nicole Bojanowski at Clos Gravillas. Not only do they produce pure Carignan from vines as old as 1911 in Le Vielh, but they also blend it with just a little Cabernet Sauvignon in Rendez-Vous au Soleil. John explained that 5 per cent of Cabernet Sauvignon in the blend is just right, since it makes the wine deeper, longer, and racier, but 10 per cent is too much. Domaine de Nizas Vieilles Vignes is another rewarding example, as is Le Cas from Mas Conscience.

In the valley of the Agly, old Grenache vines are responsible for the soaring interest in, and success of, the area. Grenache, not only Noir but also Gris and Blanc, was originally used for *vin doux naturel*, but with the sad but steady decline in that market, these old vines have come into their own for table wines. The parallel appellation may be Côtes du Roussillon Villages, but for that you need specific proportions of specific grape varieties and wines of a certain alcohol level, which imposes too many constraints on these innovative wine growers.

Nor is this diversity confined to the Midi. Until this year, Sauvignon Vert was for me merely a textbook grape variety. I had never tasted it, but you can now find an example in the Loire Valley – and delicious it is, too, with some intriguing herbal notes and a richness that is unusual in northern Sauvignon Blanc. In the Lot Valley, close to Cahors, Domaine Eugénie is making an eminently drinkable blend of Cabernet Sauvignon and Ségalin (a cross of Jurançon Noir and Portugais Bleu), neither of which is allowed in the appellation of Cahors.

Although there are constraints of yield, grape variety, alcohol level, and technique for *vins de pays*, they are generally much less restrictive than for appellations. Consequently, you can find Chenin Blanc in the Midi, Pinot Noir in western France, and Chardonnay in Alsace. Syrah has not yet been planted in Bordeaux, and it is unlikely to be, since the new Vin de Pays de l'Atlantique does not allow it. Jean-Claude Mas of Domaines Paul Mas would argue that Cabernet Franc has enormous potential as a Vin de Pays d'Oc, since it ripens properly in the Midi and you obtain ripe but fresh flavours with good balancing acidity, something that can be elusive further north in the Loire Valley.

In Corsica, there has been some intensive research on long-lost grape varieties. Antoine Arena makes Bianco Gentile as a *vin de table*, since the variety, although recognized as having considerable potential, is not yet permitted in the appellation. He is also taking Vermentino, the classic white variety of Patrimonio, to greater heights that do not conform to the appellation regulations. He believes that Vermentino can resemble Chenin Blanc and, accordingly, has produced a delicious *demi-sec* with rich, peachy flavours. Nor do his experiments stop there. A *rancio* wine, following almost forgotten Corsican traditions, had an affinity with oloroso sherry.

Grapevine

• **Vin de Pays de la Haute Vallée de l'Orb** remains in line for an appellation, eventually, but these things move slowly. The growers' *syndicat* is still discussing specific criteria for submission to the INAO. Similarly, further east in the Gard, Vin de Pays de la Duché d'Uzès is another aspiring appellation, centred on the enchanting town of Uzès and covering about 130 communes, producing wines with more specific regional characteristics than the broader Vin de Pays des Cévennes, which tends to resemble Vin de Pays d'Oc. Usually Vin de Pays de la Duché d'Uzès is a blend, rather than a pure varietal.

• **Vin de Pays des Côtes de Thongue** has no aspirations for an appellation, but it too continues to grow in importance and quality, with a growing number of reputable estates making a reputation for an area that has no parallel appellation.

• **Vin de Pays d'Ardaihou,** a little-known and rarely encountered *vin de pays* situated in the Hérault on the coast to the west of Agde, has been suppressed, but since the coastal plain is hardly suitable viticultural land, no one is likely to notice its disappearance.

• A new *vin de pays* has been recognized in northern France: Vin de Pays des Côtes de Meuse, covering a handful of villages south of the city of Metz, in a department that is not usually known for its wine production. The little-known wine region of the Côtes de Toul is nearby, and together they have formed a promotional organization, Vignobles de Lorraine. These are some of the most northern vineyards in France, planted with Pinot Noir, Gamay, Chardonnay, and Auxerrois. With global warming, who knows what their future might be?

Once upon a time, *vin de table* used to imply the very worst of wines, but no longer. The clue is the reputation of the producer. Take René Rostaing's Viognier Les Lézardes, where Viognier is grown outside the appellation of Condrieu and therefore has no legal recognition. Another example is the maiden vintage of Clos Montels. Hélène Mir was the previous owner of Domaine des Belles-Eaux near Pézenas, which is now owned by the large insurance company AXA. In 2004, she made just 2,400 bottles of a delicious Syrah/Carignan blend. It is a humble *vin de table*, since it was simply not worth the hassle of going through the bureaucratic hoops of *labellisation* for an appellation.

Of course, the key example of disregard of authority rests with Eloi Dürrbach of Domaine de Trévallon. If he could have been persuaded to plant a few vines of Grenache Noir, his wine would enjoy the appellation of Coteaux Les Baux, but he has fiercely and quite rightly maintained his refusal to bow to officialdom, and so it is a humble *vin de pays* but, nonetheless, one of the great wines of France.

Grapevine

• **Vin de Pays de la Petite Crau** has been renamed Vin de Pays des Alpilles, which will certainly provide a more distinctive regional image for anyone familiar with the dramatic bauxite hills of the Alpilles around Les Baux.

• **We may hear more** of the wines of the Ile de France, which are produced from scattered pockets of vineyards in the Paris suburbs. At the moment there is no more than a total of 11 or 12 ha, made up of tiny plots, usually run by individual town councils, with the wine used for official or charitable purposes, but Christian de la Guéronnière, president of the Association des Vignobles Franciliens and originally from Pomerol, has aspirations for a *vin de pays*. One example is the tiny vineyard on the hill below the château of St Germain-en-Laye, to the west of Paris, overlooking the Seine, and the most famous is the vineyard of Montmartre in the shadow of the Sacré Coeur.

• *Copeaux*, or oak chips, have finally been allowed in France, following European Union legislation, for *vins de pays* and *vins de table*, but not for appellation wines. The Institut Cooperative du Vin in the Hérault reckons that the difference in cost between *copeaux* and barrels is €0.01–0.025 per litre for *copeaux*, as opposed to €0.10–0.30 per litre for real oak barrels.

GREATEST WINE PRODUCERS

1. Domaine de Trévallon (Bouches du Rhône)
2. Domaine de Clovallon (Oc/Haute Vallée de l'Orb)
3. Domaine Gauby (Côtes Catalanes)
4. Domaine La Grange des Pères (Hérault)
5. Mas de Daumas Gassac (Hérault)
6. Mas des Chimères (Coteaux du Salagou)
7. Domaine Antoine Arena (Ile de Beauté)
8. Producteurs Plaimont (Côtes de Gascogne)
9. Domaine Chabanon (Oc)
10. Domaine La Croix Belle (Côtes de Thongue)

FASTEST-IMPROVING PRODUCERS

1. Jean-Louis Denois (Oc)
2. Domaine Magellan (Côtes de Thongue)
3. Ampelidae (Vienne)
4. Domaine de Ravanès (Côtes de Thongue)
5. Domaine Gravillas (Côtes du Brian)
6. Mas Conscience (Oc)
7. Domaine de Puechamp (Cévennes)
8. Domaine Camp Galhan (Duché d'Uzès)
9. Domaine de Montplézy (Côtes de Thongue)
10. Vignobles Guillaume (Franche-Comté)

NEW UP-AND-COMING PRODUCERS

1. Domaine des Vents (Côtes Catalanes)
2. Domaine des Crès-Ricards (Mont-Baudile, Oc)
3. Domaine des Trémières (Oc)
4. Les Trois Poules (Côtes de Thongue)
5. Mas Lumen (Cassan)
6. Domaine Marie du Fou (Vendée)
7. Mas Cal Demoura (Oc)
8. Domaine Lacoste (Hérault, Oc)
9. Les Trois Terres (Oc)
10. Domaine de Canteperdrix (Cassan)

BEST-VALUE PRODUCERS

1. Producteurs Plaimont (Côtes de Gascogne)
2. Domaine Condamine l'Evêque (Oc)
3. Mas Montel (Oc, Gard)
4. Domaine de Perdiguier (Coteaux d'Enserune)
5. Domaine de l'Orviel (Oc, Cévennes, Duché d'Uzès)
6. Domaine Camp Galhan (Duché d'Uzès, Oc)
7. Domaine Cazes (Côtes Catalanes)
8. Domaine de la Grangette (Oc, Côtes de Thau)
9. Domaines Paul Mas (Oc)
10. Domaine Granoupiac (Oc)

GREATEST-QUALITY WINES

1. **Vin de Pays de l'Hérault Cuvée Emile Peynaud 2002** Mas de Daumas Gassac (€90)
2. **Vin de Pays de l'Haute Vallée de l'Orb Pinot Noir Les Pomarèdes 2005** Domaine de Clovallon (€13.50)
3. **Vin de Pays d'Oc Cuvée Passerillée Vendange d'Octobre 2004** Domaine Lacoste (€20.60)
4. **Vin de Pays des Cévennes Antarès 2004** Domaine de Puechamp (€12.50)
5. **Vin de Pays de l'Hérault L'Etincelle 2005** Mas Cal Demoura (€14)
6. **Vin de Pays des Coteaux d'Enserune Cuvée d'en Auger 2000** Domaine de Perdiguier (€14)
7. **Vin de Pays de l'Ile de Beauté Grotte di Sole Blanc Demi-Sec 2004** Domaine Antoine Arena (€16.50)
8. **Vin de Pays d'Oc Trélans 2003** Domaine Chabanon (€23)

⑨ **Vin de Pays de l'Hérault Le Cas 2005** Mas Conscience (€10)

⑩ **Vin de Pays de Cassan Belcanto 2001** Domaine de Canteperdrix (€9)

BEST BARGAINS

① **Vin de Pays des Côtes Catalanes Aquilon Rouge 2004** Domaine des Vents (€7.50)

② **Vin de Pays des Cévennes Fontanalba 2005** Domaine de Puechamp (€5.80)

③ **Vin de Pays du Mont Baudile Cousin Cousine Alicante 2005** Domaine des Crès-Ricards (€7)

④ **Vin de Pays des Coteaux du Salagou Blanc 2004** Mas des Chimères (€7)

⑤ **Vin de Pays des Côtes de Gascogne Premières Grives 2005** Domaine du Tariquet (€6)

⑥ **Vin de Pays d'Oc Cuvée Jericho 2005** Mas Montel (€6)

⑦ **Vin de Pays du Comté Tolosan Symphonie Moelleux 2005** Domaine de Perchade (€6.50)

⑧ **Vin de Pays des Coteaux d'Ensérune 2004** Domaine de Perdiguier (€6)

⑨ **Vin de Pays des Côtes de Thongue Cabernet Franc 2005** Les Trois Poules (€5.40)

⑩ **Vin de Pays du Comté Tolosan 2004** Domaine Bellevue-la-Forêt (€2.60)

MOST EXCITING OR UNUSUAL FINDS

① **Vin de Pays de l'Hérault 2004 Clos des Estivencs Cuvée Reginae** Domaine Lacoste (€19.60) *From a producer who is better known for Muscat de Lunel. His first red wine, a pure Carignan, has style and balance after 13 months in oak.*

② **Vin de Pays de Vendée Pinot Noir Très Noir 2005** Château Marie du Fou (€8.50) *An unlikely source of Pinot in western France with some delicious varietal flavours.*

③ **Vin de Table Bianco Gentile 2005** Domaine Antoine Arena (€13) *One of the indigenous Corsican grape varieties that is enjoying a small revival.*

④ **Vin de Pays du Jardin de la France Sauvignon Gris 2005** Domaine de Saulzaie (€8.50) *Yet another unusual grape variety that does not feature within an appellation.*

⑤ **Vin de Pays d'Oc Doux Caprice de l'Engarran 2005** Domaine de l'Engarran (€20 per 50-cl bottle) *From passerillé Grenache Noir, a light and delicious Banyuls-style wine. The first vintage, it is 100 per cent Grenache Noir.*

⑥ **Le Rappu Vendange Tardive** Clos Nicrosi (€11) *Not even vin de table, hence lack of vintage, but moût de raisin partiellement fermenté. Mainly Aleatico, found more commonly on Elba than Corsica, with some Grenache and Nielluccio to make an intriguingly sweet wine with an aroma of fruit cake.*

⑦ **Vin de Pays des Coteaux de Narbonne 2004** Domaine Romilhac (€9.50) *Equal parts of Grenache Noir and Merlot, and refreshingly without a trace of oak.*

⑧ **Vin de Pays des Cévennes Petit Verdot 2005** Domaine l'Orviel (€5.50) *A satisfying expression of a grape variety that is rarely found as a monocépage.*

⑨ **Vin de Pays de l'Hérault Pico 2005** Domaine du Poujol (€6) *An intriguing blend of Vermentino and Carignan Blanc.*

⑩ **Vin de Pays du Lot 2005** Domaine Eugénie (€3.70) *Another unlikely blend: Cabernet Sauvignon and Ségalin, making a rounded, spicy wine. An attractive alternative to Malbec in the Cahors area.*

Germany

Michael Schmidt

German oak is experiencing a revival of its fortunes in the wine cooperage industry.

MICHAEL SCHMIDT

Growers in the Pfalz, Rheingau, Baden, and the Ahr region have woken up to the fact that wood from their own "back yard" can bring added value to their products, not only in terms of quality and flavour, but also promotion and marketing. Though the term "industry" needs to be put into a rather small perspective, the handful of German coopers who possess the necessary expertise have experienced a healthy swelling of their order books for barrels "made in Germany".

For many years, large consignments of wood from the country's vast oak forests have found their way over the borders, mainly into France, but, since the "burgundization" of Spätburgunder from the mid-1980s, a local following has also gathered pace. Werner Näkel from the village of Dernau in the Ahr Valley was one of the first to give his Pinots a serious, albeit French, oaking. Little did he know then that, only a couple of miles away, wooden treasure slumbered in the forest of Grafschaft and Bölingen. Today oak trees from this source not only supply the staves for the local cooperative Mayschoss-Altenahr, but also Schloss Johannisberg in the Rheingau.

The idea for this venture came from Hans Hösch of the Rheinhessen village of Hackenheim, whose family has been involved in the cooperage business for four generations. Another cooperage benefiting from the trend for native wood is that of the Gies family in Bad Dürkheim in

MICHAEL SCHMIDT has been involved with the wines of Germany for more than three decades, and he visits estates and producers in his native country several times a year. Back in Britain he runs his own wine school (www.wineschmidt. co.uk) in Surrey and Hampshire. He is a judge at the International Wine and Spirit Competition and has worked as a consultant on a number of publications, including advising on the selection of recommended wines for the German chapter of *Sotheby's Wine Encyclopedia* (Dorling Kindersley, 1988–2005).

the Pfalz region, only a stone's throw from one of the company's most prestigious clients, the Knipser Estate in Laumersheim. For more than 150 years, most of the supplies used by Gies for their range of 225- to 10,000-litre barrels have come from Johanniskreuz in the Pfälzer Wald, a vast forest expanse with ancient oak plantations. Also among their 130 or so customers is organic producer Gerhard Roth, of Wiesenbronn in Franken, who supplies them with wood from his local Steigerwald forests. All the winemakers mentioned, together with other well-known oak users such as Lingenfelder and Ziereisen, believe that there is a special affinity between their wines and wood from the same area.

The cohabitation of oak and wine in a totally different way is at the heart of a research project conducted at the renowned wine village of Ayl in the Saar region. The Institute for Forestry at the University of Freiburg planted oak and poplar seedlings with Riesling and Sauvignon Blanc on the Rauberg site in 2005. The study will investigate the influence of their joint cultivation on the growth, development, and yield of the vines, the quality of the resulting wine, and the growth and development of the trees. Further objectives of the project, named Arbustum, are to investigate the competition of the two different plant species in the rhizosphere (root sphere of the soil) for water, nutrients, and space. The trial also aims to quantify the effects of the partnership arrangement on respective photosynthetic activities in the phyllosphere, as well as on the formation of mycorrhiza, a symbiotic association between the roots of the plants and fungi. The ultimate purpose of the project is to simulate conditions as they would have occurred almost two millennia ago, when the Romans first introduced the vine into the heavily wooded environment.

Grapevine

• "Liebfraumilch producer becomes member of VdP" would make a mischievous headline for the admission of Rheinhessen grower Gutzler to the ranks of Germany's premium wine estates in 2006. In addition to some holdings in the Grosse Gewächse sites Westhofener Kirchspiel and Morstein, the family also owns the Liebfrauenstift Kirchenstück. This vineyard in Worms was the original source of Liebfraumilch before it became a brand name, indiscriminately extended to include grapes from any place, any time, anyhow.

• **Though recent statistics** show a 0.2 per cent decline in German vineyard plantings, mainly due to continuing contraction in the Mosel region, black varieties gained another 3 per cent between 2003 and 2005, putting them at an overall share of almost 37 per cent. With an increase of 770 ha, Regent has taken over as the fastest mover from Dornfelder, which seems to be slowing down after a period of growth to over 8 per cent of the country's total area under vine. The leader Spätburgunder continues to expand, with the addition of 640 ha taking its share to 11.4 per cent.

SAUVIGNON GAINING MOMENTUM

A devotee of noble sweet bordeaux wines from the early beginnings of my imbibing career, in 1976 I found mention of a mysterious German "Sauternes" by what can only be described as the most respected German wine writer of that time, Ernst Hornickel. I managed to track down this envisaged rarity, only to find to my great disappointment that the Gräflich Wolff-Metternisches Weingut in the Baden village of Durbach did not grow any Semillon at all, but merely produced a Sauvignon Spätlese on its Schloss Grohl estate. Impressive nevertheless, considering that Sauvignon was not classified in the German wine law of 1971 and therefore not a permitted variety.

The most likely explanation that a blind eye was turned by the authorities can probably be found in the fact that the original cuttings for the tiny 0.2-ha plot of Sauvignon on the Herrenberg site were given in the 1830s to the then owner of Schloss Grohl, the Freiherr Zorn von Bulach, by his friend and the "King" of Sauternes himself, Marquis de Lur-Saluces of Château d'Yquem. In the mid-19th century, the variety is reported to have enjoyed a fair degree of popularity with growers in Württemberg and the Pfalz, albeit under the name of Muscatsylvaner. Following a 50-year absence from the country's vineyards, the go-ahead was given for some experimental plantings in 1986, and initial results were such that today there is almost a scramble for cuttings of Sauvignon from vine nurseries: 600,000 alone in 2005. From 30 ha nationwide in 2001, the variety

has snowballed to an estimated 200 ha in 2006. The Sauvignon Blanc Trophy of Germany's leading wine magazine for the 2005 vintage saw 115 entries from seven different regions. Fortunately, however, there is no word of German "Sauternes" any more, and almost all the wines are styled in the restrained and mineral mould of Loire and northern Italian renditions rather than the more exotic and aromatically pungent style of New Zealand.

MITTELRHEIN MYSTERY

In the 1950s, the banks of the River Rhine between Bonn and Bingen still sported an impressive 2,500 ha of vine plantings. Now, with less than 500 ha, the Mittelrhein is one of the smallest wine-growing regions of Germany. It's not all bad news, however, since most of what survived is located on steep slopes with prime exposition and is eminently suitable for the production of exquisite Riesling. A breathtaking combination of romantic villages, ancient castles, and a spectacular landscape has been rewarded with world cultural-heritage status in 2002 for this stretch of the river, with further beneficial effects for both tourism and wine sales.

But all is not well in the valley. A rift appears to exist between Bacharach and Boppard, which has nothing to do with geology and everything to do with politics. Bacharach has long been the frontrunner, with growers like Ratzenberger, Jost, Bastian, and Lanius setting an admirable standard justly rewarded by membership of the regional section of the VdP (association of German premium wine producers). However, since the mid-1990s a band of young growers from Boppard has crept up along the railings and – reading between the carefully drafted lines of highly respected wine journalists – has in some instances even overtaken the old guard. My own conclusions are that, in the hands of Didinger, Müller, Perll, and, *primus inter pares*, Florian Weingart, the wines from the Fässerlay, Feuerlay, and Ohlenberg vineyards of Boppard have achieved a class simply demanding recognition by the VdP. But any mention of this in the company of a high-ranking VdP member and it's as if their Riesling Trocken had been spiked with lemon juice!

From the VdP Mittelrhein itself, mutterings may be heard of yields too high and prices too low, and it cannot be denied that customers of the Boppard boys benefit from an outstanding price:quality ratio. Some say that the downriver upstarts are not interested in becoming members. A well-informed insider not wishing to be named even made reference to mysterious sectarian differences between the two clans. I suggest that changes in attitude are needed on both sides. The VdP Mittelrhein is not served well by boycotting half the region's best growers; and ignoring advice from the Federal Board of the Association, as well as the country's leading wine writers, suggests that a radical overhaul may be required. The shooting stars from Boppard need to realize that a Lone Ranger mentality is no long-term business concept and that a reasonable increase in prices would be just reward for their hard graft.

TIMES OF CHANGE

In the latter part of 2006, announcements were made of the retirement of two of the most important figures (and adversaries) of the German wine scene. While in the case of Prinz Salm, longtime president of the VdP, it would be justified to speak of an orderly and well-executed withdrawal from duty, the retreat of Achim Goering as head of the DWI (German Wine Institute) was hasty and forced by discontent within the ranks of the powerful cooperatives and merchant bottlers. The departure of the latter clearly spelled a change of direction, though continuing quarrels between regional sections, as well as strong criticism of president of the German wine growers' association Norbert Weber, a close ally of Goering, did not bode well.

In stark contrast, Prinz Salm leaves his house in order. The handing over of the baton to his successor Steffen Christmann in 2007 was well organized, the future aims of the VdP are clearly defined, and the support of a newly founded network of successors-designate to the present heads of VdP estates shows a canny knack of fostering evolution rather than provoking revolution. At the time of writing, the DWI was under interim leadership and there was no inkling as to who would be elected as the new boss. For the sake of German wine, it is to be hoped that the new brooms in both organizations will sweep in the same direction.

Opinion:

German Riesling instead of claret?

What appears a statement bordering on sacrilegious or ridiculous may, in the context of market forces and financial speculation, come much closer to the truth than comfortable for the real Riesling enthusiast. With the reputation of the 2005 bordeaux elite acquiring mythical proportions, demand gathered the momentum of an avalanche among a new class of obscenely rich, who need the best of everything. Former dedicated but now financially outmuscled buyers of top clarets were, or pretended to be, appalled by the greed of the prime château owners, and word began to spread of a switch of allegiances to a vinous alternative.

The rise of Riesling in Germany to new heights of sublime quality had not gone unnoticed, and the 2005 vintage saw an unprecedented *en primeur* campaign, particularly in the two most important export markets of the USA and the UK. The swift increase in sales in both countries could be regarded as final recognition of the successful efforts of German producers to reinstate Riesling to its rightful place in the hierarchy of fine wines. As a dedicated follower of the great white hope, I am delighted by this newly found international admiration. What does worry me is the notion that the newly acquired celebrity status may be due as much again to a protest reaction of jilted bordeaux wine luvvies: not too many palates will readily adapt to a hasty change from tannin to acidity.

It would be a shame to think that these swift conversions were solely triggered by motives of financial speculation. Though even right at the top of the quality pyramid there may be more estates and vineyards to choose from in Germany, quantities of Riesling's finest renditions are infinitely smaller than the output of Bordeaux's best, and it would not take much to send the price of, let's say, a Westhofener Morstein Grosses Gewächs from Keller or Wittmann into orbit. Unnecessary fuel is added to this fire by the unhealthy ambition of some patriotic journalists to see fiscal par restored between claret's and Riesling's greatest, just as it existed on the wine lists of fine-wine merchants and exclusive gentlemen's clubs more than a century ago. I say, let's not!

Finally, from the corner of the producers, we can hear the ring of the all-too-familiar alarm bells: the quality of the 2005s and 2006s is good, oh so good, but the quantity is tiny, oh so tiny. Prices will have to rise. The starting pistol has been fired, the usual suspects are out of their blocks, and the true wine lover limps off, having been shot in the foot once again.

Vintage Report

Advance report on the latest harvest

2006

A year of extreme changes in terms of weather and vegetation presented growers with some of the most challenging conditions for many a vintage. Following a long winter, a cold and wet spring delayed development of the vines but topped up water levels to an optimum degree. May was warm and dry, June and July hot with occasional showers, and vines were two weeks ahead in annual average vegetation until they were slowed down by a cool, rainy August. Indian summer conditions in September resulted in healthy grapes with excellent ripeness levels, raising hopes of another vintage of the century. These expectations could have been totally dashed by the arrival of flood-like rains in late September/early October. All hands were called on to bring in most of the grapes before any serious damage could be done. Stringent selection procedures were applied to any material affected by rain or rot, with some areas seeing a reduction of their crop by up to 40 per cent. Early predictions expect to see these uncompromising concessions to quality rewarded with excellent results, but with quantity well below average for the second year running, prices will have to rise.

Updates on the previous five vintages

2005

Vintage rating: *Red: 92 (provisional), Dry white: 89, Sweet white: 97*

Early predictions for 2005 raised expectations of another vintage of the century, combining the fruit of 2004 with the body and power of 2003, comparisons being drawn with the great 1959 and 1947 vintages! Warm weeks in the spring facilitated a problem-free flowering period. Despite ample rainfall in the summer, almost uninterrupted sunshine in September and October led to an early ripening of the grapes. All 13 regions were unanimous in reporting excellent physiological ripeness with an optimum ratio of sugar and acids. However, incidents of rot caused by humid conditions led to a few problems in the Pfalz and, to a lesser extent, in Rheinhessen. Mosel, Nahe, Mittelrhein, and Franken excelled. A smaller-than-average crop of 9 million hl put many smaller estates under financial pressure.

2004

Vintage rating: *Red: 85, White: 91*

Despite the adverse weather conditions experienced by some regions in the spring, the eventual harvest total of 10–11 million hl proved slightly above average for the past 10 years. Summer showers provided ample water supplies, avoiding a repeat of the 2003 stress syndrome. Phenological data showed that developments followed the pattern for an average year. The final ripening period began towards the end of August with grapes in a very healthy state and very little sign of any disease. In the autumn, a much more drawn-out ripening period than 2003 proved a bonus to growers looking for more fruit and less alcohol. Stable pH values, sound acidity levels, and an almost simultaneous occurrence of physiological and sugar ripeness resulted in lively, refreshing wines, filling a gap left by the blockbuster 2003.

2003

Vintage rating: *Red: 94, Dry white: 85, Sweet white: 96*

A record-breaking vintage with the driest and warmest growing conditions in Germany since 1540! The starting gun for the harvest was fired in early August, 102° *Oechsle* for a *Spätlese* reported by the middle of that month, the first *Trockenbeerenauslese* grapes gathered at the end of September, and the earliest frozen berries for *Eiswein* picked on 24 October. Several growers reported must weights of over 300° *Oechsle* for their TBAs. Harvest conditions were ideal, and most grapes achieved at least *Spätlese* level. Mainly due to the lack of precipitation, quantity was down by 20 per cent, with an estimated 8 million hl total. Expectations of a vintage of the century did not materialize, as many producers struggled to find the right balance between alcohol, fruit, and acidity.

Grapevine

• **Germany's oldest vines** grow in the southern part of the Pfalz region. Planted around the time of the Thirty Years War, the Traminer vines are estimated to be between 350 and 400 years old, and despite having stems the size of small tree trunks, they still produce grapes, albeit on an irregular basis. The site lies at the foot of the Rietburg castle near the small village of Rhodt.

• **Generally believed to be** the ancestor of today's white version, for many years the dark-berried Red Riesling survived only as an object of genetic research in the nurseries of viticultural institutes. Impressed by the taste of an experimental vinification, Rheingau grower Ulrich Allendorf decided to reintroduce the variety on a small but nevertheless commercial scale. The first harvest of grapes from 2,500 vines planted at the prime site Winkler Hasensprung is expected in 2008.

2002

Vintage rating: *Red: 81, White: 92*

An even growing season with an almost perfect balance of sunshine and precipitation was spoilt somewhat by heavy rains from the end of September onwards. Low autumn temperatures prevented the spread of rot seen in the warmer and more humid conditions of October 2000. Patient growers were rewarded with grapes of *Auslese*, *Eiswein*, and *Trockenbeerenauslese* quality.

2001

Vintage rating: *Red: 92, White: 90*

Favourable weather conditions until the end of August led to well-advanced degrees of ripeness, but September rains dashed hopes for an outstanding vintage. Fine weather in October and November rewarded patient growers with *Auslese* grape material. Red-wine producers in the Ahr, Pfalz, Baden, and Württemberg reported an almost-perfect balance of phenolic and sugar ripeness. A big freeze in mid-December led to copious amounts of *Eiswein*.

GREATEST WINE PRODUCERS

1. Keller (Rheinhessen)
2. Dönnhoff (Nahe)
3. Egon Müller (Saar)
4. JJ Prüm (Mosel)
5. Emrich-Schönleber (Nahe)
6. Geltz-Zilliken (Saar)
7. Knipser (Pfalz)
8. Leitz (Rheingau)
9. Fürst (Franken)
10. Wittmann (Rheinhessen)

FASTEST-IMPROVING PRODUCERS

1. Schäfer-Fröhlich (Nahe)
2. Weingart (Mittelrhein)
3. Friedrich Becker (Pfalz)
4. Schnaitmann (Württemberg)
5. Reinhold Haart (Mosel)
6. St Urbanshof (Mosel, Saar)
7. Stodden (Ahr)
8. Salwey (Baden)
9. Fürst Löwenstein (Franken, Rheingau)
10. Pawis (Saale-Unstrut)

NEW UP-AND-COMING PRODUCERS

1. Ziereisen (Baden)
2. Van Volxem (Saar)
3. Kühling-Gillot (Rheinhessen)
4. Korrell-Johanneshof (Nahe)
5. Martin Waßmer (Baden)
6. Hartmut Schlumberger (Baden)
7. Kistenmacher-Hengerer (Württemberg)
8. Zimmerling (Sachsen)
9. Hofmann (Franken)
10. Kriechel (Ahr)

BEST-VALUE PRODUCERS

1. Merkelbach (Mosel)
2. August & Thomas Perll (Mittelrhein)
3. Matthias Müller (Mittelrhein)
4. Didinger (Mittelrhein)
5. Weingart (Mittelrhein)
6. Manz (Rheinhessen)
7. Ullrichshof (Pfalz)
8. Gerhard Klein (Pfalz)
9. Knab (Baden)
10. Wachtstetter (Württemberg)

GREATEST-QUALITY WINES

① **Saarburger Rausch Riesling Trockenbeerenauslese 2005** Geltz-Zilliken, Saar (est. €1,000+ per half-bottle, to be auctioned)

② **Scharzhofberger Riesling Auslese Lange Goldkapsel 2005** Egon Müller, Saar (€320 per half-bottle)

③ **Westhofener Morstein Riesling Grosses Gewächs 2005** Keller, Rheinhessen (€44)

④ **Laumersheimer Kirschgarten Spätburgunder Auslese Trocken Grosses Gewächs 2003** Knipser, Pfalz (€30)

⑤ **Oberrotweiler Henkenberg Grauer Burgunder Spätlese Grosses Gewächs 2005** Salwey, Baden (€15.50)

⑥ **Chardonnay Spätlese Trocken 2005** Rebholz, Pfalz (€18)

⑦ **Weißer Burgunder Auslese Trocken *** Barrique "R"** R & C Schneider, Baden (€18)

⑧ **Bürgstadter Centgrafenberg Frühburgunder Trocken "R" 2004** Fürst, Franken (€51)

⑨ **Homburger Kallmuth Asphodill Silvaner Trocken Großes Gewächs 2005** Fürst Löwenstein, Franken (€20)

⑩ **Neipperger Schlossberg Lemberger Trocken Grosses Gewächs 2004** Graf Neipperg, Württemberg (€25)

BEST BARGAINS

① **Riesling Qualitätswein Trocken 2005** Knebel, Mosel (€5.60 per litre bottle)

② **Schloss Fürstenberg Riesling Spätlese 2005** Weingart, Mittelrhein (€7)

③ **Kreuzhalde Gewürztraminer Qualitätswein Trocken 2005** Winzergenossenschaft Wasenweiler, Baden (€4.30)

④ **Lemberger Trocken 2005** Kistenmacher-Hengerer, Württemberg (€5.50)

⑤ **BB Weißer Burgunder Qualitätswein 2005** Winzergenossenschaft Bischoffingen, Baden (€5.50)

⑥ **Cuvée Gaudenz Rotwein Trocken 2003** Knipser, Pfalz (€7.80)

⑦ **Grauer Burgunder Tafelwein Trocken 2005** Ziereisen, Baden (€7.30)

⑧ **Erdener Treppchen Riesling Auslese 2005** Merkelbach, Mosel (€7.50)

⑨ **Spätburgunder Rotwein Trocken 2003** Diefenhardt, Rheingau (€6.40)

⑩ **Frühburgunder Trocken "S" 2004** Gerhard Klein, Pfalz (€9.50)

MOST EXCITING OR UNUSUAL FINDS

① **Grosskarlbacher Burgweg St Laurent Spätlese Trocken 2003** Knipser, Pfalz (€20) *The Knipser brothers have been at the forefront of German reds for years, but with their 2003s they have found a new dimension. I picked the St Laurent as an illustration of their perfect craftsmanship, even with a so-called lesser variety.*

② **Kanzemer Altenberg Riesling Alte Reben 2005** Van Volxem, Saar (€28) *Not Riesling as we know it! Extremely low yields from old vines produce a wine that almost defies description, but notes of flint, smoke, and minerality on a creamy texture certainly banish the grape's acidity to a mere supporting role.*

③ **Divino Pinot Blanc Beerenauslese Barrique Aged 2002** Winzergenossenschaft Nordheim, Franken (€29.80) *We don't think of Beerenauslese and* barrique *as suitable bedfellows, but Pinot Blanc does not have the acidity of Riesling, and this combination is as exquisite and luscious as many a fine oak-raised Sauternes.*

④ **Cuveé Fleurs des Rosées Sekt NV** Staadter Sektkellerei Hausen, Saar (€10) *A Cabernet Sauvignon Sekt from the Saar(!), albeit with a shot of Pinot Blanc, certainly qualifies as unusual, though my first reaction was trepidation rather than excitement. Needlessly so: it was the best Cabernet sparkler I have ever tasted.*

⑤ **Tempranillo Qualitätswein Trocken 2002** Leiner, Pfalz (€23) *Cabernet, Merlot, and Syrah have got a foothold in Germany now, but there is only one Tempranillo, and the jury appears still to be out on this one; unusual enough to be included.*

⑥ **Steingrübler Gutedel Tafelwein Trocken 2005** Ziereisen, Baden (€6) *The favourite quaffer of many German wine pros. This is Ziereisen's de-luxe edition of an often maligned variety, earthy and with a firm grip.*

⑦ **Röttinger Feuerstein Tauberschwarz Trocken "R" 2004** Hofmann, Franken (€15) *Autochthonous black grape of the Tauber Valley brought back from the brink of extinction, earthy and*

spicy in its simpler renditions, but coaxed to a very respectable standard by Hofmann.

⑧ **Viognier Qualitätswein Trocken 2005** Fritz Waßmer, Baden (€17.50) *Following several growers' success with "copies" of Côte Rôtie in the Markgräflerland, at least one of them now has Condrieu in his sight. The southernmost outpost of the Baden region has always been Pinot rather than Riesling country, and the northern Rhône is just a few miles down from Burgundy, after all.*

⑨ **Freyburger Edelacker Blauer Zweigelt Qualitätswein Trocken 2003** Lützkendorf, Saale-Unstrut (€16) *Even the asphyxiating conditions of the area's Bolshevist past did not manage to curb the Lützkendorfs' enthusiasm for nonconformist wine, and with this taut Zweigelt exhibiting aromas of herbs and spices, they successfully continue to push the boundaries of their region's northerly exposure.*

⑩ **Niederhäuser Pfaffenstein Würzer Auslese 2005** Mathern, Nahe (€6.75) *Würzer, a cross of Gewürztraminer and Müller-Thurgau, survives in the Nahe and Rheinhessen, and if you like your Auslese sweet and mild with spicy aromas and a gentle scent of rosewater, this is it!*

Grapevine

• **German goats do roam** vineyards indeed. In *Wine Report 2006*, I reported on the rampage of black rot in abandoned vineyards. The European Union was willing to support grubbing-up of the affected areas on condition that they would never be planted with vines again. Many growers wanted to keep their options open and did not take up the offer. In a unique trial, the Federal Biological Institute released a herd of goats into a severely affected plot. The greedy animals devoured any grasses, weeds, and leaves that could possibly act as hosts for the spores of the fungus, eliminating the pest and leaving only the stumps of the vines for easy removal.

Italy overview

Nicolas Belfrage MW & Franco Ziliani

Controversy has broken out in light of suggestions from Professor Mario Fregoni that varietal wines should be made only from the named grape variety.

Fregoni, one of the most illustrious of Italy's wine academics, of the University of Piacenza, has published a paper called "Mongrel viticulture undermines sense-experience", in which he laments the fact that so many of Italy's self-declared varietal wines are not actually made with *vitigni in purezza* but are allowed, under the EU-inspired rules governing their DOCG, DOC, or IGT to blend in up to 15 per cent of other grapes, which in practice often means the invasive character-bending bordeaux varieties plus Syrah. Worse still, of all the hectarage planted to DOC and DOCG grapes in Italy, only 4 per cent is devoted to single varieties; and, of the 370 native Italian grape types registered for DOC(G) production, only 60 – that is, 16.2 per cent of the total – are planted *in purezza*.

Fregoni concludes: "Respect for grape varieties, as for terroir, is rarely found. European and Italian viticulture is mongrelized, the fruit of vineyard mixes and vinous blends of considerable variability. The consumer is thus precluded from a sensorial perception of the variety declared on the label. The future of indigenous varietals is consequently under threat."

Fregoni proposes nothing less than a unilateral renunciation on the part of Italy of the EU regulation that permits blending of other varieties up to 15 per cent in a declared "varietal" wine, as well as the adoption of a purely Italian provision requiring varietal wines to consist of 100 per cent of the stated variety. Given the forces ranged against him – not only the legal blenders but also those who, in supposed 100 per cent varietals like Barolo or Brunello di Montalcino, do it "under the table" as it were – he is very unlikely to get his wish. The result of this failure, he writes, will be a "confusion of varietal names and tastes such as to erode our genetic inheritance, which is of such enormous historic and commercial value, and the standardization of organoleptic characteristics".

Wine tourism

According to figures released by the producers' organization Coldiretti, cellar-door sales in Italy are growing apace. Coldiretti estimates that, out of a total sales value for wine in Italy of €9 million, something like €1 million is accounted for by sales to tourists. In Italy, there are 21,000 wine producers who sell at the cellar door – a phenomenon that is rapidly expanding to include bottled wines. The practice of visiting cellars for a taste and a purchase has been much abetted by the now annual ritual of throwing open thousands of cellar doors on a designated date – cantine aperte (open cellars). Wine tourists are further helped by the demarcation of 147 Strade del Vino (wine roads) with routes running through no fewer than 540 Città del Vino (officially designated wine towns). This is good news for producers, who tend to sell at retail price, thereby collecting the tranche that usually goes to the middleman. Good news, too, for buyers, who can taste before they buy and understand a bit more about the processes by which their favourite tipple is made. (Visit www.cittadelvino.com for more information.)

Prices set to rise

After several years of price stagnation, due largely to a falling market, especially for premium wines, wine prices in the coming year are likely to increase by not less than 10 per cent. This, at any rate, is the view of the Unione Italiana Vini (UIV) after several years of producers absorbing increases on bottles, cartons, corks, capsules, labels, and energy. "Despite the current difficulties in the market," UIV president Andrea Sartori commented, "price rises are absolutely essential for our members, whose margins over the past few years have been steadily falling." On the positive side, fruit quality is generally up following the 2006 harvest. On the other hand, after two years in which prices have in some instances actually gone down, grape prices are surging strongly.

Italy still leads in Germany

Despite many cries of pain from Italian wine producers over the past few years, moaning that the German market for their products has collapsed, it turns out that Italy is still the leading exporter of wine to its northern neighbour by a margin. In 2005, according to the Federal Office of Statistics at Wiesbaden, Germany imported 463 million litres of wine from Italy at a value of €516 million. France came trailing in second with 212 million litres at a value of €380 million, followed by

Spain with 180 million litres. It would appear that the New World has a long way to go to equal its performance in the British market, where Australia, the USA, South Africa, and Chile, not to mention France, are all ahead of Italy in terms of exports.

Alternative-closures debate sparked

A brouhaha of interesting proportions has blown up over the use of alternative closures in Italy. According to a decree of 1993, it is forbidden to use any closure other than cork for DOCG wines. UK importer David Gleave of Liberty Wines recently wrote to Minister of Agriculture Paolo De Castro, inviting him to rethink the legal situation. According to Gleave (whose letter may be viewed at www.libertywines.co.uk), since his company started using alternative closures in 2000, sales have increased exponentially. Italy being the only country to ban alternatives, Gleave opines that it is in grave danger of relegating itself to a progressively lower level in international esteem, as well as of losing sales.

Gleave's position is partially supported by the president of the UIV, Andrea Sartori, who commented that his organization would appeal to the government to liberalize laws on alternative closures and containers for DOC wines, although it would "naturally exclude DOCG wines from any modification".

Piero Mastroberardino, president of Federvini (the other major wine producers' organization), was both more cautious and more radical, saying that, while he personally did not like alternative closures, there was a case for them in the lower echelons of the "quality pyramid". "There are DOCGs", he commented, "that, for their wide diffusion and modest price, would perhaps benefit from alternative closures. But there are other DOCGs, indeed some IGTs, that should continue to use cork."

Wine Report's inclination would be to allow individual consortia and indeed producers to make their own decisions as to how they want to present themselves. Blanket laws are too heavy.

Opinion:
The tangled web Italians weave

As 2007 dawned, the number of Italian DOC(G)s and IGTs stood at 465, and counting. Of these, 34 were DOCG (including the likes of bog-standard Chianti, which hardly deserves the honour, as distinct from Chianti + name of zone, such as Rufina), 313 were DOC, and 118 were IGT.

How on earth is anyone, even the greatest "expert", supposed to keep track of all that lot? *Campanilismo* – pride in one's local produce – is all very well, but Italians seem to have an almost suicidal urge to go to ridiculous extremes. It must be obvious to anyone who has studied the world market that one of the reasons New World wines are doing so well today is because ordinary drinking folk can glance at the label and have some understanding of how the liquid smells and tastes. Not much chance of that when you're looking at a bottle of Terradeiforti Valdadige Inantio, one of a batch of new DOCs crowned in 2006. What happens in the Italian brain upon reading that message is not known (probably depends on where in Italy the brain comes from), but at least Italians can pronounce it. Citizens of Wichita, Kansas, or Kyoto, Japan, would be flummoxed on all counts and swiftly move on to the Chilean Merlot. And yet Angelo Rossi, director of the Terradeiforti consortium (the zone, in the virtual certainty that you didn't know, straddles southern Trentino and northwestern Veneto), has said of the switch from DOC Valdadige subzone Terradeiforti to Terradeiforti Valdadige DOC (can you figure the difference?): "It is a result of fundamental importance for our territory." Presumably he meant: for our local politicians.

Bad enough to have more DOC(G)s than make marketing sense, and for this number to be actually growing… It should instead be slashed by three-quarters. But what in the name of the gods is the point of having nearly 120 IGTs? There should be no more, or hardly, than there are regions – that is, 20. After all, IGT conveys little, compared with DOC, in terms of quality control and almost nothing in terms of terroir. It's mainly a device for dragging top producers out of the *vino da tavola* bracket while staying in line with EU regulations. An example of a recent absurdity in this respect is the new "Montecastelli", a made-up brand name if ever there was one, and maybe that's not a bad thing, except that there already exists for Tuscany as a whole an IGT that does everything Montecastelli is supposed to do for the province of Pisa: it's called Toscana, a name that actually conveys something to most wine bibbers. So why duplicate?

Northern Italy

Nicolas Belfrage MW & Franco Ziliani

Masi Agricola, together with private-equity group Alcedo Sgr and possibly other partners, is aiming at the constitution of an axis of wine production.

NICOLAS BELFRAGE MW

FRANCO ZILIANI

The proposed 'axis' would be based in northeast Italy and is set for quotation on the stock market within two to three years. Masi, owned by the Boscaini family, has opened its doors to an influx of capital from financiers and industrialists. The Boscaini family retains 72.5 per cent of the capital. The plans would see Masi as a provider of marketing, sales, technical assistance, and so on for smaller producers, brought together through acquisition or by joint venture and sharing a spirit of the Veneto and neighbouring regions. The idea would be to provide a complete range of the wine products of the northeast.

NICOLAS BELFRAGE MW was born in Los Angeles and raised in New York and England. He studied in Paris, Siena, and London, taking a degree at University College London in French and Italian. Nick has been specializing in Italian wines since the 1970s and became a Master of Wine in 1980, the first American citizen to do so. He is the author of the double-award-winning *Life Beyond Lambrusco* (Sidgwick & Jackson, 1985), *Barolo to Valpolicella* (Mitchell Beazley, 1999), and *Brunello to Zibibbo* (Mitchell Beazley, 2001). Nick is a regular contributor to *Harpers Wine and Spirit Weekly* and *The World of Fine Wine*.

FRANCO ZILIANI is a freelance writer who has specialized in Italian wines since 1985. He is a regular contributor to the English periodicals *Harpers Wine and Spirit Weekly*, *Decanter*, and *The World of Fine Wine* (where he is also a member of the editorial board), the Californian magazine *Wine Business Monthly*, the Italian periodicals *Il Sommelier Italiano*, *AIS Lombardia News*, *LaVINIum*, and *VQ*, and the Italian weekly magazine *Il Corriere Vinicolo* (the official organ of Unione Italiana Vini). Franco publishes a weekly wine newsletter, *Bvino*, which is mailed to 28,000 wine enthusiasts, and a wine blog, *Vino al Vino* (www.vinoalvino.org).

Fontanafredda up for sale

During the late autumn of 2006, the rumour started circulating: Barolo's biggest and most prestigious winery, Fontanafredda, with more than 110 ha of prime vineyard and a turnover of €30 million, was up for sale. Banker-proprietors Monte dei Paschi di Siena, in charge since 1931 when they took over from the bankrupt royal family of Mirafiori, were offering the estate to the likes of GIV or Campari, or anyone with the rumoured asking price of around €300 million sloshing around in their current account. Other possible purchasers were whispered to speak Italian with a Tuscan accent, and a foreign takeover was by no means ruled out. According to the president of the bank, Giuseppe Mussari, wine "is not strategically or functionally at the heart of the business of the bank".

Did it really take 75 years to work that one out?

Record figures for Cavit

Cavit, the giant Trentino cooperative, has announced a turnover of €172.1 million for the 2005/06 financial year, up 6.5 per cent on the previous year, with a net profit of €6.4 million. Not everything was roses in the Cavit garden, however, since an ill-tempered split occurred between them and one of their historically most important fruit suppliers, La Vis, when Cavit decided to exclude the rapidly expanding La Vis from its governing council over a commercial spat (Cavit taking exception to La Vis selling wine to a customer of Cavit). The battle of the titans is on.

Grapevine

• **The name Tocai,** historically used to describe one of Friuli's classic grapes, is no longer legally printable on labels. It was going to be replaced by the second half of the classic name Tocai Friulano – that is, "Friulano" – just as Alsace's Tokay-Pinot Gris is to lose the first half of its name, but that has now been thrown into doubt by a ruling in a court of Rome, which held that "Friulano" is too geographical a name to be applied to a grape variety. The protagonists of the drama, of course, are the producers of the famous sweet wine of Hungary, whose grapes have nothing to do with either Pinot Gris or Tocai Friulano, but who seem to think the public are too stupid to make the distinction (perhaps they're right).

• **The most recent case** of Pinot Grigio fiddling, uncovered by the Fraud Squad of Verona together with the *carabinieri* of the Antisophistication Nucleus of Padua, involves a certain 'Mr FS' of Sona in the province of Verona, who was recently arrested before managing to commercialize some 210,000 litres of phoney liquid. The wine has been confiscated, and Mr FS is presumably in the clink, but as long as the public continues to demand 'Pinot Grigio' whether or not it comes from vines of that type, the FSs of this world will thrive. Provided, that is, they don't get caught.

Opinion:
To oak or not to oak

The question of whether to allow *trucioli* (pronounced 'troo-cho-lee') or oak chips to play a part in winemaking has much exercised the Italian vinous mentality in past months. The practice may have been given the affirmative nod by the European Commissioner for Agriculture, Mariann Fischer Boel, but that doesn't mean Italians are agreed on using it.

Viticulturist Professor Attilio Scienza of the University of Milan opined: "There is today a growing tendency to use substances that modify the characteristics of wine. Wood chips bring only an added sensation, a banal appendage, to wine, while *barriques* are containers that provoke an oxy-reductive reaction, which gives it important characteristics. I hope that this oenological practice will not be allowed in … DOC wines, and that where it is used there will be a specific indication … on the label."

Dr Giacomo Tachis, a Piemontese though he made his name in Tuscany, dismisses chips with the remark: "You might as well make an infusion of wood and add it as flavouring to the wine." But Ezio Rivella, ex-president of Italian oenologists and ex-head of Banfi Montalcino, begs to differ. He ridicules the "visceral and hysterical reactions of those, far removed from the reality of production, who would set Italy up as the defender of the *barrique*", a technology imported only about 30 years ago from France and that purists have widely blamed for distorting the character of certain Italian classics.

"Once again," moans the weekly wine journal *Il Corriere Vinicolo*, "Italy has seized the occasion to flagellate itself, pursuing thus its mad self-harming course towards the void. The world of wine seems to have gone mad. And all this because of a practice used by New Worlders for some time, a practice that has in no small way helped them to create and diffuse the so-called 'international taste' … bringing tangible success to American and Australian wines."

In any case, says Angelo Gaja of Barbaresco, "What is the point of authorizing *vini da tavola* [or IGTs] to use chips [while forbidding them to DOCs] when there is no official method of analysis by which to distinguish a *barriqued* wine from one with chips?" This seems the crux of the problem. Mario Ubigli, director of the Institute for Experimental Agriculture of Asti, recently confirmed that at present "there is no possibility of an analytical control" of chips versus *barrique*. Ubigli expresses his hope that the practice will not spread to DOC/Gs (implying that in IGTs it would be acceptable?). But, if it does, there is apparently nothing anyone can do about it.

Vintage Report

Advance report on the latest harvest

2006

In terms of quantity, Piemonte was up 10 per cent on the previous year. Early spring was cold, and the vegetative cycle was delayed, but flowering occurred in good conditions. The thermometer then climbed, the vine caught up, and rains were regular, so there were few problems despite some very high temperatures. August was cool, but September was fine until mid-month, when there were three days of heavy rainfall. A similar phenomenon occurred a week later, but there was little or no rot. Producers began picking Nebbiolo for Barolo/Barbaresco soon after the second rainy period, and the weather remained fine until the end of the vintage. Thanks to the adequate but not excessive heat of the summer, sugar levels were contained, and the general feeling was that these will be wines of good balance and complexity, capable of ageing very well.

The story in Lombardy was similar to that in Piemonte, although quantity levels did not change significantly. The great heat of July was tempered by the cold and rains of August, with September coming to the rescue with mostly fine weather broken by short periods of violent precipitation. The whites of Oltrepò Pavese, the Cabernets and Merlots of Franciacorta, and the Nebbiolos of Valtellina all fared very well. If there was a question mark, it was over Barbera, whose thinner skin rendered it vulnerable to September rains.

On the whole, growers were pleased with results in Alto Adige and Trentino, where volume was up around 10 per cent and the important grapes – the majority that didn't suffer from the low level of rot that occurred briefly in some vineyards towards the third or fourth week of September – were nicely balanced with firm acidity and fine, delicate aromas. Most of the reds escaped botrytis, and wines should be complex and balanced.

Results in the Veneto were highly satisfactory in terms of quality, if on a similar level to 2005 in terms of quantity. There were plenty of healthy bunches to be laid down to dry for Amarone, and they, like the Garganegas for Soave, benefited from the changeable autumn temperatures. Early-picked whites, such as Pinot Grigio, were juicy and nicely acidic.

In Friuli, the weather in spring and early summer led to a fall in quantity of about 10 per cent year on year. Flowering was extended and subject to adverse conditions, which reduced the number of berries per bunch and hence bunch weight, while in early summer the great heat reduced berry size. Nonetheless, Friulians were well pleased with the results in terms of balance, aroma, and flavour.

In Emilia Romagna, early-picked whites and late-picked reds like Lambrusco and upper-altitude Sangiovese fared very well for quality, though quantity was similar to that of 2005. There were some heavy rains a week apart in mid-September, but fine weather preceding, between, and following made up for the lapse.

Updates on the previous five vintages

2005

Vintage rating: *Red: 87, White: 89*

Not a bad year; a number of good wines have emerged, though little of great note. The biggest problem, perhaps, was the fall in quantity compared with 2004: in the north, between 10 and 25 per cent. Quality, however, was also down on 2004, with wines just that bit more dilute and less complex, without being bad. As a matter of fact, there were some quite good drinking wines, but nothing much that you'd be inclined to lay down.

2004

Vintage rating: *Red: 92, White: 90*

This vintage has largely lived up to its promise as (with 2001) one of the best of the century, not that that's saying too much (yet). Following two difficult years, 2004 – a year of measured heat and rainfall, with the added bonus of fine weather at harvest time – came up trumps for both quantity and quality, whites as well as reds. The whites of Friuli, Alto Adige, Trentino, Veneto, Lombardy, and Piemonte show great finesse and brightness, with rich, intense fragrances and aromas. Reds are marked by solid structure, good varietal characteristics, balance, and excellent ageing potential. Piemontese reds Nebbiolo, Dolcetto, and Barbera showed a significant increase in sugar levels, and acid levels were ideal, the wines combining the best of traditional structure with modern roundness, fruit, and balance.

2003

Vintage rating: *Red: 88, White: 82*

One of the shortest harvests in the past 50 years, following the absolute shortest, 2002. The year was marked by high temperatures and drought, the good news being that grapes remained universally healthy; the bad being that many were raisined, baked, or overconcentrated. A very early harvest, whites being picked in many cases in the first half of August, reds not much later. Those who go in for mega-wines will like the 2003s, but balance was not easy to come by and was achieved, when it was achieved, in well-tended, deep-rooted vineyards. Barolo and Barbaresco attracted some raves, as did Valpolicella and other reds, but it was a year, when all is said and done, for careful selection.

2002

Vintage rating: *Red: 70, White: 80*

In retrospect, from certain points of view, not as bad as we thought at the time, nor certainly as bad as the international pundits have painted it. In Piemonte, it's true, many Barolos/Barbarescos were produced in tiny quantities or not at all, due to hail damage or general lack of ripeness, but Nebbiolos of lesser denominations, as well as Barberas and Dolcettos, often benefited from the addition of grapes from great vineyards normally reserved for the *crus*. A similar comment could be made in Valpolicella – wines not as big as usual but drinking nicely now. As for whites, some growers in Soave were declaring 2002 to be the best year for a decade, and indeed there was plenty of freshness and nerve, if less alcohol, in whites of other northern zones: Gavi, Alto Adige, and Friuli.

2001

Vintage rating: *Red: 94, White: 90*

The first year of the new millennium had points of excellence to rival those of the previous six. There were predictions of Barolos and Barbarescos at the highest quality levels, possibly capping the achievements of the previous six years. Other Piemontese wines were excellent too, with Barberas and Dolcettos of great concentration and structure. Nebbiolo (Chiavennasca) in Valtellina was also splendid. Very good year, too, for the whites of Friuli and for the Soaves of Veneto, as well as for the reds of Valpolicella.

Lists compiled by Franco Ziliani.

GREATEST WINE PRODUCERS

1. Giacomo Conterno (Barolo)
2. Bruno Giacosa (Barolo & Barbaresco)
3. Giuseppe Mascarello (Barolo)
4. Cavallotto (Barolo)
5. Roberto Voerzio (Barolo)
6. Ca' del Bosco (Franciacorta)
7. Triacca (Valtellina)
8. Tenuta San Leonardo (Trentino)
9. Vie di Romans (Friuli)
10. Jermann (Friuli)

FASTEST-IMPROVING PRODUCERS

1. Bartolo Mascarello (Barolo)
2. GD Vajra (Barolo)
3. Comm. GB Burlotto (Barolo)
4. Sobrero (Barolo)
5. Lupi (Liguria)
6. Arpepe Pellizatti Perego (Valtellina)
7. Enrico Gatti (Franciacorta)
8. Pojer & Sandri (Trentino)
9. Il Roncus (Friuli)
10. Collavini (Friuli)

NEW UP-AND-COMING PRODUCERS

1. La Crotta di Vegneron (Aosta Valley)
2. Pugnane (Barolo)
3. Massimo Rivetti (Barbaresco)
4. Sella (Lessona, Piemonte)
5. Ottaviano Lambruschi (Liguria)
6. Conti Vistarino (Oltrepò Pavese)
7. Il Mosnel (Franciacorta)
8. Casata Monfort (Trentino)
9. Eugenio Rosi (Trentino)
10. Pfannenstielhof (South Tyrol)

BEST-VALUE PRODUCERS

1. Cantina Rizzi (Barbaresco)
2. Sordo Giovanni (Barolo)
3. Manzone Fratelli (Barolo)
4. Monchiero Fratelli (Barolo)
5. Brezza (Barolo)
6. Massimo Rivetti (Barbaresco)
7. Quinto Chionetti (Dolcetto di Dogliani)
8. Romano Dogliotti La Caudrina (Moscato d'Asti)
9. Fattoria Cabanon (Oltrepò Pavese)
10. Cavalleri (Franciacorta)

GREATEST-QUALITY WINES

1. **Barolo Monprivato 2001** Giuseppe Mascarello, Piemonte (€45)
2. **Barolo Vignolo Riserva 2000** Cavallotto, Piemonte (€35)
3. **Barolo Ginestra Vigna Casa Matè 2001** Elio Grasso, Piemonte (€27)
4. **Barbaresco Martinenga 2003** Cisa Asinari Marchesi di Gresy, Piemonte (€30)
5. **Barbaresco Rabajà Riserva 2001** Bruno Giacosa, Piemonte (€90)
6. **Vignamare 2001** Lupi, Liguria (€20)
7. **Franciacorta Satèn 2001** Ca' del Bosco, Lombardy (€40)
8. **Valtellina Prestigio 1999** Triacca, Lombardy (€25)
9. **Trento Giulio Ferrari Riserva del Fondatore 1997** Ferrari, Trentino (€60)
10. **Vintage Tunina 2004** Jermann, Friuli (€35)

BEST BARGAINS

1. **Ghemme 2001** Mazzoni, Piemonte (€12)
2. **Barolo Vigna Fraschin 2001** Manzone Fratelli, Piemonte (€18)
3. **Barolo Solanotto Altinasso 2001** Cavalier Bartolomeo, Piemonte (€18)
4. **Barolo Vigna Castellero 2001** Barale Fratelli, Piemonte (€20)
5. **Dolcetto d'Alba Villero 2005** Sobrero, Piemonte (€6)
6. **Barbera d'Alba Cannubi Muscatel 2004** Brezza, Piemonte (€8)
7. **Barbera d'Alba Vigna del Cuculo 2004** Cavallotto, Piemonte (€10)
8. **Grignolino del Monferrato Casalese 2005** Canato, Piemonte (€5.50)
9. **Rosso di Valtellina 2004** La Maroggia, Consorzio Produttori Maroggia, Lombardy (€7.50)
10. **Riviera Ligure di Ponente Vermentino Lunghèra 2005** Durin, Liguria (€10)

MOST EXCITING OR UNUSUAL FINDS

1 Barbaresco Boito 2001 Cantina Rizzi, Piemonte (€20) *Barbaresco produced in the traditional manner: grapes in contact with the skins for 15–20 days, two years' ageing in large oak barrels of 25–50 hl.*

2 Barbaresco Froi 2003 Massimo Rivetti, Piemonte (€15) *Aged in large 25-hl barrels, this Barbaresco comes from a small producer worthy of being followed. Even from a hot year like 2003, it succeeds in achieving great freshness, balanced acidity, and a juicy but compact mouthfeel.*

3 Barolo Carobric 2001 Paolo Scavino, Piemonte (€45) *Barolo Carobric is not a single-vineyard Barolo but derives from an acronym of three vineyards: CAnnubi, ROcche di Castiglione, and BRICco del Fiasco. It brings together the nervous, perfumed character of Rocche di Castiglione, the tannic breadth of Fiasco, and the warmth and harmony of Cannubi.*

4 Barolo Brunate 2001 Poderi Marcarini, Piemonte (€30) *Absolutely elegant aromas, creamy, fresh, consistent, and great purity: rose, chocolate, tar, liquorice, leather, gamey, strawberries and cassis, just like a great Pinot Noir. Great richness, savoury, perfectly balanced, silky tannins, very large and consistent in the palate. Fantastic earthy finish that never ends: a great Barolo.*

5 Barolo Rocche di Castiglione 2001 Oddero, Piemonte (€35) *Luscious, pure fruit, silky and velvety tannins; perfect balance between fruit and tannins. Splendid to drink now, but with a great future.*

6 Dolcetto di Diano d'Alba Vigna del Pinnacolo 2004 Gigi Rosso, Piemonte (€6.50) *From the Moncolombetto vineyard, at an altitude of 500 m (1,640 ft), on dry, chalky soil, this is a special Riserva Dolcetto di Diano d'Alba that convinces and surprises for the richness of its structure and for its marked mineral character.*

7 Franciacorta Decennale 1996 Ca' del Bosco, Lombardy (€60) *With 20 per cent Pinot Noir, matured in oak and given a very lengthy refinement in bottle, this is a Franciacorta of impressive structure. Despite its long stay on the yeast, it is surprisingly fresh and drinkable – a joy to drink.*

8 Alto Adige Pinot Bianco Vorberg 2004 Cantina Produttori Terlano, South Tyrol (€10) *From grapes grown at 500–900 m (1,640–2,950 ft) altitude, this outstanding white, fermented and aged in large oak barrels, is destined to evolve extremely well and to last for decades, as with so many of the extraordinary white wines of this exemplary South Tyrolean cooperative.*

9 Prosecco di Valdobbiadene Vecchie Viti NV Ruggeri, Veneto (€13) *Made with grapes selected from 80–100-year-old vineyards, this is a Prosecco that surprises with its complexity, elegance, and marked personality. In no way inferior to a good champagne-method wine.*

10 Collio Bianco Broy 2005 Collavini, Friuli (€20) *With 40 per cent Chardonnay, 40 per cent Tocai Friulano (or just Friulano), and 20 per cent Sauvignon, this is a white wine of class. The Friulano and Chardonnay grapes undergo a light appassimento, after which they are crushed and blended with the Sauvignon and fermented in Allier barriques, where the wine remains until the spring. The result is a wine of notable complexity.*

Central & Southern Italy

Nicolas Belfrage MW & Franco Ziliani

Feudi di San Gregorio of Sorbo Serpico in Campania has announced that Vincenzo Ercolino has yielded his presidential post to Edoardo Narduzzi.

NICOLAS BELFRAGE MW

FRANCO ZILIANI

Feudi di San Gregorio is one of southern Italy's most famous wineries – indeed, one of the biggest successes of recent years in all of vinous Italy – and it was Ercolino, with the help of his wife and two brothers (the latter subsequently moving on in circumstances never quite clarified), who presided over the establishment of the extremely costly vineyard-cum-production facility in the mountains east of Naples. They poured in millions, the source of which was never convincingly revealed, and Feudi rapidly rose to rival southern Italy's most respected

NICOLAS BELFRAGE MW was born in Los Angeles and raised in New York and England. He studied in Paris, Siena, and London, taking a degree at University College London in French and Italian. Nick has been specializing in Italian wines since the 1970s and became a Master of Wine in 1980, the first American citizen to do so. He is the author of the double-award-winning *Life Beyond Lambrusco* (Sidgwick & Jackson, 1985), *Barolo to Valpolicella* (Mitchell Beazley, 1999), and *Brunello to Zibibbo* (Mitchell Beazley, 2001). Nick is a regular contributor to *Harpers Wine and Spirit Weekly* and *The World of Fine Wine*.

FRANCO ZILIANI is a freelance writer who has specialized in Italian wines since 1985. He is a regular contributor to the English periodicals *Harpers Wine and Spirit Weekly*, *Decanter*, and *The World of Fine Wine* (where he is also a member of the editorial board), the Californian magazine *Wine Business Monthly*, the Italian periodicals *Il Sommelier Italiano*, *AIS Lombardia News*, *LaVINIum*, and *VQ*, and the Italian weekly magazine *Il Corriere Vinicolo* (the official organ of Unione Italiana Vini). Franco publishes a weekly wine newsletter, *Bvino*, which is mailed to 28,000 wine enthusiasts, and a wine blog, *Vino al Vino* (www.vinoalvino.org).

and enduring wine producer, Mastroberardino of nearby Atripalda. The new president is quoted as saying that he "hopes to realize wines of the highest quality by bringing into harmony the complex relationship between terroir and product". We wish him luck in this noble endeavour, which will be in marked contrast to the efforts of the Ercolino era.

DOCG status for Morellino di Scansano

Morellino di Scansano wines will, from the 2007 vintage on, enjoy DOCG status. Whether anyone will take any notice is doubtful, DOCG as a general category being undermined in the public eye by the continuing presence in its ranks of cheap Chiantis, Vernaccias, Gavis, Barbarescos, and the like. In one respect, however, the promotion is likely to have an effect: producers will see it as an excuse to move the price up. Whether the consumer will pay the new price is another matter.

Attack at Pantelleria

Salvatore Murana – the most celebrated of the producers of the sweet wines from dried Muscat di Alessandria grapes called Moscato Passito di Pantelleria, from the cinder-dark but curiously captivating volcanic island of that name off the coast of Tunisia – has suffered a second attack on his establishment in 10 years. The attackers burned a plastic tunnel where the grapes of the 2006 harvest were being dried, dousing it with naphtha. The first attack came in 1996, when some 15 greenhouses were lacerated and a wooden cross left by way of macabre warning. Murana, president of the island's consortium, professes himself mystified by this treatment, as do the local *carabinieri*. It is the second assault on members of the Consorzio in a few months. Could this, local producers worried, be a return of the feuding that tore apart the island's wine production in the 1990s?

Grapevine

• **Edoardo Valentini** of Loreto Aprutino in Abruzzo, one of the great personalities of postwar Italian oenology, passed away in June 2006. It was Valentini who demonstrated that great wine, not just ordinary wine or even merely good wine, could be made with Abruzzo's indigenous varieties, Montepulciano and Trebbiano, grown on high trellises or *tendone*. His methods were artisanal in the highest degree (he never filtered, not even whites, and bottled everything by hand), but he was a perfectionist who never sold a bottle he did not consider worthy, and indeed he sold more than 90 per cent of his annual production in bulk, mainly to a nearby cooperative (Roxan), of which he was a member of the council for years.

Opinion:
An Italian wine No. 1 in the world?

Readers of *Wine Report* may not be the most slavish of followers of US magazine *Wine Spectator*, with its scores that never dip far below 80 and its quirky valuations (such as the awarding of 100 points – presumably the status of absolute perfection – to the 2000 Barolo vintage, an opinion that virtually no Barolo producer or serious wine writer would share). On the whole, unless they've been singled out for praise, Italian winemakers would agree with their colleagues from Alba that the "expectorator" is inclined to bizarre judgments, though they may not say so above a whisper. But the Italian wine industry in general, and Brunello di Montalcino producers in particular, were "over the moon" when, late in 2006, they learned that one of their number had been declared by the said publication to be the number-one wine in the world. It proves, they say, that Italian wine is capable of reaching the greatest heights, and it finally lays to rest the notion that Italians, for all their flair and passion in other pursuits, are not world-beaters when it comes to wine.

The wine in question is the 2001 Brunello di Montalcino Tenuta Nuova from Casanova di Neri – proprietor Giacomo Neri, winemaker Carlo Ferrini. Sadly, not everyone who wishes Italian wine well regards the valuation as sound or even desirable. Franco Ziliani writes: "The affirmation of Brunello Tenuta Nuova 2001 as 'best wine in the world' not only does not fill me with enthusiasm but seems to me the umpteenth exercise in inspired marketing on the part of the famous American institution. The wine that was crowned, in fact, is not one of those that arouse my passion and have me swearing that from that beautiful Tuscan commune it is possible to obtain, from 100 per cent Sangiovese, wines among the best of Italy and the world … This Brunello represents that modernist new wave that, in my opinion, is undermining the identity and the credibility, if not the appreciation, of Montalcino and its vinous symbol. Brunello aged in small oak barriques, scented with wood, softened, rounded out, rendered user-friendly and sufficiently seductive to please the palate of that American market that consumes 35 per cent of the denomination says very little to me, as a non-American, except that truly great wine, indeed great Brunello, is something quite different. Confronted with a wine and a style that I do not recognize as genuine, that I feel to be alien to my way of thinking, and that I consider harmful to the image of Italian wine, how can I rejoice?"

Vintage Report

Advance report on the latest harvest

2006

The experience of west-central Italy – Tuscany, Umbria, Lazio – was largely similar to that of northern Italy. Quantity was slightly up compared with 2005, quality being distinctly higher and perhaps better even than that of 2004. Things got off to a slow start in the cool spring, but the extreme heat of June and July soon put that right, and by August the vines were bursting with healthy fruit, requiring some fairly rigorous bunch-thinning on the part of those so inclined. The cool weather of August slowed things down again, but, despite September's sporadic rain, the grapes remained largely healthy, and early- and late-picked varieties fared well, with the only question mark being over those grapes picked towards the last week of September. In general, however, quality was really good, both Sangiovese- and Cabernet/Merlot-based wines being balanced and lacking in some of that excessive power and concentration that seem to have marked the production of recent years. There should be plenty of interesting bottles for laying down from 2006.

In central Italy east of the Apennines, things were not quite so rosy in quantity terms, with a loss of some 10 per cent compared with 2005, although growers were well pleased with the quality both of whites – mainly Verdicchio and Trebbiano, which boasted good balancing acidity and a nice array of perfumes – and reds, mainly Montepulciano and Sangiovese, from which it is even possible to hope for some outstanding wines in future.

Campanians did very nicely thank you out of 2006, with an increase of 10 per cent in terms of quantity and – if these things can be quantified – of more like 25 per cent in terms of quality. White wines have proved to combine freshness of acidity with complexity of aroma, and we can look forward to some fine Greco di Tufos, Falanghinas, and Fianos. Aglianico, one of the latest-ripening varieties in Italy, benefited from a long, warm autumn with marked day–night temperature shifts, and there should be some humdingers for laying down.

Puglia once again suffered from adverse conditions in the month of September, especially in the south in respect of the two principal varieties, Primitivo and Negroamaro. There was on-off sun-rain in September, which compromised the health of some grapes and, though the final quality of the red wines of the Salento peninsula is actually pretty good, it is down some 30 per cent compared with 2005 in quantity terms. This keeps happening in Puglia as never before, and one begins to wonder whether global warming has got it in especially for this corner of the universe.

Both Sicily and Sardinia suffered volume-wise by more than 10 per cent, mainly due to heat and drought, although the final judgment in respect of quality was that some pretty good wines have resulted.

Updates on the previous five vintages

2005

Vintage rating: *Red: 86, White: 88*

In the centre-west there were some difficult conditions to contend with in September – mainly in the form of rain, but in parts also of hail. This was a year for the early pickers, though, because if growers thought things were not ideal before October, they found they became a lot worse afterwards. The first 10 days of October were wet, and anything picked after that time was compromised. There are some decent wines, obviously mainly from early-gathered grapes, but they are not of the long-lived variety, more for drinking up. A similar picture prevailed east of the Apennines in the Marche and Abruzzo, where the 30 per cent of wines that are good all come for early-picked grapes. Further south the picture was brighter, with some very agreeable reds and whites from Puglia and Campania. Sicily and Sardinia, on the other hand, fared very well, with points of excellence.

2004

Vintage rating: *Red: 95, White: 90*

In central Italy and most of the south, all the factors for exceptional wine were in place: growth stages all normal, slow and gradual sugar accumulation, good balance of components in the fruit, and appropriate yield ratio between grapes and wine. There were no hot spells during the summer months, no frosts in the spring or later, and humidity levels stayed normal. What was needed, however, in particular for late-maturing varieties, was an exemplary September, bestowing sunny days, a touch of rain, and good diurnal temperature differences. Which was precisely what central viticultural areas west of the Apennines, and some southern areas, received. In Tuscany, Brunello di Montalcino was given the first maximum rating of five stars since 1997, and it was a similar story in Chianti Classico and Montepulciano. In Tuscany, Romagna, the Marche, Lazio, Campania, and Sardinia, the judgment was "exceptional". Only along the eastern coast, towards the south – in Abruzzo, Molise, and especially Puglia – was quality compromised to some extent by vintage-time rain.

2003

Vintage rating: *Red: 88, White: 80*

A year of drought and very high temperatures, with little relief in the evenings. Vineyards worst affected were towards the centre, these conditions being more normal in the south – for example, Puglia's principal reds, Negroamaro and Primitivo, especially those planted to *alberello*, thrived in the conditions. But it was too much for most whites, which tended to emerge flabby and overweight, and many reds, especially those lacking deep roots or planted in well-drained soil. Sugar ripening was very advanced in many places, but it was not necessarily accompanied by polyphenolic ripeness, which made for too many unbalanced wines. As in the north, the classic wines will need careful selection.

2002

Vintage rating: *Red: 67, White: 79*

The shortest vintage in quantity for 50 years, qualitatively 2002 has proved not as bad as predicted. White wines like Verdicchio are fresh and fragrant, with plenty of nerve. Sangiovese in Tuscany had a poor time of it, but there is so much Merlot and Cabernet these days that they can compensate. Lower-than-average temperatures, plenty of rain, and freak weather conditions made a mess of things along the east coast, but modern techniques saved a lot that would have gone down the pan in 1992.

2001

Vintage rating: *Red: 93, White: 93*

A good year virtually everywhere. Marginally better, perhaps, than 1997, although that vintage received much more hype. Perhaps 2001 was less anomalous than 1997, with wines more in the mainstream but at a higher-than-normal level, whereas 1997s in retrospect seem almost too ripe, too much of a good thing. In Chianti Classico, the level was very good from the start, and the emerging wines confirm that it is a year of excellent aroma, concentration, and balance. In the south, Puglia and Sicily enjoyed ideal conditions. All in all, a very satisfactory outcome for both whites and reds.

Lists compiled by Franco Ziliani.

GREATEST WINE PRODUCERS

1. Case Basse Soldera (Montalcino)
2. Fattoria di Felsina (Chianti Classico)
3. Fontodi (Chianti Classico)
4. Fattoria San Giusto a Rentennano (Chianti Classico)
5. Fattoria Poggio di Sotto (Montalcino)
6. Lisini (Montalcino)
7. Avignonesi (Montepulciano)
8. Agricole Vallone (Puglia)
9. Librandi (Calabria)
10. Palari (Sicily)

BEST-VALUE PRODUCERS

1. Tenuta Il Poggione (Montalcino)
2. Contucci (Montepulciano)
3. Col d'Orcia (Montalcino)
4. Cantina Colonnara (Marche)
5. Contesa Rocco Pasetti (Abruzzo)
6. Ciavolich (Abruzzo)
7. Di Meo (Campania)
8. Tenuta Zicari (Puglia)
9. Botromagno (Puglia)
10. Carrozzo (Puglia)

FASTEST-IMPROVING PRODUCERS

1. Fattoria Selvapiana (Chianti Rufina)
2. Tenute Silvio Nardi (Montalcino)
3. Altesino (Montalcino)
4. Salicutti (Montalcino)
5. Mastrojanni (Montalcino)
6. Fattoria Uccelliera (Montalcino)
7. Castello di Cacchiano (Chianti Classico)
8. Ormanni (Chianti Classico)
9. Rodano (Chianti Classico)
10. Mustilli (Campania)

GREATEST-QUALITY WINES

1. **Chianti Classico Vin San Giusto a Rentennano 1999** Fattoria San Giusto a Rentennano, Tuscany (€50)
2. **Brunello di Montalcino Ugolaia 2000** Lisini, Tuscany (€50)
3. **Brunello di Montalcino 2001** Gorelli Le Potazzine, Tuscany (€30)
4. **Brunello di Montalcino 2001** Eredi Fuligni, Tuscany (€40)
5. **Brunello di Montalcino 2001** Fattoria Poggio di Sotto, Tuscany (€60)
6. **IGT Toscana Fontalloro 2003** Fattoria di Felsina, Tuscany (€30)
7. **IGT Toscana Flaccianello della Pieve 2003** Fontodi, Tuscany (€30)
8. **Costa d'Amalfi Furore Bianco Fiorduva 2005** Marisa Cuomo, Campania (€35)
9. **IGT Salento Graticciaia 2001** Agricole Vallone, Puglia (€35)
10. **IGT Val di Neto Rosso Magno Megonio 2004** Librandi, Calabria (€25)

NEW UP-AND-COMING PRODUCERS

1. Il Colle di Carli (Montalcino)
2. Mocali (Montalcino)
3. Tenuta di Sesta (Montalcino)
4. La Palazzetta (Montalcino)
5. Terredora (Campania)
6. Di Prisco (Campania)
7. D'Alfonso del Sordo (Puglia)
8. Cefalicchio (Puglia)
9. Vetrere (Puglia)
10. Gulfi (Sicily)

BEST BARGAINS

1. **Chianti Classico 2004** Ormanni, Tuscany (€8)
2. **Brunello di Montalcino 2001** Canalicchio Franco Pacenti, Tuscany (€23)
3. **Vin Santo del Chianti Classico 1999** Villa Calcinaia, Tuscany (€25)
4. **Rosso di Montalcino 2004** Gianni Brunelli, Tuscany (€14)
5. **IGT Toscana Salvino 2004** Podere Erbolo, Tuscany (€7.50)
6. **Brut Metodo Classico Rosé NV** Velenosi, Marche (€12.50)
7. **Greco di Tufo 2005** Di Meo, Campania (€9)
8. **IGT Salento Rosato 2005** Taranta Vetrere, Puglia (€5)
9. **IGT Puglia Bombino Rosato 2005** Rivera, Puglia (€5)
10. **IGT Murgia Pier delle Vigne 2001** Botromagno, Puglia (€10)

MOST EXCITING OR UNUSUAL FINDS

1. **Rosso di Montepulciano 2004** Crociani, Tuscany (€6) *From a 10-ha vineyard of medium impasto, this is a Rosso di Montepulciano that combines great typicity and drinkability, very much the child of its three varietal parents: Prugnolo (Sangiovese), Canaiolo, and Mammolo. It is aged for eight months in oak barrels.*
2. **Vino Nobile di Montepulciano Santa Venere 2003** Triacca, Tuscany (€13) *From the Swiss family Triacca, a leader among wines of Valtellina, comes this Vino Nobile di Montepulciano of classic style and impeccable personality, made from Sangiovese with 5 per cent Colorino.*
3. **Brunello di Montalcino 2001** Gianni Brunelli, Tuscany (€30) *The classic style of the 2001 Brunellos is truly a reference point,* combining wonderful expression of terroir with the best characteristics of pure Sangiovese. The wine receives a medium-long maceration on the skins and is aged in medium-large oak barrels, with no barriques.
4. **Brunello di Montalcino 2001** Capanna, Tuscany (€25) *This small estate, positioned in the north of Montalcino, regularly turns out some of the most authentic wines of the denomination. Thanks to soils of a very stony make-up and to temperatures that tend to be lower than the average for Montalcino, Capanna produces a Brunello of distinct youthfulness yet capable of ageing very well – a wine of clean, precise lines, quintessential, with no concession to prevailing fashions.*
5. **Vin Santo del Chianti Classico 1999** Castello di Cacchiano, Tuscany (€25) *A Vin Santo that follows the classic recipe for the genre: Malvasia Bianca del Chianti with long, loose-knit bunches, drying for four months on wooden slats, very long ageing in small barrels, called caratelli, of oak but also of chestnut, mulberry, ash, juniper, and cherry. The barrels are 0.5–1 hl, with staves 35 mm thick, and they are untoasted to avoid bitter flavours. The result is a wine of superior class, full of flavour, clean and fresh.*
6. **Vin Santo del Chianti Classico 1998** Rocca di Montegrossi, Tuscany (€35) *Malvasia del Chianti grapes from massal selection material planted in the 1970s, rich in aroma and thick of skin – such is the foundation of this extraordinary Vin Santo, aged for six to seven years in 50–100-litre caratelli of oak, cherry, and blackberry. The drying takes place*

with the bunches hung one by one on special nets mounted on rails. The wine is still youthful but has enormous potential for excellent evolution.

7 Sannio Fiano 2005 Mustilli, Campania (€8) *An interesting oenological case history: this wine shows that a great variety like Fiano di Avellino can offer excellent results in the Sannio Beneventano zone (until now best known for Greco di Tufo and Falanghina), and not only in Irpinia. This rich, complex wine, full of personality, from the terroir of Sant'Agata dei Goti, amply demonstrates the thesis.*

8 IGT Murgia Ponte della Lama Rosato 2005 Cefalicchio, Puglia (€7.50) *A surprising rosato from a part of Puglia (Canosa in the province of Foggia) not normally known for top wines. It is made from Uva di Troia (90 per cent) and Montepulciano grapes*

cultivated in Alta Murgia and is notable for its aromatic range, its well-judged alcoholic content, and its clean, characterful style.

9 IGT Salento Rosso Malia 2003 Duca Guarini, Puglia (€12) *A rare example of Malvasia Nera vinified unblended and not mixed, as is traditional in the Salento peninsula, with Negroamaro. The wine is surprising for its freshness, bright acidity, and lively articulation on the palate, despite coming from an extremely hot vintage.*

10 IGT Val di Neto Efeso 2004 Librandi, Calabria (€20) *From one of the best southern Italian estates, this is a unique white wine. It is made from the native Calabrian variety Mantonico, from which Librandi has for years been making the sweet wine Passule. It has a lively aroma and vivacity and is a wine of great persistence.*

Grapevine

• **Trentino cooperative** Cantina La Vis e Valle di Cembra, already one of the 10 biggest producers in the land in terms of turnover, has entered (with its wholly owned subsidiary Casa Girelli) into a joint venture with Baglio Chitarra of Trapani, western Sicily. The companies' aim is the production and commercialization

of traditional Sicilian wines. The brand La Mura, already known in the USA and the UK, will feature wines made from Sicily's Grillo and Nero d'Avola grapes. The Trentino giant will invest €1 million over the course of three years to build a new winery and to support the La Mura brand.

Spain

John Radford

Portugal is working on it; France has toyed with it, thrown it out, brought it back in and thrown it out again, and eventually approved it, and so has Spain.

JOHN RADFORD

Vino de la Tierra de Viñedos de España, the new nationwide classification for regional table wines from (almost) any part of Spain, was approved in the summer of 2006. The idea behind it is to allow winemakers to compete on equal terms with unregulated New World wine producers. Under the previous (Europe-wide) rules, wines blended from more than one area lost the right to use any kind of geographical appellation (except "Produce of Spain") and were forbidden to mention a grape variety or vintage date. The new legislation allows for all these details to be included, with the legend "Viñedos de España" on the label.

The first vintage to be bottled under the new regulations is 2006, and we may expect to see wines labelled simply "[Brand name] Tempranillo 2006, Vino de la Tierra Viñedos de España", with the back label giving further details, which could include the specific region from which the wine originates. Not every part of Spain is included in the scheme, however. *Autonomías* included are Andalucía, Aragón, Illes Balears, Canarias, Castilla-La Mancha, Catalunya, Extremadura, Madrid, Murcia, Valencia, and

JOHN RADFORD is a writer and broadcaster with more than 30 years' experience of the culture, landscapes, architecture, food, and wine of Spain. He is the author of *The New Spain* (Mitchell Beazley), which won four international awards, a new edition of which was published in September 2004, and *The Wines of Rioja* (Mitchell Beazley Classic Wine Series), which was published in November 2004 and won the Livre Gourmand Best European Wine Book at Versailles in 2005. He was awarded the Premio Especial Alimentos de España in 2006 by the Spanish government for his coverage of Spanish wines. He co-wrote *Cook España, Drink España* with Spanish celebrity chef Mario Sandoval, published in 2007, and he is also the chairman of the Spanish committee of the *Decanter* World Wine Awards.

Navarra, although the Navarra towns of Andosilla, Aras, Azagra, Bargota, Mendavia, San Adrián, Sartaguda, and Viana are specifically excluded, because they are all within the DOCa Rioja Baja subzone. Apart from the whole of the (rest of the) Rioja wine-production zone, other exclusions are Galicia, Castilla y León, Asturias, Cantabria, and the Basque Country – most of the northwest of the country. The new classification covers all still wines, late-harvest, fortified, and *aguja* ("spritzig") wines but, perhaps significantly, not sparkling wines, and the regulations stipulate that they may be sold in bottle or bag-in-box up to 5 litres' capacity. By the time this edition is published, we should have had the opportunity to see what the marketing people have been able to do to address the export business.

Interestingly, a survey conducted by the Federación Español del Vino (FEV) revealed the following reactions by wine producers in Spain: "Good news for the wine industry", 23 per cent; "Absolutely against it", 4 per cent; "Each to his own", 46 per cent; and "As long as it avoids confusion with Vino de Mesa", 27 per cent – so it seems to have strong support, with the inevitable diehards.

Grapevine

• **A new Rioja website** has been launched to serve the UK, which emerged as Rioja's biggest importer in 2005, taking almost one-third of all the region's exports (245,000 hl/€100 million). Exports to the UK increased again in 2006, when volume rose by 17 per cent and value by 31 per cent. Consequently the OIPVR launched www.winesfromrioja.co.uk, believed to be the first UK-only website created by a Spanish wine region.

• **DO Toro wines** are about to become a benchmark for Spanish red wines. The bold, concentrated, heavily extracted style, the high alcohol (up to 14.5 per cent ABV), the blockbusting fruit of the Tinto Fino, and the ability of the wines to drink well at two or three years old are, apparently, what everyone's looking for within Spain and in export markets. Certainly, the wines have come from nowhere to have the biggest growth in sales of any Spanish wine region. Fetch the Rolls-Royce, Parker…

• **Jacques and François Lurton** have made wine in DOs Rueda and Toro for a number of years, but now they're making them both in the same building. The two DO zones overlap slightly at the town of Villafranca del Duero, where the two brothers have built a new *bodega*. It is the first and only winery in Spain permitted to make two different DO wines. The law stipulated that the *bodega* had to have two separate cellars – one for Rueda and one for Toro – and the grapes will, of course, come from vineyards registered with the appropriate CRDO. There are many companies that make several different wines, but never before in the same building.

NEW VARIETIES FOR RIOJA

In the 2006 edition of *Wine Report* we catalogued some of the changes likely to be made by the new interprofessional regulator in Rioja (OIPVR, established in 2004). Rumours then spoke of additions to the permitted white-grape varieties. However, in January 2007, the OIPVR voted unanimously to permit new varieties for both red and white wines. Some are historic varieties (h) that died out in the early 20th century; some have succeeded (s) in other parts of Spain; and some are, not to put too fine a point on it, market-grabbers (m). *White varieties:* Tempranillo Blanco (h), Maturana Blanca (h), Turruntés (h), Verdejo (s), Sauvignon Blanc (m), and Chardonnay (m – sigh!). *Black varieties:* Maturana Tinta (h), Maturana Parda (h), and Monastel de Rioja (h). The last is no relation to Monastrell or Moristel.

In practice, the historic varieties will take years to come to maturity if, indeed, growers will bother with these ancient, low-yielding vines. Cynics have suggested that the addition of "historic" varieties is nothing more than a smokescreen to cover up the relentless march of "international" varieties.

Any plantations of the newly approved varieties must be matched by grubbing-up of established vineyards, with much of Rioja's Viura and Malvasia likely to disappear as a result. Significantly, "experimental" varieties such as Cabernet Sauvignon, Merlot, and Syrah have not (yet) been approved, but we are informed that there are more "unspecified" varieties yet to come.

The new regulations also exclude the use of oak chips in ageing of wines, and the *crianza* regulations remain unchanged despite the national wine law of 2003, which reduced the time in cask required for *gran reserva* reds.

Grapevine

• **Castilla y León** is still the only region to have taken advantage of the VCIG/VCPRD regulations enshrined in the 2003 national wine law, but the Organos de Gestión are now fully organized, and the details have been published. The final number of producers is as follows: Arribes, 11 *bodegas*; Tierras de León, 33; Zamora, 8; Arlanza, 10; and Benavente, 7. Interestingly, 60 *bodegas* in the region are also members of the Vino de la Tierra Castilla y León, which seems to indicate that the "maverick" tendency is alive and well.

• **Moving away from the Ministry,** the Consejo Regulador for DO La Mancha has converted itself into an interprofessional organization, following the example of Rioja in 2004. The idea behind it is to become independent of the local department of agriculture, and to ensure that quality control is emphasized at least as much as regulation.

REAL MADRID

DO Vinos de Madrid seems finally to have come of age. Last year we celebrated the fabulously expensive Divo by Ricardo Benito, but visits this year show that most of the *bodegas* are now turning out world-class wines, and investment is flooding into the region. Even 10 years ago Madrileño wines consisted mainly of slightly oxidized whites made from Malvar and unexciting reds from Garnacha, but all that has changed. In a brief two-day tour of local *bodegas*, plus a visit to the Salón de los Vinos de Madrid, the wines showed extremely well, even those from "industrial" *bodegas* and whites from Malvar and Albillo, which have real, fresh fruit and lipsmacking acidity. Carlos Falcó, the Marqués de Griñón, has launched El Rincón from his Madrid estate, and other stars include Qubél from Gosálbez Orti, Tagonius from a new *bodega* established by the Foxá Hotel Group, and Tejoneras from a brand-new *bodega* called Nueva Valverde. Confidence is riding high, even though, as one winemaker said, shaking his head, it would be nice if "we could persuade the people of Madrid to order a bottle of wine from Madrid!"

THE PONCE OF MANCHUELA

Manchuela is something of a forgotten DO, on the eastern fringe of Castilla-La Mancha, once the haunt of gloomy co-ops and wines that were seen (if they were seen at all) as sub-La Mancha in quality. As with so many regions, however, new *bodegas* are coming into the business, mostly small and privately owned, and geeing up the old co-ops (80 per cent of production) to take a bigger interest in export-quality wines. There is great potential in the Bobal grape (yet another variety once dismissed as suitable for bulk wines only), exemplified by one particular *bodega*, Ponce, which was founded in 2005 and is turning out wines of exemplary quality (see Clos Lojen in the lists below). Meanwhile, the dear old co-ops are still turning out something drinkable for small change (see Villavid in the lists).

GREAT WHITE HOPE

Ribeiro and Valdeorras are gradually coming out of the shadow of their neighbour Rías Baixas, in Galicia. Last year we reported on an upsurge in interest in white wines within and without Spain, and the trend has continued. This has proved helpful for the Godello, Galicia's "other" world-class white grape, which has been winning medals all over Europe (see Valdesil in the lists). Ribeiro likes to remind people that it was exporting wine 100 years before its upstart neighbour was granted the DO, but, as always, it's taken modern winemaking and an almost forgotten variety to bring the area back to the fore.

FOURTH PAGO ON THE WAY?

Finca Guijoso, the 65-ha estate belonging to Sanchez-Muliterno, is tipped to become the fourth DO Pago. The estate grows mainly "international" varieties plus Tempranillo, and the vineyards are at 1,000 m (3,280 ft) altitude. The estate is situated near

Bonillo in the Sierra de Alcaraz in Albacete, Castilla-La Mancha, just a few kilometres from Manual Manzaneque's Finca Elez, one of the first two DOs de Pago, created in 2003. Quite a few private estates are in the running to accede to this status, but for some reason Castilla-La Mancha seems much more sympathetic to its applicants than some of the other regions, perhaps because it was this region that started the Pago ball rolling in 1999/2000.

NEW DO ON ITS FEET

DO Uclés, created in 2005, bottled its first wines under the new label (the 2005 vintage) in April 2006. There are eight *bodegas* in the zone, making wine under DO Uclés or declassifying it to DO La Mancha, according to the origin of the grapes. The new DO was the result of an initiative by the founding *bodegas*, following the creation of DO Ribera del Júcar (also a subdivision of DO La Mancha) in 2001–03, and it seems likely that other areas within DO La Mancha with access to higher-quality vineyards may follow. Uclés is authorized to grow Cencibel (Tempranillo), Garnacha, Cabernet Sauvignon, Merlot, and Syrah. There is a sliding scale of production according to the age of the vines – from 8,000 kg/ha (approximately 56 hl/ha) for six-year-old vines, down to 5,000 kg/ha (35 hl/ha) for vines over 40 years old. Only 1,500 ha of vineyards are classified for the DO, on either side of the Altomira mountain range at high altitudes, and only red wines are included.

Grapevine

• **Valtiendas** will become the sixth VCPRD, if all goes to plan. It was formerly a Vino de la Tierra zone in its own right, covering 22 towns and villages in the province of Segovia, directly to the south of DO Ribera del Duero, but it was absorbed into the Vino de la Tierra Castilla y León, in which *bodegas* were able to hone their skills with Cabernet and Syrah as well as the native Tempranillo/Tinto Fino. Early results show well, although the prices of the wines are perhaps dangerously close to those of its northern neighbour.

• **Has anybody heard of Cangas?** It's a small area in the southwest of Asturias (much better known for its excellent cider), with six villages plus the town of Cangas del Narcea,

about 80 km (50 miles) southwest of the capital, Oviedo. They grow Mencía as well as some pretty obscure local varieties: Albarín Negro, Verdejo/Berdejo Tinto, and Carrasquín Tinto for reds, and Picapoll Blanco, Albillo, and Albarín Blanco for whites. We are assured that Albarín Blanco and Verdejo/Berdejo are no relation to similarly named grapes in neighbouring Galicia and Castilla y León. Some 80 per cent of the vineyard is black grapes, but the wines are fairly rustic. The whites, however, have some character, as you'd expect this far north, and may have a future outside the region (see Monasterio de Corias in the lists). The prices, however, may mean that local pride is more important than export potential.

Opinion:
Whose palate counts?

We keep reading articles by fellow wine writers bemoaning high alcohol levels in wine and wishing for the days of "light luncheon claret" at 11.5 per cent ABV, which, allegedly, had "subtlety, style, depth, complexity [insert adjective of your choice], rather than palate-busting power". A while ago we visited a cooperative in DO Cariñena at which winemaker Javier Domecque (no relation) described his brief for Bombero – a red wine from old-vine Garnacha destined for Laithwaites in London. Tony Laithwaite (not a man known for his mistakes) had specified low yields, 15 per cent ABV alcohol, and a retail price of £4.99, and for the past four years it has been his bestselling red wine in the UK, as well as winning medals in professional (blind) tastings. In the autumn of 2006, González Byass launched an addition to its supermarket Altozano range from La Mancha. It's a Shiraz (so labelled) with a purple screwcap, and it too is 15 per cent ABV. We presented it at a blind tasting to WSET students, those who will be the next generation of wine-trade management, and they went longitudinally ape over it. It retails in the UK at £4.99 and in Spain at €4.50. So who's right? The pundits or the people who vote with their wallets?

"Industrialization" of viticulture?

Many modern vineyards, especially in the dry south of Spain, use drip-irrigation systems with sophisticated technology. Dendrometers monitor the roots, and a computer determines how many drops of water are needed to maintain the vine's vigour without giving it an easy time. Water-stress methods irrigate only one root per plant, allowing the others to dry, which confuses the vine about whether it's in a drought situation or not and prevents it from completely closing its stomata, which would slow down or stop photosynthesis. In a wine world where "naturalness" and everything from organic to biodynamic viticulture is increasingly popular, how "natural" can a wine be when its grapes were grown in such a heavily managed way? The pioneer of this technology in Spain, Carlos Falcó, would point out that the world-class wines he's making at Malpica and El Rincón would not exist if the vines had been left to fend for themselves in the arid soils of Toledo and Madrid.

Vintage Report

Advance report on the latest harvest

2006

Winter rains in the north provided plenty of water for a good start to the vegetative cycle, and the spring was warm and dry, providing ideal conditions for flowering. Summer was rather hotter than most growers would have liked, with drought in places, and comparisons were being made with the searing heat of 2003. In the event, however, those temperatures did not materialize, but they did effectively prevent the risk of cryptogams in the run-up to the vintage, as well as providing excellent sugar levels. Eventually there were sufficient rains, although some parts of the vineyard did ripen unevenly and the crop had to be gathered by hand selection. In Rioja, in spite of sporadic spring hailstorms, the CRDOCa is very upbeat about the prospects for quality, but several individual growers have suggested that, while 2006 will be good, it's unlikely to hit the heights of 2004 and 2005.

Updates on the previous five vintages

2005

Vintage rating: *Red: 90, White: 90*

In a repeat of 1994/95, nature delivered two *excelente* harvests in a row: 2005 was characterized by low rainfall in the early part of the year and then oppressive heat, with drought in many places during the ripening season and, paradoxically, outbreaks of hail in June, especially in Aragón. Late rains in the north interrupted the harvest, but the resulting grapes were dry and healthy and the summer heat had reduced the risk of cryptogams.

2004

Vintage rating: *Red – Rioja: 90, others: 80; White: 90*

This was an "isometric" split, with the northwest and central south doing well and the north-central and northeast having a fair amount of dull and cloudy weather, although the latter part of the ripening season was warm and sunny in most areas, giving yields slightly up on 2003. Rioja, particularly, came through with its second *excelente* year of the century.

2003

Vintage rating: *Red: 90, White: 90*

High levels of summer heat right across Spain brought the harvest forward by anything up to 10 days. Parts of Rioja suffered very badly, and vineyards with irrigation survived the best. Penedès harvested excellent reds with the exception of Syrah, which had suffered from the heat, and quantity was down almost everywhere.

2002

Vintage rating: *Northeast – Red: 60, White: 60;*
Southwest – Red: 80, White: 70

The 2002 vintage in Spain divided roughly into a southwest/northeast divide, with the former having the better time of it. Damp conditions in Catalonia extended to rain during the harvest with resultant rot, while in the south, La Mancha picked very healthy fruit in excellent conditions.

2001

Vintage rating: *Red: 90, White: 90*

Excellent quality throughout Spain, with Rioja and Ribera del Duero showing particularly well, and the south (La Mancha, Valdepeñas, etc.) making what may become some very long-lived wines. These wines are starting to drink very well indeed. Good whites, too, particularly in Rías Baixas and Rueda, for early drinking.

GREATEST WINE PRODUCERS

1. Alvaro Palacios (Priorat, Bierzo, Rioja)
2. Mariano García (Ribera del Duero, Toro, Rioja, Castilla y León)
3. Peter Sisseck (Ribera del Duero)
4. Xavier Ausás, Vega Sicilia (Ribera del Duero, Toro)
5. Alejandro Fernández (Ribera del Duero, Toro, La Mancha)
6. Carlos Falcó (Dominio de Valdepusa, Pagos de Familia)
7. Miguel Torres (Penedès, Catalunya)
8. Marcos Eguren (Rioja, Toro)
9. Telmo Rodríguez (ubique)
10. Benjamín Romeo (Rioja)

FASTEST-IMPROVING PRODUCERS

1. Vinos Jeromín (Vinos de Madrid)
2. Nuestra Señora de la Cabeza (Manchuela)
3. Villavid (Manchuela)
4. Campante (Ribeiro)
5. Martín Códax (Rías Baixas)
6. Pazo de Señorans (Rías Baixas)
7. Valdesil (Valdeorras)
8. Algueira (Ribeira Sacra)
9. Dinastía Vivanco (Rioja)
10. San Roque (Vinos de Madrid)

NEW UP-AND-COMING PRODUCERS

1 Nueva Valverde (Vinos de Madrid)
2 Gosálbez Orti (Vinos de Madrid)
3 Irius (Somontano)
4 Antion (Rioja)
5 Tagonius (Vinos de Madrid)
6 Regina Viarum (Ribeira Sacra)
7 Pérez Hidalgo (Sierras de Málaga)
8 Vagal (Valtiendas)
9 Cortijo de Jara (Cádiz)
10 Anfora Enix (Ribera del Andarax)

BEST-VALUE PRODUCERS

1 Nuestra Señora de la Cabeza (Manchuela)
2 San Alejandro Co-op (Calatayud)
3 San Gregorio Co-op (Calatayud)
4 Cortijo de Jara (Cádiz)
5 González Byass (Castilla)
6 Félix Solís (Valdepeñas, Ribera del Duero)
7 Casa de la Viña (Castilla)
8 Laderas del Pinoso – El Sequé (Utiel-Requena)
9 Naia (Rueda)
10 Castro Martín (Rías Baixas)

Grapevine

• **Dehesa del Carrizal** (formerly DO La Mancha) was promoted to DO Pago status in March 2006, only the third in Spain, and all of them in Castilla-La Mancha, so Spain currently has 3 DOs de Pago, 2 DOCA/DOQs, 62 DOs, and 5 VCPRDs – 72 QWPSR zones in all. The number of "official" VdlTs (that is, those that belong to AVIMES) is 37, but there are a further "unofficial" 20, plus some regional names that have no official sanction. But, this being Spain, nobody takes any notice. With the rise of the VCPRDs and regional VdlTs, many will not survive.

GREATEST-QUALITY WINES

1 **Rioja La Viña de Andres Romeo 2003** Benjamín Romeo (€70)
2 **Rioja Aurus 2002** Finca Allende (€100)
3 **Rioja Cirsión 2003** Roda (€125)
4 **Bierzo Tares P3 2003** Dominio de Tares (€35)
5 **Ribera del Duero M2 de Matallana 2003** Telmo Rodríguez (€16.50)
6 **Rioja 2002** Señorío de San Vicente (€26)
7 **Rioja Trasnocho 2002** Fernando Remirez de Ganuza (€48)
8 **Ribera del Duero Unico 1995** Vega Sicilia (€160)
9 **Ribera del Duero 2002** Aalto (€30)
10 **Rioja Dalmau 2001** Marqués de Murrieta (€45)

BEST BARGAINS

1 **Manchuela Dulce Nombre de Jesús Tempranillo 2004** Villavid (€2.08)
2 **Vino de la Tierra Castilla y León Tempranillo 2004** Casa de la Viña (€2.90)
3 **Valdepeñas Viña Albali Reserva 1999** Félix Solís (€3.25)
4 **Vinos de Madrid Qvod 1 Blanco Albillo 2005** Don Alvaro de Luna (€3.46)
5 **Alicante Laderas de El Sequé 2004** Laderas del Pinoso (€3.90)
6 **Bierzo 2004** Peique (€4.50)
7 **Navarra 2004** Inurrieta Sur (€4.60)
8 **Rueda Blanco Joven 2004** Hermanos Lurton (€4.92)
9 **Navarra Crianza 2002** Principe de Viana (€5.28)
10 **Pla de Bages Abadal Cabernet Sauvignon Rosado 2004** Masíes d'Avinyó (€6.10)

MOST EXCITING OR UNUSUAL FINDS

① **Vino de la Tierra Cádiz Cortijo de Jara Roble 2005** Puertanueva (€3.40) *Until 2002 they grew Palomino and sold it to the sherry houses but replanted in 2003 with Tempranillo, Merlot, and Syrah. Tremendous potential and excellent value.*

② **Vino de la Tierra Castilla y León Altozano Shiraz 2005** González Byass (€4.50) *The controversial 15 per cent ABV addition to this supermarket range, made in Otero in the province of Toledo. This is the first release; it promises to ruffle a few feathers.*

③ **Vino de la Tierra Castilla y León Vagal 940 Cuvée Joana 2005** Vagal (€5.50) *The "940" refers to the altitude of the vineyards in the province of Segovia, which will become the VCPRD Valtiendas. The bodega is run by two brothers and their sister Joana, and the wine is 100 per cent Tinto Fino.*

④ **Manchuela Clos Lojen Bobal 2005** Ponce (€6) *Bodegas y Viñedos Ponce was founded in 2005 to exploit plantations of 30- to 70-year-old Bobal vines and to prove that Bobal is a world-class grape. Production is very low, but the quality potential is extraordinary.*

⑤ **Sierras de Málaga Vega del Geva Roble 2005** Pérez Hidalgo (€7.50) *Founded in 2001 (first vintage 2004), this small bodega has 4 ha growing Syrah, Cabernet Sauvignon, and Merlot, and the wine has six months in French and American oak.*

⑥ **Montsant Etim Old Vines Grenache 2002** Falset-Marça (€8.40) *This company is a combination of two original co-ops but has raised its game considerably since DO Montsant was created in 2001. The Etim range, in particular, is performing particularly well.*

⑦ **Vino de la Tierra Cangas Viña Grandiella 2005** Monasterio de Corias (€8.50) *Something of a curiosity: the Vino de la Tierra Cangas came into being in 2001, but little has been seen outside the region. Production is mainly red, but at these northern latitudes the whites are probably better. This old monastic vineyard makes its white mainly from Albarín Blanco. The price may be optimistic.*

⑧ **Vinos de Madrid Tejoneras Alta Selección 2005** Nueva Valverde (€8.50) *A brand-new bodega sitting amid a vast hunting estate. They grow mainly Garnacha (up to 50 years old) but with new plantings of Tempranillo and Shiraz in a smart but small winery. The winemaker is half-Australian, and it shows in his wines.*

⑨ **Priorat Badaceli 2003** Cal Grau (€16.70) *At last, a Priorat wine that delivers that wonderful combination of concentration, power, and elegance without asking the usual Priorat price. The main grapes are Cariñena (55 per cent) and Garnacha (35 per cent), with a little Cabernet Sauvignon.*

⑩ **Vinos de Madrid El Rincón 2004** Marqués de Griñón (€19.50) *This is the latest vintage of Carlos Falcó's project at his estate in the province of Madrid. Using the same vineyard technology that has done so well at Malpica, he is growing Syrah and Garnacha. The wine is quite an eye-opener, even among the newly resurgent Vinos de Madrid.*

Sherry

Julian Jeffs QC

There has been talk of growing sales as one false dawn
follows another, fuelled by the optimism of Andalusia.
But this time there is slight cause for encouragement,
as the slowdown is reduced to 2.6 per cent.

JULIAN JEFFS QC

If the sun is ever going to rise, it will take
some time to do it. And does it matter?
The export markets of the late 1970s may
not come again for half a century, but that
is just history repeating itself. It always does.
The peak of 1875 collapsed abysmally, and
things started to look up only in the 1920s.
The story was the same: low prices and
even lower quality.

In the meantime, the sherry shippers have
developed new markets for old products.
Manzanilla has taken off in Spain, while sherry vinegar is to be found
all over Europe and is a favourite with French chefs. It has become so
important that the words "y Vinagre de Jerez" have been added to the
title of sherry's governing body. It is now available as an aged reserve.
These products were always there, just waiting to be developed. But the

JULIAN JEFFS QC became a Gray's Inn barrister in 1958, attained Queen's Counsel
in 1975, and retired from practice in 1991, although he continued as a Deputy
High Court Judge until 1996. His love of sherry began in 1956, when he was a
sherry shipper's assistant in Spain, and this led to a passion for writing when his
book *Sherry* (Faber & Faber) was published in 1961. He began a two-year stint as
editor of *Wine and Food* in 1965, and in 1971 he created Faber & Faber's radically
new Wine Series. Over the next 40-odd years he commissioned many of the most
respected, long-lasting, and definitive works on wine. He held this position until
2002, when Faber & Faber sold the Wine Series to Mitchell Beazley. Julian has
been chairman (1970–72), vice president (1975–91), and president (1992–96) of
the Circle of Wine Writers, winning the Glenfiddich Wine Writer award in 1974
and 1978. His books include *The Wines of Europe* (Faber & Faber, 1971), *The Little
Dictionary of Drink* (Pelham, 1973), and *The Wines of Spain* (Faber & Faber, 1999).

lesson has at last been learned. The shippers are sailing on a new tack. The new age-classified and vintage wines have given sherry the quality image it always deserved and these more highly priced wines are now prized, and they are bargains compared with table wines of similar ages. One shipper – Bodegas Tradición – makes nothing else. Sales of these wines increased by 56 per cent between 2003 and 2004, a trend that still continues. They, too, were always there but were never exploited, the shippers relying on their bulk sales of cheap wines. Now sherry is being appreciated for the great wine it undoubtedly is. The future is indeed bright, but quite different.

VOS and VORS wines

The list of age-dated wines listed in *Wine Report 2006* is now out of date. Not only are there additions and omissions, but even the names of some of the *bodegas* have changed; and no list is up to date for long. Emilio Lustau has already indicated its intention to give up VORS and to concentrate on VOS. The current list is shown below.

Shipper	Style	Classification	Name
Alvaro Domecq	Amontillado	VORS	AD
	Palo Cortado	VORS	1730
	Oloroso	VORS	1730
	Oloroso	VORS	Alburejo
	Pedro Ximénez	VORS	1730
Barbadillo	Amontillado	VOS	Principe
	Amontillado	VORS	Barbadillo
	Palo Cortado	VORS	Barbadillo
	Oloroso	VORS	Barbadillo
	Oloroso	VORS	San Rafael
	Oloroso Dulce	VORS	Barbadillo
Beam Global España	Amontillado	VORS	51-1ª
	Amontillado	VORS	Harveys
	Palo Cortado	VORS	Capuchino
	Oloroso	VORS	Harveys
	Oloroso	VORS	Sibarita
	Pedro Ximénez	VORS	Harveys
	Pedro Ximénez	VORS	Venerable
Bodegas 501	Amontillado	VOS	Miranda
	Amontillado	VORS	Gades
Dios Baco	Amontillado	VORS	Baco Imperial
	Palo Cortado	VORS	Baco Imperial
	Oloroso	VORS	Baco Imperial
Emilio Hidalgo	Palo Cortado	VORS	Privilegio
	Pedro Ximénez	VORS	Santa Ana
Emilio Lustau	Amontillado	VOS	VOS Lustau
	Palo Cortado	VOS	VOS Lustau
	Oloroso	VORS	VORS Lustau

Shipper	Style	Classification	Name
Federico Paternina	Amontillado	VORS	Fino Imperial
	Oloroso	VORS	Victoria Regina
	Pedro Ximénez	VORS	Vieja Solera
Garvey	Oloroso	VOS	1780
	Oloroso	VORS	1780
	Pedro Ximénez	VOS	1780
	Pedro Ximénez	VORS	1780
González Byass	Amontillado	VORS	Amontillado del Duque
	Palo Cortado	VORS	Apóstoles
	Oloroso Dulce	VORS	Matusalém
	Pedro Ximénez	VORS	Noé
Hidalgo-La Gitana	Amontillado	VOS	Pastrana
	Amontillado	VOS	Wellington
	Amontillado	VORS	Solera Especial
	Amontillado	VORS	Viejo Hidalgo
	Palo Cortado	VORS	Wellington
	Oloroso	VORS	Vaedro
José Estévez	Oloroso	VOS	Don Gonzalo
	Oloroso	VORS	Covadonga
	Oloroso	VORS	Majestad
M Gil Luque	Amontillado	VORS	De Bandera
	Palo Cortado	VORS	De Bandera
	Oloroso	VORS	De Bandera
	Pedro Ximénez	VORS	De Bandera
Osborne	Pedro Ximénez	VORS	Viejo
Pedro Romero	Amontillado	VORS	Don Pedro Romero
	Palo Cortado	VORS	HDPRV
	Oloroso	VORS	El Alamo
Pilar Plá Pechovierto	Amontillado	VORS	1830
	Oloroso	VORS	1/7
	Oloroso	VORS	1/14
Sanchez Romate	Amontillado	VORS	La Sacristia de Romate
	Oloroso	VORS	La Sacristia de Romate
	Pedro Ximénez	VOS	La Sacristia de Romate
Sandeman Jerez	Amontillado	VOS	Royal Esmeralda
	Oloroso	VOS	Royal Corregidor
	Pedro Ximénez	VOS	Royal Ambrosante
Tradición	Amontillado	VORS	Tradición
	Palo Cortado	VORS	Tradición
	Oloroso	VORS	Tradición
	Pedro Ximénez	VOS	Tradición
Valdespino	Amontillado	VORS	Coliseo
	Palo Cortado	VORS	Cardenal
	Oloroso	VOS	Solera 1842
	Oloroso	VORS	Su Majestad
Williams & Humbert	Amontillado	VORS	Jalifa
	Amontillado	VORS	Solera Especial
	Palo Cortado	VOS	Dos Cortados
	Pedro Ximénez	VOS	Don Guido

Opinion:
The price of quality

Under EU law, the *consejo regulador* can no longer set a minimum price for sherry, and it appears that some shippers are again selling wines at uneconomically low prices. This can only be destructive, and it is to be hoped (probably in vain) that the big buyers will insist on quality and will be prepared to pay for it. One solution may well be to limit sales to a smaller proportion of stocks held, and this is certainly being considered. A new hope lies in the development of fresh markets. Publicity campaigns in the United States and Canada are beginning to bear fruit and new markets may be built up in the Far East, particularly in Japan and China, since sherry goes very well with Eastern foods.

Grapevine

• **A marriage has taken place** in Sanlúcar. The small but excellent *bodega* of Gaspar Florido has been bought by the larger and also excellent Pedro Romero. It should be a very happy union. But another excellent *bodega* – Herederos de Argüeso – has left family ownership and has been bought by a wealthy construction company. The wines are unchanged, and the intention is to continue as before, but tongues wag and suggest that the beautiful old *bodegas* down by the river, where the demand for holiday flats is enormous, will one day disappear, and the wines will be moved to another, less valuable, site.

• **Bodegas Valdivia,** mentioned in *Wine Report 2007*, is now fully operational and being marketed in the UK. It intends to specialize in age-dated sherries and at present lists three: the Sacromonte range of 15-year-old amontillado, oloroso, and Pedro Ximénez.

• **Bodegas Pilar Aranda** has changed its name to Alvaro Domecq SL after some legal wrangling, but it continues to use the trademark "1730", since the mark Domecq was sold. Alvaro Domecq, a great bullfighter and a former mayor of Jerez, sadly died in 2005, but his family continues to own the *bodega*, so the Domecqs are active again with their own wines. We wait to see if they will emulate the success of the great Pedro.

Vintage Report

Advance report on the latest harvest

2006

Vintage rating: *98*

The consistently high ratings of sherry vintages must be a source of envy to nearly all other wine growers. It has happened again. While 2005 was a year of drought with a small, top-quality vintage, 2006 had below-average rainfall but enough to bring the yield to about average with very good quality. This was improved by a storm just before the vintage (not an unusual occurrence), which gave the grapes just the water they required. The vintage began on 20 August, a fortnight before the traditional date, and is the ninth consecutive vintage to have started in August, which says something for global warming. The *Baumé* was 12.1 degrees. Production was 66.3 hl/ha, giving 113,295 butts that qualified for the DO. This is still a shortfall for sales of 120,000, but it's an improvement on 2005. There was plenty of free-run juice.

Updates on the previous five vintages

2005

Vintage rating: *98*

A remarkably tactful vintage, producing a very small yield of top-quality must. Since earlier vintages had been rather too abundant, this was good news for the shippers but less good news for the growers. The rainfall was very low indeed. After a hot July punctuated by Levante winds, which dried the grapes, the vintage started early, on 14 August, producing very small but exceedingly ripe and healthy grapes, their health demonstrated by the low gluconic acid content. The average *Baumé* was 11.93 degrees. Production was 66 hl/ha, and a total of 97,000 butts qualified for the DO. So why not a rating of 100? This would have been justified were it not for the fact that, owing to the small size of the grapes, there was not a lot of free-run juice for finos.

2004

Vintage rating: 90

At 740 mm (29 in), rainfall was well above average (600–620 mm [23.6–24.4 in]) but was well distributed throughout the year. A damp spring caused mildew in some vineyards around Sanlúcar and Trebujena, but July and August were very mild with no Levante winds to dry out the grapes and reduce yields, so they were harvested in excellent condition. Total production was 81.62 hl/ha, with 66.6 granted the DO, giving 138,244 butts. The maturity was excellent and the quality very good, with an alcoholic strength of 11.3 per cent.

2003

Vintage rating: 95

A yield of 64 hl/ha provided 138,000 butts of wine. Rainfall was above average at 760 mm (30 in) but happened at the right times. After a hot summer, some of the grapes were overripe, but the maturity was generally good, with an alcoholic strength of 12 per cent.

2002

Vintage rating: 95

A yield of 64 hl/ha provided a total of 137,888 butts. Rainfall 594 mm (23 in). Quality: excellent – good maturity with an alcoholic strength of 11 per cent.

2001

Vintage rating: 95

A yield of 72 hl/ha provided 152,102 butts. An early vintage. Rainfall: 474 mm (18½ in). Quality: exceptional – the grapes had a perfect level of maturation.

Grapevine

• **The name Domecq** has been the greatest in Jerez since 1730 and showed up proud and prominent on its huge *bodegas*. But following the sale of the *bodegas*, the name is gradually being wiped out, its place taken by Beam Global España, and many tears have been shed. But the wines and spirits, whether for the marks owned by Beam Global or those owned by Pernod Ricard, are still made in the old way and in the same place.

• **Vintage sherry,** from small beginnings by González Byass, has begun to take off and has also been available from Tradición, Harvey, Sandeman, Lustau, and Real Tesoro.

GREATEST WINE PRODUCERS

1. González Byass (including Croft and Wisdom & Warter)
2. Beam Global España (Domecq, Harvey)
3. Osborne
4. Garvey (including de Soto and Sandeman)
5. Barbadillo
6. Hidalgo-La Gitana
7. José Estévez (including Valdespino and Real Tesoro)
8. Emilio Lustau/Luis Caballero
9. Williams & Humbert
10. Sanchez Romate

FASTEST-IMPROVING PRODUCERS

1. Alvaro Domecq
2. Pedro Romero
3. Dios Baco
4. Pilar Plá Pechovierto
5. José Estévez/Valdespino
6. Bodegas 501
7. Emilio Hidalgo
8. Williams & Humbert

NEW UP-AND-COMING PRODUCERS

1. Alvaro Domecq
2. Tradición
3. Rey Fernando de Castilla
4. Pilar Plá Pechovierto (El Maestro Sierra)
5. Gutiérrez Colosia
6. Ferris
7. Dios Baco
8. M Gil Luque
9. Valdivia

BEST-VALUE PRODUCERS

1. González Byass/Wisdom & Warter
2. Beam Global España
3. Williams & Humbert
4. Emilio Lustau
5. José Estévez
6. Bodegas 501
7. Gutiérrez Colosia
8. Federico Paternina

GREATEST-QUALITY WINES

This selection has been hard to make, since there are now so many top-quality wines, but I have aimed to include wines of every style, which are listed in order of price, bearing in mind that a good age-dated wine must necessarily be more expensive than a good fino.

1. **San León Manzanilla** Herederos de Argüeso (€5.10)
2. **Coquinero Fino Amontillado** Osborne (€7)
3. **Tio Pepe Fino** González Byass (€7.60)
4. **Pastrana Manzanilla Pasada** Hidalgo-La Gitana (€11)
5. **Amontillado del Duque VORS** González Byass (€40)
6. **Amontillado 51-1ª** Beam Global España (€48)
7. **Tradición Palo Cortado VORS** Tradición (€50)
8. **Don Pedro Romero Palo Cortado Viejisimo** Pedro Romero (€53.85)
9. **Fino Imperial Amontillado VORS** Federico Paternina (€72)
10. **Añada Millennium 2000 Oloroso** González Byass (€120)

BEST BARGAINS

What is a bargain? Generally, with sherry, as with anything else, you get what you pay for, but sometimes you are surprised and would have expected to pay more. Happily there are many such and those listed are just a selection.

① **Las Medallas Manzanilla** Herederos de Argüeso (€3.64)

② **Fino San Patricio** Garvey (€5.20)

③ **Obispo Gascon Palo Cortado VSOP** Barbadillo (€14.48)

④ **Sacromonte Amontillado Seco 15 Years** Valdivia (€30)

⑤ **Sacromonte Oloroso 15 Years** Valdivia (€30)

⑥ **Royal Corregedor Oloroso VOS** Sandeman (€30)

⑦ **Matusalém Oloroso Dulce VORS** González Byass (€36)

⑧ **Noé Pedro Ximénez VORS** González Byass (€36)

⑨ **Palo Cortado VOS** Emilio Lustau (€38)

⑩ **Oloroso VOS** Emilio Lustau (€38)

MOST EXCITING OR UNUSUAL FINDS

① **Añada Millennium 2000 Oloroso** González Byass (€120) *This añada is actually not one at all: it is a blend of añadas drawn from the best vintages from each of the 10 decades of the 20th century. The result is stunning.*

② **Harveys Orange Aperitif** Beam Global España (€11) *Is this a sherry at all? Its base certainly is: a blend very similar to the company's famous Bristol Cream. Orange flavourings for sherry are traditional; wines of this kind used to be sold as jerez aromatizado. Although described as an apéritif, it is also a most agreeable drink with which to end a meal.*

③ **Victoria Regina Oloroso VSOP** Federico Paternina (€72) *When the old Diez Hermanos bodegas were sold and then sold again, there were fears that some of their great wines would be lost and gone for ever, as happened with other buyouts. But this one, like Fino Imperial (above), survived and is as fine as ever: a classic old, dry oloroso.*

④ **Antique Sherry Pedro Ximénez** Rey Fernando de Castilla (€31.25) *By the standards of Pedro Ximénez this is remarkably light, both in colour and in flavour, so it does not cloy. It is very complex and has an almost bitter finish, showing its age.*

⑤ **Noé Pedro Ximénez VORS** González Byass (€36) *Another example of how good a really old Pedro Ximénez can be. This is in the dark, traditional, rather viscous style, but it shows its age in a glorious, sharp finish.*

Grapevine

• Since 1995, 2,904 ha of vines have been planted or replanted – 28 per cent of the total. But most sherry is still made from 30-year-old or older vines.

• In the year 2004/05, there were 532,427 butts of sherry maturing in the *bodegas*. This rose to 535,379 in 2005/06, amounting to 2,676,895 hl.

• **Exports to the UK** amounted to 18,199,941 litres in 2005, rising to its traditional place as the top export market, overtaking the Netherlands with 14,354,001 litres. Spain was the third-largest market, with 13,512,042 litres.

Portugal

Charles Metcalfe

Even the French are now realizing that the way to sell large amounts of wine these days is to create a brand and market it for all it's worth.

CHARLES METCALFE

But it's a penny that has not yet hit the floor in Portugal – with certain notable exceptions, such as port, Vinho Verde, and Mateus Rosé. And there is a bunch of Alentejo reds – including Monte Velho, Tinto da Anfora, and Periquita – that have established good images and sales. However, most producers are happy to put their name on the label and hope customers will become familiar enough with it to carry on buying.

It's no surprise that Sogrape, creator of Mateus, has been first to pursue new brands. (Sogrape was never going to be huge in the Anglophone world…) Callabriga, originally the name of a Sogrape estate in the Douro, is steadily moving in a multiregional direction. First step was the rebranding of the Douro red from Quinta de Callabriga to Callabriga (which meant they could use grapes from outside the estate). Then came an Alentejo Callabriga. Now there are a Dão Callabriga and

CHARLES METCALFE's new book, *The Wine and Food Lover's Guide to Portugal*, was published in June 2007. Past careers as an opera singer, investment analyst, tour guide, security guard, and freelance cook provided the perfect preparation for founding Britain's second consumer wine magazine (*Wine International*) and the International Wine Challenge. Having served a 12-year term as drinks expert on Richard and Judy's *This Morning*, Charles will talk to anybody and everybody about wine – from vast corporations, to local wine societies. His palate is much in demand in tasting competitions, and he has judged in Australia, France, Germany, Italy, New Zealand, Portugal, South Africa, and Spain, as well as being co-chairman of the International Wine Challenge, the biggest wine competition in the world. He writes sporadically for a number of publications and occasionally embarrasses his children by popping up on TV programmes as a drinks presenter.

two reserve Callabrigas (Douro and Alentejo). The common theme is Aragonez/Tinta Roriz/Tempranillo, blended with other varieties appropriate to the region. The Douro has Touriga Franca and Touriga Nacional; the Alentejo, Alfrocheiro and Alicante Bouschet; and the Dão, Touriga Nacional and Alfrocheiro. Another brand Sogrape has extended is Grão Vasco, which used to be only Dão, but now has Douro and Alentejo versions too.

Another couple of eye-catching brand extensions are Peter Bright's companions for BrightPink: BrightWhite and BrightRed. They come, like BrightPink, in shiny aluminium bottles, and now in a 25-cl size as well.

Berardo buys into Sogrape … and Aliança

The Portuguese wine industry was shaken in July 2006 when a third of Portugal's largest wine company, Sogrape, was bought by Madeiran entrepreneur Joe Berardo. He bought the stake from the Carmo family, one of the founding families that set up Sogrape in 1942. Although he immediately announced that his intentions were not hostile, Berardo received a frosty reception from the majority owners, the Guedes family. Since then, there has been an uneasy standoff, made no better by Berardo's announcement that he wants to float his wine-holding company on the stock market and make a public offering of up to 49 per cent of the shares.

Eight months later, Berardo paid €11 million for 60 per cent of Caves Aliança in Bairrada, one of Portugal's largest wine companies and a member of G7, Portugal's elite group of large wine exporters. His portfolio now includes 86 per cent of Bacalhôa Vinhos de Portugal, 45 per cent of Quinta do Carmo, and 20 per cent of Henriques & Henriques. The combined group will be Portugal's largest wine company.

Grapevine

• **The end may be near** for Portugal's DOC-in-waiting classification, Indicação de Proveniência Regulamentada (IPR). There are now only four regions waiting for final confirmation of (or rejection from) the top wine-region status of DOC. They are Biscoitos, Graciosa, and Pico in the Azores, and Lafões in the Beiras.

• **Changes in DOCs** include the creation of the DOC Trás-os-Montes in Portugal's northeastern corner, with the former IPRs Chaves, Planalto-Mirandês, and Valpaços as subregions, the absorption of the Alcobaça DOC into the Encostas de Aire DOC, and the creation of Madeirense DOC for the fledgling Madeira unfortified-wine industry.

• **The former Trás-os-Montes VR region** has been split and renamed. The area occupied by the Douro and port DOCs becomes VR Duriense; the rest of the region is VR Transmontano.

• **Spurred on** by the success of its Spanish Tempranillo rosé, Sogrape is looking for another European rosé. The word is that it will be from the south of France, probably Syrah.

Opinion:
Portugal must sort out its regions

There has just been another reorganization of Portugal's wine regions, but it leaves questions unanswered. The reshuffle showed that IPR regions don't necessarily make the grade to DOC, and that there are still too many DOC regions. Portugal has moved from 33 VQPRD regions (26 DOCs and 7 IPRs) to 29 VQPRD regions (25 DOCs and 4 IPRs). The four IPRs left are Biscoitos, Pico, and Graciosa in the Azores, and Lafões, in the extreme north of the Beiras. A few producers bravely struggle to make wines on the Azores, but they hardly merit three separate DOCs. One Vinho Regional (VR) would be more to the point. And the Lafões wines aren't said to be up to much, either. Best off tucked into the Beiras.

Three of the former IPRs (Chaves, Valpaços, and Planalto-Mirandês) have been united in one new DOC, Trás-os-Montes. If wine producers there want to, they can label their wines with the subregion name as well as Trás-os-Montes, but Trás-os-Montes is a simpler proposition for the consumer, already befuddled by all those initials. (This is what happens in the Alentejo and Ribatejo, and it works perfectly well.) As for DOCs, Alcobaça has been quietly absorbed into Encostas de Aire (good decision), and the fledgling table-wine industry of Madeira got its own DOC. There aren't many producers, and some of their offerings aren't great, but rules and regs are all controlled by the local Madeira Wine Institute.

There's a rumour that the Ribatejo and the Estremadura have been courting, with the intention of merging both regions into a Lisboa VR, and creating two DOCs, Estremadura and Ribatejo, with all the current DOCs as subregions. It could happen soon. The same sort of thing has apparently been happening in the Beiras, but these talks are less advanced. A similar move in the Algarve would make sense, too.

Best would be if all nine DOC regions in Estremadura merged into one super-DOC (as in neighbouring Ribatejo), with optional subregions on the labels. The Estremadura really needs to get exports moving. The Torres Vedras co-op (yes, that's one of the six DOCs) has gone bust already, and life is not rosy for other co-ops. It would be easier if export markets had only the name "Estremadura" to learn. The same approach would be constructive in the Algarve. The very name "Algarve" would be a more powerful sales tool than most in Portugal. To have four DOCs down there is surely misguided.

That would leave Portugal with 13 DOCs, 10 VRs, and no IPRs – better for big and small companies alike. And Portugal might sell more wine.

Vintage Report

Advance report on the latest harvest

2006

All over Portugal, growers enjoyed good winter rains, with rare snowfalls in the Ribatejo and Alentejo. Spring was dry – warm in most of Portugal, though cold in the Alentejo – and flowering and fruit set were correspondingly successful. In the Douro, parts of the Pinhão and Rio Torto valleys were hit by savage hailstorms in mid-June, and some growers lost up to a third of their crop. Elsewhere, summer was hot and dry, with occasional rainfall that refreshed the vineyards.

Only in Bairrada, the Alentejo, and the Douro Superior did the heat get too much for the vines, and ripening was delayed by vines shutting down. In the Minho, Dão, Terras do Sado, and Ribatejo, those who were not expecting high yields picked in early to mid-September and made good, if not great, wines. Those whose grapes were not ripe (and picked) by the time of the autumnal equinox (23 September) got caught by rain that started on 21 September. This was particularly significant in Dão, where early-ripening varieties such as Alfrocheiro and Jaen were excellent (picked before the rain), whereas the later-ripening Aragonez, Touriga Nacional, and Tinto Cão were not as good. Good white wines were made in the Minho, Bairrada, Dão, Ribatejo, and Terras do Sado before the rain. The Moscatels in the Setúbal peninsula have been particularly successful.

In Bairrada, the summer heat stopped Baga ripening. When the rain came, yields were high, the grapes were unripe, and rot set in, so 2006 was not great for Bairrada reds. In the Douro, despite mid-August rain, the hot weather continued, sugar levels shot up, and some grapes raisined. Quantities were lower than expected, and the resulting wines are aromatic but without great structure. Everything looked good in the Alentejo by early August – then the heat was turned up. Some grapes were already ripe, with high sugar levels, and these were picked fast. Others (such as Aragonez) were not, and vines stopped ripening just to stay alive. For those who had patience (and harvesting machines or pickers), late September was cooler, but still dry, and the harvest finished well, in some cases in late October. The Aragonez never really caught up, and most have slightly green, underripe flavours. Algarve producers had similar problems with the reds, but the whites are excellent.

Overall Portuguese wine production was 7.3 million hl, almost exactly in line with the 10-year average.

Updates on the previous five vintages

2005

Vintage rating: *83*

The winter of 2004/05 was the driest on record. Flowering and fruit set were successful, but berries and bunches remained small. Hail cut a swathe through vineyards on the northern margins of the Douro in June. The summer months (especially July) were warmer than average, and by early August many growers were predicting catastrophe, with vines losing their leaves and grapes drying up on the vine. However, rain at the end of August and the beginning of September helped swell the grapes, especially in the north. For the Alentejo and the south, this was too little, too late, since the harvest was already well under way. Cool, clear weather continued into October. But, with production down by as much as 30 per cent, some concentrated but often fiercely alcoholic and unbalanced wines have been made. Further north and towards the coast, some excellent wines have been made by quality-conscious producers in Dão, Bairrada, and the Douro. At 7.5 million hl, overall production was just above the 10-year average.

2004

Vintage rating: *88*

Rain in August and early September caused sporadic outbreaks of rot, but the weather took a significant turn for the better just before the harvest. Some fantastic wines have been made. In Dão and the Douro, Touriga Nacional has performed especially well. Overall, 2004 has produced some wonderfully well-balanced reds with alcohol, intensity, and acidity, which should hold them in good stead for years.

Grapevine

• **Quinta do Noval** has released its first Douro red. The vintage is 2004, made entirely from grapes grown on the estate. The blend is 70 per cent Touriga Nacional, with 20 per cent Tinto Cão and 10 per cent Touriga Franca, and it will retail for around €45. A second wine, Cedro do Noval, will sell for about €15. The only well-known port group not to have released a Douro wine is the Fladgate Partnership (owners of Taylor's, Fonseca, Croft, and Delaforce). When will they crack?

• **Quinta de Pancas,** a quality pioneer in Alenqer, was bought in May 2006 by Companhia das Quintas, a subsidiary of Portuvinus, the steadily growing wine company headed by Miguel Melo Azevedo (the other company Portuvinus owns is Caves Borlido).

• **António Gonçalves Faria,** maker of some of Bairrada's finest wines, died in August 2006. He had recently retired from his work at the Estação Vitivinicola in Bairrada, and was hoping to devote more time to his wines.

2003

Vintage rating: *85*

At the end of July, the entire country sustained nearly three weeks of extreme heat. Photosynthesis slowed and the maturation process came to a standstill. By the start of September, the harvest was under way throughout much of southern Portugal, but sugar readings remained unusually low. However, as the warm weather continued, *Baumés* suddenly rose. Those who got their timing wrong made unbalanced wines with high pH and surprisingly low alcohol. The Alentejo, Dão, and parts of the Douro suffered most heat damage, whereas Bairrada enjoyed its best and most trouble-free vintage for a decade. The best wines will tend to be those from late-ripening varieties. With the exception of reds from Bairrada and parts of the Douro, wines from 2003 are forward and early maturing.

2002

Vintage rating: *65*

By early September, the grapes were generally in good condition, but it rained for five full days in the middle of the month. The unsettled weather continued into October, spelling disaster for Bairrada and Vinho Verde, where many growers watched their grapes rotting on the vine. Some excellent wines were made in the Douro by those who harvested early, and there are small quantities of good wine from the south. But for most producers, 2002 is a vintage they would rather forget. The overall size of the harvest is about average at 6.6 million hl.

2001

Vintage rating: *85*

The 2001 harvest produced a hefty crop, although cool weather led to some uneven ripening in the north. Warm weather in early September saved the day, and some high sugar readings were recorded. Torrential September rain in the Alentejo brought *Baumés* down but, nonetheless, Moreto (usually an insipid grape) was harvested at 14 degrees *Baumé*. In the Dão and Alentejo, the harvest dragged on into late October. However, with total production at 7.6 million hl, 2001 seems to have matched quantity with quality.

GREATEST WINE PRODUCERS

1. Niepoort (Douro)
2. Quinta do Crasto (Douro)
3. Quinta do Vale Meão (Douro)
4. Quinta da Pellada (Dão)
5. Wine & Soul (Douro)
6. Sogrape (Douro, Dão, Alentejo)
7. Luis Pato (Beiras)
8. Prats & Symington (Douro)
9. Quinta dos Roques (Dão)
10. Herdade do Mouchão (Alentejo)

FASTEST-IMPROVING PRODUCERS

1. Quinta do Passadouro (Douro)
2. Quinta do Vale de Raposa (Douro)
3. Dão Sul (Dão)
4. Quinta do Portal (Douro)
5. Quinta da Chocapalha (Estremadura)
6. Quinta do Mouro (Alentejo)
7. Lavradores de Feitoria (Douro)
8. CARM (Douro)
9. Manuel dos Santos Campolargo (Bairrada)
10. Caves Transmontanas (sparkling wines)

NEW UP-AND-COMING PRODUCERS

1. Poeira (Douro)
2. Caves do Freixo (Bairrada)
3. Filipa Pato (Beiras)
4. Rogenda (Beira Interior)
5. Dona Maria (Alentejo)
6. Pilheiros (Douro)
7. Quinta da Murta (Bucelas)
8. Herdade da Mingorra (Alentejo)
9. Quinta do Barranco Longo (Algarve)
10. Quinta dos Termos (Beira Interior)

BEST-VALUE PRODUCERS

1. Adega Cooperativa de Borba (Alentejo)
2. Casa Santos Lima (Estremadura)
3. Casa Ermelinda Freitas (Terras do Sado)
4. Falua (Ribatejo)
5. Adega Cooperativa San Isidro de Pegões (Terras do Sado)
6. DFJ Vinhos (Estremadura, Ribatejo)
7. Adega Cooperativa Regional de Monção (Minho)
8. Sogrape (Douro, Dão, Alentejo)
9. Bacalhôa Vinhos de Portugal (Terras do Sado, Alentejo)
10. UDACA (Dão, Beiras)

GREATEST-QUALITY WINES

1. **Douro Charme 2004** Niepoort (€123)
2. **Douro Vinho da Ponte 2004** Quinta do Crasto (€95)
3. **Douro 2003** Quinta do Vale Meão (€84)
4. **Dão 2004** Quinta da Pellada (€38)
5. **Douro Pintas 2004** Wine & Soul (€70)
6. **Douro Barca Velha 1995** Sogrape (€175)
7. **Douro Vinha Maria Teresa 2003** Quinta do Crasto (€100)
8. **Douro Reserve 2004** Quinta do Passadouro (€30)
9. **Alentejo Tonel 3-4 2001** Herdade de Mouchão (€90)
10. **Douro Curriculum Vitae 2004** Quinta do Vale Dona Maria (€55)

BEST BARGAINS

1. **Vinho Verde Muralhas de Monção Alvarinho 2005** Adega Cooperativa Regional de Monção (€3.25)
2. **Beira Interior Rogenda Reserva 2004** José Joaquim Afonso (€5)
3. **Douro Branco Reserva Castello d'Alba 2004** Vinhos do Douro Superior (€4)
4. **Alentejo Reserva Branco 2004** Herdade do Esporão (€7)
5. **Dão Duque de Viseu 2002** Sogrape (€4)
6. **Obidos Reserva 1998** Quinta das Cerejeiras (€10)

⑦ **Palmela Reserva Quinta da Mimosa 2003** Casa Ermelinda Freitas (€8)

⑧ **Terras do Sado Colheita Seleccionada 2003** Adega Cooperativa San Isidro de Pegões (€8)

⑨ **Alentejo Alentex 2004** Enoforum (€2.70)

⑩ **Tinto da Anfora Grande Escolha 2003** Bacalhôa Vinhos de Portugal (€16)

MOST EXCITING OR UNUSUAL FINDS

① **Estremadura Aurius 2003** Quinta do Monte d'Oiro (€40) *Ex-metal trader José Bento dos Santos made his name with immaculate Syrahs in Alenquer. This is different: 50 per cent Touriga Nacional, 30 per cent Syrah, and 10 per cent each of Touriga Franca and Petit Verdot.*

② **Moscatel de Setúbal Trilogía NV** José Maria da Fonseca (€120) *JM da Fonseca is famous for its Setúbal Moscatels, young and old, made from white and black members of the Muscat family. How do you grab the world's attention when you are so well known? You take some of your 1965 Moscatel, add 15 per cent of the 1934, 15 per cent of the 1900, and blend. Fabulous, intense, essence of Muscat.*

③ **Alentejo JB Garrafeira 2004** Dona Maria (€80) *Júlio Bastos sold the family wine business, Quinta do Carmo, and built a magnificent new winery with the proceeds. This is made from 2.2 ha of ancient Alicante Bouschet vines.*

④ **Beira Interior Rogenda Reserva 2003** José Joaquim Afonso (€5) *José Afonso grows Touriga Nacional on granite soil in the top eastern corner of the Beiras, and Rui Moura Alves (wizard of Bairrada) helps him turn the grapes into this ripe, splendidly aromatic, herby red.*

⑤ **Beira Interior Fonte Cal Reserva 2004** Quinta dos Termos (€5.50) *In the valley of the River Zêzere, between the Serra da Estrela and Spain, is a local white grape called Fonte Cal. This mineral, complex dry white wine has notes of honey, apple, quince, and greengage.*

⑥ **Madeirense Latadas Branco 2005** Seiçal (€10) *The best wine so far from the new Madeirense DOC (for unfortified wines made on Madeira). Pure, citrous Verdelho from Seiçal in the north.*

⑦ **Vinho Licoroso Chico Maria 1998** Adega Brum (€12.50) *Luis Brum is the guardian of the vinous flame of Biscoitos, on the island of Terceira in the Azores. He makes this almost dry, lightly fortified wine from pure Verdelho. It's a unique style, clean and tangy, with high acidity and nutty intensity.*

⑧ **Beiras Vinhas Velhas de Santa Maria 2003** Quinta de Foz d'Arouce (€35) *This is an estate that can ripen Baga every year, and it's not in Bairrada, but about 30 km (19 miles) further south. Sixty-year-old Baga vines give this astonishingly perfumed, densely tannined red, with notes of orange peel and herbs.*

⑨ **Douro 2004** Quinta do Noval (€45) *The latest great port name to come up with an unfortified Douro DOC red – a blend of Touriga Nacional, Tinto Cão, Aragonez, and something less local. The Touriga dominates, with sweet, herby, liquorice aromas and dark, firm tannins.*

⑩ **Dão Callabriga 2004** Sogrape (€12) *The most successful of the three Callabriga regional wines so far. It has the trademark Callabriga Aragonez backbone, with Touriga Nacional and Alfrocheiro added – all red fruits and bergamot perfume.*

Port & Madeira

Richard Mayson

Where will it end? The wave of mergers and takeovers is continuing in Oporto with two major players having changed hands.

RICHARD MAYSON

The Barros Almeida group, which includes port shippers Kopke, Feist, and Hucheson, has been bought outright by Sogevinus, the drinks arm of the Spanish bank Caixanova. Sogevinus, which already owns Cálem, Burmester, and Gilberts, has effectively doubled its sales volumes with this deal, making it the fifth-largest port shipper, with around 11 per cent of the market.

The Symington family, now the second-largest of the port shipping groups (see below), has further reinforced its hold on the Douro with the purchase of all the vineyards, wineries, lodges, bottling installations, and maturing stocks belonging to Cockburn, Martinez Gassiot, and CR&F brandies. Cockburn became part of Jim Beam Global on the break-up of Allied Domecq, following its takeover by Pernod Ricard. The new North American

RICHARD MAYSON writes and lectures on wine, dividing his time between London, Portugal, and a family business in the Peak District. He speaks fluent Portuguese, having been brought up in Portugal, and is regarded as one of the most respected authorities on port, sherry, madeira, and the wines of Spain and Portugal. His interest in the subject goes back to his university days, when he wrote a thesis on the microclimates of the vineyards of the Douro Valley. His books include *Portugal's Wines and Wine Makers* (Ebury Press, 1992), *Port and the Douro* (Faber & Faber, 1999), and *The Wines and Vineyards of Portugal* (Mitchell Beazley), which won the André Simon award for the best drinks book published in 2003. A second, fully revised edition of *Port and the Douro* was published by Mitchell Beazley in 2004, and Richard is currently preparing a book on the wines of Madeira and a third edition of *Portugal's Wines and Wine Makers*. He also owns a vineyard in the Alto Alentejo region of Portugal and launched his first wine, Pedra Basta, in 2007.

owners subsequently approached a number of port shippers looking to divest themselves of their Portuguese assets while retaining the brands. The Symington family will now own and manage the former Cockburn's vineyards and wineries, assuming responsibility for all Cockburn's staff and producing Cockburn's port for Beam Global.

At the time of writing it was announced that C da Silva is being acquired by La Martiniquaise, which already owns Gran Cruz. This now makes it the largest port shipper in volume terms. There is continuing speculation that one other small port firm is also looking either to sell up or merge.

Low *benefício* expected to push up prices

The 2006 *benefício* (the port production limit) was set below annual sales for the fifth year in a row. The Instituto dos Vinhos do Douro e Porto (IVDP) set a *benefício* of 123,500 pipes, equivalent to 9.5 million 9-litre cases. But, with annual sales of 10.4 million cases, shippers expect that a shortage of young port may force prices to rise. The total shortfall in production over the past five years amounts to 4.6 million cases. However, a modest price rise is seen by many shippers as a positive move, with parts of the port trade having been damaged by deep discounting in recent years (see *Wine Report 2007*). Jorge Monteiro, president of the IVDP, pointed out that "the sustainability of both the trade and the Douro producers may be at risk if the negative tendency of prices is not inverted [i.e., reversed] with care".

Four declarations in 2004

Quinta do Noval was the first shipper to declare the 2004 vintage and one of only a handful of companies to opt for a full declaration (the others were Ramos Pinto, Real Companhia Velha, Poças, and Borges). Most shippers declared second-label or single-quinta wines. Christian Seely, managing director of Axa Millésimes, which owns Noval, was upbeat about 2004, describing it as "more typically Noval" than 2003, which was universally declared.

Douro's 250 years celebrated

The Douro Demarcated Region celebrated its 250th anniversary in 2006. The Douro is arguably the oldest delimited wine region in the world. The anniversary was marked by a series of events, including exhibitions, concerts, conferences, and tastings running from 31 August to the end of the year. On 10 September 2006, 250 years to the day since the Royal Charter established the Companhia Geral da Agricultura das Vinhas do Alto Douro, the president of the Republic, Professor Anibal Cavaco Silva, presided over a commemorative ceremony in the Casa do Douro, Régua.

Opinion:
All change in the Douro

Over half the port trade has changed hands in the past decade as the multinationals (once owners of major brands like Croft, Delaforce, and Sandeman) have made their exits. Cockburn, the only brand still owned by a multinational (Jim Beam Global), has probably undergone the most radical and unexpected shake-up of all, with the Symington family having bought all the company's assets. All that remains with Jim Beam Global is the brand – still leader in the UK market with Cockburn's Special Reserve. In Vila Nova de Gaia, the newly slimmed-down Cockburn now employs just three staff.

The deal puts the Symington family in an incredibly strong position, with the largest vineyard holding in the Douro, now extending to nearly 1,000 ha between 23 *quintas*. It is worth making a tally of just what comes in the deal. It includes the pioneering Vilariça vineyard high in the Douro Superior, Cockburn's pride and joy when it was first laid out in the late 1970s to supply the Special Reserve brand. Downstream are *quintas* Vale Coelho and Telhada (two of the most peaceful properties in the Douro) and the historic Quinta do Tua. The only estate that remains attached to Cockburn (but is still owned by the Symingtons) is the magnificent Quinta dos Canais, which was bought as recently as 1989 and was completely replanted a decade ago.

Cockburn's former owners, Allied Domecq, spent huge amounts on vineyards but almost nothing on winemaking, which took place in a number of dingy facilities last upgraded in the 1960s. By contrast, the Symingtons and Taylor/Fonseca (who subsequently acquired Croft and Delaforce and formed the Fladgate Partnership) spent millions upgrading existing facilities and building brand-new central wineries. While managers focused on global branding and distribution, from the 1970s onwards Cockburn, Sandeman, Croft, and Delaforce have all produced some pretty poor vintage ports. This has done nothing for their reputations. By contrast, the reputations of Graham, Dow, Warre, Taylor, and Fonseca have never been higher.

The multinationals never really got to grips with the supply side of the business. Decisions were taken by brand managers and accountants. Family-run firms are not necessarily a prerequisite to success in the port business, but two family groups – Symington Family Estates and the Fladgate Partnership – have capitalized on three decades of remote mismanagement by the multinationals. It now remains to be seen how the Symingtons manage the unusual situation where they are effectively supplying Jim Beam Global with wine for Cockburn brands outside the family's control.

Vintage Report

Advance report on the latest harvest
2006

Port – Following the extreme drought of 2005, heavy winter rain went some way towards replenishing groundwater reserves. The spring was warm and dry, and flowering took place in excellent conditions. May and early June were dry and hot, except for a hailstorm on 14 June that damaged vineyards in the Pinhão and Torto valleys. Some vineyards lost 30 per cent of their crop. July was very hot, with temperatures at the Symington family's Quinta do Vesúvio reaching 40°C (104°F) on all but seven days in the month. August was much cooler, and a significant amount of rain fell in the middle of the month. Apart from vineyards damaged by hail, the grapes were looking very healthy until the start of September, when there was another unexpected burst of heat that shrivelled the grapes. Young vineyards were badly affected, whereas older vines, with deeper root systems, withstood the extreme conditions. Picking began in the Douro Superior on 11 September and in the Cima Corgo a week or so later. However, the weather broke on the 13th, and more persistent rain fell after the 20th, which took its toll on grapes picked during the latter part of the vintage. As a result, 2006 is extremely variable in the Douro, with the best wines produced from older vineyards and warmer sites where picking took place early.

Madeira – The best harvest in over a decade for the island's principal grape variety, Tinta Negra Mole, which accounts for more than 80 per cent of production. The harvest began at the end of August, and the grapes ripened unusually rapidly due to the arrival of the Leste (a hot, dry wind from the Sahara) in early September. With production up by 18 per cent on 2005, quality was matched by quantity.

Updates on the previous five vintages
2005

Vintage rating: *Port: 80, Madeira: 95*

Port – The harvest was one of the earliest on record after the driest and warmest growing season in living memory. Picking began in the Douro

Superior as early as 22 August, followed by the Cima Corgo on 5 September. There was a high incidence of raisined berries in younger vineyards, which produced unbalanced wines. Yields were significantly down in some parts of the region. Despite the challenging conditions, small quantities of good, concentrated wine have been made from the older vineyards best placed to withstand the drought.

Madeira – The island enjoyed an outstanding harvest, with no shortage of high-quality fruit. The shippers have already set aside their best *lotes* for colheitas and vintage madeiras, the latter to be released in 20 years' time. Expect some outstanding Verdelho and Bual.

2004

Vintage rating: *Port: 87, Madeira: 88*

Port – After rain in early and mid-September, the sunshine returned in the nick of time. Sugar levels rose suddenly and continued to rise as temperatures exceeded 30°C (86°F). With yields down slightly on the previous year, the overriding feature of 2004 is the balance of the musts. Some fine single-*quinta* ports have been declared.

Madeira – Some fine wines were made from all parts of the island. This was another dry year, with the hottest temperatures for nearly 30 years at the end of July. Vineyards on the north side suffered from excess humidity in August, but well-ventilated sites on the south side yielded the best grapes. Bual (of which there was no shortage) proved to be outstanding.

2003

Vintage rating: *Port: 94, Madeira: 90*

Port – An abnormally hot growing season produced some very promising wines. Yields were above average, and ports of a very high standard were made throughout the Douro. One leading shipper has described it as a "textbook year". A vintage was unanimously declared in the spring and summer of 2005.

Madeira – An exceptional year, with a large production of healthy, generally disease-free grapes. This was an excellent year for Tinta Negra Mole and Verdelho, both of which registered good levels of ripeness. For Verdelho it was the best harvest for 10 years. Both Sercial and Bual produced some good wines, but for Malvasia it was a year with low production and some localized disease problems.

2002

Vintage rating: *Port: 70, Madeira: 85*

Port – Near-perfect growing season ruined by rain during the harvest. Those who managed to pick before the rain (mostly in the Douro Superior) made small quantities of good wine. A handful of single *quintas* declared, but for most producers 2002 was a damp squib. Wines made towards the end of the harvest were dilute and dreary, proving difficult to sell.

Madeira – This vintage saw a large production and particularly good-quality Tinta Negra Mole on the south side and excellent quality with large volumes of Bual from Calheta at the extreme west. Bual and Tinta Negra Mole in the Campanário district in the southwest suffered from a difficult vintage due to persistent fog in the last four weeks or so before the vintage. Malmsey and Sercial were inconsistent. Verdelho was excellent but limited in volume.

2001

Vintage rating: *Port: 85, Madeira: 75*

Port – With flowering taking place under optimum conditions and groundwater supplies thoroughly replenished, there was a large crop. Temperatures were uneven during August, but rain at the end of the month helped swell the grapes. Yields were up by 30 per cent on 2000 in the A/B-grade vineyards. Overall, 2001 proved to be a useful year in which a number of single *quintas* have produced some fine vintage ports for drinking over the medium term.

Madeira – There was a big production of Tinta Negra Mole, but the volume of Malmsey was reduced due to *coulure* at flowering. Sercial and Verdelho from the northern vineyards had particularly bad weather during flowering, which resulted in a greatly reduced vintage for these two varieties. Bual did not suffer as much, and volumes were normal.

Grapevine

• **Fonseca Terra Prima Organic Reserve,** the first fully certified organic port from a major shipper, is made from organically farmed grapes grown in the Pinhão Valley and fortified with organic spirit. Fonseca has also bottled small quantities of organic vintage port from Quinta do Panascal, where it has been experimenting with organics since 1992.

• **The Symington family** has acquired Quinta do Bom Retiro Pequeno from the Serodio family. Wine from this estate, in the lower reaches of the Rio Torto, has made up a significant part of Warre vintage port since 1935.

GREATEST WINE PRODUCERS

1. Graham
2. Fonseca
3. Quinta do Noval
4. Henriques & Henriques (madeira)
5. Taylor
6. Dow
7. Cossart Gordon (madeira)
8. Niepoort
9. Barbeito (madeira)
10. Warre

FASTEST-IMPROVING PRODUCERS

1. Croft
2. Delaforce
3. Quinta de la Rosa
4. Quinta do Crasto
5. Cálem
6. Quinta do Portal
7. Poças
8. Justino Henriques (madeira)
9. Rozès
10. Quinta da Pacheca

NEW UP-AND-COMING PRODUCERS

1. Quinta de Roriz
2. Quinta Vale Dona Maria
3. Quinta de Ventozelo
4. Quinta do Portal
5. Quinta do Vallado
6. Quinta da Prelada
7. Quinta do Silval
8. Porto Heredias
9. Wine and Soul
10. Quinta do Tedo

BEST-VALUE PRODUCERS

1. Smith Woodhouse
2. Martinez
3. Gould Campbell
4. Warre
5. Croft

GREATEST-QUALITY WINES

1. **Ramos Pinto Quinta do Bom Retiro 20 Year Old Tawny Port** (€40)
2. **Fonseca Guimaraens Vintage Port 2004** (€35)
3. **Dow's Quinta Senhora da Ribeira Vintage Port 2004** (€35)
4. **Quinta de Roriz Vintage Port 2004** (€40)
5. **HM Borges Boal 1977** (€65)
6. **Niepoort 30 Year Old Tawny Port** (€115)
7. **Quinta do Vesúvio Vintage Port 1994** (€55)
8. **Graham's Vintage Port 1983** (€65)
9. **Justino's Malmsey 1933** (bottled 2006) (€165)
10. **Pereira d'Oliveira Boal 1973** (bottled 2002) (€115)

BEST BARGAINS

1. **Warre's Bottle Matured LBV 1995** (€17)
2. **Smith Woodhouse Bottle Matured LBV 1992** (€20)
3. **Croft Quinta da Roeda 2004** (€30)
4. **Henriques & Henriques 15 Year Old Verdelho Madeira** (€25 per 50-cl bottle)
5. **Niepoort LBV 2001** (€16)
6. **Warre's Warrior Reserve Port** (€12)
7. **Ramos Pinto Collector Reserve Port** (€10)
8. **Croft LBV 2000** (€12)
9. **HM Borges Colheita Madeira 1995** (€12 per 50-cl bottle)
10. **Graham's Six Grapes Reserve Port** (€12)

MOST EXCITING OR UNUSUAL FINDS

1 Henriques & Henriques Grand Old Boal (€432) *Intense peaty nose (with more than a hint of Irish whiskey), very fine and focused, spicy, leathery, and incredibly powerful. A wine originating from the 1820s, aged in cask followed by demijohns and bottled as late as the 1960s. Still released sparingly by the shipper.*

2 Taylor's Vargellas Vinhas Velhas 2004 (€150) *Tiny production (4 pipes, or 2,200 litres) from the oldest vines on Taylor's flagship quinta – powerful and dense, yet promising elegance and a long life ahead.*

3 Fonseca Terra Prima Organic Reserve Port (€12) *The first port made from organically grown grapes to be commercialized by a mainstream shipper: a big, bold, and immensely satisfying reserve ruby.*

4 Delaforce Colheita 1964 (€75) *Fine, attractive, savoury-nutty aromas; quite dry and refined in style; savoury-sweet flavours. Very well-balanced, carefully crafted colheita.*

5 Pereira d'Oliveira Bastardo 1927 (€260) *Produced from a grape that is virtually extinct and bottled only in 2005, having spent more than 70 years in cask: singed, off-dry, astringent, but not without charm.*

6 Cossart Gordon Sercial Colheita 1988 (€25) *Good Sercial madeira is becoming quite scarce, especially a relatively young wine that is as expressive as this: fine, delicate, dry, with a hint of marmalade. A worthy trophy winner in the Decanter World Wine Awards.*

7 Sandeman's 40 Year Old Tawny Port (€120) *Clean, delicate, and high-toned; restrained sweetness, with a lovely candied-peel finish. Most 40-year-olds are considerably more unctuous, but this wine has unusual poise and balance in its category.*

8 Cossart Gordon Bual Colheita 1995 (bottled 2005) (€20) *Very expressive for a young madeira: quite pungent, yet smooth, with just the right amount of richness balanced by spicy astringency. A taste of vintage madeira without the price tag.*

9 Quinta da Pacheca Vintage Port 2003 (€45) *I have never rated the wines from this large Baixo Corgo estate before, but this soft, sweet, fleshy vintage port has real charm. Not a long-term keeper, but a lovely wine nonetheless.*

10 HM Borges Boal 1977 (€65) *Fine, pure, lifted aromas, with a hint of green tea; delicate, leafy flavours, with some richness mid-palate yielding to a long, fresh, sinewy finish. Very expressive. A truly wonderful young vintage madeira from a small shipper whose wines are rarely seen.*

Grapevine

• **SPR Vinhos,** the group that includes Rozés and São Pedro das Aguias, has invested €5 million in a new winery at Quinta de Monsul near Lamego. The group is 100 per cent owned by Vranken Pommery Monopole.

• **With wine-related tourism** gaining ground in the Douro, Quinta do Vallado near Régua has been converted into a hotel.

Great Britain

Stephen Skelton MW

Though global warming is not having much effect in UK vineyards on budburst or harvest dates (neither having changed for 50 years) or even on sugar levels, it does seem to be changing the regularity and size of yields.

STEPHEN SKELTON MW

Although the official figures show average yields over the past few years to be just below the long-term average, these statistics are bedevilled by changes in the varietal makeup of our vineyards (average yields were bound to be higher when Seyval Blanc was the most widely planted grape) and by the number of very young vineyards that appear in the statistics. If you take a very light crop from a young vineyard, it still has to be recorded, which lowers the overall average. With the large number of vineyards planted in 2003 and 2004 now coming into their first yields, the effect is quite significant.

Established vineyards and wineries all over the UK had their biggest tonnages to date: Three Choirs recorded 760 tonnes of its own and contract fruit; Chapel Down, around 600 tonnes; New Hall, 295 tonnes; Stanlake Park, 135 tonnes; Camel Valley, 48 tonnes from its own vineyards

STEPHEN SKELTON MW established the award-winning Tenterden Vineyards in 1977 and made wine there for 22 years. His wines have won the Gore-Browne Trophy for the Best UK Wine on three occasions. He is currently a consultant to a number of UK vineyards and wineries. Stephen was a director of the United Kingdom Vineyards Association (UKVA) between 1982 and 1998 and chairman from 1998 until 2003. Having written on wine, winemaking, and viticulture since 1986, he published *The Vineyards of England* in 1989 and rewrote and updated this work under the new title of *The Wines of Britain and Ireland* (Faber & Faber, 2001). This book won the André Simon Award in 2002. Stephen became a Master of Wine in 2003, also winning the Mondavi prize, which is awarded to the candidate gaining the highest marks in the written part of the examination.

plus another 147 tonnes for other growers; Sharpham, 60 tonnes for themselves and another 60 for contract customers; RidgeView, 44 tonnes from its own vineyards plus another 58 tonnes under contract; Yearlstone, 51 tonnes, including contracts; Bob Carr at Brightwell Vineyard, 32 tonnes; Plumpton College, 25 tonnes; and so it goes on. My estimate is that we will be close to – or perhaps even over – the largest UK yield to date, which was in 1992 with 26,428 hl, or around 3,700 tonnes of grapes (3.5 million bottles).

Grapevine

• **Gusbourne Vineyard** near Tenterden in Kent recorded its first yield and sent 30 tonnes of grapes "perfect in terms of cleanliness, acids, and sugars" to be processed by Mike Roberts at RidgeView. Owner Andrew Weeber was highly pleased with his crop: 4.94 tonnes/ha from his first 6 ha. The total planted area is now 15 ha, with another 6 ha planted during 2007.

• **Pebblebed Vineyard** in Cornwall seems to have found favour with the Italians. Its wines can now be found in three restaurants in Piedmont, including a Michelin-starred eatery near Turin, which serves its 2005 rosé with an upmarket version of fish and chips. The vineyard is now nudging 9 ha and is the largest organic vineyard in the UK.

• **The German variety** Frühburgunder (Early Burgundy) has been planted in several vineyards in the UK and until recently was always called Early Pinot Noir. Keen Wine Standards Board (WSB) officials suddenly became concerned about this apparent attempt to "pass off" the variety as a noble Pinot and demanded that growers call it what it was: Frühburgunder. After lengthy negotiations, it has been agreed that UK growers can adopt the French nomenclature, and wines made from it will be called Pinot Noir Précoce.

• **Bob Lindo and son Sam** of Camel Valley have been expanding and improving both visitor and winery facilities with more temperature-controlled tanks, an air-conditioned specialist vineyard tractor, and a huge terrace from which visitors can admire the vineyards.

• **Will Davenport** has landed what must be one of the best sales coups of the year by being chosen by the Prince of Wales as supplier of an English sparkling wine under the Duchy Originals label. The wine is a 2004 cuvée, organic (as are all Davenport wines), and it hit the shelves in late 2006. Will also picked up the 2006 Soil Association's Best Wine award for his 2005 Limney Horsmonden Dry.

• **The Rolls-Royce of champagne presses** – the Coquard PAI – is one of those winery fixtures seldom seen outside top wineries in Reims and Epernay. There is one at Montana in New Zealand and another in Italy, but that's about it – until the Roberts clan at RidgeView decided to install one. This revolutionary press manages, by the use of a novel hydraulic pressing system and the gravity of the grapes within the machine, to press and break up the cake in quick stages without undue damage to the grapes. It was purchased with the help of a DEFRA-EU grant.

Opinion:
A sparkling future for English wine?

The changes occurring in the English (and to a lesser extent, Welsh) wine scene are remarkable. With the area under vine occupied by sparkling-wine varieties having doubled in three years and even more planting in the pipeline, will shelf space be found for all this wine, or will there be a glut of grapes looking for a home?

Although by no means the first in the UK to produce bottle-fermented sparkling wines, Nyetimber was unique in two aspects: it used classic champagne varieties, and its wines were aged *sur lattes* for a minimum of four years, giving the wines a nutty, toasty elegance reminiscent of vintage champagne. Its success in the IWSC competition in 1997 with its 1992 Chardonnay-based Blanc de Blancs, which won a gold medal and the English Wine Trophy, and in 1998 with the 1993 Pinot Noir/Chardonnay-based Classic Cuvée, which won a gold, the English Wine Trophy, and the trophy for the best non-champagne sparkling wine, put both Nyetimber and English sparkling wine firmly on the wine map.

Amid further successes in both national and international competitions, Nyetimber got the stamp of royal approval when rumour had it that the Queen and her guests drank it to toast the new millennium. The city fathers also served it at Her Majesty's jubilee lunch at the Guildhall. This helpful publicity fanned the flames, and the story has never been far away from the airwaves and the press.

In 1990, official WSB figures showed a total area under vine of the three champagne varieties – Chardonnay, Pinot Noir, and Pinot Meunier – of 57 ha, or 6 per cent of the total. By 2003, this had risen to 94 ha, or a shade under 11 per cent of the total. By summer 2006, the area was 198 ha, a rise of 3½ times in 15 years; these three varieties now represent almost 23 per cent of the total UK vine area. Although the top two slots are still occupied by "old" varieties – Seyval Blanc at number 1 with 94 ha, and Reichensteiner at number 2 with 93 ha – both these varieties dropped by around 24 per cent in the same period and will be (officially) overtaken by the next time the figures are published. Müller-Thurgau and Schönburger, once at the top of the charts, both dropped by 28 per cent and will very soon disappear from the top 10 altogether.

In fact, the official WSB figures tell only part of the story, and they often lag behind reality, especially in times of rapid decreases or (as in this case) rapid increases in vineyard area. The actual area under sparkling-wine varieties is probably nearer 275 ha, and Pinot Noir and Chardonnay undoubtedly occupy the top two slots.

What all this means in terms of the market for the product is anyone's guess – hence the question at the top of the page. The current output of English sparkling wine (from all grape varieties) for sale – as opposed to being put away for ageing – is probably no more than 250,000 bottles, or 15 per cent of the current total production of 1.6 million bottles. A fair chunk – maybe up to 50 per cent of this – is sold at the farm gate or to local shops, hotels, and restaurants and never gets anywhere near a high street or supermarket. However, by 2008–10 most of the currently planted vines will be cropping, and there will be a flood of grapes looking for winery space. If all the currently planted vines crop well and we get a fair crack of the weather whip, there are potentially around 1.5 million bottles' worth of sparkling grapes to be vinified. Nyetimber has a new winery in mind to cope with its 80 ha, Denbies doesn't take outside fruit, Chapel Down is almost up to its limit, Three Choirs likewise – so where are the rest going?

As far as shelf space goes, a log-jam of wine is less likely to occur since the time spent *sur lattes* is critical from the quality point of view, as well as delaying the moment of truth when the wine must be marketed. However, every bottle has to find a market, and if history is anything to go by, this might be a tough call. Today's relatively high shelf prices for English sparkling wine are probably unsustainable once the product goes mainstream, and the current high-street/multiple-grocer price range of £15–21 must surely fall. Supermarket wine buyers are not known for their altruism, and if they sense that there's an overhang of stock, they will offer facings, but only at a lower price. One leading supermarket buyer, who already sells more than his/her fair share of English wine, thinks there is a good market there, but at sub-£15 (bear in mind that there is a slew of champagne on offer at £10–15), which means a trade price (ex VAT, but including duty) of £5.50–8.50. Can anyone in the UK make bottle-fermented sparkling wine profitably at that price?

Spending money (on vineyards, wineries, and stock-building) is the easy half of creating a lasting business. The hard part is persuading already harassed wine buyers that yours is a must-have product and that they should pay a price that reflects your costs. Wine buyers have limitations on shelf space, targets to aim for, margins to make, and sales rates to maintain. The industry must concentrate on quality, continue winning prizes, and keep convincing the wine-buying public that English sparkling wine really is worth buying. Only if enough hands reach out and grab bottles off shelves will a long-lasting niche be created. I seriously hope that the industry, collectively, can rise to the occasion.

Vintage Report

Advance report on the latest harvest

2006

With the vines having come through a mild winter and frost-free spring, flowering took place in ideal weather during the hottest July since records began. With 11 days when the temperature soared over 30°C (86°F) in this month alone, the prospects seemed excellent for a very fine vintage. Then, as if to remind us that nothing in UK viticulture should be taken for granted, August, September, and October, while remaining warmer than average, turned out to be much wetter too. The end result of this was a very large harvest with yields in some cases well over the top end of projections, sugars and acids that were lower than expected, and unfortunate outbreaks of downy mildew to start with and then botrytis in the later stages. Taken together, these factors turned the year into a disappointment after what had looked like being a dream year.

On first tasting, super-fruity varieties such as Bacchus and Schönburger seem lighter and less vibrant than usual, and some reds are on the lighter side. On the sparkling front, however, base wines made from Chardonnay, Pinot Noir, and Pinot Meunier seem ideal, with acids requiring no adjustment and some nice, clean, pure wines.

Updates on the previous five vintages

2005

Vintage rating: *Red: 86, White: 90, Sparkling: 86*

Yet another strange year for UK growers. Despite what felt like a cool, somewhat damp summer with on/off sun and rain, September and October turned into very good months, and sugar levels ended up even better than those achieved in 2003, the hottest year on record. A few vineyards got caught by frost in May, but in general, yields were above average, very clean, and certainly better-than-average quality. Sugar/acid balances seem to be perfect.

2004

Vintage rating: *Red: 85, White: 89, Sparkling: 88*

Despite the large yields, many of the 2004s have turned into really typical UK-grown wines with a good balance of fruit and acidity. A high proportion of the silver medals awarded in the 2005 UKVA Wine of the Year Competition went to 2004s. The best wines made from the Bacchus grape variety have good flavour with sufficient length for their style and have the typical freshness and fragrance this variety brings.

2003

Vintage rating: *Red: 92, White: 90, Sparkling: 93*

An amazing year for UK winemakers. A trouble-free spring was followed by great summer weather, with temperatures hitting 35°C (high 90s F), but the autumn was the clincher. September and October were very warm, sunny, and almost completely dry. Grapes were harvested at unheard-of sugar levels, with potential alcohol levels of 11–13 per cent in many vineyards. All competent growers appear to have made extremely good wines, with reds and sparklings from traditional varieties (that is, traditional champagne varieties) the stars. It was certainly the best year for black varieties that anyone can remember. In general, the 2003s are very good, with some in the "excellent" category.

2002

Vintage rating: *Red: 82, White: 85, Sparkling: 90*

The overall crop was smaller than average, but an Indian summer resulted in exceptional quality, especially with the harder-to-ripen varieties, such as Chardonnay, and the successful black varieties: Pinot Noir, Rondo, Regent, and Dornfelder. Natural sugar levels, which usually languish around 7–9 per cent, were well up into double figures in many cases. Several winemakers made completely natural wines – that is, without chaptalization.

2001

Vintage rating: *Red: 75, White: 82, Sparkling: 82*

This was a very fair year. No spring frosts and a good flowering combined to produce a larger-than-average crop. Temperatures were higher in 2001 than for centuries, and this was reflected in an early harvest of clean, ripe grapes. Reds had more colour than usual, and the generally tough-to-ripen varieties, such as Riesling and Pinot Blanc, did well. Chardonnay and Pinot Noir for sparkling wine put in good performances, and this should be reflected in the wines.

GREATEST WINE PRODUCERS

1. Nyetimber
2. English Wines Group (Chapel Down)
3. Sharpham
4. RidgeView
5. Denbies
6. Camel Valley
7. Three Choirs
8. Stanlake Park
9. Astley
10. Nutbourne

FASTEST-IMPROVING PRODUCERS

1. Yearlstone
2. Astley
3. Brightwell
4. Heart of England
5. Plumpton College
6. New Hall
7. Bookers
8. Glyndwr
9. Warden Abbey
10. Wyken

NEW UP-AND-COMING PRODUCERS

1. Bow-in-the-Cloud
2. a'Beckett's
3. Court Lane
4. Wroxeter Roman
5. Hoopers
6. Thelnetham
7. Ickworth
8. Down Lane
9. Throwley
10. Worthenbury

BEST-VALUE PRODUCERS

1. English Wines Group (Chapel Down)
2. RidgeView
3. Denbies
4. Three Choirs
5. Camel Valley
6. Stanlake Park

GREATEST-QUALITY WINES

1. **Pinot Reserve Sparkling 2002** Chapel Down (£24.99)
2. **Pimlico 2003** RidgeView (£24.95)
3. **Blanc de Noirs Pinot Meunier 2003** Nyetimber (£29.95)
4. **Blanc de Blanc 2001** Bookers (£21.95)
5. **Bacchus Dry 2005** Camel Valley (£10.95)
6. **Reserve Ortega 2003** Throwley (£8.50)
7. **Triassic 2005** Astley (£8.50)
8. **Ortega 2004** Denbies (£11.99)
9. **Rosé 2005** Camel Valley (£9.95)
10. **Bacchus 2005** Sharpham (£12.50)

BEST BARGAINS

1. **Brut NV** Chapel Down (£14.99)
2. **English Rosé 2005** Chapel Down (£9.99)
3. **Flint Dry NV** Chapel Down (£6.99)
4. **Bloomsbury 2004** RidgeView (£17.95)
5. **Chalk Ridge NV** Denbies (£4.99)
6. **Coopers Brook 2004** Denbies (£5.99)
7. **Dart Valley Reserve 2005** Sharpham (£7.50)
8. **Willow Brook 2005** Three Choirs (£5.75)

MOST EXCITING OR UNUSUAL FINDS

① Blanc de Noirs Pinot Meunier 2003 Nyetimber (£29.95) *This is the first 100 per cent Pinot Meunier wine from Nyetimber and, judging by the quality of this wine, I hope not the last. Although aged for just two years on the lees, it still has Nyetimber's hallmark yeasty nose and palate.*

② Pimlico 2003 RidgeView (£24.95) *The balance between acidity and sweetness in this wine is sheer perfection. A very, very satisfying and pleasurable glass of sparkling wine.*

Grapevine

• **The IWSC** (International Wine and Spirit Competition) Yarden Trophy for the best non-champagne went to an English sparkler, the 1998 Nyetimber Classic Cuvée, for the second year running (and the third time in nine years). Last year it was won by RidgeView with its 2002 Bloomsbury. Nyetimber previously won the trophy in 1998 with its 1992 Classic Cuvée.

• **Sharpham Nouveau:** Beaujolais Nouveau may have had its day, but in south Devon the annual release of Sharpham Vineyard's New Vintage in early November is treated with equal fervour. Only five weeks after picking, 250 cases of the wine, based on Madeleine Angevine 7672, were bottled and on their way to local pubs and restaurants.

• **In the UKVA national competition,** Sharpham picked up a gold medal and the Jack Ward Trophy for the best wine of the previous vintage with its 2005 Bacchus, plus five silver medals and two bronzes. Its Cabernet/Merlot-based red, Beenleigh, continues to defy economic gravity and sells out at £25 a bottle.

• **Plumpton College** handled 25 tonnes of grapes in 2006, its largest harvest to date. The winery has been re-equipped with new tanks, temperature-controlled rooms for barrel storage and malolactic fermentation, a must chiller, and a scraped-surface heat exchanger for cold stabilization. A new visitor centre will open in 2007, all part of the college's £1-millon investment in wine and the sciences. Plumpton sells its 2005 oaked Ortega to the Michelin-starred Hakkasan restaurant in London.

• **Jersey's only commercial vineyard,** La Mare, one of the oldest in the UK, is spending £1.3 million on a new winery and new visitor and conference facilities. Its largest harvest was in 2006, with 42 tonnes of grapes (plus 46 tonnes of apples for its cider and "calvados"), and its new winery will include a fully automated bottling and labelling line.

• **Peter Dart,** new(ish) owner of Stanlake Park (ex-Valley/Thames Valley Vineyards), is raiding the piggy bank to the tune of £75,000 to install a state-of-the-art Costral bottling line complete with depalletizer and screwcap facility. In 2006, Stanlake Park made wine for 25 other vineyards, and winemaker Vince Gower (whatever happened to John Worontschak?) reports that he didn't have an empty tank in the winery.

Belgium, Netherlands & Scandinavia

Fiona Morrison MW & Ronald de Groot

Denmark is becoming more professional, even boasting a growers' organization; ambition is low in Belgium; and although wine production in the Netherlands continues to grow, it suffers from a lack of regulation.

FIONA MORRISON MW   RONALD DE GROOT

BELGIUM

Belgium seems quite happy to remain a tiny player on the wine-production stage, with a couple of hundred small producers making a few hectolitres of wine to sell to friends, local restaurants, or at open days in their cottage-garden-like vineyards.

In spite of a decade or so of serious wine growing, very few producers aspire to expanding their vision beyond their own region. Apart from Genoels-Elderen, which has found commercial success with its Chardonnays and Pinot Noirs, the only consistent high achiever on the wine scene is Peter Colemont, whose Clos d'Opleeuw vineyard is only 1 ha. There are only a dozen or so producers, such as Meerdael, Boschberg, and Domein Tempelberg, who have gained a respectable reputation and are consolidating their initial plantings with the release of new wines.

FIONA MORRISON MW has spent more than 20 years in the wine trade around the world and speaks several languages. She became a Master of Wine in 1994 and is now a freelance wine journalist and lecturer. She is married to Jacques Thienpont, a wine négociant and owner of Le Pin in Pomerol, and together they divide their time between Bordeaux and Belgium, making, tasting, and promoting wine. RONALD DE GROOT is owner and editor of the leading Dutch wine magazine *Perswijn*. He organizes tasting events for professionals and consumers and is a freelance contributor to various media. As a wine consultant, he is a member of the KLM Royal Dutch Airlines tasting panel. He is also a member of one of Europe's leading tasting panels, the Grand Jury Européen.

THE NETHERLANDS

Wine growing in the Netherlands is increasing quite rapidly, although it is still a mini-winemaking country. Visiting vineyards is becoming a very popular tourist activity, and vines are being planted in every province, even on Ameland, one of the Wadden islands in the north – quite an extraordinary place to plant vines. There are now 150 ha of vines in the Netherlands, with 100 ha in production; by 2010 the number of professional wine growers is expected to rise to about 100. Total output is currently 400,000 bottles, most of which are sold at the winery or to local customers and restaurants. Only a few wineries sell nationally, such as De Linie, the Apostelhoeve, and Fromberg. De Linie wines have been chosen by KLM for business-class flights.

No appellations for Netherlands

No agreement has been reached on official appellations for the Netherlands. Nederlandse Landwijn, the Dutch equivalent of Vin de Pays, is the only classification. Classic grapes and hybrids are both authorized for use. Several organizations see themselves as *the* representative body, but the top producers don't want to belong to an organization. Unity is a distant prospect. The only region where there is discussion about a possible appellation is the southern part of Limburg, which would warrant one because of its unique terroir and microclimate. There is no prospect of a change in the national rules in the near future.

Medal success for Gelderland

For the first time, the province of Gelderland, Netherlands, was awarded most medals in the national wine competition, winning 10 out of 24. Among the winners were De Colonjes in Groesbeek, Hof te Dieren and De Gulder Akker in Azewijn (two bronze medals each), and one each for De Heikamp in Wijchen, the Oogsthoek in Zelhem, and Wageningse Berg. The latter was also the winner of the only silver medal, for its Regent Barrique 2005.

DENMARK & SWEDEN

Winemaking in Denmark and Sweden is becoming more professional. In the wake of EU recognition as a wine-producing country in 2005, **Denmark** now has its own wine growers' association, with an annual tasting held by the Danish Sommelier Society. To be a professional grower farmers have to register their vineyards with the Danish Plant Directorate.

One wine that found fame recently was Dons, which featured on BBC international news in 2006 as Denmark's first commercially produced wine. Dons is a sparkling wine produced by Sven Moesgaard, who also makes red and white wines in his vineyard, Skaersoegaard. Moesgaard attributes the secret of his success in growing vines so far north to the "white nights" – the long summer days that bring extra sunlight.

In **Sweden**, growing grapes is an even more challenging proposition. There are a few established producers today – Blaxta Vineyards, famous for its icewines, and Akessons, which has been producing sparkling wines since 1985 – but bureaucracy, lack of information on cold-climate grape growing, and the difficulties of selling local wines have hindered further development.

One of the most successful growers, Lauri Pappinen, owner of Gutevin winery on the island of Gotland, has decided to go it alone, creating his own restaurant, shop, and guest house to sell and publicize his wines. His example has inspired Gunnar Dahlberg, owner of Wannborga winery on the neighbouring island of Oland, to follow the same route.

There are now around 50–100 small vineyards in southern Sweden, almost all run by amateurs producing a little wine for family and friends. The leap to commercial production is hindered by the behemoth wine monopoly Systembolaget, which will not promote local wines except as special listings, since volumes are not large enough. Today there are about 12.5 ha of commercial vineyards, with around 92,000 bottles produced annually. It will be a long time before Swedish wines become more than a tiny niche product – and an expensive one at that: Sweden's most famous wine, Blaxta Vidal Ice Wine, costs SEK 1,924 (£140) a bottle.

Grapevine

• **Classification of Belgian appellations** and table wines was concluded in 2006, with three VQPRD zones for still wines in Flanders, plus a table-wine and a sparkling-wine designation. In Walloon, there are now two sparkling-wine appellations: a VMQPRD for Walloon and one for *crémant* produced in a specific region of Walloon.

• **Genoels-Elderen,** the best-known Belgian wine estate, has started to make its own grappa. This is distilled to about 68 per cent, then stored in oak barrels for several years to let the alcohol concentration drop naturally.

• **Clos des Agaises at Haulchin,** in Hainault, near Mons, Belgium, has won considerable acclaim since its launch last year. The 6-ha vineyard, planted between 2002 and 2005 with 60,000 Chardonnay vines, is overseen by Raymond Leroy, a Montpellier-qualified oenologist. The Cuvée Ruffus won top prize at the Brussels Mega Vino competition and is currently sold out.

• **Some 70 Dutch producers** are registered officially as "professional wineries", but this number is misleading. Registration at the Productschap in The Hague, part of the Ministry of Agriculture, is compulsory for growers with 0.1 ha (10,760 sq ft) of vines. The number of "real" professionals is no more than about 30. To make a living, a plot of at least 3–4 ha is needed.

Opinion:
Belgium needs to raise its game

In spite of efforts by the Federation of Belgian Wines & Spirits to legalize production and create appellations, many growers do not feel the need to be part of such a grouping. This means there is no structure in which quality, cooperation, and ambition are nurtured. A handful of professional or semi-professional wine growers have a vision beyond their borders, but most are content as amateurs. This makes it difficult to gather information, statistics, or even wine samples. The recent success of Belgian sparkling wines has captured the public's attention and it will probably be these wines, priced at €12–15, that will build domestic wine consumption.

Global warming has led to a steady recent improvement in red wines, with Pinot Noir showing more concentration and depth. Also, the overly oaked Chardonnays from Genoels-Elderen have been toned down; since this estate sets the benchmark for many Belgian wines, this is good news.

However, there are still far too many insipid wines with dirty aromas or too much sulphur. That these wines have any market at all is testament to the Belgians' support for a fledgling industry. This year, in our tastings we expected to see the positive effects of the 2005 vintage, but we were rather disappointed. Perhaps the vines are too young to show vintage character; but it is careful winemaking rather than a successful harvest that marks out the best Belgian wines.

Netherlands: hybrids or classics?

The dispute about what to plant continues in the Netherlands. The wine-growing scene seems split into two camps: those who plant only *Vitis vinifera*, and those who see the future in hybrids. For people who like to make red wines, hybrids seem to be the only solution, since classic varieties do not ripen early enough. In light of this, our tastings of the Netherlands' reds were not very encouraging; in particular, older Regent wines had not aged well.

There is pressure from groups around the University of Wageningen to plant hybrids such as Rondo and Regent, but can these grapes produce quality wine in the long term? Auxerrois, Riesling, Müller-Thurgau, Pinot Blanc, or Pinot Gris are a sure bet, but they restrict growers to whites.

Shorter extraction times might improve red wines, balancing some producers' powerful, tannic wines. Also, rosé is quite fashionable in the Netherlands. As in every "new" wine country, it will take time to plant the right grapes in the right spots, but the market will eventually correct this.

Vintage Report

Advance report on the latest harvest

2006

Belgium – In 2006, a mild, damp winter replenished the water table after the late summer drought of 2005. An average spring with mild temperatures helped the initial stages of growth, but it was the perfect summer weather at the beginning of June and through most of July that gave a great boost to the grapes during flowering. By the time the dull August weather came along, the vines were well advanced, so the lack of sunshine did not harm the grapes. Overall, 2006 was warmer and sunnier than 2005, and the harvest was a week or so earlier than usual. Quantities were up slightly on 2005 for the white grapes, and quality is good for red wines and very good for whites.

Netherlands – A very difficult summer had a negative effect on the 2006 harvest. July was extremely hot, with two heat waves in a row, which stressed the vines. Wet weather in August resulted in a lot of disease. A splendid autumn, with great weather in September and October, brought a lot of relief. Early-ripening grapes could not fully enjoy the advantages, but later-ripening ones, such as Riesling and Pinot Gris, showed very well.

Updates on the previous five vintages

2005

Vintage rating: *Belgium – Red: 89, White: 86;*
Netherlands – Red: 83, White: 85

Belgium – A wonderful spring resulted in an exceptional flowering. The summer, however, was disappointing; between 15 July and the end of August, the weather was wet and cloudy with relatively little sunshine. Luckily, the end of August and the month of September were excellent and turned the harvest from an average one to one of very good potential.

Netherlands – A slightly cooler summer forced producers to harvest a bit later than normal, but the grapes were generally ripe. Sugar and acidity were well balanced, producing quite powerful wines. Spring frosts and rain during flowering reduced the harvest by 20 per cent. In general, it was quite a good vintage for Dutch growers.

2004

Vintage rating: *Belgium – Red: 87, White: 83;*
Netherlands – Red: 80, White: 82

Belgium – A mild winter and an unsettled spring, but good weather during flowering. The summer was disappointing, with dull weather and quite a lot of rain. However, the Indian summer in September and October brought a fairly abundant crop of decent quality.

Netherlands – The season was cool, making it difficult for the grapes to ripen. In September and October, the grapes caught up to some extent, but rain disturbed the harvest. The wet weather contributed to a larger harvest than normal. Wines are more elegant in character and more "nervous", with higher acidity, but they are quite acceptable in quality. This is a vintage for lovers of a fresher style.

2003

Vintage rating: *Belgium – Red: 81, White: 85;*
Netherlands – Red: 83, White: 86

Belgium – A wonderful vintage on paper because of the high amount of sunshine during summer and autumn. However, northern grape varieties are used to dealing with excess water, and several vineyards suffered from hydric stress; the wines are not as concentrated and rich as the summer heat might have suggested, but there are some very good ones.

Netherlands – This was a very good vintage with a few exceptions. The wonderful summer and autumn brought powerful wines, with some excellent examples with real complexity and more alcohol than usual. Vines on sandy soils suffered from drought, which stressed the vines, so there were some mixed results here. In general, as in other countries, there is less acidity, so wines are ripening faster.

2002

Vintage rating: *Belgium – Red: 79, White: 81;*
Netherlands – Red: 82, White: 84

Belgium – Another vintage saved by the sunny late-summer weather after mixed weather during a long growing season. Some attractive wines made people sit up and take notice of Belgian wines.

Netherlands – Quite a good vintage, with well-balanced wines, good acidity, and nice power. Saved by good autumn weather.

2001

Vintage rating: *Belgium – Red: 68, White: 69; Netherlands – Red: 69, White: 68*

Belgium – The reverse of recent vintages, the cool, wet weather during harvest created problems after a better-than-usual summer. Wines lacked concentration, and many were not very clean.

Netherlands – Quality was not very good because of bad weather during summer and autumn. It rained nearly every day in September. Wines tend to be unbalanced, less concentrated, lean, and thin.

GREATEST WINE PRODUCERS

1. Peter Colemont, Clos d'Opleeuw (Gors-Opleeuw, Belgium)
2. Apostelhoeve (Maastricht, Netherlands)
3. Genoels-Elderen (Riemst, Belgium)
4. Lindener, Domein Tempelberg (Lubbeck, Hageland, Belgium)
5. Domein Cohlenberg (Borgloon, Haspengouw, Belgium)
6. Kleine Schorre (Schouwen-Duiveland, Netherlands)
7. Wijnhoeve de Colonjes (Groesbeek, Netherlands)
8. Pietershof (Crindalaer, Belgium)
9. Roelof & Ilse Visscher, Hof van Twente (Bentelo, Netherlands)
10. John & Wilma Huisman, De Reestlandhoeve (Balkbrug, Netherlands)

FASTEST-IMPROVING PRODUCERS

1. Peter Colemont, Clos d'Opleeuw (Gors-Opleeuw, Belgium)
2. John & Wilma Huisman, De Reestlandhoeve (Balkbrug, Netherlands)
3. Kleine Schorre (Schouwen-Duiveland, Netherlands)
4. Lindener, Domein Tempelberg (Lubbeck, Hageland, Belgium)
5. Wijngaard de Oorsprong (Zuid-Beveland, Netherlands)
6. Aldenyck (Maasvallei, Belgium)
7. Pietershof (Crindalaer, Belgium)
8. Boekenderhof (Limburg, Netherlands)
9. Roelof & Ilse Visscher, Hof van Twente (Bentelo, Netherlands)
10. Paul & Anne Vleminckx, Meerdael (Oud-Heverlee, Belgium)

NEW UP-AND-COMING PRODUCERS

1. Pietershof (Crindalaer, Belgium)
2. Kluisberg (Bekkenvoort, Belgium)
3. Paul & Anne Vleminckx, Meerdael (Oud-Heverlee, Belgium)
4. John & Wilma Huisman, De Reestlandhoeve (Balkbrug, Netherlands)
5. Wijnhoeve de Colonjes (Groesbeek, Netherlands)
6. Elzenbosch (Assent, Belgium)
7. Kleine Schorre (Schouwen-Duiveland, Netherlands)
8. Roelof & Ilse Visscher, Hof van Twente (Bentelo, Netherlands)
9. Lindener, Domein Tempelberg (Lubbeck, Hageland, Belgium)
10. Philippe Grafé, Domaine du Chenoy (Belgium)

BEST-VALUE PRODUCERS

1. Aldenyck (Maasvallei, Belgium)
2. Kleine Schorre (Schouwen-Duiveland, Netherlands)
3. John & Wilma Huisman, De Reestlandhoeve (Balkbrug, Netherlands)
4. Apostelhoeve (Maastricht, Netherlands)
5. Wijnhoeve de Colonjes (Groesbeek, Netherlands)
6. Roelof & Ilse Visscher, Hof van Twente (Bentelo, Netherlands)
7. Paul & Anne Vleminckx, Meerdael (Oud-Heverlee, Belgium)
8. Pietershof (Crindalaer, Belgium)
9. Wijngaard de Oorsprong (Zuid-Beveland, Netherlands)
10. Elzenbosch (Assent, Belgium)

GREATEST-QUALITY WINES

1. **Chardonnay 2005** Clos d'Opleeuw, Belgium (€21)
2. **Sparkling Zwarte Parel 2004** Genoels-Elderen, Belgium (€16.50)
3. **Riesling 2005** Apostelhoeve, Netherlands (€9)
4. **Auxerrois 2005** Apostelhoeve, Netherlands (€9)
5. **Regent 2005** Vidaigne, Belgium (€7)
6. **Pinot Blanc 2005** Kleine Schorre, Netherlands (€8.50)
7. **Vlaamse Landwijn Pinot Blanc 2005** Aldenyck, Belgium (€7.50)
8. **Chardonnay 2005** Pietershof, Belgium (€8.20)
9. **Reestland Wit 2005** De Reestlandhoeve, Netherlands (€7.90)
10. **Johanniter 2004** Wijngaard de Oorsprong, Netherlands (€6.95)

BEST BARGAINS

1. **Auxerrois 2005** Apostelhoeve, Netherlands (€9)
2. **Sparkling Zwarte Parel 2004** Genoels-Elderen, Belgium (€16.50)
3. **Vlaamse Landwijn Pinot Blanc 2005** Aldenyck, Belgium (€7.50)
4. **Pinot Blanc 2005** Kleine Schorre, Netherlands (€8.50)
5. **Cabernet Colonjes 2004** Wijnhoeve de Colonjes, Netherlands (€8 per 50-cl bottle)
6. **Reestland Wit 2005** De Reestlandhoeve, Netherlands (€7.90)
7. **Chardonnay 2005** Pietershof, Belgium (€8.20)
8. **Müller-Thurgau 2005** Apostelhoeve, Netherlands (€9)
9. **Regent Barrique 2003** Wijnhoeve de Colonjes, Netherlands (€10.50)
10. **Regent Rosé 2005** Hof van Twente, Netherlands (€10.80)

MOST EXCITING OR UNUSUAL FINDS

1. **Chardonnay 2005** Clos d'Opleeuw, Belgium (€21) *Rich, yellow colour; ripe and round. Lovely nose with mineral, fruit (pears, quince, and Cox apple flavours), and a touch of oak. Rich and round in the mouth, this serious wine has obviously benefited from the 2005 harvest. In a league of its own.*
2. **Sparkling Zwarte Parel 2004** Genoels-Elderen, Belgium (€16.50) *Belgium has just made sparkling-wine production official, and a string of good crémant-style wines has appeared in the past year. This is the leader so far.*
3. **Riesling 2005** Apostelhoeve, Netherlands (€9) *One of the few successful Rieslings grown here, made by the Netherlands' top producer. A little young and harsh still. Good nose, a touch of*

sweetness, quite well made; spicy, still with some acidity and green notes.

④ **Johanniter 2004** Wijngaard de Oorsprong, Netherlands (€6.95) *The nose is quite rich if a little stinky. Lychees, peaches, some good acidity. Light and quite fine, although a slight sweetness is present.*

⑤ **Vlaamse Landwijn Pinot Blanc 2005** Aldenyck, Belgium (€7.50) *Quite attractive lemon-yellow colour, with some good varietal character. There is interest here, and the wine is well made, with some richness and good lychee fruit.*

⑥ **Pinot Blanc 2005** Kleine Schorre, Netherlands (€8.50) *From a large professional vineyard that has shown good results from the start. Not much mineral character, but good apple and pear fruit, fresh and lively, well balanced.*

⑦ **Chardonnay 2005** Pietershof, Belgium (€8.20) *Good Chard aromas with some nice tropical-fruit character and some richness.*

The wine is round, quite full, and creamy. Slightly on the sweet side.

⑧ **Regent 2005** Vidaigne, Belgium (€7) *Dark, rich colour, good concentration, 13 per cent ABV. Grown on iron sandstone, clay, and lime, near Ypres. Typical bitter-cherry and damson flavours of Regent, well structured and well made, with good richness and some depth.*

⑨ **Rosé 2005** Boekenderhof, Netherlands (€9.50) *New vineyard from ambitious Stan Beurskens. The vines are too young to make a quality red wine, but for rosé it is less of a problem. Nice and fruity, not complex, but easy drinking.*

⑩ **Pinot Noir Vroege Loonse 2005** Domein Cohlenberg, Belgium (€7.50) *Very pale and lacking concentration. Light on the nose, with some slight aromas of bitter cherries and a touch of Pinot sweetness. Quite good in the mouth, with classic Pinot cherry aromas. Lacking a little bit of depth. Good effort.*

Grapevine

• **Sparkling-wine sales increased** considerably in 2006 in Belgium, as more growers, including Meerdael, Genoels-Elderen, and Domaine Schorpion, improved the quality of their wines. The rising star in sparkling wines is Clos des Agaises near Mons, a vineyard that was planted only three years ago.

• **A new website for lovers** of Belgian wines has just been created by sommelier Vincent De Coninck at www.belgianwines.com. The site lists 22 different wines and two *digestifs* (including a rather alarming-sounding endive liqueur) that are available for purchase online.

• **Organic viticulture** is beginning to make inroads in Belgium. The best wine featured in the influential *Test Achat* magazine recently was Hageling Bio, made by an organic grower in Tienen in Hageland. Owned by Hugo Bernar, the estate also serves as a nursery for organic vines, importing plants from Germany, Hungary, and Switzerland. Most vines are hybrids, such as Bianca, Phoenix, Regent, Rondo, Sirius, and Blue Muscat.

Luxembourg

David Furer

Luxembourg's quality leader Abi Duhr has delineated his wines from those of his family with the increased production of his Château Pauqué line of wines.

DAVID FURER

In addition to establishing distinct differences in house styles (Mme Aly Duhr is among Luxembourg's best, yet adheres to classic parameters), Duhr has raised prices significantly for his 2005 vintage. All Pauqué wines are from the best parcels of the Grevenmacher Fels, of which he owns 1.4 ha and rents another 0.6 ha.

Crémant is the way forward

It seems that *crémant* is the direction forward for a growing number of Luxembourg producers. Johnny Vesque opened an expanded facility in Cep d'Or in April 2007. "We need more room for the *crémants* because we're now at 60,000 bottles a year and want to age them longer than the current 18 months." A multi-use gallery for the arts and social affairs and a *vinothèque* were constructed. A separate cellar for oak-ageing, both *barriques* and fuder (especially for Rieslings), and 500- to 2,000-litre tanks for microvinification were installed. All vinification techniques will be monitored by computer, and gravity flow

DAVID FURER is the author of *Wine Places* (Mitchell Beazley, 2005) and a contributor to *Hugh Johnson's Pocket Wine Book* and the *Which? Wine Guide*, a contributing editor to *Santé*, a writer for *The Wine News*, *Gourmetour*, *Vinforum*, *Australia & New Zealand Wine Business Magazine*, *Harpers Wine and Spirit Weekly*, *Decanter*, *Gourmet Traveller Wine*, and Merrick's Media travel titles, among others. He has led wine classes and guest lectured at the University of Chicago, Oxford and Cambridge universities, at Volkshochschulen in Germany, and California's Professional Culinary Institute. Generic trade organizations from Spain, Germany, Slovenia, and France, as well as restaurants in London and Chicago, have retained his services as a consultant. He is a Certified Wine Educator, an Advanced Sommelier, and a Certified Sherry Educator.

will be *de rigueur* for the reds. As further evidence of its push towards quality, Cep d'Or regrafted much Rivaner in place of Pinots Blanc and Gris. The consummate salesman's export markets now include Belgium, the Netherlands, Germany, France, the UK, Denmark, and Sweden.

New rules on blending

Spurred by producers' requests for greater flexibility, the government is to allow *assemblage* of multiple varieties within the Marque Nationale system, although it still bars Rivaner or Elbling for *premier cru* or *grand premier cru* designations. Whether this will spur a growth of *cuvées* of the best wines or the most simple remains in the hands of the producers. It will certainly encourage more branded wines.

First Sauvignon on the way

Contrary to my previous assertion, Sylvaner is allowed in a wine marked *grand premier cru*. Schram & Fils's 2005 has a pleasant mix of herb, mineral, and primary fruit character but suffers from a quick, cool fermentation. Luxembourg's first Sauvignon Blanc is expected from Ahn's Ley-Schartz in time for the 2008 vintage. Hoping to out-Muscat Charles Decker, Cep d'Or harvested its first Muscat à Petits Grains in 2006. Decker himself has planted some Siegerrebe, Würzer, and St Laurent, and has Savagnin and Muscat Rosa on the way. He'll also release a Crémant Blanc de Noirs from a four-vintage blend in late 2007. It's very unusual to have four years blended into a *crémant*; they are mostly single- or double-vintage wines.

Grapevine

• **Yves Sunnen's** biodynamic success continues with his successful 2006 harvest. Good timing for vineyard treatments, even in the face of spring peronospera, assured only minimal difficulties. Enough people on hand made for a quick and correct harvest. At this writing, his 2005 stock was sold out – a sure sign that biodynamics work in a marketing sense.

• **The commune of Stadtbredimus** (including Greiveldange), Schwebsange (including Wintrange) in the Wellenstein commune, and Wasserbillig are undergoing the final government-decreed environmental analysis and will begin a *remembrement* (vineyard restructuring) in 2007. Remerschen in the Schengen commune will begin soon – probably in 2008. According to Charles Konnen, director of the Office of Remembrement, 99 ha of land will be affected, but much of this will be public infrastructure and not only vineyards.

• **Marc Gales** was approached by the new owner of Luxembourg's Simon craft brewery, Betty Fontaine, to co-market a Heritage brand hybrid: *crémant* beer. In two months they sold what was projected for its first year. A special glass was created for the product, and Belgian breweries are considering cooperating with Gales and Fontaine on this product for their market.

Opinion:
Quality confirmed

Prodded by a comment made by one of Luxembourg's most vocal producers, I staged a mostly blind tasting of Moselle Rieslings, Pinot Gris, and *crémants* in Remich, Luxembourg, with the support of the IVV and the Marketing Board. All Moselle wineries were welcome to contribute what they wished. Assisting me were the able palates of Telecran's wine specialist Claude François and sommelière Dominique Rizzi of Mondorf's Jangeli restaurant, both recognized leaders in the Luxembourg wine community. Mostly the results confirmed what was already known: standouts included Hartmann, Gales, Rochers, Duhr, and Bastian. There were, however, a few surprises, such as the lovely still wines from Kohll-Leuck, a Pinot Gris from Schram, and Vinsmoselle's new Crémant Blanc de Pinot Noir, CULT.

Bumping against the quality barrier

Contrary to my comments in *Wine Report 2007* on the immutability of Luxembourg's Top 10 list, Schumacher-Knepper's strong 2005 showing, along with its progressive marketing of older vintage wines, threatens to displace one of the current 10. Efforts to improve quality have also been seen at Desom, while Cep d'Or's remodelling and restructuring of its facility, Häremillen's quality spikes, and the Pinot Noirs of Henri Ruppert all merit attention. Kohll-Leuck is steadily climbing upwards, and there are rumblings of new developments at the venerable but still sleeping Domaine Mathes. A greater willingness to experiment with new varieties/clones, lower yields, and longer hang time, along with sensitivity to competition from the New World, are helping younger growers and/or those with the vision or capital to break out of Luxembourg's traditional straitjacket.

Grapevine

• **After a bizarre 2003 Crémant,** due to the vagaries of the hot vintage, Alice Hartmann is back on form with its stellar 2004 Crémant. Hats off to its German winemaker Hans-Jörg Befort for keeping one of Luxembourg's finest wineries on track and for expanding the number of Rieslings, all from the Wormeldange Koeppchen, from two to three with no slip in quality. HJ Befort has also purchased 0.15 ha of 40-year-old Trittenheimer Apotheke in the heart of Germany's middle Mosel, joining its white St Aubin *blanc* for a triumvirate of European regions in its high-quality portfolio.

Luxembourg's Rieslings, Pinot Gris, and *crémants* are the best the Moselle can offer, and export efforts should focus on countries other than France and Germany, both of which produce far larger quantities. Luxembourg's style, uniqueness, and relative obscurity provide it with opportunities to export to the UK, Scandinavia, Japan, and North America.

Reset your watches

Showing that even a stopped clock is correct twice a day, highly commendable wines were made by underperformers Desom and Schumacher-Lethal with their ageworthy Pinot Gris 2005, and Max Lahr with his *à point* Auxerrois Heiligenhaueschen 2005.

More time on the lees for some *crémants*, please. The benefits of extended *sur lie* ageing are evident in the *crémants* of A Gloden at 4–5 years on the lees, Kox's Age de Raison at 6.5 years, and Schumachers Knepper and Lethal, with their 2002 at 3+ years on the lees. Some are great with less, as evidenced by those from Hartmann, Rochers, Krier Frères, and Gales, but the consumer also deserves diversity.

All too often I've gone into Luxembourg cellars asking for older wines to taste along with new releases, only to be told that they have sold out. Often these same producers tell me, when comments are made about the extreme youthfulness of their new releases, that their wines need to be enjoyed with some age. Well, if you want to assure the buying public of your wines' ageworthiness, keep some on hand for those interested, and raise your prices by 10–20 per cent annually for each year cellared.

Grapevine

• **Hampshire-based UK importers** Vine Associates launched a range of 26 wines from the Grand Duchy at London's Sheraton Belgravia hotel in September 2006. Sixty-nine attendees from various sectors tasted 10 wineries' bottlings, capping the hotel's month-long promotion of Luxembourg's relatively undiscovered wines and foods.

• **The Luxembourg Wine Marketing Board** conducted its first study of consumer habits in an informal blind tasting of six white wines. The wines were selected by wine controller Marc Kuhn, and the survey was designed by market-research company Quest. The project will be staged at several forthcoming public gatherings before the results are tabulated and quantified.

• **Following the 2006 harvest,** Jean-Louis Modert left his position marketing the wines of Vinsmoselle to work in Luxembourg's other major business, banking. Ruth Latin-Herber is now in charge of marketing and communication at Vinsmoselle.

• **The idea for a cross-border Schengen appellation** with France and Germany, proposed by Vinsmoselle, seems to have been discarded as unworkable and not in the region's best interests. Good riddance.

Vintage Report

Advance report on the latest harvest

2006

A relatively dry winter led to a rapid flowering two days earlier than usual. Spring frost didn't show. Heavy rains came at the end of May/early June, with patchy June hailstorms destroying up to 60 per cent of some crops in Remerschen and Wormeldange. Muscat and Gewürztraminer were affected by relatively humid conditions later in June, but July was perfect: its dry conditions deterred powdery mildew and were ideal for prevention of oidium. However, August's rainfall was three times higher than normal. September saw great weather, with the harvest beginning on 21 September and Rivaner seeing some rot. For those who employ it, skin contact was limited because, in some cases, 30–60 per cent of grapes were affected by mould.

Even being harvested two weeks earlier than normal on average, Riesling has a higher-than-normal level of acidity, and serious selection was required. Pinot Gris showed high acidity and possibly some green notes due to an early-ish harvest. Pinot Noir will be solid, not outstanding, for both still and *crémant* wines, with a loss of up to 25 per cent of Pinot Noir and Riesling due to rot. Musts of botrytized grapes often required clarification to minimize the risk of the development of vinegar. Nearly all grapes were harvested by 18 October in what IVV viticulturist Serge Fischer described as "one of the shortest harvests of the last decade", down about 9 per cent from normal.

Updates on the previous five vintages

2005

Vintage rating: *Red (Pinot Noir): 88, White: 93*

Spring frosts and later hail left damaged berries in the north, lowering yields by up to 40 per cent. July was wet, August cool and cloudy. An almost perfect harvest began on 19 September. Mildew didn't pose major problems, and most growers used sexual confusion against moth infestation, limiting the need for insecticides. Musty notes from the mould *esca* and from a bit of botrytis have appeared in a few Pinots Blanc and Gris, though most are terrific. Nearly all whites are showing well, with excellent balance; many have good-to-great ageing potential. Best are Riesling and Gewürztraminer. The Pinot Noirs will be better than 2004, though not quite at the level of 2003. Expect good to great *crémants*. Many great icewines were produced.

2004

Vintage rating: *Red (Pinot Noir): 85, White: 88*

Overall, a good year both for quantity and quality, comparable to 1998. IVV reported above-average health for grapes. A dry autumn with cool nights and warm days followed a fairly dry summer, ensuring a classic vintage. The harvest began on 4 October for *crémant* base wines. Chilly nights supported retention of acidity and aromatic complexity. The high levels of malic v. tartaric acid in many whites may ensure a reasonably long life, though with an excessively sour character. Those who left Riesling on the vine to mature fully have been rewarded with great wines. Gewürztraminers are very good across the board; Pinot Noirs range from average to good quality.

2003

Vintage rating: *Red (Pinot Noir): 90, White: 85*

A long, hot, dry summer meant very ripe grapes with low natural acidity, particularly for those who did not take care in the vineyard. This was the first year Luxembourg was allowed to acidify, so inexperienced producers made disharmonious wines. Auxerrois was harvested by the end of September, allowing for some acid retention, though even the best won't be drinking much beyond this printing. There are a few difficult Pinot Blancs and many difficult Pinot Gris due to excessive residual sugar coupled with high alcohol, but most will offer pleasure for the near to mid-term. Riesling and Pinot Noir are mostly excellent, maintaining regional character despite the heat. Some Rieslings have a bit more residual sugar than usual, but those with enough acidity are ageing well. There are many expressive *vendanges tardives* and *vins de paille*, and some terrific icewines from Riesling and Auxerrois. This vintage will put Luxembourg Pinot Noir on the map, if you can find any. With their heavy fruit nose and palate, especially from those with a large percentage of Riesling or Pinot Gris, this year's *crémants* are best avoided.

2002

Vintage rating: *Red (Pinot Noir): 83, White: 92*

The grapes were ripe, but the high acidity levels of many 2002s meant longer fermentation for grapes from more northerly, limestone-influenced soils. Since nearly all work in Luxembourg is done in steel tank, wines are now emerging from their shells, with the sweeter ones needing more time. Pinot Blanc, Riesling, Auxerrois, Gewürztraminer, and Chardonnay are all interesting to great; many Pinot Blancs are only now beginning to open. Most Pinot Gris and Pinot Noirs rank as only okay, as they tend towards leanness. Good icewines were harvested in early January. Most of the fine *crémants* have been drunk.

2001

Vintage rating: *Red (Pinot Noir): 80, White: 89*

Alternating hot and cold summer periods with much rain through September devastated quality hopes for early ripeners like Auxerrois. The best wines are classic, with crisp freshness and intriguing fruit; many still need a few years. Good Pinot Blanc and Gewürztraminer, as well as the icewines harvested in December. Simple but pleasant, Pinot Noirs are drinking well or fading fast. Several good to excellent *crémants* were made, but most are now long gone.

GREATEST WINE PRODUCERS

1. Mme Aly Duhr & Fils
2. Alice Hartmann
3. Gales
4. Clos des Rochers
5. Krier Frères
6. Mathis Bastian
7. Château Pauqué
8. A Gloden & Fils
9. Thill Frères
10. Charles Decker

FASTEST-IMPROVING PRODUCERS

1. Schumacher-Knepper
2. Cep d'Or
3. Desom
4. Häremillen
5. Kohll-Leuck
6. Vinsmoselle

NEW UP-AND-COMING PRODUCERS

1. Cep d'Or
2. Schumacher-Knepper
3. Krier-Welbes
4. Mesenburg-Sadler
5. Henri Ruppert
6. Häremillen
7. Kohll-Leuck
8. Desom
9. Kayl-Noesen
10. La Chaumière

BEST-VALUE PRODUCERS

1. Gales
2. Mme Aly Duhr & Fils
3. Mathis Bastian
4. Vinsmoselle
5. A Gloden & Fils
6. Krier-Welbes

GREATEST-QUALITY WINES

1. **Riesling Domaine & Tradition 2005** Mme Aly Duhr & Fils (€8)
2. **Pinot Gris Nussbaum 2005** Mme Aly Duhr & Fils (€6)
3. **Riesling Vieilles Vignes 2005** Château Pauqué (€9)
4. **Riesling Paradäis Vendange Tardive 2005** Château Pauqué (€24)
5. **Riesling Remerschen Kreitzberg 2005** Charles Decker (€8)
6. **Pinot Blanc Remerschen Kreitzberg 2005** Charles Decker (€8)
7. **Crémant Brut 2004** Alice Hartmann (€14)
8. **Riesling Wormeldange Koeppchen Sélection du Château 2005** Alice Hartmann (€12)
9. **Pinot Gris Wintrange Felsberg 2005** Schumacher-Knepper (€7)
10. **Riesling Domaine & Tradition Fût 12 2005** Mathis Bastian (€8)

BEST BARGAINS

1. **Pinot Gris Nussbaum 2005**
Mme Aly Duhr & Fils (€6)
2. **Riesling Nussbaum 2005**
Mme Aly Duhr & Fils (€7)
3. **Pinot Blanc Wintrange Felsberg 2005** Schumacher-Knepper (€6)
4. **Pinot Gris Wintrange Felsberg 2005** Schumacher-Knepper (€7)
5. **Pinot Gris Foulschette Tradition du Domaine 2005**
A Gloden & Fils (€7)
6. **Pinot Gris Wellenstein Foulschette 2005** Gales (€7)
7. **Pinot Blanc Remerschen Kreitzberg 2005** Charles Decker (€8)
8. **Crémant Brut St Cunibert 2004**
Krier Frères (€7)
9. **Pinot Gris Wellenstein Foulschette 2005** Caves St Remy Desom (€6)
10. **Riesling Wormeldange Weibour 2005** Bernard Massard (€5)

MOST EXCITING OR UNUSUAL FINDS

1. **Pinot Gris Primerberg 2005**
Stronck-Pinnel (€4 per half-bottle) *Made with 100 per cent botrytis-affected grapes, and unusual in that it's made in a dry style, since it fermented through October 2006. Somewhat volatile and alcoholic, but no one can accuse J-Pierre Stronck of resting.*
2. **Crémant Riesling Brut 2004**
Linden-Heinisch (€9) *Unusual style made with botrytized grapes – a style choice Jean Linden-Heinisch seems to be clutching to his breast.*
3. **CULT Crémant Blanc de Noirs 2004** Vinsmoselle (€12) *The latest from Luxembourg's mighty cooperative is by far the best sparkling wine it has produced. Priced competitively, though relatively highly by Luxembourg*

standards. Smaller producers may look to this as a wedge to raise prices on their bubblies, nearly all of which are sold at less than €10.
4. **Chardonnay Ahn Hohfels 2004**
Schmit-Fohl (€8) *Luxembourg's first Chardonnay planting dates to 1989, with further plantings from 2000.*
5. **Riesling Ahner Vogelsang Barrique 2005** Ley-Schartz (€9) *Aged in second- and third-fill barrels, this is noteworthy not only for showing little in the way of oak influence but also for its ability to mimic Sauvignon Blanc – a grape unexpected here until 2008. Is there something we're not being told or does this merely portend good things to come?*
6. **Pinot Noir en Barrique 2005**
Henri Ruppert (€12) *From Dijon 777 clones, this early effort by Ruppert has a long way to go.*
7. **Riesling Grevenmacher Fels 2005** Château Pauqué (€8) *Reminiscent of a German middle-Mosel Riesling from someone who knows his way around such wines.*
8. **Crémant Pinot Noir Rosé 2004**
Cep d'Or (€7) *Macerated for four days, this "nearly red" is vibrant red with a hint of pink and has big raspberry flavours, more than a hint of tannin, and medium length.*
9. **Sylvaner Bech-Macher Kurschels 2005** Schram & Fils (€5) *From 0.2 ha planted in 1984, roughly equal parts white and red, producing this dry wine. Rivaner was previously planted here, and from tasting this and the previous vintage, the Sylvaner is better.*
10. **Coup de Foudre 2005** Pundel Sibenaler (€7) *Equal parts Rivaner, Riesling, and Pinot Gris, and aged in large oak casks, this is the first conscious Luxembourg entry into New World-style blended branding.*

Switzerland

Chandra Kurt

Swiss wine consumption has dropped again over the last year, in what seems to be an unstoppable trend.

CHANDRA KURT

Consumption fell to 2.7 million litres in 2006, or 36 litres per head, a considerable drop from 41 litres per head in 2000. Swiss wine has been hit harder than foreign wine: consumption of Swiss white wine has declined by 8 per cent, red wine by 5 per cent.

An advertising campaign for Swiss wines has been suggested as a means of both reversing this trend and increasing consumption. One proposal is for a tax of 5 rappen (cents) per litre to be allocated to advertising, which would amount to SF 13 million per year.

Swiss have their chips

The news that the Swiss government (even though it is not a member of the EU) has agreed with the USA that certain substances, including oak chips and liquid tannins, can be permitted in Swiss wine caused a furore in the media. The aim of the agreement is to improve trade between the two countries, but the Swiss media have criticized the fact that there is no obligation to mention the use of oak chips on wine labels.

CHANDRA KURT is the author of several wine books, including the bestseller *Weinseller*, which she has been publishing for nine years. Chandra is a freelance wine writer and contributes on a regular basis to leading newspapers such as *Cash*, *Al dente*, and *Schweizer Familie*, as well as leading wine publications such as *Hugh Johnson's Pocket Wine Book*. In 2004, her first fiction book, *Wine Tales* (Orell Füssli), was published; it was translated into Italian in 2005. In 2006, she won three awards: the Lanson prize for originality for the book *Weintipps* (Werd-Verlag, 2006); the Swiss government's Goldene Rebschere 2006 award for her work in the wine business; and Best Book of the Year 2006 from the Italian sommeliers' association for *Racconti del Vino*. Chandra works as a wine consultant for Swiss International Airlines and several Swiss retail institutions. Chandra's website is www.chandrakurt.com.

Busy bees

Worldwide, there are only 38 ha of Amigne grapes, all in the Swiss canton Valais. Of these, 27 ha are in the Valais commune of Vétroz. Amigne, which was brought to Switzerland by the Romans 2,000 years ago, is one of the specialities of the country. Confusion has been caused in the past, however, by the lack of information on the label as to whether the wine was dry or sweet. Now Amigne producers are using bee illustrations on labels to indicate the amount of residual sugar: one bee is 0–8 g/l; two bees, 9–25 g/l; three bees, more than 25 g/l.

Grapevine

• **The University of Neuchâtel** has launched a new, freely accessible database. The Swiss Vitis Microsatellite Database (SVMD) is a standardized database of microsatellite genotypes of virtually all grape varieties, rootstocks, and wild grapevines that grow in Switzerland (see www.unine. ch/nccr/svmd).

• **Cabernet Dorsa,** a little-known Cabernet Sauvignon/Dornfelder cross, is finding its way into blended wines in east Switzerland. Created in 1971 in Germany (Staatliche Lehr- und Versuchsanstalt Weinsberg), its growing popularity is due to the complexity and deep colour it gives to the wines.

• **Swiss Wine Communication,** the failed government wine-promotion office, has been relaunched as Swiss Wine Promotion (SWP). SWP houses the PR offices of the six Swiss wine regions, along with the export association SWEA (Verband der Schweizer Weinexporteure). In charge are Robert Crüll (president), David Escher, and Monique Perrottet.

• **Discounter Denner** has launched its first wine bar, D-Vino, in Zürich, with more bars planned over the next few years. All Denner's 250 wines can be drunk by the glass. The price per glass is calculated by adding SF 25 to the price of the bottle and dividing by seven.

• **More than a dozen Swiss producers** have launched new low-alcohol wines (less than 9 per cent) as a result of the 2005 law reducing permitted blood alcohol levels for drivers to 0.5 per cent.

• **Vin Vaudois** is the new official label for wines produced in Vaud under the AOC regulations. Vaud is the first region to apply such a logo, and it's expected that other regions will follow suit.

• **RAC Changins** and FAW Wädenswil, the two principal Swiss research stations in viticulture and oenology, have merged and are now administered by Agroscope (ACW).

• **Wines with noticeable residual sugar** are appearing more often, especially in the eastern part of Switzerland around the areas of Schaffhausen, Zürich, and Aarau. They seem to be easier to sell than bone-dry wines. This trend affects red Pinot Noirs as much as white Chardonnays and Pinot Gris.

• **Research station FAW Wädenswil** has launched a new harvesting machine that not only harvests automatically but presses the grapes immediately to shorten the time between picking and pressing. The machine will be tested in Germany and Chile during 2007 (see www. beverages.ch).

Opinion:
The effect of globalization

The globalization of the wine world is having a marked effect on Switzerland. Despite the fact that Switzerland is not a member of the EU and retains its neutrality, it has been affected by globalization as much as any other country. Switzerland is well known for its consumption of high-priced wines and has a very developed wine market. Wines from all over the world are available in supermarkets and discount stores, which account for around 70 per cent of sales. Around half of the wine sold is foreign, mainly from France, Spain, and Italy. New World wines were popular briefly a few years ago, but the trend is now towards buying European wines, especially Italian.

"Natural" v. "industrial" wines

A lively debate is taking place in Switzerland over the differences between "natural" wines and "industrial" wines. The problem is not that mass-produced wines are not good (we all know that they are perfectly well made); it's more that a consumer cannot tell from the label whether the wine comes from a small, artisanal producer or an industrial operation.

Don't lose the terroir!

The divide between commercial and terroir-driven wines is reflected in Swiss wine styles today. The last year has seen more "modern" wines launched than ever before. The danger is that producers – or even regions – are tempted to make wines to please the consumer. The Parker influence is strong, and many wines are produced in the style he is thought to prefer, even though they are not at all typical of the country. On the other hand, the quality of the top producers of terroir-proud regions like the Valais is better than ever. Tradition and market-driven wine production walk side by side in Swiss vineyards, just as they do on the supermarket shelves.

Grapevine

• **The second edition** of the official Swiss wine guide, *Guide des Vins Suisse*, has been published. Produced by Ringier, Zürich, it has more than 540 pages outlining 600 wine growers and their wines (www.guide-des-vins-suisses.ch).

• **Vetropack,** the biggest Swiss glass factory, has bought a majority share in the Ukraine packaging company Gostomel Glass Factory, near Kiev. Vetropack has plans to expand into Eastern Europe.

Vintage Report

Advance report on the latest harvest

2006

Of 15,000 ha of Swiss wines, 8,500 are planted with black grapes, and in 2006 almost 1 million hl of wine were harvested. It looks as if the quality is similar to the rather good 2005s, especially for reds. Very good results are expected in the Valais, the Ticino, and the Bündner Herrschaft (Grisons), where weather conditions were generally better. In the Grisons, 1.6 million litres of red and 440,000 litres of white wine were produced. The main grape (Pinot Noir) reached an average level of 100° *Oechsle*. In the Ticino, Merlot reached an average of 89° *Oechsle*, 0.4 higher than 2005. On the 1,000 ha of Ticino vines, 5.6 million litres of wine were produced (85 per cent Merlot). The main white grape became Chardonnay, with 230,000 kg (226 tons).

The Valais, the biggest canton in terms of production, harvested 40.9 million litres (247,000 hl red and 162,000 hl white) of wine from an area of 5,200 ha. With 10.2 million litres, Chasselas makes up a quarter of the total harvest in the Valais, and it seems that the decline of Chasselas/Fendant has ended. The Valais was lucky in 2006. Despite a lot of rain at the end of August, the autumn was long and warm. There was no rot, and black varieties were mature and healthy at harvest. Late-harvest wines are going to be very interesting, since they reached an *Oechsle* level of 200°.

The Waadt harvest was the smallest for 25 years (down 1.1 million litres). The total is 27.18 million litres (19.49 million litres white, 7.69 million litres red). Quality-wise, 2006 is being compared to 2002. The average Chasselas degrees *Oechsle* are 74.01, Gamay 85.32, and Pinot Noir 89.32.

Updates on the previous five vintages

2005

Vintage rating: *Red: 92, White: 91*

As in most parts of Europe, 2005 turned out to be a very special vintage. The overall quality is very good but quite limited, so wines sold out more quickly than usual. Unlike the 2003 vintage, higher-quality wines show good ageing potential (especially red wines) and are marked by elegance and overall balance. In 2004, wines were generally marked by delicacy, fruitiness, and liveliness, whereas in 2003 they showed concentration and maturity: 2005 seems to have taken the best out of these two vintages.

2004

Vintage rating: *Red: 90, White: 90*

Most producers were happy that 2004 was not as hot as 2003. Though similar in quantity to 1998 and 2001, quality was far better, and wines were more balanced than the extreme 2003s. In the Valais, red wines have very good structure and balance. In the Vaud, the Chasselas had a lively, fruity freshness. Red wines in Geneva appear to have the edge on quality: the Pinot Noirs of the Drei-Seen-Region reached 90° *Oechsle*, while Chasselas was lower at 72°. The wines from Bündner Herrschaft had higher sugar levels due to the Föhn (the region's warm autumn wind): 98° *Oechsle* for Pinot Noir and 73–78° for Müller-Thurgau. In general, reds and whites are harmonious and balanced. In the Ticino, Merlot reached an average of 86.6° *Oechsle*.

2003

Vintage rating: *Red: 91, White: 88*

Although many of the 2003 results are outstanding in quality and aroma, cellar work needed flexibility and skill. Wine quality is extraordinary. Pinot Noir reached an average 106° *Oechsle*, Müller-Thurgau 83°. In general, most of the varieties had *Oechsles* over 100, a quality level not seen since 1947. It was also a very early harvest – a month earlier than usual in the Grisons. Due to a difficult, very hot summer, there are two types of quality. Wine growers with more experience knew how to manage the high sugar levels, but a lot of the smaller growers produced overalcoholic wines with an overcooked taste. When buying wine, you have to know who did a good job in the cellar.

2002

Vintage rating: *Red: 90, White: 85*

Quality varies from good to excellent, with wines that are more elegant than full-bodied. In some regions, quantity dropped by as much as 30 per cent over 2001, showing that growers reduced quantity to increase quality.

2001

Vintage rating: *Red: 89, White: 85*

A climatically difficult year produced a small crop of variable quality. In the Valais, the quality was very good indeed, while it was just average for the rest of the Romandie. It was excellent in Schaffhausen and the Grisons.

GREATEST WINE PRODUCERS

1. Daniel & Martha Gantenbein (Fläsch)
2. Jean-René Germanier (Bon Père, Germanier SA, Vétroz)
3. Hans-Ulrich Kesselring (Schlossgut Bachtobel, Ottoberg)
4. Fromm Weingut (Malans)
5. Luigi Zanini (Besazio)
6. Werner Stucky (Rivera)
7. Daniel Huber (Monteggio)
8. Christian Zündel (Beride)
9. Charles & Jean-Michel Novelle (Satigny)
10. Marie-Thérèse Chappaz (Fully)

FASTEST-IMPROVING PRODUCERS

1. Denis Mercier (Sierre)
2. Domaine du Daley (Lutry)
3. Daniel Marugg (Weingut Marugg, Fläsch)
4. Simon Maye & Fils (St Pierre-de-Clages)
5. Thomas & Barbara Studach (Malans)
6. Peter Wegelin (Malans)
7. Ruedi Baumann (Baumann Weingut, Oberhallau)
8. Stéphane Reynard & Dany Varone (Domaine Cornulus, Sierre)
9. Chanton Weine (Visp)
10. Jacques Tatasciere (Domaine de la Rochette, Cressier)

NEW UP-AND-COMING PRODUCERS

1. Weingut Bisang (Dagmersellen)
2. Weingut Reblaube (Uetikon am See)
3. Nicolas Bonnet (Domaine de la Comtesse Eldegarde, Satigny)
4. Didier Joris (Chamoson)
5. Baumann Weingut (Oberhallau)
6. Weingut zur Sonne (Christian Obrecht, Jenins)

7. Bad Osterfingen (Familie Meyer, Osterfingen)
8. Jürg Saxer (Weingut Bruppach, Neftenbach)
9. Domaine du Centaure (Dardagny)
10. Johanniterkeller (Twann)

BEST-VALUE PRODUCERS

1. Provins (Sion)
2. VOLG Weinkellereien (Winterthur)
3. Zweifel (Zürich)
4. Vins Rouvinez (Sierre)
5. Caves Fernand Cina (Salgesch)
6. Philippoz Frères (Leytron)
7. Weingut Pircher (Eglisau)
8. Davaz Weine (Fläsch)
9. Jean-René Germanier (Bon Père, Germanier SA, Vétroz)
10. Henri Cruchon (Echichens)

GREATEST-QUALITY WINES

1. **Cabernet Sauvignon/Cornalin 2004** Jean-René Germanier, Bon Père, Germanier SA, Vétroz (SF 33)
2. **Cayas 2004** Jean-René Germanier, Bon Père, Germanier SA, Vétroz (SF 33)
3. **Platinum 2003** Guidi Brivio, Ticino (SF 80)
4. **Pinot Noir 2004** Daniel & Martha Gantenbein, Fläsch (SF 46)
5. **Bianco del Ticino 2004** Castello Luigi, Luigi Zanini, Besazio (SF 95)
6. **Ermitage Grain Noble 2003** Marie-Thérèse Chappaz, Fully (SF 44 per 50-cl bottle)
7. **Heida Mario Nr 6 2003** Chanton Weine, Visp (SF 40 per 50-cl bottle) (sweet)
8. **Montagna Magica 2004** Daniel Huber, Monteggio (SF 51)
9. **Chardonnay 2005** Zweifel, Zürich (SF 25)
10. **Pinot Noir Der Andere 2005** Schlossgut Bachtobel, Ottoberg (SF 29)

BEST BARGAINS

1. **Müller-Thurgau 2005** Schlossgut Bachtobel, Ottoberg (SF 14)
2. **Pinot Noir 2004** Denis Mercier, Sierre (SF 15.50)
3. **Blauburgunder 2005** Fromm Weingut, Malans (SF 18)
4. **Pinot Noir 2005** Caves Fernand Cina, Salgesch (SF 14)
5. **Gamay de Vétroz 2005** Cave de la Madeleine, Vétroz (SF 11.50)
6. **Fragolino Rosso Brut NV** Delea, Losone (SF 9.50)
7. **Fendant Stockalper 2005** Provins, Sion (SF 12.90)
8. **Federweiss 2005** Weingut Marugg, Fläsch (SF 15.50)
9. **Vinzel Tradition 2005** Vincent Beetschen, Bursins (SF 9.50)
10. **Chasselas 2006** Neuchâtel Blanc, Grillette, Cressier (SF 11.80)

MOST EXCITING OR UNUSUAL FINDS

1. **Valais Domaine Evêché Diolinoir 2003** Provins, Sion (SF 28) *The large cooperative Provins took over the diocese vineyard of Sion two years ago. One of their wines is a pure Diolinoir, a Valais speciality.*
2. **Riesling 2005** Daniel & Martha Gantenbein, Fläsch (SF 45) *This Swiss couple produce the best Pinot Noir in the country and the most exciting Riesling, with grapes sourced from Dr Ernst Loosen.*
3. **Chardonnay 2005** Fromm Weingut, Malans (SF 28 per half-bottle) *Georg Fromm is not only one of the best producers of the Grisons but is also successful in New Zealand with the La Strada Winery. His Swiss Chardonnay is a great example of balance and liveliness.*
4. **Malbec 2005** Charles Steiner, Schernelz (SF 28) *A new wine in the Steiner family range. This medium-bodied, dark wine is sweet on the nose, with aromas of strawberry jam, pink pepper, and some dark chocolate. The tannins are soft and well balanced. Elegant finish. A striking contrast to an Argentine Malbec – but a charming one.*
5. **Sauvignon Blanc 2005** Schlossgut Bachtobel, Ottoberg (SF 20) *A crisp, fresh, and energetic Sauvignon Blanc with grassy and exotic fruit notes. Perfect to start an evening or quench your thirst. Best young.*
6. **Cornalin 2004** Denis Mercier, Sierre (SF 33) *A dark wine made from a variety found only in the Valais. Fruit-driven and lively, the wine has firm tannins that surround the fruity heart of the wine with delicacy. Very charming finish.*
7. **Completer 2004** VOLG Weinkellereien, Winterthur (SF 23.50) *One of Switzerland's oldest grapes, Completer is mainly found in eastern Switzerland. Its high acidity gives the wine an interesting energy. The wine has aromas of curry, Muscat, and honey and is full-bodied and complex. Decanting recommended.*
8. **Pinot Blanc 2005** Familie Meyer, Bad Osterfingen, Osterfingen (SF 16.50) *Not comparable to a Pinot Blanc from Alsace, but it's modest, fruit-driven, aromatic, and very pleasant. The freshness and clean minerality are wonderful.*
9. **Müller-Thurgau 2005** Baumann Weingut, Oberhallau (SF 12.60) *Shows aromas of roses and pears. Clean and light body, with medium acidity and no wood aromatics. A good everyday wine.*
10. **Chas 2005** Domaine du Crepon, Villeneuve (SF 17.50) *A new-generation Chasselas. No malo (which is against Swiss tradition). As a result, the wine is full of freshness, with citrus aromas and a steely finish. Wakes up the palate.*

Austria

Philipp Blom

After the giddiness of expansion comes redefinition. Austria's wines have shown their worth internationally, but top growers have taken note of stylistic criticism.

PHILIPP BLOM

Of particular note have been the comments regarding the turbo-charged offerings created out of a mixture of excitement, experimentation, and extreme ideas.

A constructively sober mood is now setting in among the country's top growers. It is possible to make world-class wines here – as many outside the traditionally terroir-oriented regions already realize – but is it possible to create world-class wines that can be made *only* here? The techniques, data, and grape varieties are all there, but in some regions tougher questions are being asked about which of these are appropriate for their wines and for their region.

This rethink has created a raft of fascinating wines designed to sound out local terroir and get away from the additional magic wrought in the cellar. One aspect of this development (helped by EU money) has been a lively discussion about organic and biodynamic viticulture, and already the density of "natural" winemaking is exceptional.

There are also several initiatives based on the terroir idea. Following the lead of the Weinviertel, the Mittelburgenland has created its own DAC (controlled region of origin) initiative based on Blaufränkisch, while on the western shore of Lake Neusiedl, the Leithaberg group aims to explore and promote the terroir of the Leitha hillsides.

PHILIPP BLOM is a writer and journalist (*Wine & Spirits Magazine, Hugh Johnson's Pocket Wine Book*). His book *The Wines of Austria* was published by Faber & Faber in 2000 and appeared in a revised and extended edition in 2006. Among his other books are *To Have and to Hold: An Intimate History of Collecting* (Penguin, 2002), *Encyclopédie: The Triumph of Reason in an Unreasonable Age* (Fourth Estate, 2004), and *Luxor* (Tisch 7, 2006), a novel. He lives in Vienna.

Another welcome sign of a maturing market, this time for export, is a strategic shift among top producers, who are becoming less concerned about continuing expansion. International demand continues to be strong, but there is more concentration on the main export markets and a less gung-ho approach: "Let's put it this way – we're not exactly preparing to conquer China," as one grower remarked.

One last element in this puzzle is the emergence of medium- or larger-scale producers who can offer well-made wines at internationally competitive prices. This had been lacking in the Austrian wine landscape – and with it a second tier to shore up the country's exports against changing fashion. Now, new or renewed brands are filling the vacuum left by the continuing lacklustre qualitative performance of the country's giants.

Grapevine

• **Carlo Wolf,** the driving spirit behind the astonishing revival of Schloß Halbturn, has unexpectedly parted ways with his employers. The vines and the modernized cellars, however, are still in good hands: François-Xavier Gaboriaud and Markus Sieben form an excellent and dedicated team. The reign of a Frenchman and a German in a Burgenland cellar is a topic hotly debated among some of their neighbours.

• **The indefatigable Fritz Miesbauer,** having taken over the Weingut der Stadt Krems in 2002 and dramatically improved quality, is now holding the reins in the vineyards and cellars of the historic Stift Göttweig, a beautiful baroque abbey more famous for its architecture and altarpieces than the quality of its wines until now.

• **The Mittelburgenland,** with its flagship varietal Blaufränkisch, was the second region after the Weinviertel to announce a DAC (controlled region of origin), followed shortly afterwards by the small Traisental region with a white DAC for Grüner Veltliner and Riesling. Other regions are on the verge of declaring, while a third group is either too divided about what to include in the DAC or, like the Wachau, largely uninterested.

• **Mayer am Pfarrplatz,** the traditional Viennese producer, has a new owner, local marketing tycoon Hans Schmid, who is planning to renovate the cellars and the image of this historic house, which has plenty of potential.

• **Willi Klinger** is the new director of the Austrian Wine Marketing Service, following the dynamic Michael Thurner. Willi was formerly manager of Freie Weingärtner Wachau and global export manager for Angelo Gaja. This position carries some political influence, and Mr Klinger's international stature will be an asset.

Opinion:
Finding Austrian terroir

Regional authenticity are buzzwords in Austrian cellars at the moment, but the idea of specific terroirs is clearly defined in only a few regions, notably Wachau, Kremstal, and Kamptal, as well as parts of Styria and the Burgenland. In some other regions, a particular terroir is at times defined by one wine of one outstanding grower with little or no opportunity for comparison. It is one thing to demonstrate wine's aromatic profile in a vertical tasting, but to establish a terroir it has to be clear that it expresses itself consistently. Cellar technique is too often substituted for the uncertain business of trusting a terroir, particularly in regions eager to create a profile.

It may be true that only a selected few can afford to bet on terroir and vintage characteristics: those depending on wholesalers and cellar-door sales are all too often expected to produce reliably round and aromatically consistent wine, more house brand than vintage. On the positive side, there is a rethinking of style across the board, accompanied by a new openness to experimentation with cultivation methods (particularly organic and biodynamic), different and generally more traditional vinification techniques, and vintage variation – all in pursuit of real individuality.

Even outside the traditionally defined terroirs along the Danube, some pioneers have done much to explore and advance the idea. The Moric initiative in Mittelburgenland, for instance, has revealed very clear profiles for Blaufränkisch from the villages of Neckenmarkt and Lutzmannsburg, while the fascinating story of Schloß Halbturn in the Burgenland continues (see Grapevine). Some of the methods they employ are iconoclastic: black grapes are trodden in traditional Bordelais manner, then cold-soaked and heated up for quick fermentation. The results are so unusual for the region and so positive that some colleagues are now experimenting in this direction. The efforts of the Leithaberg group, in Neusiedlersee-Hügelland, to define its terroir are beginning to bear fruit.

The battle for authenticity is dominated by the Wachau, which has the most clearly terroir-based public image. Elsewhere, there are barbed remarks about making a cult of terroir while allowing irrigation, but wine styles and winemaking techniques are still so dominant in some emerging regions that in some producer marketing groups the wines made by members definitely have a group character, but no discernible terroir profile.

All these initiatives are steps in the right direction, but it will take many more vintages to really define the idea of terroir in many parts of Austria.

Vintage Report

Advance report on the latest harvest

2006

Nothing was normal in 2006. A long, cold, and snowy winter turned into a wet, cool spring with very little sun. The cool, rainy weather affected fruit set for early-blossoming varieties, especially Grüner Veltliner, reducing yields. Other varieties, such as Riesling, were hardly affected. In mid-June, summer set in suddenly with record-breaking temperatures and warm winds, a change demanding a great deal of skilful canopy and green-cover management to cope adequately with both rain and dry heat – a test especially for the growing crop of organic and biodynamic producers in the country.

August was cool and exceptionally rainy, but September and October brought one of the most beautiful autumns in living memory, with hot days and cold nights, leading to a rush of ripening and compressing ideal harvest times for many varieties into a small window only, far less staggered than in other years. Only some Rieslings and grapes for sweet wines were still on the vines in early November.

In Lower Austria, especially Wachau, Kremstal, and Kamptal, producers are delighted with grape quality, despite the exceptionally low yields of Grüner Veltliner. The ideal weather during the late ripening and harvest periods has created wines with mature fruit balanced by high acidity, and the first finished wines are very encouraging, especially with a view to ageing. The autumn warmth was good news, too, in the other regions of Lower Austria.

In Burgenland, yields were "average to good", with outstanding grape qualities. The sustained warmth allowed Blaufränkisch grapes in particular to achieve full ripeness while maintaining high levels of acidity. International black varieties such as Cabernet Sauvignon also fared very well, while Zweigelt struggled with its tendency to flabbiness. Once again, some interesting Pinot Noir was harvested, while among the white varieties Chardonnay responded particularly well. The dry, warm weather did nothing to help botrytis for the nobly sweet wines, and growers had to be very patient to get any results.

Influenced by the climate of the Adriatic, Styria had a warmer August than other regions, and a good deal of rain in the third week of September. This created problems with rot, and rigorous selection was necessary. The fine weather in late September and October, however, created expressive aromas, good news especially for Gelber Muskateller, but also for Chardonnay and Sauvignon Blanc.

Not an easy year, 2006 will produce some exceptional wines. A rare aromatic balance in the material and a continuing discussion about wine styles and terroir will result in some stylistic milestones with excellent ageing prospects.

Updates on the previous five vintages

2005

Vintage rating: *Dry white: 86, Red: 91, Sweet white: 92*

As ever, the scores are misleading, since they ignore the great quality differences in this vintage, ranging from very mediocre to outstanding, especially for dry whites. After an endlessly rainy autumn, some top growers had to accept yields of only 30 per cent of normal to ensure perfectly ripe and healthy material, producing some exceptional wines.

Expect pure fruit, elegant acidity, and good ripeness for leading white wines in Lower Austria. Early-ripening red wines are likely to have done well, too. In Styria, vineyards may have suffered from Mediterranean low-pressure systems more than the rest of Austria, but with equivalent quantitative losses, producers were able to achieve full ripeness and good fruit for their wines. It is certainly a vintage that emphasizes terroir over sheer fruit extract. For once, early ripeness was not an advantage in the Burgenland, where growers had to wait for harvesting and also had to deal with substantial botrytis infections. This was good news for sweet wines, and there will be outstanding TBAs, if only in very small quantities.

2004

Vintage rating: *Dry white: 93, Red: 88, Sweet white: 87*

Simple scores misrepresent 2004, since the quality of wines depended on individual producers' care in the vineyard, and results vary widely. The climate was far from ideal, even if a beautiful August and early September rescued much of what had been written off. If there are some great wines in the making, it shows that the producers are masters of their craft. Only the grapes of those producers relying on low yields from the start could achieve full physiological ripeness, and these produced beautiful, clean, and strongly varietal wines with pronounced acidity. It was a particularly elegant vintage for Grüner Veltliner and Riesling, as well as for Chardonnay and Sauvignon Blanc, but quantities were small. Among the red wines, early ripeners like Zweigelt had a clear advantage, showing dense, fine tannins indicative of considerable potential. Varieties such as Blaufränkisch often benefit from a good, elegant acidity, while other, hotter grapes, such as Cabernet Sauvignon and Syrah, are likely to be fully ripe only in exceptional circumstances.

2003

Vintage rating: *Dry white: 92, Red: 94, Sweet white: 85*
Marked by two heat waves, in May and in late summer, this is an
exceptional year, and harvests began in August, the earliest recorded date,
and under ideal conditions, though younger vines especially suffered from
drought. Growers who dealt well with the excessive heat (by leaving leaf
canopies etc) could bring in a dream harvest.

This is a perfect year for red wines, and while conditions would have
allowed another charge of blockbusters, many producers opted for denser,
more structured wines. Growers who protected their grapes from sun stress
also harvested white wines of astonishing freshness with beautiful acidity
and great ageing potential.

2002

Vintage rating: *Dry white: 93, Red: 90, Sweet white: 97*
In Lower Austria, this year will be remembered for its autumn rains and
floods that made many terraced vineyards collapse. Red wines are well
balanced with ripe tannins, and the prevalent botrytis was good news
for nobly sweet wines.

Styrian growers made expressive Sauvignon Blancs and Chardonnays, and
in Lower Austria this difficult vintage proved to possess the seeds of true
greatness for producers who practised rigorous grape selection and who
harvested late. Wonderfully balanced Rieslings and, to a lesser extent, Grüner
Veltliner, especially in the Wachau and the Kamptal, show great elegance,
depth, and enormous potential. In the best cases this is a classic vintage.

2001

Vintage rating: *Dry white: 89, Red: 90, Sweet white: 85*
After a hot summer, September came with never-ending rain. The weather
finally changed in October. These difficult conditions also brought with
them a very work-intensive harvest, sorting out the healthy grapes from
others. Two frosty periods in December, finally, allowed an icewine harvest.
This was a real year to demonstrate conscientious vineyard work and good
vinification; in general, it is marked by clarity and balance, with the reds
less powerful than 2000 but possessing more charm. A good crop of
botrytis wines was harvested, too. Will evolve quite quickly.

GREATEST WINE PRODUCERS

1. Alzinger (Wachau)
2. Willi Bründlmayer (Kamptal)
3. Gross (South Styria)
4. Hirtzberger (Wachau)
5. Emmerich Knoll (Wachau)
6. Kracher (Neusiedlersee)
7. FX Pichler (Wachau)
8. Prager (Wachau)
9. Tement (South Styria)
10. Ernst Triebaumer (Neusiedlersee-Hügelland)

FASTEST-IMPROVING PRODUCERS

1. Bauer-Naturnaher Weinbau (Donauland)
2. Höllmüller (Wachau)
3. Undhof Salomon (Kremstal)
4. Geyerhof (Kremstal)
5. Weingut der Stadt Krems (Kremstal)
6. Judith Beck (Burgenland)
7. Vorspannhof Mayr (Kremstal)
8. Birgit Eichinger (Kamptal)
9. Schloß Halbturn (Neusiedlersee)
10. Freie Weingärtner Wachau (Wachau)

NEW UP-AND-COMING PRODUCERS

1. Josef Bauer (Donauland)
2. Kloster am Spitz (Neusiedlersee-Hügelland)
3. Gabi Mariell (Neusiedlersee-Hügelland)
4. Sepp Muster (South Styria)
5. Claus Preisinger (Neusiedlersee)
6. Fam. Rixinger (Wachau)
7. Rudi Sax (Kamptal)
8. Heinrich Sigl (Wachau)
9. Franz Schneider (Donauland)
10. Rainer Wess (Wachau)

BEST-VALUE PRODUCERS

1. Günter Brandl (Kamptal)
2. Willi Bründlmayer (Kamptal)
3. Buchegger (Kamptal)
4. Emmerich Knoll (Wachau)
5. Schloß Gobelsburg (Kamptal)
6. Roman Pfaffl (Weinviertel)
7. Peter Schandl (Neusiedlersee-Hügelland)
8. Heidi Schröck (Neusiedlersee-Hügelland)
9. Ludwig Hiedler (Kamptal)
10. Alois Gross (South Styria)

GREATEST-QUALITY WINES

1. **Grüner Veltliner Smaragd Kellerberg 2004** FX Pichler, Wachau (€30)
2. **Riesling Smaragd Steinertal 2003** Alzinger, Wachau (€15.50)
3. **Sauvignon Blanc Zieregg 2003** Tement, South Styria (€28)
4. **Cuvée Comondor 2003** John Nittnaus, Neusiedlersee (€30)
5. **Blaufränkisch Dürrau 2002** Weninger, Mittelburgenland (€35)
6. **Nouvelle Vague Chardonnay TBA Nr 8 2002** Kracher, Neusiedlersee (€48)
7. **Riesling Heiligenstein Lyra 2002** Willi Bründlmayer, Kamptal (€25)
8. **Riesling Smaragd Singerriedel 2002** Hirtzberger, Wachau (€45)
9. **Riesling Smaragd Wachstum Bodenstein 2002** Prager, Wachau (€30)
10. **Cuvée Salzberg 2000** Heinrich, Neusiedlersee (€45)

BEST BARGAINS

1. **Riesling Steinhaus 2005**
Rudi Sax, Kamptal (€6)
2. **Blaufränkisch/Cabernet 2005**
Ernst Triebaumer, Neusiedlersee-Hügelland (€9)
3. **Zweigelt Goldberg 2005**
Werner Achs, Neusiedlersee (€9)
4. **Grüner Veltliner Pichlpoint Smaragd 2005** Höllmüller, Wachau (€12)
5. **Riesling Hinterberg 2005**
Bauer-Naturnaher Weinbau, Donauland (€8)
6. **Grüner Veltliner Federspiel 2005** Gritsch, Wachau (€6)
7. **Blaufränkisch Weinberg 2004**
Kopfensteiner, Mittelburgenland (€9)
8. **Riesling Kirnberg Smaragd 2005** Heinrich Sigl, Wachau (€6)
9. **Grüner Veltliner Pichlpoint Federspiel 2005** Schmelz, Wachau (€7)
10. **Grüner Veltliner Gaisberg 2005** Birgit Eichinger, Kamptal (€11)

MOST EXCITING OR UNUSUAL FINDS

1. **Riesling Smaragd Achleiten 2005** Rudi Pichler, Wachau (€25)
Very pure and deep, exuberant and expressive, with aromas of peach and almond. Great persistence.
2. **Cuvée Imperial 2003** Schloß Halbturn, Neusiedlersee (€23)
A wine in the best, classic French style from the Burgenland! This cuvée of Cabernet Sauvignon, Blaufränkisch, Merlot, and Cabernet Franc has great elegance.
3. **Riesling Beerenauslese 2005** Hirtzberger, Wachau (€37)
A marvel of a wine. Immensely pure and long, with an endlessly intriguing interplay of aromas.
4. **Grüner Veltliner Stockkultur 2005** Prager, Wachau (€30)
The virgin harvest from this experimental gobelet planting of various old clones by Toni Bodenstein produced a wine of monumental promise.
5. **Ruster Ausbruch Turner 2005** Heidi Schröck, Neusiedlersee-Hügelland (€38) If a wine could dance, this would be it: fantastic balance and delicacy, wonderfully understated fruit, and true sophistication.
6. **Riesling Tradition 2004** Schloß Gobelsburg, Kamptal (€16) This wine has already become a classic, but with this vintage, Michi Moosbrugger has succeeded in combining depth, structure, and purity that set a new standard.
7. **Moric Blaufränkisch Neckenmarkt 2002** Alte Reben, Mittelburgenland (€38)
A red wine from Austria that has become emblematic for the region's terroir: darkly expressive yet fresh on the palate, with delicate tannins and great length.
8. **Pinot Noir Dechant 2004** Loimer, Kamptal (€20) Wonderfully fine spice, nutmeg, and dry leaves; lively fruit, tarry edge, delicate acidity, and lingering berry notes.
9. **Riesling Bruck Smaragd 2005** Gritsch, Wachau (€12) Intense and mineral, elderflower and almond, great depth and harmony. Keeps on growing.
10. **Riesling Loibenberg Smaragd 2005** Stierschneider, Wachau (€14) A fine, aromatic wine, with notes of lime blossoms and delicate minerality – a perfect expression of the Loibenberg terroir.

Eastern & Southeastern Europe

Dr Caroline Gilby MW

Russia has been flexing its political muscles over its neighbours and unilaterally banned all wine from both Moldova and Georgia on 27 March 2006.

DR CAROLINE GILBY MW

The Russian health minister claimed that the Moldovan and Georgian wines were contaminated with heavy metals and pesticides, and that they endangered the Russian consumer. Little hard evidence was produced to support Russia's action, not least because many grape growers in these countries are far too poor to afford agrochemicals anyway. Several commentators believe that wine is being used as a political football to punish both countries for daring to look West. Deputy Foreign Affairs Minister Valeriu Ostalep claimed a clear link between the timing of the ban and political disputes with Russia over the breakaway Transnistria region. "It came immediately after we changed the system of monitoring border controls with Ukraine," he stated.

For Moldova, this situation has been desperate. It was already the poorest country in Europe, with a minimum monthly salary of US$32, and yet the most heavily dependent on wine in the world. Wine accounted for 25 per cent of export earnings in 2005, worth around $312 million, with CIS states taking $300 million and more than 85 per cent of that going to Russia. Until the embargo, Moldova was Russia's top supplier, though

DR CAROLINE GILBY MW is a freelance writer specializing in Eastern Europe and viticulture. She contributed to *Wines of the World* and *The Oxford Companion to Wine*, and has been published in *Decanter*, *Harpers Wine and Spirit Weekly*, *Off Licence News*, and *New Scientist*. She is on the editorial board of the *Journal of Wine Research*. She has a PhD in plant sciences but left science to become senior wine buyer for a major UK retail chain. She lectures for the WSET Diploma and judges at international wine shows, as well as working as a consultant to the wine trade.

market share had recently dropped to 45 per cent in the face of the growing competition from Western Europe and the New World.

The problem that Moldova seems reluctant to recognize is that much of its sales have been of very low-quality, semi-sweet wine sold to Russia on price alone – shipments so huge that many wineries have dedicated railway connections. The Western world's wine markets are already saturated, and there is no obvious gap for Moldova to fill. It certainly won't make much headway unless it tackles its winemaking styles, widespread poor quality, and the ever-present issues of fragmented landholdings and poorly tended vines.

To make these changes requires investment in equipment, vineyards, and expertise. However, around 20 per cent of all bank credit has been going to wineries, based on guarantees against Russian wine sales, and funds have dried up. Even before the ban, some wineries were beginning to realize that this Russian gravy train could not last and had started to make changes in vineyards and equipment. The influx of European and heavily promoted New World wines is changing Russian taste, so this loss of market was a problem waiting to happen, albeit accelerated by Russian tactics to bring Moldova to heel.

In the meantime, Moldovan workers and growers are suffering, and reports suggest that as much as 50 per cent of the industry may be bankrupted. Signs of a resolution to the ban were announced on 29 November 2006 after a meeting between presidents Putin and Voronin. They agreed to allow resumption of exports in bottle from Moldova to Russia, subject to new control measures. The industry is still unclear as to how this will work in practice and how long it will take.

Georgia has been exporting 80 per cent of its wine to Russia, and the ban is causing widespread panic and economic difficulties. It's clearly a bigger issue than wine, since a ban on mineral water was announced in May, and sources reckon that the situation in Chechnya is the underlying cause. Many wineries are struggling financially and, having large stocks from the last vintage, have bought only limited quantities of the best grapes in 2006, so prices have collapsed.

A government-backed scheme to persuade local businesses to help the industry by buying grapes appears to have taken up around 4,000 tonnes out of an estimated 140,000-tonne harvest. Much of the surplus is reported to have been made into concentrate. Lado Uzunashvili (consultant to Pernod Ricard-owned GWS) says, "It is ironic that this is happening when the overall quality of Georgian wine has reached a high level, and the country was ready to present 'Brand Georgia' to the world."

The Russian situation may well be a huge opportunity for Bulgaria, and there have been reports of Russians hunting for wine supplies across the country and also of Moldovans moving to Bulgaria. Exports of Bulgarian bottled wine to Russia were up by 75 per cent even before the ban. Shipments from Romania have also increased, and there are stories of massive increases in exports from Moldova to Romania, since this was cheaper than making wine in Romania in 2006.

Moldova briefly imposed a ban on all exports of bulk wine in November, in an apparent attempt to head off the threat of action by the Russian president of Ukraine. Ukraine was hit very hard by winter frost, losing up to 80 per cent of the grape crop in the south, and has seen significant wine and grape shipments from Moldova to compensate. Sales from two Ukraine wineries to Russia were recently stopped amid claims that they were re-exporting Moldovan wine.

Russia itself was also hit by frosts of −32°C (−25°F), leaving it short by around 3.8 million hl. Russian winemakers are allowed to blend in 40 per cent of imported material, and there are huge volumes being shipped from Spain, Chile, and Argentina. "Where it's all going and under what labels is anyone's guess. If a wine is brought in unstabilized or unfiltered, it is exempt from most taxes, and if processed in Russia it's considered Russian," said one source.

Grapevine

• **Michel Rolland,** the renowned winemaker and oenologist, has become chief winemaking consultant to Telish Wine Cellars in Bulgaria. He is involved in a project that will include 200 ha of new vineyard and construction of a winery, due to have finished by June 2007.

• **Leading Tokaji producer** István Szepsy has parted company with Királyudvar to concentrate on his own eponymous winery, working with his son and daughters. His plans include focusing on a range of dry wines reflecting terroir, increasing the range to nine or 10, and working on vineyard management of Furmint to improve consistency of ripening.

• **Recaş Winery,** Romania, has invested a further €3 million in winery and vineyard improvements. The winery now has fully automatic temperature control. Hartley Smithers, senior winemaker at Casella in Australia, made the wine for the second year running in 2006.

• **Jidvei in Romania** has completely renovated its winemaking facilities in a €7-million project, part funded by SAPARD. The winery already had the biggest single vineyard in Romania, at 936 ha, and is continuing to buy land for further planting.

• **Terra Tangra** in Bulgaria launched its first wines in 2006, made from French clones planted three years ago. Its 300 ha of vineyards will be certified organic from 2007.

• **Egon Muller's** Kastel Bela project in Slovakia has started to buy land for its own vineyards, but will not start planting until a big enough parcel to retrellis has been put together.

TAX STAMPS IN RUSSIA

The Russians have caused their own problems by delays in supplying new bar-coded tax stamps, which are applied at the customs warehouse on arrival in Russia, rather than at source. Since 50 per cent of alcohol sold in Russia is reckoned to be illegal, a new computerized tracking system was introduced, intended to reduce fraud. Inevitably, crashes and problems with software caused chaos. Stock taxed under the old system had to be sold off or withdrawn by the end of June 2006, but failure to make new tax strips available in time resulted in shop shelves empty of wine and spirits in the summer – and distributors going out of business. Sales of beer have increased, and it was no surprise to hear stories of deaths caused by bootleg vodka.

EXPANDING EU

The EU continues to exert major influence across the region, and Bulgaria and Romania have swelled its ranks, joining in January 2007. Wine producers from countries joining last time round can warn them that it may not be easy under the new regime. Import restrictions will be relaxed, which will increase competition, especially from New World countries previously hampered by punitive local duties. Romania has already become a net importer of wine – notably cheap wine from Spain and Italy – and this seems likely to increase.

Availability of labour may also become an issue, since it will be easier for workers to move across borders to find better-paid work. In the longer term, this will force wages up or wineries will have to mechanize. Substantial subsidies available through the EU's SAPARD programme have driven massive investments in wineries and vineyards in these countries, but the funds will dry up. It will become almost impossible to plant new vineyards and change varieties, so there was a last frantic rush to get vines in the ground and projects approved before the end of 2006.

Grapevine

- **In Bulgaria,** textile and dairy magnate Eduardo Miroglio from Piedmont has invested more than €11 million in a winery, hotel, and vineyard complex near Sliven. So far, 180 ha have been planted, and plans include a number of Italian varieties new to Bulgaria. As part of acquiring the land, 1,300 plots were consolidated.

- **A new wine office** has been set up in Hungary, and a fund of HUF 8 per litre, previously paid as excise duty, will to be used to fund wine promotions. However, an error in the legislation meant that funds could not be collected. This should be rectified by early 2007.

- **The Cyprus Vine Commission** organized the first-ever national Cyprus wine competition in March 2006, judged by a panel of international tasters. The aim is to encourage competition between local producers to raise standards and also to help foster a sense of pride in local wines in a market under increasing pressure from imports. Petritis 2004 (featured in *Wine Report 2007*) was the top-scoring dry wine.

Opinion:
Stamp out fraudulent wine

Fake or fraudulent wines continue to blight wine industries across Eastern Europe and must be stamped out. In theory, these practices are illegal, but enforcement is ineffectual. Sometimes called "secondary" wines, these are made by adding sugar and water back to grape skins after the first fermentation to stretch the crop and produce some sort of alcoholic drink that can be sold as cheap wine. Sources claim that the grape harvest in Bulgaria is routinely overdeclared to "legitimize" these practices (by as much as 50 per cent, according to one source). Stands at the annual wine fair Vinaria in Bulgaria in March 2006 were openly selling artificial colourings for wine.

Bulgaria is not the only country affected by this problem; there are reports of desperate producers in Moldova also returning to such practices. A recent check in Romania analysed 289 million litres of wine and found 29 per cent to be either fake or cases of "passing off" as something they weren't. In Ukraine, politicians have claimed that as much as 75 per cent of wine sold in the country is faked and have drafted a bill for tighter controls on wine sales. Georgia has suffered heavily from counterfeiting, with a recent FAO study reporting that 90 per cent of Georgian wine on export markets is fraudulent. The government has reacted by shutting down labs that were issuing fake certificates, and putting in place a new regulatory body and "passport" system to improve traceability. Its embassies take legal action wherever possible, recognizing that Georgia's reputation is being undermined.

Grapevine

• **Slovenia has been lobbying** for a change in EU priorities, pointing out that funds available for distillation are almost double the amount available for wine promotion. The country is also moving towards integrated production and has a new wine district called Stajerska Slovenija, which replaces five smaller areas. This means that Podravje has just two districts instead of seven, which should make supply and marketing easier.

• **Franz Weninger,** the leading Soproni producer (Hungary), has completed a new cellar and has converted to biodynamic cultivation. He reports earlier ripening and greater complexity in this year's harvest.

• **In Moldova,** a group of leading wineries is working together to form a generic association. This includes Acorex, Dionysos-Mereni, Château Vartely, DK Intertrade, Purcari, and Bostavan.

At the same time, "home-made" wines should be eliminated, because many drinkers still believe these wines (often sold by the roadside in plastic bottles) are more authentic than commercial wines. This undermines efforts to raise the quality and profile of wine in the domestic market. In Bulgaria, it is estimated that 120 million litres of home-made wine are still produced, and in Macedonia an estimated 35 per cent of grapes go into home-made wine and *rakia*. In Moldova, hybrids like Isabella and Lidia are still used for home-made wine, vinified semi-sweet. This means that efforts to get growers involved in tasting the end product are hampered by a huge gulf of understanding. Ironically, this is all happening at a time when the region's top producers are really finding their feet and making some very exciting wines that show a true sense of place.

Supermarkets spreading east

Last year's *Wine Report* warned about the rise of Western supermarket chains across Eastern and Southeastern Europe and the global sourcing trends that will follow. This pattern is continuing, with Metro announcing sales increases of more than 15 per cent in Eastern Europe, especially in Russia, Romania, and Ukraine. Tesco, already number 1 in Hungary, is expanding across the region, announcing plans for 20 stores in Turkey in 2007/08, and is sourcing from Italy for stores across Poland, Hungary, and the Czech Republic. Producers claim ever-greater demands from supermarkets in terms of listing fees, funded promotions, distribution fees, and volume rebates. In Romania, it is now essential for producers to employ their own merchandisers to open cartons and stock shelves to ensure that brands are on sale – in spite of paying so much up front.

Grapevine

• **Leading Cyprus producer** Sophocles Vlassides is experimenting with native Maratheftiko, trialling cold soaks and extended maceration, as well as working in the vineyard to tackle the variety's propensity for excess vigour and uneven berry set.

• **Halewood Wine Cellars** has brought in Aussie winemaker Stephen Bennett, who has previously worked for other wineries in Romania. It has also hired a new vineyard manager, Valentin Resdeman, a native Transylvanian who has just returned after six years at Katnook in Coonawarra. New plantings at Cernavodă include Shiraz, Sangiovese, Semillon, and Viognier.

• **Bulgarian *garagiste*** Santa Sarah is producing its first Pinot Noir in 2006; owner Ivo Genowski made an amazing Mavrud icewine in early 2006, with guidance from Jürgen Hoffman of Reh Kendermann.

• **Cyprus continues to be free** of phylloxera, but trials with rootstocks are likely to be in place soon – in particular to tackle problems of chlorosis in Shiraz.

Vintage Report

Advance report on the latest harvest

2006

This year has generally seen substantial improvement in quality over 2005 across the region. Most areas experienced a cool August, retaining plenty of acidity, followed by a warm September bringing good ripeness levels.

Moldova, southern Ukraine, and Russia were hit badly by severe winter cold, with temperatures dropping to −30°C (−22°F) and damaging up to 80 per cent of vines in some places. Crop levels in Moldova were just 2.75 tonnes per hectare, and a total of 200,000 tonnes – well below normal. Near Purcari some black grapes (Merlot, Malbec, and Shiraz) were virtually wiped out. Sugar levels at harvest were very high, but financial issues resulting from the ban meant problems with disease where spraying had not been carried out. In Georgia, summer rains brought high disease pressure, and in some areas black grapes are showing green acidity. In Russia, the growing season was hot and dry, so there was little disease and the limited crop is reported to be very high in quality. The Czech Republic was also hit by severe winter cold, affecting Neuberger, Müller-Thurgau, and Muscat. Grüner Veltliner had poor fruit set and produced only a third of the normal crop. August was rainy, but a warm September rescued the season and the result is very high-quality, healthy fruit with good acidity. Terrific results are reported in Slovakia.

Slovenia reports the best year since 1943, with fruit showing good sugar levels, body, and balanced acidities due to cool nights in August and September. Quantities are down by 25–50 per cent. Reports suggest that it was an average year in Croatia with some hot spells and rain before and during harvest.

Hungary also reports excellent quality due to the warm September and October, accompanied by cool nights, giving fruit with excellent body, ripe flavours, and plenty of acidity. In Tokaj, *aszú* formation is good but low in quantity due to drought. Quality already seems much better than 2005 for dry, late-harvest, and *aszú* styles.

In Bulgaria, quality is very good on the whole, with some producers claiming the best vintage of the past decade, while others have had patchy results, depending on vineyard management. The north suffered from some frost damage, though the south avoided this. A mild spring and warm summer followed, with some rain towards the end of October. Romanian producers regard 2006 as a significant improvement over 2005. There was some hail damage reported in Drăgăşani, but grapes are very healthy with good sugar levels and little rot this year.

The crop in Cyprus has suffered from considerable drought stress, giving very small berries and high tannin levels. Some vines shut down and had ripening problems, requiring careful tannin management during vinification. Whites fared better, though snow in November for the first time in 20 years caused problems with Xynisteri at high altitudes.

Updates on the previous five vintages

2005

Vintage rating: *Red – Bulgaria, Romania, Turkey: 70; Slovenia, Hungary, Georgia, Cyprus, Moldova: 85; White: 80; Sweet: 85*

A variable year across the region, with producers in most countries reporting a late and difficult harvest. A cool summer and damp August caused delayed ripening and brought disease pressure.

In Romania, the vintage was disappointing, with low sugars and high acid. The crop was 55 per cent below 2004, and cellars were empty by harvest time in 2006. Best results were around Recaş and Cotnari, where there was less rain and whites fared better than reds.

In Bulgaria, harvest volumes were down by 30 per cent and quality was below 2004. Where wineries own vineyards, they report some nicely balanced wines, though with lower alcohol. Vineyards in the south (Sakar, Liubimetz) and southwest (Strouma Valley) enjoyed a warm summer. In Turkey, quality was low, due to downy mildew and because wineries fighting for supplies forced picking too early.

In Hungary, quality was satisfactory where wineries were able to spray professionally and select fruit. In the south, Villány had higher rainfall than normal, which affected early-ripening varieties; later varieties were better, giving slow-maturing but potentially long-lived reds. Szekszárd and Sopron picked late, but produced some very good reds, while in Tokaj a warm autumn rescued a poor season. This allowed botrytis development for producers in the north of the region, who are very optimistic about the quality of *aszú* wines.

Both Macedonia and Moldova bucked the trend across the region, with a much better season than 2004. Clean, healthy fruit, with good natural sugar, flavour development, and acidity, similar to 2003, are reported. In the Czech Republic, the damp summer was rescued by a warm autumn, giving good sugars and plenty of aromatics. Cyprus produced a small harvest but with fresh aromatic whites and promising reds.

In Georgia, hopes of an excellent vintage were dashed by heavy rain and devastating hailstorms in late August. Careful fruit selection was essential, but overall quality is promising, especially for Saperavi, which is showing excellent varietal character.

Western Slovenia saw a harvest similar to 2004, though selection was vital with better-than-expected quality in the reds, and whites that are ripe but fresh. Eastern Slovenia had problems with achieving full ripeness. Croatia had rains mid-harvest, so wines will be mediocre overall, especially whites, though Plavac Mali should have good structure.

2004

Vintage rating: *Red: 75, White: 80, Sweet: 80*

This vintage was at least two weeks later than normal, and professional vine management paid off because fungal disease pressures were high. Low yields were crucial in achieving full ripeness in many areas.

In Romania, reds are lighter than 2003, but whites are fresh, with good aromatics. The Bulgarian harvest was smaller than 2003, and reds are less ripe, though the whites are notably fresh. In Hungary, whites and rosés showed good fruit levels and crisp acidity, but reds ripened well only on favoured sites. In the south, conditions were difficult, with decent results only with ultra-low yields and meticulous selection. In Tokaj, there were good levels of botrytis but without great concentration, so wines are elegant and fruity, but mainly at lower *puttonyos* levels.

In the west of Slovenia, whites are fruity and fresh, while reds have good colour and fruit except for some green tannins in Cabernet. In the east, grapes were low in sugar with high acid, except where yields were severely reduced. Croatia reported a slightly better-than-average vintage, though less tannic than normal, with some botrytis development for sweet wines.

Wines in the Czech Republic and Slovakia showed good aromatics, especially where growers picked late, and botrytis development in November enabled production of sweet wines.

Georgia reports a very good vintage: expressive and well-balanced whites, and reds with fine, well-matured tannins. It was a difficult year in both Moldova and Russia. Disease pressures were high and Moldovan whites are very high in acid.

2003

Vintage rating: *Red: 95 (Ukraine & SE Romania: 75),*
White: 90, Sweet: 90

The hot, dry summer across Europe meant that most countries reported particularly good results for reds and a very early start to the harvest.

In Bulgaria, quality was very good, with high levels of sugar and polyphenols at harvest but with unusually high acidity. In Romania, western areas reported a warm, dry summer with good quality. In Moldova, the harvest was generous and of high quality, the best vintage for five years. Slovenia had a very early vintage with extremely high-quality reds, though some whites suffered from low acidity. Tokaj saw a lower *aszú* yield than expected, but it is generally regarded as a good to very good year, though without the balancing acidity of 1999 and not as rich in sugar as 2000. Dry and late-harvest wines show very good to outstanding results. The rest of Hungary reports excellent reds and intense fruit flavours in whites, though low acidity in some varieties. In Croatia, 2003 is a year with lots of extract, alcohol, and excellent quality. Cyprus also reports one of the best vintages in recent years and good quantities. In Slovakia, picking Riesling was delayed until October but with excellent results.

2002

Vintage rating: *Red: 75 (Hungary & Slovenia: 90), White: 80, Sweet: 90*

A mixed year, ranging from outstanding in Transylvania to below average in areas such as northern Bulgaria and southeastern Romania, which were hit by heavy rains.

In Hungary, wines are very concentrated. Reds, especially from the south, continue to show well. In Tokaj, hopes for a great *aszú* vintage were dashed by rain in October, but wines are nicely balanced, especially for fruit harvested early. In Romania, most areas are showing very good quality but heavily reduced yields due to drought at flowering. It was not a successful year for either Bulgaria or Macedonia. In Cyprus, quality was good, though low in quantity. Slovenian production was down 20–30 per cent, but overall quality was high in both reds and whites.

2001

Vintage rating: *Red: 80, White: 75, Sweet: 75*

A rain-soaked September caused mould development and poor flavours for some Tokaji producers, though some decent *aszú* wines have been made with ultra-careful selection. Elsewhere in Hungary, early whites picked before the September rain were above average, and reds picked late were sound, too. In Romania, it was a good ripe year, though yields were slightly lower than 2000. Bulgaria suffered from a second year of drought, reducing crops by as much as 50 per cent due to shrivelling. Some producers report good wines, but vines in poor condition shut down and failed to ripen.

GREATEST WINE PRODUCERS

1. Szepsy (Hungary)
2. Királyudvar (Hungary)
3. Domaine de Disznókő (Hungary)
4. Oremus (Hungary)
5. Malatinszky Kúria (Hungary)
6. Gere Atila (Hungary)
7. Weninger (Hungary)
8. Marjan Simčič (Slovenia)
9. Edi Simčič (Slovenia)
10. Château Belá (Slovakia)

FASTEST-IMPROVING PRODUCERS

1. Santa Sarah (Bulgaria)
2. Dobogó (Hungary)
3. Vylyan (Hungary)
4. Carl Reh (Romania)
5. Georgian Wines & Spirits (GWS) (Georgia)
6. Damianitza (Bulgaria)
7. Belvedere Group (Domaine Katerina, Domaine Sakar, Trinity) (Bulgaria)
8. Jeruzalem-Ormož (Slovenia)
9. Tsiakkas (Cyprus)
10. Sodap (Cyprus)

NEW UP-AND-COMING PRODUCERS

1. Patricius (Hungary)
2. Bessa Valley (Bulgaria)
3. Valley Vintners (Bulgaria)
4. Miroglio (Bulgaria)
5. Casa DaVino (Romania)
6. Prince Stirbey (Romania)
7. Vlassides (Cyprus)
8. Kyperounda (Cyprus)
9. Villa Liubimetz (Bulgaria)
10. Logodaj (Bulgaria)

BEST-VALUE PRODUCERS

1. Pannonhalmi Apátsági Pincészet (Hungary)
2. Château Vincent (Hungary)
3. Recaş (Romania)
4. Carl Reh (Romania)
5. Nyakas (Budai) (Hungary)
6. Nagyréde (Hungary)
7. Telish Wine Cellar (Bulgaria)
8. Maxxima (Bulgaria)
9. Jeruzalem-Ormož (Slovenia)
10. Aurvin (Moldova)

GREATEST-QUALITY WINES

1. **Tokaji Aszú 6 Puttonyos 2002** Szepsy, Hungary (HUF 19,500)
2. **Tokaji Aszú Esszencia 2000** Château Dereszla, Hungary (HUF 16,000)
3. **Tokaji Aszú 6 Puttonyos 1999** Királyudvar, Hungary (HUF 18,900)
4. **Tokaji Aszú 6 Puttonyos Kapi 1999** Domaine de Disznókő, Hungary (HUF 16,095)
5. **Hétfürtös Edes Elet Tokaji Cuvée 2001** Arvay és Társa, Hungary (HUF 11,000)
6. **Villány Cabernet Franc 2003** Malatinszky Kúria, Hungary (HUF 12,840)
7. **Kopar Cuvée 2003** Gere Atila, Hungary (HUF 9,126)
8. **Teodor Rdece Reserve 2002** Marjan Simčič, Slovenia (€24)
9. **Duet Lex 2002** (previously sold as Riserva) Edi Simčič, Slovenia (€38)
10. **Kékfrankos Spern Steiner 2004** Weninger, Hungary (HUF 5,300)

BEST BARGAINS

1. **Tricollis 2006** Pannonhalmi Apátsági Pincészet, Hungary (HUF 1,100)
2. **Extra Brut 2000** Château Vincent, Hungary (HUF 2,670)
3. **Budai Sauvignon Blanc 2006** Nyakas, Hungary (HUF 1,590)
4. **Sivi Pinot 2006** Jeruzalem-Ormož, Slovenia (€5)
5. **Petritis 2004** Kyperounda, Cyprus (CYP 3.25)

⑥ **Pinot Noir 2005** Recaş, Romania (RON 12)

⑦ **Tokaji Szamarodni 2003** Szepsy, Hungary (HUF 7,300)

⑧ **Mylitta 2004** Dobogó, Hungary (HUF 2,860)

⑨ **Ats Cuvée 2004** Royal Tokaji, Hungary (HUF 2,500)

⑩ **Melnik 55 2005** Logodaj, Bulgaria (BGN 6)

MOST EXCITING OR UNUSUAL FINDS

① **Claret 2004** Château de Val, Bulgaria (BGN 16) *Based on the local wedding tradition of blending all the guests' wines, expat Val Markov makes this from a blend of at least eight varieties, including Saperavi and Pamid, growing in his family's century-old vineyards.*

② **Cuvée Charlotte 2003** SERVE, Romania (RON 70) *Corsican Count Guy de Poix has set out to show what Romania is capable of with this beautifully crafted and complex blend of Cabernet, Merlot, and local Fetească Neagră.*

③ **Pinot Noir 2004** Vylyan, Hungary (HUF 3,600) *A blend of Pinot Noir from 12-year-old vines and virgin fruit from recently planted burgundian clones. One of the best Pinot Noirs to come out of Hungary so far.*

④ **Sipon Ice Wine Prestige 2003** Curin, Slovenia (€120) *This amazingly luscious and intense wine beat a lineup of excellent Tokajis to win the regional trophy in this year's Decanter World Wine Awards.*

⑤ **Saperavi Reserve 2005** Georgian Wines & Spirits, Georgia (GEL 20) *A great snapshot of the potential of Saperavi, which needs careful handling to tame its fierce tannins and acidity and show off its wonderful fruit character.*

Winemaker Lado Uzunashvili has brought all his Australian experience back to raise standards in Georgia.

⑥ **Shiraz Reserve 2003** Vlassides, Cyprus (CYP 6.25) *Davis-trained young winemaker Sophocles Vlassides has taken winemaking on Cyprus to new heights with this ripe, spicy, and concentrated wine, showing there's a lot more to Cyprus than cheap bulk wine and imitation "sherries".*

⑦ **Pinot Noir La Cetate 2006** Carl Reh, Romania (RON 30) *Romania has carved a reputation for its Pinot Noir, though historically very little was actually planted in the country, and that was mainly sparkling clones. A new generation of decent red-wine clones is coming into crop, and this young Pinot is a lovely example.*

⑧ **Brumariu Ice Wine 2003** Dionysos-Mereni, Moldova (MDL 500) *Moldova's first commercial icewine – a lusciously concentrated Riesling with lovely varietal perfume, made from grapes picked at −15°C (5°F). Winemaker Costia Stratan produced this based on stories from pre-Soviet times of late-harvest wines made from grapes picked after the first frosts, mainly for home consumption.*

⑨ **Maratheftiko 2003** Vasa, Cyprus (CYP 5.65) *This tiny but beautiful winery is showing what can be done with Cyprus's local Maratheftiko. This is a fine, elegant, and surprisingly fresh wine.*

⑩ **Novac 2004** Prince Stirbey, Romania (RON 50) *The first release of a rediscovered grape variety from one of Romania's few real boutique wineries, this deep-coloured red has an amazing aroma of wild herbs and very supple, silky tannins.*

Greece

Nico Manessis

Shortly after designating the export of olive oil as a priority, the government of Prime Minister Kostantinos Karamanlis devoted the same attention to wine exports.

NICO MANESSIS

In an unprecedented action (instead of a chorus of broken promises), Minister of Rural Development and Foods Evangelos Basiakos stepped in to help wine exports to Russia after Prime Minister Mikhail Fradkov's visit to Greece. Other targeted markets are China, which is holding the summer Olympic Games in 2008, and India. Meanwhile, as reported in *Wine Report 2005* and *2006*, exports to the USA are now showing an increase in quantity and value and are set to grow in the near future as new, non-ethnic mainstream distribution agreements come into effect. Another positive development has taken place in Denmark. Danish professionals are remarkably well informed about Greek geography and the distinctive flavours of Greek grapes, and by spreading the word to their fellow countrymen, they have propelled Greek wine to its current cult status.

NICO MANESSIS is the author of *The Illustrated Greek Wine Book* (Olive Press, 2000) and the three editions of *The Greek Wine Guide* (Olive Press, 1994, 1995, 1996). He is currently working on a new book. He lectures on Greece in a variety of fora, such as the Université du Vin in France, the Ecole du Vin de Changins in Switzerland, and the Le Monde Institute in Greece. He has been writing articles on the wines of his native Greece in the international press for more than 12 years. Nico is a contributor to *Hugh Johnson's Pocket Wine Book* and is the wine critic for Athens's *Insider* magazine. Nico often judges in wine competitions in England, France, Spain, Switzerland, Germany, Cyprus, and Greece, and he is chairman of the Greek panel at the *Decanter* World Wine Awards. He is based in Geneva, where he is a member of the Académie Internationale du Vin. In 2007, Nico was honoured for his past and ongoing international contribution to Greek wine by the Wine Producers Association of the Northern Greece Vineyard (ENOABE; for more information, see www.wineroads.gr).

Demand soars for premium wine

Production of limited-release, premium wines began in Greece about 10 years ago. Although several of these exceptional wines now enjoy iconic status, retail prices remain reasonable at €10–25 and seem unlikely to increase. Mostly reds, the wines – from Aghiorghitiko, Merlot, Syrah, Cabernet Sauvignon, and now Xinomavro (or blends of these) – have one thing in common: demand has become insatiable. This new trend is fuelled not by "wine snobs" who buy trophy labels from France or the New World, but by wine lovers from all parts of the country.

The price of Domaine Kosta Lazaridi's new wine, made with French consultant Michel Rolland (see *Wine Report 2007*), is as yet unknown. I am willing to predict that it will be shrewdly priced at €15–20, and not overpriced just because it carries Monsieur Rolland's signature.

Xinomavro: greatness at last

Of approximately 150 indigenous black grapes in Greece, Xinomavro was the most abused: unsuitable pruning, poor clones, and inappropriate vinification techniques produced wines light in colour but as tough as nails. Although Xinomavro has an inimitable aroma, the palate of this tannic, high-acid grape was often disappointing. Also, after bottle ageing, the colour could change, alarmingly, to orange-brown. However, one quality that Xinomavro does have is staying power. Naoussa vintages such as 1985, 1992, 1993, 1997, and 2001 have aged magnificently, picking up complexity and nuances not found in any other grape. It has a warm-fruit Pinot Noir-like "sweet" nose, with a Nebbiolo tannic bite. Improvements have come from changes in vineyard and cellar. Growers use specific clones and higher canopies to produce phenolically ripe grapes with higher ABVs, and vinification techniques include cold soaks, longer macerations, and lees stirring.

The rustic peasant has been transformed into a polished gentleman, so much so that we can now speak of a new style of wines. The Ghi ke Uranos 2005 made by 27-year-old Apostolos Thimiopoulos is an eye-opener, with its depth and balanced structure. The Argatia Xinomavro 2005 (see my Most Exciting or Unusual Finds list) is grape specialist Haroula Spinthiropoulou's professional triumph. Both these estates are found at the extremes of the Naoussa appellation.

Further north, in cooler-climate Amyndeo, Alpha Estate has been trying all sorts of innovative farming and winemaking approaches. Its Xinomavro 2006 balances fruit and tannic grip with elegance. Perhaps best of all, these three pioneers are markedly different in how they mirror their terroir. This is a timely wake-up call for the Xinomavro "triangle" – Goumenissa, Amyndeo, and Naoussa.

Opinion:
Wine supremo needed

After a frenzied 20 years of changes, the dust has settled and new challenges have emerged. Our qualitative revolution remains inward-looking and misses many opportunities to grab the attention of internationally respected commentators and increase the presence of Greek wine on the world market. Our selling point is quality in a niche market. We should be publicizing our dozens of indigenous grapes and fascinating blends, such as cask-fermented Assyrtiko/Semillon, now sweeping medals in competitions. The way forward is to highlight the quality in the bottle and put less emphasis on the historical aspect of Greek wine.

All this has to be communicated effectively, with long-term planning and vigorous execution – not last-minute improvisations that may work at home but are ineffectual and comical abroad, to say the least. None of the new generation of winemakers who brought about this revolution has stepped forward to be a leader. More than ever, Greece needs a wine supremo with a long-term mandate. A lot is happening in Greek wine today that is going unreported, and this unrealized potential is everyone's loss.

Grapevine

• **Michael Jones,** a graduate from Plumpton College with two New Zealand harvests under his belt, has joined Gabriele Beamish (an ex-lecturer at Plumpton College) as assistant winemaker at Gentilini on the island of Cephalonia.

• **Wine and Spirit Professional Consultants** (WSPC) (see *Wine Report 2006*), a wine-education school in association with the Wine & Spirit Education Trust, has had 490 students gain wine qualifications since opening its doors.

• **The local authority in Nemea** and the Nemea Wine Producers Association have collaborated on a joint initiative to restore and convert the town's 19th-century school into a tasting centre showcasing the region's 30 wineries (see www.pelopnet.gr).

• **Chateau Nico Lazaridi,** the Drama-based winery, has invested in partnership with local vine grower Nikos Asimomitis in a new winery boasting a tasting room, wine shop, and luxury suites at Mau, Pano Mera, on the cosmopolitan island of Myconos. This new joint venture is named Ampelones Myconou.

• **Tatsis Bros,** the Goumenissa estate, is adding biodynamic principles to its organically farmed vineyards. Like many biodynamic practitioners, they don't fully understand why biodynamics works. Pericles Tatsis says: "It works, our grapes are healthy even in difficult vintages, and we find a shift in the wines – they are more linear." A producer to watch, Tatsis has moved into a new winery.

Vintage Report

Advance report on the latest harvest

2006

A year of unusually extreme weather patterns. Global warming is now a favourite farmers' topic. Flowering was later than usual and was followed by cool, intermittent showers into late spring. June was sunny and warm, but July was one of the coolest on record, with farmers complaining that it was not hot enough. Nemea had the rare experience of low nocturnal temperatures. August was hot and dry, with excellent conditions, although black grapes were two weeks behind average, and some suffered vine stress due to drought. Due to timely winter rains, Santorini managed a record-breaking fourth vintage of exceptional quality, though the quantity was average. September was cool with intermittent showers, heavier in Naoussa and Goumenissa. Hailstorms struck high Aighialia in late September. On the islands, whites were harvested a week later than usual, and black grapes two to three weeks later. Mantinia's Moschophilero is less aromatic than 2005. Amyndeo benefited from the slow maturity cycle, which added fragrance to both colours. On Crete, the tougher-skinned Mandelari grape rather outperformed the softer-tannined Kotsifali. Early impressions indicate that wines are not as uniform as the splendid 2005s. There are, however, exceptions in many regions, highlighting the levels of high quality now attained by the top names, even in a year of such climatic contrasts.

Updates on the previous five vintages

2005

Vintage rating: Red: 90, White: 89

After the abundance of the two previous vintages, nature corrected itself with a yield drop of up to 15 per cent. Summer had no extreme weather, and sunny days with cool nights produced ripe, healthy grapes. Conditions during picking were textbook, with the exception of Nemea, which experienced heavy rain towards the end of harvesting. The northern vineyards of Naoussa, Amyndeo, Epanomi, Kavala, and Drama did particularly well in reds and whites. In the Peloponnese Patra, Mantinia did best. The dessert Muscats of Rio Patra are among the most fragrant and balanced in recent years. In the upper part of Nemea, wines harvested prior to the rain have deep colour, with more body than the more delicate 2004s. Santorini made super-concentrated, bone-dry whites. Cretan dry whites, especially those made with central Crete's spicy Vilana grape, are astonishing for their levels of ripeness and freshness. Samos Muscats are perfumed and have real backbone, and they should age magnificently.

2004

Vintage rating: *Red: 88, White: 92*

Harvest started a week later than average for white grapes, and two or three weeks later for black. White grapes ripened fully. International grape varieties were of a rarely seen homogeneous quality. Delicate indigenous whites are more concentrated, with natural high acidity. It is a rare and outstanding vintage for all white wines, including the sweet specialities. A dry and sunny October saved the red-wine harvest. Reds have good colour and elegant tannins, and they are very fragrant. Across the board there is a more northern-latitude climatic imprint, not unlike the 1997 vintage, though with far more complete and distinctive wines.

2003

Vintage rating: *Red: 90, White: 88*

Unhurried ripening benefited from a moderate summer with no heat waves. In all but two regions – Naoussa and Goumenissa – both international and indigenous grape varieties produced exceptionally healthy, ripe, and balanced grapes, with some appellations producing wines the likes of which have rarely been seen. The island vineyards of Santorini and Cephalonia are the best. Reduced grape yields in central Crete produced whites and reds showing the unrealized potential of Greece's southernmost island. Muscats from Limnos and Samos are terrific. Eastern Macedonia produced outstanding wines, especially from imported varieties. The finicky, late-ripening Xinomavro, affected by yields that were far too high, struggled to ripen fully in Naoussa and Goumenissa. Re-energized Amynteo experienced the finest vintage since 1994. Nemea, in the Peloponnese, produced deep-coloured, fruity wines from the lower-altitude valley subregions. The quality from the hillside vineyards is exceptional. The delicate and aromatic light whites of Patras show uniform consistency and terroir expression.

2002

Vintage rating: *Red: 75, White: 85*

Drama, Kavala, and Epanomi wines are all very good, vibrant, and fruity. Elsewhere, a contrast of extremes was the case. Santorini harvested a fraction of its usual tonnage. Naoussa was a washout, with unripeness and widespread rot. Nemea was a disaster, although a couple of higher-elevation vineyards produced healthy grapes, albeit in small amounts and with less colour and body than usual. The unprecedented shortfall resulted in strong domestic demand for red wine, pushing up prices. Mantinia had little rot, good aroma, and satisfactory, if lower, levels of ripeness. Rhodes, which has the easternmost island vineyards, experienced the best vintage in years.

2001

Vintage rating: *Red: 90, White: 89*

Another very good vintage. Lower yields and higher acidities encouraged wines of notable quality in both colours. Crete, Cephalonia, and Santorini produced superb, crisp dry whites. Following the previous year's heat wave, which had stressed Savatiano vines to their limits, Attica vineyards equipped with drip irrigation excelled. Mantinia had one of its finest harvests, with a quantity and quality not seen since 1998. Standout reds are to be found everywhere. Naoussa wines are delicious, without the overripe, jammy fruit found in the previous vintage. Those of Goumenissa are a little less ripe, though delicate. Nemea produced atypical wines, the best of them characterized by an inspired combination of class and ethereal edge. Balanced Samos Muscats are a delight.

Grapevine

• **Katoghi,** the first winery to plant Cabernet Sauvignon back in 1963, has now entered wine tourism in style, with the opening of the Katoghi-Averoff Suite Hotel beside the winery in Metsovo (Epiros). Guests can enjoy a health spa, wine-derived beauty products, and a restaurant specializing in organic game, trout, and the renowned local cheese specialities. This picturesque village is now accessible from the new Egnatia national highway via the port of Igoumenitsa and is set to become a year-round destination.

• **France's ENTAV** (Etablissement National Technique pour l'Amélioration de la Viticulture) has licensed the Bakasietas nursery in a research-and-development agreement. Jean-Michel Boursiquot, the successor to the father of modern ampelography Pierre Galet, visited all the major appellations, marking vines for clone identification and eventual certification.

GREATEST WINE PRODUCERS

1. Gerovassiliou
2. Gaia Wines
3. Alpha Estate
4. Tselepos
5. Biblia Chora
6. Ktima Mercouri
7. Parparoussis
8. Sigalas
9. Oenoforos
10. Samos Cooperative

FASTEST-IMPROVING PRODUCERS

1. Mountrihas
2. Lyrarakis
3. Pavlidis
4. Karipidis
5. Tatsis Bros
6. Wine Art Estate
7. Douloufakis
8. Tetramythos
9. Argatia
10. Papayanakos

NEW UP-AND-COMING PRODUCERS

1. Dryopi
2. Mitravela
3. Dougos
4. Tetramythos
5. Kokkalis
6. Manousakis
7. Liapis
8. Douloufakis
9. Manolesakis
10. Palivos

BEST-VALUE PRODUCERS

1. Semeli Nemea
2. Lyrarakis
3. Katoghi-Strofilia
4. Samos Cooperative
5. Oenoforos

6. Domaine Kosta Lazaridi
7. Creta Olympias
8. Mountrihas
9. Tsantalis
10. Douloufakis

GREATEST-QUALITY WINES

1. **Alpha Estate 2005**
   Alpha Estate (€22)
2. **Gaia Estate 2005**
   Gaia Wines (€20)
3. **Ghi ke Uranos 2005**
   Thimiopoulos (€16)
4. **Ovilos White 2006**
   Biblia Chora (€14)
5. **Avaton 2003** Gerovassiliou (€21)
6. **Merlot 2005** Chateau Julia (€15)
7. **Assyrtiko Santorini 2006**
   Canava Arghyrou (€10)
8. **Cava 2003** Ktima Mercouri (€22)
9. **Mikroklima Nemea 2003**
   Papaioannou (€29)
10. **Thema Ktima 2005**
    Pavlidis (€12.50)

BEST BARGAINS

1. **Dafnios Kotsifali/Syrah 2006**
   Douloufakis (€5.50)
2. **Novus 2006** Lyrarakis (€5.50)
3. **Mavro se Kokkino Nemea 2006**
   Mitravela (€6)
4. **Chardonnay/Sauvignon Blanc 2006** Mikros Vorias Oenoforos (€6.50)
5. **Xerolithia 2006**
   Creta Olympias (€6.70)
6. **Roditis 2006** Liapis (€7)
7. **Limnia Ghi Muscat 2006**
   Hatzigeorghiou (€7.40)
8. **14-18H Agiorgitiko Rosé 2006**
   Gaia Wines (€7.80)
9. **Sparkling Rosé NV**
   Amyndeo Cooperative (€8)
10. **Mantinia Fumé 2004**
    Ktima Tselepou (€10)

MOST EXCITING OR UNUSUAL FINDS

1 **Gerontoklima Rematias 2003** Antonopoulos (€22) *A most striking wine made from the obscure Ionian island speciality, Vertzami. Sourced from the high vineyards of Lefkada. Plenty of life ahead.*

2 **Xinomavro 2005** Argatia (€20) *Leading grape scientist's new venture with clonal matchmaking between variety and different soil types. Organic. Showing the way forward for this great grape.*

3 **Omega 2003** Alpha Estate (€19 per 50-cl bottle) *Late-harvest Gewurztraminer/Malagousia blend with a pronounced lemony, smoky aftertaste and Rhine-like freshness. Unfiltered. Continues the no-compromise standards this estate is rapidly becoming known for.*

4 **Epiloges Debina 2006** Zitsa Cooperative (€6.50) *Proof that organically farmed vines, in this cooler mountainous region of Epiros, have more aroma and taste different. Charged with a lemon-grass punch, revealing a previously unknown character of the high-acid, fruity Debina grape.*

5 **Refosco/Aghiorghitiko 2004** Chateau Julia (€17) *Not one to rest on its laurels, this shrewdly managed estate launches an original blend with 20 per cent Aghiorghitiko taming the bursting-with-fruit, low-yield, terroir-laden, inky-black Refosco.*

6 **Cabernet Franc 2004** Giardino Ktima Hristou Florou (€18.70) *Since very little Cabernet Franc is planted in Greece, this is quite a surprise. Made by an artisan in the Kilkis, it's fragrantly spicy, with tobacco-leaf and sappy tannins. Dense. Approachable, and with the stamina to age.*

7 **Sangiovese 2005** Karipidis (€13.50) *Currently the most successful variety on the scene from a host of recently imported black grapes up and down the country, including Touriga Nacional, Petit Verdot, and Nebbiolo. A rich, broad style from this ever-improving producer.*

8 **Aidani Santorini 2006** Canava Arghyrou (€10 per 50-cl bottle) *The aromatic glory of the Cyclades brought into the 21st century through skin contact and low-temperature fermentation. Floral-scented, delicate terpenes, minerally, elegant dry finish. Nothing remotely like it.*

9 **To Dakri tou Pefkou Retsina NV** Kechri (€10.50) *Cask-fermented Assyrtiko with a feather-light touch of pine resin. The bonus is the fresh ginger on top of the yeasty aftertaste. A textured, fun wine. What will they think of next?*

10 **Kotsifali 2006** Lyrarakis (€4.50) *Not new per se, just reinvented through rigorous vineyard selection. From Alagni, a high plateau on central Crete, this hitherto-unknown high-potential grape (with a spoonful of Syrah) now makes an accessible, warm-fruited wine with melt-in-the-mouth tannins. Great value.*

Lebanon

Michael Karam

The main story for Lebanese producers in 2006 was the summer fighting between Israel and the Lebanese militant group Hezbollah.

MICHAEL KARAM

Ramzi Ghosn, co-owner of Massaya, summed it up: "Two weeks into the war, I walked in the vineyards and could smell that vegetal aroma of ripening grapes. But ... I realized there was a very good chance I would not be able to pick them. There were tears in my eyes."

That was in July. By mid-August a ceasefire was brokered as the first Chardonnay raced to maturity, and producers breathed a sigh of relief. They went on to harvest a bumper crop, taking advantage of the lower prices and buying extra grapes from the main *négociants* in the western Bekaa.

A prolonged military campaign would have wiped out the harvest, while an indefinite sea blockade would have deprived most of Lebanon's 20 major producers of vital oenological products and packaging material. Even more devastating would have been the damage done to all the progress that Lebanon's wine producers have made in the past 10 years in terms of building awareness, improving their product, and penetrating new markets.

London peace initiative fails

As the bombs fell, there were well-meaning attempts to use wine as a unifying force. Illi Adato, a London-based Israeli wine-culture promoter,

MICHAEL KARAM has lived in Lebanon since 1992. He is a business journalist and wine writer. His articles have appeared in *Decanter*, *Harpers Wine and Spirit Weekly*, and *The Spectator*. He is a contributor to *The Oxford Companion to Wine* (Oxford University Press) and is the author of *Wines of Lebanon* (Saqi, 2005), which won the Gourmand award for the Best New World Wine Book 2005; *Château Ksara: 150 Years of Wine Making 1957–2007* (Vinehouse Media, 2007); and *Arak and Mezze: The Taste of Lebanon* (Saqi), which will be published in 2007.

proposed a joint tasting – Wine in the Name of Peace – at Vinopolis, featuring Israeli and Lebanese wines.

Adato had secured participation from both sides: Château Musar, Château Kefraya, and Vin Nakad from Lebanon, and the Israeli Dalton, Tabor, and Recanati wineries. However, as the Lebanese producers witnessed the ever-expanding destruction wrought on their country, they had no choice but to pull out.

In the event, not one winery was directly hit, though there were some close shaves. One of Domaine Wardy's vineyards was slightly damaged when a shell landed 200 m (650 ft) from Château Ksara but failed to explode.

Le Hochar de nos jours?

Ramzi Ghosn, who refused to leave Massaya as the shrapnel fizzed around the vines, showed the coolness under fire that made Serge Hochar the darling of the wine world a generation earlier and typified Lebanon's resilience to conflict.

Ghosn's French partners – Dominique Hébrard and the Brunier brothers – were kept up to date on developments and a 4x4 was kept nearby in case he had to make a run for it. But there were also personal reasons why he stayed. In 1975, at the outbreak of the Lebanese civil war, his family had to flee the estate – supposedly for one week. For the seven-year-old Ghosn, it would be 17 years before he would return.

Political instability hits sales

In 2006, Lebanon exported around 2.2 million bottles – a year-on-year increase of 13 per cent – with the UK once again the biggest importer. However, as 2006 came to a close, political instability returned. Producers were already factoring in a 15 per cent loss in business due to a war that had wiped out the crucial summer tourist season, when, as the lucrative Christmas and New Year season loomed, the nation ground to a halt as Hezbollah and its allies sought to topple the government with a massive and prolonged demonstration outside parliament.

Lebanon's wine producers were already operating in a fragile economic environment (Lebanon's total debt stands at US$39.4 billion, a year-on-year increase of 6.9 per cent – a debt-to-GDP ratio of 190 per cent), and its image as regional party central evaporated faster than you could say Bacardi Breezer. Brand Lebanon, which nearly two years ago oozed with promise, looked very brittle. The summer war, gangster-style hits on Cabinet ministers in broad daylight, and the sight of soldiers behind razor wire defending a holed-up government were not good for business, and business is what makes Lebanon.

RED TAPE BURDEN

Lebanese producers now have to pay LL 75,000 (£25) per analysis for mandatory testing of all new wines at "approved" government labs to satisfy EU export regulation VI (1). The same procedure must be followed for every wine exported. Producers have to send a sample to the lab along with a VI (1) form and a copy invoice. All this has to be stamped by the lab, forwarded to the Ministry of Agriculture for its stamp, and then sent to customs and excise. So, for example, if Château X produces three reds, two whites, and a rosé and sends one container of a selection of each wine each week, it pays LL 23,400,000 (£7,800) a year for the privilege.

The producers' main objection is that the results of every analysis are different, creating potential difficulties should any tests be conducted abroad. This has forced one producer to send his own independent European analyses with his sample and to insist that the labs use his results. In effect, he is paying to have his own analyses certified to ensure accuracy and consistency.

Then there is the issue of the pallets: Lebanese export regulations now require all pallets destined for foreign markets to be fumigated, which costs producers LL 210,000 (£71) per container. The annual fumigation cost to Châteaux X is LL 10,920,000 (£3,692), bringing the total of the new charges to LL 34,320,000 (£11,492) – an extra LL 660,000 (£221) per container.

While the regulations are seen as a financial irritant, reducing flexibility, producers console themselves by acknowledging that the regulations will deter the export ambitions of all but the most credible producers.

NWI DELAYED AGAIN

The advent of VI (1) should have accelerated the establishment of the much-needed National Wine Institute. Intended to be responsible for all areas of grape growing and wine production, it would protect and guarantee the name and quality of Lebanese wine.

In September 2006, Charles Ghostine, general manager of Château Ksara and the UVL representative tasked with lobbying the government, announced triumphantly that the Institute's "file" had reached the Cabinet. Having already been approved by the ministries of economy, agriculture, and industry, it looked as if the hard work had been done. Then, at the 11th hour, it was decided that the Ministry of Social Affairs should have its say, effectively sending the file to the back of a very long queue.

Elsewhere, the UVL is working with the EU to implement the widely used Geographic Indication (GI) system as a guarantee of the quality and the specific character of wine (and other agricultural products), while protecting product names from misuse and imitation.

Grapevine

• **Elie Issa,** co-owner of Domaine des Tourelles, says he wants to make a Syrah varietal. The winery, which also makes the famous Le Brun *arak*, has been in innovative mood lately. In 2006, it released Marquis des Beys, its premier red, a blend of Cabernet Sauvignon and Syrah. Now Issa feels that the Syrah is so good that it can go it alone.

Opinion:
Leadership

As Lebanon descends into increasing political chaos and hovers on the cusp of economic meltdown, it is time for the UVL to show some teeth. There have been disappointments in recent years, notably the cancellation of the OIV conference and the continued stalling of the establishment of the National Wine Institute, and while these setbacks were not the fault of the UVL, the association still has to prove that it can genuinely represent all Lebanon's wine producers. Significantly, only half of Lebanon's wine producers are members. The summer 2006 war did generate some short-term solidarity, and the UVL's new website should create positive activity by giving Lebanese wine better exposure and encouraging those who have not joined the UVL to do so. However, a prolonged political crisis, no National Wine Institute, and the very real threat of inflationary bedlam if the lira goes under will not help Lebanon's cause. The UVL needs leadership and vision of the highest level if Lebanon is to retain its image of a small but perfectly formed wine nation.

Diverse terroir

While producers with wineries outside the Bekaa Valley still use Bekaa grapes, almost all of them have planted vines in their own areas and are waiting patiently to go it alone. By 2009, we should have wines made with grapes from Jezzine, Mount Lebanon, Kififane, Bhamdoun, Rashmaya, and the north. The taste of the different terroirs will add a new dimension to Lebanese wine.

Producers are also experimenting with new terroir in the Bekaa, especially in Hermel, north of Baalbek, where the stony soil has produced interesting results. Time may prove that the western Bekaa, with its abundance of water, does not necessarily provide Lebanon's best grape-growing region.

Buy Lebanese!

Ultimately, promoting Lebanese wine promotes Lebanon. Chile, Argentina, and South Africa, once beyond the pale, now invoke images of rolling vineyards, summer dining, and beautiful people. Wine can wash away a lot of bad memories, and given the hostilities of 2006, now more than ever is the time to launch an international generic campaign. Sadly, with no finance for such a venture, it probably remains a pipe dream. More viable would be a national marketing campaign emphasizing the quality of Lebanese wine, educating consumers on the health benefits of drinking wine over, say, whisky or *arak*, and stressing the economic importance of buying Lebanese. It should also target the tourist. Posters for Lebanese or Bekaa wine should be among the first images visitors see when they arrive at Beirut airport.

A national strategy

The quality of Lebanese wine has improved dramatically since the mid-1990s. Producers are working with a wider range of grapes, including "noble" varieties, but they know there is still work to be done. They are discovering that the Bekaa's flat vineyards generally give grapes with low alcohol, low polyphenolic maturation, and high acidity, while the slopes tend to produce grapes with high alcohol, a high level of polyphenolic maturation, but low acidity. To help producers grow grapes with lower alcohol and higher acidity that can reach full polyphenolic maturation, there should be a UVL/government-sponsored strategic planting of clones and rootstock, selected according to the needs of the Bekaa's individual terroirs, employing irrigation (until recently a dirty word in Lebanon) where necessary. An extension of such a programme to all Lebanon's terroirs would paint a more detailed picture of Lebanon's viticultural potential and produce better results in the bottle.

A different strategy

Since 9/11, the number of non-Arab tourists has dropped by 90 per cent. With a little imagination and vision, Lebanon could kick-start its stalled wine-tourism initiative. During the summer, when Lebanon hosts its celebrated international music festivals, a mixed itinerary of music and wine could reap a lucrative harvest and promote Lebanon, its wine, and its festivals to a wider international audience.

Grapevine

• **The UVL** finally has a website: www.lebanonwines.com. It outlines the background, mission, and activities of the UVL, provides links to the sites of its members, and offers other useful data about Lebanon and Lebanese wine: varieties, climatic conditions, etc. There is also a press section, in which the latest UVL and UVL-member news will be posted and where general and media enquiries will be processed.

• **Château Belle-Vue**, the Bhamdoun winery established by ex-Merrill-Lynch executive Naji Boutros and his American wife Jill, released its first wines – both 2003 – in November 2006. Currently, they are available only to members of the Château Belle-Vue wine club. The grapes – Cabernet Sauvignon, Cabernet Franc, Syrah, and Merlot – are grown in Bhamdoun and harvested at a yield of 1 kg (2.2 lb) per vine.

Vintage Report

Advance report on the latest harvest

2006

A very good homogeneous year for Lebanon's black grapes – especially Cabernet Sauvignon, Syrah, and Merlot – all of which produced powerful tannins, good colour, and excellent structure – including the Cinsault and Grenache, which traditionally prefer a gentler summer. There was less rain than 2005 and less than average for the Bekaa Valley, but the cycle ran like clockwork. Even the war, which began on 12 July, came at the "best" time: it could have happened during the pruning and treatment seasons, which would have meant the loss of the entire crop. The 14 August ceasefire came just one day before producers wanted to start picking. The white grapes did not have a spectacular year; the consensus among Bekaa producers was that they would have been better suited to a cooler summer. However, farmers in the southern Lebanese town of Jezzine – altitude 1,300 m (4,265 ft) – said their Semillon and Muscat were the "best yet".

Updates on the previous five vintages

2005

Vintage rating: *Red: 80, White: 89*

A tough year, the most humid in nearly half a century, especially in July and August. The winter was long and wet, which impacted negatively on the lower-lying areas of the Bekaa, where the grapes took longer to ripen. In other areas, the grapes raced to maturity. The time span was phenomenal and reflected the performance of the various terroirs on the Bekaa plateau. However, any interesting results of this freakish summer were negated by excessive mildew, which affected the black grapes especially. In contrast, it was a good year for whites, which had plenty of acidity and pleasant floral aromas. The reds had a mixed year. The traditional early ripeners – Cabernet Sauvignon, Merlot, and Syrah – all ripened well but were hit by mildew, while Cinsault and Grenache were helped by a cooler September that allowed them to compensate for the humidity. Indeed, they may prove to be the better grapes. That said, the wines may yet surprise.

2004

Vintage rating: *Red: 90, White: 85*

At the beginning of the harvest, the grapes had low sugar content and medium acidity levels, but a sudden heat wave, two weeks later, changed everything, producing grapes with higher sugar but still maintaining medium acidity. It was as though there were two harvests in the same year, and fermentation was affected accordingly. Generally, grapes picked in the first two weeks of the harvest were fruity, round, and mellow, with floral aromas, but Cabernet Sauvignon, one of the Bekaa staples, was different: it was powerful, intense, concentrated, and leathery, with red fruits. "Second-phase" grapes, especially Carignan and Cinsault, developed more of a red-fruit character in smell and taste, while smooth tannins became more obvious and the palate more velvety.

2003

Vintage rating: *Red: 91, White: 85*

A unique harvest came on the back of the wettest winter in 15 years and a 10-day heat wave in May, both of which contributed to a marvellous balance between acidity and sugar content and an exceptional concentration of phenol compounds due to dry weather in September. The whites were aromatic with high acidity, producing vivid gunflint notes, finishing with a pleasant, mild, and unctuous taste, while the reds produced intense colour. They were more tannic than former vintages, but with balanced, mellow tannins, supple, and not astringent. All the different varieties were exceptionally fragrant, producing full-bodied and powerful wines.

Grapevine

• **Château Musar** is establishing an Old Wine division to respond to increased demand from Canada, the USA, Europe, and Japan for its older vintages, especially the rare whites made from the Lebanese Merweh and Obaideh grapes. The details still have to be finalized, but owners Serge and Ronald Hochar want to classify all wines 10 years and older as Old Wines. They have also decided to release vintages as old as the 1956 red and the 1954 white, both of which come with price tags higher than US$1,000.

• **Château Ksara** took the lion's share of Lebanese wine exports in 2006 with an impressive 40.5 per cent market share of all Lebanese wines sold abroad – a 16 per cent year-on-year increase and an 80 per cent growth in its UK sales. Massaya, part of Lebanon's new generation of wine producers, exports 80 per cent of the 300,000 bottles it produces each year and reported a 23 per cent year-on-year increase in foreign sales, mostly in the UK.

2002

Vintage rating: *Red: 91, White: 85*

After four successive years of drought, there was a long, cold, rainy winter, followed by a mild July and a hot August. The vines took longer to ripen their grapes and had high levels of sugar, acidity, and tannin. Grape maturity levels varied from vineyard to vineyard, forcing growers to be selective. Fermentation went perfectly but, against all the odds, was very slow – therefore much longer – and the wines have turned out to be much bigger, riper, and fuller than expected.

2001

Vintage rating: *Red: 80, White: 70*

The crop was good, albeit 15 per cent down, with ripe fruit but without much tannin or acidity. Fermentation progressed well, and the malolactic fermentation followed easily and naturally. The wines were easy and fruity, with good alcohol levels.

GREATEST WINE PRODUCERS

1. Château Musar
2. Château Ksara
3. Château Kefraya
4. Massaya
5. Clos St Thomas
6. Domaine Wardy
7. Domaine des Tourelles
8. Vin Nakad

FASTEST-IMPROVING PRODUCERS

1. Massaya
2. Château Ksara
3. Clos St Thomas
4. Domaine des Tourelles
5. Cave Kouroum
6. Château Kefraya
7. Château Ka
8. Château Belle-Vue
9. Karam Winery
10. Domaine Wardy

NEW UP-AND-COMING PRODUCERS

1. Château Ka
2. Château Khoury
3. Château Belle-Vue
4. Karam Winery
5. Nabise Mont Liban
6. Kfifane Winery

BEST-VALUE PRODUCERS

1. Château Ksara
2. Château Kefraya
3. Massaya
4. Domaine Wardy
5. Clos St Thomas
6. Fakra
7. Heritage
8. Domaines des Tourelles
9. Nabise Mont Liban

GREATEST-QUALITY WINES

1. **Château Musar 1988** (LL 150,000)
2. **Château Musar 1991** (LL 75,000)
3. **Château Musar 1995** (LL 53,000)
4. **Château Musar 1996** (LL 38,000)
5. **Château Musar White 1999** (LL 17,000)
6. **Comte de M 2001** Château Kefraya (LL 40,000)
7. **Selection 2003** Massaya (LL 18,000)
8. **Cuvée du Troisième Millénaire 2003** Château Ksara (LL 35,000)
9. **Château St Thomas 2002** Clos St Thomas (LL 30,000)
10. **Château Ksara 2002** (LL 20,000)

BEST BARGAINS

1. **Reserve 2003** Massaya (LL 30,000)
2. **Cuvee Réserve 2002** Château Musar (LL 10,000)
3. **Marquis des Beys 2004** Domaine des Tourelles (LL 30,000)
4. **Cuvée de Printemps 2004** Château Ksara (LL 8,000)
5. **Le Fleuron 2004** Heritage (LL 5,000)
6. **Rosé du Printemps 2005** Domaine Wardy (LL 8,000)
7. **Les Emirs 2003** Clos St Thomas (LL 12,300)
8. **Blanc de Blancs 2003** Heritage (LL 11,000)
9. **Château Kefraya 2002** (LL 20,500)
10. **Cloud 9 2004** Karam Winery (LL 11,000)

MOST EXCITING OR UNUSUAL FINDS

1. **Syrah/Cabernet Sauvignon 2003** Cave Kouroum (LL 26,000) *A fistful of Syrah at a whopping 14.5 per cent alcohol, with notes of strawberry, chocolate, pepper, and tobacco.*
2. **Rosé 2004** Domaine des Tourelles (LL 8,000) *Chocolate and strawberries dominate this cracking rosé made from Cabernet Sauvignon and Syrah.*
3. **Plaisirs du Vin 2000** Heritage (LL 13,000) *Cinsault/Cabernet Sauvignon blend from a producer who knows that Cinsault can give excellent results.*
4. **Syrah de Nicolas 2004** Karam Winery (LL 15,000) *Only 5,000 bottles of this sumptuous wine were produced, but they demonstrate that south Lebanon has the terroir to compete with the Bekaa.*
5. **Classic Red 2005** Massaya (LL 8,000) *Cinsault, Cabernet, and Syrah make up this fruity favourite. Excellent chilled.*
6. **La Renaissance 2003** Château Belle-Vue (LL 30,000) *A blend of Cabernet and Merlot that is full-bodied, fruity, and mouthfilling; a good wine to age.*
7. **St Michael 2006** St Michael Winery (LL 6,000) *One hundred per cent Grenache and 100 per cent delightful summer quaffing from this tiny winery in Masser el Chouf. Superb home-made organic wine – soft and supple.*
8. **Chardonnay 2005** Clos St Thomas (LL 17,000) *An unoaked Chardonnay that is perfumed, flinty, and fabulous.*
9. **Rosé du Printemps 2005** Domaine Wardy (LL 8,000) *Lebanon produces impressive rosé wine. This is one of the very best and up there with Domaine des Tourelles.*
10. **Cuvée Réserve White 2005** Château Musar (LL 9,000) *Made with Lebanese indigenous grape Obaideh, this is the more accessible cousin of the Château white. Maybe not to all tastes, it has acidity and notes of fruits and nuts.*

Israel

Daniel Rogov

The onset of war between Israel and the Hezbollah forces of Lebanon in July 2006 cast a mood of gloom not only on consumers but on the wineries as well.

DANIEL ROGOV

During the two-month war period, wine consumption fell by 40 per cent, partly because most restaurants and pubs in the north were shut down. Missiles falling on a nearly hourly basis on the Galilee ensured that wineries with vineyards near the Lebanese border (for example, Dalton and Galil Mountain) could not tend their vineyards during the crucial time before harvest. As a result, the harvest was delayed in some cases, and some vines were destroyed by missiles.

It is said that even in catastrophe one can find humour, and if the war brought about any smiles whatever it was in seeing petite winemaker Na'ama Mualem of the Dalton Winery violating military orders, donning a helmet and flak jacket, and making her way to the vineyards directly on the border to check the status of the grapes. On a truly positive note, during the war, communication between Israeli and Lebanese winemakers and wine critics continued (primarily by e-mail), with both sides expressing genuine concern for the fate of their colleagues.

Yet more changes at Carmel

Carmel, the largest winery in the country, continues to go through a series of major managerial changes, aimed largely at bringing the company out

DANIEL ROGOV is the wine and restaurant critic for the Israeli daily newspaper *Haaretz* as well as for the Israeli edition of the *International Herald Tribune*. He is the author of *Rogov's Guide to Israeli Wines* and is a regular contributor to *Hugh Johnson's Pocket Wine Book*. Rogov also publishes wine and gastronomic reviews and articles on his website, Rogov's Ramblings (www.stratsplace.com/rogov/home.html).

of its economic morass. For the third time in three years, CEOs have been replaced, and along with that, almost entirely new management teams have moved in. What seems clear now is that Carmel is planning to sell its facility in Rishon le Tzion and shift major operations to its wineries at Zichron Ya'akov and Ramat Dalton in the north of the country, both locations far better suited to receiving and processing grapes from the Galilee and the Golan Heights. The move seems logical from both the winemaking and economic points of view, since the sale of the property in Rishon le Tzion will ease Carmel's debt burden and give the company breathing space. The best news from Carmel is that the team of talented winemakers stays in place, and its top-of-the-range wines (the Single Vineyard and the Regional Series) show ever-increasing excellence.

International wine exposition and competition

Between 13 and 15 June 2006, the country held its first international wine exposition, IsraWinExpo. Organized in a thoroughly professional manner, 68 local wineries and each of the major importers participated. The exposition, open to the trade and press during the day and the public during the evening, was a broad success, its international aspect provided by the impressive attendance of foreign journalists and buyers. The exposition is scheduled to be a biennial event.

Parallel to IsraWinExpo was Terravino, billed as an international competition. All in all, 401 wines were entered (more than half Israeli), and 170 medals or awards were distributed. To a great many, including this critic, Terravino reinforced the hypothesis that most such competitions are organized largely for the profit of the organizers, with the medals perhaps helping to sell wine but not reflecting the quality of the winners.

Grapevine

• **In an attempt** to increase exports, the Ministry of Agriculture and the Ministry of Trade and Industry allocated US$1.3 million two years ago to promote Israeli wines abroad. The results were poor, and several wineries have withdrawn from the programme, deciding to go it on their own or with one or more private, primarily US-based consortia that are striving, so far without signs of success, to increase sales in the American market.

• **Reflecting overproduction** or the inability to sell their wines at relatively high prices within Israel, several wineries are now exporting the same wines under different labels that imply the existence of wineries that exist only on paper. Ella Valley Vineyards, for example, is exporting wines under the Hai label, and Efrat under the Kinneret label, both at prices far lower in the United States than for the same wines within Israel.

Opinion:
Grape confusion

In some cases there is little control over what goes into a bottle of wine. Bottles labelled as Cabernet Sauvignon may have aromas and flavours remarkably similar to those found in wines containing large amounts of Carignan or Argaman grapes. No less important, it seems (although it cannot at this stage be proved) that a few medium-sized and boutique wineries are using table grapes and labelling their wines as those of noble varieties.

Unification needed

There are currently six government or quasi-government agencies involved in the local wine trade – the Israeli Wine Institute, the Ministry of Agriculture, the Ministry of Trade and Industry, the Standards Institute, the Wine and Grape Board, and the Association of Grape Growers. Often working at cross-purposes and rarely communicating with one other, this situation almost guarantees that the industry has no central marketing arm, very limited control over labelling procedures, and no reliable source of data concerning either production or grape varieties under cultivation. No one in the country can reliably say, for example, how much of any variety is planted either in a specific region or in the country as a whole. What continues to be needed is a central body that will ensure proper standards, issue reliable data, and promote marketing both locally and abroad. Perhaps the most important step would be to establish a new wine institute that could function via fully fledged and enforceable new regulations. Such a body should also have a public-relations function, publishing and distributing educational, promotional, and statistical materials, and should have a major presence at wine fairs and seminars. The new institute should conduct serious research on determining which grapes are best suited to different subregions within the country, and encourage an atmosphere of cooperation between local wineries.

Appellation system

Finally, after more than a decade of discussion, it appears that the country is on its way to a proper appellation system. Although the land area of Israel is a mere 20,700 sq km (7,992 sq miles) (which is 5 per cent of the land area of California), like many wine-growing nations or regions that have a long north–south axis the country has a large variety of microclimates. In the north, snow falls in winter and conditions are comparable to those of Bordeaux and the northern Rhône Valley; yet within a few hours' drive one arrives at the Negev Desert, where the climate is similar to that of north Africa. The country is currently divided into five broad vine-growing regions (Galilee, Shomron, Samson, Judean Hills, and the Negev), but these regions are so badly defined that it is virtually impossible to know where any one ends and any other begins. The appellation system being developed at this time by a joint effort of the wineries and faculty members of the Ben Gurion University in Be'er Sheva and the Hebrew University's Faculty of Agriculture in Rehovot will function not so much to limit the specific grapes that may be planted but to more accurately identify regional and subregional areas and to ensure that labelling procedures are more reflective of reality.

Grapevine

• **There is puzzlement** over the proliferation of series of wines released by some wineries. At least two of the larger wineries (Barkan and Binyamina) now boast no fewer than eight different series, some containing as many as nine different wines. This phenomenon has also spread to the boutique wineries, with at least one producer (Ramim) producing under 100,000 bottles annually but boasting more than 20 different labels. Moreover, at least two wineries are now using labelling procedures that imply that the wines in a specific series are from an independent winery (for example, Binyamina's The Cave and Efrat's Tepperberg series).

• **Some wineries** have concluded that the solution to the wine glut, which impacts on Israel as it does on most wine-producing countries of the world, is to focus on raising local wine consumption. One step in this direction is the introduction of Carmel's Young Selected series: five red and white wines, all semi-dry, that the company hopes will tempt the young away from beer and soft drinks and into the world of wine.

• **Rumour has it** that two of the better small wineries in the country, Flam and Amphorae, may be switching to kosher production. If this is the case, they will be joining others who have gone the same path, not out of religious belief but in an attempt to increase sales to the observant Jewish market in Israel as well as in the USA.

• **The proliferation** of boutique and artisanal wineries may be slowing down. More than 150 such wineries are now on the scene, with nearly 50 per cent of those reporting substantial losses and decreasing sales. Data released recently by the Ministry of Trade and Industry reveal that the eight largest wineries in the country – Carmel, Barkan, Binyamina, The Golan Heights Winery, Efrat, Recanati, Galil Mountain, and Tishbi – continue to control 95 per cent of the market.

Vintage Report

Advance report on the latest harvest

2006

An especially dry winter, a cold, rainy April, and rains during mid-harvest in October (five times the seasonal norm) led to an extended harvest lasting from August to November, with surprisingly low yields. Probably better for reds than whites, but not an exciting year, and many top-of-the-range series and single-vineyard wines will not be released from this vintage.

Updates on the previous five vintages

2005

Vintage rating: *Red: 90, White: 90*

One of the most promising years in the past decade, with a prolonged harvest of overall high quality, exceptionally good in many parts of the country for reds and whites alike. Barrel tastings and some wines already released reveal wines of excellent balance, structure, and ageing potential.

2004

Vintage rating: *Red: 89, White: 91*

A short and hectic harvest but an excellent crop. Barrel tastings and early releases show greatest strength for whites but good concentration and intensity for reds. The best wines will be elegant and cellar-worthy.

2003

Vintage rating: *Red: 90, White: 90*

An excellent vintage for both reds and whites, with advance tastings revealing many intense and concentrated but elegant and ageworthy reds. Whites released are drinking nicely now and will cellar comfortably until 2008 or later.

2002

Vintage rating: *Red: 84, White: 80*

Prolonged heat spells made this a problematic year, both quality- and quantity-wise. Some good and even very good reds and whites, but nearly all are destined for early drinking.

2001

Vintage rating: *Red: 87, White: 85*

This was one of the earliest harvest years in recent history. Overall, a better year for reds than whites, with the whites now fully mature or beyond their peak, and the better reds drinking very well now and promising to cellar for four to five years longer.

GREATEST WINE PRODUCERS

1. Golan Heights Winery (Katzrin, Yarden, Gamla)
2. Castel
3. Yatir
4. Margalit
5. Clos de Gat
6. Flam
7. Galil Mountain
8. Carmel (Ltd Edn, Single Vineyard)
9. Chateau Golan
10. Ella Valley

BEST-VALUE PRODUCERS

1. Galil Mountain
2. Golan Heights Winery
3. Tabor
4. Dalton
5. Amphorae
6. Recanati
7. Saslove
8. Barkan
9. Tishbi
10. Efrat

FASTEST-IMPROVING PRODUCERS

1. Tabor
2. Efrat
3. Barkan
4. Dalton
5. Binyamina
6. Galil Mountain
7. Benhaim
8. Rota
9. Ben Hanna
10. Kadita

NEW UP-AND-COMING PRODUCERS

1. Pelter
2. Vitkin
3. Assaf
4. Odem Mountain
5. Savion
6. Smadar
7. Avidan
8. Tulip
9. Agur
10. Ruth

GREATEST-QUALITY WINES

1. **Katzrin 2003** Golan Heights Winery (NIS 165)
2. **Cabernet Sauvignon Yarden 2003** Golan Heights Winery (NIS 140)
3. **Limited Edition 2003** Carmel (NIS 155)
4. **Cabernet Sauvignon 2004** Margalit (NIS 180)
5. **Grand Vin Castel 2004** Castel (NIS 180)
6. **Clos de Gat 2003** Clos de Gat (NIS 160)
7. **Yatir Forest 2004** Yatir (NIS 155)
8. **Merlot Reserve 2004** Flam (NIS 160)
9. **Yiron 2003** Galil Mountain (NIS 130)
10. **Eliad 2003** Chateau Golan (NIS 155)

BEST BARGAINS

1. **Cabernet Sauvignon Bazelet 2005** Tabor (NIS 59)
2. **Merlot Bazelet 2004** Tabor (NIS 59)
3. **Cabernet Sauvignon 2005** Galil Mountain (NIS 55)
4. **Classico 2005** Flam (NIS 69)
5. **Merlot Gamla 2005** Golan Heights Winery (NIS 55)
6. **Cabernet Sauvignon 2005** Recanati (NIS 60)
7. **Barbera 2005** Dalton (NIS 55)
8. **Cabernet Sauvignon 2005** Dalton (NIS 55)
9. **Carignan 2004** Vitkin (NIS 60)
10. **Chardonnay 2005** Galil Mountain (NIS 50)

MOST EXCITING OR UNUSUAL FINDS

1. **Rosé 2005** Galil Mountain (NIS 55) A blend of 65 per cent Sangiovese, 22 per cent Cabernet Sauvignon, and 13 per cent Syrah. Medium-bodied and crisp, perhaps the best rosé ever from Israel.

2. **Pinotage Reserve 2004** Barkan (NIS 80) Medium- to full-bodied, with generous but not exaggerated wood and tannins that yield to reveal blackberry, black-cherry, and plum flavours. Good balancing acidity, and a moderately long finish.

3. **Late Harvest Sha'al Single Vineyard Gewurztraminer 2004** Carmel (NIS 70) Made from grapes from the upper Golan Heights, some affected by botrytis. Medium-bodied, with generous sweetness set off by good balancing acidity, and on the nose and palate honeyed apricot, cinnamon, and rose-petal flavours. Rich, spicy, and elegant.

4. **Shiraz/Grenache T-Selection 2004** Pelter (NIS 110) Full-bodied, with generous tannins well balanced by the influence of ageing in French oak casks for 14 months. Distinctive, ripe, and luxurious, with near-sweet plum, blueberry, and citrus peel intertwined beautifully with spicy, herbal, and pomegranate aromas and flavours.

5. **Cabernet Franc 2004** Vitkin (NIS 145) This 90/10 blend of Cabernet Franc and Petit Verdot finely balances wood, moderately firm tannins, and vegetal, fruity, and spicy characteristics. Distinctly Mediterranean.

6. **Shiraz 2004** Kadita (NIS 135) Rich, ripe, and generous; full-bodied, with soft tannins. Plum, blueberry, black cherry, and spices. Power and grace come together in a long finish.

7. **Blanc de Blanc Brut NV** Pelter (NIS 170) A delicious méthode champenoise sparkling wine showing toasted white bread, a long mousse that goes on and on, and grapefruit and lime fruits backed up by hints of cloves, ginger, and roasted nuts.

8. **Barbera 2004** Recanati (NIS 70) Excellent balance between gentle oak, acidity, and a tempting array of plum, black-cherry, and currant fruits matched nicely by overtones of freshly turned earth, chocolate, and a hint of white truffles.

9. **Moscato Golan 2006** Golan Heights Winery (NIS 35) Made in the style of Moscato d'Asti. Generously sweet, with good balancing acidity and remarkably floral on the nose. Aromas and flavours of green apples, ripe white peaches, tropical fruits, and a hint of grapefruit, all with a nice fuzziness. Not complex but fun.

10. **Viognier 2005** Amphorae (NIS 70) Unoaked and with no malo, this medium-bodied, lively wine offers crisp tropical fruits, peaches, melon, and a floral accent. Lightly spicy, aromatic, generous, and delicious.

South Africa

Cathy van Zyl MW & Tim James

Falling grape prices, exports squeezed … and still
the Cape has new wineries opening at the rate of
nearly one per week.

CATHY VAN ZYL MW and TIM JAMES

There was plenty of gloom about –
especially in the more volume-oriented
parts of the industry – as the grapes
ripened in the Cape vineyards for
harvest 2007. Expectations of a
bumper crop didn't help (in what
other agriculture industry does the
prospect of a big harvest add to a
farmer's depression?). In fact, many
grape growers were faced with the disheartening task of being paid –
minimally – to drop their crops.

Industry giant Distell announced the likelihood of "vineyard
mothballing": putting vine production on temporary hold through severe
pruning and low maintenance, avoiding vineyard costs as well as the
expense of vinifying grapes into already overstretched tank storage space.

Another major producer, the squirm-inducingly named Company
of Wine People (producers of big brand Arniston Bay and the more
prestigious Kumkani range, among others) paid its shareholder grape
farmers ludicrously little to abandon their crops while, rumour had it,
coping with alarmingly huge debts. Early in 2006, export-oriented,

CATHY VAN ZYL MW and TIM JAMES both work on the rigorously independent
wine-journalism project Grape, which they founded as a magazine in 1999 but
is now the website www.grape.co.za, for which Tim takes major responsibility.
Both also taste for the *Platter Wine Guide*, and Cathy particularly is in increasing
demand as a judge on the competition circuit and is also involved in wine
education. In 2005, she became South Africa's first Master of Wine to have
qualified while remaining in the country. In addition to Grape, Tim James writes
for various local and international publications, including *The World of Fine Wine*,
and consults to *The World Atlas of Wine*.

big-volume Coppoolse Finlayson had been forced to sell up, and it was surely only a matter of time before financial exigencies took a further toll among both large and small producers.

The factors producing all this? International glut, of course, and European supermarket power taking advantage of the desperation of suppliers everywhere to squeeze profits – this at a time when the local currency had hardened to a point that seriously cut margins and damaged exports (leading, incidentally, many producers to start wooing the local customers they had tended to airily ignore when the rand was lower and the export market was laying golden eggs). A relative softening of the currency in 2006 gave some respite, at least.

Le rouge et le noir

South Africa's re-entry into the international market after 1994 revealed a comparative shortage of black varieties, and growers overcompensated for this by ripping up and overgrafting white vines and planting virtually whatever black grapes they could lay their hands on (especially Syrah). Now white grapes are so scarce that in 2006 Sauvignon Blanc became the most expensive variety, a first for a white variety. Semillon was the only other variety to raise its average price over the previous year's, and Chenin has substantially climbed overall in recent years. Prices for black varieties have, though, collapsed: sexy Shiraz (with a tenfold increase in vineyard area in the past decade or so) suffered most, down by more than 20 per cent in 2006 compared with the previous year alone.

There will be no trouble meeting the demand for red wine over the next five years, announced the statisticians of SAWIS (SA Wine Industry Information and Systems), with no perceptible irony, but there will be a definite shortage of white wines after 2007. That timing coincides with an expected return to positive figures in the growth of exports. The big brands tend to dominate the statistics, but smaller, prestige wineries have been doing extremely well overseas. The benchmark 2007 *Platter Guide* rated 62 more wineries than the previous edition and a net gain of 600 wines. But the Cape is replete with trophy wine farms, not all of which are mere luxuries, and many of these and others that are overcapitalized are probably on the fringes of insolvency. For a while it looked as if simply raising the already aspirational prices of some pretty ordinary wine might help; but it won't take long for that mistake to be revealed.

NEW INDUSTRY LEADERSHIP

Restructuring at the level of industry leadership gave birth to the SA Wine Industry Council, out of the previous SA Wine and Brandy Company. Johan van Rooyen continues as CEO, with Kader Asmal MP as chairperson, promising some dynamism in dealing with the council's tasks. Which are? Confronting major wine-industry issues, including transformation, addressing growth opportunities, and "streamlining relations between the industry, government and all relevant stakeholders to stimulate competitiveness and development in the local and global market". That implies, among other things, a focus on growing wine tourism and building local markets – for which latter point read: getting the burgeoning black middle class to take its drinking responsibilities seriously and start consuming wine in a big way…

LOWER ALCOHOL DURCH TECHNIK

The flavours and textures of ultra-ripeness remain fashionable, but consumers and critics everywhere seem to be tiring of high alcohols (though standards change, and the 2007 *Platter Guide* includes some applauding of "lowish 13.5 per cent" alcohols). Local legislation has come to recognize the problem, and regulations now permit alcohol to be abstracted from wine by means of centrifuge, reverse osmosis, distillation, and nano-filtration. What the Californians happily call "rehydration" (adding water) is not permitted, although many serious winemakers claim that this is not only the cheapest but also the most sympathetic means of reducing the alcohol proportion (and, reputedly, the one occasionally used illegally until now – is this likely to change?). While many welcomed the new weapon at their disposal, most top-end producers insist that they will continue to search for all aspects of quality in the vineyard rather than resolving problems in the cellar.

IMPROVED VINEYARDS DURCH TECHNIK

Transgenic grapevines have been a focus of Stellenbosch University's Institute for Wine Biotechnology for some time. The research programme got nearer the crunch when application to the relevant national authorities was made to allow some carefully controlled field trials of GM grapevines – of the kind already happening in various countries. The research is designed to offer increased resistance to fungal and viral disease. Inevitably, the request was vehemently opposed from many quarters within and without the industry. The Wine Industry Council supports and funds GM research to enable the industry "to remain at the cutting edge of technology", while stressing that there is no prospect of genetically enhanced plants and yeasts being allowed until the practice becomes internationally acceptable. The generic marketing body WOSA, however, understandably fears that any meaningful action in this area will damage its attempts to promote the Cape as a heartland of biodiversity. Given the protests and the exigencies of the seasons, the earliest that grafting could occur, following permission, would be in spring (October) 2007.

WHAT'S IN A NAME?

The 2002 agreement between South Africa and the EU seemed a done deal – though some wondered about what had happened to the €15 million promised in partial exchange for phasing out European names like port, sherry, ouzo, and grappa. In late 2006, it was learned that the SA government had never ratified the agreement and the money would not be forthcoming. The trouble seemed to centre on a requirement of an associated free-trade agreement to phase out certain long-used trademarks. For example, the name of one of the Cape's most famous and long-established brands, Nederburg, has to go because it conflicts with that famous geographical indicator in – is it Holland… or perhaps Belgium? The stalemate became a matter for intergovernmental negotiation, to the relief of the wine authorities. On the sidelines, already irritated producers of probably the best "ports" outside the Douro were threatening to reclaim the name they had agreed to phase out totally by 2012, if the agreement was not honoured by the EU.

FOILING THE WINE SELLERS

The use of foil bags for selling wine has long exercised the tolerance of those concerned with the image of Cape wine and the sale of it in its cheapest form in these containers – affectionately or contemptuously known by the Afrikaans term *papsakke* ("soft bags"). Because of their place in the market, the bags have become associated with the financially impoverished end of alcohol abuse. The Ministry of Agriculture has agreed to effectively ban them, joining the wine industry leadership in fondly hoping that the measure will assist in solving the Cape's real problem with endemic alcoholism, when complementing other measures "directly focusing" on the problem.

Grapevine

• **Bordeaux's Madame de Lencquesaing** is eagerly awaiting the southern hemisphere's 2008 harvest, when grapes will be crushed in a new cellar on Pichon-Lalande's 125-ha Stellenbosch property, Glenelly. After the 2003 acquisition, 45 ha were quickly replanted to Cabernet Sauvignon, Shiraz, Petit Verdot, Merlot, Chardonnay, and Riesling. The first crop was vinified on a neighbouring property in 2007, but no doubt all involved with the venture look forward to the "home advantage".

• **A single vineyard** of up to 6 ha is now permitted as the smallest Wine of Origin terroir unit. Some of the registered names are splendidly idiosyncratic or inappropriate, genuinely historical, PR consultant-driven – or plain dull. Difficult to imagine CS1 or Block 12 making their way on to labels, but we can already enjoy Signal Hill's inner-city vineyard of Clos d'Oranje, Graham Beck's The Ridge, and Vergelegen's Schaapenberg (Sheep Hill), and perhaps look forward to the likes of Louis se Graf (Louis's Grave), Persephone, Pampoenland (Pumpkinland), and Bobbejaanblock (Baboon Block) – all now registered.

Opinion:
Focus on strengths

The tradition of smallish, estate-based wineries each producing a wide range – from (hopefully) delicate Riesling to (unfortunately) blockbuster Shiraz – is dying hard. True, many new producers concentrate on one or two wines, from grapes known to do well in the area, but others apparently fear being unable to meet the winery visitor's (or supermarket buyer's) every vinous need. It's a practice that ignores the slowly emerging recognition of something like terroir in the Cape, which sees certain areas increasingly recognizing their strengths – for example, Sauvignon Blanc and Semillon in Constantia, Cabernet Franc on the Helderberg, and the Rhône varieties in the Swartland. Not to mention Sauvignon Blanc in coolish Elgin. So why are ambitious producers there still trying their luck with Shiraz, even if it's clearly doomed to be inferior to their Sauvignon or their Pinot Noir? The pattern is repeated all over the Cape.

In some instances, a big range makes undeniable financial sense. Villiera somehow manages to produce an excellent sparkling wine and a pleasant enough port, with just about everything in between. It would be churlish to do other than marvel and applaud their success in meeting the demands of their target market – but Villiera's image is unlikely to soar. For others, perhaps it is the ambitious exuberance of a winemaker like

Grapevine

• **It wasn't a historic property** by Cape standards in the sense of age and fine old buildings, but Welgemeend's first releases in 1979 opened new chapters in the story of Cape wine: the first bordeaux-style blend; in Amadé the first (by a long way) "Cape blend" including Pinotage – both made by passionate amateur Billy Hofmeyr in perhaps the Cape's first "boutique" winery. Daughter Louise continued Billy's restrained, elegant style of winemaking on taking over the cellar some 15 years ago. Now vineyard manager mother Ursula gets overdue retirement, and the farm is sold – but its place in Cape history is assured.

• **Havana Hills** matures its Virgin Earth red wines under water at its Klein Karoo property. The newly fermented wine goes into barrels, which are then lowered into the farm dam for a year – it makes for softer and rounder wines, apparently. And Anthony Hamilton Russell hopes to ratchet up the terroir component by maturing his stuff in amphorae made from local clay.

André van Rensburg at Vergelegen, convinced he can do just about everything better than anyone else. But will excellent Vergelegen ever rank alongside the top Californian and French wineries while its focus is diffused? Will the world (or that part of it that values the idea of terroir) believe that an estate can excel across a broad range?

A lead is given by passionate terroirist Anthony Hamilton Russell, whose little Walker Bay empire includes six wines but three distinct labels, each with its own vineyard sources, each planned to have its own winery. There's just one pair of wines in each – a red and a white – since AHR believes that this is the maximum number consistent with the highest quality standards and, more particularly, image (something he understands as well as his soils). The best Cape producers need to concentrate and to be seen to be concentrating.

Continuing concerns

The name Riesling is officially conferred upon lowly Crouchen Blanc, while the real thing must bear the prefixed weight of "Weisser" or "Rhine" on the local market.

Strategies for "black economic empowerment" in the wine industry increasingly focus on enriching a few rather than improving the (grim) conditions of the many.

Too many wine journalists have conflicts of interest, as consultants, entrepreneurs, public-relations practitioners, and the like.

The big companies buy their way corruptly on to too many restaurant wine lists (with, clearly, some greedy restaurant connivance).

Grapevine

• **Making a change** from northern-hemisphere investment, Australia's Yalumba bought a fifth of Stellenbosch-based The Winery of Good Hope (which already features the unique Radford Dale range of wines from both countries). Along with a capital injection permitting the expansion of its production and export capabilities come 157 years of experience and worldwide distributor relationships. The Winery will also source vine material from Yalumba's commercial nursery, the largest in the southern hemisphere, for its vineyards held on long-term lease.

• **The UK's Tony Hindhaugh** found wine fame around the world with the broadcast of *The Grape Escape*, a reality TV series following his acquisition and revamping of Eaglevlei in Stellenbosch. The youthful entrepreneur's key message to viewers is: "Making wine is easy, selling it is the difficult part." Having a TV series dedicated to your brand does help. Hindhaugh has also turned Eaglevlei into a multifaceted tourism destination. The wines have not been exactly acclaimed – but it is early days yet.

Vintage Report

Advance report on the latest harvest
2007

Official estimates put 2007 crop levels up on 2006, but anecdotal evidence is contradictory: warmer areas seem up, while cooler, or more temperate, zones are down. But there's no confusion about quality, with claims that it is on a par, or higher, than 2006, aided by a cold winter, enabling most vines to go into proper dormancy, and good rains. Some growers were concerned about the milder-than-usual temperatures in the weeks before the harvest, believing they were retarding ripening. A heat wave at the end of January ended the anxiety of those who like everything picked before late summer, while some rain and cooler temperatures in February countered the potential stress to later-ripening varieties and also, some say, favourably affected physiological ripeness. Early-March rains followed by warmer weather were good for noble rot, but also for less desirable fungal infections, and slight damage was widely reported. Sauvignon Blanc (unless caught by the heat wave) and Chardonnay appear most promising of the whites, while black berries were smaller, giving excellent skin-to-fruit ratios and boding well for colour, concentration, and structure.

Updates on the previous five vintages
2006

Vintage rating: *Red: 90, White: 95*

Despite wind causing havoc with berry set, heat accelerating sugar ripeness, fire and smoke contaminating vineyards, and power cuts downing must coolers, pumps, and tank jackets, winemakers were more than happy with fruit quality. A standout vintage for whites, particularly Sauvignon and Chenin Blanc; red wines are fleshier and less tannic than the more austere 2002. Only Shiraz, the biggest victim of the winds, seems to need cherry-picking.

2005

Vintage rating: *Red: 85, White: 85*

A tricky, short harvest, early-season rain causing mildew and excessive vigour in many vineyards; a heat wave sent sugar levels rising in others. Generalizations are almost impossible. The yield just topped 1.2 million tons, about 12 per cent less than 2004. Reds all round are concentrated, if alcoholic; full, firmly structured wines came from the coastal regions. Whites are mostly average.

2004

Vintage rating: *Red: 88, White: 88*

Long, predominantly healthy harvest, with one of the largest-ever crops. Cool conditions during flowering caused uneven berry set, prompting much green-harvesting to ensure even ripening. Shiraz and Merlot pleasing, also Chardonnay and Sauvignon Blanc.

2003

Vintage rating: *Red: 95, White: 90*

Quality-wise, the vintage stands well above many in the past 25 years, with well-structured, generous reds and fine whites. Yields, too, were up – some 12 per cent on 2002.

2002

Vintage rating: *Red: 75, White: 80*

Downy mildew and excessive botrytis a result of prolonged winter rains; accelerated ripening promoted by February heat waves; many juggled late-maturing whites/early-ripening reds. Shiraz was the best performer under the difficult conditions.

Grapevine

• **Stormhoek** (owned by Orbital Wines in London, based in Wellington) used Internet-based marketing techniques such as viral e-mails and blogging to come from nowhere (via more Web exposure than any other wine in the world, they say) to build substantial international retail markets. Latterly, it set about consolidating its position as a quality producer among its loyal followers abroad by incorporating fruit quality and winemaking skill messages in its campaigns.

• **South African winemaking families** are spreading their wings and acquiring vineyards in far countries. Pioneer Clive Torr bought a share in a Burgundy domaine a decade back, and more recently Tom Lubbe invested in Roussillon, and Eben Sadie in Priorat. Then, in 2006, Bruce Jack and Wilhelm Coetzee of Flagstone Winery joined forces with UK-based Ed Adams MW to produce a Spanish wine label for the global market. The range, which is available in foreign-wine-starved South Africa, has wines from Montsant, the Jumilla highlands, and Jumilla. And the Griers of Villiera now have some 22 ha under vine and a cellar in Roussillon's Fenouillèdes, launching their first wines from this venture late in 2007. French locals are reportedly delighted with the Griers' respect for their traditions, while South African wine lovers will be delighted with some new flavours available locally.

GREATEST WINE PRODUCERS

1. Vergelegen
2. Sadie Family
3. Boekenhoutskloof
4. Hamilton Russell Vineyards
5. Thelema
6. Rustenberg
7. Cape Point Vineyards
8. Steenberg
9. Kanonkop
10. Rudera

FASTEST-IMPROVING PRODUCERS

1. Chamonix
2. Hartenberg
3. Klein Constantia
4. Scali
5. Lammershoek
6. La Motte
7. Nederburg
8. Durbanville Hills
9. Robertson Winery
10. Rijk's

NEW UP-AND-COMING PRODUCERS

1. Oak Valley
2. Solms-Delta
3. Tulbagh Mountain Vineyards
4. The Foundry
5. Capaia
6. Tokara
7. Ataraxia
8. Quoin Rock
9. Vilafonté
10. Sterhuis

BEST-VALUE PRODUCERS

1. Pecan Stream (Waterford)
2. Perdeberg Cooperative
3. Alto Estate
4. Du Toitskloof
5. Buitenverwachting
6. Paul Cluver
7. Little River (De Meye)
8. Guardian Peak
9. Villiera
10. De Krans

GREATEST-QUALITY WINES

1. **Vergelegen White 2005** Vergelegen (R193)
2. **Syrah 2004** Boekenhoutskloof (R200)
3. **Columella 2004** Sadie Family (R395)
4. **Palladius 2005** Sadie Family (R275)
5. **Isliedh 2005** Cape Point Vineyards (R120)
6. **Mountain Reserve Sauvignon Blanc 2005** Oak Valley (R100 ex cellars)
7. **Chardonnay 2005** Hamilton Russell Vineyards (R180)
8. **Cape Vintage Reserve 2001** JP Bredell (R205)
9. **Weisser Riesling Noble Late Harvest 2005** Paul Cluver (R60)
10. **Chenin Blanc 2005** De Morgenzon (R110)

BEST BARGAINS

1. **Sauvignon Blanc 2005** Chamonix (R52)
2. **Petit Chenin 2006** Ken Forrester (R29)
3. **Cabernet Sauvignon/Shiraz 2004** Pecan Stream (Waterford) (R40)
4. **Chenin Blanc 2006** Perdeberg Cooperative (R16 ex cellars)
5. **Alto Rouge 2004** Alto Estate (R55)
6. **Relishing Red NV** De Krans (R20)
7. **Shiraz 2004** Little River (De Meye) (R27)
8. **Two Cubs Cape Blend 2005** Knorhoek (R39)
9. **Weisser Riesling 2005** Paul Cluver (R60)
10. **Gewurztraminer 2005** Paul Cluver (R54)

MOST EXCITING OR UNUSUAL FINDS

1 **Solms Hegewisch Africana 2005** Solms-Delta (R123) *From Syrah dried (on the vine) in convincing Amarone style; intense, rich, with sour-cherry notes. Varietal character is not the point of this vino da meditazione, but interest and character are.*

2 **Eszencia NV** Signal Hill (R2,000) *The first from the Cape following Tokaji's model of the ultimate elixir; from Furmint, Chenin, and Sauvignon; 480 g/l sugar, huge compensating acidity, alcohol well below the local threshold to be officially "wine".*

3 **Ashbourne 2004** Ashbourne (R235) *Anthony Hamilton Russell in cooler-climate Walker Bay is responsible for this unique take on Pinotage: the Cape's most bordeaux-like and elegant example.*

4 **TMV White 2005** Tulbagh Mountain Vineyards (R125) *Cleverly oaked, Chenin-led blend offering perfume, power, poise, and palatability. Heady, with attention-grabbing oxidative notes, this pushes South Africa's Chenin envelope.*

5 **Cape Tawny Vintner's Reserve 1980** Boplaas (R150) *Not a vintage misprint but a satiny melange of nuts and maraschino cherries from 15 years' slumber in old oak.*

6 **Nebbiolo 2005** Steenberg (R110) *One of a handful of local varietal bottlings, this Constantia example raises the quality bar with each vintage. Taut, juicy acidity and a touch of sweet fruit hint at Italian origins.*

7 **Hannibal 2004** Bouchard Finlayson (R130) *Pinot Noir/ Chardonnay master Peter Finlayson lavishes care, and one-third new French barrels, on this Sangiovese/ Pinot-dominated blend, when crossing the Alps with Nebbiolo, Mourvèdre, Barbera, and Shiraz.*

8 **Solms Hegewisch Koloni 2005** Solms-Delta (R93) *The second of this exciting new producer's wines from desiccated grapes. An aromatic marriage of Riesling and Muscats d'Alexandrie and de Frontignan. Big, powerful, and just off-dry.*

9 **Auction Reserve Weisser Riesling 2005** Hartenberg (R80) *Sold at the 2006 Cape Winemakers Guild Auction, a most successful experiment: a lightly wooded, just-dry version of a grape always sensitively treated at this estate; winningly balanced and rather fine.*

10 **Babiana Noctiflora 2005** Armajaro (R70) *Relished for both its splendid name (referring to a local plant species) and its character. Part of a wave of fascinating white blends from the Perdeberg area, it's a cunning, old-oaked blend of Chenin and Viognier – fruity and rich, but not excessively so.*

Grapevine

• **While the grape glut** and falling prices saw much battening down of hatches, some were laying plans – and bricks – for the future. Anticipating an upturn, owners such as Dave Hidden of Hidden Valley Wines and grape growers like Tjuks and Johan Roos, business partners to The Winery of Good Hope, forged ahead with the construction of state-of-the-art facilities. Hidden Valley Wines' new multimillion-rand home came on-stream for the 2007 harvest, while The Winery, which has a long-term lease on the Roos' vineyards and cellar, will take grapes into the new cellars only in 2008.

California

Dan Berger

California's major wine regions are beginning to formally recognize the differences between themselves – and in marketing terms, as well as in wine styles.

DAN BERGER

Napa Valley has always been the key wine-country area, but it has only a tiny percentage of the state's wine-grape acreage, and other districts, some making more diverse wines, aren't happy that the "wine country" designation has been ceded to Napa by default.

Three top North Coast regions created marketing organizations in 2006 to help put across the message that they too make superb wines. The largest self-funded marketing effort was approved in Sonoma County, which hired a full-time marketing director. Similarly, efforts began in Lake County (north of Napa) and Mendocino County, which sells more than 80 per cent of its fruit to other regions upgrading their wines.

The three county areas can also make exciting wines – and more diverse than Cabernet-centric Napa. But even Napa's image eroded in 2006, when a retasting was staged of the original 1976 Judgment of Paris tasting in which Napa Cabs beat the French again. However, this time, it wasn't a Napa wine that won; it was the Ridge 1971 Cabernet from Santa Cruz Mountains.

DAN BERGER contributes a nationally distributed wine column weekly to Creators Syndicate; publishes his own weekly newsletter on wine, *Dan Berger's Vintage Experiences*; and writes trade-magazine articles for US magazines *Cheers*, *Beverage Dynamics*, and *Wines and Vines*, as well as *Off Licence News* and *Decanter* in London. He is a speaker at major wine symposiums around the world and is a judge at numerous wine competitions in the United States and abroad. He also coordinates the Riverside International and Long Beach wine competitions in southern California.

The marketing efforts of the three North Coast regions should have the greatest impact in Sonoma, with its Chardonnays, Pinot Noirs, Sauvignon Blancs, and Zinfandels. Mendocino already has one "concept wine" in place. To focus attention on its stylish Zinfandel-based blends, nearly a dozen wineries now make a superior blend called Coro, which began with the 2001 vintage.

Now other areas are considering campaigns to raise their images, such as Central Coast Pinot Noir paradises Santa Lucia Highlands, Santa Rita Hills, Santa Maria Valley, and Edna Valley.

Distribution chaos

A Supreme Court ruling that seemed a victory for consumers in their quest to buy wines from tiny, family-owned wineries in other states has worked to broaden distribution of some limited-production wines. However, the ruling has created new and confusing regulations that have frustrated wine collectors and, combined with Transportation Safety Administration restrictions, left some wine-transport issues unresolved.

The Supreme Court ruled that states couldn't discriminate in the shipping of wine: if a state permitted wineries to ship in-state, it could not prohibit out-of-state wineries from doing the same.

Most states opted to liberalize their shipping laws, but what replaced them in most instances was a permit system that required wineries to pay for a permit to ship into each state. Moreover, left out of this permit system was the consumer, who discovered that it wasn't possible to ship home wine purchased at a winery unless the winery did the shipping. In addition, some states (such as Virginia) heeded the wholesalers' desires and imposed additional restrictions on local wineries.

Direct shipping remains a confusing issue.

Grapevine

• **The giant E&J Gallo Winery,** in an effort to simplify its image in the market, switched the name of its Gallo of Sonoma wines to "Gallo Family Vineyards".

• **Mega-Purple** and other so-called colour additives to wine were widely used in 2006 as winemakers sought to darken the colour of red wines that were perceived by some marketing executives as too light. A pernicious side-effect of the use of such colour-fixing agents is that they also add sugar (legally, since it is a wine concentrate) as well as flavours of their own to the doctored wines.

• **Sales of Riesling** continue to rise in California. From an admittedly small base, Riesling sales in supermarkets and other scannable locations are up markedly, and some large wineries (like Brown Forman's Fetzer and Jekel) are scrambling to fill the need.

Opinion:
Percentage points and sameness

The winemaker was frustrated as he said it: "Fourteen is the old 13, and soon the 'new 14' will be 15." He was referring to alcohol levels in many of California's more expensive wines, which have increased over the past decade by a full percentage point. Some wines are fast approaching two points higher than the previous optimum.

The main reason for this pernicious trend is that the number-mongers seem spellbound by more powerful wines, even though such intensity plays havoc with the flavours of food, which was once a mandatory companion for wine. "The wines that get high scores are 'walking around' wines," said the winemaker. "You can't drink them with a meal." It's true. But winemakers know that if they want a 90+ score from one of the power scorers, they must make bigger wines.

Problems began, mainly with Cabernet, soon after the "long hang-time" vintage of 1997, which was inappropriately certified as great by some top reviewers. (Most 1997s are now dying an ugly death.) Now the trend towards blacker, denser red wines has invaded Pinot Noir production, partly due to the use of newer French clones that ripen faster and make for a wine that is most certainly un-Pinot-like.

For decades, California wines were, region to region and varietal to varietal, distinctively different and proudly so. However, since about 1997 a disappointing sameness has crept into the wines. Pinot Noirs now taste as much like Syrah as anything, and terroir has become not only absent, but a term used by the self-anointed experts as an excuse for what they see as bad winemaking.

After many years of success in making top-rate wines, many winemakers decided to fix what wasn't broken. Their justification for ultra-concentration: they must pick late to achieve "physiological maturity" – as if grapes need to reach a magical point before great wine can be made. However, ripeness is a range, not a point. By waiting so late, winemakers are destroying California's uniqueness as a diverse wine-growing region. The consumer who appreciates uniqueness now faces a sea of identicalness.

Vintage Report

Advance report on the latest harvest
2006

For the second year in a row, winter rains and a cool, rainy spring posed early problems, with the potential for botrytis. Most growers had to spray to fight the problem, and leaf removal was then essential because of excessive ground moisture, which accelerated unwanted canopy growth. The weather was cool almost the entire summer, but between late July and the first week of August, a sustained heat wave caused vines to shut down photosynthesis. Ten days of heat were followed by cooler-than-usual weather, so acid levels in most grape varieties stayed higher than normal. The cool weather pushed the harvest back nearly a month. Harvest was erratic, with some whites harvested later than some reds. Pinot Noir, which suffered a tiny crop in 2005, rebounded to near-normal levels. Quality was rated as superb, with great natural acids.

Updates on the previous five vintages
2005

Vintage rating: 97

A cool, wet spring lasted until mid-June, leaving some North Coast areas with mildew problems. Late spring was also cool, and similar temperatures lasted until early summer. Sufficient heat finally came, but the harvest was odd, with

Grapevine

• **Napa Valley** vintner Al Brounstein, founder of Diamond Creek Vineyards, died at age 76; and Sonoma County wine pioneer Rodney Strong died at age 78, following a stroke.

• **Kendall-Jackson winery** owner Jess Jackson continued to gobble up prestige brands. He acquired the Robert Pecota Winery in the Napa Valley and Murphy Goode in Sonoma County, as well as three significant projects that had been owned by Legacy Estates Group: Arrowood

Winery in Sonoma Valley, Byron in California's Central Coast, and Freemark Abbey in Napa Valley.

• **Immigration restrictions** at the California–Mexico border made harvesting grapes difficult for some growers in 2006. A stringent crackdown on undocumented workers coming into the USA made it hard for some growers to find sufficient numbers of pickers, and some varieties' harvest dates were delayed.

some black grapes (such as Pinot Noir) being picked before whites. It was a large and healthy crop for the most part, but in some coastal strips (such as the Sonoma Coast and Russian River Valley), Pinot Noir tonnage was only a fraction of normal. However, the cool weather provided excellent acid levels, and overall quality was rated to be exceptional.

2004

Vintage rating: *94*

A warm spring got vines off to a fast start. But two months of cooler weather followed, then two weeks of dry summer heat. That made for one of the earliest harvests in decades, running three to four weeks ahead of normal. The first grapes, for sparkling wine, were picked on 23 July. Quality was rated as excellent. Tonnage declines of about 5 per cent were reported in most Napa and Sonoma regions.

2003

Vintage rating: *93*

Early rains and late heat spikes contributed to lower overall yields. The result was a slightly erratic vintage of good quality, good colour concentration, and intensity of flavour. Heat in March led to shatter, reducing crop size. Then a cold May left the crop a month behind schedule. Dramatic heat spikes in September moved the harvest forward closer to a normal schedule. There was a rush to get everything harvested, and much came in at the same time. Reds had good acid, high sugar, and low pH.

2002

Vintage rating: *92*

No prolonged summer heat, just many short heat spells late in the season, resulting in excessively high sugars in many varieties. The heat spells occurred after a relatively cool summer, so sugars rose quickly. Some awkward reds; whites survived better, since the slightly cooler summer left Chardonnay, Sauvignon Blanc, and Pinot Gris with good acids. Rated higher by some.

2001

Vintage rating: *93*

A warm summer followed by a cooling trend in September brought acids back up. Some fruit was harvested early, leading to better acidity structure. An excellent vintage with great potential for reds that will be aged.

GREATEST WINE PRODUCERS

1. Navarro
2. Stag's Leap Wine Cellars
3. Dutton Goldfield
4. Morgan
5. Au Bon Climat
6. Gary Farrell
7. Robert Sinskey
8. Gundlach Bundschu
9. Kenwood
10. Chimney Rock

FASTEST-IMPROVING PRODUCERS

1. Matanzas Creek
2. Savannah-Chanelle
3. Stryker Sonoma
4. DuMOL
5. Hahn Estates
6. Londer
7. Scott Harvey Wines
8. Dry Creek
9. Graziano/Saint Gregory/Enotria
10. Charles Krug

NEW UP-AND-COMING PRODUCERS

1. Sonoma Coast Vineyards
2. Alma Rosa
3. Campion
4. Joel Gott
5. Moshin
6. Hook and Ladder
7. Holdredge
8. Tolosa
9. Copeland Creek
10. Papapietro Perry

BEST-VALUE PRODUCERS

1. Fetzer
2. Sutter Home
3. Pepi
4. Windy Ridge
5. McManis
6. Castle Rock
7. Taft Street
8. Forest Glen
9. Kendall-Jackson
10. Windmill

GREATEST-QUALITY WINES

1. **Chardonnay 2004** HdV, Los Carneros ($55)
2. **Morelli Lane Vineyard Zinfandel 2005** Dutton Goldfield, Russian River Valley ($40)
3. **Muscat Blanc 2005** Navarro, Anderson Valley ($16)
4. **Tondre's Grapefield Pinot Noir 2005** Morgan, Santa Lucia Highlands ($55)
5. **Lot 1 Cabernet Sauvignon 2003** Louis M Martini, Napa Valley ($95)
6. **Cabernet Sauvignon 2003** Spottswoode, Napa Valley ($110)
7. **Earthquake Pinot Noir 2004** Marimar Torres, Don Miguel Vineyard, Russian River Valley ($47)
8. **Beeson Ranch Zinfandel 2003** Dry Creek Vineyard, Dry Creek Valley, Sonoma County ($30)
9. **Sauvignon Blanc 2005** Matanzas Creek, Sonoma County ($20)
10. **Pinot Noir 2005** Papapietro Perry, Leras Vineyard, Russian River Valley ($48)

BEST BARGAINS

1. **Fleur Pinot Noir 2005** Mahoney, Carneros ($12)
2. **Syrah 2004** Cycles Gladiator, Central Coast ($9)
3. **The Tillerman 2003** (Cabernet/Sangiovese blend) Hook and Ladder, Russian River Valley ($16)
4. **Edelzwicker 2005** (Gewurztraminer/Riesling blend) Navarro, Anderson Valley ($11)
5. **Cotes du Crows 2005** (red Rhône blend) Morgan, Monterey County ($18)
6. **Sangiovese 2003** Vino Noceto, Shenandoah Valley ($16)

⑦ **Petite Sirah 2004**
Guenoc, California ($9)

⑧ **Pinot Grigio 2005**
Tamas Estate, California ($10)

⑨ **Petite Sirah 2004** Parducci,
Mendocino County ($10)

⑩ **Chardonnay 2005** Windy Ridge,
Central Coast ($11)

MOST EXCITING OR UNUSUAL FINDS

① **The Rat Carignane 2005**
Roshambo, Dry Creek Valley ($25)
*Dramatic cranberry/cherry aroma,
with a hint of Beaujolais Nouveau
spice, and superb fruit in the mouth.*

② **Albariño 2005** Tangent, Edna
Valley ($17) *Tangerine, lime, and
white-pepper aroma, with a brilliant
spice note in the mid-palate. Good
acid and dry, but the wine is so
succulent it seems as if there is
a tad of sugar.*

③ **Aglianico 2003** Seghesio, Russian
River Valley ($39) *Dense, dark colour
and remarkably Italianate nose of
dried roses, tar, and spice. Thick
tannins, but a rather sweet finish.*

④ **Gewurztraminer 2005** Zmor,
Russian River Valley ($35) *Barrel-
fermented, 100 per cent malolactic,
dry. Rose petals, spice, and gardenia
aroma; weighty entry (like Viognier in
texture); pleasingly bone dry to
complement Asian food.*

⑤ **Deviation NV** Andrew Quady,
California ($30 per half-bottle)
*Fortified Orange Muscat flavoured
with scented geranium and
damiana (from the leaves of the
damiana shrub). Exotic, sweet, and
unctuous. (Is this an aphrodisiac?)*

⑥ **Ozymandias 2004** Daniel Gehrs,
Santa Barbara County ($36) *This
Cabernet/Syrah blend offers
blueberry and blackberry fruit with a
note of tobacco. Penetrating regional
character of the cool Central Coast
with a note of olives and tea.*

⑦ **Eleganza 2005** Daniel Gehrs, Santa
Barbara County ($28) *This blend of
barrel-fermented Chardonnay and
stainless-fermented Viognier has
a minty/earthy aroma, hints of
camomile tea, and not much oak.*

⑧ **Las Brisas Vineyard Vermentino
2005** Mahoney, Carneros ($14)
*Striking aroma of fresh white peach,
blossom/floral notes, and a dry but
not austere finish.*

⑨ **Charbono 2004** Robert Foley,
Napa Valley ($35) *Deep plum, racy
underbrush notes, with a solid core
of fruit; quite complex. Should age
a decade. From Gary Heitz's highly
regarded Charbono vineyard south
of Calistoga.*

⑩ **Frivolo Moscato Bianco 2005**
Vino Noceto, Shenandoah Valley
($12.50) *This blend of 75 per cent
Muscat and 25 per cent Orange
Muscat is only 7.5 per cent alcohol
and has substantial sweetness, but
it is balanced by good acidity and
a hint of spritz. Delightful to serve
with fruit salad.*

Grapevine

• **Ridge Vineyards'** 1971
Cabernet Sauvignon came
first in a blind tasting staged
concurrently in the Napa Valley
and London, in a restaging of the
famed 1976 Judgment of Paris
tasting, in which California wines
finished first in both red and
white evaluations. What was most
compelling, however, were tasters'
reactions after evaluating (not
competitively) a range of recent
reds from both Bordeaux and
California. Most tasters on both
sides of the Atlantic agreed that,
although California's 1970s wines
had held up remarkably well, the
structure of the recent (21st-
century) wines was such that few
held any hope they'd hold up for
a decade, let alone 30 years.

Pacific Northwest

Paul Gregutt

The ongoing lawsuit filed by Costco Wholesale Corp against the Washington State Liquor Control Board (WSLCB), first filed in February 2004, continues to slog its way through the courts.

PAUL GREGUTT

Costco, the nation's largest wine retailer, is headquartered in Seattle, Washington. The company initially charged the WSLCB with "establishing and supporting monopoly power, imposing a trust, fixing prices, limiting production, regulating transportation, conferring privileges and immunities, lending state credit, and discriminating against out-of-state wineries and brewers".

In broad terms, the suit has sought to overturn post-Prohibition laws that prevent Costco from purchasing wine directly from producers, receiving volume discounts, and discount pricing – tactics that it applies to virtually every other consumer product in its stores.

Early in 2006, US District Court Judge Marsha Pechman ruled in Costco's favour, throwing out key parts of the existing laws and provoking appeals from the state and the Beer and Wine Wholesalers Association. Among the rulings: the state discriminated by allowing Washington wineries to ship directly to retailers while prohibiting out-of-state wineries the same access. The state immediately caved in and now allows all domestic wineries, with proper licensing, to ship directly to Washington retailers.

PAUL GREGUTT writes regularly on wine for *The Seattle Times*, *Yakima Herald-Republic*, *Walla Walla Union-Bulletin*, *The Spokane Spokesman-Review*, *Pacific Northwest* magazine, and *Wine Enthusiast* magazine. He is a member of the *Wine Enthusiast* tasting panel and the author of the critically acclaimed *Northwest Wines* (Sasquatch Books, 1996). His new book – *Washington Wines and Wineries: The Essential Guide* – was published in October 2007 by the University of California Press. Online, you'll find him at paulgregutt.com.

The judge also tossed out the laws banning quantity discounts, extension of credit, and central warehousing. These rulings are all on appeal, with a final decision expected sometime in 2007/08.

Controversy over new AVAs

Washington State gained its ninth appellation with the official certification of the Rattlesnake Hills AVA in March 2006. A subregion of the Yakima Valley AVA, it covers 68,500 acres and includes 17 wineries, 29 vineyards, and approximately 1,500 bearing acres. The new appellation has already become Washington's most contentious.

Some vintners and growers feel that its boundaries exclude certain vineyards that should have been included. Others contend that it detracts from the reputation (already a bit tattered) of the Yakima Valley appellation. Several of the most prestigious wineries located within the new AVA do not plan to use it on their labels. Gail Puryear of Bonair Winery, who spearheaded the Rattlesnake Hills application process, disagrees with critics who say that the existing Yakima Valley appellation is sufficient. "The Yakima Valley AVA is not an AVA at all," he insists, "it is a landform. I estimate that 95 per cent of the AVA is unplantable. The Rattlesnake Hills AVA", he says, "has more in common with Red Mountain [another subappellation] than Prosser Flats [the valley floor]."

Whether or not Puryear's arguments convince critics, the push to define more and more AVAs in the Pacific Northwest continues to gain momentum. Washington's nine AVAs pale beside Oregon's 15, which include six new Willamette Valley subregions: Dundee Hills, Eola-Amity Hills, Chehalem Mountains, Yamhill-Carlton District, Ribbon Ridge, and McMinnville.

Chehalem Mountains, the last of the six to be approved, was officially blessed by the TTB (Alcohol and Tobacco Tax and Trade Bureau) in 2006. Supporters such as Ken Wright, who has worked on the appellation project for the past decade, argue that the value of these new AVAs is that "they provide insight to the expected aromas, flavours, and textures of the wines they produce". Others, this writer included, believe that the jury is still out on whether anyone but the winemakers can really spot the differences.

Acquisitions

Seattle-based wine company Precept Brands, founded in 2003, has quickly become Washington's third largest. Apart from developing proprietary brands, Precept has gone on an acquisition spree recently, adding the Magnificent Wine Company and Waterbrook to its portfolio. The former is the brainchild of Charles Smith, the rock impresario turned winemaker whose Walla Walla boutique, K Vintners, is best known for its single-vineyard Syrahs.

Smith started Magnificent four years ago with a simple concept: to market a $10-dollar red with the engaging name of House Wine. With its crude black-and-white label – a childlike block drawing of a house – House Red sold like hot cakes, and spun off a House White, along with a Red Table Wine and a White Table Wine. Sales are currently around 100,000 cases annually, and Precept expects to triple that number within a couple of years.

Walla Walla's Waterbrook Winery, founded in 1983 by Eric and Janet Rindal, is best known for its affordable Merlots and Chardonnays. Production has reached roughly 30,000 cases annually, most in the $12–15 price range. Eric Rindal, who no longer makes the wines, will continue as "brand ambassador".

The state's biggest winery group, Ste Michelle Wine Estates, has continued its buying spree by acquiring Oregon's Erath Winery. In a deal similar to its 2005 agreement with Spring Valley Vineyards, Ste Michelle purchased the Erath name and inventory. Founder Dick Erath will continue to farm the winery vineyards under a long-term sales contract. Erath Winery is the first Oregon property to join the Ste Michelle portfolio.

Grapevine

• **Master of Wine David Lake,** who began making wine at Columbia Winery in 1979, has retired. Working closely with grower Mike Sauer, Lake was the first in Washington State to produce varietal Syrah, Cabernet Franc, and Pinot Gris. He experimented widely with different grapes and clones, pioneered vineyard designates, and worked tirelessly to create elegant, ageworthy wines styled for the European palate. He hopes to continue his involvement in the wine industry, including judging and winemaking.

• **Norm McKibben and Jean-François Pellet,** the managing partner and winemaker of Pepper Bridge winery, have founded MPM Vintners, a custom-crush facility in Walla Walla. Offering turnkey winemaking services, MPM becomes the anchor tenant for the refurbished Crown Cork & Seal Building, now owned by the Port of Walla Walla. With the number of Walla Walla wineries already approaching 100, this new facility seems likely to add still more new labels to retail shelves.

• **Allen Shoup's** Long Shadows Vintners has added Tuscany's Ambrogio and Giovanni Folonari to its growing stable of international winemakers. The Folonari team is producing a Columbia Valley Super-Tuscan-style red called Saggi. A new, $4.2-million Long Shadows winery, which Shoup describes as "a state-of-the-art, no compromise production facility", has opened a few miles west of Walla Walla. After working in cramped, borrowed space for the past few years, resident Long Shadows winemaker Gilles Nicault will be able to sort, crush, and ferment wines according to each visiting winemaker's preferred methods.

Opinion:
Time to overhaul the WSLCB

Washington State Governor Christine Gregoire has asked the Washington State Liquor Control Board to provide her with an independent review and analysis of projected revenue growth, the impact of increased sales on public safety, operational and policy efficiencies, and possible organizational restructuring.

The laws governing the purchase, sale, and distribution of beer, wine, and spirits in Washington were set 75 years ago. They are hopelessly out of date. The state is caught in the untenable position of having to both regulate and sell these products, opening it up to charges of being a state-run monopoly. It also finds itself trying to manage its thousands of stores profitably, while not appearing to promote the use of alcohol, which would be politically incorrect.

It has a burgeoning, multibillion-dollar wine industry under its supervision (one of the few agricultural success stories in the state), yet state liquor stores cannot hold wine tastings, distribute educational materials, or even sell corkscrews!

There are some 500 wineries in Washington, close to 1,000 in the Pacific Northwest, double that number in California, and hundreds more scattered across the rest of the country. Almost none of them is benefiting from laws that make their products extremely difficult to market, distribute, ship, and sell.

Online shopping is here to stay. The current regulations are confusing, haphazardly applied, and often irrelevant. A complete and thorough overhaul of how to redesign the system to manage all these issues is a daunting task to be sure, but the current situation is jamming up the courts and making criminals of consumers who just want a glass of wine with their dinner.

Never mind the sizzle, let's see some steak

Washington has (finally) begun to recognize that wine touring has the potential to bring significant tourist dollars to the eastern half of the state. Last spring, the Washington Wine Commission scraped together funding for a test branding effort behind their slogan, "Washington State – the Perfect Climate for Wine".

Tampa, Florida, was chosen for a 12-week blitz of print, radio, and outdoor advertisements, along with trade tastings and Washington wine-themed promotions. Calling it an "overwhelming success", Robin Pollard, the Commission's executive director, pointed to a 45 per cent increase in Washington wine sales in the region following the campaign. Follow-up efforts are planned for the coming year.

Less successful was the Department of Tourism's effort to come up with a suitable slogan for the state. "Say WA" – the numbingly stupid result of a year's worth of test marketing and a budget close to $1 million – sank without trace shortly after it was introduced to a thoroughly puzzled public. The fact is that what Washington State needs, apart from enlightened liquor laws, is more, much more, of the amenities that make California wine touring so popular.

Until five years ago you couldn't find a decent meal in Walla Walla, the epicentre of eastern Washington wine touring. Quality lodging is equally rare and sells out months in advance. There are virtually no tasting rooms anywhere in Washington with good selections of wines from multiple wineries. Want to do an appellation-focused tasting room? Forget it – the law won't allow it. Want to have a restaurant in your tasting room? Sorry, can't do that either. If Washington wants to bring in tourists, it has to offer major-league attractions, and the place to begin is by taking off the legal handcuffs on doing basic business. The great wines are here already, and consumers are eager to explore this beautiful, unspoiled wine country. The state needs to get out of its own way.

Sink the ark!

The world needs more quality wines at everyday prices, not more wines named after critters, vehicles, and other gimmicks. Finding sound, flavourful wines in the lower price ranges is the hardest challenge any wine writer faces. Many frogs must be kissed (along with emus, roosters, kangaroos, jackaroos, crocodiles, cockatoos, swans, loons, penguins, fish, and koala bears) before you uncover a prince or princess.

Whether a wine is named after a critter, a river, a little black dress, or a tree stump matters little to me. What I want for my six or eight bucks is really quite simple. If a wine is labelled Chardonnay, it should taste like Chardonnay, not like microwave popcorn or vanilla syrup. If it is labelled Merlot, it should taste like something (with cheap Merlot, you tend to be grateful for almost any flavour at all). If it is going to call itself Syrah (or Shiraz) or Cabernet, well, it had better be an honest representation of those glorious grapes.

So, enough with the critter wines, oh corporate marketing mavens! Instead of hunting for the next cute animal label, think what kind of success you could have if you spent the marketing money on improving the actual wine. Don't believe me? Pick up a bottle of Precept's House

Wine. It sells hundreds of thousands of cases. Charles Smith scribbled the label idea on a napkin (I was there). It has no animal, no story, and no primary crayon colours (in fact, no colours at all). Just good wine at a good price. That's what really sells.

Quick shots across the bow (and barrel)

Let's get serious about defining and/or limiting the use of the term "Reserve" on wine labels. Certainly there is no more abused, misleading, and frequently worthless adjective on a wine label than "Reserve" – unless you already know and trust the reputation of the producer. The Washington Wine Quality Alliance (WWQA), a voluntary organization of wineries and grape growers, has set out guidelines for its members. Among them: reserve wines must be among the higher-priced wines produced by the winery and can apply only to the greater of 3,000 cases or 10 per cent of the winery's production of the given variety or blend. A good start, and one that California, with industrial wineries churning out hundreds of thousands of cases of reserve this and that, might wish to emulate.

Lose the plastic corks! Is there anything more ugly and off-putting than some lime-green, lemon-yellow, or hot-pink piece of plastic in your wine bottle, even if it is designed to match the lime-green lizard, lemon-yellow truck, or hot-pink babe on the label? These plastic monstrosities are not just ugly, they're almost impossible to remove, and good luck trying to force one back in once you've pried it loose! Dump the plastic and switch to screwcaps – or better yet, use the gorgeous glass stoppers being employed by Oregon's Sineann winery.

Stop shipping wines in Styrofoam. There are plenty of recyclable alternatives. Styrofoam is clogging up our oceans and consuming more and more landfill. The wine industry, which has dedicated itself to organic practices, sustainable viticulture, environmental sensitivity, and wildlife preservation, should make every effort to reduce, if not eliminate, the use of Styrofoam for its packaging.

Grapevine

• **Due to open soon** is a combination Novelty Hill/Januik Winery in the burgeoning Woodinville wine district, just outside Seattle. Mike Januik is the winemaker for both wineries, which have shared production facilities since Novelty Hill was established in 2000. The new 3,000-sq-m (33,000-sq-ft) facility is adjacent to Columbia Winery and across from Ste Michelle.

Vintage Report

Advance report on the latest harvest
2006

Washington – A cool, wet spring and late budbreak were followed by a long, warm summer with close to record-setting heat accumulations in the warmest sites. The harvest began very early, with some white grapes being picked in late August. A cool spell in mid-September slowed things down and allowed for more hang time for black grapes, but a late October freeze caught some wineries flat-footed. If they waited too long to pick, they found trouble. Overall, acids are up a bit from 2005 and crop levels are moderate. Look for exceptional white wines and dark, muscular, ageworthy reds.

Oregon – A warm, dry growing season throughout Oregon allowed growers to increase yields and maintain quality. September brought heat spikes to some sites, then intermittent rains and cooler weather overall, compressing the harvest. Quality in the Willamette Valley will be site-dependent. Winemakers are calling it a combination of 1998's ripeness and 1999's depth and three-dimensionality. In eastern Oregon's Columbia Gorge, Columbia Valley, and Walla Walla Valley AVAs, the vintage mirrored Washington's.

Updates on the previous five vintages
2005

Vintage rating: *Washington – Red: 94, White: 92; Oregon – Red: 90, White: 88*

Washington – An unusually long harvest led to extra hang time and fully ripe tannins. Warm sites (Wahluke Slope, Red Mountain) fared especially well. Whites are plump, juicy, and balanced. The reds are luscious, rich, and textural; yields are down, flavour concentration way up. The best vintage since 1999, and more accessible early on.

Oregon – A late, cool, rather wet vintage yielded finished wines with less alcohol than in recent hot years. The reds are light and fragrant, with plenty of natural acidity. For Pinot Noir, the vintage marks a welcome return to finesse and elegance. Eastern Oregon sites in the Columbia Gorge and Walla Walla Valley AVAs had an exceptional vintage in line with Washington's.

2004

Vintage rating: *Washington – Red: 84, White: 78;*
Oregon – Red: 90, White: 84

Washington – A severe January freeze wiped out most Walla Walla grapes. Elsewhere, a very hot summer turned cool and wet at harvest, causing rot problems and making what began as a very early vintage into one of the latest on record. The best producers made excellent, concentrated red wines, especially Merlot, Syrah, and Cabernet, but more generic bottlings are spotty. White-wine grapes were more prone to rot.

Oregon – A difficult start led to dramatically reduced yields. The best Pinots show ripeness, fine colour, bright raspberry and mulberry fruit, and complex, elegant flavours.

2003

Vintage rating: *Washington – Red: 90, White: 88;*
Oregon – Red: 86, White: 86

Washington – A dry, scorching-hot summer cooled off during harvest. White wines are ripe and fruity, with forward, precocious flavours and lower acid levels. Merlot shows superb colour, complexity, and balance. Cabernet Sauvignons are dark and concentrated; Syrahs are packed with juicy fruit.

Oregon – A cold, wet spring; a brutal July heat wave; cold, wet weather at harvest; and finally a late-season heat wave! Red wines are deeply extracted, ripe and tannic, but blocky and one-dimensional, with high levels of alcohol.

Grapevine

• **The North Prosser Business Park,** a 32-acre "wine village" currently under development, debuted in 2006. It is already home to more than a dozen wineries, including Yakima Valley stalwarts such as Willow Crest and Thurston Wolfe, and newcomers Olsen Estates, Bunnell Family Cellar, and Milbrandt Winery. The Olsen and Milbrandt families, both experienced growers with substantial vineyard holdings, are part of an encouraging trend in Washington: grape growers moving into winemaking.

• **Washington's eighth AVA** is the Wahluke Slope, a hot-climate growing area located in central eastern Washington. The region's best-known vineyards belong to the Milbrandt brothers, who will be opening their own winery in 2007. Many of the state's smallest boutiques purchase grapes from one or more of their vineyards, which are especially noted for their ripe, citrous Syrahs.

• **The next two Washington AVAs** likely to be officially designated are Lake Chelan (in north-central Washington) and Ancient Lakes, east of Wenatchee. Both regions have applications currently on file with the federal government. Lake Chelan is home to more than 15 wineries, whose tasting rooms and newly planted vineyards surround the lake, a favourite tourist destination.

2002

Vintage rating: *Washington – Red: 88, White: 90; Oregon – Red: 78, White: 86*

Washington – A record crop with high sugars, high acidity, and high extract. The white wines were juicy and crisp; the reds immediately accessible and loaded with bright, fresh fruit flavours. Not for keeping.

Oregon – A cold, wet year. Many Pinots are ungenerous and unyielding, with strong scents of tomato leaf and beetroot, and earthy, hard tannins.

2001

Vintage rating: *Washington – Red: 92, White: 90; Oregon – Red: 89, White: 87*

Washington – Red wines are structured to age well over the medium term; they are stylistically midway between the classic, austere 1999s and the broadly fruity 2000s. The white wines are unusually ripe and tropical. Drink up.

Oregon – The best reserve and single-vineyard Pinots can continue to improve, but many of the 2001s were soft, forward, and simple. Drink up.

GREATEST WINE PRODUCERS

1. Quilceda Creek (Washington)
2. Leonetti Cellar (Washington)
3. Cayuse (Washington)
4. DeLille (Washington)
5. Betz Family (Washington)
6. Sineann (Oregon, Washington)
7. Andrew Will (Washington)
8. Cadence (Washington)
9. Beaux Frères (Oregon)
10. Cristom (Oregon)

FASTEST-IMPROVING PRODUCERS

1. J Bookwalter (Washington)
2. K Vintners (Washington)
3. Three Rivers (Washington)
4. Rex Hill (Oregon)

5. Dunham Cellars (Washington)
6. Pepper Bridge (Washington)
7. Woodward Canyon (Washington)
8. Reininger (Washington)
9. Chateau Ste Michelle (Washington)
10. Boudreaux Cellars (Washington)

NEW UP-AND-COMING PRODUCERS

1. Fielding Hills (Washington)
2. Buty (Washington)
3. Mark Ryan (Washington)
4. Abeja (Washington)
5. Syncline (Washington)
6. Fidélitas (Washington)
7. Gorman (Washington)
8. Lachini (Oregon)
9. Beresan (Washington)
10. Scott Paul (Oregon)

BEST-VALUE PRODUCERS

1. Columbia Crest Two Vines (Washington)
2. Barnard Griffin (Washington)
3. Columbia Crest Grand Estates (Washington)
4. L'Ecole No 41 (Washington)
5. Townshend (Washington)
6. Covey Run (Washington)
7. Owen Roe (Oregon, Washington)
8. Snoqualmie (Washington)
9. Balboa (Washington)
10. Rulo (Washington)

GREATEST-QUALITY WINES

1. **Cabernet Sauvignon 2003** Quilceda Creek, Washington ($95)
2. **Armada Vineyard Syrah 2003** Cayuse, Washington ($65)
3. **Reserve Red 2003** Leonetti Cellar, Washington ($100)
4. **Cabernet Sauvignon 2004** Fielding Hills, Washington ($30)
5. **Abbott Claim Vineyard Pinot Noir 2005** Ken Wright, Oregon ($50)
6. **Annie Camarda Syrah 2002** Andrew Will, Washington ($58)
7. **Ethos Syrah 2003** Chateau Ste Michelle, Washington ($29)
8. **La Cote Rousse Syrah 2004** Betz Family, Washington ($45)
9. **Dead Horse Red 2004** Mark Ryan, Washington ($42)
10. **Chaleur Estate Blanc 2005** DeLille, Washington ($33)

BEST BARGAINS

1. **Riesling 2005** J Bookwalter, Washington ($16)
2. **Oak Ridge Vineyard Gewurztraminer 2005** Sineann, Oregon ($18)
3. **Semillon/Sauvignon Blanc 2005** Buty, Washington ($21)
4. **Viognier 2004** Townshend, Washington ($10)
5. **Meritage White Wine 2005** Three Rivers, Washington ($19)
6. **Semillon 2005** L'Ecole No 41, Washington ($15)
7. **Snapdragon White Blend 2005** Isenhower, Washington ($18)
8. **Pinot Gris 2005** Ponzi, Oregon ($17)
9. **In The Buff Chardonnay 2005** Wineglass Cellars, Washington ($13)
10. **Cabernet Sauvignon 2005** Balboa, Washington ($16)

MOST EXCITING OR UNUSUAL FINDS

1. **Bionic Frog Syrah 2004** Cayuse, Washington ($65) *Certified biodynamic, Cayuse makes in-your-face wines with a full complement of what vigneron Christophe Baron calls "good funk". Wild herb, beef blood, and silage aromas enhance a thick and meaty Syrah, lifted and intriguing all through the long finish, which keeps adding new scents and flavours as it sails along.*

2. **Camerata Red Wine 2004** Cadence, Washington ($50) *This is a beautiful rendition of 100 per cent Cabernet Sauvignon from a single Red Mountain vineyard – Tapteil. It shows the power of the grape, the structural verticality, the austerity – yet it is ripe enough to stand alone and shine.*

3. **Cuvée Elena Grenache/ Mourvèdre/Syrah 2004** Syncline, Washington ($35) *A southern-Rhône-inspired blend of Grenache, Mourvèdre, and Syrah, the Cuvée Elena has great concentration, and a tarry, jammy mid-palate that pushes the fruit into maximum richness and intensity.*

❹ **Old Vine Zinfandel 2005** Sineann, Oregon ($36) *This perennial favourite, from century-old vines, is more restrained in this vintage, the alcohol down to a welcome 14.8 per cent. Complex, soft, plummy fruit carries itself with the grace of old vines, which quietly show a winning bouquet of scents and lightly liquorous flavours, laden with plums, cherries, dates, and figs.*

❺ **Dry White Riesling 2005** Woodward Canyon, Washington ($25) *Woodward Canyon makes very little Riesling, but what it makes is wonderful. Dense and powerful, this bone-dry Riesling (from DuBrul vineyard grapes) strikes me as Australian in style, the perfect pairing of New World fruit and an almost austere minerality. It shows what elegance Washington Riesling can achieve when handled properly from vineyard to vat.*

❻ **Bésoleil Red Wine 2004** Betz Family, Washington ($40) *A Grenache-based blend that includes 19 per cent Mourvèdre and 12 per cent Syrah. It's a sure sign of the resurgence of Grenache in Washington vineyards, which all but eliminated the cold-sensitive grape a decade ago. The interest in all things Rhône-ish has brought it back.*

❼ **Roussanne 2005** Doyenne, Washington ($31) *This is pure Roussanne from Red Mountain's Ciel du Cheval vineyard. Fresh, juicy, and ripe, it is bursting with floral scents and citrous acids, along with sweet honeysuckle and juicy lime. Another indication that Washington is the true home of the West Coast Rhône Rangers.*

❽ **Fries Vineyard Semillon 2005** L'Ecole No 41, Washington ($20) *Semillon is probably the least-known great grape in Washington, usually relegated to some cheap table-wine blend. L'Ecole treats it right, bottling three different versions: this one is best of all, with bright, rich, and polished fruit, tasting of figs, melon, and white peaches.*

❾ **Counoise 2003** Morrison Lane, Washington ($25) *Counoise? Though best known (if at all) as a minor ingredient in Châteauneuf-du-Pape, it's a surprise winner in Washington, making a deliciously spicy wine with light fruits running from watermelon to strawberry to plum.*

❿ **Cuvée M White Table Wine 2005** Ribbon Ridge, Oregon ($20) *This fascinating white wine is two-thirds Chardonnay, the rest a beguiling blend of Pinot Blanc, Auxerrois, Ehrenfelser, Scheurebe, Sylvaner, and Ruländer! The Alsatian grapes were planted 20 years ago as the owner's "personal" vines. They add wonderful tangy, peppery flavours reminiscent of Grüner Veltliner.*

Atlantic Northeast

Sandra Silfven

The big story for this region is about all the money and expertise pouring into new and established wineries, as well as the wines that prove these steps are paying off.

SANDRA SILFVEN

A home-grown Sonoma-style Cabernet Sauvignon from Indiana (Oliver), a sweepstakes-winning dry Riesling from Ohio (Ferrante), and an Alsace-style dry Gewurztraminer from Michigan (Peninsula Cellars) are proof that the region is serious about quality (see the Top 10 lists).

In Virginia, former Washington Redskins president John Kent Cooke and his wife Rita opened Boxwood in Middleburg, employing architect Hugh Newell Jacobsen, viticulturist Lucie Morton, and oenology icon Dr Richard Vine. The seriously financed Acorn Hill Farm also opened in Virginia, and Crossing Vineyards in Bucks County, Pennsylvania. On New York's Long Island, Bedell owner Michael Lynne remodelled the winemaking facility and hired John Irving Levenberg from Paul Hobbs Winery in Sonoma as winemaker. He also hired Pascal Marty as consulting oenologist. Marty also consults for Pine Ridge in Napa, which would lead one to guess (nobody is talking) that his expertise is being tapped for development of the Broadfields and Charles John vineyards on Long Island, owned by Leucadia National Corp, the parent company of Pine Ridge. Leucadia shocked the locals by removing thousands of grapevines to replant at a much higher density. Levenberg explains: "Higher density is where we should be going, because, unlike California, this is a region with plenty of water, and you want the vines to be competing for water."

SANDRA SILFVEN lives in Dearborn, Michigan, and has worked in reporting and editing positions at *The Detroit News* for more than 30 years. She has written about wine for most of her career, and she produces the **Michigan Wine Report** for Detroit News Online (www.detroitnews.com/wine).

Champagne master Claude Thibaut is not only consulting for Andrew Hodson at Veritas in Virginia, but making a Virginia *blanc de blancs* under the Thibaut & Janisson label, with partner Manuel Janisson. Thibaut says that he sees good potential for sparkling-wine production from Chardonnay grapes in Virginia, but world-class? Thibaut reminds you that he started the production of J for Jordan and consulted for Iron Horse when nobody believed in Sonoma County.

In Maryland, where sales of state wines in 2006 were up 18 per cent versus 2 per cent for all wines, two properties were raising eyebrows: the new Sugarloaf Mountain, with Morton consulting and UC Davis grad Carl DiManno making the wine; and Black Ankle, where Morton and Bordeaux's Lucien Guillemet were consulting.

Grapevine

• **In New York,** Cornell University oenologist for 19 years and Riesling champion Dr Thomas Henick-Kling left to become the new director of the National Wine and Grape Industry Centre at Charles Sturt University in New South Wales, Australia. Also, Dr G Stanley Howell retired. He shepherded the Michigan wineries during the 37 years he spent in the horticulture department at Michigan State University.

• **In Virginia,** South African Stephen Barnard is back making wine at Keswick after a short stint at Rappahannock Cellars, where he grabbed the 2006 Virginia Governor's Cup for Rappahannock's 2005 Viognier Reserve. Andy Reagan moved from Chrysalis in the north to Jefferson Vineyards in Charlottesville, and Mark Bunter, with a wealth of California experience, replaced him at Chrysalis. Miguel Martin of Spain joined Palmer in New York.

• **Three new grape varieties,** developed and tested by Bruce Reisch and Thomas Henick-Kling of Cornell University in Geneva, NY, were rolled out: Noiret and Corot Noir (black) and Valvin Muscat (white).

• **Icewine production** all over the northeast and Ontario was stalled by the warm November and December in 2006. Wineries, including Mazza in Pennsylvania and Ferrante in Ohio, grabbed a window of opportunity in mid-January 2007 to pick what was a greatly reduced harvest.

• **Jim Trezise,** president of the New York Grape & Wine Foundation since its inception in 1985, was presented with the Wine Industry Integrity Award by the Lodi-Woodbridge Winegrape Commission, an honour that doesn't often go outside the West Coast.

• **Wölffer Estate winemaker** and general manager Roman Roth earned raves for the roll-out of his own brand, The Grapes of Roth, with aged, unfiltered, select lots of Merlot from Long Island's North Fork.

• **Michigan's Bryan Ulbrich** left Peninsula Cellars to devote his attention to his own label, Left Foot Charley, opening a winery and tasting room in Traverse City.

FALLOUT FROM SHIPPING RULING

The 2005 US Supreme Court ruling on interstate shipping forced states to readdress their alcohol laws and gave wholesalers a chance to increase their foothold. Virginia wineries, with lawmakers under pressure from wholesalers, initially lost their right to self-distribute to local shops and restaurants. Now they are sorting out a convoluted law that lets them self-distribute 3,000 cases a year if they first sell the wines to a "virtual" distributor set up in the Virginia Department of Agriculture. New Jersey and Indiana lost the right to self-distribute. Maryland lets small in-state and out-of-state wineries (those producing fewer than 11,500 cases) sell directly to restaurants and retailers. Massachusetts adopted similar legislation. Pennsylvania wineries kept their right to own satellite stores and self-distribute, but at this writing, they were unsure how the forced resignation of Jonathan Newman would affect them. Newman was the celebrated chairman of the Pennsylvania Liquor Control Board who streamlined the wine-buying experience for consumers.

LEGEND DIES

Willy K Frank, son of vinifera pioneer Dr Konstantin Frank and a giant in the northeast in his own right, suffered a stroke and died unexpectedly on 7 March 2006, at the age of 80, on a sales trip to Florida. Beloved for his gregarious personality and workaholic creed, he had run Dr Frank Vinifera Wine Cellars in Hammondsport, NY, since 1985. He was responsible for streamlining the business, narrowing the focus from his father's 60 wines to a dozen or so. Frank also founded Chateau Frank, a separate label and facility for sparkling-wine production.

Other notables who will be missed: Charles L "Monty" Stamp, founder of Lakewood Vineyards in New York and a pillar of that state's wine industry; Dr Thomas Quilter, a champion of the Ohio wine industry at Shamrock Vineyards; entrepreneur Joseph Zafarana of Zafarana Vineyards in Michigan, whose generosity to his community was on a par with his passion for wine; and Ray Blum of Ackerly Pond, founder of Peconic Bay Winery and one of the biggest growers on Long Island, New York.

Grapevine

• **New York wineries** in the Finger Lakes and Long Island have banded together to create signature wines that typify their terroir. Tierce Dry Riesling is made by Anthony Road, Red Newt, and Fox Run in the Finger Lakes; Merliance is a Merlot by Pellegrini, Raphael, Sherwood House, Shinn, and Wölffer on Long Island.

• **Benmarl,** founded in 1957 in Marlboro, NY, by Mark Miller, who helped father the modern New York wine industry, was sold to Victor and Barbara Spaccarelli, who have overhauled the winemaking facility and put in more vineyards to preserve the historic brand. Eric Miller, owner of Chaddsford near Philadelphia, is Mark Miller's son.

• **Windham Winery in Virginia,** which was sued by Wyndham Estate Winery in Australia, has changed its name to Doukenie, which is Greek for "duchess".

Opinion:
Web-smart

My annual rant about overoaked whites, reds released too young, untamed viticulture, and lack of marketing savvy plays on. But many of these problems are being addressed in multistate conferences and on the university level, at schools such as Cornell in New York, Ohio State, Penn State, and Purdue in Indiana. The east has indeed awakened to the economic impact of this industry, but there's another wrinkle now: e-commerce. With the new and growing business of selling wine over the Internet, wineries can no longer be lax about outdated, visually unappealing, slow-to-load, too-tricky, or too-lame websites. Michigan's Larry Mawby says a website can no longer be just a billboard: "It has to be interactive and give people information before they even ask a question. It used to be that your label was the most important selling point. Now it's your website." Sakonnet in Rhode Island already sells 20 per cent of its production online.

Recognizing the value of e-commerce, the New York State Department of Agriculture & Markets awarded 114 wineries grants of up to $2,500 for the purchase of age-verification software, shopping-cart and online payment processing programs, and assistance with graphics.

Wineries getting it right include: Rhode Island's sakonnetwine.com, for its details (not just price, but number of cases produced, and alcohol and residual-sugar levels); Pennsylvania's valavineyards.com, for its depth of content, visual appeal, and humour; and Virginia's veritaswines.com, for speed, easy purchasing system, and the food and tourism components.

It's an old gimmick in the newspaper business: a story has to have multiple points of entry to grab readers – from maps to information boxes. It's the same for winery websites. They're the perfect place to beef up interest in a wine club and newsletter. Why not start a blog, too?

Grapevine

- **Massachusetts voters,** in autumn 2006, rejected an initiative to allow wine sales in supermarkets. As archaic as the issues sound, apparently voters were swayed by pitches that supermarket sales would increase illegal purchases by minors and add to car accidents, and that "package" liquor stores did a better job of policing sales. It was the most expensive ballot issue in the state's history.

- **The new Frederick Cellars** in Maryland purchased Catoctin Vineyards and moved the operation to a historic ice house in downtown Frederick. Robert Lyon, who founded Catoctin in 1982, stays as winemaker.

Vintage Report

Advance report on the latest harvest

2006

The winter was mild, but a cold snap in April damaged vineyards in Michigan, Ohio, and New York. The growing season was plagued by humidity and rain, as well as temperatures that were cooler than usual. Spraying and leaf-pulling were mandatory. Whites appear excellent for aromatics, acidity, and fruit expression, while reds were more difficult, with much blending and other cellar work expected. New York finally saw a fairly large crop after two years of light harvests.

Updates on the previous five vintages

2005

Vintage rating: *Red: 92, White: 90*
One of the best vintages in the past 10–15 years. It was superb across the region because of the long, hot summer and autumn. Whites were riper and richer than usual (atypical for the region); reds were a joy, with sugars higher than usual, wonderful tannic structure, and upfront fruit.

2004

Vintage rating: *Red: 85, White: 89*
In a smaller-than-average vintage with challenges from the weather, the whites are exciting, with bracing acidity and enough fruit to carry the day. Reds are on the lighter side.

2003

Vintage rating: *Red: 74, White: 88*
It was a small vintage that yielded some stunning, crisp whites, but reds had low sugars, diluted acids, and light tannins. Many were declassified.

2002

Vintage rating: *Red: 90, White: 94*

Most states, with the exception of Virginia and New York's Finger Lakes, were thrilled with the quality of all the whites and, almost uniformly in the northeast, the reds. Flavours are rich and intense for whites, concentrated with balanced acids for reds.

2001

Vintage rating: *Red: 92, White: 94*

Except for New Jersey, which was deluged with rain at harvest, this was an excellent vintage for both reds and whites. Fruit, tannins, and wood are integrating nicely in the premium Cabs and Merlots.

GREATEST WINE PRODUCERS

1. Dr Konstantin Frank (New York)
2. Bedell (New York)
3. Wölffer (New York)
4. Lenz (New York)
5. Paumanok (New York)
6. L Mawby (Michigan)
7. Linden (Virginia)
8. Barboursville (Virginia)
9. Chaddsford (Pennsylvania)
10. Sakonnet (Rhode Island)

NEW UP-AND-COMING PRODUCERS

1. Brys Estate (Michigan)
2. Longview (Michigan)
3. Mastropietro (Ohio)
4. Thirsty Owl (New York)
5. Crossing (Pennsylvania)
6. Maize Valley (Ohio)
7. Delfosse (Virginia)
8. Chateau O'Brien (Virginia)
9. St Michaels (Maryland)
10. Silver Decoy (New Jersey)

FASTEST-IMPROVING PRODUCERS

1. Heron Hill (New York)
2. Ferrante (Ohio)
3. Anthony Road (New York)
4. Ravines (New York)
5. Veritas (Virginia)
6. Chateau Chantal (Michigan)
7. Kinkead Ridge (Ohio)
8. Shady Lane (Michigan)
9. Manatawny Creek (Pennsylvania)
10. Flickerwood (Pennsylvania)

BEST-VALUE PRODUCERS

1. Firelands (Ohio)
2. Fox Run (New York)
3. Leelanau Cellars (Michigan)
4. Lakewood (New York)
5. Domaine Berrien Cellars (Michigan)
6. Pinnacle Ridge (Pennsylvania)
7. Debonne (Ohio)
8. Tomasello (New Jersey)
9. Mount Nittany (Pennsylvania)
10. Terra Cotta (Ohio)

GREATEST-QUALITY WINES

1. **Riesling Reserve 2005** Dr Konstantin Frank, New York ($30)
2. **Old Vines Merlot 2001** Lenz, New York ($55)
3. **Merlot 2001** The Grapes of Roth, New York ($50)
4. **Manigold Vineyard Gewurztraminer 2005** Peninsula Cellars, Michigan ($20)
5. **Cabernet Sauvignon Grand Vintage 2002** Paumanok, New York ($39)
6. **Creekbend Vineyard Cabernet Sauvignon 2004** Oliver Winery, Indiana ($40)
7. **Cabernet Franc 2005** Linden, Virginia ($27)
8. **Ingle Vineyard Riesling 2005** Heron Hill, New York ($25)
9. **Cabernet Franc 2004** Kinkead Ridge, Ohio ($17)
10. **Merican 2002** Chaddsford, Pennsylvania ($40)

BEST BARGAINS

1. **Whole Cluster Riesling 2005** Chateau Grand Traverse, Michigan ($13)
2. **Vidal Blanc Ice Wine 2005** Tomasello, New Jersey ($18)
3. **Cabernet Sauvignon 2003** Firelands, Ohio ($11)
4. **Chambourcin 2005** Pinnacle Ridge, Pennsylvania ($12)
5. **Viognier 2005** Bellview, New Jersey ($14)
6. **Seyval/Chardonnay NV** Chateau Lafayette Reneau, New York ($9)
7. **Ballet of Angels NV** Sharpe Hill, Connecticut ($12)
8. **Vidal Blanc 2005** Sakonnet, Rhode Island ($11)
9. **White Catawba 2005** Lakewood, New York ($7)
10. **Riesling 2005** Debonne, Ohio ($9)

MOST EXCITING OR UNUSUAL FINDS

1. **Blanc de Blancs 1999** Chateau Frank, New York ($35) *The best sparkling wine I tasted from the northeast – a fitting tribute to the late Willy Frank.*
2. **Martini-Reinhardt Selection Riesling 2005** Anthony Road, New York ($26) *Incredible Pfalz style, with structure and minerality.*
3. **Taste White 2005** Bedell, New York ($25) *Bold – from the label to the flavours, a blend of Chardonnay, Gewurztraminer, Viognier, and Riesling. It has tremendous aromatics and structure.*
4. **Meritage 2005** Ravines, New York ($25) *Flavour intensity that matches the human intensity of owner-vintner Morten Halgren. I'd like to taste it five years from now.*
5. **Meditazione 2004** Channing Daughters, New York ($40) *Not many wineries have the grapes or guts to try such an exotic, dry, full-bodied, aromatic blend (seven white varieties fermented together), inspired by Italy's vino da meditazione.*
6. **Marsanne 2005** Domaine Berrien Cellars, Michigan ($15) *A rarity in the USA, let alone Michigan, and it's impressive.*
7. **Meritage 2005** King Family, Virginia ($25) *So ripe and jammy, you'd think the fruit came from Alexander Valley.*
8. **Chambourcin 2005** Keswick, Virginia ($17) *Big, spicy, oaky, jammy hybrid behaves like a Zinfandel.*
9. **Petit Verdot 2005** Veritas, Virginia ($25) *Truly a standout for ripe fruit, elegance, and supple tannins.*
10. **Dry Riesling Golden Bunches 2005** Ferrante, Ohio ($15) *Finally, an Ohio Riesling, a dry one at that, ready for the world stage.*

Other US States

Doug Frost MW

With each of the 50 states enacting its own individual set of laws at the end of Prohibition in 1934, it was all but inevitable that legislative chaos would prevail.

DOUG FROST MW

And in the wake of the Granholm v. Heald case, in which the Supreme Court held that at least some of these laws discriminate against wineries in other states, it was equally inevitable that individual solutions would be just as messy. However, hardly any states had the same system before Granholm and at least some are now collaborating, if only to quell the increasing number of lawsuits that numerous states are facing.

Kansas has created a particularly bizarre set of new rules. Consumers there are now welcome to have wines shipped directly to their homes, provided that they have visited the winery. Kansas consumers can purchase wines from wineries that they haven't physically visited, as long as the winery buys a Kansas licence and produces no more than 380,000 litres of wine annually. The winery will send the wine to a Kansas retailer, who will then pay applicable taxes. If the winery produces in excess of 380,000 litres annually, the consumer must arrange for the winery to buy a different licence from the state, then deliver the wine to a wholesaler, who will then deliver it to the consumer's specified retailer for pick-up and payment of taxes.

Perhaps the consortium of wholesalers, retailers, and legislators who dreamed up this Byzantine pathway might be able to explain it without breaking into laughter, but it's hard to believe that even those individuals actually believe it's a reasonable solution. The notion of treating wineries differently based on their size is a barely concealed attempt to continue

DOUG FROST MW is the author of two wine books, including *On Wine* (Rizzoli International Publications, 2001). He is one of only three people in the world to hold the titles of both Master Sommelier and Master of Wine.

the practice Granholm abolished: allowing in-state wineries to be encouraged and out-of-state wineries to be prohibited.

Doug Caskey of the Colorado Wine Industry Development Board defends his state's decision to allow only wineries producing less than 76,000 litres to ship into the state directly. "The economic reality is that large wineries can afford to navigate the spiffs and expenditures of the three-tier system. Just because few states have wineries that produce more than 20,000 gallons annually, or whatever number a state uses to define a small winery, imposing size limits on direct shipment or self-distribution is not an attempt to inhibit trade. It is an acknowledgment that we are not starting with a level playing field."

Admissions such as this, that new regulations are intended to provide an economic advantage to a state's wineries and to disadvantage wineries from outside the state, indicate why these laws are likely to be overturned. The entire thrust of Granholm was that a state cannot provide an advantage to its own wineries if doing so prevents competitors in other states from fairly accessing the marketplace.

Tracy Genesen, legal counsel for the Coalition for Free Trade and one of the lawyers who successfully brought the Granholm case to the Supreme Court, was asked if she thought the Kansas law would pass muster. "I would love to mount a legal challenge to the Kansas direct shipping law," she responded. "The problem is that the wine industry does not take on all of the irrational and discriminatory laws that exist out there. They tend to choose those egregious state laws in bigger markets."

Grapevine

• **Illinois's first AVA** was approved in December 2006. Shawnee Hills AVA in southern Illinois is a 20-mile ridge bounded by the Ohio and Mississippi rivers. There are 15 wineries in the AVA, and the quality of the wines from the region seems to bode well for the future.

• **The Kansas State Fair** will sell Kansas wine by the glass in July 2007 for the first time in the state's history, a dramatic improvement in a state that was once ardently opposed to alcohol.

• **About 40 small wineries** have opened in Kentucky, some with help from tobacco settlement money

distributed by the state Agriculture Development Board. Some of these wineries have been built by growers who themselves have turned away from tobacco towards grapes.

• **The University of Minnesota** continues to play an invaluable part in the creation of cold-hardy hybrids. The school's advisers are now recommending primarily four grapes: Frontenac (a consistently productive black grape), Frontenac Gris (a lighter-coloured and peachy mutation), La Crescent (an extremely hardy and aromatic white), and Marquette (a promising black variety).

THE STATE OF THE UNION

The 30 states covered in this chapter all select from a menu of potential solutions, but with many existing obstacles, US wine legislation is still a crazy quilt. Here is a guide to the rules in the rest of the USA.

Alabama: Recently adopted direct sales and distribution for the state's own wineries, in effect allowing its wineries to act as retailers. Some legal minds believe that the state is likely to become a target of lawsuits from both out-of-state wineries and retailers. Otherwise, the state allows direct shipping, provided that a consumer obtains the prior consent of the Alcohol Beverage Commission (fat chance) and has the wine shipped to a state store.

Alaska: Allows direct sales and distribution to consumers in most communities in the state, but most areas of the state aren't served by the state-mandated common carriers.

Arizona: Utilizes some of the Kansas methodology; the state allows consumers to ship to themselves if they have physically purchased the wine at a winery. A new law allows direct shipping only for wineries producing less than 76,000 litres annually. Michigan's high-quality Black Star Farms is suing to change that rule.

Arkansas: Has yet to confront reality. Only in-state wineries and retailers are allowed to ship to the state's residents, but a lawsuit has challenged that. The solution is still in play; wholesalers are suing to prevent all direct shipping, including by the state's wineries. The wholesalers lost the suit in August 2006 but are appealing, and direct shipping is still banned under a court-imposed two-year stay. Arkansas wineries retain the right to ship during that stay, but consumers are still prevented from bringing wines into the state themselves. Violation of the law stipulates up to 90 days in jail for any wine-fixated Arkansans.

Colorado: Has offered a permit since July 2006 that allows all non-Colorado wineries to ship to its consumers directly. Wineries must pay excise taxes on a monthly basis. A physical visit to the winery is no longer required, and there are no quantity limits. These requirements appear to be moving towards relaxed enforcement.

Florida: Since August 2005, the Florida Division of Alcoholic Beverages and Tobacco has been enjoined from enforcing any of the direct shipping laws. Consumers are expected to self-report taxes owed, and wineries are expected to calculate and pay excise taxes monthly. But Southern's servants in the Florida House have passed a bill that allows limited direct shipping except for wineries producing more than 100,000 cases per year.

Georgia: Allows consumers to ship limited amounts of wine to themselves as long as they have physically visited the winery from which they purchased the wine. Wineries with no representation in the state are allowed to purchase a special shipping licence from the state to facilitate direct sales. However, Georgia is also host to some of the most Draconian franchise rules: the state allows wineries little freedom in ending a wholesaler relationship regardless of the wholesaler's incompetence or inactivity.

Idaho: Now issues shipping permits to wineries outside the state. The law is relatively liberal, though the state offers little flexibility to wineries currently represented by wholesalers.

Illinois: In flux. Thus far, the state has remained wedded to the concept of reciprocity. Once the only method by which consumers were legally able to enjoy the benefits of direct shipping, reciprocity (in which certain states allow other states to direct ship, so long as each is open to the other) is now discredited as a result of readings of Granholm. Near the end of 2006, an Italian winery brought suit to extend the impact of Granholm to foreign wineries. The fortunes of that suit seem dubious, especially in a state so closely controlled by wholesale forces.

Iowa: Notion of reciprocity still holds. While the common wisdom is that Granholm vacated the principle of reciprocity, Iowa legislators recently held that there was a "consensus" that reciprocity was still an effective means of handling multistate wine commerce. As if.

Kansas: See main body of text above.

Kentucky: After drafting laws that allowed consumers to ship wines only if they had visited the winery from which the wine was shipped, the state has done an about-face. As of January 2007, the state has created out-of-state licences for wineries. Like other states, Kentucky restricts the permits to "small farm wineries" or those that produce no more than 190,000 litres annually.

Louisiana: Allows for shipping permits to out-of-state wineries, as long as they are not currently represented by any wholesaler. And consumers are allowed to ship wine to themselves, as long as they are present at the winery when they purchase it. But in order to protect itself against the possible impact of the Costco case, the state has ended sales by in-state wineries to the state's consumers.

Minnesota: Prior to a court ruling of April 2006, the state prevented out-of-state wineries from even communicating with consumers via the Web. But, as a result of Granholm and other cases, the state is fairly wide open to direct shipping and sales.

Mississippi: Remains one of the few places where direct shipping is prohibited by every means. In-state wineries have no direct access to consumers, and state-controlled stores handle all wine sales.

Missouri: Retains its reciprocal status, though reciprocity as a concept is probably negated by Granholm. California's Rafanelli winery and one Indiana winery and retailer have sued for wider access to the state marketplace. With Missouri's robust wine industry, the likely outcome is that the state will open its borders more completely so that Missouri wineries can enjoy access to other states' markets.

Montana: Utilizes the usual on-site sales requirements for its wine consumers. There is now a regulation under which consumers can buy a "connoisseur's permit" and provide a shipping label to a "foreign winery" in order to have wine sent to them.

Nebraska: Wineries wishing to ship into Nebraska now have to buy an annual permit for $500. There are few out-of-state wineries that would find it advantageous to spend $500 to access a few mail-order customers in a low-population state.

Nevada: Limits how much wine a consumer is allowed to receive per year (12 cases), in this instance from all wineries combined. How a winery is supposed to have this information is not stated by the regulators. And wineries that have shipped more than 25 cases per year must arrange for representation by a wholesaler.

New Mexico: Retains its reciprocal status with the other states that chose that route, but now allows consumers to order and receive as much wine as they wish.

North Carolina: Wineries can ship if they have a state permit, and consumers now have access to something called a Purchase Transportation Permit. If wineries exceed 1,000 cases, they have to utilize a wholesaler.

North Dakota: Its reciprocal status is vulnerable to lawsuit, and the state's three wineries can ship freely. So once the lawyers are done with more populous states, North Dakota will show up in their crosshairs.

Oklahoma: Laws here are particularly vulnerable. Its nearly 40 wineries have some freedom to ship, while other wineries are limited to shipping one bottle at a time to customers. The state's wholesalers have won the first round in a legal battle to rescind Oklahoma wineries' ability to ship. Sometime during 2007, lawmakers are expected to sort out the mess.

South Carolina: Now offers winery licences for $300 per year that allow wineries to ship directly to consumers.

South Dakota: Considers all direct shipping illegal, but on-site sales are theoretically tolerated as long as consumers bring no more than five bottles in at a time.

Tennessee: Consumers must be confused by the process. Theoretically, they are allowed to order and receive five bottles at a time from out-of-state wineries, while they are allowed 15 bottles from an in-state winery. There are several suits pending.

Texas: In May 2006, the Texas Alcoholic Beverage Commission (TABC) agreed to a preliminary injunction preventing the TABC from interfering with sales or shipments of wine from out-of-state wineries or retailers to Texas consumers.

Utah: Virtually everything about wine is illegal in Utah, including sending e-mails offering wine for sale.

Wisconsin: Has allowed direct wine sales from reciprocal states. In the wake of Granholm, at least as of this writing, the state is discouraging or forbidding nearly all direct sales. Some legislative remedy is expected.

Wyoming: Offers shipping licences and limits consumers to no more than two cases per year from any single winery, while in-state wineries are allowed three cases per year. Sometime in 2007, the legislature will tackle that disparity.

Grapevine

• **In New Mexico,** key vintner Kent Callaghan of Callaghan Vineyards is pulling out some classic varieties such as Cabernet. "It's been good that we've had these challenging years in terms of rain," explains Callaghan. "The Mourvèdre, Petit Verdot, and Tempranillo came through great. But the Cabernet Sauvignon was not good. So we're taking out Cabernet and putting in Tempranillo. The Merlot will go to Petite Sirah and Tempranillo. I think I'm going to get rid of the Zinfandel, too," says Callaghan.

• **Texans' love affair** with Rhône varieties continues. While Texas viticulturists often endure challenging conditions — 1.5 m (yes, 5 ft!) of rain during the 2005 growing season stands as a notable example — the Syrah and Viognier vineyards may have settled into a somewhat predictable situation for growers. "I think there's a trend," says Kim McPherson of McPherson Cellars and Cap Rock Winery. "One year the crop is heavy, and the next year it's on the light side. In 2005, Viognier and Syrah presented a fairly generous crop. In 2006, both crops were very light."

Opinion:
Breaking down barriers

Most observers have been surprised, if not shocked, by the rapidity with which barriers to direct shipping are falling in most states. While the previously noted rules and regulations for the 30 states in this survey must seem extraordinarily arcane to an outsider, these represent an enormous leap forward for most consumers.

And contrary to the wholesalers' worst fears, the youth of America is not running wild in the streets, swilling Lafite and Latour. Nor have the wholesalers gone bankrupt. Direct shipping to consumers, now allowed in 33 states, amounts to only 1–2 per cent of all wine sales in the USA. If direct shipping were so deleterious to wine, why is California's wine industry thriving, since the state has allowed direct wine sales and self-distribution to retailers and restaurants for more than 30 years?

The new frontier appears to be the battle over retailers' access to each state's consumers. Today there are only 12 states that allow other states' retailers to ship to their consumers. Many legal experts believe that it will be difficult for most states to prevent an onslaught of lawsuits demanding they open their borders to other states' retailers. In the meantime, states are hurriedly drafting laws to allow other states' wineries to ship wine, in the perhaps vain hope that wine consumers will be satisfied with that.

For the purposes of this report, that is enough. Wineries are being handed access to the entire country's consumers at a far more rapid pace than many of us believed possible. And that will probably bring unprecedented sales growth and diversity to the US market as more states nurture thriving wineries.

Grapevine

• **Ed Swanson of Cuthills Vineyards** in Nebraska has created a very promising Tempranillo/Riparia crossing, and the first bottlings of the wine show pretty cherry fruit, balanced acidity, and a tannic grip missing from most cold-hardy experimental hybrids. He is now working on a black Muscat and has also bred a riparian Tempranillo/Syrah crossing and a riparian Tempranillo/Zinfandel crossing.

• **The heavily Mormon state** of Idaho now has 23 wineries, 1,000 acres of vines, and continued growth in the industry with showcase wineries such as Blue Rock Vineyards and the Winery at Eagle Knoll. Both Coeur d'Alene Cellars and TimberRock wineries are new ventures in the Panhandle area, but each utilizes only grapes from Washington's Columbia Valley.

Vintage Report

Advance report on the latest harvest

2006

A challenging year for many of the states in this survey. Missouri and
Illinois had struggles with the weather in 2006. Vignoles and Seyval Blanc
will not see the successes of 2005, but Norton and other reds look very
good. Illinois had similar challenges, with insufficient ripeness. Like most of
the Midwest, Wisconsin had rain problems; everything was perfect until the
wet harvest. New Mexico, Arizona, and Texas had mixed results at best. The
year was wet at the wrong times, "spectacular for rain" in New Mexico but
"too hot and too dry" in Texas "without physiological ripeness", though
Lubbock and the Texas High Plains did better than Texas Hill Country.
Colorado's crop was small but very good, while Idaho had an excellent
vintage, with powerful reds, good whites, and high hopes for great
icewines. The East Coast, too, was in better shape than some previous
harvests; Georgia and the Carolinas had a good to great vintage.

Updates on the previous five vintages

2005

Georgia and the Carolinas saw a cooperative harvest. In Missouri, Kansas,
and Illinois, whites are difficult because of rain in August. Reds did well
because of a lot of sunshine and limited rainfall during September and
through to the end of October. Wisconsin saw a good crop, but inclement
weather contributed to a lack of intensity. In Texas, Hill Country experienced
a damaging spring hailstorm, reducing the crop, and fungal pressure close
to harvest further reduced crop size, but Texas had one of the finest
vintages in a decade. Arizona and New Mexico both saw some bumper
crops, while the growers on Colorado's Western Range are elated with the
quality of their crop. Idaho's vintage started out with 66 cm (26 in) of rain
in June and July alone, but the season turned out far better than feared,
with very good ripeness to the tannins.

2004

Rain was the main story of the vintage, whether it's the trio of hurricanes to hit the southeastern USA in rapid succession, or the torrents that struck Texas, with rains of a remarkable 1.5 m (5 ft) in accumulation over the summer. Missouri experienced many of the moisture and mildew problems of other regions in the south and southeast. Colorado's vineyards saw significant losses due to spring frost, and the same cold spell created problems in Nebraska. Idaho growers, however, were delighted with the vintage and Wisconsin growers were reasonably happy.

2003

The theme in most areas is spring damage. In central Texas, eastern Wisconsin, and Missouri, freeze and frost damage created very small crops, in some cases a third of the normal size. The wines, however, are often good. Missouri's whites are in short supply, but the reds are very good. Wisconsin's whites are excellent. Texas lost a lot of its crop, both reds and whites, but Colorado saw a very big and very high-quality crop. Idaho's wines were big and perhaps a bit too hard.

2002

Idaho's reds were slightly high in alcohol. Missouri's reds were intense and concentrated. In New Mexico, it was yet again a drought year, and the wines show good concentration as a result. Georgia and the Carolinas were victims of excessive rains. All vineyards were cooler than normal and the wines a mixed bag. Texas saw cooler-than-normal temperatures and higher-than-normal precipitation.

2001

In Idaho, even ripening and a warm, quick year resulted in good quality in whites and reds. White wines are even crisper than usual, and the reds show balance and length. Some lovely white wines were made in Missouri, though the Vignoles was difficult. Some reds are a bit stingy, but some Nortons are delightful. For New Mexico, this was year four of the drought, and forest fires raged throughout much of the area.

GREATEST WINE PRODUCERS

1. Stone Hill Winery (Missouri)
2. Augusta Winery (Missouri)
3. Gruet Winery (New Mexico)
4. Callaghan Vineyards (Arizona)
5. Montelle Winery (Missouri)
6. Carlson Vineyards (Colorado)
7. Pend d'Oreille Winery (Idaho)
8. Flat Creek Estates (Texas)
9. McPherson Winery (Texas)
10. Galena Cellars (Illinois)

FASTEST-IMPROVING PRODUCERS

1. Ste Chapelle Winery (Idaho)
2. Childress Vineyards (North Carolina)
3. Bookcliff Vineyards (Colorado)
4. HolyField Winery (Kansas)
5. S Rhodes Vineyards (Colorado)
6. Kiepersol Estate (Texas)
7. Crown Valley Vineyards (Missouri)
8. Fredericksburg Winery (Texas)
9. Persimmon Creek Vineyards (Georgia)
10. Llano Estacado (Texas)

NEW UP-AND-COMING PRODUCERS

1. Blackstock Vineyards (Georgia)
2. Sutcliffe Vineyards (Colorado)
3. Alto Vineyards (Illinois)
4. Rockhouse Vineyards (North Carolina)
5. Dry Comal Creek (Texas)
6. Coeur d'Alene Cellars (Idaho)
7. Somerset Ridge (Kansas)
8. Raffaldini Vineyards (North Carolina)
9. Garfield Estates (Colorado)
10. Woodrose Winery (Texas)

BEST-VALUE PRODUCERS

1. Wollersheim Winery (Wisconsin)
2. Milagro Winery (New Mexico)
3. Les Bourgeois (Missouri)
4. Alto Vineyards (Illinois)
5. Cuthills Vineyards (Nebraska)
6. Llano Estacado (Texas)
7. St James Winery (Missouri)
8. Cap Rock Winery (Texas)
9. Adam Puchta Winery (Missouri)
10. Fall Creek Vineyards (Texas)

GREATEST-QUALITY WINES

1. **Late Harvest Vignoles 2005** Stone Hill Winery, Missouri ($30)
2. **Moscato Bianco 2005** Flat Creek Estates, Texas Hill Country ($16)
3. **Blanc de Noir NV** Gruet Winery, New Mexico ($14)
4. **Tre Coloré 2005** McPherson Winery, Texas ($20)
5. **Reserve Riesling Ice Wine 2004** Ste Chapelle Winery, Idaho ($20)
6. **Dry Vignoles 2005** Montelle Winery, Missouri ($13.50)
7. **Seyval Blanc 2005** Augusta Winery, Missouri ($8)
8. **Ice Wine 2005** Wollersheim Winery, Wisconsin ($47)
9. **Padre's 2004** Callaghan Vineyards, Sonoita, Arizona ($28)
10. **Ddraig Goch 2004** Sutcliffe Vineyards, Colorado ($38)

BEST BARGAINS

1. **Vignoles 2005** HolyField Winery, Kansas ($18)
2. **Cream Sherry NV** Stone Hill Winery, Missouri ($15)
3. **Adagio NV** Bookcliff Vineyards, Colorado ($14)
4. **Norton Port NV** Adam Puchta Winery, Missouri ($23)
5. **Touriga 2005** Silver Coast Winery, Georgia ($15)
6. **Chambourcin Estate 2003** Augusta Winery, Missouri ($16)
7. **Chambourcin 2004** Stone Hill Winery, Missouri ($15)
8. **Chambourcin 2003** Alto Vineyards, Illinois ($14)

⑨ **Vidal Blanc 2005** Cedar Creek Winery, America ($8.50)

⑩ **Vintner's Select Vignoles 2005** St James Winery, Missouri ($11)

MOST EXCITING OR UNUSUAL FINDS

① **A*C*E 2004** Blackstock Vineyards, Georgia ($25) *Mourvèdre, Touriga, and a little Merlot from the vineyard that has been one of the most important sources for quality grapes in the southeast and is now producing its own quality wine.*

② **Syrah 2005** Garfield Estates, Grande Valley, Colorado ($21) *Either Syrah seems to be the most forgiving of grapes, or the western slopes of Colorado harbour very good sites for it.*

③ **Sangiovese 2003** Childress Vineyards, North Carolina ($25) *I remain unconvinced that Sangiovese can be great on America's eastern shores, but I still like this wine very much.*

④ **Tempranillo Hybrid 2005** Cuthills Vineyards, Nebraska ($15) *Dedicated vintners such as Ed Swanson are creating new grapes that offer the best opportunities to produce quality reds in the northern Plains.*

⑤ **Dry Gewurztraminer 2005** Fredericksburg Winery, Texas ($14) *Not a keeper, but a fun and quenching drink for immediate consumption.*

⑥ **Laughing Cat Gewurztraminer 2005** Carlson Vineyards, Colorado ($12) *There seems to be a shade more acidity in this version, but none of the floral and peachy element has been lost.*

⑦ **Malbec 2003** Pend d'Oreille Winery, Idaho ($28) *A benchmark leader in Idaho wine takes Malbec's fat and easy nature and adds some manly bulk and girth.*

⑧ **Vermentino 2004** Raffaldini Vineyards, North Carolina ($13) *Italian grapes continue to show promise in the southeast, even if they are relatively neutral versions. No matter; they are clean, tangy, and refreshing.*

⑨ **Oktoberfest NV** Somerset Ridge, Kansas ($9) *A new winery in Kansas is experimenting with vinifera but having success with hybrids — and in taming the high acidity in hybrids with sweet fruit.*

⑩ **Syrah 2003** Coeur d'Alene Cellars, Idaho ($28) *It's unfortunate that so many of Idaho's wineries are partially or wholly dependent on Washington fruit, but that's pretty good fruit to rely on.*

Grapevine

• **Jack Kroustalis,** credited with helping start North Carolina's wine industry, died in March 2006. He was one of the first to push the state's growers to move beyond the Muscadine grape and plant European varieties. He opened his winery, Westbend Vineyards, in 1988, when there were only a few wineries in the state. Today North Carolina boasts more than 50 wineries.

• **While the state of Texas** still has dry counties in which alcohol is not supposed to be sold, it is nonetheless focused on wine sales and wine tourism. The Texas Hill Country Wine Trail has become an active magnet for local and regional tourism. And Texas has added another AVA to its seven: Texoma AVA, nestled against the Oklahoma border.

Canada

Tony Aspler

The Canadian wine press finally got a chance to taste the long-awaited wines of Ontario's newest winery, Le Clos Jordanne.

TONY ASPLER

This co-venture between Constellation/Vincor International and burgundy shippers Boisset concentrates on Pinot Noir and Chardonnay sourced from four vineyards on the Niagara Escarpment around the town of Jordan. (The original name, Le Clos Jordan, was disputed by Jordan, the Sonoma winery.)

Winemaker Thomas Bachelder, late of Lemelson Vineyards in Oregon, and his associate Isabelle Meunier showed off the 2003 and 2004 vintages of Le Clos Jordanne Pinot Noir and the 2004 vintage of Chardonnay. These terroir-driven wines were enthusiastically received by the critical audience, and for this reviewer they were the best Pinots he has tasted in Canada.

Like their burgundian models, the wines are tiered as Village Reserve, Single Vineyard, and Grand Cru and range in price from C\$35 to C\$60.

TONY ASPLER is the most widely read wine writer in Canada. He was the wine columnist for *The Toronto Star* for 21 years and has authored 11 books on wine and food, including *Vintage Canada*, *The Wine Lover's Companion*, *The Wine Lover Cooks*, and *Travels with My Corkscrew*. His latest book is *Canadian Wine for Dummies*. Tony is a member of the North American advisory board for the Masters of Wine, creator of the annual Ontario Wine Awards competition, and a director of the Independent Wine & Spirit Trust. He is also a director of the Canadian Wine Library and serves on Air Canada's wine-selection committee. At the Niagara Grape & Wine Festival 2000, Tony was presented with the Royal Bank Business Citizen of the Year award. Tony also writes fiction, including a collection of wine murder mysteries featuring the itinerant wine writer-cum-detective Ezra Brant: *Blood Is Thicker than Beaujolais*, *The Beast of Barbaresco*, and *Death on the Douro*. His latest book is *The Wine Atlas of Canada* (Random House, 2006). Tony is the co-founder of the charitable foundation Grapes for Humanity (www.grapesforhumanity.com). Find him online at tonyaspler.com.

Much of the interest centred on whether Constellation would proceed with the ultra-modern winery that the renowned Canadian architect Frank Gehry had designed for the project. Constellation's president and COO Rob Sands was noncommittal: "We've had some very light vintages [in Ontario]. We haven't had a full chance to get up to full production. The Gehry winery is a nice idea, but it's just a façade … We're going to have to wait a couple of years to see if it really makes sense and make a decision at that time."

Thomas Bachelder expects to make 10,000 cases of the 2006 vintage.

No agreement in BC

In an industry-wide vote in September 2006 a proposed operating agreement between the British Columbia (BC) government and the new BC Wine Authority was defeated by the larger wineries. The agreement, drafted by the interim board of the Wine Authority, which includes representatives of all factions of the winery industry, required a double majority approval from both the larger wineries representing the bulk of BC wine production and the smaller wineries representing the largest number of wineries. The smaller wineries had sought a wine standard based on 100 per cent BC-grown wines and not VQA, which, they pointed out, is a brand. Larger wineries cited concerns about diluting VQA requirements for their lack of support.

Grapevine

• **The BC government** announced a C$50,000 grant to the BC Wine Institute in late 2006 to plan a new BC wine and culinary centre in Vancouver. Agriculture and Lands Minister Pat Bell said that the new centre would become a central destination for local and visiting wine and food lovers to discover and celebrate the province's food and wine.

• **Fifteen Canadian judges** assessed close to 1,000 wines from all over the world to determine the best buys available in Canada under C$25. The first International Value Wine Awards, organized by *Wine Access* magazine, were held at Hotel Arts in Calgary in June 2006. See www.wineaccess.ca for the results.

• **Remoissenet Père et Fils,** the Burgundy *négociant*, has been purchased by a group of North American investors. Real-estate developers Howard and Edward Milstein of New York and wine importer Todd Halpern of Toronto bought the company, which is based in Beaune, with Maison Jadot taking a minority interest.

• **Donald Ziraldo and Karl Kaiser** have both resigned from Inniskillin, the winery they founded in 1974. Their departure happened a few months after the takeover by Constellation Brands of Vincor, Canada's largest wine conglomerate. Ziraldo, the supersalesman, and Kaiser, the winemaker, put Canada on the international wine map in 1991, when their Vidal Icewine 1989 won a Prix d'Honneur at Vinexpo. Although officially retired, Kaiser will still consult on the company's icewine production.

French vines in hot water

It looks like the phylloxera story in reverse. A nursery in France has supplied grapevines to BC that were infected with the European disease *bois noir*. The Canadian Food Inspection Agency has confirmed that the pestilence currently affecting European vineyards has been detected in vineyards in Osoyoos in the extreme south of BC's wine-growing region.

"This is a very, very, very serious thing," says David Bond, executive director of the Association of BC Winegrowers. "My members are scared silly about it." Chuck Lemmon, a spokesman for the Canadian Food Inspection Agency, has said that the entire shipment of 2,000 vines from the French nursery will be destroyed and new rules governing the importation of vines from France and Germany will come into effect in 2007. To ensure that no more insects carrying the *bois noir* infection will enter Canada, all imported plants from France will have to be hot-water treated.

Most expensive wine in the world

Royal DeMaria, "Canada's Icewine Specialists" in Ontario, has sold a half-bottle of Chardonnay Icewine 2000 for C$30,000. Yes, you read that right – the world's most expensive wine!

The Chardonnay Icewine is just one of the 18 different varieties of icewine Royal DeMaria has marketed from its own vineyard. Among other firsts, the company – owned by Joseph DeMaria – has the distinction of producing the world's only Meritage Icewine (in 2002), which used to be the world's most expensive icewine. This product was introduced at C$395 per half-bottle, but as stocks diminished, the price rose to C$5,000.

A step up in price from Royal De Maria's Collector's Series, which ranges from $1,800 to $5,000 a half-bottle, the Chardonnay inaugurates a series honouring Niagara grape grower Billy Myers, a farmer of 40 years.

At this writing, DeMaria has sold one bottle and is following up on three other sales. "As usual," he says, "I increase the price point as the sales increase. Although the 2000 Chardonnay Icewine is at C$30,000 now, I can guarantee that by the last bottle, this icewine will have a price tag of C$500,000 a bottle." Let's hope there are no TCA problems.

Grapevine

• **The latest BC vineyard** census shows 6,630 acres of wine grapes under vine – a rise of 21 per cent in two years. Along with the increase has come an explosion of new wineries. At the time of writing, there are 120 operating wineries in the province, with a further 50-odd seeking licences. Most are smallholdings, averaging just over 7 acres of vineyard. The most widely planted red is Merlot, in spite of *Sideways*, and the predominant white is still Chardonnay.

Opinion:
Who needs a winery?

When I visit Napa, my first port of call is the Napa Wine Company – a great stone barn of a place that operates as a custom crush house for some 80 brands of wine. Here you can taste the products of 25 wineries you may never have heard of, some of which produce just 200 cases a year.

The original facility was built in 1877 for the Nouveau Medoc Winery, and in 1977 it was amalgamated into a second winery constructed in 1892. The expanded property was used for the large-scale production of jug wines and was eventually taken over by Inglenook. In 1993, the Pelissa family, long-time Napa growers, purchased the winery and completely renovated it, transforming it into a custom crush facility. Many of California's cult wines were born here. The last time I was there, I tasted Jones Family Vineyard Cabernet 2000 and Showket Vineyard Cabernet Sauvignon 2000, both made by the legendary Heidi Peterson Barrett, who made the wines for Screaming Eagle until 2005. I also got to taste Crocker & Starr Stone Place Cabernet Blend 2003 made by Pam Starr, the winemaker for Spottswoode, and Joel Gott's Plekan Ranch Syrah 2003, made from Sonoma County fruit.

In addition to visiting winemakers who fashion their own wines under its ample roof, the Napa Wine Company has its own resident winemaker, Rob Lawson, who makes Cabernet Sauvignon, Pinot Blanc, Sauvignon Blanc, and Zinfandel from the Pelissa family's 600 acres of organic vineyards. The wines are available for sale, as are those of his visiting winemakers, on the company's website: www.napawineco.com.

Why am I telling you all this? Because this is precisely what we should have in Ontario and BC – a custom crush house where winemakers who don't own or have access to a licensed winery can make small batches of high-quality wines from purchased grapes. You don't need bricks and mortar to make good wine. A simple change in the regulations would make this concept possible. The nearest we come to this in Canada at present are Howard Soon's excellent Sandhill Small Lots label in BC, using fruit from the Burrowing Owl Vineyard and produced at the Calona facility, and Charles Baker's 2005 Riesling, produced at Stratus from Chef Marc Piccone's tiny Vineland vineyard in Ontario. Soon has been Calona's long-time winemaker, and Baker works as the sales and marketing director for Stratus winery.

So, first we need a change in the law and then we need a far-sighted entrepreneur to invest in a custom crush facility. Who knows what Canadian icon wines could be produced under these conditions?

Vintage Report

Advance report on the latest harvest

2006

Ontario – After the disastrously short 2005 harvest, the mild winter and spring provided a very good crop that was evenly distributed on the vines, allowing for greater consistency of ripening. A long, hot summer meant good physiological ripeness and high sugars in the early-ripening varieties (Chardonnay, Pinot Noir, Baco Noir, Gamay, Pinot Blanc) and the mid-season varieties (Riesling, Sauvignon Blanc, Gewurztraminer, Merlot, Cabernet Franc). Ample summer rains kept the vines healthy, the fruit appropriately sized, and the ground saturated with water.

Wet weather at harvest swelled the grapes, making cluster weights 50 per cent larger than the previous year. Some winemakers used reverse osmosis on bordeaux varieties, but Chardonnay and Pinot Noir performed well, making it something of a burgundian year in Ontario. However, 2006 augurs well for a perfect icewine vintage: a warm, hot, high-sugar summer with an ample crop, followed by a cool slowdown during September/October to preserve acidity and delay physiological ripeness (preventing breakdown), followed by −8°C temperatures early in December. Some wineries picked on 6 December.

British Columbia – The 2006 grape-growing year was virtually seamless in BC. Coming through a mild winter, the vines entered blossom time on schedule despite extended cooler spring weather and, buoyed by the previous year's lighter crop, set a heavier crop than average. A warm, sunny summer brought on *véraison* in very good time, and an extended, generally sunny and warm autumn allowed all varieties to reach full ripeness in their order, creating a comfortably paced harvest. The crop was 25–30 per cent larger than in 2005, and in isolated cases, where a larger-than-advisable crop of Shiraz was left on the vine, there was a challenge reaching full ripeness. An early-winter freeze in the last week of November permitted the daytime harvest of a larger-than-average icewine crop. Across the board, 2006 produced fruit of excellent quality, which will be reflected in generous amounts of high-quality wines.

Updates on the previous five vintages

2005

Vintage rating: *Ontario – Red: 93, White: 91;*
British Columbia – Red: 90, White: 92

Ontario – For the Ontario wine industry it has been the best of times and the worst of times. The 2005 harvest, thanks to the hottest, driest growing season on record, has produced the best fruit the wineries have ever seen, particularly for bordeaux varieties. But because of the horrendously cold winter and early spring that preceded it, killing off buds and splitting vines, quantities were down drastically. A normal Ontario harvest produces an average of 50,000 tonnes of grapes. This year, the growers were lucky that they reached 26,000 tonnes. Not only was it the earliest harvest on record for table wines, but it was the earliest harvest in the province's history for icewine. Henry of Pelham picked on 24 November.

British Columbia – A clement fall with mixed sun and a few brief rain showers allowed the grapes to reach full maturity over a period that extended to early November for the latest varieties.

The spread-out harvest period allowed for longer hang times, which resulted in intense flavour characteristics shown by early wine samples. Another contributing factor to the favourable flavour profiles was a smaller crop, down anywhere from 10 to 30 per cent, depending on location and variety. This is believed to be mainly due to rainy conditions during the blossom period, which resulted in smaller berries and cluster weights.

Early wine tastings and winemaker comments indicate a vintage of well-balanced wines with fewer of the 15 and 16 per cent alcohol readings that popped up here and there in recent vintages.

2004

Vintage rating: *Ontario – Red: 85, White: 92;*
British Columbia – Red: 91, White: 92

Ontario – A cool, elongated growing season began with so much rain that winemakers gloomily predicted another 1992. But Nature smiled in the autumn, and throughout September and into the first week of October the sun shone and rescued the harvest. Tonnage was about normal after the previous year's disastrously low grape production. The earlier-ripening varieties – Pinot Noir, Chardonnay, Pinot Gris, and Gewurztraminer – showed better than the bordeaux varieties. This year is better for whites, with lively acidity.

British Columbia – Summer weather was very good until a dramatic shift to cool, moist conditions began in August and continued for a month.

Grapes were slowed in ripening, but the cooler weather gave the vines the time they needed to pack the fruit with flavour and intensity without generating excess sugar and low acid; some outstanding white wines resulted. On the downside, the cool, moist conditions caused some scattered fungus problems, resulting in up to 20 per cent crop loss in some instances. The return of warm, sunny conditions in the third week of September continued through into November, allowing black varieties to complete the ripening process and produce good-quality wines.

2003

Vintage rating: *Ontario – Red: 85, White: 90;*
British Columbia – Red: 94, White: 91

Ontario – The Indian summer encouraged maximum ripeness, but it also woke up the ladybugs. The horrendously cold winter reduced the tonnage of grapes to below 50 per cent of normal yields. Some varieties, such as Sauvignon Blanc and Merlot, were down to 25 per cent of the 2002 harvest, but the quality of the fruit was good because of Nature's Draconian thinning.

British Columbia – A record grape crop following the hottest and sunniest year ever. The 2003 red wines are potentially even better than the highly lauded 2002s. Bill Dyer at Burrowing Owl used extended maceration on his Cabernet Sauvignon for the first time.

2002

Vintage rating: *Ontario – Red: 86, White: 85;*
British Columbia – Red: 94, White: 94

Ontario – Yields were slightly down from predicted levels, but the quality and concentration of fruit were excellent. Winemakers say that 2002 will be one of the best vintages on record, particularly for red wines.

British Columbia – It is likely that 2002 will go on record as being the best vintage yet, surpassing 1998 by having more moderate heat for further flavour development and allowing white wines to retain natural acid balance.

2001

Vintage rating: *Ontario – Red: 88, White: 83;*
British Columbia – Red: 89, White: 94

Ontario – A vintage compromised by the presence of ladybugs, which affected the flavour of some wines. Some Sauvignon Blanc was harvested

almost two weeks earlier than usual. Rains in late September and October slowed down some of the mid-season harvesting, which helped the reds.
British Columbia – A high-end vintage for most whites. Red wines also did well, with excellent fruit ripeness and a softer-than-average tannin structure in all but the latest-ripening varieties.

GREATEST WINE PRODUCERS

1. Jackson-Triggs (BC)
2. Sumac Ridge (BC)
3. Blue Mountain (BC)
4. Stratus (Ontario)
5. Henry of Pelham (Ontario)
6. Burrowing Owl (BC)
7. Quails' Gate (BC)
8. Malivoire (Ontario)
9. Château des Charmes (Ontario)
10. Tawse (Ontario)

FASTEST-IMPROVING PRODUCERS

1. Peller (BC)
2. Hester Creek (BC)
3. Flat Rock (Ontario)
4. Golden Mile (BC)
5. Nk'Mip (BC)
6. Closson Chase (Ontario)
7. Thornhaven (BC)
8. Coyote's Run (Ontario)
9. Tantalus (BC)
10. Fielding (Ontario)

NEW UP-AND-COMING PRODUCERS

1. Le Clos Jordanne (Ontario)
2. Dunham & Froese (BC)
3. Noble Ridge (BC)
4. Le Vieux Pin (BC)
5. Norman Hardie (Ontario)
6. Thirty Bench (Ontario)
7. Huff (Ontario)
8. Herder (BC)
9. Therapy (BC)
10. Mountain Road (Ontario)

BEST-VALUE PRODUCERS

1. Colio (Ontario)
2. Calona (BC)
3. Jackson-Triggs (Ontario)
4. Lakeview (Ontario)
5. Gehringer Bros (BC)
6. Greata Ranch (BC)
7. Hawthorne Mountain (BC)
8. Peller (BC)
9. Magnotta (Ontario)
10. Hernder (Ontario)

GREATEST-QUALITY WINES

1. **Le Grand Clos Pinot Noir 2004** Le Clos Jordanne, Ontario (C$60)
2. **First Growth Cabernet Sauvignon 2002** Reif Estate, Ontario (C$50)
3. **SLC Sauvignon Blanc/Semillon 2004** Mission Hill Family Estate, BC (C$30)
4. **Syrah 2003** Burrowing Owl, BC (C$30)
5. **Quam Qwmt Merlot 2003** Nk'Mip, BC (C$30)
6. **Black Paw Vineyard Pinot Noir 2004** Coyote's Run, Ontario (C$36)
7. **Riesling 2005** Tantalus, BC (C$19.90)
8. **Proprietors Grand Reserve Red Meritage 2004** Jackson-Triggs, BC (C$25)
9. **Pinnacle 2003** Sumac Ridge, BC (C$50)
10. **Paul Bosc Estate Riesling Icewine 2002** Château des Charmes, Ontario (C$60 per half-bottle)

BEST BARGAINS

1 **Classic Ehrenfelser 2005**
Gehringer Bros, BC (C$12.99)

2 **Sauvignon Blanc 2005** Henry of
Pelham, Ontario (C$14.95)

3 **Artist Series Pinot Gris 2005**
Calona, BC (C$14)

4 **Private Reserve Rosé 2005**
Sumac Ridge, BC (C$11)

5 **Riesling Icewine 2003** Magnotta,
Ontario (C$39.95)

6 **Trius Merlot 2004** Hillebrand,
Ontario (C$14.95)

7 **Proprietors Reserve Cabernet
Franc Rosé 2005** Jackson-Triggs,
BC (C$14.95)

8 **Bench Chardonnay 2004** Stoney
Ridge, Ontario (C$12.85)

9 **Pinot Noir 2004** Arrowleaf, BC
(C$16)

10 **Pinot Blanc 2005** Hester Creek,
BC (C$13)

MOST EXCITING OR UNUSUAL FINDS

1 **Fume Blanc 2005** Peninsula
Ridge, Ontario (C$26.95) *An oak-
aged Sauvignon that resembles a
white bordeaux – smoky, grassy,
green plum flavours with a floral
grace note.*

2 **Okanagan Malbec 2004**
Inniskillin, BC (C$24) *One of the
most impressive Malbec varietals,
with distinctive berry flavours,
depth, and elegance.*

3 **Pinot Noir 2005** Henry of Pelham,
Ontario (C$24.95) *Unfiltered. Firmly
structured, succulent cherry fruit;
well made, with a tannic finish.*

4 **Pinotage 2004** Lake Breeze, BC
(C$24) *Canada's original Pinotage
producer has continued to develop
its heft and flavour intensity.*

5 **Paul Bosc Estate Chardonnay
2004** Château des Charmes, Ontario
(C$19.95) *Spicy, clovey, toasty oak,
apple on the nose; dry, full-bodied,*
*apple and lemon flavours with a
whisper of oak; good length.*

6 **Minus 9 Ehrenfelser Icewine
2005** Gehringer Bros, BC (C$48)
*This icewine encapsulates
Ehrenfelser's outgoing floral and
fruity characteristics.*

7 **Small Lots Series Barbera 2003**
Sandhill Vineyards, BC (C$30) *Rich
red-plum flavours with exciting
aromatic highlights make this an
outstanding red wine.*

8 **Proprietors Grand Reserve
Merlot 2002** Jackson-Triggs,
Ontario (C$24.95) *Cedar, blueberry,
and vanilla bouquet; full-bodied, well-
extracted ripe fruit, firmly structured;
tannins are there but pliant.*

9 **Schonburger 2005** Kettle Valley,
BC (C$20) *Fully developed as a
food wine, the concentration and
complexity were built by skin
contact before fermentation and
barrel fermentation.*

10 **Meritage Reserve 2002**
Creekside, Ontario (C$34) *Vanilla
oak with red berries and tobacco-
leaf nose; medium-bodied, sweet
blackcurrant and blackberry fruit,
well-integrated oak, firm structure;
good length. Very bordeaux-like.*

Grapevine

• **Former Blues Brother and
Ghost Buster** Dan Aykroyd is
launching a portfolio of Ontario
wines under his own name in
2007: the Dan Aykroyd Signature
Reserve Series of super-premium
offerings and the Dan Aykroyd
Discovery Series of mid-priced
wines. The first wine released
was the Signature Reserve VQA
Niagara Peninsula Vidal Icewine
2005, which was made available
in 2007. A Chardonnay, Riesling,
and Gewurztraminer and a series
of reds, including a Cabernet
Sauvignon, will follow.

Chile

Peter Richards

After years of infighting and internal divisions, 2007 heralded a new dawn for Chilean wine as its two major winery associations decided to join forces.

PETER RICHARDS

In phoenix-like fashion, from the ashes of Viñas de Chile and Chilevid has risen Vinos de Chile. The new association incorporates 91 wineries, representing the vast majority of Chilean wine exports and overall sales. The deal is a major step forward for the industry. Interestingly, what appears to have paved the way for the eventual detente was the successful genesis of Wines of Chile, a joint project between the two that has achieved impressive results in promoting Chilean wines abroad.

The news has been warmly welcomed by the wineries, though tangible results are now expected. As one industry insider commented: "Now we just need the government to step up to the plate (and cough up), so we can raise the presence of Chile globally on a generic level."

Strong peso hits profits

After years of optimism and bullish growth, a new atmosphere of caution and uncertainty has settled over the Chilean wine industry as ongoing currency woes (strong peso, weak dollar) continue to ravage profits.

PETER RICHARDS is one of the UK's youngest award-winning wine writers. TV credits include *Saturday Kitchen* (BBC1), *Daily Cooks* (ITV1), *Taste* (Sky One), and UKTV Food's *Great Food Live* and *Food Uncut*. Peter has published two books on wine: *Wineries with Style* (Mitchell Beazley, 2004) and *The Wines of Chile* (Mitchell Beazley, 2006). His writing portfolio includes *The Guardian*, *Daily Mail*, *Decanter*, and *Wine & Spirit*, and he also has a column in *The Liberal*. Chile is a specialist focus for Peter, who has lived and worked there and is now a regular visitor to the country, covering the region for many wine publications, as well as judging in wine competitions (in 2006 he became the youngest regional chairman – for Chile – at the *Decanter* World Wine Awards). Peter lives in London.

The situation shows no sign of imminent improvement. Most wineries have adopted an attitude of grim-faced stoicism, cutting costs and waiting it out. Others – such as the Concha y Toro group – have pushed up prices on key brands.

Initial reaction from the UK market on these price rises appears, significantly, to be positive. And promotional body Wines of Chile is no doubt delighted that Chile is finally moving into the premium sector with its biggest-hitting brands.

Producers remain cautious, however. Most are concerned about what price hikes will mean for volume sales and key contracts. Stocks are high and harvests are more and more plentiful. Consolidation talk remains prevalent.

While it is certainly not all gloom and doom, and the industry should yet emerge from this difficult period the stronger for it, Chile is undoubtedly experiencing growing pains.

No Silva lining

Respected viticultural consultant Eduardo Silva has ruffled a few feathers by announcing that "at least 20 per cent" of Chile's vineyard is not profitable because the market is "not capable of absorbing all the grapes produced".

In a no-nonsense wake-up call to the industry, Silva estimated that, given current market conditions, Chile could sell a maximum of 550 million litres, some 250 million litres less than it produces at present.

From a commercial point of view, Silva recommended three remedial courses of action for producers: cultivating export markets, educating the Chilean consumer, and selling off current backlogs of stock at low prices.

Silva also urged producers to address the issue from a viticultural point of view. Measures recommended included carrying out detailed classifications and profitability analyses of vineyards, as well as improving viticultural practices all round.

Grapevine

• **This year's foot-in-mouth award** goes to Laurent Dassault, part-owner of the high-profile Altaïr joint venture, who let slip to a Chilean newspaper that the top-dollar wine was "a good product but poorly focused". The comment did not go down very well with the winery itself or, indeed, with his partners in the venture, San Pedro, who, many industry insiders believe, are now looking to assume full ownership of Altaïr.

• **There is excitement in Bío-Bío** as the Córpora group announced that it has acquired the locally based Canata winery as part of a major expansion drive in the southerly region. The deal makes Córpora by far the biggest quality player in Bío-Bío, and further growth is planned.

STINK OVER PULP FACTION

Vigorous protests have been taking place in Chile's southerly Itata region following the controversial opening of a massive new wood pulp and paper plant in Nueva Aldea. Local residents have filed a series of lawsuits claiming that foul emissions are causing sickness, while wine growers in the vicinity are up in arms, claiming that the plant will ruin their business.

Local wine producer Fernando Giner of Casas de Giner is at the forefront of the protests. "We are located just 500 metres from the plant, and I believe that gas emissions, including dioxins, represent a very real danger to the quality of the wines and the health of the vines," he said. Another local producer, Itata Wines, blamed the recent loss of an 80,000-bottle deal with Sweden on Itata's image being tarnished by the plant.

The irony of the situation is that part of the land on which the factory is built was previously a respected vineyard run by Fundación Chile, a project with the aim of encouraging local wine growers to improve quality in the region.

GALLO NOT CHICKEN

Chile is no stranger to outside forces establishing themselves within its narrow confines, though the larger global drinks groups (Diageo, Pernod Ricard, LVMH) have tended to prefer Argentina.

But the situation is changing. US giant Gallo has entered into a venture with Colchagua-based Bisquertt, which is now making the Chilcaya brand on Gallo's behalf. Constellation already has a foothold in Chile courtesy of its stake in Veramonte. In addition, Australian producer Lindemans, part of the mighty Foster's Group, recently announced it was to market a Chilean wine under its brand (sourced from its subsidiary venture in Chile, Dallas Conté).

Persistent rumours have also been doing the rounds about other big-name Chilean wineries engaged in takeover talks with significant foreign players.

CHILEANS INVESTING ABROAD

Over the years, Chile has tended to be the target of foreign investors rather than investing abroad itself – but now telling news to the contrary has emerged.

The most significant new item has been Montes announcing a new venture in Napa. Fruit is being sourced from growers in around 10 different areas and vinified in the Artesa winery, and the wines are expected for release in 2008 – both red blends with mainly Cabernet Sauvignon and some Syrah. Export director Carlos Serrano comments: "It was a big challenge for us, but we like challenges. People ask us, 'Why Napa?' We say, 'Because it's there.'"

Furthermore, Argentina has become a notable stomping ground for Chilean wineries in recent years, and developments suggest the gap across the Andes is becoming narrower by the day. Both Santa Carolina and Misiones de Rengo have announced that they are incorporating Argentine wines into hitherto all-Chilean brand lines – a trend originally started in low-key fashion by the likes of Concha y Toro and San Pedro.

Opinion:
Stop the musical chairs

The annual carnival that is the winemaker transfer market in Chile takes place year round but usually hits a peak in the months before Christmas, coinciding with the start of the summer growing season. New winemakers are paraded to much fanfare; optimism is expressed; so, too, is sadness at the departure of the previous incumbent.

It is a well-worn routine in Chilean winemaking circles, but it creates an inherent instability at the heart of Chilean winemaking and risks undermining the experience and stability critical to success in this business.

Some of the more significant recent moves include Irene Paiva leaving San Pedro as the winery was joined by consultant Paul Hobbs and former Los Vascos winemaker Marco Puyo. Ed Flaherty went from Via to the Southern Sun group (Tarapacá et al). Aurelio Montes Jr left Ventisquero to join his father, Aurelio Montes Sr, in their eponymous winery. Tabalí, Calina, Santa Carolina, Garcés Silva, Chocalán, Viña Casablanca, Matetic, Casa Rivas, and Casas del Bosque all have new head winemakers.

No one in their right mind would argue that a winemaker should be denied better pay or better opportunities. Nor is it tenable to argue that all winemakers who have been in their jobs a long time are necessarily good. But Chile is at a delicate stage in its evolution as a wine nation, and it needs to build up experience in its winemakers, consolidating knowledge and fine-tuning its vineyards and winemaking practices – as well as communicating an image of stability and expertise to the world.

This is achieved only by having stable winemaking teams with a sound knowledge of their patch (Cono Sur and Concha y Toro are prime examples). If further knowledge or perspective is needed, there are plenty of opportunities for wineries to hire consultants, or for winemakers to do vintages around the world. Playing musical chairs with winemakers is not in Chile's best long-term interests.

Grapevine

- **Three significant investments of late.** The first was the surprise takeover of Viña Leyda by San Pedro via its subsidiary Tabalí. Then came the news that O Fournier, which owns wineries in Spain and Argentina, had sealed a deal to make wine in Chile from the 2007 vintage (white from San Antonio, red from Maule). Finally, Vosne-Romanée producer Louis-Michel Liger-Belair announced that he would be making his first Chilean wines from 2007.

Vintage Report

Advance report on the latest harvest

2007

A very early budbreak in coastal vineyards raised concerns about the risk of frost (which didn't materialize) but also that the vines may not have undergone a proper dormancy. This was followed by a deluge in mid-February, which even saw some hail and snow in the Andes foothills. Although these early-season rains did not significantly affect the quality of the harvest, it was enough to put producers firmly on their toes, especially since weathermen had been predicting a recurrence of El Niño (late-season rain) for this year. High temperatures in late January and February pushed maturity of early varieties ahead of schedule – Sauvignon Blanc from coastal areas was picked up to two to three weeks earlier than 2006. Slightly cooler weather in March meant that things normalized, and producers were optimistic about the quality of Chardonnay and Pinot Noir. Initial conclusions would be that this is an unusual and heterogeneous year, with volumes slightly down on the large harvest that was 2006.

Updates on the previous five vintages

2006

Vintage rating: *Red: 91, White: 92*

Cold, dry, and long was the summary of the 2006 vintage, with some of the best quality produced in aromatic whites, while reds generally show a fresh style. It was a moderately challenging year for growers, who had to be patient and judge their harvest times well to achieve quality. Overall crop size was about 10–15 per cent up on 2005. The reds are not predicted to have quite the density and power of the 2005 vintage due to larger berry sizes, but in general quality seems good.

2005

Vintage rating: *Red: 96, White: 93*

Chile's most hyped vintages in recent times have been the odd years: 1999, 2001, 2003. While 2005 is no exception to this rule, it is different to its predecessors in character – this was not simply a hot, dry year but instead a long, moderate season that led to a late harvest and wines showing notable freshness, complexity, and natural balance. Reds fared the best and are considered to offer good to outstanding quality; whites are good to very good.

2004

Vintage rating: *Red: 89, White: 86*

An uneven vintage that gave good, if variable, results. A hot summer and rainy autumn meant that this was something of a pressurized harvest in which good vineyard management was crucial. Alcohol levels tend to be quite high and, while the wines generally show good concentration and often notably ripe character, this has resulted in some imbalance, especially in whites from coastal appellations like Casablanca and San Antonio. One to drink sooner rather than later.

2003

Vintage rating: *Red: 93, White: 92*

Generally a very successful vintage, with concentrated, ripe reds and characterful whites. This was a warm year with a dry, long autumn, and the wines tend to reflect this in their maturity and intensity. A classic warm Chilean vintage that gave consistent quality and good to excellent wines across the board.

2002

Vintage rating: *Red: 79, White: 84*

It pays to be circumspect with the 2002 vintage. Performance was patchy due to localized late-season rains, especially in the south. Some dilution is evident, and in general the wines are not ageing well. Though some good quality was produced, choose only top producers and wines.

Grapevine

• **Another Norwegian-owned venture** is taking shape in Chile. Dan Odfjell did it in Maipo, now banker Alex Vix has bought 4,000 ha in southern Cachapoal, just over the hill from Apalta. Consultant Patrick Valette has been hired, and there are plans for a 6-million-litre winery and 600 ha of vines by 2009, mainly reds. Possibly the only thing the project now lacks is a name.

• **After falling out of business** with Jorge Coderch, Michel Laroche's itinerant Chilean brand has finally found a home. Laroche has bought the Villard winery and vineyards in Casablanca — though Villard will continue to make wines under his brands.

GREATEST WINE PRODUCERS

1. Concha y Toro
2. Montes
3. Cono Sur
4. Errázuriz
5. Almaviva
6. Emiliana Orgánico
7. De Martino
8. Miguel Torres
9. Casa Marín
10. Santa Rita

BEST-VALUE PRODUCERS

1. Concha y Toro
2. Cono Sur
3. Emiliana Orgánico
4. Ventisquero
5. Misiones de Rengo
6. Casas del Bosque
7. Viña Leyda
8. La Rosa
9. San Pedro
10. Montes

FASTEST-IMPROVING PRODUCERS

1. Matetic
2. Santa Carolina
3. Viña Leyda
4. Córpora
5. Anakena
6. Cousiño Macul
7. Casa Silva
8. Aquitania
9. Caliterra
10. Los Robles

GREATEST-QUALITY WINES

1. **EQ Syrah 2004** Matetic, San Antonio (CLP 22,000)
2. **Almaviva 2001** Almaviva, Maipo (CLP 59,900)
3. **Cipreses Vineyard Sauvignon Blanc 2005** Casa Marín, San Antonio (CLP 19,000)
4. **Ocio Pinot Noir 2004** Cono Sur, Casablanca (CLP 29,000)
5. **20 Barrels Sauvignon Blanc 2005** Cono Sur, Casablanca (CLP 12,000)
6. **Neyen 2003** Neyen, Colchagua (CLP 32,000)
7. **Lot 21 Pinot Noir 2005** Viña Leyda, San Antonio (CLP 22,000)
8. **Purple Angel 2003** Montes, Colchagua (CLP 29,000)
9. **20 Barrels Chardonnay 2005** Cono Sur, Casablanca (CLP 12,000)
10. **Casa Real Reserva Especial Cabernet Sauvignon 2001** Santa Rita, Maipo (CLP 30,000)

NEW UP-AND-COMING PRODUCERS

1. Loma Larga
2. Korta
3. Candelaria
4. Kingston
5. Quintay
6. Los Maquis
7. La Reserva de Caliboro (Erasmo)
8. Polkura
9. Chocalán
10. Viña Santa Cruz

Grapevine

• **Organizers** of the first-ever Carmenère al Mundo competition were surprised and delighted that more than 200 wines were submitted, from as far afield as Uruguay, Bolivia, and France. Chilean winery Casa Silva took the title.

• **Following the lead** of Real Madrid and Boca Juniors, Santiago football club Colo Colo is launching a range of wines. Made in association with San Pedro, the range runs from a basic wine, sold in Tetra Pak, to a "Special Edition" Cabernet Sauvignon 2005.

BEST BARGAINS

1. **Pinot Noir 2006** Cono Sur, Central Valley (CLP 4,000)
2. **Casillero del Diablo Merlot 2005** Concha y Toro, Central Valley (CLP 3,500)
3. **Alta Tierra Syrah 2004** Falernia, Elqui (CLP 8,500)
4. **Cantaluna Cabernet Sauvignon 2004** Cantaluna, Colchagua (CLP 3,500)
5. **Syrah Reserva 2004** Casas del Bosque, Casablanca (CLP 4,500)
6. **Corralillo Syrah 2005** Matetic, San Antonio (CLP 12,000)
7. **Limited Release Gewurztraminer 2006** Cono Sur, Bío-Bío (CLP 1,900)
8. **Sunrise Merlot 2005** Concha y Toro, Central Valley (CLP 1,700)
9. **Cahuil Pinot Noir 2005** Viña Leyda, San Antonio (CLP 10,500)
10. **Chileno Gold Sauvignon Blanc 2005** Ventisquero, Casablanca (CLP 4,500)

MOST EXCITING OR UNUSUAL FINDS

1. **Reserva Superior Syrah/ Grenache/Viognier 2005** Gracia, Cachapoal (CLP 12,000) *Grenache is a rarity in Chile, but in this Rhône-style blend it shines alongside the Syrah and Viognier.*
2. **Carmenère Reserva 2005** Falernia, Elqui (CLP 9,000) *Carmenère made using some Amarone-style dried grape fermentation to add richness and depth. Intriguing.*
3. **Yaquil Vineyards Malbec/Syrah 2003** Candelaria, Central Valley (CLP 10,000) *Unusual but successful blend from this new Colchagua outfit.*
4. **Pangea 2004** Ventisquero, Colchagua (CLP 30,000) *First release of this Apalta-grown Syrah/ Cabernet made in conjunction with former Grange winemaker John Duval.*
5. **Blanc de Blancs 2003** Valdivieso, Curicó (CLP 5,500) *Sparkling Chilean wine isn't on most people's radar, but this well-balanced version shows there are good things available.*
6. **Novas Chardonnay/Marsanne/ Viognier 2005** Emiliana Orgánico, Casablanca (CLP 7,000) *Highly unusual blend for Chile, but a fleshy, spicy, excellent one.*
7. **Syrah 2005** Loma Larga, Casablanca (CLP 20,000) *Another very promising Syrah from a new producer in coastal Casablanca.*
8. **Single Vineyard Chardonnay 2005** De Martino, Limarí (CLP 10,000) *Limarí is being hotly tipped as Chile's best region for Chardonnay; this nutty, vibrant wine shows why.*
9. **Castillo de Molina Sauvignon Blanc 2006** San Pedro, Elqui (CLP 5,500) *A unique blend sourced mainly from Elqui, with 10 per cent from Leyda, making for a vibrant, zingy white.*
10. **Corralillo Merlot/Malbec 2004** Matetic, San Antonio (CLP 12,000) *Sleek, spicy proof that these Bordelais varieties can work in coastal Chilean vineyards.*

Grapevine

• **Chile now has** its very own biodynamic wine producers' association, formed on the advice of Californian consultant Alan York. The purpose of the group, which includes Antiyal, Emiliana Orgánico, Seña, and Matetic, is to encourage the spread of biodynamics in Chile and to work with scientists to validate the theories behind this still-contentious method of agriculture.

Argentina

Tim Atkin MW

Argentina's vineyards continue to increase in size, according to the Instituto Nacional de Vitivinicultura, confirming that the industry is booming after the difficult economic times of 2002 and 2003.

TIM ATKIN MW

The latest statistics show new plantings of 5,931 ha in 2005, taking the national total to 218, 589 ha (up 2.79 per cent on 2004). This is still some way short of the 300,000 ha that existed in the late 1970s, but today's vineyards are planted with more suitable varieties and, crucially, are located in a broader range of microclimates, taking advantage in particular of higher altitudes closer to the Andes.

Mendoza continues to dominate the viticultural landscape, with 69.96 per cent of plantings. After much warmer San Juan (21.98 per cent) and La Rioja (3.84 per cent), no area has more than 2 per cent of plantings. Only Río Negro (1.32 per cent), Catamarca (1.09 per cent), and Salta (0.89 per cent) are statistically significant. It is a sign of Argentina's traditional approach to viticulture (and to high yields and abundant water for irrigation) that nearly 60 per cent of these vineyards are planted on overhead trellises (*parrales*).

Argentina's varietal diversity is as strong as ever, but the move away from basic grapes such as Criolla continues. The most planted varieties

TIM ATKIN MW is the wine correspondent of *The Observer* and wine editor at large of *OLN* and *Class* magazines. He has won more than a dozen major awards for his wine writing, including five Glenfiddichs and four Lanson Wine Writer of the Year gongs. He first visited Argentina in 1994, since when he has returned to the country on eight occasions to taste its wines, dance the tango badly, and marvel at the thickness of its steaks. Tim judges wines all over the world and is co-chairman of the International Wine Challenge, the world's biggest blind-tasting competition.

are currently Malbec (22,462 ha), Bonarda (18,033 ha), Cabernet Sauvignon (16,928 ha), Syrah (11,678 ha), Torrontés (8,106 ha), Tempranillo (6,099 ha), Chardonnay (5,155 ha), Chenin Blanc (3,027 ha), and Ugni Blanc (2,603 ha). Of these varieties, only Chenin Blanc, Ugni Blanc, and Torrontés (very slightly) have lost plantings since 1990, which gives an indication of how many hectares of Criolla have been grubbed up. As you'd expect, the major increases have been for Bonarda, Malbec, Syrah, and, especially, Cabernet Sauvignon.

Wines of Argentina Awards

The first Wines of Argentina Awards, held in Mendoza in February 2007, had a British feel to them, with a lineup of judges that included Jancis Robinson MW, Oz Clarke, Peter Richards, Adrian Atkinson, Beverley Blanning MW, Joe Fattorini, and Robert Joseph, as well as UK-based sommelier Henri Chapon. Completing the panel were four Argentine judges: Pedro Marchevsky from Dominio del Plata, Daniel Pi from Trapiche, Roberto de la Mota from Bodegas Mendel, and Carlos Tizio from Monteviejo.

Nearly 500 wines were blind-tasted, categorized by price (above and below £10) and grape variety/varieties. Gold trophies were awarded to nine wines: Familia Zuccardi Alma 4 Chardonnay Roble 2003, Pulenta Estate La Flor Sauvignon Blanc 2006, Bodega Felix Lavaque Quara Torrontés 2006, Luigi Bosca Gala 3 Viognier 2006, Tittarelli VOSA Reserva Especial Tempranillo 2004, Norton Privada 2003, Santa Ana La Mascota Cabernet Sauvignon 2005, Domaine Vistalba Fabre Montmayou Malbec Gran Reserva 2005, and Finca Don Domenico de Huanacache Syrah 2006. A further 15 wines won gold medals.

Grapevine

• **The UK's ethically minded Co-operative Group,** which leads the world in promoting Fairtrade wines, has expanded its range to include its first bottles from Argentina. The four wines are all sourced from the La Riojana Co-operative, which received Fairtrade accreditation in May 2006. The project, which will benefit a community of workers in the village of Tilimuqui, will initially focus on providing a regular water supply to the 97 inhabitants. The four wines are a Torrontés/Chardonnay, a Bonarda/Shiraz, a Pinot Grigio, and a Shiraz.

• **Trapiche, Argentina's largest producer,** has selected the second lineup of its Malbec Single Vineyard wines. The three varietals, all from the 2004 vintage, were whittled down from 90 samples and were chosen by chief winemaker Daniel Pi and his team. The three wines came from Viña Carlos Gei Berra in Lunlunta, Viña Victorio Coletto in El Peral, and Viña Pedro Gonzalez in El Cepillo. All three wines were aged for 18 months in French oak and are labelled with the name of the grower. Pedro Gonzalez was also chosen in 2003.

Opinion:
The UK lags behind the USA

Is the UK missing out on what Argentina has to offer? The question may sound a little silly, given that British judges constituted the majority of the tasters at the first Wines of Argentina Awards and that the country's first generic office overseas has just opened in the UK. There's also the small fact that the UK is still Argentina's second-largest export market, with 1.645 million cases in 2006 (source: CAUCASIA Wine Thinking).

It is true that the UK remains some way ahead of other major buyers of Argentine wine (Brazil, the Netherlands, Canada, and Denmark), but it is slipping further and further behind the number-one export market, the United States. And while the USA is steadily increasing imports (1.876 million cases in 2004, 2.26 million in '05, and 2.586 million in '06), the UK struggled to sell Argentine wine in 2006 (down from 2.072 million in '05).

When you look at the price that consumers are prepared to pay for Argentine wine, however, the picture is even more dramatic – at least it is if you're an Argentine winery owner. The average case price to the trade in the UK is US$19.67, which puts the UK a miserly 13th in the list of Argentina's 15 largest export markets. Only Russia and Paraguay pay less for their Torrontés, Syrah, and Malbec.

The figures are even more significant when you isolate the UK and the United States. Americans pay an average of US$29.29 per case, which is nearly US$10 more than we Brits do. The total FOB (free on board) prices for the two nations in 2006 were US$75.759 million and US$32.355 million respectively. In other words, any winery that wants to export will get a much higher price for its wines in the USA (and Mexico, Canada, Finland, and Sweden) than in the UK.

The appreciation of top Argentine wines is much, much greater in the USA than it is in the UK, where South America's largest producing nation is still regarded, above all, as a source of sub-£6 red. Argentina is not the only country to suffer from the competitiveness of the UK wine trade – and the apparent unwillingness of consumers to spend more than an average of £4 on a bottle of wine – but it is struggling to make headway in the UK. Part of the reason is that it does not have a perceived top end in the way that Australia, New Zealand, the United States, and even Chile do. This is something James Forbes and his team at Wines of Argentina (UK) need to address as a matter of urgency – otherwise, the top Argentine producers are going to go elsewhere.

Vintage Report

Advance report on the latest harvest

2007

It was always going to be difficult for the 2007 vintage to follow 2006, widely regarded as one of the best ever in Argentina. But purely in numerical terms, the signs are that it has surpassed it, with Mendoza and San Juan, the two provinces that account for 94 per cent of the country's total crop, reporting increases of 2.3 per cent and 8.12 per cent on 2007. To a certain degree, the increase can be explained by new plantings, but in high-production areas the crop suffered less from adverse weather conditions (particularly hail), and hail nets were also introduced.

The overall growing season was characterized by warmer-than-usual daytime temperatures (1.8°C [3.25°F] above average) and colder nights (1°C [1.8°F] below average). It was also marked by higher relative humidity, helping prevent problems with sunburned bunches but creating other, bunch-rot-related headaches for growers. On 16 February, a particularly cold snap in Mendoza (when temperatures fell to 2–3°C [35.6–37.4°F] at night) caused what Bodega Catena Zapata describes as a "hormonal shock" in many vineyards, "significantly quickening the ripening process". Picking was, therefore, two to four weeks earlier than usual, depending on the region.

The vintage was marked by higher-than-average rainfall and several violent hailstorms. In San Rafael, 5,000 ha were hit by a storm at the end of January, while 3,000 ha in Mendoza lost 50–100 per cent of their grapes. Even so, initial quality predictions are good to very good, if not as high as in 2006. As much as anything, this is a reflection of more modern viticultural practices. At this stage, 2007 looks like being a winemakers' vintage.

Updates on the previous five vintages

2006

Vintage rating: *Red: 97, White: 95*

The 2006 vintage is being hailed as one of the finest ever in Argentina, producing red wines with deep colour, soft tannins, and intense flavours. The whites are also very good, especially from higher-altitude vineyards in areas such as the Uco Valley. In Mendoza, a cool, snowy winter was followed by warmer-than-average temperatures in spring and summer.

Higher-than-normal levels of humidity meant that the vines did not suffer from heat stress. Pronounced diurnal-temperature variation promoted slow grape maturation and well-balanced wines. In January, temperatures in Mendoza varied between 10°C and 32°C (50–90°F). On the minus side, Mendoza suffered from a large hailstorm on 27 December 2005, which hit the subregions of Perdriel and especially Vistalba. A second, less damaging storm in the first week of March affected the areas of Medrano and the central eastern region. Yields are up on 2005, with some wineries talking about an increase of 20 per cent. Reacting to a potentially large crop, many of the leading producers used fruit thinning in December and January to reduce yields by as much as 50 per cent.

2005

Vintage rating: *Red: 93, White: 92*

A cooler ripening season and a late harvest produced elegant, full-coloured wines with intense fruit flavours and a slightly lower degree of alcohol than usual. January and February were cool. There were fears that rains in January might pose problems, but good work in the vineyards avoided this. Much more serious, at least in Perdriel, were the hailstorm and heavy rains that came on 14 February. March was somewhat warmer, bringing on complete ripeness of the grapes, which were harvested in good condition and with no sign of dehydration. In San Juan, several producers rated 2005 as one of the best-ever vintages, with Syrah vines showing particularly well. The best Malbecs and Chardonnays are most impressive in 2005, especially from high-altitude vineyards, where late autumn was dry and sunny, yet comparatively cool.

2004

Vintage rating: *Red: 94, White: 90*

The winter of 2003 was particularly warm and dry and much affected by the Zonda, the warm wind from the mountains to the north, which causes humidity to drop dramatically. This led to irrigation starting earlier than usual, partly because of a lack of snow in the Andes. Nevertheless, bunch formation was good, as were flowering and fruit set. The summer was also hot and dry, with temperatures remaining high during the nights. Some rain fell at the end of January, leading to a rapid spurt in growth. In February, temperatures fell and there was a little more rain. In order to minimize the effects of botrytis, the picking of white grapes began on 8 February. For the black grapes, however, picking was later than usual, due to delays in achieving optimal phenolic ripeness. The white wines are full of flavour, with crisp acidity, while the best reds are outstanding, with deep colour, full tannins, and good ageing potential, thanks to thicker skins and intense varietal character.

2003

Vintage rating: *Red: 97, White: 94*

The official position on the 2003 vintage in Mendoza is that the white wines are "very good" and the reds "outstanding". Spring was cool and dry, but the summer was the hottest on record, with rainfall well below average. Some vineyards suffered from sunburn, which called for carefully managed irrigation. The autumn was cooler, and grapes were picked in ideal conditions. Opinions are divided as to whether the wines are as good as those from the excellent 2002 vintage, but some vineyard managers, such as Alejandro Sejanovich at Catena Zapata, think that 2003 outperformed 2002 in some vineyards. Cabernet Sauvignon was the star variety in 2003, although some high-altitude Malbecs are outstanding, too.

2002

Vintage rating: *Red: 98, White: 94*

Considered in Mendoza to be the best vintage for 10 years or more, with plentiful water for irrigation and close to ideal conditions. The ripening period was long, with cool, dry weather, leading to wines with concentrated fruit flavours. In Salta, in the north, the vintage took place 10 days earlier than usual. There are many outstanding wines from this vintage, with the best reds showing fruit concentration, deep colour, ripe tannins, and marked ageing potential. The top reds are still drinking very well and will continue to improve for five to eight years or more.

Grapevine

• **Familia Zuccardi,** arguably the most innovative producer in Argentina, has planted a number of new varieties in its Santa Julia Innovación vineyards: Trincadeira, Greco di Tufo, Fiano di Avellino, Albariño, Petit Manseng, and Vermentino. This follows its success with other off-the-wall varieties such as Carmenère, Ancellotta, Caladoc, and Marselan.

• **Wines of Argentina,** after four years of working with various PR companies in the UK, opened its first office outside Argentina in September 2006. The director is James Forbes, previously a senior buyer at the Oddbins off-licence chain, where one of his responsibilities was purchasing South American wines.

GREATEST WINE PRODUCERS

1. Catena Zapata
2. Alta Vista
3. O Fournier
4. Terrazas
5. Pascual Toso
6. Bodega Lurton
7. Viña Cobos
8. Pulenta Estate
9. Yacochuya
10. Noemia

FASTEST-IMPROVING PRODUCERS

1. Trapiche
2. Kaikén
3. Navarro Correas
4. Etchart
5. Tittarelli
6. Familia Zuccardi
7. Finca Flichman
8. Susana Balbo
9. Graffigna
10. Altas Cumbres

NEW UP-AND-COMING PRODUCERS

1. Kaikén
2. Chakana
3. Bodega Chacra
4. Viña Melipal
5. Familia Schroeder
6. Saurus
7. Familia Cassone
8. Finca de Altura
9. Eral Bravo
10. Alma 4

BEST-VALUE PRODUCERS

1. Finca Flichman
2. Bodegas Callia
3. Familia Zuccardi
4. Argento
5. Pascual Toso
6. Doña Paula

7. Trivento
8. La Riojana Co-operative
9. Norton
10. Finca La Celia

GREATEST-QUALITY WINES

1. **Catena Alta Chardonnay 2003** Catena Zapata, Mendoza (AP 120)
2. **Gala 3 2005** Luigi Bosca, Mendoza (AP 100)
3. **A Crux Malbec 2004** O Fournier, Valle de Uco (AP 120)
4. **Magdalena Toso 2002** Pascual Toso, Mendoza (AP 200)
5. **Gran Corte VII 2004** Pulenta Estate, Alto Agrelo (AP 105)
6. **Chacayes 2004** Bodega Lurton, Mendoza (AP 180)
7. **Cobos Malbec 2003** Paul Hobbs, Luján de Coyo (AP 270)
8. **Viña Victorio Coletto Single Vineyard Malbec 2004** Trapiche, Mendoza (AP 180)
9. **Cheval des Andes 2003** Terrazas/ Château Cheval Blanc, Mendoza (AP 200)
10. **Nicolás Catena Zapata 2002** Catena Zapata, Mendoza (AP 320)

BEST BARGAINS

1. **Sauvignon Blanc 2006** Chakana, Agrelo (AP 25)
2. **Finca La Higuera Pinot Gris 2006** Bodega Lurton, Mendoza (AP 30)
3. **Viognier 2006** Trivento, Mendoza (AP 25)
4. **Crios de Susana Balbo Torrontés 2006** Susana Balbo, Cafayate (AP 40)
5. **Misterio Malbec 2005** Finca Flichman, Mendoza (AP 25)
6. **Oak Aged Malbec Reserva 2005** Finca Flichman, Mendoza (AP 40)
7. **Malbec 2006** Argento, Mendoza (AP 40)

⑧ **Barrel Select Malbec 2003**
Norton, Mendoza (AP 45)

⑨ **Syrah 2005** Pascual Toso,
Mendoza (AP 30)

⑩ **Grande Reserve Malbec Terroir
Selection 2004** Alta Vista,
Mendoza (AP 75)

MOST EXCITING OR UNUSUAL FINDS

① **Fairtrade Argentine Torrontés/
Chardonnay 2006** Co-operative
Group (AP 20) *The best of the
Fairtrade wines produced by La
Riojana, signalling a new, ethical
departure for Argentina. Grapey
and perfumed, with Torrontés in
the driving seat.*

② **Barbera 2005** Norton, Mendoza
(AP 25) *An unoaked take on a
classic Piedmont grape, this has
the tannins and the slight rusticity
you expect from the grape, as well
as the fruit sweetness.*

③ **Bonarda 2006** Argento, Mendoza
(AP 40) *Meaty, deeply coloured,
and packed with sweet plum and
blueberry fruit, this is a classic
glugging red at a great price.*

④ **Synthesis The Blend 2004**
Sophenia, Mendoza (AP 80) *This
Uco Valley winery already has a
great reputation for its whites, but
this refined, sweetly oaked Malbec/
Cabernet/Merlot blend is stunning.*

⑤ **Torrontés Late Harvest 2005**
Etchart, Salta (AP 40) *The best of
a number of dessert wines made
from Argentina's most distinctive*
white grape. The sweetness is
perfectly judged, with enough
acidity for balance.

⑥ **Extra Brut 2005** Santa Julia,
Mendoza (AP 60) *The addition
of 11 per cent Viognier adds
interest to this flavoursome Pinot/
Chardonnay fizz, making it one of
the better Argentine sparklers.*

⑦ **Estate Reserve Merlot 2004**
Canale, Río Negro (AP 70) *Evidence
that southerly, cool-climate Río
Negro has a bright future with
Merlot, this is textured and fleshy
with attractive chocolate and
green-pepper notes.*

⑧ **Clos de los Siete 2005** Clos
de los Siete, Mendoza (AP 85)
*The best vintage yet of this
brilliant-value blend of 50 per cent
Malbec, 30 per cent Merlot, 10
per cent Cabernet Sauvignon, and
10 per cent Syrah, with considerable
complexity at the price.*

⑨ **Zuccardi Q Tempranillo 2003**
Familia Zuccardi, Mendoza (AP 55)
*Already established as one of
Argentina's best Tempranillos,
the Zuccardi 2003 is a step up
on previous vintages, with sweet,
spicy fruit and lovely texture.*

⑩ **Tesco Finest San Juan
Argentinian Shiraz 2005**
Bodegas Callia, San Juan (AP 55)
*It's good to see a major retailer
getting behind the up-and-coming
region of San Juan, especially for
its most promising grape, Shiraz.
Ripe and fleshy with a touch of oak.*

Grapevine

• **Two of the world's biggest
drinks groups** have made substantial
investments in existing projects in
Argentina recently. LVMH, owner of
Terrazas, has spent US$18 million on
a new facility in Agrelo, while Diageo
has invested US$6 million in its
existing winery in the suburbs of
Mendoza. A third big investment,
this time in the comparatively
unfashionable region of La Rioja, is
Chanar Muyo, where the owners
have spent US$8 million on a new
winery, restaurant, and guest house.

Australia

Huon Hooke

Drought … frost … fires. Grape glut and depressed prices. There seems to be no end of woes for Australia's grape growers at present.

HUON HOOKE

It's almost a classic chain reaction. First, there's been a drought for several years – the exact number depends on which region is under discussion. But soil moisture levels are very low in just about every region except Margaret River, underground water tables having fallen gradually over many years and showing no sign of replenishing (Coonawarra is simply the most graphic region thus afflicted: you can actually see the sinking water level). Restricted spring growth (RSG) is a reality in many vineyards, with stunted, sick-looking foliage the outward sign.

Irrigation water is critically low in many areas, especially the Murray River-dependent Riverland and Sunraysia, where allocations have been repeatedly cut this year (70 per cent of normal at time of writing and likely to be cut further), and if rain doesn't fall soon – and it's not forecast to – allocations will be zero next season, which will guarantee that vines and fruit trees will simply die. Mildura's rainfall is never high, but this season

HUON HOOKE is coauthor of *The Penguin Good Australian Wine Guide*, the country's most respected buyer's guide. He is a wine-marketing and production graduate of Roseworthy Agricultural College and has been a weekly columnist for the John Fairfax Group of newspapers since 1983. Huon writes columns in the Good Living section of the *Sydney Morning Herald* and the *Good Weekend* magazine of the *Herald* and Melbourne's *The Age*. He is also contributing editor of Australian *Gourmet Traveller Wine* magazine and writes for various other publications, such as *Decanter* and *Slow Wine*. He has been judging in wine competitions since 1987 and judges eight to 10 shows a year in Australia and abroad. Huon has judged in New Zealand, South Africa, Chile, Belgium, Slovenia, Canada, and the USA. He currently chairs several Australian competitions and is a senior judge at Adelaide and Sydney.

they've had just 20 per cent of the average. Unless there is major rain in May (which looks very unlikely), there will be no irrigation water allocation at all in the Murray-Darling system in the 2007/08 season. Trees and vines cannot live without irrigation in this region, and the death of entire vineyards means not one but many years of hardship for growers.

Frost is the less anticipated symptom of drought. Lack of cloud cover in late spring meant very cold nights and frosts that killed the tender new growth. Not just once, but repeatedly. This means that the growth from the secondary buds is also killed, and next season's crop will be affected because bunch primordiae were burned. Yarra Valley, Heathcote, Goulburn Valley, King and Alpine valleys, Riverland, and many other regions were affected. The Victorian Wine Industry Association estimated that 35–40 per cent of grapes had been lost right across the state. Early forecasts of loss were about A$40 million.

However, there is potentially some good news in all this gloom: most of Australia's approximately 300,000-tonne grape surplus is in the cooler regions, where the combination of drought and frost is taking

Grapevine

• **Farewell to two** of Australia's greatest wine identities, who passed away during 2006: Len Evans and John Middleton. Evans was our best-known wine man: a wine-company owner, marketer, promoter, judge, artist, raconteur, and all-round wine man, cofounder of the Rothbury Estate and Petaluma, a *Decanter* magazine Man of the Year, a formidable palate, educator, and proselyte for quality. He died on 17 August at the age of 75. Former medico Dr John Middleton, the irascible creator, owner, and chief winemaker of Yarra Valley icon Mount Mary, died in June at the age of 82. In 2005, US critic Robert Parker lambasted flagship Mount Mary wine Quintet, a blend of all five bordeaux black grapes, despite the fact that innumerable wine lovers and critics with different tastes (self included) rate it as one of Australia's greatest wines. Middleton disliked wine competitions, writers, and "serial wine tasters" who taste many wines at a time. He did not believe anyone could taste more than a handful of wines at a sitting. "Alcohol is an anaesthetic," he would say, "and anaesthetics quickly render the palate insensible."

• **With wine and grapes** in oversupply, Australians have seen branded varietal Chardonnay for A$2.99 a bottle, and BWS – a Woolworths liquor subchain – had a perfectly quaffable cleanskin Chardonnay for A$1.99 – the Aussie equivalent of Two Buck Chuck.

• **Bob Oatley**, the founder of Rosemount who precipitated the sale of Southcorp to Foster's a couple of years ago, has re-entered the wine industry. Oatley and his family, who made millions from selling Rosemount to Southcorp, have bought the Montrose winery in Mudgee (formerly owned by Orlando Wyndham) in which to vinify the grapes from their several hundred hectares of Mudgee vineyards.

the heaviest toll. It is likely that, while the short-term pain will be great, the balance between supply and demand will be restored substantially sooner because of the reduced 2007 crop.

Lousy vines in Yarra Valley

The Yarra Valley has had a triple whammy in the 2006/07 season: after devastating frosts and drought came the news that the vine aphid phylloxera had been discovered in the region for the first time. Phylloxera, one of the most dreaded grapevine afflictions, has been in several Victoria wine regions since the late 1800s, but the Yarra had managed to avoid it. Foster's discovered the small infestation in its 32-ha vineyard on St Huberts Road at Coldstream on 1 December. A quarantine zone 5 km (3 miles) in radius has been declared around the site, and the infected vines will be destroyed on-site. And what variety are they? Merlot (groan!).

Adelaide Hills expansion

The Adelaide Hills wine region has a green light to expand, following the removal of a moratorium on building new wineries. There has been a temporary ban on wineries and cellar-door facilities in the Hills for the past five years because of environmental considerations: the Hills are an important part of the catchment for the Adelaide water supply, and it was felt that run-off could be polluted by winery waste. Just how dangerous winery waste – which is mostly grape residue – could be was a moot point. Now the Hills, which is among Australia's finest wine regions and one of the most attractive to visit, is likely to get at least six new wineries, taking the total to 14.

Grapevine

• **Shiraz/Viognier** will soon appear on wines distributed in the EU. Until the new Australia–EU wine-trade agreement, our winemakers were not legally allowed to label Shiraz/Viognier blends as such in the EU unless they contained at least 5 per cent Viognier.

• **A proposed bypass** threatens the vineyard of Parker Coonawarra Estate, the flagship producer of Terra Rossa First Growth red wine. The bypass is planned for the region's main town, Penola.

• **Yellow Tail** notched up yet another major achievement in the USA in 2006. It became the top-selling wine overall, by retail value, according to "The US Wine Market: Impact Databank Review and Forecast". Yellow Tail, produced in the Riverina by family-owned Casella Wines, registered sales of US$621 million, which was about 3 per cent of the total US$21 billion Americans spent on retail wine purchases. This capped Yellow Tail's 2003 achievement, when it became the biggest-selling imported wine by volume in the USA.

Opinion:
Smoke threat

Smoke-tainted grapes will be a big issue following the widespread bushfires in the 2006/07 summer. Most of northeast Victoria's vineyards, as well as much of the Yarra Valley, were affected by bushfire smoke in the early summer. The King and Alpine valleys, which lost millions of dollars because of bushfire smoke tainting grapes in 2003, were in the firing line again. Smoke lingering over vineyards leaves a residue on the grape skins, a guaiacol compound not too different from the 4EG (4-ethyl guaiacol) caused by Brettanomyces, which even in small amounts leaves an objectionable taste in wine. It can be treated by reverse osmosis, but this is expensive and not 100 per cent effective. After years of drought, Australian forests are tinder-dry, leading to an unusually high bushfire threat. In addition, air humidity levels, even at night, are abnormally low, giving rise to what some say are unprecedented conditions for wild fires.

A related issue is controlled fuel-reduction burns, conducted by fire brigades and government departments such as Western Australia's Conservation and Land Management (CALM). This organization persists with hazard-reduction burns in the weeks preceding harvest, when grapes are vulnerable to smoke tainting. In regions such as Pemberton, this has already led to significant income loss for some growers, and there is no sign of CALM changing its ways. A solution agreeable to both parties must be worked out, and soon.

Show samples should come from retailers

The Wither Hills controversy in New Zealand has implications for Australia, because of the widespread practice of batch bottling. Most, if not all, large-volume Australian wines are bottled in batches, some of them many batches in a year, and there is no guarantee that all batches are similar, let alone identical. Tasting a shop-bought bottle of inexpensive big-brand Australian wine with a gold medal or trophy sticker can lead one to wonder how any panel of competent judges (and most Australian shows are competently judged) could score the wine so highly. You don't have to be a cynic to ask whether the judges tasted a bottle from a different batch. The temptation for winemakers to put together a special blend for shows and wine critics must be considerable. The Australian Society for Viticulture and Oenology recommends that all wine shows conduct random audits, in which a bottle taken from the winery warehouse is compared with the show entry, and many shows now do this. Ideally, however, they should buy the audit samples from retailers.

Growers v. wineries

Truth is the first casualty in any war, and so it is in the battle between growers and wineries.

It's more than 20 years since the last grapevine-pull, but growers in the Riverland, Australia's largest grape-growing region, are seriously considering uprooting vines, starting with the less popular varieties. It has been estimated that a quarter of the region's 1,300 growers face ruin. The current wine surplus is very serious, with estimates ranging from 200 million to 900 million litres.

There seem to be fibs on both sides as the big wine companies seek to overstate the surplus in an effort to drive down grape prices. Grower spokesman Chris Byrne says that at least 25 per cent of the region's growers will be unsustainable within the next five years, since costs outstrip returns. He also says that it costs an average A$350 to grow a tonne of grapes, but returns were as little as A$100 in the 2006 vintage. One thing is certain: wineries have not paid fair prices for grapes, and growers would be better off dropping them on the ground than selling them for below production cost and caving in to the big companies' game.

Grapevine

• **Cullen Wines** of Margaret River has become the first Australian winery and vineyard to be certified carbon-neutral. Always environmentally aware, winemaker Vanya Cullen has announced that all the carbon used and the carbon dioxide emissions created are offset by planting an appropriate number of trees. Cullen has converted all its vineyards to biodynamic farming, and Vanya is an active promoter of the philosophy.

• **The number** of Australian wine producers has doubled in the past eight years, according to the latest edition of the industry's bible, *The Australian and New Zealand Wine Industry Directory.* The total is now 2,008, compared with 998 in 1998. In fact, there are almost certainly a lot more, since we wine scribes often receive tasting samples and mail from wineries that are not listed in the directory.

• **The Sydney-based** *Wine Dogs* book phenomenon continues to gather momentum. *Wine Dogs USA Edition* (A$49) is the biggest yet, with 536 pages, 450 dogs, and more than 300 wineries covering 10 states. Go to the website (www.winedogs.com) and watch the movie of Parker rating his own bulldog out of 100.

Vintage Report

Advance report on the latest harvest

2007

This was a season most Australian *vignerons* would prefer to forget. Universal drought, widespread and repeated frosts, and bushfires early in the season – even hail at Christmas in some Yarra Valley vineyards – all added up to overall yields slashed by what looks, at time of writing, to be somewhere between 30 and 35 per cent down on 2006. While catastrophic for many small growers, causing an unprecedented cash-flow crisis, it will soon help bring the oversupply into something approaching balance. The vintage was so early – a month in places – that winemakers were wondering what to do with their spare time. Quality is very variable: some hotter regions such as Barossa Valley found the season too hot and dry, with reds being tough and tannic without much fruit, while cooler regions such as Tasmania and southern Victoria have some good to very good wine, but little of it. Mornington Peninsula, Hunter Valley, and Margaret River look to have had the most successful vintages. The King and Alpine valleys suffered more than most: yields are down by 70 to 80 per cent, and as in 2003, bushfire smoke taint again made much of the fruit unusable. Bring on 2008…!

Updates on the previous five vintages

2006

Vintage rating: *Red: 92, White: 90*

The great paradox in this wide, brown land in 2006 was that in Western Australia it was one of the latest harvests on record, and in the eastern states one of the earliest. In the east, the hurried ripening was brought on by drought conditions and hotter summer-to-autumn temperatures – generally good for red wines, but not great for whites. In the west, the cool, overcast conditions delayed harvest, so that reds are very chancy but whites can be superb. Most of the top wineries will make some 2006 red, but in much-reduced quantities. One exception to the eastern states' white-wine rule was Clare and Eden Valley Rieslings, which are very good, although unlikely to live as long as the stellar 2005s and 2002s. In most of Victoria, New South Wales, and South Australia, the 2005/06 season was the fourth successive season of drought, although the large size of the crop belied this fact. Overall, a good to very good season.

2005

Vintage rating: *Red: 95; White: 96*

This is an outstanding vintage, the best since 2002 and possibly 1998. It gave benchmark wines of all the classics: Rieslings in the Clare and Eden valleys, Semillons in the Hunter Valley, Shiraz in the Barossa, Cabernet in Coonawarra, and Pinot Noir in Tasmania and the Yarra Valley. The whites proved outstanding, although the reds could be their equal; already, 2005 Pinot Noirs from the cooler southern districts have greatly impressed. Western Australia is the only real glitch: mid-vintage rain upset ripening, and winemakers were less enthusiastic than elsewhere. Some very good wines have already been released, however. Production equalled the 2004 record, although high yields in the high-quality regions were not a problem as in 2004.

2004

Vintage rating: *Red: 93, White: 86*

Initial expectations for the 2004 reds have been upgraded as the wines appear on the market, revealing 2004 as a very good red year, especially in South Australia. Original estimates for a massive crop were trimmed after a combination of severe mid-February heat, especially in South Australia, and crop thinning, but it was still a record harvest. Southern Victoria had high yields and avoided temperature extremes. Yarra Valley quality is good, despite a wet end to the vintage: whites are very good, but lower yields would have made it a top red year, too. Coonawarra had big yields, and while quality is mostly good, overcropped vineyards struggled to ripen. Clare had a good vintage despite suffering in the February heat, and the Rieslings are good but forward. McLaren Vale and the Barossa made excellent Shiraz, and the Adelaide Hills had a decent vintage overall. The Hunter made very good Semillon and Chardonnay, but reds are light.

2003

Vintage rating: *Red: 87, White: 83*

As the 2004s have gone up in our estimations, the 2003s have slipped further. Many of the reds appear to be drying out already, with unbalanced tannins and fading fruit. Universally, 2003 was a year of reduced yields caused by drought, with small bunches of small berries. Rain close to harvest resulted in berry split, further cutting yields in several regions, stretching from Tasmania to central Victoria to McLaren Vale, and smoke taint from January bushfires in northeast Victoria added insult to injury.

Some noted "big red" regions such as Heathcote, Barossa, and McLaren Vale struggled to attain flavour ripeness despite very high alcohols. There are some reds with unripe tannins. The best wines are Shiraz and Chardonnay, with patches of excitement created by Clare and Eden Valley Riesling and Coonawarra Cabernet. Southern Victoria had a very good vintage. Late rain spoilt the Tasmanian vintage and, to a lesser degree, the Great Southern in Western Australia. Margaret River was variable and only fair.

2002

Vintage rating: *Red: 94, White: 95*

Record cool temperatures during the summer brought South Australia an outstanding vintage, especially for white wines in Clare and the Barossa – and even McLaren Vale, not noted for fine dry whites. The Riverland had a great year with some fine whites and reds showing superb colour and varietal flavour. There is a slight question mark over flavour ripeness for reds in cooler areas such as Eden Valley. The Hunter Valley, Mudgee, Orange, Hilltops, and Riverina all had an excellent vintage, while southerly regions like Tasmania and southern Victoria were able to ripen their grapes fully. Southern yields were miserly, especially in cool regions such as Tasmania, Yarra, Mornington, and Geelong. Western Australia was less favoured, but whites are good.

GREATEST WINE PRODUCERS

The brands that qualify the umbrella company for inclusion are listed after the regions.

1. Giaconda (Beechworth)
2. Henschke (Eden Valley)
3. Paringa Estate (Mornington Peninsula)
4. De Bortoli (Yarra Valley)
5. Shaw & Smith (Adelaide Hills)
6. Voyager Estate (Margaret River)
7. Balnaves (Coonawarra)
8. Foster's (national) Penfolds, Seppelt, Wynns, Coldstream Hills, Devil's Lair
9. Hardys (national) Hardys, Houghton, Brookland Valley, Yarra Burn
10. Lion Nathan (national) Petaluma, Stonier, St Hallett, Knappstein, Mitchelton

FASTEST-IMPROVING PRODUCERS

1. De Bortoli (Yarra Valley)
2. Thorn-Clarke (Barossa Valley)
3. Oakridge (Yarra Valley)
4. Zema Estate (Coonawarra)
5. Harewood (Great Southern)
6. Moorooduc Estate (Mornington Peninsula)
7. Pizzini (King Valley)
8. Mistletoe (Hunter Valley)
9. Port Phillip Estate (Mornington Peninsula)
10. Sandalford (Margaret River)

NEW UP-AND-COMING PRODUCERS

1. John Duval (Barossa Valley)
2. SC Pannell (McLaren Vale)
3. PHI (Yarra Valley)
4. Savaterre (Beechworth)
5. Spinifex (Barossa Valley)
6. Bellarmine (Pemberton)
7. YarraLoch (Yarra Valley)
8. Tapanappa (South Australia)
9. Prancing Horse (Mornington Peninsula)
10. Grampians Estate (Grampians)

BEST-VALUE PRODUCERS

The brands that qualify the umbrella company for inclusion are listed after the regions.

1. Trentham Estate (Murray Valley)
2. Westend (Riverina) Three Bridges, Richland
3. De Bortoli (Riverina) Deen De Bortoli, Sacred Hill, Windy Peak, Gulf Station
4. Peter Lehmann (Barossa Valley)
5. Simon Gilbert (Mudgee) Prince Hill, Acrobat
6. Bellarmine (Pemberton)
7. Nugan Estate (Riverina) Cookoothama, Talinga Park
8. Orlando Wyndham (national) Jacob's Creek, Jacob's Creek Reserve, Richmond Grove, Wyndham Estate
9. Hardys (South Australia) Stepping Stone, Leasingham, Banrock Station, Oomoo
10. Cheviot Bridge/Long Flat Wine Company

GREATEST-QUALITY WINES

1. **The Tally Reserve Cabernet Sauvignon 2004** Balnaves, Coonawarra (A$80)
2. **Reserve Pinot Noir 2004** Paringa Estate, Mornington Peninsula (A$90 ex cellars)
3. **Johann Georg Old Vine Shiraz 2004** Kalleske, Barossa Valley (A$90)
4. **Shiraz/Viognier 2005** Clonakilla, Canberra (A$78)
5. **Reserve Chardonnay 2005** Coldstream Hills, Yarra Valley (A$45)
6. **Yattarna Chardonnay 2003** Penfolds, Adelaide Hills (A$130)
7. **Hannah Cabernet Franc/Merlot 2004** Wantirna Estate, Yarra Valley (A$115 ex cellars)
8. **Quintet 2004** Mount Mary, Yarra Valley (A$85 ex cellars)
9. **Riesling 2005** Crawford River, Henty (A$30)
10. **Limited Release Botrytis Semillon 2004** McWilliams, Riverina (A$27 per half-bottle)

BEST BARGAINS

1. **Riesling 2006** Peter Lehmann, Eden Valley (A$15)
2. **Shotfire Ridge Quartage 2004** Thorn-Clarke, Barossa Valley (A$23)
3. **Watervale Riesling 2005** Richmond Grove, Clare Valley (A$19)
4. **Shiraz/Viognier 2005** Terra Felix, Tallarook (A$15)
5. **Selection 23 Sauvignon Blanc 2006** Zilzie, Murray Valley (A$11)
6. **Semillon/Sauvignon Blanc 2006** Salisbury, Murray Valley (A$11)
7. **Baldivis Estate Chardonnay 2005** Palandri, Western Australia (A$12)
8. **Chardonnay 2004** Cookoothama, Riverina (A$15)
9. **d'Arry's Original Shiraz/ Grenache 2004** d'Arenberg, McLaren Vale (A$21)
10. **Oomoo Grenache/Shiraz/ Mourvèdre 2005** Hardys, McLaren Vale (A$15.50)

MOST EXCITING OR UNUSUAL FINDS

① **Nebbiolo 2004** Arrivo, Adelaide Hills (A$55) Co-owners Peter Godden, a key scientist at the Australian Wine Research Institute, and Sally McGill, a long-time Italian wine importer, probably have Australia's only vineyard dedicated solely to Nebbiolo, from which they fastidiously craft a lovely fruit-driven wine using no new oak and winemaking techniques aimed at achieving good extract but soft tannins.

② **Fortuna 2006** Freeman, Hilltops (A$30) The super-Friulian blends such as Vintage Tunina and Terre Alte inspired former oenology professor Brian Freeman to blend Pinot Gris, Riesling, Sauvignon Blanc, Chardonnay, and a smidgen of Aleatico from his high-altitude vineyard near Young in central New South Wales. Older barrels were used in order to highlight the fruit.

③ **Coronamento Reserve Nebbiolo 2002** Pizzini, King Valley (A$110) Pizzini is the first Aussie winery to do well with this grape, and the 2002 is their first reserve bottling – a multilayered, richly textured, powerful, if rather oaky, wine. Italy's Alberto Antonini is their consultant.

④ **Syrah 2005** Luke Lambert, Yarra Valley (A$28) This is a challenging, innovative Shiraz with 3 per cent Viognier. Ignore the slightly stinky bouquet, which reflects a wild-yeast ferment with 35 per cent whole bunches and absence of fining or filtration. The wine is delectable in the mouth and grows as you sip.

⑤ **Tempranillo/Sangiovese/Shiraz 2006** Pindarie, Barossa Valley (A$25) Pindarie burst on to the market in 2006 with an excellent, inexpensive Shiraz from mature vines. This eccentric blend works: it's concentrated, dark-plum juicy, young and not complex, but has flavour and texture to burn.

⑥ **864 Riesling 2005** Oakridge, Yarra Valley (A$50 per half-bottle) Made by freezing grapes in a refrigerated shipping container, this makeshift icewine is delicious. With high acidity, relatively restrained sugar, and heightened aromatics, it's a fine alternative to the super-sweet Riverina blockbusters.

⑦ **MT Tempranillo 2005** Pondalowie, Bendigo (A$24) This is a deliciously gluggable unwooded young Tempranillo made in an early-drinking style by a couple who also make wine in Portugal (MT stands for the Portuguese minha terra). Bright cherry, sarsaparilla, and liquorice flavours.

⑧ **Nullo Mountain Riesling 2005** Louee, Mudgee (A$18) An exciting, enterprising addition to the Mudgee region, this vineyard was planted at 1,100 m (3,600 ft) and yields a startlingly refined, delicate, cool-tasting Riesling. Made by Mudgee's widely experienced David Lowe.

⑨ **Estate Grown Sauvignon 2006** De Bortoli, Yarra Valley (A$22) Influenced by a couple of Sancerre growers, this heralds a new dawn for this grape in Australia: solidsy juice, wild yeasts, old-barrel ferment, and lees-contact techniques lend extra layers of flavour to the fruit without sacrificing varietal integrity.

⑩ **Roussanne 2005** Tallarook, Central Victoria (A$27.50) Winemaker Martin Williams MW uses a variety of techniques such as wild-yeast ferments in older barrels and lees contact to make a series of white wines that push the envelope. This is multidimensional, full of peach/stone fruit, nutty, buttery complexities, and more richness and interest than the grape usually displays.

New Zealand

Bob Campbell MW

Acting on a tip-off, wine writer Michael Cooper bought a bottle of Wither Hills 2006 Sauvignon Blanc and compared it with a sample that he and his panel had just given five stars in a review for *Cuisine* magazine.

BOB CAMPBELL MW

The samples tasted sufficiently different for Cooper to have them chemically analysed. Sure enough, the alcohol level of the wine submitted to the magazine was 14.3 per cent ABV, while the purchased wine was 13.7 per cent ABV. There were also differences in the acidity and residual sugar levels of the samples.

Wither Hills 2006 Sauvignon Blanc had earned a creditable two gold medals, one silver medal, and a five-star rating in local

wine competitions and reviews. Manager/winemaker Brent Marris acknowledged that there were differences, but he claimed inevitable batch variation in large-production wines. More than 100,000 cases of the wine had been made. As a result of the ensuing furore, Marris resigned as chief judge of the Air New Zealand Wine Awards and handed back medals earned by the wine.

Marris is unrepentant, claiming he was the victim of a rigid interpretation of wine-show entry requirements demanding samples be identical to the wine in the marketplace. An audit by NZ Winegrowers failed to find any evidence that superior batches had been deliberately prepared for wine shows. Marris has a point. Strict interpretation of the rules would, for example, mean that any cork-sealed wine was ineligible. I can guarantee

BOB CAMPBELL MW lives in Auckland, where he is group wine editor for ACP Media and wine editor for five magazines within that publishing company. He writes for publications, including *Wine Spectator*, in seven countries, and has judged at wine competitions in seven countries. Bob established his own wine school in 1986, and 18,000 people have graduated from his wine diploma course.

that, if you open 20 bottles of a wine under cork, there will be significant differences, thanks to a variation in air uptake and variable reactions between wine and cork.

However, the rule is necessary to safeguard the integrity of wine shows and to protect the interests of anyone relying on results. In the past 10 years, two wineries have been caught entering wines that were dramatically different from wine under the same label in the marketplace. Both suffered from the public outcry that followed. Wither Hills is guilty of a minor infringement by comparison.

All local wine shows plan to increase the audit of show entries to prevent any manipulation of show samples. But when does batch variation cross the line between significant and insignificant? Wine-show judges will need to decide. Winery lawyers may disagree.

Regional integrity … coming soon

Until recently, New Zealand had no appellation or label-integrity system that guaranteed the authenticity of any region, subregion, district, or vineyard shown on wine labels. In December 2006, the government passed the Geographical Indications (Wine and Spirits) Registration Act, which will eventually provide the framework and legal clout necessary to define and register the boundaries of wine-growing regions.

Although the Act has been passed, it depends on regulations to make it work. These are expected to be in place by December 2007. Then "interested parties" (mainly grape growers and winemakers) will need to apply for registration of defined land areas with special attributes in relation to wine. These may include factors that influence wine flavour, history, reputation, or structure.

The New Zealand model is similar to Australia's Wine Integrity Program except that the Australian system is managed by the Australian Wine Spirit & Brandy Corporation, while ours is managed by the Intellectual Property Office of New Zealand. In other words, theirs is sensibly run by wine people, while ours will be run by bureaucrats with the help of wine people – a distinct disadvantage in my view.

Although those involved in developing this piece of legislation hope that the gradual creation of defined wine areas will be an orderly process, I think it's rather more likely that a little chaos – and a lot of friction – will result, with lawyers and journalists the likely beneficiaries.

Labels to conform to EU standards

The New Zealand Wine Act has increased the minimum percentage for label information on grape variety, vintage, and area of origin from

75 per cent to 85 per cent from the 2007 vintage, effectively bringing local requirements in line with the EU.

If a label features a single variety, it must be made from at least 85 per cent of that variety. If it's a blend of, say, Cabernet Sauvignon and Merlot, these two varieties must comprise at least 85 per cent of the total. If a label claims that the wine is a combination of grape variety, vintage, and origin, the combination must be 85 per cent of that wine. For example, if the wine claims to be a 2008 Marlborough Pinot Noir, 85 per cent of the wine must be from the 2008 vintage and from Marlborough and from Pinot Noir.

USA the largest export market?

The world's largest wine market may soon become New Zealand's largest export market, as burgeoning sales are expected to take the USA into the lead by value in 2007 and ahead by volume in 2009, according to NZ Winegrowers. Export sales to the UK rose 4 per cent in 2006 but were beaten by an 11 per cent rise in US sales. Average earnings per litre from the US were NZ$9.60, while the more competitive UK market returned only NZ$8.87. "The return may be greater from the USA, but the cost of doing business there is significantly greater than in the UK," commented one winemaker.

Sauvignon Blanc: too much of a good thing

The NZ Winegrowers Annual Report shows total wine sales enjoying steady growth, with export earnings cracking through the NZ$500-million barrier for the first time, and total volume now exceeding 100 million litres. Exports increased 18 per cent in value and 12 per cent in volume on the previous year.

But a note of warning was sounded over the country's increasing dependence on Sauvignon Blanc. NZ Winegrowers CEO Philip Gregan says, "There is some concern about having all our eggs in one basket. We need to keep up the impetus with Sauvignon Blanc but achieve good growth with other varieties such as Pinot Noir and Syrah."

Sauvignon Blanc exports grew by 18 per cent on the previous year. At present, 72 out of every 100 bottles sold overseas are Sauvignon Blanc. In 2006, Sauvignon Blanc production grew by 50 per cent and, for the first time, was greater than all other varieties combined.

Pinot Noir has overtaken Chardonnay as the second most exported variety, with a spectacular surge of 55 per cent on last year's figures.

Opinion:
Pinot Gris – a leaky life preserver

The success of Marlborough Sauvignon Blanc distracts attention from the mediocre performance of the country's next two most widely grown grape varieties, Chardonnay and Riesling.

It's fair to say that the much-abused brand Chardonnay had it coming. A flood of cheap, bland Australian Chardonnay dulled the lustre of one of the world's greatest white grape varieties. After a rapid rise, Chardonnay sales have begun to fall. The decline has been slowed by discounting – an action that has done little to lift Chardonnay's long-term image.

Riesling has, despite desperate cries of "the Riesling Renaissance is coming", simply never performed. That is a pity, because the best examples are truly world-class wines. New Zealand Riesling continues to be the country's best-value wine, although that's cold comfort to winemakers trying to sell it at a profit.

Just as things were starting to look a little grim for any winemaker not producing Marlborough Sauvignon Blanc, along came Pinot Gris. For many wine drinkers it was love at first sip, although I'm still not sure why. Some believe that Pinot Gris trades on the fashionable status of its close relative, Pinot Noir. I wonder whether it's popular simply because it's inoffensive.

Whatever the reason, Pinot Gris has become the new Sauvignon Blanc. Winemakers and wine growers have been furiously planting vineyards with an abandon that resembles the Sauvignon Blanc planting frenzy in Marlborough recently. The increase in Pinot Gris production between 2005 and 2006 was 122 per cent.

Will Pinot Gris bring fame and fortune to the New Zealand wine industry? I don't think so. It's a second-division grape variety. New Zealand Pinot Gris is not significantly different from or superior to wines made in many other countries. The multitude of styles being made in New Zealand already frustrates many wine drinkers.

The love affair will soon be over. Grüner Veltliner, anyone?

Vintage Report

Advance report on the latest harvest

2007

"Quantity down; quality good to excellent" just about sums up the New Zealand vintage in 2007. Cool, wet conditions during flowering reduced potential crop size by up to 20 per cent, according to several winemakers, although a spokesman for wine-industry body NZ Winegrowers estimates that the harvest will set a new record thanks to an expanded vineyard area.

Marlborough Sauvignon Blanc appears to be one of the biggest losers. The rising price of Sauvignon Blanc grapes dropped suddenly once growers realized that volume would be down. However, the lower crop and perfect ripening conditions mean that quality will be very good indeed, and better than the generally excellent 2006 vintage.

Since 1991, odd vintages have been relatively lacklustre in Hawke's Bay. Savvy consumers buy the region's even vintages. That spell appears to have been broken this year, with good volumes (except Sauvignon Blanc and Pinot Noir) and good to outstanding quality. The best vintage since 2002, according to several growers. Results in Gisborne mirror those of Hawke's Bay.

Central Otago has suffered a crop shortfall of 20–30 per cent through poor flowering, according to one leading producer. A very similar vintage to 2005, with small berries producing intense and sometimes tannic Pinot Noir.

Updates on the previous five vintages

2006

Vintage rating: *North Island – Red: 80, White: 86;*
South Island – Red: 86, White: 90

This was the largest-ever New Zealand vintage, thanks to an increase of 18 per cent in vineyard area. Flowering and fruit set occurred very early throughout the country. Early flowering increased the risk of damage by late winter frost, but there were no reports of frost damage. The weather after flowering was near-perfect in every region until late in March, when most experienced heavy rain, the fallout of tropical cyclone Wati, which dissipated before reaching New Zealand. By that time, most white grape varieties had been harvested from Hawke's Bay and further north. Winemakers in these regions then had to decide whether to harvest their first black grapes under pressure or to wait in the hope of a return to fine weather. Those who waited fared better.

Most South Island regions – in particular Central Otago – had an exceptionally early harvest. Marlborough's Sauvignon Blanc crop enjoyed very good ripening conditions and produced many exceptional wines.

A long, dry autumn throughout most of the country favoured growers who were prepared to wait. A generally excellent vintage.

2005

Vintage rating: *North Island – Red: 86, White: 80; South Island – Red: 79, White: 87*

The vintage yielded 139,400 tonnes of grapes, down on 2004 due to wet, cold weather during flowering. A long, dry Indian summer brought Auckland/Northland its best-ever harvest in quality terms. The Hawke's Bay vintage was dogged by rain, particularly in the early stages. There are deep colours and good flavours in red wines, but most winemakers admit that whites were less successful. Martinborough suffered from rain, but the wines generally, and Sauvignon Blanc in particular, are very good indeed. Some Canterbury producers were affected by frost at the beginning of October and generally poor flowering. Quality is average to good. A below-average year for Central Otago Pinot Noir, with a few obvious exceptions.

2004

Vintage rating: *North Island – Red: 80, White: 78; South Island – Red: 72, White: 78 (except Sauvignon Blanc: 70)*

Generally a cool vintage with heavy February rain. Central Otago was hit by frost at the beginning and the end of the season. Marlborough Sauvignon Blanc is variable, with many dilute and high-acid wines. Warm, dry weather at the end of the vintage helped compensate for difficulties early in the season. Hawke's Bay has produced some excellent reds, although Cabernet Sauvignon struggled to ripen fully in some districts.

Grapevine

• **Gypsy Dancer,** a small Central Otago-based Pinot Noir specialist owned by the high-profile American Gary Andrus, has been placed in receivership by the Bank of New Zealand. Andrus, founder of Archery Summit Winery in Oregon and Pine Ridge Winery in the Napa Valley, purchased his first Central Otago vineyard in 2002 and claims to have invested US$6.5 million in the project. Two low-yielding vintages in 2003 and 2004 were an added financial burden, with around half the expected tonnages of grapes.

2003

Vintage rating: *North Island – Red: 60, White: 65;*
South Island – Red: 75, White: 80

All regions except Central Otago and Nelson suffered frost damage,
ranging from minor in Auckland to severe in Hawke's Bay. The North
Island suffered from generally wet conditions, while the South Island was
relatively dry, with drought in some areas. Many grape growers in frost-
affected areas tried to recover some production by harvesting later-ripening
grapes from "second set", but this often resulted in unsatisfactory wines
with varying ripeness levels. The crop of Marlborough Sauvignon Blanc
was significantly reduced by frost, although quality was good, with some
outstanding wines made.

2002

Vintage rating: *North Island – Red: 83, White: 85;*
South Island – Red: 88, White: 88

A long, hot, dry spell of autumn weather resulted in many outstanding
wines. Gisborne enjoyed a vintage that several winemakers called the
best ever. Hawke's Bay produced many good whites and reds. A high crop
of Sauvignon Blanc in Marlborough led to some variation in quality, but
the best wines were exceptional. Canterbury had a cool, late vintage with
average to above-average wines; Central Otago boasted some of the
region's best-ever reds.

GREATEST WINE PRODUCERS

1. Villa Maria Estate
2. Felton Road
3. Craggy Range
4. Dry River
5. Neudorf
6. Cloudy Bay
7. Trinity Hill
8. Saint Clair
9. Astrolabe
10. Kumeu River

FASTEST-IMPROVING PRODUCERS

1. Johanneshof
2. Muddy Water
3. Pernod Ricard
4. Peregrine
5. Escarpment
6. Daniel Schuster
7. Kaituna Valley
8. No. 1 Family Estate
9. Amisfield
10. Forrest Estate

NEW UP-AND-COMING PRODUCERS

1. Bell Hill
2. Richardson
3. Dog Point
4. Delta
5. Greystone
6. Passage Rock
7. Carrick
8. Aurum Estate
9. Wooing Hill
10. Tresillian

BEST-VALUE PRODUCERS

1. Mount Riley
2. Spy Valley
3. Villa Maria Estate
4. Pernod Ricard
5. Morton Estate
6. Wither Hills
7. Coopers Creek
8. Mission Estate Winery
9. Seifried Estate
10. Babich

GREATEST-QUALITY WINES

1. **Homage Syrah 2004** Trinity Hill, Hawke's Bay (NZ$110)
2. **Pinnacle Pinot Noir 2005** Peregrine, Central Otago (NZ$150)
3. **Le Sol Syrah 2004** Craggy Range, Hawke's Bay (NZ $69.95)
4. **Riesling 2003** Cloudy Bay, Marlborough (NZ$29)
5. **Pioneer Block 6 Sauvignon Blanc 2006** Saint Clair, Marlborough (NZ$24.95)
6. **Single Vineyard Keltern Chardonnay 2005** Villa Maria Estate, Hawke's Bay (NZ$35)
7. **Riesling 2006** Greystone, Waipara (NZ$24)
8. **Gewurztraminer 2005** Lawson's Dry Hills, Marlborough (NZ$21.95)
9. **Single Vineyard Taylors Pass Pinot Noir 2005** Villa Maria Estate, Marlborough (NZ$55)
10. **Single Vineyard Taylors Pass Pinot Gris 2006** Villa Maria Estate, Marlborough (NZ$29.95)

BEST BARGAINS

1. **Sauvignon Blanc 2006** Mount Riley, Marlborough (NZ$15.95)
2. **Sauvignon Blanc 2006** Saint Clair, Marlborough (NZ$20.95)
3. **Pinot Noir 2005** Delta, Marlborough (NZ$23)
4. **Private Bin Gewurztraminer 2006** Villa Maria Estate, East Coast (NZ$16.95)
5. **Riparian Riesling 2006** Coopers Creek, Marlborough (NZ$17)
6. **Pinot Noir 2005** Triplebank, Marlborough (NZ$22.95)
7. **Terroir Riverpoint Gewurztraminer 2005** Montana, Gisborne (NZ$24.95)
8. **Pinot Gris 2006** Waipara Hills, Waipara (NZ$23)
9. **Reserve Pinot Gris 2006** Shingle Peak, Marlborough (NZ$21.95)
10. **Sauvignon Blanc 2006** Wither Hills, Marlborough (NZ$19.95)

MOST EXCITING OR UNUSUAL FINDS

1. **Chardonnay 2004** Bell Hill, North Canterbury (NZ$60) *I'm not alone in saying that this is the best New Zealand Chardonnay I've tasted. From limestone soils in a tiny vineyard and an exciting new region. Reminds me of a good Montrachet.*
2. **The Cox Block Pinot Gris 2005** Tresillian, Canterbury (NZ$25) *First wine from a new vineyard 22 km (14 miles) east of Christchurch. One of the best New Zealand*

examples made to date, it boasts pronounced pear and peach fruit flavours with impressive purity.

3 Gewurztraminer 2006 Johanneshof, Marlborough (NZ$30) *Moderately sweet Gewurztraminer with a totally seductive silken texture and delicate floral/rose-petal characters. This small producer tops the charts every year. This is their best yet.*

4 Reserve Syrah 2005 Passage Rock, Waiheke (NZ$50) *Gimblett Gravels in Hawke's Bay is the source of New Zealand's best Syrah, but this wine, made from grapes grown on Waiheke Island in Auckland's harbour, is a stunner.*

5 Sauvignon Blanc 2006 Astrolabe, Marlborough (NZ$19.95) *Year after year, Astrolabe Sauvignon Blanc is among the country's top 10 examples of the variety, at a price that puts it at the head of the list in value. This vintage is probably the best they've made.*

6 Pinot Noir 2005 Carrick, Central Otago (NZ$42) *My top-rated Pinot Noir in a tasting of 43 Central Otago wines from this vintage.*

Lush, rich, dense fruit-bomb style with appealing layers of black-fruit flavours.

7 Riesling 2006 Greystone, Waipara (NZ$24) *A new and exciting first taste from an ambitious Waipara vineyard covering 40 ha. Taut, elegant wine, beautifully balanced by racy acidity.*

8 Tempranillo 2005 Trinity Hill, Hawke's Bay (NZ$29.95) *Trinity Hill makes New Zealand's only Tempranillo, although others plan to follow its lead. The best example since the first in 2001.*

9 Pinot Noir 2005 Wooing Tree, Central Otago (NZ$34.95) *Dense wine with strong plum-fruit flavour and an appealing silken Musigny-like texture. Quite long and plump. One of the brightest stars of the vintage.*

10 Number One Cuvée Blanc de Blancs NV No. 1 Family Estate, Marlborough (NZ$38) *Champagne-like méthode with masses of bready yeast autolysis character, a soft texture, and a lingering finish. Intensely flavoured sparkler with great character.*

Grapevine

• Marlborough wine producer **Forrest Estate** has released a controversial low-alcohol "Doctor's Riesling", with a prescription-style statement suggesting the wine might be better for your health than normal Riesling. At 8.5 per cent ABV, the wine has 60 per cent less alcohol than average, according to Dr John Forrest. A spokesman from the Alcoholic Liquor Advisory Council (ALAC) claimed that Forrest had "completely overstepped the mark. The name of the wine suggests that it must be good for you." He did concede that, if a man drank a whole bottle of Forrest Doctor's Riesling, he would still be within the acceptable guideline

of four standard drinks a day. Women are not so lucky. They could drink only half a bottle. (The wine, incidentally, is very good indeed.)

• New Zealand **Vineyard Estates** is developing an appetite for buying wineries. In recent years, the company has merged with Waipara Hills and bought the high-profile Waipara winery, Canterbury House. Its latest acquisition is the 75,000-case Marlborough winery Mud House. The enlarged company now has the capacity to produce wine from more than 5,500 tonnes of grapes, including the crop from its own 350 ha of vineyards.

Asia

Denis Gastin

Not only are the wineries in Asia multiplying in number (now approaching 800 in 12 countries) and scale, but increasingly, the industry is attracting major stakes from some of the region's largest food and beverage players.

DENIS GASTIN

Brewers Suntory and Sapporo have well-established wine operations in Japan. In Thailand, the family behind Singha beer has a major stake in the industry with its PB Valley Khao Yai winery, and the founders of the Red Bull energy drink have graduated from a marginal presence with a pop wine cooler (Spy) to a serious range of table wines under the Monsoon Valley label. The owners of two of China's best-known alcoholic beverage brands, Tsingtao beer and Moutai spirits, have added further momentum to this trend in recent years with modest moves into wine production. And now, underlining the reality that wine has become a mainstream beverage in Asia, there are manoeuvres into wine by two more of the region's biggest beverage companies.

Big moves in India

Without doubt, the biggest triumph for Maharashtra State's bold wine-industry growth strategy thus far is the move by giant beer and spirits conglomerate the UB Group (now incorporating long-time sector player

DENIS GASTIN is a feature writer and Australian correspondent for Japan's liquor-industry newspaper, *The Shuhan News*, and for *Wine Review* magazine in Korea. He is a regular columnist for *Australian & New Zealand Grapegrower & Winemaker* and contributes to various other journals and to wine reference books, including *The Oxford Companion to Wine* and *The World Atlas of Wine*. His particular interests are the more unusual aspects of winemaking, the more remote and least understood regions of the wine world, and the groundbreaking work that some of the industry champions have been doing with exotic grape varieties and new wine styles.

Shaw & Wallace) to set up a very large winery at Baramati. This follows the decision in December 2005 by the government of this state, where two-thirds of the Indian wine industry is concentrated, to double the excise tax on imported wine, on top of an earlier incentive deal that includes a 100 per cent exemption from excise duty for 10 years for new wine ventures, simplified licensing provisions, and sales tax relief. Almost 40 new wine-producing ventures have started in Maharashtra since the first incentive package was launched in 2001. But the UB Group's operation is expected to dwarf all of them. The greenfield Four Seasons winery will kick off bottling imported bulk wine, but plans are already under way to plant more than 120 ha of vines to provide fruit for its own wines. A further 80 ha are to be planted as land becomes available, and up to 320 ha are to be drawn on through contract growers. The winemaking operation will be overseen by Abhay Kewadkar, formerly of Grover Vineyards.

Grapevine

• **The tally of Asia's wineries** now stands at almost 800 in 12 countries. More than half of them are in China, in 26 provinces – virtually all of them established since the late 1970s and over 100 of them less than 10 years old. Almost a quarter are in Japan, concentrated principally in Yamanashi and Nagano. Numbers are expanding rapidly in India – now with around 50 wineries. Other Asian countries in which there is an established winemaking tradition are Thailand, Korea, Vietnam, and Indonesia. Fledgling operations can be found in Taiwan, Sri Lanka, Bhutan, Myanmar (Burma) and, most recently, Cambodia.

• **Asian winery names** are now popping up much more frequently on the award lists at international wine competitions and at international wine-trade fairs. At the 2006 London IWSC, for example, Japanese wines won four silver medals and seven bronze. Indian wines won five bronze, and Thai wines won one silver and two bronze.

• **The 2nd Asian Wine Competition** was held in China's Shaanxi province in April 2006 in conjunction with the 4th International Advanced Vine & Wine Seminar, with entries being judged by an international panel of experts. Seven gold medals and eight silver medals were awarded. Wines from the newer, less humid regions of inland China stood out among the prizewinners, especially wines from Ningxia (two gold and one silver) and Xinjiang provinces (two gold and two silver) in the northwest, and Yunnan province (two gold and one silver) in the southwest.

• **Chateau Indage** is forging new wine frontiers in India. In collaboration with the Himachal Pradesh State Government, it has planted Chardonnay and Pinot Noir in the Himalayan foothill districts of Shimla and Kullu. This is on roughly the same latitude as southern California, but MD Ranjit Chougule hopes that the cooler climate and higher altitude (1,800 m [5,900 ft]) will result in this region emerging as India's Burgundy. The first wines are expected from the 2008 vintage. Indage has also entered into contract planting arrangements in Karnataka, Andhra Pradesh, and Orissa states in the south and east of the subcontinent.

... AND ALSO IN JAPAN

As 2006 drew to a close, Japan's largest beverage business, Kirin Brewery Co, launched an ultimately successful bid to acquire a controlling 50.1 per cent stake in Mercian Corporation, itself a diversified beverage producer that is also the nation's largest producer of wine. Kirin offered a 40 per cent price premium to existing Mercian shareholders to achieve this, but both parties are describing the move as a "business alliance" rather than a takeover. The objective, they say, is to add value to both businesses but, particularly, to consolidate Mercian's position as the nation's leading wine producer, as well as to enable Mercian to push past Suntory as Japan's leading wine merchant, drawing on wineries owned by both companies in California and France.

CHINESE WINEMAKERS HEAD FOR THE HILLS

The southwest highland province of Yunnan is rapidly becoming the new frontier for the wine industry in China. Table grapes have been growing here since Christian friars brought vines from France in the mid-1800s for their early missions. Now extensive plantings of Cabernet Sauvignon, Merlot, Grenache, Italian Riesling, and Chardonnay have been added to the descendants of the original vines (principally a purple grape known locally as Rose Honey and a white grape known as Crystal – both now believed to be extinct in France) to serve a cluster of recently established wineries. The biggest among them are

Yunnan Hong, Yunnan Taiyanghun (Sun Spirit), Yunnan Gaoyuan (Plateau) and Shangri-la. The main concentration of new plantings is on the plateaus among the mountain ranges south of the provincial capital, Kunming, not far from the border with Vietnam and Laos. This is now the highest-altitude (at around 2,000 m [6,500 ft]) and lowest-latitude (24°) wine-producing region in China. Wines made from Rose Honey and Crystal varieties won medals at the 2nd Asian Wine Competition and are being promoted as unique Chinese wines.

GETTING SERIOUS IN THAILAND

The Thai Wine Association is to be congratulated on its determination to ensure authenticity in locally produced wine – something that is missing in most Asian wine-producing countries. The association, a collaborative industry body set up by the seven leading wineries in 2004, has a charter that sets the standard for wines that can be called Thai and manages compliance through independent laboratory testing of members' wines and visits to participating wineries by an independent authority to ensure that quality and safety standards accord with the charter. To qualify for the TWA's seal, the wine must be made solely from Thai grapes, and if they make up less than 90 per cent, this must be specifically declared on the label. A wine can be labelled as a single variety only if it contains a minimum of 75 per cent of that variety. Most wineries are now declaring on their labels all varieties used in any blends.

BROADENING AND DEEPENING IN JAPAN

The maturing Japan Wine Competition, held annually at Kofu in Yamanashi Prefecture, is demonstrating the growing regional and varietal diversity in the Japanese domestic wine spectrum, as well as the pace at which a distinct Japanese wine identity is taking shape.

Entries in the 2006 competition were from 23 prefectures, and consisted of 49 different varieties – some standalone, some only in blends. Only 23 were European varieties and included grapes such as Zweigeltrebe (9 entries), Kerner (20), Müller-Thurgau (8), Dornfelder, and Lemberger. Japan's own vinifera grape, Koshu, lays the core claim to producing a unique Japanese wine: there is enough Koshu being made in Japan to justify a category of its own at the competition (112 entries, a quarter of the total).

Some of the more adventurous contemporary efforts to find unique Japanese wine styles include varietal blends such as Koshu and Chardonnay. With the reds, there is a growing focus on Muscat Bailey A (29 entries), a hybrid variety that is sometimes blended with Merlot. Black Queen and Kai Noir (with 8 and 9 entries respectively) are two Japanese hybrids (75 entries in total) that are increasingly appearing as straight varietals or in blends. Even more adventurous are the experiments with the wild mountain grape varieties (Yamabudo), which have come a long way since Hokkaido's Tokachi Winery began to work with the local *Vitis amurensis* vines in the 1970s. Two very promising recent appearances are Shokoshi (a crossing of three strains of Yamabudo) and Yama Sauvignon (a crossing of *Vitis coignetiae* with Cabernet Sauvignon).

Grapevine

• **Thailand's Village Farm Winery** persists in the view that true premium red wine must involve Cabernet Sauvignon. However, the variety stubbornly refuses to perform in Thailand, even in the hands of Village Farm's Bordeaux-based winemaker, Jacques Bacou. Accordingly, the winery brings in its Cabernet from France. This is fully indicated on the label, with the 2005 Chateau de Brumes Le Prestige, for example, declared as 70 per cent locally grown Shiraz and 30 per cent French Cabernet.

• **India's Sula Vineyards** is the first winery in Asia to commit fully to screwcap closures, beginning with the Sula 2006 Sauvignon Blanc and followed by Chenin Blanc, Late Harvest Chenin Blanc, and Blush Zinfandel. An even bolder move has been the progressive adoption of

screwcap closures for its red wines, beginning with Red Zinfandel. By the end of 2007, all Sula's non-sparkling wines will be sealed with screwcaps – right through to their premium Dindori Reserve Shiraz.

• **Sula also continues** to set a cracking pace of expansion. In late 2006, it acquired a derelict sparkling-wine facility with a capacity for 350,000 bottles and recommissioned it in February 2007, boosting the company's total capacity to 2.5 million bottles. Winery capacity growth is also being matched with vineyard expansion: an extra 200 ha of vines were planted in 2006, including 40 ha of Merlot. A further 160 ha are planned by the end of 2008, bringing the total area under winery management or under contract to 650 ha.

Opinion:
Action needed on integrity

Label integrity and formal industry winemaking standards are the compelling issues of the moment in Asia. Progressives in the industry understand that international standards must be met if broader consumer respect is to be won. But much of the traditional end of the industry still seems motivated by the convenience afforded by ambiguous production and labelling codes – and the practices of the few are damaging the status of the increasing number who are deadly serious. Government remains very much in the background.

A basic issue is origin. Some efforts are being made to reduce the scope for ambiguity by introducing regional AOC systems in parts of China and Japan. But a bigger issue is country of origin: labelling practices condone the use of imported bulk wine, imported grape must, and imported grapes in "local" wine. Grape varieties are increasingly stated on labels, but most countries have no rules governing this or vintage declarations. Alcohol-content levels stated on labels are unreliable.

Change is on the way, though. China's decision to ban a local concoction known as "half-juice wine" from hijacking the name "wine" is commendable, especially since government action was urged by the industry itself. There was an industry-standards code promulgated at the end of 2006, but compliance will remain a big issue. In Myanmar, one of the newest wine countries in Asia, there is a determined effort to get it right at the outset, with an industry charter that has been written in collaboration with the relevant local ministry. But the benchmark has been set in Thailand, where the newly established Thai Wine Association has set rigorous production and labelling standards, with an equally rigorous audit process to ensure compliance.

Back to the vineyard

Another big constraint on producing good wine in Asia is the slow emergence of a genuinely wine-focused viticultural tradition. Most traditional grape growers are not yet confident enough to commit to the different viticultural practices required for good wine, and wineries are limited (by land ownership laws, among other things) in the extent to which they can do this themselves. With heavy investment in modern winery equipment now behind them, the next challenge for most Asian winemakers lies in the vineyards, with yield management and ripeness the priority targets.

Vintage Report

Advance report on the latest harvest
2007

India – Because of the 2006 vintage experience, some vineyards in Maharashtra pruned earlier than usual, bringing on harvests as early as Christmas Day, and the major wineries picking early reported generally satisfactory yields and good fruit quality. Further south in Bangalore, where harvests will last through to May, lower yields are expected due to a drier winter than usual but with good fruit concentration.

Thailand – Early-pruned vineyards suffered from prolonged rain that again delayed flowering and affected fruit set: for some, yields will be even lower than the severely reduced levels of 2006. Colder-than-usual weather from mid-November to January slowed ripening, however, and growers were hoping that dry weather would extend longer than usual to allow vines to catch up and deliver quality fruit.

Updates on the previous five vintages
2006

China – A good year in Shandong, with much less fungal disease than normal, and good fruit ripeness generally. Hebei got off to a good start with a mild winter, but heavy rainfall and prolonged humidity in spring and early summer caused some fungal disease and some loss of volume in the early-picked white grapes. Harvesting of reds was delayed by some weeks, resulting in better fruit flavours and colours, with reasonable yields. There were severe early frosts in Shanxi, so yields were down by up to 20 per cent, but the rest of the season went without setbacks and fruit was fully ripened.

Japan – A cold spring complicated budburst in Yamanashi and parts of Nagano, and a long rainy season with reduced sunshine didn't help. Yields were average, but fruit struggled to achieve moderate ripeness, and colour for the reds. Nagano experienced some losses due to fungal disease. But most of northern Honshu and Hokkaido achieved good yields and quality fruit.

India – A record monsoon in Maharashtra delayed pruning. Yields were lower than usual, though adequate grape-sugar levels were achieved in most districts while maintaining satisfactory acid levels. Further south, in Bangalore, conditions were generally more favourable, permitting slower bunch maturation and delivering aromatic whites and concentrated reds.

Thailand – Prolonged rain after pruning reduced flowering and affected fruit set. It also caused some early fungal disease. As a result, yields were down to as little as half 2005 levels in some vineyards, though the generally dry and cool weather from mid-December through to harvest and radical canopy and bunch management ultimately helped vineyards deliver grapes with good colour and flavours in most regions.

2005

China – For the second year running, Shandong province had heavy summer rains that caused widespread fungal disease and great difficulty reaching acceptable ripening. Combined with early frosts, yields were well down, forcing the larger wineries to look to other regions, especially in the west, for fruit. Hebei province fared much better, since it was spared the worst of the rains and enjoyed higher temperatures.

Japan – A difficult vintage overall, due principally to a shortage of sunshine days and generally lower temperatures, making ripening difficult. Rain was less of a problem than usual late in the vintage, so some patchy recoveries were made and fungal damage was generally contained. In Yamanashi, Koshu didn't ripen well. Conditions were little better in Nagano: quality in Merlot varies among producers, and Chardonnay was good rather than excellent.

India – Late monsoon rains affected early-pruned vineyards, causing lower yields, especially for Sauvignon Blanc. Later-pruned vineyards were unaffected and benefited from a cooler-than-normal ripening period.

Thailand – In Khao Yai, rain finished early after pruning in September, resulting in good fruit set and no disease. Mild weather throughout the vintage produced very good results in both early- and later-ripening varieties. It was an exceptional vintage in the Chao Phraya Delta region: very little rain, no disease, and cool weather from November through to harvest in February. Volume was low, but sugar levels were higher than usual. At Loei, in the north, Chenin Blanc was the best in 10 years.

2004

China – Heavy rains in July and August caused widespread mildew throughout the north and northeast, especially in Shandong and Hebei provinces, and much fruit was picked far too soon. Huailai was generally affected less by summer rains than other parts of Hebei. Conditions in Shanxi were much better, with good sugar and acid levels and few losses to disease. The northwest was, as usual, dry throughout, but yields were lower.

Japan – The year began well with prolonged warm, dry weather after *véraison*, which saw good early fruit development. But a blitz of typhoons late in the season caused many wineries to take fruit early. For others, fungal disease caused losses in quality and volume. As usual, the valleys fared worst and the more elevated and inland locations did best.

India – A very good year for whites in Maharashtra and quite good for reds. Cool weather extended until mid-February, longer than usual, resulting in slower ripening and more complex flavours. Conditions were very favourable around Bangalore, adding to the region's growing reputation for consistency.

2003

China – Very wet conditions in Hebei and Shandong produced big berries with low sugar and acid levels in most white varieties, though late-maturing reds were generally of good quality. Fungal disease was a problem in most regions and was particularly devastating in parts of Shanxi province. Even in the west, where conditions are generally more amenable, colder and wetter weather than usual impacted adversely on quality. Overall, 2003 was not a good year.

Japan – Extensive summer rainfall severely dented yields and kept sugar levels low in all the major regions. A few of the later-picked varieties saw some recovery when rains eased late in the harvest in Yamanashi and the Komoro district of Nagano. But overall it was a poor year, and the wines generally suffer from suppressed natural flavours and colours.

India – Vintage was over early in Maharashtra. Warmer weather throughout the ripening period and a weaker monsoon saw fruit ripening early, relatively free of disease. Sauvignon Blanc and more aromatic wines are not as intense as in some years, but the reds have lots of flavour and colour. In Bangalore, conditions were close to ideal.

2002

China – Grapes ripened very late in Hebei province, but wineries that could delay picking produced wines with good flavour and colour. Grape growers in Shandong province made even better use of the cooler, drier conditions, achieving desired sugar levels and robust colouring, with very little rot.

Japan – Conditions were very good in Yamanashi and Nagano – a few typhoons in the early summer but no damage to vines or fruit. With sustained sunshine and little rain late in the season, vineyards enjoyed much lower rot levels, encouraging growers to wait for optimal ripeness before picking.

India – A weaker-than-usual monsoon season delivered drier-than-normal conditions, which favoured even ripening patterns and made rot more manageable. The white varieties came off well in Bangalore, as did most of the reds. In Maharashtra, it was an excellent year overall.

GREATEST WINE PRODUCERS

1. Château Mercian (Japan)
2. Dragon Seal (China)
3. Suntory (Japan)
4. Grace Winery (Japan)
5. Sapporo (Japan)
6. Great Wall (China)
7. Manns Wine (Japan)
8. Changyu (China)
9. Dynasty (China)
10. Indage (India)

FASTEST-IMPROVING PRODUCERS

1. Grover Vineyards (India)
2. Katsunuma Winery (Japan)
3. Coco Farm (Japan)
4. Weilong (China)
5. Okuizumo (Japan)
6. Siam Winery (Thailand)
7. Hayashi Noen (Japan)
8. Kuzumaki (Japan)
9. Takahata (Japan)
10. Kizan (Japan)

NEW UP-AND-COMING PRODUCERS

1. Suntime (China)
2. Sula (India)
3. Domaine Sogga (Japan)
4. Tsuno Wines (Japan)
5. Shanxi Grace (China)
6. GranMonte (Thailand)
7. Yamazaki (Japan)
8. PB Valley (Thailand)
9. Asahi Yoshu (Japan)
10. Shidax Château TS (Japan)

BEST-VALUE PRODUCERS

1. Dragon Seal (China)
2. Château Mercian (Japan)
3. Sula (India)
4. Grace Winery (Japan)
5. Siam Winery (Thailand)
6. Tsuno Wines (Japan)

7. Weilong (China)
8. Shanxi Grace (China)
9. PB Valley (Thailand)
10. Izutsu (Japan)

GREATEST-QUALITY WINES

1. **Kikyogahara Signature Merlot 2002** Château Mercian, Japan (¥18,000)
2. **Chairman's Reserve 2004** Shanxi Grace, China (Rmb 388)
3. **Domaine Rubaiyat 2003** Marufuji Winery, Japan (¥4,305)
4. **Huailai Reserve Cabernet Sauvignon 2005** Dragon Seal, China (Rmb 140)
5. **Solaris Shinshu Chikumagawa Merlot 2003** Manns Wine, Japan (¥3,675)
6. **Hokushin Chardonnay 2005** Château Mercian, Japan (¥6,300)
7. **Primavera Unwooded Chenin Blanc/Colombard 2006** GranMonte, Thailand (THB 780)
8. **La Réserve Cabernet Sauvignon/Shiraz 2004** Grover Vineyards, India (Rp 440)
9. **Cuvée Misawa Chardonnay 2004** Grace Winery, Japan (¥6,300)
10. **Dindori Reserve Shiraz 2005** Sula, India (Rp 650)

BEST BARGAINS

1. **Unfiltered Chardonnay 2005** Tsuno Wines, Japan (¥2,800)
2. **Sauvignon Blanc 2005** Grover Vineyards, India (Rp 410)
3. **Cabernet Sauvignon 2006** Dragon Seal, China (Rmb 45)
4. **Monsoon Valley Shiraz Special Reserve 2005** Siam Winery, Thailand (THB 430)
5. **Sawasdee Khao Yai Shiraz 2005** PB Valley, Thailand (THB 320)
6. **Niya Chardonnay 2003** Suntime, China (Rmb 80)
7. **Sparkling Brut NV** Sula, India (Rp 475)

8 **Vineyard Rosé 2004**
Shanxi Grace, China (Rmb 68)

9 **Nagano Merlot 2004**
Château Mercian, Japan (¥3,007)

10 **Solaris Juventa Rouge 2003**
Manns Wine, Japan (¥2,100)

MOST EXCITING OR UNUSUAL WINE FINDS

1 **Late Harvest Chenin Blanc 2005** Sula, India (Rp 225) *One of only two Indian late-harvest Chenin Blancs. A quality dessert wine at a price that represents unbeatable value.*

2 **Marselan Dry Red 2004** Sino-French Demonstration Vineyard, China (Rmb 368) *A top example of this experimental variety (from a crossing of Cabernet Sauvignon and Grenache), delivering the firm Cabernet-like structure with a soft and rich Grenache fruit overlay.*

3 **Chenin Blanc 2004** Shanxi Grace, China (Rmb 128) *First release of this variety by Grace, and also believed to be China's first Chenin Blanc.*

4 **Kai Noir 2006** Grace Winery, Japan (¥2,210) *Made from a rare local hybrid (Black Queen x Cabernet Sauvignon) that is valued in blends, particularly to add colour. Not surprisingly, this wine impresses with its dense purple tones with soft, almost Beaujolais-style aromas but with a firm finish.*

5 **Pino de Bali NV (White)** Hatten Wines, Indonesia (Rp 65,000) *An oak-aged fortified wine made from tropically grown Belgia grapes. Very well structured, it delivers warm raisin and nutty aromas and flavours with a soft vanillin overlay.*

6 **Pinot Noir 2006** Dragon Seal, China (Rmb 80) *This winery is one of very few in Asia producing a straight Pinot Noir; it was the first in China. This version exhibits pleasing varietal characteristics.*

7 **Napa Mieng Shiraz Premium 2004** Mae Chan Winery, Thailand (THB 580) *From relatively new vineyards near Changrai in the Golden Triangle, and a different style of Shiraz from those in the more southerly locations in Thailand: more Old World than New World.*

8 **Village Cellar Chenin Blanc 2005** Village Farm Winery, Thailand (THB 590) *A quality drink, but a rather intriguing wine. It is not a typical Chenin Blanc. The elevated and very rocky soils might explain some of its musky and granitic aromas and flavour, but the small proportion of Muscat undoubtedly is a major contributor, too.*

9 **Cabernet Gernischt Dry Red 1999** Helan Mountain Wine Co, China (Rmb 258) *This mysterious Cabernet-family vine has been growing in China since the end of the 19th century but has only recently begun to turn up on labels. This one is an excellent example of what can be achieved with it, and it can't fail to attract attention for this grape.*

10 **Dry Red Wine 2002** Yunnan Taiyanghun (Sun Spirit) Wine Co, China (Rmb 118) *A quality Cabernet-based offering from one of China's newest wineries in one of its newest regions – Yunnan province, in the southwest, abutting the border with Vietnam and Laos.*

Grapevine

• **The 2008 Beijing Olympics** are being viewed as a great opportunity to showcase Chinese wines. The Organizing Committee for the Games has selected COFCO Wines & Spirits (Great Wall) as the official (and exclusive) supplier with rights to use the official marks and be part of Olympic themes and activities.

Organic & Biodynamic Wines

Monty Waldin

You'd be hard-pressed to find a mainstream wine magazine published during the past 12 months that did not mention the B word. No, not Bordeaux, or Burgundy, or even Beaujolais, but biodynamics.

MONTY WALDIN

Every wine-producing country, and all the major wine-producing regions, now possess at least one flagship estate either dabbling in or fully committed to biodynamics.

Even the most negative press on biodynamic wines, such as Barquín and Smith's "Objections to Biodynamics" in the rarefied pages of *The World of Fine Wine* (issue 12, 2006), accepts that wines from biodynamic vineyards generally differ, in a positive way, from those of their conventional peers. What Barquín and Smith object to is the apparent lack of scientific proof that it is the use of the nine biodynamic preparations (500–508), as opposed to the more conscientious approach to farming in general (common among biodynamic vine growers) that accounts for any qualitative differences in

MONTY WALDIN While working on a conventionally farmed Bordeaux château as a teenager, Monty Waldin realized that the more chemicals were applied to a vineyard, the more corrective treatments became necessary in the winery. When the opportunity arose to write about wines for both trade and consumer magazines, he specialized in green issues. His first book, *The Organic Wine Guide* (Thorsons, 1999), has now been joined by *Biodynamic Wines* (Mitchell Beazley, 2004). This is the first guide dedicated to the world's biodynamic wine producers. Monty's interest in biodynamism was stimulated in 1999 by six months working on the Fetzer family's biodynamic Home Ranch vineyard in California's Mendocino County, where livestock husbandry and vegetable growing were integral to the vineyard. Previous winemaking experience in Chile and Bordeaux contributed to his *Wines of South America* (Mitchell Beazley, 2003) and *Discovering Wine Country: Bordeaux* (Mitchell Beazley, 2005) books. Monty moved to Tuscany to learn Italian while preparing his latest book, *Discovering Wine Country: Tuscany* (Mitchell Beazley, 2006).

the crops. Biodynamic growers shrug at such observations, but there are structural issues that the biodynamic community does need to deal with.

While European organic growers proved adept at harvesting juicy subsidies for conversion (Italy, France, Spain, Austria) because organic certification was regulated by government, the biodynamic (Demeter) fraternity chose in the main to operate a private standard (in Italy, Spain, and Portugal, for example), uncontrolled by any designated national body. This meant that no subsidies could be paid for official biodynamic conversion.

This lack of subsidy is one reason that the biodynamic wine movements in Italy, Spain, and Portugal remain stubbornly flat-footed, despite these countries' ongoing history of integrating livestock and other crops (olives, tree fruit) in wine production and relying on indigenous, rather than imported, grape varieties – massive pluses in biodynamics, since each farm should be self-sustaining. The situation is not helped by the fact that the biodynamic folks running these organizations are often spiritual scientists (officially known as anthroposophists, unofficially as the biodynamic ultras) opposed, in the main, to the production or consumption of alcohol.

In Australia, the internecine rivalry between the two main biodynamic groups has prevented wine growers from entering the certification programme "due to the politics". And the Australian group controlling the rights to the official (Demeter) biodynamic certification symbol isn't even recognized by the biodynamic movement's global parent organization, Demeter International. Inconveniently, this is based in Germany, the world's biggest importer of wine and the world's biggest consumer of bio products.

In New Zealand, too, wine growers practising biodynamics have so far opted out of the national Demeter association in favour of organic certification, not because of philosophy but to gain easier access to foreign markets (the EU). The wine standard they have finalized has no official biodynamic input.

In the USA, an apparently testy relationship exists between the official biodynamic certification body Demeter USA and the Josephine Porter Institute for Applied Biodynamics (JPI), the body Demeter USA designated to make the nine biodynamic preparations, use of which is mandatory in biodynamic farming. Although Demeter USA certification is not recognized as part of the US government's National Organic Program (NOP), at least growers now get organic certification thrown in at no extra cost via Demeter USA's offshoot Stellar Certification, which is recognized as NOP.

Demeter USA's recent decision to withdraw funding from JPI for purely financial reasons has spurred JPI to call a "Future of the Preparations" conference to discuss whether it should stay as a non-profit organization or become an "irrevocable trust". Another possibility is to run it as a Community Supported Agriculture (CSA) farm. The best-quality biodynamic preparations are made on farmland surrounded by uncultivated areas such as woodland and freshwater streams, which JPI has.

A more harmonic picture of biodynamics emerges in South America, where Alvaro Espinoza has created a biodynamic wine association to promote biodynamics and to encourage a cross-fertilization of ideas and vineyard information. The association currently has four members. In Argentina, growers in the north and south (see Grapevine below), albeit with non-Argentine origins (Denmark/Italy at Bodega Noemía; Switzerland/ USA at Colomé) are pooling resources to organize staff training.

Grapevine

• **Henschke began converting** its Keyneton vineyards (including Hill of Grace, Mount Edelstone, and the Home Gardens) to biodynamics from October 2006 by using the sequential spraying technique. This involves spraying the earth-building horn manure 500 in the afternoon, and the solar-attracting horn silica 501 the following morning, with the aim of bringing earth and sun forces into balance. Creeping saltbush (*Atriplex semibaccata*) and wallaby grasses (*Danthonia spp.*) have been sown to attract beneficial predators like ladybirds and wasps respectively.

• **Edgehill in McLaren Vale,** with 24 acres of certified organic vineyards, is converting another 40 acres, having invested in machinery for under-vine weeding, a task previously largely done by hand. Edgehill extended its wine range in 2006 with the Battle of Bosworth War of the Rosé Cabernet.

• **Argentina's two most** biodynamically inclined but geographically distant *bodegas,* Noemía de Patagonia in the south and (non-certified) Colomé in the north, coordinated a combined staff biodynamic training programme focusing on cosmic rhythms and the nine biodynamic preparations (500–508). Bodega Noemía's recently acquired 6-ha Pirri vineyard is in bio conversion from 2006, while its 5-ha winery vineyard at Valle Azul has full certification from 2006.

• **While Concha y Toro** has dropped its organic vineyard programme due, it says, to having trialled organics on varieties planted on the wrong sites, its offshoots are expanding theirs. Cono Sur now has more than 100 ha under organic management (not all of it yet certified) and Emiliana Orgánico (the former Viñedos Orgánicos Emiliana) has more than five times that amount with full biodynamic certification.

• **The Association Bien Boire,** which manages the most comprehensive online database of France's organic vineyards (around 800) now has English content: see www.organic-wine.bien-boire.info.

• **In Burgundy,** wineries either in conversion to or newly certified organic include Julien Brocard's Domaine de la Boissonneuse and Domaine A&O de Moor (Chablis); Domaines Amiot-Servelle, Henri Gros, Rossignol-Trapet, and Thibault Liger-Belair (Côte de Nuits); Domaine Christian Perrin (Côte de Beaune); and Domaines N Rousset and EARL Tripoz (Mâconnais).

Europe, ideological differences emerge to confuse at almost every turn.
Should the five solid biodynamic compost herbal preparations be stored
moist or dried? Should vineyards be forced to get these preparations
on to the farm/vines in time-consuming form as solid compost, risking
overfertility (the traditional Rudolf Steiner way) or as a quick-fix, White-
Russian-via-Australia-inspired tea that risks producing topsoils more
suited to vegetables than vines (the so-called Alex Podolinsky method)?

Should biodynamic vineyards be defined by their "biodynamicness" –
the official view of Demeter France, which handles biodynamic certification
in France and which is government-accredited – or by how truly their
wine reflects the terroir – the view of the unofficial biodynamic wine
cheerleader Nicolas Joly of the Loire's Clos de la Coulée de Serrant?

Perhaps, even, they should do both.

A third and arguably more pragmatic group is emerging in France in
the form of the succinctly titled Syndicat International des Vignerons en
Culture Biodynamique or SIVCBD (logo: Biodyvin).

Not only does the SIVCBD embrace the distinctly un-French idea of
having members from outside France (there is even one German member),
is is also working towards a winemaking standard flexible enough to take
account of the various and non-contiguous needs of growers coping with
the canicule of Corsica or the chill of Champagne.

In a world of increased climatic extremes, the effects of which
biodynamic farming is (pace Barquín and Smith) supposed to modify, this
pragmatic approach to standard-setting could prove a globally useful,
and even global, model.

Warning on organic imports

Patrick Holden, director of the UK's most media-savvy organic body,
the Soil Association, warned at its AGM of a watering down in organic
standards due to a massive increase in demand for organic products –
especially from the all-powerful supermarkets. While this warning was
more likely to be of interest to Britain's dairy farmers than foreign wine
growers, Holden made a more pertinent one (from a wine perspective)
by targeting rising imports of organic products and the environmental
damage that this causes.

He said that organic standards will have to become tougher if "we're
not to lose sight of our commitment to promote sustainable farming".
In other words, the environmental benefits of going organic (which are
hotly disputed anyway) make no sense if they are outweighed by the
environmental cost of getting bottles to market. And the UK is the
world's biggest non-wine-producing wine consumer.

CURRENT STATUS OF CERTIFIED ORGANIC VINEYARDS

Country or region	Hectares certified organic	Percentage of vineyards	Year	Comments
Europe	<82,000	<2.2	2005	*Around half of Europe's organic vineyards are found in Italy, a reflection partly of the subsidy-hungry nature of Italian farmers, who were paid handsomely to convert to organics, but also of Italy's polycultural or extensively farmed vineyards, a legacy of postwar sharecropping. Such vineyards, although becoming less prevalent, are inherently suited to organic farming. It is also easier for Italian farmers to commercialize a range of crops from a smallholding (wine grapes, olives, fruit, nuts, vegetables) via a powerful and well-organized cooperative movement.*
Argentina	<2,500	<2.0	2007	*Argentina's organic vineyards are found in Mendoza (75%), La Rioja (20%), Salta province (3%), and Patagonia (2%).*
Australia	<1,100	<0.6	2007	*While flagship organic projects like Penfolds Clare Valley Organic remain static or go backwards (like at least one of M Chapoutier's three joint ventures here), the likes of Cullen (WA), Edgehill (SA), the five-vineyard-strong Organic Vignerons Association (SA), Sergio Carlei (VIC), and Ngeringa (SA), plus new arrivals like Gemtree (SA) and Krinklewood (NSW), are taking organics forward.*
Austria	2,000	3.5	2006	*Around 100 Austrian wineries are certified organic, comprising around 1,800 ha of vineyards. The number of biodynamic estates continues to nearly double (albeit from a low base), from 8 (77 ha) in 2005 to 15 (119 ha) in 2006, with 9 more in conversion (69 ha).*
Canada	<150	<1.5	2006	*The main organic players are the part-Boisset-owned Le Clos Jordanne in Niagara (ON), with 50 ha of Pinot Noir and Chardonnay, and Summerhill Pyramid Winery in Okanagan Valley (BC) with 20 ha. Newly planted vineyards include Baccata Ridge (North Okanagan, BC), and Zovi & Bishop (Saltspring Island, BC).*
Chile	<2,000	<1.9	2006	*Chile's organic vineyards are concentrated in Maipo Valley (33%), Colchagua Valley (20%), and the emerging Maule Valley (15%).*
England	<20	<0.5	2006	*The UK's half-dozen certified organic vineyards are confined to England, but only Chevelswarde, Davenport, and Sedlescombe ferment and bottle their own wines.*
France	17,900	<2.0	2006	*Agence Bio, France's office for organic statistics, estimates the market for organic produce at €1.568 billion in 2005, with supermarkets accounting for 40%. Sales of wine from organically grown grapes were worth €189 million, of which 33% was sold by specialist retailers, 25% by supermarkets, and 42% direct from the winery. Wine is France's most popular organic farm-gate purchase at €81 million, compared to €80 million for fruit and vegetables, €33 million for bread/flour, and €30 million for dairy products.*
Germany	<2,500	<2.5	2007	*The main regions for organic vineyards are Baden-Württemberg (652 ha) and Rheinland-Pfalz (1,222 ha, mainly Rheinhessen rather than Pfalz).*
Greece	<1,200	5.5	2005	*Greece's organic vineyards account for more than 10% of its organic farm area, the highest in the EU.*

Country or region	Hectares certified organic	Percentage of vineyards	Year	Comments
Italy	<50,000	5.5	2006	*The main areas for organic vineyards are the Veneto and the southern Italian regions of Puglia and Sicily. Biodynamic vineyards are far less significant in Italy than in France: fewer than 20 wine-grape vineyards held the official biodynamic Demeter certification in 2005.*
New Zealand	<300	<2.0	2007	*After several attempts, New Zealand's organic grape growers and winemakers finalized a set of organic standards in 2006, with benchmarks for both grape growing and winemaking.*
Portugal	<1,100	<0.5	2005	*Portugal's organic statistics include a proportion of non-wine grapes. Portugal has around 100 organic wine-grape growers, but fewer than a dozen make wine commercially.*
Slovenia	<250	<0.5	2007	*Slovenia's organic standards conformed to EU norms even before the country's accession to the EU in 2004. Entry to the Eurozone should encourage a rise in both organic wine exports and quality.*
South Africa	<350	<0.35	2006	*South Africa is (finally) drawing up its own national organic legislation, which should follow the European model in recognizing the term "wine from organically grown grapes" but not unsulphited or "organic" wine.*
Spain	<20,000	<1.9	2006	*Cooperatives in La Mancha and estate wineries in Rioja and Penedès continue to drive Spain's organic wine scene. Organic sherry-style wines exist, but not organic versions of sherry itself.*
Switzerland	<350	<2.5	2006	*More than 10% of Swiss farmland is certified organic, while 10% of Switzerland's biodynamic farms are vineyards (100 ha).*
Uruguay	27	<0.2	2007	*The organic wine movement lacks inspiration here, since Uruguay's first and only certified organic wine producer, Vinos de La Cruz, produces lacklustre wines from a 27-ha portion of its 65-ha vineyard.*
USA: California	3,500	<2.0	2007	*California's organic vineyard grew by 7% between 2005 and 2006. Green tax breaks for solar power have encouraged wineries like Grgich Hills (Napa), which gained the capacity to become 100% solar powered in 2006. Grgich also became the biggest biodynamically farmed (but still only organically certified) vineyard in the state (366 acres). New biodynamic (Demeter-certified) vineyards include Quivira (26 ha) and Porter Bass (8 ha).*
USA: Oregon	388	<7.0	2006	*The big player here is King Estate (174 ha), followed by Cooper Mountain (48 ha), Cornucopia (47 ha), Sokol Blosser (32 ha), Croft (18 ha), Brick House (11 ha), Bergström (9 ha), and Cattrall (9 ha).*

Grapevine

• **Pesticide residues** were found in 96 per cent of samples of surface water and in 61 per cent of samples from the underlying water table, France's Institute for the Environment (IFEN) reported in August 2006 after 10,000 water samples were drawn nationwide. France is the EU's biggest user of pesticides, 20 per cent of which are used by vineyards, even though vines account for just 3 per cent of French farmland. Eighty per cent of the chemicals used on vineyards are fungicides.

Opinion:

Time to recognize some hybrids

Wines made from fungal-resistant hybrid crossings with the same "unfoxy" quality characteristics as *Vitis vinifera*, such as those developed in Germany, should be officially recognized across the EU as being eligible for quality-wine status. So far, only the Bundesortenamt (Federal Plant Patent Office) in Germany has given Regent, Solaris, and Johanniter such status. Over a dozen hybrids are accepted as *Vitis vinifera* equivalents in Germany, while in the UK, quality-wine status is recognized in Orion, Phoenix, Regent, and Rondo. These vines offer one solution to the use of copper in the vineyard, for which no effective alternative acceptable to organic rule-makers has been found.

Global standards required

A globally recognized organic grape-growing standard is desirable for those who believe there are too many contradictions in the way certification bodies operate – for example, tolerance of parallel production (when only part of a vineyard is farmed organically). Swiss certification bodies such as IMO (Institut für Marktökologie, which certifies Antiyal and Emiliana Orgánico in Chile, for example) are much stricter over the issue of parallel production than other European certification bodies, setting wider "buffer zones" between organic and conventionally farmed parcels.

Sadly, a world organic grape-growing standard is unlikely to appear while growers in Europe continue to argue over, for example, exactly how many kilograms of copper per hectare per year may be used on downy mildew. A global winemaking standard seems even further away, especially in the EU, where no organic winemaking standard exists, so wines must be described as "made from organically grown grapes" and not as "organic wines".

Perhaps the EU could adopt the winemaking rules of the United States' National Organic Program, which do permit the term "organic wine" if no sulphur dioxide is used during winemaking. This could happen from January 2009, when the EU updates its organic norms (2092/91), dating from 1991. The new norms will cover transformed food products for human consumption, such as wine. With typical clarity, the EU did not mention wine specifically in the field of application, but did not exclude it either.

An umbrella study group called ORWINE, with members from Italy, France, Germany, Switzerland, and the International Federation of Organic Agriculture Movements (IFOAM), is being financed by the EU, in the hope that organic winemaking rules can be agreed between member states.

GREATEST WINE PRODUCERS

1. Domaine Leroy (Burgundy, France)
2. Domaine Marcel Deiss (Alsace, France)
3. Domaine Zind Humbrecht (Alsace, France)
4. Ferme de la Sansonnière/ Marc Angeli (Loire, France)
5. Domaine Huet (Loire, France)
6. Nikolaihof (Wachau, Austria)
7. Domaine Leflaive (Burgundy, France)
8. Domaine Pierre Morey (Burgundy, France)
9. Domaine des Epeneaux/Comte Armand (Burgundy, France)
10. Emiliana Orgánico (Central Valley, Chile)

FASTEST-IMPROVING PRODUCERS

1. Château Moulin du Cadet (Bordeaux, France)
2. Le Clos Jordanne (Niagara, Canada)
3. Edgehill (McLaren Vale, Australia)
4. Sokol Blosser (Oregon, USA)
5. Domaine de la Boissoneuse (Chablis, France)
6. Davenport Vineyards (East Sussex, UK)
7. Bonterra Vineyards at McNab & Butler Ranches (California, USA)
8. Quinta da Côa (Douro, Portugal)
9. Gautherot, Vouette & Sorbée (Champagne, France)
10. Emidio Pepe (Abruzzo, Italy)

NEW UP-AND-COMING PRODUCERS

1. Grgich Hills (Napa Valley, California)
2. Hochkirch (SW Victoria, Australia)
3. Meinklang (Burgenland, Austria)
4. Quivira (Dry Creek Valley, California)
5. King Estate (Willamette Valley, Oregon)
6. Bergström (Willamette Valley, Oregon)
7. Tulbagh Mountain Vineyards (Western Cape, South Africa)
8. Kiltynane Estate (Yarra Valley, Australia)
9. Domaine La Capitaine (Begnins, Switzerland)
10. La Raia (Piedmont, Italy)

BEST-VALUE PRODUCERS

1. Domaine Huet (Loire, France)
2. La Riojana Cooperative (La Rioja, Argentina)
3. Emiliana Orgánico (Central Valley, Chile)
4. Stellar Organics (Western Cape, South Africa)
5. Domaine de la Grande Bellane (Rhône, France)
6. Château Moulin du Cadet (Bordeaux, France)
7. Domaine de Pajot (Gascony, France)
8. La Distesa (Le Marche, Italy)
9. Domaine Zusslin (Alsace, France)
10. Domaine Petit Roubié/Jacques Frélin (Languedoc-Roussillon, France)

Grapevine

• **New Zealand's** biodynamic association is applying for government funds to finance an advisory extension. A similar recent programme in Australia, where members of biodynamic associations were paid as accredited "workplace trainers", led to an explosion of interest among wine growers (and other farmers) in organics and biodynamics.

GREATEST-QUALITY WINES

1. **Clos de la Roche 2000** Domaine Leroy, Burgundy, France (€415)
2. **Altenberg de Bergheim 2000** Domaine Marcel Deiss, Alsace, France (€61)
3. **Gewurztraminer Grand Cru Hengst 2004** Domaine Zind Humbrecht, Alsace, France (€49)
4. **Vouvray Clos du Bourg Demi-Sec 1996** Domaine Huet, Loire, France (€22)
5. **Steiner Hund Riesling Reserve 2001** Nikolaihof, Wachau, Austria (€40)
6. **Anjou Blanc La Lune 2001** Ferme de la Sansonnière, Loire, France (€21)
7. **Chevalier-Montrachet 2000** Domaine Leflaive, Burgundy, France (€310)
8. **Côte Rôtie 2003** Domaine Clusel-Roch, Rhône, France (€29)
9. **The McNab 2004** Bonterra Vineyards, Mendocino, California (US$35)
10. **G Colchagua Valley Tinto 2003** Emiliana Orgánico, Chile (CLP 48,500)

BEST BARGAINS

1. **Grüner Veltliner 2005** Meinklang, Burgenland, Austria (€5.40)
2. **Adobe Cabernet Sauvignon Colchagua Valley Tinto 2005** Emiliana Orgánico, Chile (CLP 4,300)
3. **Vin de Pays du Comté de Grignan Rouge 2005** Domaine du Jas, Rhône, France (€3.10)
4. **Era Nero d'Avola 2005** Cantine Volpi, Sicily, Italy (€2.95)
5. **Le Quartre Cépage Blanc 2005** Domaine de Pajot, Gascony, France (€3.20)
6. **Vouvray Le Mont Sec 2005** Domaine Huet, Loire, France (€15)
7. **Battle of Bosworth Chardonnay/Viognier 2006** Edgehill, McLaren Vale, Australia (A$18)
8. **Clos Liebenberg Riesling 2002** Domaine Zusslin, Alsace, France (€14)
9. **Coteaux d'Aix en Provence Rouge Cuvée Valeria 2003** Domaine les Bastides, Provence, France (€12.50)
10. **Verdicchio dei Castelli di Jesi Classico Superiore Gli Eremi 2004** La Distesa, Le Marche, Italy (€10)

Grapevine

• **Tulbagh Mountain Vineyards** is spreading a paste made from fermented lion manure around its vineyard boundary because the scent deters grape-eating baboons. Aloe vera teas are also being used on the vines to minimize heat stress.

• **Mike Benziger** of the Benziger Family Winery in Sonoma said that 2006 was the first year in 10 years that his horn manure 500 preparation, which is buried in the ground between autumn and spring, did not make the transformation from cow manure to humus by the spring equinox of 20 March (of the 31 days in March, it rained 26 days). Benziger had to leave it in the ground for another six weeks. German growers reported similar problems.

• **The Organic Trade Association (OTA)** in the USA reported that sales of wine made from organically grown grapes rose 28 per cent between 2004 and 2005, hitting US$80 million. The volume of organically produced wine sold doubled between 2003 and 2006, and it is expected to rise 17 per cent annually to 2008.

MOST EXCITING OR UNUSUAL FINDS

1 Begnins Gamaret en Barrique 2004 Domaine La Capitaine, Begnins, Switzerland (€14) *Red wine from Gamaret, a Swiss crossing of Gamay x Reichensteiner, showing perky colour, polished fruit, and polite tannins.*

2 Rosso di Montalcino 2004 Salicutti, Tuscany, Italy (€18) *You'll struggle to find Sangiovese with such an unselfconsciously pallid colour, clarity of flavour, and typicity of texture in Montalcino's overhyped, overpriced Brunello zone.*

3 Preliminaire Still Blanc de Noir 2005 Kiltynane Estate, Yarra Valley, (A$42) *Whole-bunch-pressed, wild-yeast- and barrel-fermented still white from Pinot Noir.*

4 Burgenland Red 2004 Meinklang, Burgenland, Austria (€5.40) *Who says Austria can't make juicy, classy reds from the likes of the oft-scorned Zweigelt (65 per cent), Blaufränkisch (20 per cent) and St Laurent (15 per cent)?*

5 Syrah/Mourvèdre 2003 Tulbagh Mountain Vineyards, Western Cape, South Africa (R250) *A cracking advertisement for why Rhône-style reds, not bordeaux-style ones, are likely to be South Africa's organic red-wine future.*

6 Authentis Brut Millésimé Cumières 2001 Duval-Leroy, Champagne, France (€60) *Toasty, structured, oak-aged, mono-cru champagne sourced from Vincent Laval's premier cru vineyards in Cumières.*

7 Live-a-Little Really Ravishing Red 2004 Stellar Organics, Western Cape, South Africa (R21) *This wine marks a new era for Fairtrade organic wines, which, until now, have targeted the consciences of* the eco-conscious rather than more mainstream wine drinkers' palates.

8 Vin de Pays d'Oc Orion Rouge 2004 Domaine Petit Roubié/Jacques Frélin, Languedoc-Roussillon, France (€3.75) *France's biggest shipper of organic wines specializes in pile-it-high-and-sell-it-cheap wines; and why not, with a growing global wine surplus?*

9 Limney Horsmonden Dry 2005 Davenport Vineyards, East Sussex, UK (£6.80) *As well as making a small amount of traditional-method sparkling wine for Prince Charles's Highgrove Estate, Will Davenport makes the UK's most consistently appealing still white wines (barely off-dry in this case).*

10 Regent Oak Matured Red 2004 Sedlescombe Organic Vineyard, East Sussex, UK (£12.95) *England's oldest organic vineyard shows that, although global warming may make Britain a red-wine paradise, carefully selected interspecific crossings like Regent play their part, too.*

Grapevine

• **Former Fetzer boss** Paul Dolan, whose 68-acre Dark Horse estate in Mendocino now has full Demeter biodynamic certification, has sold his Cypress Hill vineyard "because it wasn't going to produce the quality we were looking for". He has purchased, with partners Tim and Tom Thornhill, a 62-acre benchland property called Upper Home Ranch. Currently in its second year of organic certification, it will eventually go into the biodynamic programme. Dolan is also converting another 40-acre Chardonnay vineyard, Ghionda Rose, from certified organic to biodynamics.

Wine & Health

Beverley Blanning MW

Each year brings more research reinforcing the widely accepted view that moderate consumption of alcohol has a beneficial effect on general health.

BEVERLEY BLANNING MW

While it has long been thought that wine and other alcoholic drinks complement a healthy lifestyle, several recent studies have quantified the extent to which moderate drinking contributes to good health. These studies show that even those with very healthy lifestyles can reduce their risk of ill health by moderate drinking.

Last year, this report spoke of the young; this year, there is more to report on the elderly. Studies from around the world are now showing more and more positive health outcomes for older people from moderate drinking. It appears likely that this sector of the population has the most to gain and least to lose from enjoying a daily glass of wine.

There is still a frustrating lack of research differentiating between wine and other drinks. However, a common assumption persists that red wine is the best option for health. While this does seem plausible at a marginal level, it is too early to be sure of this, and it has certainly not been proved that individual wines have significantly greater health benefits than others.

BEVERLEY BLANNING MW is a wine writer based in London. She writes for a number of publications and tastes and travels widely. She also lectures, judges at international wine competitions, and organizes tasting events. Beverley became a Master of Wine in 2001, specializing for her dissertation on the effects of wine on cardiovascular health.

Alcohol as part of a healthy lifestyle

Several pieces of research stemming from a study of US male health professionals have pointed to the importance of alcohol, and wine in particular, as part of a healthy lifestyle. These have reinforced the view that moderate daily consumption of alcohol is one of the five key habits for a healthy lifestyle. The others are: not smoking; 30 minutes of exercise daily; avoiding obesity; and following a healthy diet, rich in fruits, vegetables, grains, and fish.

Compared to non-drinkers, moderate drinkers have been shown to have a 37 per cent lower risk of coronary heart disease (CHD) and a 63 per cent lower risk of myocardial infarction (heart attack) compared with those enjoying a similarly healthy lifestyle but not drinking. Looking at risks associated with ischaemic stroke, populations following a healthier lifestyle but with no alcohol consumption would have their risk of stroke reduced by 44 per cent compared to 69 per cent for those consuming alcohol. The conclusion is that moderate alcohol consumption lowers risk of CHD, heart attack, and ischaemic stroke, even for those with an already very healthy lifestyle. This finding refutes the suggestion that moderate drinkers enjoy better health only because of their already healthy lifestyle.

Grapevine

• **Italian scientists** claim to have discovered high levels of the sleep hormone melatonin in some wine grapes, perhaps explaining why drinking a glass of wine can have a relaxing, or even soporific, effect. Iriti and colleagues found high levels of melatonin in Nebbiolo, Merlot, Cabernet Sauvignon, Sangiovese, and Croatina grapes.

• **A large study** of non-smoking adults in the USA by Arif et al concludes that moderate drinking reduces the odds for obesity, although the reasons for this are not known. Furthermore, those who drink more frequently seem to show the least obesity. The authors comment: "The consistency of the inverse relationship observed between obesity and frequency of drinking suggests that the beneficial effect of drinking on obesity is present when the alcohol is consumed in moderate amounts on a regular basis."

• **Physician visits** were 43 per cent higher among non-drinkers, compared to low-risk drinkers, in a random sample of adults aged 20–64 in Germany.

• **Health warnings** on alcoholic drinks are now compulsory in France. The French government has implemented a health warning directed at pregnant women on all alcoholic drinks. The UK is working towards increasing the amount of information available on labels, including units of alcohol and a health message.

PATTERN OF DRINKING IS KEY

People who drink moderately, frequently, and in a stable pattern appear to enjoy the best health outcomes. This is the message coming through from several studies on drinking patterns. A Dutch study found that moderate drinkers who did not change their alcohol intake significantly over time had the lowest all-cause mortality rate. A Danish study found that less frequent consumption was related to a higher risk of death than more frequent patterns. Similar results had been found in an earlier study in the USA, which showed that small amounts of alcohol consumed several times a week reduced risk to a greater extent than the same amount consumed on fewer occasions.

A study of healthy middle-aged men and women in Denmark, published in 2006, shows the importance of distinguishing between men and women when it comes to health outcomes associated with alcohol. In this study, by Tolstrup et al, development of CHD was monitored over a period of around six years. The results were analysed in terms of amount and pattern of drinking, and showed marked differences between women and men: for men, the greatest inverse relationship was seen between high frequency of drinking (daily) and risk of CHD; for women, those who drank at least one day a week had a lower risk of CHD than women who drank less frequently than this; but, unlike men, greater frequency was not associated with reduced risk. For women, greatest reduction in risk of CHD was generally seen at the highest levels of consumption, over 14 drinks a week. The authors point out that little is known about drinking patterns among women, but they caution that these results may be limited to post-menopausal women (of the women in the study, only 17 per cent were pre-menopausal). Alcohol consumption is believed to increase oestrogen levels, thereby offering post-menopausal women protection from risk of CHD. Mukamal et al previously found that drinking frequency is inversely associated with risk of myocardial infarction for both men and women. In any event, this highlights once more growing evidence that there may be significant differences between the sexes when it comes to alcohol consumption.

ELDERLY BENEFIT MOST FROM DRINKING?

Research published by the American Geriatrics Society found that women in their 70s who consume one or two alcoholic drinks daily are more likely to be in good health than non-drinkers. The study, of Australian women aged 70–75, compared the health of non-drinkers with those who drank one to two drinks three to six times per week. The non-drinkers were more likely to die sooner and were generally in poorer health, physically and mentally, compared to the drinkers.

Further studies show that the incidence of dementia is less likely in elderly moderate drinkers. A study of an elderly Chinese population, by Deng et al, showed reduced incidence of dementia for light to moderate drinkers compared with non-drinkers. These results appeared to be especially good for wine and spirits drinkers. A study of cognitive function in Hispanics over 65 years of age, by Lindeman et al, showed higher scores for moderate drinkers. The multitude of studies analysing cognitive dysfunction and alcohol consumption consistently show that light to moderate alcohol consumption protects against cognitive dysfunction, including dementia.

Further evidence of the benefits of wine in particular comes from a New York study by Pasinetti et al, where mice bred to develop Alzheimer's disease were fed water, alcohol in water, or wine (Cabernet Sauvignon) to the equivalent of the USDA's recommendations for moderate consumption. After a seven-month period, the mice were tested in a maze, after being alcohol-free for three days. The mice that had been drinking wine escaped from the maze significantly faster than those drinking water or alcohol in water. The researchers concluded that the red wine had slowed the symptoms of Alzheimer's.

The so-called Mediterranean diet, combined with moderate alcohol consumption, may lower the risk of developing Alzheimer's disease, according to recent research conducted on elderly residents of Manhattan, New York. Scarmeas and colleagues followed 2,258 elderly people for four years. Those adhering most closely to the Mediterranean diet had a lower risk of developing the disease.

A study by Mukamal et al of risk of myocardial infarction in US adults over the age of 65 showed that the lowest risk was seen among the heaviest-drinking group, that is those consuming more than 14 drinks per week. Even breaking the results down into those drinking 14–20 and over 21 drinks did not materially affect the results. The benefit was consistent across wine, beer, and spirits.

NEGATIVE EFFECTS OF BINGE DRINKING

A study on Finnish twins concluded that binge drinking in middle age significantly increased the likelihood of dementia in later life. The twins provided information about drinking habits between 1975 and 1981 and were assessed for signs of dementia 25 years later, when all were over 65 years of age. Binge drinking, defined as five bottles of beer or a bottle of wine on one occasion at least monthly, was associated with a significantly increased risk of dementia.

Research conducted at 45 hospitals in the USA measured relative risk of death following myocardial infarction, depending on patterns of drinking; 1,919 patients (94 per cent male) were followed up for a median of 3.8 years. Mukamal et al found that binge drinkers, defined as those consuming three or more drinks within two hours (around 42 g [1.5 oz] alcohol), had a twofold higher risk of mortality compared with those who did not binge. Interestingly, this relationship was irrespective of total consumption or of beverage type. The authors concluded that, although alcohol consumption following myocardial infarction was inversely associated with mortality, binge drinking completely negated this effect.

SENSIBLE-DRINKING MESSAGE NOT GETTING THROUGH

A survey among Scottish supermarket shoppers concludes that there is "considerable confusion" among consumers about what constitutes sensible drinking, suggesting that the message on sensible drinking – which has not changed since 1995 in the UK – is still not getting through. Whether this is due to consumer apathy or lack of clarity in communication is unclear, but it seems that there is work to be done by the drinks industry if this state of affairs is to improve.

On a more positive note, a 2006 study from Datamonitor suggests that binge drinking is declining in the UK, with consumption now approaching that of other European countries. However, the British average of 6.3 units on a night out is still high and exceeds the European average of 5.1 units.

The Institute of Alcohol Studies, funded by the European Commission, has published a report, *Alcohol in Europe: A Public Health Perspective*, listing 52 recommendations with the aim of reducing alcohol-related harm across the EU. It recommends that alcohol health warnings and suggested labels "should not promote an alcoholic product by any means that are likely to create an erroneous impression about its characteristics or health effects".

LIVER CIRRHOSIS RISING IN BRITAIN

A study of mortality from cirrhosis in Europe between 1950 and 2002 published in *The Lancet* shows that the number of deaths increased greatly in Britain over the period. The figures showed that liver cirrhosis doubled in men in Scotland between the periods 1987–91 and 1997–2001 and rose by more than two-thirds in England and Wales. These relative increases are the steepest in Western Europe. The authors of the study point to increased alcohol consumption and obesity as the probable cause of the increase. Most other European countries experienced declining deaths from cirrhosis. A further report from the UK's National Health Service noted that hospital admissions for alcoholic liver disease more than doubled between 1995/96 and 2004/05. The figure increased from 14,400 to 35,400.

CANCER

An international team led by Dr Paolo Boffetta of the International Agency for Research on Cancer in Lyon has concluded that 3.6 per cent of all cancer cases worldwide are alcohol-related, leading to 3.5 per cent of all cancer deaths. The problem is especially marked in Central and Eastern Europe. The authors state: "A causal link has been established between alcohol drinking and cancers of the oral cavity, pharynx, oesophagus, colon, rectum, liver, larynx, and breast." More than 60 per cent of alcohol-related cancers in men were in the upper digestive tract; for women, 60 per cent were in the breast.

A study published in the journal *Cancer* by Genkinger et al has concluded that, contrary to previous suggestions, there is no link between moderate alcohol consumption and risk of ovarian cancer. The study included more than 500,000 women and showed similar results for wine, beer, and spirits. The study showed that there was no observed increase in incidence at higher consumption levels.

A Danish study of post-menopausal women has shown that the association between breast cancer and alcohol intake was present mainly in women with low folate intake. However, a meta-analysis by scientists at the University of Bristol concluded that there is no link between low dietary folate and breast cancer. It is possible that the link is relevant only for drinkers, but the inconsistent conclusions suggest that more research is needed to clarify this issue.

A study in the *International Journal of Cancer* by Stanford et al shows that men who drink more than four glasses of red wine a week appear to reduce their risk of prostate cancer dramatically – by 50 per cent. The authors found no effect from consumption of beer or spirits and no consistent effect from white wine. Stanford suggests that the findings may be attributable to the antioxidant resveratrol in red wine, known to have potent anti-cancer properties.

DAILY RED-WINE INTAKE REDUCES PLASMA VISCOSITY

Blood that is more viscous moves more slowly and tends to clot more easily. Higher blood viscosity is associated with greater risk of atherosclerosis. A recent Norwegian study by Jensen et al of 80 healthy, non-smoking volunteers showed that those who drank a single glass of red wine every day for three weeks had reduced plasma viscosity at the end of this period and for three weeks afterwards.

WINE BENEFITS FOR DIABETICS

In an Italian study of people with type 2 diabetes mellitus who had suffered a heart attack, subjects were advised to consume a Mediterranean diet and to exercise. In addition, half the group was advised to consume one small glass of red wine daily. After a year,

those who had drunk wine showed significantly better cardiac performance and higher HDL (good) cholesterol compared to the other half.

WINE THE BEST CHOICE OF BEVERAGE

A study of Melbourne adults by Baglietto et al investigated deaths from all causes over a 10-year period and sought to identify associations between volume of alcohol consumed, frequency of drinking, and beverage choice. The J-curve was observed for both men and women. The lowest mortality was associated with moderate wine consumption for men and for women. Beer was associated with increased risk for men. Greater frequency of consumption was inversely associated with risk of dying in men.

SEARCH FOR "BEST" HEALTH WINE

A much-publicized UK report emerged at the end of 2006. London scientist Roger Corder and colleagues found that the most potent anti-atherosclerotic polyphenols in wine were procyanidins. They compared the level of procyanidins in different wines from around the world, focusing on areas with known longevity of population. The authors found that wines from the Gers in southwest France and the Nuoro province of Sardinia – areas known for great longevity – had the highest levels of procyanidins. The authors attribute this finding to the polyphenol-rich Tannat grape used in southwest France and to the "traditional winemaking" methods followed in these regions (by which they mean extended maceration of the wine with skins and seeds).

Opinion:

Current practices that should stop

- Sensationalist media reporting of issues relating to wine and health.
- Ban on ingredient labelling – of particular interest to vegetarians, buyers of organic food, and those with allergies.
- Misleading information on wine bottles relating to the health risks of wine.

Things that should be happening

- Clearer dissemination of information about the meaning of moderate drinking and, especially, binge drinking.
- Up-to-date and unbiased reporting of the benefits of moderate wine consumption and the dangers of binge drinking.
- International standardization of the definitions of a unit of alcohol and moderate consumption. Both vary enormously from country to country, causing consumer confusion over safe or desirable consumption levels.
- Unit labelling on bottles to indicate the number of units per bottle – of increasing importance with rising alcohol levels in wine.
- A move to precise per cent alcohol measures on labels.
- Greater focus on research into the different effects of drinking on women's health, especially breast cancer.
- Greater focus on the effects of drinking on different age groups.
- More research distinguishing between wine and other drinks.
- More research on patterns of consumption. Specifically, given the focus on the dangers of binge drinking, there is a need to understand how wine is now consumed compared to its traditional patterns.
- Research on the benefits of red versus white wine, and different types of red wine identified in research where possible.

Grapevine

- **UK retailer Sainsbury's** launched Red Heart in December 2006, a wine the supermarket claims is "actually good for your heart" (although, as readers of *Wine Report* will already know, actually, they all are!). The company also claims that the wine has 32 per cent more antioxidants than "other leading red wines", but it seems reluctant to give more details on how it derives these figures or what research it has used in coming up with the product.

TOP WINE HEALTH BENEFITS

1 Increased longevity from regular, moderate consumption for men over 45 and post-menopausal women.

2 Significant protection from cardiovascular diseases with moderate consumption.

3 Drinkers, especially wine drinkers, have lowered risk of many other diseases, including stress-related illnesses and the common cold.

TOP WINE HEALTH HYPES

1 Drinking is good for you – it always depends on individual circumstances.

2 The benefits of consumption are accrued equally by young and old; recent studies indicate that the elderly benefit the most.

3 Resveratrol is the most important beneficial agent in wine.

4 Wine is necessarily a better option than beer or spirits – all alcoholic drinks can be beneficial.

5 Red wine is significantly better than white in providing health-related benefits.

6 The idea that regular, moderate consumption of wine is an acceptable substitute for improving health outcomes in place of changing diet and other lifestyle factors, such as regular exercise.

TOP WINE HEALTH DANGERS

1 Most dangers come from excessive consumption. Excessive will mean different things for different people. Risks include:
- alcoholism;
- risk of accidents;
- violent crime;
- domestic violence;
- child abuse;
- suicide and depression;
- severe damage to every system in the body.

2 Increased risk of breast cancer, even at low levels of consumption. This is of greatest significance to young women, who have less to gain from the protective effects of alcohol against cardiovascular disease.

3 Increased risk of health problems for women drinkers at relatively low consumption levels.

4 Ignorance of sensible drinking levels, especially underestimating the dangers of excessive drinking and what constitutes a binge.

5 Increasing levels of dangerous consumption among the young, who appear to have little, if anything, to gain in terms of health benefits and much to lose.

TOP WINE HEALTH MYTHS

1 Drinking is bad for you.

2 Drinking is good for you.

3 Drinking any alcohol while pregnant significantly increases the risk of FAS.

Grape Varieties

Dr François Lefort

Research into grapevines is bearing fruit everywhere in the world of viticulture, and this year we report on a host of new varieties.

DR FRANÇOIS LEFORT

Some of the grapes listed below could become the mainstays of future generations, finding places in new appellations that could be created in northern Europe and the USA as a result of global warming. These new varieties, which can be planted now, have passed stringent evaluation programmes, are better adapted to particular climates or soils, and are selected for aroma or resistance/tolerance to diseases such as grey mould, oidium, or downy mildew. However, they are not being widely planted, mainly because of restrictions placed on appellations in Europe. Some have been used in France to make *vins de pays*, in some cases so successfully that the wines sell for higher prices than AOC wines.

Grapes produced by the extensive breeding programmes of the USSR are currently being tested in the West, particularly in the USA and Denmark. The former Soviet republics are continuing their research into grapevines, focusing mainly on cold-hardiness. New varieties from Belarus, Estonia, Hungary, Latvia, and Russia, some of which can stand winter temperatures as low as –40°C (–40°F), are detailed below.

Agra: Very early-ripening white variety produced by Latvian breeder Pauls Sukatnieks with a small cluster of medium-sized berries. It needs winter protection in the Latvian and the Belarusian climate but can stand temperatures as low as –25°C (–13°F).

DR FRANÇOIS LEFORT is a professor at the University of Applied Sciences of Western Switzerland in Geneva. He has been working on the diversity of grapevine varieties for many years. François is the creator of the Greek Vitis database and the coauthor of the Bulgarian Grapevine database. He is now more involved in describing new pathogens affecting grapevines and other plants.

Jubileinaja Novgoroda: Early-ripening white-wine variety developed by A Kuzmin at the Central Genetic Laboratory in Michurinsk in Russia. It produces fruity pineapple flavours and displays good botrytis resistance in the cool, wet conditions of north Russia. It is also being tested at Roogojka farm by Professor Kivistik from Rapina Gardening College in Estonia.

Kosmonauts: Very early-ripening red-wine interspecific hybrid with large clusters of large white berries. It can be used as a table grape or for making *blanc de noir* wines. It was developed by Dr Romuald Loiko at Samokhvalovitchy in Belarus. Needs to be grown with winter protection in Belarus.

Meda: Cold-hardy variety withstanding winters to −30°C (−22°F); developed by Latvian breeder Pauls Sukatnieks. It has medium clusters of small to medium seedless berries, making it suitable for table grapes.

Muscat Melnik: Blue-skinned Muscat variety with medium-sized clusters of small to medium berries developed at the Central Genetic Laboratory in Michurinsk, Russia. It produces a white Muscat-flavoured wine and needs winter protection in northern Russia. It is also grown in Bulgaria.

Reform: New Hungarian wine-grape variety displaying small berries with a rather neutral aroma. It produces small clusters of small to medium-sized berries. It is also being tested in Denmark.

Sirvinta: Red-skinned variety developed by Lithuanian breeder Roberts Galaitis. An extremely early-ripening variety, it needs winter protection in Latvia. It produces small to medium-sized clusters with fruit-flavoured berries.

Skujinsh 675 (Moskovskiy Ustoichiviy): ([(Pearl of Csaba x Amurskiy) x Alpha]; Professor Skujinsh). This white-wine variety was named after Latvian breeder Skujinsh from the Tymiryazev Academy of Agriculture (TCXA) in Moscow. It is also known in Russia as Moskovsky Ustoichiviy. This variety is very early-ripening, and its promising wine displays fruity flavours. It is under quarantine trials in the USA and Denmark.

Sukribe: Very productive white variety from Pauls Sukatnieks, displaying large clusters of large berries. It is cold-hardy down to −30°C (−22°F) and is grown without winter protection in the Baltic.

Varajane Sinine: Native Estonian variety ("early blue" in Estonian), discovered by Jaan Kivistik of the Rapina Gardening College, who evaluated it for many years. It is a very early-ripening variety with medium clusters and can be grown without winter protection in Latvia.

Veldze: White selection from Latvian breeder Pauls Sukatnieks, producing large clusters. Cold-hardy down to −20°C (−4°F).

Vidzeme Skaistule: With blue lavender berries in small clusters, this variety is a selection obtained by Andrash Fazekash, Vidzeme, Latvia. It is very cold-hardy (resistant to −35°C [−31°F]) and a very early-ripening variety (end of August in Latvia). It is an aromatic variety with a fruity Gewürztraminer-like flavour.

Zilga: (Dvietes 4-2-108 [Smuglyanka (*Vitis amurensis*) x [Dvietes Zilas (*Vitis labrusca*) x Jubileinaja Novgoroda (*Vitis vinifera* x *Vitis labrusca*)]]; P Sukatnieks, 1964). The most cold-hardy selection developed by Latvian breeder Pauls Sukatnieks, this can stand winters as cold as −40°C (−40°F). It is a very vigorous and productive grapevine with small to medium-sized clusters of blue berries.

New grapes being tested in Estonia

Roogoja Farm, a collective farm until 1990, specializes in plant breeding. It is testing about 30 winter-hardy grape varieties, mostly from ex-Soviet Union breeders or breeding institutes. Grapes are grown in plastic greenhouses without heating but are covered during spring nights to protect them from frost. Flowering takes place in the middle of June, and some varieties may be harvested as early as mid-August. To resist winter frosts as low as −25 to −30°C (−13 to −22°F), shoots are cut hard back in autumn and covered with peat. These tests involve the grapes listed below.

Belaja Rannaja: (Ukraine) Green variety that ripens early.

CGL 2-05-43: (A Kuzmin, Russia) Dark-blue variety that ripens very early.

Guna: (P Sukatnieks, Latvia) Black, early-ripening variety, surviving −30°C (−22°F) but requiring pollination.

Hübriid 1-2-6: (E Petersons, Latvia) Yellowish-green, early-ripening variety grown in a thick bush.

Jalta 343: (Magarach Institute, Ukraine) Yellowish-green, variety that ripens early.

Jubileinaja Novgoroda: (A Kuzmin, Russia) Yellowish-green, very early-ripening variety that may survive −30°C (−22°F) in winter. Growing period of 110 days.

Krasa Severa: (J Filippenko, Russia) Yellowish-green, early-ripening variety that survives −25°C (−13°F). It produces sparse, thin clusters of berries.

Krasavets: (A Kuzmin, Russia) A black variety that is hard to grow but produces an abundant harvest.

Madeleine Angevine: Old French variety with yellowish-green berries that ripens early. It has a growing period of 110–125 days and needs pollination.

Malingre Seemik: (I Mitsurin, Russia) Green variety; early ripening.

Rosova Taifi: (central Asia) Greenish-yellow variety; late-ripening but hard to grow.

Russkaja Korinka: (J Filippenko, Russia) Yellowish-green variety with small seedless berries. Ripens very early and survives −26°C (−14.8°F).

Supaga: (P Sukatnieks, Latvia) Yellowish-green early-ripening variety; survives −25°C (−13°F) and gives an abundant harvest.
Veina: (P Sukatnieks, Latvia) Light-green, early-ripening variety that survives −20°C (−4°F).

These varieties can be obtained from Kivistik Roogoja Farm, Karla küla Kose vald, 75101 Harjumaa, Estonia (e-mail kivistik@trenet.ee).

Missouri programme bears fruit

Keith Striegler of the State Fruit Experiment Station in Mountain Grove, Missouri, has been testing 77 different varieties imported from Eastern European countries since 1993, evaluating their adaptability and productivity in Missouri as part of the Missouri Wine Grape Importation Program. After extensive screening for cold-hardiness, physiological character, fruit yield, and wine quality, experimental wines were made in 2003 and submitted to the Missouri wine industry for assessment. As a result of this programme, grapes that could soon be found in Missouri are: Toldi, SK77-12/6, Viorica, M 36-13/38, K38, Pitos, CSFT 194, CSFT195, M 36-12/110, BV 19-88, Kristaly, Ovidiopolki, XIV 1-86, Odessia, and Muscat (white); and XIV 11-57, T Ranij, L 4-9-18, Mi 5/106, M 39-9/74, Kozma 525, I 55/8, Nero, and Golubok (black). Parentages were not reported.

Recent French varieties

The French institute for agricultural research, INRA, has released many new grape varieties in the past 20 years. Some, such as Marselan, have already found favour with French growers and consumers. Folignan, initially bred as a wine grape, was honoured in 2005 by becoming one of the few varieties used in cognac production. Others are not so successful, being restricted to *vins de table* and *vins de pays*, or even totally ignored, in spite of their good winemaking qualities. Here is a selection.
Aranel: (= INRA 1816-106; Grenache Gris x Saint Pierre Doré; INRA Montpellier, Paul Truel, 1961) White variety authorized for *vins de table* and *vins de pays*.
Arinarnoa: (Merlot x Petit Verdot; INRA Bordeaux, Durquety) Black variety for *vins de table* and *vins de pays*, recommended since 1985 in west and southwest France. It reached 5.8 ha in 1994. Resistant to grey mould.
Arriloba: (Raffiat de Moncade, a white variety, x Sauvignon; INRA Bordeaux, Durquety) White variety for *vins de table* and *vins de pays*, cultivated on 15 ha in 1994. It is tolerant of grey mould because of its thick skin and is also well suited to mechanical harvesting.

Caladoc: (= INRA 1510-104; Grenache Noir x Cot; INRA Montpellier, Paul Truel, 1958) Black variety authorized for *vins de table* and *vins de pays*.

Chasan: (= INRA 1527-78; Listan Blanc x Chardonnay Blanc; INRA Montpellier, Paul Truel, 1958) White variety authorized for *vins de table* and *vins de pays*. Cultivated only in the Landes region (southwest France).

Chenanson: (= INRA 1509-149; Grenache Noir x Jurançon; INRA Montpellier, Paul Truel, 1958) Black variety authorized for *vins de table* and *vins de pays*; recommended for planting since 1985.

Egiodola: (Fer x Abouriou; INRA Bordeaux, Durquety) Early black variety for *vins de table* and *vins de pays*. Last estimated planting area was 280 ha in 1994. It is tolerant of grey mould and gives tannic wines.

Ekigaïna: (Tannat x Cabernet Sauvignon; INRA Bordeaux, Durquety) Black variety for *vins de table* and *vins de pays*, covering only 2 ha in 1994. It gives coloured, weakly acidic wines.

Ganson: (= INRA 1509-73; Grenache Noir x Jurançon; INRA Montpellier, Paul Truel, 1958) Black variety authorized for *vins de table* and *vins de pays*.

Gramon: (= INRA 1740-774; Grenache Noir x Aramon Noir; INRA Montpellier, Paul Truel, 1960) Black variety authorized for *vins de table* and *vins de pays*.

Liliorila: (Baroque Blanc x Chardonnay Blanc; INRA Bordeaux, Durquety) White variety for *vins de table* and *vins de pays*; only 0.5 ha planted in 1994. It gives strong aromatic wines of low acidity.

Marselan: (= INRA 1810-68; Cabernet Sauvignon x Grenache Noir; INRA Montpellier, Paul Truel, 1961) Black variety authorized for *vins de table* and *vins de pays*.

Monerac: (= INRA 1740-1142; Grenache Noir x Aramon Noir; INRA Montpellier, Paul Truel, 1960) Black variety authorized for *vins de table* and *vins de pays*.

Perdea: (Raffiat de Moncade, a white variety, x Chardonnay Blanc; INRA Bordeaux, Durquety) White variety for *vins de table* and *vins de pays*; 3.5 ha planted in 1994. Tolerant of grey mould. Gives aromatic wines.

Portan: (= INRA 1508-25; Grenache Noir x Portugais Bleu; INRA Montpellier, Paul Truel, 1958) Black variety authorized for *vins de table* and *vins de pays*.

Ségalin: (= INRA 1377-174; Jurançon Noir x Portugais Bleu; INRA Montpellier, Paul Truel, 1957) Black variety authorized for *vins de table* and *vins de pays*.

Semebat: (Baroque Noir x Cot; INRA Bordeaux, Durquety) Black variety for *vins de table* and *vins de pays*; 4.4 ha cultivated in 1994. It is tolerant of grey mould and gives coloured and full-bodied wines.

AOC status for INRA grape

Folignan (= INRA 8476; Ugni Blanc x Folle Blanche; INRA Bordeaux, 1965) is more resistant to grey mould than Ugni Blanc. Authorized for table wines in 1996 in west and southwest France, it produced fairly uninteresting dry white wines but had very good potential for making aromatic cognac. It was authorized as a variety for cognac production in 2005 in AOC Cognac areas but must not represent more than 10 per cent of the AOC Cognac land surface. It covered only 20 ha in 2006 but will certainly increase in the near future. Folignan is the first variety created by INRA to be planted in an AOC vineyard.

Swiss creations

Swiss wine growers have much greater scope for planting different varieties for appellation wines than France, Italy, or Spain. Varieties created by the federal agricultural research institute Agroscope Changins have found their way into bottles in Geneva, Vaud, Valais, and Neuchâtel. A selection is listed below.

Carminoir: (Pinot Noir x Cabernet Sauvignon; Agroscope Changins, 1982) Black variety very resistant to grey mould but requires good soil. It produces coloured, full-bodied, tannic wines.

Charmont: (Chasselas x Chardonnay; Agroscope Changins, 1965) White variety giving slightly aromatic round wines with more body than Chasselas.

Diolinoir: (Rouge de Diolly, now identified as Robin Noir x Pinot Noir; Agroscope Changins, 1970) Black variety giving coloured, tannic wines.

Doral: (Chasselas x Chardonnay; Agroscope Changins, 1965) White variety selected to replace Chasselas, an old French table variety widely grown in Switzerland for wine production. It gained some aromatic characteristics from its Chardonnay parent and is well suited to producing mellow wines.

Gamaret: (Gamay x Reichensteiner [= Müller-Thurgau x (Madeleine Angevine x Weisser Calabreser)]; Agroscope Changins, 1970) Black variety giving coloured, tannic wines.

Garanoir: (Gamay x Reichensteiner [= Müller-Thurgau x (Madeleine Angevine x Weisser Calabreser)]; Agroscope Changins, 1970) Black variety giving coloured, tannic wines.

OIV opens its files

The OIV (Office International de la Vigne et du Vin) has published some very interesting information about grape varieties free of charge on its website (www.oiv.int/uk/accueil/index.php).

The database includes an updated list of cultivated varieties, along with common synonyms, in most of the main wine-producing countries (Argentina, Australia, Austria, Belgium, Canada, Chile, Cyprus, Czech Republic, France, Germany, Italy, Morocco, Republic of South Africa, Slovenia, Spain, Switzerland, and the USA). See http://news.reseau-concept.net/images/oiv/Client/ListeCepageOIV_112006.pdf.

Another very useful and comprehensive tool is a detailed description of 500 wine grapes of the world (see http://news.reseau-concept.net/images/oiv/client/des_cep_monde.pdf). The information is given in four languages (English, French, German, and Spanish).

Widest-cultivated white grape varieties
Global, wine grapes only.

Grape variety	Acres in 2006*	Main countries
1. Airén	756,300	Spain
2. Chardonnay	473,640	USA, France, Italy
3. Ugni Blanc	375,840	France, Italy, Argentina
4. Rkatsiteli	264,850	Ukraine, Georgia, Moldova
5. Sauvignon Blanc	207,600	France, Moldova, USA
6. Riesling	139,550	Germany, Ukraine
7. Macabeo	123,000	Spain, Argentina, Australia, Morocco
8. Muscat of Alexandria	118,230	Spain, Chile, Algeria
9. Welschriesling	113,700	Canada, Germany, USA, Slovenia, Czech Republic
10. Muscat Blanc	109,550	Greece, Spain, Italy, France, Portugal, Australia, USA

* Estimated. Source: Patrick W Fegan, Chicago Wine School, 2007.

Widest-cultivated black grape varieties
Global, wine grapes only.

Grape variety	Acres in 2006*	Main countries
1. Cabernet Sauvignon	709,530	France, Chile, USA
2. Merlot	700,380	France, Italy, USA
3. Grenache	511,650	Spain, France, Italy
4. Tempranillo	501,900	Spain, Argentina, Portugal
5. Syrah	376,850	France, Australia
6. Carignan	261,250	France, China, Tunisia
7. Bobal	219,800	Spain
8. Pinot Noir	219,335	France, USA, Germany
9. Sangiovese	188,000	Italy, Argentina, USA
10. Monastrell/Mourvèdre	185,300	Spain, France, Australia

* Estimated. Source: Patrick W Fegan, Chicago Wine School, 2007.

Widest-cultivated grey/rosé grape varieties
Global, wine grapes only.

Grape variety	Acres in 2006*	Main countries
1. Pinot Gris	67,650	Italy, Germany, USA
2. Criolla Grande	57,400	Argentina
3. Cereza	44,800	Argentina
4. Gewürztraminer	41,150	Moldova, France, Ukraine
5. Grenache Gris	5,900	France
6. Roditis	2,500	Greece
7. Catawba	2,100	USA
8. Grolleau Gris	1,400	France

* Estimated. Source: Patrick W Fegan, Chicago Wine School, 2007.

Fastest-growing white grape varieties
The greatest global increase in recent plantings of white (wine only) grape varieties.

Grape variety	Acres in 2005*	Acres in 2006*	% increase**
1. Sauvignon Blanc	199,900	207,600	3.9
2. Chardonnay	458,900	473,640	3.2
3. Riesling	135,400	139,450	3

* Estimated. ** Some increases may reflect improved data collection rather than an actual increase in acreage. Source: Patrick W Fegan, Chicago Wine School, 2007.

Fastest-growing black grape varieties
The greatest global increase in recent plantings of black (wine only) grape varieties.

Grape variety	Acres in 2005*	Acres in 2006*	% increase**
1. Syrah	357,700	374,150	4.6
2. Pinot Noir	215,500	219,335	1.8
3. Cabernet Sauvignon	701,300	709,530	1.2
4. Merlot	694,400	700,380	0.9

* Estimated. ** Some increases may reflect improved data collection rather than an actual increase in acreage. Source: Patrick W Fegan, Chicago Wine School, 2007.

Fastest-growing grey/rosé grape varieties
The greatest global increase in recent plantings of grey/rosé (wine only) grape varieties.

Grape variety	Acres in 2005*	Acres in 2006*	% increase**
1. Pinot Gris	63,800	67,650	6
2. Gewürztraminer	39,600	41,150	3.9

* Estimated. ** Some increases may reflect improved data collection rather than an actual increase in acreage. Source: Patrick W Fegan, Chicago Wine School, 2007.

BEST WINES FROM NEW VARIETIES OR NEW CLONES

❶ **Båtels Vitt 2005** Lauri Pampinen, Gute Vingård AB, Sweden (SEK 192) *White wine (12 per cent ABV) from Madeleine Angevine (Madeleine Royale x Précoce de Malingre; Vibert, 20th century).*

❷ **Nuits Rouges Gamay/Gamaret 2005** Grégory Favre, Domaine d'En Bruaz, Switzerland (SF 5) *Red wine (12.5 per cent) from Gamay Noir (70 per cent) and Gamaret (30 per cent) (Gamay x Reichensteiner [= Müller-Thurgau x (Madeleine Angevine x Weisser Calabreser)]; Agroscope Changins, 1970).*

❸ **Lukase Reserv 2004** Lauri Pampinen, Gute Vingård AB, Sweden (SEK 368) *Red wine (12 per cent ABV) from Rondo (= Geisenheim 6494-5; Saperavi Severnyi [= Vitis amurensis x Précoce de Malingre?] x St-Laurent [= Pinot St-Laurent]; BAFZ Geilweilerhof, 1965).*

❹ **Nordlund 2005** Jens Michael Gundersen, Nordlunfvin, Denmark (DKK 349) *Red wine (11.5 per cent ABV) made from Rondo, Léon Millot (Léon Millot = Kühlmann 194-2 [Vitis riparia x Vitis rupestris] x Goldriesling; Kühlmann, 1911), Regent (Gf 67-198-3; [Silvaner x Müller-Thurgau] x Chambourcin [= Joannes Seyve 26205]; BAFZ Geilweilerhof), and Castel (which of the five Castel interspecific hybrids is not stated).*

❺ **Gamaret 2005** Domaine du Vieux-Clocher, Caves Leyvraz & Stevens, Switzerland (SF 15) *From Gamaret (Gamay x Reichensteiner [= Müller-Thurgau x (Madeleine Angevine x Weisser Calabreser)]; Agroscope Changins, 1970).*

❻ **Vin de Pays du Lot Cuvée La Treille du Roy Rouge 2005** Château Eugénie, France (€5) *Red wine (12 per cent ABV) made from Ségalin (INRA 1377-174; Jurançon Noir x Portugais Bleu; INRA Montpellier, Paul Truel, 1957), Cabernet Sauvignon, and Merlot.*

❼ **Vin de Pays de Cassan Chenançon Noir 2005** Alexandre Fouque, Domaine de la Tour Penédesses, France (€6) *Red wine from Chenançon (= INRA 1509-149; Grenache Noir x Jurançon; INRA Montpellier, Paul Truel, 1958).*

❽ **Vin de Pays des Bouches du Rhône Arinarnoa 2006** Patrick Henry, Domaine de l'Isle St-Pierre, France (€3.90) *Red wine (12.55 per cent) from Arinarnoa (Merlot x Petit Verdot; INRA Bordeaux, Durquety).*

❾ **Johanniter 2006** Domaine des Bossons, Caves Leyvraz & Stevens, Switzerland (SF 9.80) *From Johanniter (FR 177-68; Riesling x [Seyve Villard 12-481 x (Ruländer x Gutedel)]; Staatlichen Weinbauinstitut Freiburg, 1968). Good resistance to fungal diseases.*

❿ **Vin de Pays des Terroirs Landais Blanc 2005** Domaine de Labaigt, France (€3.50) *White wine (12 per cent ABV) from Arriloba (Raffiat de Moncade, a white variety, x Sauvignon; INRA Bordeaux, Durquety).*

BEST WINES FROM UNUSUAL, OBSCURE, OR REDISCOVERED GRAPE VARIETIES

This year's list reflects the tremendous efforts that wine growers in southwest France have made to revive old local varieties, such as Oeillade, Aspiran, Abouriou, Fer Servadou, Négret de Banhars, and even Lledoner Pelut, which disappeared during the phylloxera epidemic. To revive the taste of these legendary wines also meant persuading professional and government bodies to permit the propagation of these little-

known grapes and authorize them for wine production, although they are less competitive and agriculturally less well adapted than superior clones of classic varieties. Still, they are worth tasting.

1 **Vin de Table de Sologne Evidence 2003** Claude & Julien Courtois, Domaine Les Cailloux du Paradis, France (€15 per 50-cl bottle) *Matured 36 months before release. Exceptional organic white (12 per cent ABV) from Menu Pineau (or Petit Pineau), an old variety of unknown origin from Sologne.*

2 **VDQS Estaing Cuvée St-Jacques 2005** Les Vignerons d'Olt, France (€6) *Red wine (12 per cent ABV) from a blend of an old and almost forgotten variety, Fer Servadou (30–35 per cent), with Cabernet Franc and Cabernet Sauvignon. This is the smallest appellation in France on 13 ha cultivated by 14 wine growers, 10 of whom are in the wine cooperative.*

3 **VDQS Estaing Cuvée des Coustoubis 2005** Les Vignerons d'Olt, France (€4.90) *Red wine (12 per cent ABV) from a blend of old varieties Abouriou, Négret de Banhars (5 per cent), and Fer Servadou, with Pinot Noir and Gamay. This is the only wine made using Négret de Banhars; only 1.5 ha remain in France.*

4 **Vin de Table de St-Georges d'Orques Le Mailhol Rouge 2005** François & Laurence Henry, Domaine Henry, France (€35) *Red wine (12.5 per cent ABV) from old, rare varieties Oeillade Grise, Oeillade Noire, Aspiran Noir, Aspiran Gris, Morrastel Noir à Jus Blanc, Terret Noir, and Terret Gris, which were common in the region before phylloxera.*

5 **Vin de Pays des Collines de la Moure Blanc 2005** François & Laurence Henry, Domaine Henry, France (€7.50) *White wine (13.5*

per cent ABV) from Chardonnay (70 per cent) and Terret Blanc (30 per cent), an old local variety.

6 **Coteaux du Languedoc Pic St-Loup Blanc 2004** Mas de Mortiès, Duchemin-Jorcin Vignerons, France (€9) *White wine (12.5 per cent ABV) made from 80 per cent Roussanne and 20 per cent Rolle.*

7 **Vin de Pays des Coteaux du Libron Lledoner Pelut 2005** Domaine la Colombette, France (€15) *Red wine (14 per cent ABV) from Lledoner Pelut, an old variety grown in the Languedoc region, perhaps of Catalan origin.*

8 **Coteaux du Languedoc Pic St-Loup Soleil d'Automne 2005** Jocelyne Thérond, Mas de Gourdou, France (€6) *White wine (15.5 per cent ABV) from Grenache Blanc and Clairette.*

9 **Coteaux du Languedoc Blanc 2005** Eric Fabre, Château d'Anglès, France (€10) *White wine (14.5 per cent ABV) made from four old French varieties: Bourboulenc, Marsanne, Roussanne, and Grenache Blanc.*

10 **Coteaux du Languedoc Picpoul de Pinet 2005** Michèle & Philippe Vaillé, Domaine St Paul de Fannelaure, France (€4.80) *White wine (13.4 per cent ABV) made from Piquepoul Blanc. Production limited to 8,000 bottles.*

Grapevine

- Grapevine varieties recommended or authorized for different uses in regions of viticulture in the EU are listed in the 1981 European Union regulation 3800/81 and its 19 additional regulations (1981–99). See http://europa.eu.int/smartapi/cgi/sga_doc?smartapi!celexapi!prod!CELEXnumdoc&numdoc=31981R3800&model=guichett&lg=en.

Classic Wine Vintage Guide

Serena Sutcliffe MW

When one is seeing and opening a great number of old bottles, one gradually builds up an overview of what holds good in terms of received wisdom and what is, quite frankly, second-hand nonsense!

SERENA SUTCLIFFE MW

I am sure this is true of any profession, but experience counts for a great deal in the wine world, where there is a certain amount of mythology and smoke. Much energy is expended in discussion about the "level" the wine reaches in the bottle. Many are obsessed by having the "level in the neck", which is barely credible in old wines. Line up several bottles of the same 40-year-old wine, stored side by side, and you may well get three different levels. Then taste them and you may not necessarily find that the highest level tastes the best. It is also a fallacy that a high level will always deliver a perfect wine – I have tasted wines that are clearly "stewed" through hot storage, but the bottles looked wonderful. Heat does not necessarily shrink the liquid. It is particularly

SERENA SUTCLIFFE MW A Master of Wine and head of Sotheby's International Wine Department, Serena is considered one of the world's leading authorities on wine. A former chairman of the Institute of Masters of Wine, Serena was made a Chevalier dans l'Ordre des Arts et des Lettres by the French government in 1988. She was elected to the Académie Internationale du Vin in 1993, and in 2002 she received the New York Institute of Technology's Professional Excellence Award. In 2006, she received the Lifetime Achievement Award from the Society of Bacchus America, and was awarded the title of Chevalier dans l'Ordre National de la Légion d'Honneur for her seminal work in promoting and selling French wines.

Serena is an internationally recognized wine writer and renowned taster, and she writes regularly for many international publications. Besides heading Sotheby's worldwide wine auctions, she is also a member of Sotheby's European Board and is a regular lecturer and broadcaster in Europe, the United States, and Asia. Her book *The Wines of Burgundy* appeared in its eighth edition in 2005.

noticeable that old red burgundy with low levels can be marvellous – it seems very resistant to air, more so than a Cabernet-based wine, which is interesting. And, of course, sweet wines with low levels seem pretty impervious to major change, thanks to the defensive qualities of sugar.

Do large formats taste younger than bottles? In principle, yes, but there are many other factors at work, from storage to the actual day you taste and whether the wine felt *bien dans sa peau* at that particular moment. Recently, for instance, a jeroboam of Mouton 1982 tasted softer and more velvety than a more powerful magnum – fascinating. And imperials can sometimes taste less interesting than the other formats because they have just not moved at all and remain very one-dimensional. On the whole, magnums are my prize pick.

Some collectors take old wines with them as generous contributions to dinners, but this is a disaster: the movement of sediment greatly increases the smell and taste of volatile acidity. Many stand their bottles upright for a week before a dinner, but you should keep the bottles horizontal if they have been so for years to avoid disturbing the sediment.

PEAKING VINTAGES

BORDEAUX

1997 Provides lovely drinking now.

1994 Peaking.

1993 Peaking.

1992 Peaking (if you bothered to get them at all).

1991 Peaking.

1987 Peaking.

1985 Peaking, except for First Growths, top Seconds, and top Right Banks.

1984 Mostly unpleasant, as well as past their best.

1983 Mostly at their peak, except for gems like Margaux, Palmer, and Pichon-Lalande.

1982 Many have peaked, except for First Growths, Super-Seconds, top St-Emilions, and Pomerols. Gruaud-Larose excellent.

1981 Drink now.

1980 Mostly too old.

1979 Peak, but top wines still drinking well. Try Haut-Brion!

1978 Peak, but top wines still drinking well, *pace* Ausone, Lafite, Pichon-Lalande.

1977 Forget it.

1976 Peaked. Lafite and Ausone still looking good.

1975 Mostly peaked. Exceptions include Pétrus, Latour, La Mission Haut-Brion, Pichon-Lalande, Cheval Blanc, Mouton.

1974, 1973, and 1972 Enough said.

1971 Peaked. Top Pomerols still glorious, *viz* the heavenly, "roasted" Pétrus. La Mission Haut-Brion is excellent.

1970 Mostly peaked. Exceptions include Pétrus, Latour, La Mission Haut-Brion, Trotanoy, La Conseillante, Pichon-Lalande, Ducru-Beaucaillou, Palmer, Giscours, Beychevelle.

1969 and 1968 Don't even think about it.

1967 Peaked a long time ago. Pétrus still good.

1966 Mostly peaked. Exceptions include Latour, Cheval Blanc, Pétrus, Haut-Brion, La Mission Haut-Brion, Mouton.

1964 Mostly peaked. Exceptions include Pétrus, Latour, Haut-Brion, La Mission Haut-Brion.

1962 Peaked, although the Firsts are still good. Mouton is glorious.

1961 Most wines still wonderful. That small crop gave the vital concentration.

1959 The top wines are still magic.

RED BURGUNDY

1997 Delicious drinking now.

1994 Drink now, because that dry finish will intensify.

1992 Delicious now, but hurry.

1990 *Grands crus* have further to go.

1989 *Grands crus* have further to go, *premiers crus* lovely.

1988 The very top wines mostly have further to go.

1987 Should have been drunk.

1986 As above. Even Jayer is at its best.

1985 Mostly at, or over, its peak, except for top *grands crus* such as Drouhin's Bonnes Mares, La Tâche, and all DRC and Jayer.

1984 Don't go there.

1983 A very few are hanging on.

1982 As above, for different reasons.

1981 Peaked.

1980 Past their peak and even those brilliant Jayers should be drunk. La Tâche still amazing.

1979 Peaked.

1978 There are still some wonders at the top. They have a signature gaminess. DRC splendid.

1977 Treat them as if they were never there.

1976 Peaked a long time ago, with the odd, rare exception.

1975 Should not be mentioned in polite society.

1974 Unpleasant and old.

1973 Peaked a long time ago.

1972 One or two survivors, *viz* de Vogüé's Musigny Vieilles Vignes.

1971 Stay with DRC or similar here.

1970 It is all over now.

1969 Some survivors at *grand cru* level. Rousseau exceptional.

1966 A few still live gloriously on – Romanée-Conti is mind-blowing.

1964 A few terrific wines at *grand cru* level.

1962 A few top wines are still magnificent.

1961 As above.

1959 As above.

WHITE BURGUNDY

1999 You can start on the lesser wines.

1998 Many are ready.

1997 Very nice drinking now.

1996 Some greats, some looking flat.

1994 Mostly at their peak.

1993 As above.

1992 As above. They matured faster than many believed.

1991 Mostly at their peak.

1990 Some top wines still have a bit to go, others are glowing right now.

1989 As above.

1988 Mostly at their peak or over it.

1987 Peaked.

1986 Mostly peaked. Some *grands crus* are lovely right now.

1985 Many of the top wines are so fat and full they will stay around for ages, such as the Bâtards of Ramonet and Niellon. I prefer it to 1986.

1984 Peaked a very long time ago.

1983 Some tremendous wines at the top. They seemed alcoholic and heavy when young, but, boy, are they marvellous now. Some of the greatest white burgundies of my life come from this vintage, such as Corton-Charlemagne from Latour and Bonneau de Martray.

1982 Virtually all peaked a long time ago.

1981 Peaked a long time ago.

1980 As above.

1979 Virtually all peaked some time ago.

1978 As above, but some gems live on, *viz* Chablis Les Clos from Drouhin, which now looks like a Côte d'Or wine.

1976 Peaked, but there are some stunners still about at *grand cru* level.

1973 Peaked, with the odd surprise at *grand cru* level.

1971 Peaked, with some stunners left.

1970 As above.

1969 As above.

1967 It starts getting esoteric from here, but the odd surprise.

1966 Mostly history, but DRC's Montrachet makes history.

1964 Peaked a long time ago, with a few exceptions hanging on.

1962 Peaked, of course, with a few marvellous exceptions.

1961 As above.

RED RHONE

2002 Drink quickly, if from the south.

1997 Drink from now.

1994 In my view, start drinking up.

1993 Peak.

1992 Peak.

1991 Peaked for the south, fine for the north.

1990 Excellent, the best will keep.

1989 As above.

1988 As above.

1987 Peaked, so drink now.

1986 As above.

1985 At peak, although the best will keep.

1984 Peaked.

1983 Peaked for the south, but the top wines from the north still have life in them.

1982 Peaked everywhere, although the north is better.

1981 Peaked for the north, a few good ones left in the south.

1980 Peaked.

1979 Peaked, but the best still drinking well.

1978 At its peak, mostly, with some amazing wines at top level.

1976 Peaked some time ago, but Hermitage La Chapelle lives on to delight.

1972 As above.

1971 As above, but throw in Rayas, too, as well as Chave's glorious Hermitage.

1970 Peaked, but great Hermitage La Chapelle.

1969 Peaked, but glorious La Chapelle, with Chave and Rayas still in there.

1967 Peaked, but tremendous La Chapelle.

1966 As above.

1964 As above.

1962 As above.

1961 The top wines are still out of this world (La Chapelle et al).

1959 As above.

PORT

2000 Wonderful, but keep.

1997 Don't touch – too young.

1994 As above.

1992 As above.

1991 As above.

1985 Lovely drinking now, as evinced by Dow.

1983 As above.

1982 Drinking well now and over the next few years.

1980 As above.

1977 Drinking very well now, but the best will keep further.

1975 Drink up fast.

1970 Fabulous vintage, glorious now but will stay that way for ages.

1966 Excellent wines right now but will keep, of course. The fruit in them is quite beautiful. Taylor's is magnificent.

1963 Huge, powerful wines, for drinking or keeping.

1960 Beautiful now.

1958 Mostly peaked, but don't say that to Noval Nacional! Extraordinary wine.

1955 Superb now and not about to fall off the perch.

1950 Drink up, but the Nacional is eternal.

1948 Great now.

1947 Drink now.

1945 Still there, after all these years. Mammoth. Graham is great.

GERMANY

2000 For early drinking.

1999 Drink up at the bottom end.

1996 Broach and enjoy.

1995 Broach and enjoy.

1994 Peak.

1993 Approaching peak, but the best will mature in splendid fashion.

1992 Peak.

1991 Peak.

1990 Excellent, and the best will age beautifully.

1989 As above.

1988 As above.

1987 Peaked.

1986 Mostly peaked.

1985 Mostly at peak.

1984 Dreadful vintage.

1983 Mostly peaked, but some wines beautifully present.

1982 Peaked a long time ago.

1981 As above.

1980 Forget it.

1979 A very few survivors.

1976 Tremendous, with a plethora of fantastic sweet wines still vying for top honours.

1975 As above, especially for the Mosel.

1971 The tops, and still magnificent in the upper echelons.

1967 Peaked some time ago, but a few stunning survivors at TBA level.

1959 At peak – and glorious with it.

1953 Peaked, with a few beauties left.

GREATEST-QUALITY AUCTION WINES

❶ **Château Pétrus 1964** *At a wonderful Pétrus dinner in the country, where we all brought bottles and compared. The 1971 was also to die for – glorious, rich treacle – but the 1964 was a show-stopper, with its incredibly dark colour, dense, concentrated bouquet, and mouth-coating, melting taste. Lucky us – everyone stayed the night, needless to say!*

❷ **Château Mouton Rothschild 1949** *At a fabulous vertical tasting in Zürich, where the 1940s and 1950s, especially, were extraordinary. Even up against competition such as 1945, 1953, and 1959, this 1949 was magical, with haunting fragrance, heavenly fruit, and tremendous persistence – and all at 10.9 per cent alcohol! A wine to sip and dream over.*

❸ **Dom Pérignon Oenothèque 1976** (disgorged in 2003) *I have fallen in love again – this is riveting champagne. Sixty per cent Chardonnay went into the blend in this atypical, hot year. A nose of cloves, dried raisins, sultanas, and nuts. Fleshy and intoxicating, with a finish of nutmeg. You could drink this with dried galangal, all kinds of basil, chilli, and pepper – the great chefs with whom I drank this in Champagne did it proud.*

❹ **Château Calon-Ségur 1928** *What is it about these great*

St-Estèphes of the '20s? They are mind-blowing. This was bought from Sotheby's but served by an immensely generous American host. Incredible, marvellous, perfect, with so much fruit and sweetness. Crashingly good Calon – and just look at what they are doing now, too.

⑤ **Gevrey-Chambertin Clos des Ruchottes 1990** Armand Rousseau In a line-up of 1990 Gevrey grands crus at home, this was outstanding, with all the enormous breed of the climat that comes through in a Rousseau wine, plus the brilliant fruit, depth, and lingering finish. This domaine never fails – its 2004s and 2005s are en route to filling this space in the future, while the Ruchottes 2000 and 1992 are nearly as remarkable as the 1990.

⑥ **Palo Cortado Añada 1968** Gonzáles Byass This blew away the room when I spoke in Barcelona on "What Makes a Great Wine". Palo Cortado is a stupendous mystery – deep, many-layered, and utterly original. This is a chef d'oeuvre, absolutely flawless and a tribute to the skills of Gonzáles Byass. I just could not stop drinking it.

⑦ **Graham's 1970** At a Symington vintage port tasting in London, this was an irresistible 20/20 for me, with its intensely scented floral bouquet and blackberry flamboyance. The tannin and acidity balanced the great sweetness and opulence, making it one of the most complete ports ever – sheer perfection at 36 years old but with the stamina to stay.

⑧ **Clos St-Denis 1998** Domaine Dujac I could have put in Dujac's stunning Clos de la Roche 1999, but this is a greater feat: a vintage made in the vineyard. Careful sorting and date of picking both played their part in creating this extraordinary 1998 – intense, elegant, and just bursting with fabulous flavour: the essence of burgundy. It shone at the Young Lions tasting in Verona.

⑨ **Monte Bello 1991** Ridge Paul Draper showed this at a Masters of Wine tasting, and it is a superstar. A glorious, plummy bouquet leads into an immensely aromatic, complex, and multidimensional taste – a huge mouthful of tobacco, fruit, and smoky oak. The tannins just melt into the sumptuous flavour. Monte Bello is easily my favourite Californian.

⑩ **Pommard Clos des Epeneaux 1978** Comte Armand This was the era of Michel Rossignol, and only old vines went into the Clos at that time. David found this in the cellar, and no one could ask anything more of a burgundy. A gamey, wet-earth nose and wild raspberries, wild cherries, wild everything taste. Rhubarb cooked in demerara sugar, and rich, velvety, and plummy on the palate.

MOST EXCITING OR UNUSUAL AUCTION FINDS

① **Château La Tour Haut-Brion 1979** At this time, this was a second wine of La Mission, and it has long been an inside-track secret. Chocolate, spices, black fruit, and orange peel on the nose, and huge and muscular on the palate. Like liquid black cherries, silky smooth, with a fresh Kenyan coffee finish. Homeric.

② **Abadia Retuerta Selección Especial 1998** A terrific vintage and a terrific wine, last drunk in magnum over the Christmas holidays with beef Wellington. A smooth and velvety concoction from Tempranillo (75 per cent), Cabernet Sauvignon (20 per cent), and Merlot (5 per cent). All the wines made here benefited from Pascal Delbeck's meticulous research into the myriad soil types they have at this showpiece estate in Sardón del Duero.

❸ Château Lafite 1928 This might seem an unlikely choice for this section, but the wine never had the reputation of the grand Latour 1928 and was perceived to be crumbling. It was also pasteurized, as was the Cheval Blanc 1945. But at home we chanced upon a bottle (original cork, of course), and it was a big, fruity Pauillac, staying firm in the glass and with a real cassis heart to it. Low alcohol, too. A great experience – one will never fully understand wine.

❹ Collepiano Sagrantino di Montefalco 2001 Arnaldo Caprai The top wine from king of the region Marco Caprai is the 25 Anni, but the Collepiano is big enough for me, with great black-cherry fruit, chewy and succulent. The splendid 2001 has softened into real rich glycerol in the past year – I know, I have been following it around Umbria! The Sagrantino grape is one of Italy's best secrets.

❺ Quinta de Vargellas 1978 Single-quinta ports are unusual in the auction world, but what pleasure they give, especially this shining example from Taylor. Wet-damson nose and an absolutely glorious damson-jam taste. Very good after six hours' decanting, but stunning after 48 hours – more intense, more deep, utter luxury. There are no rules with

wine. Hits the luscious target with Janet Trefethen's fresh Californian walnuts.

❻ Au Jardin Les Amis Pinot Noir 1998 Bass Phillip, Victoria Specially selected by owner and maker Phillip Jones for Les Amis in Singapore: 9,000 vines per hectare, indigenous yeasts, no pumping, no filtration, 20 months in Allier and Bourgogne oak. Wild, brambly, raspberry nose, with amazing attack and definition. Concentration, mega flavour, velvety texture and elegance. Biting, pure Pinot – no one does it better.

❼ Mas de Daumas Gassac Blanc 2005 Better known for its excellent red than for its intriguing white, made of Viognier, Chardonnay, Manseng, and Chenin. Lovely lemony acidity to go with the ripeness and length. Very elegant – a leap forward in this department. Like lemon curd. The 2000 is lovely, too, composed of 15 different grape varieties.

❽ Nympha Rosso Conero 2003 Lucesole Produced from the Montepulciano grape by a small family agriturismo estate, this was a delight, sampled while looking at the hilltop village theatres of Le Marche. A few years ago, no one could create a wine like this from such humble origins – full, fruity, lusty, and perfectly in balance, in spite of its forthright 14.5 per cent alcohol.

❾ Château Doisy-Daëne 1990 The talented Dubourdieu family is responsible for this most elegant of all Barsacs, where the aim has never been to drown in sweetness but to bring out all the freshness and finesse of the fruit. Papa Dubourdieu, who made this, succeeded brilliantly with the

1990, a treat over stollen and bottled fruits brought back from the Pelion in Greece.

10 Niersteiner Hipping Gewürztraminer Beerenauslese 1976 Franz Schmitt *A treasure from a past sale, brought out at a celebratory department lunch over a pear pud. So rich and unctuous, but the spiciness of the grape prevents any cloying. It just rolls around the mouth and leaves one feeling refreshed, in spite of the great, historic ripeness of the year. The whole weight of the wine – or, perhaps, its weightlessness – is so appealing.*

BEST AUCTION BARGAINS *(hammer price)*

1 Château Saint Pierre 1989; at the London February 2006 sale (12 bottles: £180) *This Fourth Growth St-Julien just never seems to take off in price, but it is a very nice claret indeed, and I love this year.*

2 Mercurey Clos des Barraults 1999 Michel Juillot; at the London April 2006 sale (12 bottles: £70) *One of the best producers on the Côte Chalonnaise, a premier cru and the superb 1999 vintage to boot – Laurent Juillot is one to watch.*

3 Sarget du Château Gruaud Larose 2000; at the London March 2006 sale (12 bottles: £95) *A second wine of a Second Growth in a top year – it does not get much better than this.*

4 Stag's Leap Wine Cellars Cabernet Sauvignon SLV 1985; at the New York May 2006 sale (9 bottles: US$650) *Difficult to find a bargain in the excitement of the Russell Frye auction, but this was a steal.*

5 Château Suduiraut 1996; at the London June 2006 sale (24 half-bottles: £240) *Desirable halves of a stunning Sauternes in a luscious year – my perfect summer strawberries-and-cream wine.*

6 Château de Beaucastel Rouge 1998; at the New York December 2006 sale (12 bottles: US$700) *An Important New England Cellar flew, but this crept in under the wire – a boon for lovers of Châteauneuf.*

7 Château Moulin St-Georges 1995; at the New York October 2006 sale (12 bottles: US$375) *This is a great year for St-Emilion, and maybe people do not know that this is owned and made by Ausone's brilliant Alain Vauthier.*

8 Meursault Blanc 2003 J-F Coche-Dury; at the New York October 2006 sale (9 bottles: US$550) *This is a gift for this magician's Meursault, when even his Bourgogne Blanc is a treat.*

9 Volnay Les Champans 1995 Marquis d'Angerville; at the London December 2006 sale (12 bottles: £260) *I adore this particular* climat *in the excellent d'Angerville estate, and this is mouth-watering wine.*

10 Bonnezeaux Cuvée Zenith 2003 René Renou; at the London November 2006 sale (9 half-litre bottles: £100) *When are people going to wake up to the delights of sweet Loire wines, with the Chenin's characteristic sugar and acidity providing fireworks on the palate?*

Wine Auctions & Investment

Anthony Rose

It was a mixed year in which fortunes were made and lost. Prices skyrocketed, records were set, and some investors lost wines after buying *en primeur* from companies that folded due to fraud or mismanagement.

ANTHONY ROSE

The biggest story of the year was the boom in prices after a desultory period of stagnation. By February 2007, the *Decanter* Bordeaux index had soared to 143.23 compared to 119.4 in January 2006, a massive rise of 23.83 points in just over a year. This was a huge year for the auction houses, most notably in the USA, where Acker Merrall & Condit maintained its meteoric rise, breaking Sotheby's 1999 record. The UK performed well enough, with both Christie's and Sotheby's well up on the previous year, but neither could stem the oncoming tide of US auctions.

Big single-owner auctions like Acker Merrall & Condit's record sale have become an increasing focus for auctioneers, especially in the USA, where they can form a substantial part of the year's turnover. Sotheby's three great single-owner sales, featuring the cellars of Russell H Frye, Park B Smith, and "a New England collector", grossed $15.4 million (£8.6 million) in New

Because of the fluctuations in the dollar/pound exchange rate during 2006 of US$1.74 to US$1.97 = £1, we have used US$1.80 = £1 as a rough guide in this report, except where both $ and £ totals have been supplied by the auction houses.

ANTHONY ROSE is the award-winning wine correspondent for *The Independent*, and he also writes for a number of other publications, including *Wine & Spirit* magazine and *Harpers Wine and Spirit Weekly*. He specializes in the auction scene, writing a monthly column on the subject for *Decanter* and contributing to *The Oxford Companion to Wine* on auction and investment. Anthony is married to an Australian wine photographer and lives in London.

York, three-quarters of their total US sales. The strength of the global market was illustrated by the sheer breadth and variety of buyers, with Europe, Asia, and South America all pitching in.

Bordeaux enjoyed a fantastic year. Older vintages often doubled or trebled in value, while the great 1982 vintage increased more than 50 per cent over 2005 prices and the 1989s and 1990s were also vibrant. Among younger vintages, 2000 in particular has strengthened in price (see blue-chip chart), while 1995 and 1996 exploded in the wake of the release of 2005 prices, and 1996 First Growths more than doubled their 2005 prices to reach over £4,000 ($7,200) a case.

Many icon wines have performed well (see the Top 10s from Sotheby's and Christie's, p.379). The 1945 Mouton Rothschild was the year's star performer, but Pétrus, Cheval Blanc, Yquem, and DRC were all in the frame. The market for garage wines was soft, with limited demand but reasonably stable prices for the likes of Valandraud, while others fared less well. Cult Rhône was on the wane, as traditional producers such as Guigal, Chave, Beaucastel, Bonneau, Pégau, and older La Chapelle and Rayas reasserted themselves.

Super-Tuscans were also down now that Chianti Classico is back in the groove and Brunello di Montalcino is performing well. Screaming Eagle from California screeched loud and clear, with one superlot of six bottles of each of the vintages from 1993 to 2003 (except 2000) selling for $176,250 (£92,277) at Christies, New York, and a selection of Harlan Estate vintages from 1990 to 2002 selling for $32,900 (£17,200). Sine Qua Non, Marcassin, and Colgin were also in strong demand. In Australia, Penfolds 1962 Bin 60A and Clonakilla Shiraz/Viognier were among the best performers, with Langton's *en primeur* offer of Penfolds Bin 60A and Block 42 doing well.

The market for vintage port was firm for vintages such as the 1963s, all the way up to the 1970 vintage, but softer coming forward, with 1970 itself still well priced. Mature burgundy sold well, but younger burgundies were less consistent. DRC and Henri Jayer were the big draws, but the list of top names such as Rousseau, Roumier, de Vogüé, Leroy, Leflaive, and Ponsot grows longer. Top mature champagne is also growing in demand, with a case of 1964 Krug Private Cuvée selling for £6,050 ($10,890), and 1990 Dom Pérignon achieving £1,925 ($3,465).

With City bonuses going through the roof and a swathe of new buyers emerging worldwide, there was every sign that the market would remain firm throughout at least the first half of 2007. This was confirmed by the exceptional interest in the 2005 burgundies at the beginning of the year. Christie's was predicting that the demand for the rarest top wines would continue unabated into 2007, with possibly some of the more widely available wines that increased significantly in 2006 dropping back a little.

THE AUCTIONEERS

For once, the big auction news story – the historic rivalry between Christie's and Sotheby's – has been pushed into second place by the pressing question of where the power base now lies among the auctioneers, the UK or the USA? London's place as the centre of the auction-house universe has been relinquished to the USA. This is where the critical mass of the great collections are, so it's hardly surprising that the USA, buoyed by Internet auctions, has become the focal point for the global market.

Acker Merrall & Condit topped the list in 2006, bringing in a record-busting £33.5 million ($60.3 million) thanks to 11 live sales and 12 monthly online auctions. One sale alone, the entirety supplied by an unidentified West Coast collector, brought in £13.7 million ($24.7 million), breaking the previous Millennium Sale (Sotheby's with Sherry-Lehmann) record of $14.4 million (£8.5 million) in 1999.

In its best year ever, Christie's International Wine Department made £32.4 million ($58.6 million) from 44 sales in eight locations, including, in the UK and Europe, £17 million ($30.7 million) from 33 sales. Additionally, Langton's in Australia, in association with Christie's, conducted 26 sales in Sydney and Melbourne for a sale total of A$16.2 million (£6.8 million). As evidence of the greater spending power per sale in the USA, NY Wines/Christie's held 11 sales totalling £15.4 million ($27.9 million), or £1.4 million ($2.52 million) per average sale, compared to the UK and Europe's £500,000 ($900,000).

Sotheby's recorded the second-best year in its history, with global sales of £20.8 million ($37.4 million), up 28 per cent on 2005. In the USA, the cellar of Russell H Frye brought £4.3 million ($7.8 million), Sotheby's second-highest total after the Millennium Sale. Annual turnover in 2006 from 11 sales in London was £9.2 million ($17 million), up nearly 60 per cent on the previous year. Still in London, Bonhams generated £1.5 million ($2.7 million) from six sales.

US auctioneer Zachys, in its fourth year in the auction business, generated £19.3 million ($34.7 million) from 10 auctions, while Chicago-based Hart Davis Hart raised £7.7 million ($13.8 million) in six auctions. Bonhams & Butterfields' six auctions held in San Francisco raised £4.2 million ($7.5 million) and Morrell & Co's four sales (one online) brought in £2.4 million ($4.3 million). Edward Roberts International, a small Chicago house, held four auctions totalling £900,000 ($1.6 million). The rise of the Internet auction was illustrated by the California-based WineBid.com, whose online sales raised £12.5 million ($22.5 million).

WOE IS ME, SHAME AND SCANDAL IN THE FAMILY

In a year of celebration for auction houses and investors, a number of inglorious episodes came as a salutary reminder of the tried and tested principle of caveat emptor.

The first scandal was the collapse of wine merchant Mayfair Cellars, following the alleged looting by its finance director Dominic Smith of nearly £1 million ($1.8 million) of customers' wines. Smith was dismissed after the discovery of the fraud, and civil proceedings were instituted against him for breach of contract, breach of fiduciary duty, and/or deceit. Customers whose wines were still in storage were able to gain access to their stock, but some customers, whose wines had been sold on, lost their investment. The company's directors had no idea that *négociants* in Bordeaux had not been paid for the 2003 vintage, leaving hundreds of *en primeur* customers high and dry. Total losses were estimated to be in the region of £3 million ($5.4 million).

The next blot on the wine-investment landscape was the collapse of the wine exchange Uvine with £2 million ($3.6 million) of debts. Founded in November 1999 at the height of the dotcom boom, the company, run by Christopher Burr MW, had proved expensive to set up and operate and had never been profitable. Administrator Graham Wolloff reported suspected criminal conduct to the Department for Trade and Industry. In an echo of the Mayfair Cellars debacle, it emerged that Uvine had also failed to pass on to Bordeaux *négociants* money paid by their customers, mainly for bordeaux *en primeur* 2003.

At the end of the year, more than a million bottles of wine from the failed Australian investment company Heritage Fine Wines were released on to the market. Set up in Sydney by UK-born Simon Farid in 1999, Heritage collapsed in 2005 after some 3,000 investors had poured A$70 million (£29 million) into the business in the hope of cashing in on the new craze for cult Australian wines, but a fall in prices triggered the company's collapse in March 2005, leaving 2,000 creditors.

Finally, following a trial in the High Court in London, Robin Grove and Richard Gunter, directors of Vintage Hallmark plc, were disqualified for 15 years for their part in an audacious wine and spirit investment scam that targeted American doctors. Vintage Hallmark plc went bankrupt on 22 January 2003 with debts of nearly £80 million ($129 million), mostly owed to its shareholders, mainly Americans who had swapped wine and spirit investments for worthless equity.

AUSTRALIAN AUCTION NEWS

by Andrew Caillard, Langton's
In 2006, the wine-auction market continued to enjoy a strong level of bidding, clearance rates, and buyer participation. Grange, a key market indicator, rose around 15 per cent across the board, with record prices for 1971, 1986, 1990, 1991, and 1996. Henschke Hill of Grace prices also pulled up. Penfolds Bin 389 was a star performer in 2006, reaching an all-time record of A$98 (£40) a bottle.

Australian Shiraz remains king. Since 2000, the spread of small-production, single-vineyard Shirazes such as Clonakilla Shiraz/Viognier, Greenock Creek, Three Rivers, Noon, and Wild Duck Creek on the secondary wine market has been extraordinary.

Barossa Shiraz and McLaren Vale Shiraz have become recognized as classic regional styles. Clarendon Hills Astralis Syrah was classified as outstanding in 2005 because of its strong secondary-market support. In 2005, Rockford Basket Press Shiraz joined Grange and Hill of Grace in the exceptional category. Grant Burge

Meshach is now rightly regarded as one of the Barossa's top wines. Charles Melton Nine Popes has fluctuated on the market but is back on the ascendancy. Yalumba Octavius deservedly made the Langton's classification in 2005 as outstanding. Much admired by mainstream collectors, Hardy's Eileen Hardy Shiraz is in a vacuum created by the interest in single-vineyard Shiraz.

AUCTION RECORDS IN 2006

In a year in which Acker Merrall & Condit topped the auctioneers' list with a phenomenal turnover of £33.5 million ($60.3 million), records were smashed over and over again. Acker broke the record for a single auction, grossing $24.7 million (£13.7 million) in a sale of wines supplied by an unidentified West Coast collector, breaking Sotheby's (with Sherry-Lehmann) previous Millennium Sale record of $14.4 million (£8.5 million) in 1999.

At the Sotheby's Park B Smith Collection in New York, the record for a wine lot sold at auction went to the 50 cases of 1982 Château Mouton Rothschild, which sold for $1,051,600 (£557,348). After a record $170,375 (£97,357) was set for a case of wine at Christie's New York in March for a six-magnum case of 1985 Romanée-Conti, it was broken on 28 September at Christie's, Los Angeles, when a case of the legendary 1945 Château Mouton Rothschild fetched $290,000 (£154,255). The record was immediately broken again when a six-magnum case of the same wine fetched $345,000 (£183,511).

Grapevine

- **The Institute of Masters of Wine** raised more than £75,000 ($135,000) at its London auction and nearly $120,000 (£67,000) in New York for its Endowment Fund. Highlights of the London auction included: a bottle of 1982 Le Pin, which sold for £2,700 ($4,860); four imperials (6 litres each) of the 2003 vintage of Haut-Brion red and white, Laville Haut-Brion, and La Mission Haut-Brion, which went for £6,200 ($11,000); and a trip to Bordeaux that sold for £8,000 ($14,400). The New York auction saw a visit to Burgundy with fellow *Wine Report* contributor Clive Coates MW sell for $22,000 (£12,200) after some hectic bidding.

- **Langton's Classic Penfolds Wine Auction** attracted strong interest with a clearance rate of over 88 per cent. Sitting in the shadow of the 1990 and 1998 vintages, both the underrated 1991 (A$415/£173) and 1999 (A$416/£173) Penfolds Granges achieved almost identical new auction records. The fabled 1962 Bin 60A Coonawarra Cabernet/ Kalimna Shiraz achieved A$4,486 (£1,870), illustrating renewed enthusiasm for this rare wine, and the 2004 Block 42 Kalimna Cabernet, from the oldest pre-phylloxera Cabernet vineyard in the world, attracted A$461 (£192) a bottle.

- **Nearly 5,000 bottles** of fine wine amassed by Jacques Chirac during his extravagant reign as mayor of Paris sold for around €970,000 (£650,000) – nearly double the estimate.

CHRISTIE'S AND SOTHEBY'S GLOBAL TOP 10s

Christie's

1 28 September at Christie's, Los Angeles: *6 magnums of Château Mouton Rothschild 1945, $345,000 (£183,511)*

2 28 September at Christie's, Los Angeles: *12 bottles of Château Mouton Rothschild 1945, $290,000 (£154,255)*

3 2 November at Christie's, New York: *3 jeroboams of Romanée-Conti DRC 1978, $211,500 (£110,733)*

4 2 November at Christie's, New York: *50 dozen-bottle cases of Château Margaux 1995, $199,750 (£104,581)*

5 2 November at Christie's, New York: *a superlot of Screaming Eagle 1993–2003, $176,250 (£92,277)*

6 15 June at Christie's, London: *12 bottles of Romanée-Conti DRC 1978, $93,500 ($175,032)*

7 2 March at Christie's, New York: *6 magnums of Romanée-Conti DRC 1985, $170,375 (£97,357)*

8 7 December at Christie's, London: *an exceptional magnum lot from 1961 bordeaux, £88,000 ($173,272)*

9 5 October at Christie's, London: *a private collection of 100 vintages of Château d'Yquem, £88,000 ($165,000)*

10 5 October at Christie's, London: *12 bottles of Romanée-Conti DRC 1978, £79,200 ($148,500)*

Sotheby's

1 18 November at Sotheby's, New York: *50 cases of Château Mouton Rothschild 1982, $1,051,600 (£557,348)*

2 21 October at Sotheby's, New York: *a case of Château Mouton Rothschild 1945, $161,325 (£85,502)*

3 9 December at Sotheby's, New York: *12 bottles of Romanée-Conti DRC 1985, $131,040 (£67,040)*

4 18 November at Sotheby's, New York: *6 bottles of Romaneé-Conti DRC 1985, $119,500 (£63,335)*

5 20 May at Sotheby's, New York: *a double magnum of Château Lafite 1865, $111,625 (£63,626)*

6 20 May at Sotheby's, New York: *12 bottles of Romaneé-Conti DRC 1989, $111,625 (£63,626)*

7 20 May at Sotheby's, New York: *2 magnums of Château Cheval Blanc 1947, $105,750 (£60,278)*

8 21 June at Sotheby's, London: *11 bottles of Château Mouton Rothschild 1945, $84,898 (£46,000)*

9 21 June at Sotheby's, London: *a jeroboam of Château Cheval Blanc 1926, $67,918 (£36,800)*

10 18 November at Sotheby's, New York: *12 bottles of La Tâche DRC 1990, $59,750 (£31,668)*

Anomalies are due to the fluctuation in the dollar/pound exchange rate during the year of US$1.74 to US$1.97 = £1.

Grapevine

• **The Terraces Esk Valley Estate 1991** was sold for possibly the highest price ever paid for a bottle of New Zealand wine. From 1 ha of terraced vines planted in 1989 in Napier, Hawke's Bay, the blend of Malbec, Merlot, and Cabernet Franc in a balthazar (a 12-litre bottle) sold at the annual Hawke's Bay Charity Wine Auction for an astonishing NZ$11,000 (£3,760).

Exceptional growth 1999–2006

'07	'06	'05	'04	'03	Vintage	Wine	1999	2002	2003	2004	2005	2006	% growth[1]	% growth annualized[2]
1	–	3	2	1	1978	La Tâche	5,136	5,630	14,330	15,860	N/S	30,360[3]	491	28.87
2	8	8	10	3	1982	Lafleur	5,532	15,756	9,825	10,260	9,340	23,000[4]	316	22.56
3	1	1	1	0	1961	Latour	7,920	8,580	34,098	29,020	22,600	31,900	303	22
4	6	10	8	9	1989	Pétrus	6,156	14,832	11,500	8,640	12,870	23,000	274	20.7
5	4	4	0	0	2000	Margaux[5]	N/A	2,400	3,910	4,570	3,400	5,520	245	19.34
6	5	9	5	0	1982	Le Pin	11,550	15,950	27,495	18,380	24,500	39,720[6]	244	19.28
7	–	6	6	7	1978	Guigal Côte Rôtie La Landonne	2,736	6,744	6,000	5,440	N/S	9,000	229	18.53
8	7	5	0	0	2000	Mouton[5]	N/A	1,850	2,990	4,370	3,110	4,140	159	14.54
9	2	7	7	5	1982	Pétrus	7,800	19,550	16,215	14,690	20,900	15,870	104	10.67
–	3	2	1	0	1998	Le Pin	2,900	6,540	7,590	9,180	6,230	N/S	N/A	N/A

Prices in GBP per case of 12 bottles (best hammer price achieved in year indicated).

Sources: Christie's, Sotheby's.

1 Percentage growth between 1 July 1999 and 30 June 2006.
2 Annualized growth between 1 July 1999 and 30 June 2006.
3 £2,530 per bottle.
4 Magnums.
5 £1,600 en primeur in 2001.
6 £6,620 per magnum.

Blue-chip growth: 1998 vintage

'07	'06	'05	'04	'03	Wine	1999[1]	2002[2]	2003[2]	2004[2]	2005[2]	2006[2]	% growth[3]	% growth annualized[4]
1	1	2	3	3	Pétrus	3,800	7,520	6,460	7,260	9,680	15,870	318	22.64
2	3	4	4	4	Cheval Blanc	1,150	2,110	1,840	1,725	2,420	4,140	260	20.06
3	6	6	7	5	Lafite	800	1,150	1,035	1,060	1,245	2,100	163	14.77
4	7	7	9	8	Mouton	780	910	800	940	1,130	1,550	99	10.3
5	4	3	2	2	Trotanoy	800	1,740	1,550	1,210	1,470	1,550	94	9.9
6	8	8	9	10	Margaux	780	830	860	750	1,010	1,270	63	7.21
7	9	9	10	10	Latour	780	780	710	665	1,020	1,250	60	6.96
8	5	5	6	6	Haut-Brion	875	1,090	1,230	1,210	1,470	1,200	37	4.61
9	10	10	5	7	Ausone	1,150	1,420	1,725	935	1,300	1,210	5	0.73
–	2	1	1	1	Le Pin	2,900	6,540	7,590	9,180	6,230	N/S	N/A	N/A

© Anthony Rose 2007

Prices in GBP per case of 12 bottles.

Sources: En primeur prices (excluding VAT); Wine Society in bond.

1 En primeur price 1 July 1999.
2 Best auction price in year indicated.
3 Percentage growth over 1 July 1999 to 30 June 2006.
4 Annualized growth over 1 July 1999 to 30 June 2006.

Blue-chip growth: 1999 vintage

Position '07	'06	'05	'04	Wine	2000[1]	2003[2]	2004[2]	2005[2]	2006[2]	growth[3] %	annualized growth[4] %
1=	3	5	3	Pétrus	3,650	5,076	3,680	3,960	6,000	64	8.6
1=	4	2	2	Lafite	775	1,092	1,040	825	1,270	64	8.6
1=	2	3=	5	Margaux	775	912	960	858	1,270	64	8.6
4		1	6	Latour	775	900	1,080	880	1,210	56	7.7
5	-	7	10	Le Pin	3,300	N/A	3,330	N/S	5,060	53	7.38
6	6	6	4	Mouton	775	936	780	748	1,090	41	5.84
7	-	9	9	Trotanoy	550	408	410	N/S	700	27	4.1
8	5	3=	1	Haut Brion	775	1,476	960	770	940	21	3.27
9	7	8	7	Cheval Blanc	1,146	1,272	960	1,020	1,130	-1	-0.23
-	-	10	8	Ausone	1,146	1,044	N/S	N/S	N/S	N/A	N/A

© Anthony Rose 2007

Prices in GBP per case of 12 bottles.

Sources: *En primeur* prices (excluding VAT): Wine Society in bond, Pétrus Corney & Barrow, Trotanoy and Le Pin Berry Bros & Rudd.

1 *En primeur* price 1 July 2000.

2 Best auction price in year indicated.

3 Percentage growth over 1 July 2000 to 30 June 2006.

4 Annualized growth over 1 July 2000 to 30 June 2006.

Blue-chip growth: 2000 vintage

Position '07	'06	'05	Wine	2001[1]	2002[2]	2003[2]	2004[2]	2005[2]	2006[2]	growth[3] %	annualized growth[4] %
1	1	-	Le Pin	2,640	N/S	N/S	N/S	20,300	17,940	579	46.67
2	2	6	Pétrus	5,500	N/S	8,320	10,580	15,280	21,850	297	31.75
3=	8	3	Lafite	1,600	2,050	3,220	4,200	2,690	5,520	245	28.09
3=	4	1	Margaux	1,600	2,400	3,910	4,570	3,400	5,520	245	28.09
5	7	4	Las-Cases	780	N/S	1,640	1,680	1,430	2,530	224	26.52
6	3	5	Latour	1,600	2,375	3,450	3,280	3,680	5,060	216	25.88
7	10	8	Ausone	2,400	N/S	N/S	4,180	3,250	7,200	200	24.56
8	9	9	Cheval Blanc	2,500	N/S	5,290	3,900	3,820	7,480	199	24.49
9	6	7	Haut-Brion	1,600	2,095	2,990	3,000	2,970	4,600	188	23.5
10	5	2	Mouton	1,600	1,850	2,990	4,370	3,110	4,140	159	20.93

© Anthony Rose 2007

Prices in GBP per case of 12 bottles.

Sources: *En primeur* prices (excluding VAT): Wine Society in bond, Corney & Barrow, Berry Bros & Rudd.

1 *En primeur* price 1 July 2001.

2 Best auction price in year indicated.

3 Percentage growth over 1 July 2001 to 30 June 2006.

4 Annualized growth over 1 July 2001 to 30 June 2006.

Viticulture

Dr Richard Smart & Dr Caroline Gilby MW

An outbreak of phylloxera is threatening more than 70 per cent of Australia's Yarra Valley vines.

DR RICHARD SMART   DR CAROLINE GILBY MW

It was discovered in December 2006 in a Foster's-owned 32-ha vineyard in the Coldstream area, and the infested vineyard is now under quarantine. The area is particularly vulnerable to this vine-killing louse, since less than 30 per cent of vines are planted on resistant rootstocks. A control zone of 5-km (3-mile) radius has been declared around the infested vineyard, though it may take several months to find out whether the pest has spread.

DR RICHARD SMART BScAgr, MSc, PhD, DScAgr, termed by some "the flying vine-doctor", is an Australian vineyard consultant with clients in 24 countries. He is now resident in Tasmania, Australia, where Tamar Ridge Wines is his principal client. He began his career in viticulture research in Australia, spanning Israel, the USA, France, and New Zealand. Richard is the principal author of *Sunlight into Wine* (Winetitles, 1991) and is considered an authority on canopy management of grapevines. He has regular columns in trade journals *The Australian & New Zealand Wine Industry Journal* and *California's Practical Winery & Vineyard*, is published widely in scientific and other journals, and was viticulture editor for three volumes of Jancis Robinson's *Oxford Companion to Wine*.

DR CAROLINE GILBY MW is a freelance writer specializing in Eastern Europe and viticulture. She contributed to *The Oxford Companion to Wine* and Dorling Kindersley's *Wines of the World* and has been published in *Decanter*, *Harpers Wine and Spirit Weekly*, *OLN*, and *New Scientist*. She is on the editorial board of the *Journal of Wine Research*. She has a PhD in plant sciences but left science to become senior wine buyer for a major UK retail chain. She lectures for the WSET Diploma on tasting technique, vinification, and wine handling, and judges at international wine shows, as well as working as a consultant to the wine trade.

Smugglers roll their own

Growers in California have been warned that the nine viruses associated with leafroll are spreading faster than ever. One factor is that widespread uprooting of AXR1 rootstock after the phylloxera infestation has meant replanting with less resistant rootstocks, allowing the virus to spread more easily. The disease reduces ripeness, pigmentation, and cluster size, and can be transmitted by vine mealybugs, grafting, or vine to vine. There is some concern that the recent appearance of leafroll virus 3 is due to growers smuggling in cuttings from other countries.

Percentage yield

Research at Geisenheim has been looking into the use of gibberellic acid (in the form of GA3) to regulate yield and quality in minimally pruned Riesling vines where other thinning methods have failed. GA has a long history of use in table grapes to increase berry size and open up bunches, but use in wine grapes is limited because some varieties can show substantial losses in bud fertility and thus commercial yield. Weyand and Schultz compared various GA treatments on MP (minimally pruned) vines with both VSP (vertical shoot positioning) and untreated MP vines. GA3 treatment reduced inflorescence number by 30–50 per cent in the year following treatment, while berry size increased by 10–28 per cent. Yield was reduced by 26–49 per cent, similar to VSP vines, while bunch structure remained less compact than VSP vines. Analysis of sugar levels showed similar results, with VSP and GA3 treatments both superior to untreated MP, while sensory analysis showed minimal differences. The treatment seems promising for cost-effective production of quality fruit.

Definition of terroir in viticulture

Terroir remains a difficult concept to define and a challenge to study scientifically, since so many interacting factors are involved, including soil, climate, variety, and human interventions, according to Van Leeuwen and Seguin. They report that terroir is a highly important concept in viticulture because it can explain the quality hierarchy and wine style, and relate a wine's sensory attributes to its origin. The best expression of terroir is obtained in cool-climate viticulture, when the grapevine ripens its crop at the end of the growing season. Earlier-ripening varieties should be chosen in cooler climates, while later varieties will be better in warm areas to avoid grapes ripening in the heat of the summer. High quality in red wines depends on a limiting factor to reduce vine vigour, berry size, and yields. This is usually mild water deficit, though low nitrogen can also be a quality factor. In white wines, severe stress should be avoided, since it can negatively affect aromatic potential.

AUTOMATIC GRAPE-YIELD ESTIMATES

Researchers at the Agricultural Research Service (ARS) in Washington State have set up field trials in Yakima Valley to look at an automated system for estimating grape yields. It is based on tension changes in the trellis wire that supports vine canopies. It should give growers an estimate of crop yield as harvest approaches so they can adjust pruning and irrigation and plan harvesting more effectively. The system uses a load cell to detect changes in tension, along with a data logger to record and transmit information.

GLOBAL-WARMING CONCERNS AIRED

The first international Global Warming and Wine conference was held in March 2006 in Barcelona, Spain, giving experts the chance to exchange views about the seriousness of climate change for viticulture. Issues raised included depletion of water resources; increasing soil-water salinity; the need to change grape varieties to match warmer conditions; an increase in extreme weather events; the possible loss of the Gulf Stream, lowering temperatures in maritime zones in Europe; and wider infestations of pests and diseases.

GRAPEVINES ON STEROIDS

The biochemical mechanisms that control fruit ripening in grapes remain a mystery, though research in Australia may have come up with an explanation.

A joint study between the University of Tasmania and Australia's Commonwealth Scientific and Industrial Research Organisation (CSIRO) looked at the effect of a group of steroidal plant hormones called brassinosteroids, measuring levels throughout the season and testing synthetic versions. This group of compounds seems to play a role in expression of a number of genes. At *véraison*, they appear to turn off genes for photosynthesis and switch on other genes linked to flavour and sugar accumulation. Commercial treatment with brassinosteroids is unlikely to be viable at present due to their high cost.

OIV RESOLUTIONS ON VITICULTURE

Concern over the increasing threat of grapevine yellows caused by phytoplasmas has led OIV to announce a resolution calling for research into biological control of the leaf-hopper vector, maintenance of disease-free mother plantations, and training for growers in surveillance and control methods.

A resolution on wood diseases has also been published, giving recommendations for timing and practices of pruning and vineyard management to avoid cross-contamination of vines and the spread of infection. The resolution recognizes that there is a lack of knowledge about disease-causing organisms and no effective remedial control.

Opinion:

China – competition for Australia?

Late in 2006, I (RES) was talking at a field day in Tasmania and mentioning my recent visit to China. A member of the audience asked me whether I thought that China might ever compete seriously with Australia for wine export markets. This is an interesting question. Looking at the statistics, China is number five in the world in terms of grape production, following Italy, France, the USA, and Spain. Australia is number 10. However, this list includes table and drying grapes, as well as wine grapes. A list of top producers of wine in the world shows Australia at number six, following France, Italy, Spain, the USA, and Argentina. China is in number seven position.

But production statistics are only part of the picture. Australia is the fourth-largest wine exporter in the world, and China is not even in the top 10. Further, China is not listed among the top wine-consuming nations.

China is a very large grape producer, and in its own right it is a very large wine producer. For the moment, little wine is exported from China. The question is whether that might change in the future. Apple producers in Australia and New Zealand have seen the loss of export markets due to Chinese production. Might the same happen with wine?

I have now visited China about eight times over the past 15 years or so. I have had the opportunity to visit vineyards in the inland southern part of China and the northern coastal province of Shandong, and the inland regions as well.

China is one of the three sites of origin of the *Vitis* species, the others being Europe and the Americas. There are more than 10 wild grape species native to China, and one of them even has thorns! Records indicate that cultivated grapes were introduced into China during the Han Dynasty in the 2nd century BC. This is why the so-called ancient varieties of China, which are still cultivated, have so many characteristics in common with *Vitis vinifera*.

Much later, European and American grapes were introduced into China, and the first grape winery was established in the late 19th century on Shandong peninsula. Grape production is now spread around many regions of China, from north to south and east to west. Most production is with classic European varieties, but some local varieties – such as Longyan, Dragon's Eye, Niunai, and Cows Nipple – are also used.

What are the resources of China for grape growing? First we need to understand that China is a very large country – larger even than Australia. The area of China is some 9.6 million sq km (3.7 million sq miles) compared to 7.7 million sq km (3 million sq miles) in Australia. China has a wide range of climates. To the south and along the east coast the climate is typically Asian, with hot and humid summers, along with summer rainfall. While the winter is freezing, temperatures are not especially severe, at least near the coast. To the north, temperatures in summer are milder and rainfall is less but still summer dominant. In the far northwest, China is very dry. In the north, winters are severe, and for those regions with a mean January minimum temperature of less than about −15°C (5°F), the vines must be buried in winter to protect them from freezing to death.

Among the many differences between China and Australia in grape growing, the largest is obviously labour input to viticulture. Many of the holdings I saw are operated as small family farms. All operations are carried out by hand, including weed control, spraying, and vine burial. Even in large corporate vineyards there is a high labour input.

Particularly in the southern part of China, fungal disease pressure is very high, which can reduce wine quality. I am surprised there are not more hybrid grapevines grown, especially in the south, where disease tolerance would be a great virtue. Yields can be quite high. Although

Grapevine

• **Western Cape vineyards** are home to the most herbicide-resistant ryegrass in the world. Some populations of the weed are resistant not only to glyphosate and paraquat, but also to more modern selective products. Nowhere else in the world have vineyard weeds developed resistance to so many herbicides at once, probably due to repeated use of the same chemicals year after year. Glyphosate-resistant ryegrass also occurs in Australia, and its presence can cause up to 50 per cent loss in land value.

• **Researchers at Pretoria University, South Africa,** in a study of the grapevine mealybug (*Planococcus ficus*) and the longtail mealybug (*Pseudococcus longispinus*), have shown that one mealybug is all it takes to transmit the virus from a leafroll-infected grapevine to a healthy one. This finding emphasizes the importance of vector control. An integrated control programme to prevent the spread of leafroll is under trial at Vergelegen. Strategies include planting only certified planting material and long-term monitoring. The first phase has been a huge success, with a dramatic decrease in newly infected grapevines, with only 37 new diseased vines out of 44,000.

• **A disease** similar to South African Shiraz disease has been found in Australia and has also been seen in Merlot and Ruby Cabernet there. Grapevine virus A is associated with the disease in both countries.

some vineyards might claim to limit yields to 5 tonnes per hectare, one also hears stories of commercial grape growers producing towards 20 tonnes per hectare.

At the moment there are several joint ventures in China with French, American, and Italian partners. These partners have introduced modern vinification techniques that have benefited the local industry. I was impressed with retail wine prices in China. Chinese wines were selling at a good price relative to imported wines, and it would appear that the growing middle class is developing a taste for wine.

Will China ever pose a threat to Australia's export wine production? My answer is a tentative yes, but it will depend on acceptance of Chinese wine overseas. China can make quality wine, and its production will surely increase.

China is a planned economy, and the central government has recently decreed that grape production should increase in China. Using homoclime analyses, I have been able to identify many parts of China that are capable of growing premium and even ultra-premium wine, as well as commercial wine. Water and land appear to be plentiful, as is labour, and production costs are low.

One bright spot for Australia in all of this is the opportunity to sell more wine in China as the market for wine grows. There is a growing awareness of Western values, which includes wine consumption with meals.

Grapevine

• **The first international congress** on mountain viticulture took place in Val d'Aosta, Italy, in 2006, sponsored by the Centro di Ricerche, Studi e Valorizzazione per la Viticoltura Montana. It takes at least twice as many hours to tend a steep or high-altitude vineyard compared to flat or gently sloping sites. Many of these sites – such as Douro, Mosel, Wachau, Galicia, and Banyuls – are unique in their viticultural heritage. The conference aimed to highlight practical methods to help with the feasibility of keeping such sites in production.

• **The issue of hang time** has been a matter of debate for some years, and plenty of research has gone into assessing the sensory effects of

extended ripening. Now a two-year study in Napa Valley Cabernet Sauvignon vineyards has provided more concrete numbers. Grapes were harvested over a seven-week period from 23° Brix to 29° Brix and vinified into test wines. Ed Weber of UC Cooperative Extension found that for each degree of Brix over 26, a Cabernet grower's tonnage goes down about 5 per cent, meaning a loss in revenue of 5 per cent, too, based on the normal pay-by-yield approach. This information should prove useful to growers in their negotiations with winery buyers.

Wine Science

Dr Ronald Jackson

Changes in the aromatic character of opened
wine have usually been ascribed to the production
of acetaldehyde.

DR RONALD JACKSON

This was based on the assumption that
what occurs during prolonged oxygen
exposure takes place shortly after bottle
opening, but to a lesser degree – a view
repeated for so long and by so many that
it has generally become accepted as
true. However, when directly studied by
Escudero and co-workers, wines aerated
with pure oxygen developed no detectable
acetaldehyde, even after several weeks. This
should have been suspected years ago.

Singleton at Davis noted that wines often have a remarkable ability to
absorb oxygen without overt signs of oxidation. Roussis and co-workers
have directly studied the aromatic composition of wines opened and left
at room temperature for several days. They found marked decreases in the
presence of important aromatic compounds, such as ethyl and acetate
esters (fruity aromas) and terpenes (floral aromas). Ethyl esters fell by
30 per cent within one day and by 85 per cent after the second day.
After one day, reductions in acetate ester and terpene contents were
55 per cent and 85 per cent respectively. Similar but less marked losses
were noted in red wines. The presence of phenolic antioxidants, such as

DR RONALD JACKSON is the author of *Wine Science* (Academic Press, 2000),
Wine Tasting (Academic Press, 2002), and *Conserve Water, Drink Wine* (Haworth Press,
1997), and he has contributed several chapters to other texts and encyclopedias.
Although retired, he maintains an association with the Cool Climate Oenology
and Viticulture Institute of Brock University in Ontario, Canada, and has held
professor and chair positions at the botany department of Brandon University
in Manitoba, Canada.

caffeic acid, reduced but did not prevent these aromatic changes. This is the first time that aroma loss upon bottle opening has been demonstrated objectively.

Although oxidation reactions are clearly active in flavour loss, the simple escape of aromatic compounds from wine also appears to be involved. This is suggested by the loss in aromatic character when wines are stored in partially empty bottles in the absence of oxygen. The aroma and bouquet of a wine come from the presence of minute amounts of a wide range of chemicals. After bottle opening, these begin to dissipate into the surrounding air. This process liberates the chemicals we smell when tasting a wine. However, their escape also leads to the weakening of a wine's fragrance. Only a few wines, such as sherries, ports, *Beerenauslesen*, or icewines are sufficiently aromatically concentrated to retain their character for much more than an hour after pouring.

Toasty fragrance – or thiols?

Champagnes and equivalent sparkling wines are often said to possess a toasty or roasted attribute. For years, the origin of this aspect has been a mystery. Being of an unknown chemical nature, it has been difficult for producers to accurately assess how winemaking techniques affect its development. Tominaga and co-workers may now have isolated the critical compounds. Surprisingly, they seem to be volatile thiols (for example, mercaptans).

Until recently, the presence of thiols has been uniformly considered undesirable, having odours resembling that of manure, rotten cabbage, spoiled shrimps, sewer gas, skunk, etc. Tominaga had previously discovered several thiols that contribute to the varietal aroma of varieties such as Sauvignon Blanc and Cabernet Sauvignon. These workers have now isolated several other volatile thiols from ageing champagnes. These include compounds with jaw-breaking names such as benzenemethanethiol, 2-furanmethanethiol, and ethyl 3-mercaptopropionate. Despite these formidable names, they possess roasted or toasty fragrances and occur in concentrations sufficient to generate the elusive toasty fragrance so desired in premium sparkling wines.

Distinctive thiols have also been recently isolated from Sauternes wines by Bailly and co-workers. Thiols contribute to the aroma of wines made from the principal varieties used in producing Sauternes: Sauvignon Blanc and Semillon. Thus, it is not too surprising that thiols appear to donate some of the distinctive fragrant attributes of Sauternes.

BOTTLES UP OR DOWN?

Traditionally, wine bottles stoppered with cork have been stored horizontally. This keeps the cork moist, preventing the drying and shrinkage that could facilitate air ingress. Surprisingly, and contrary to what most of us would have thought, Lopes and co-workers have shown that in the short term (two years), positioning cork-sealed bottles upright does not necessarily increase oxygen ingress into the wine. In the long term, data from Skouroumounis and co-workers indicate that upright storage is ill advised if you wish to minimize browning and avoid the early development of an oxidized odour. In addition, Bartowsky and co-workers have shown that bottles of red wine stored upright are more susceptible to spoilage by acetic acid bacteria. These bacteria remain inactive in wine, except in the presence of small amounts of oxygen. Activity can be detected prior to opening by the presence of a ring-like growth at the wine/headspace interface. The consequences of vertical bottle positioning are more marked when bottles are stoppered with synthetic corks, but are absent when screwcaps are used.

BEYOND CORKS AND BOTTLES

Wine consumers are becoming accustomed to the advantages of screwcaps, even accepting them in premium estate wines. Now we have a new contender. It is Alcoa's Vino-Seal™. This is a glass-stoppering system long used in chem labs for sealing bottles. They resemble the T-cork stoppers typically used in sherries and most ports. The new glass-stoppering system is easy to open and reclose and prevents oxygen ingress. A number of wineries in Europe and the USA are beginning to use this system.

Another significant change in bottle closure may be in the offing for sparkling wines. The crown seal has started to appear on bottles of sparkling wine. Crown seals have long been used for the second, in-bottle, bubble-forming fermentation of *méthode champenoise* wines. What is new is its use on bottles released from the winery, replacing the champagne cork used to close the bottle after disgorging (removal of the yeast plug in the neck). Many Australian readers may already be familiar with this innovation, and a New Zealand producer is also investigating this

Grapevine

• **Sabella in McLaren Vale,** South Australia, has taken a different tack on oak ageing. For its 2001 Reserve Shiraz, the duration of oak ageing has been placed in the hands of the consumer. The wine has been matured without exposure to oak but has had a block of oak added to each bottle. The blocks range in weight from 2 to 4 grams. Ageing on oak occurs in the bottle until the time the purchaser opens it.

development. Being more impermeable to gas than cork, the crown seal should permit sparkling wine to retain its effervescence almost indefinitely (cork-sealed bottles of bubbly eventually lose their sparkle).

Another innovation is plastic bottles. They are the same shape as traditional glass bottles, but are made of PET (polyethylene terephthalate), the same material that is called polyester when spun into cloth. PET bottles have several advantages over glass. They require much less energy during production, are less breakable and much lighter, can easily be coloured to any specification, and are more easily recycled.

WHY ODOUR PERCEPTIONS VARY

The individuality of human odour sensitivity has long been recognized. It is well known that odour sensitivity originates in small patches of nervous tissue in the nose. Responsiveness depends on a unique group of proteins on the ends of these nerves. Individual neurons possess a single type of protein. Each protein selectively reacts with a small set of aromatic compounds. Humans can produce about 340 olfactory receptor proteins – in contrast to about 920 in mice and more than 970 in dogs. Intriguingly, humans still possess all the necessary genes, but most are non-functional. As the timing of olfactory receptor-gene inactivation correlates with the development of full-colour vision in our ancestors, this coincidence may reflect the increasing importance of vision in our evolution.

One surprising discovery in the study of olfactory genes was the degree to which individuals differ in the specific receptor proteins they synthesize. It appears that almost everyone produces a distinctive selection of these 340 receptor proteins. Ethnic groups also appear to differ in the range of receptor proteins they express. These results indicate that there are idiosyncratic as well as ethnic differences in how people may respond to wines.

Odour perception appears to be somewhat comparable to our response to musical chords. Most simple chemical odours (for example, a burnt match or white vinegar) are the equivalent of a chord, whereas complex odours (roses, apples, spices) resemble the sound of a symphony orchestra. However, in the analogy, almost everyone is tone deaf to some notes, as well as hearing some frequencies more intensely than others. In addition, any particular odour "chord" may be interpreted as seraphic, pleasant, prosaic, irritating, or repulsive, depending on personal experience and preference.

WHERE DID WINE YEAST COME FROM?

When savouring the qualities of a fine wine, one rarely ponders its microbial origin. Most consumers know that yeasts conduct the principal (alcoholic) fermentation. If questioned about where the yeasts come from, the likely response is to be that they come from grapes. Many people have the mistaken view that the matt appearance of grapes (the "bloom") is due to a yeast coating. In fact, it is caused by minute plates of wax covering the surface. Grapes do indeed possess a large yeast population, but it is invisible to the naked eye. In addition, these yeasts rarely include the "wine" yeast. Wine yeasts appear in significant numbers only on damaged grapes from which juice has escaped. This raises the question: where do wine yeasts come from if not from grapes? Some wine yeasts come from the small number of damaged grapes found in every vineyard, but most appear to come from winery equipment. Wine yeasts can survive in small amounts of dried juice on crushers, presses, fermenters, etc.

A more fundamental question concerns where the wine yeast came from before people made wine. Surprisingly, the indigenous home of the "wine" yeast appears to be oak exudate and the soil underneath oak trees. This brings up an interesting coincidence. The most southerly distribution of oak trees in Europe corresponds to the two locations where grapes were first domesticated: the northern portions of the Near East (Transcaucasia) and southern Spain. The Transcaucasian region also has the oldest archaeological evidence of wine production. Early farmers in the region also harvested acorns for both human and animal consumption. Did the juxtaposition of the beginnings of agriculture, grape domestication, and acorn collection favour the transfer of what was an "oak" yeast to grapes and its transformation into the "wine" yeast *par excellence*?

GM YEASTS ARE HERE

Van Vuuren has been working for years on perfecting a yeast strain able to induce malolactic fermentation. I was sure that the unbridled fears of transgenic organisms would prevent government agencies from registering its use. In addition, if permitted, winemakers would knuckle under to "consumer" (environmentalist) pressure and abstain from its use. I have been proved wrong on both counts.

A genetically engineered yeast, strain ML 01, has been constructed to express genes from a yeast that permits the efficient uptake of malic acid and the "malolactic" bacterium, which effectively converts malic acid to lactic acid. The result is a wine yeast that simultaneously conducts alcoholic and malolactic fermentations. This has several advantages. If the only reason for favouring malolactic fermentation is to reduce wine acidity, ML 01 will do the job. It also means that deacidification is complete when the wine has finished alcoholic fermentation. In other words, there is no need to wait (sometimes for months) for malolactic fermentation to occur under the action of malolactic bacteria.

This is of particular value if the wine is to be bottled and sold very young, as with Beaujolais Nouveau. In addition, if there is no desire to have the buttery and other flavours that frequently accompany bacterial malolactic fermentation, this is achieved with ML 01. Of minor significance is the avoidance of the potential production of constituents that produce ethyl carbamate, a potential carcinogen, if the wine is heated. Finally, by avoiding the action of malolactic bacteria, histamine production is also avoided.

BURN TREATMENT

For many people, the use of sulphur dioxide in wine production is a traditional practice. There is a growing trend, however, to reduce, if not eliminate, its addition to wine, which could have unexpected and undesirable consequences on the ageing potential of wines. Contemplating the reduced use of sulphur dioxide raises the question of when sulphur dioxide was first used in winemaking.

The ancient Egyptians, Greeks, and Romans knew of the fumigating effect of burning sulphur in buildings through its generation of sulphur dioxide. Despite this, there is no mention of burning sulphur in amphorae or wine barrels in the ancient wine texts of Cato, Columella, Pliny the Elder, or Varro. The oldest existing reference to burning sulphur in barrels to avoid problems during winemaking and storage comes from a report published in Rotenburg, Germany, in 1487. It was subsequently reprinted in *Kellerimaisterey*, published in 1537 and later. The first record of its use in English literature occurs as a citation credited to Dr Beale in 1664. As now, there was controversy over its use. The widespread adoption of sulphur dioxide in winemaking did not become established until the 1850s.

Grapevine

• **Since time immemorial,** extravagant claims have been made about commercial products, and wine is not immune. Rarely does anyone actually study these claims and publish their results, so it is intriguing to see one such product subjected to validation. The Perfect Sommelier™ purports to age wine in minutes rather than years through the use of magnets, presumably by modifying the structure of wine tannins. However, nuclear magnetic resonance (NMR), one of the main techniques used in determining tannin structure, would work only if magnetic fields did not modify the structure of tannins. Nevertheless, to be fair, the effect of the Perfect Sommelier on wine character was studied using the double-blind, randomized protocol. This procedure is the "gold standard" in psychological/medical research. Rubin and co-workers found that tasters could not distinguish between treated and untreated wines. So much for a quick fix to highly tannic wine.

• **Two years ago,** I commented in *Wine Report* on a study that compared various cleansing agents for reducing the lingering astringent sensation of one wine on the perceived taste of another. In that study, a weak solution of pectin was found to be more effective than other agents, such as unsalted crackers. Pectin, found in grocery stores, is a gelling agent for fruit preserves. This year, in a new study from Washington State University, Ross and co-workers found that unsalted crackers were more effective than pectin. Which is valid? Probably both, depending on individual responsiveness and the specific conditions of the tasting. The only way to tell which might be the most effective for you is to do your own experiment. What both studies do agree on is that water is relatively ineffective as a palate cleanser.

Opinion:
Stuck for words

Most people have great difficulty in correctly associating words with odours, especially isolated from visual clues. This is clearly evident in the incredible diversity of descriptors used in reference to wine fragrance. It is often assumed that this is due to our lack of sufficient olfactory skill (too few sensory neurons in the nose and/or insufficient space set aside in the brain to analyse olfactory information). Anatomical and physiological comparisons between ourselves and other mammals (notably dogs) suggest that we are poorly engineered to make precise and detailed verbal/odour associations. However, our olfactory skills may be poor primarily because we are not trained in odour recognition from infancy. If we were taught to associate unique terms with particular odours, as we are with colours, objects, sounds, or ideas, we might be impressed with our unused potential. Our ability to associate symbols (letters or sounds) with precise meaning is extraordinary. However, this skill takes years of training to fully manifest itself. Wine tasters and perfumers usually begin to develop their skills only in their 20s. It is clear that delaying language learning into the teens or later years results in only rudimentary language development. What would we be like if we spent an equivalent amount of time on odour acuity?

Ageing wines

Assessing the ageing potential of wine is a very imprecise science. Even seasoned wine critics can differ widely. Culture-based habituation also seems to play a major role in guesstimating ageing potential – French writers often recommend that bordeaux wines should be drunk up to 10 years younger than do their British counterparts.

Personal preferences determine how long you should age your wines. If you prefer a fresh, fruity fragrance or wines showing a distinctive varietal or stylistic character, long ageing potential is of little concern. If you don't, you'd probably prefer red wines that are several or even many years old, since they lose much of their astringency with age.

Possibly the most significant factor affecting ageing potential is storage temperature. When people ask me the best temperature for storing wines, I half-facetiously respond by asking them how long they intend to live. If you expect to live for at least the next 20 years, you can probably store your best wine at 10°C (50°F) with confidence. This is often mentioned as the ideal cellaring temperature. Otherwise, you may be buying wines for your inheritors. Although there is no formula that accurately equates maturation with temperature, a rough rule of thumb is that the ageing rate doubles with every 10°C (18°F) increase in temperature. However, above 30°C (86°F), ageing not only occurs more rapidly, but its nature changes, and not for the better. Light is also detrimental. For bottles exposed to sunlight in store windows, this clearly involves heating as well. However, light alone can activate chemical reactions that are detrimental – unless you like (or cannot detect) the smell of reduced sulphur compounds such as hydrogen sulphide (sewer gas) or mercaptans (skunky odours).

Spent copper is nothing to sniff at

It is often said that New World wines are too fruity to accompany food, whereas European wines are more subtle and food-compatible. Such differences, if they exist, may spring not so much from winemaker intent as from hitherto unsuspected consequences of vineyard procedures. For more than 150 years, Bordeaux mixture has been used to control several fungal-induced grape diseases. Its active ingredient is copper sulphate. In France and some other European countries, this has resulted in the considerable accumulation of copper in the upper layers of the soil. Copper taken up by vine roots, and subsequently transferred to the fruit, can effectively bind (make non-volatile) varietally important thiol compounds. The latter are critical aromatics found in members of the Carmenet family of grapes – Cabernet Sauvignon, Cabernet Franc, Merlot, and Sauvignon Blanc.

Copper uptake has probably compromised the flavour potential of many European wines for generations, although this situation is changing with reduced use of Bordeaux mixture. Theoretically, this should eventually result in an increase in the flavour potential of the wine. However, the tendency to reduce the use of sulphur dioxide in winemaking may offset the potential increase in wine flavour. Several varietally important thiol compounds tend to break down during wine maturation and ageing. This oxidative loss of fruit flavour is countered by the addition of sulphur dioxide. The take-home story is that changing any aspect of winemaking, even with the best of intentions, may result in sensory consequences that cannot be predicted.

Wine on the Web

Tom Cannavan

Robert Parker arrived relatively late on the website scene, launching eRobertparker.com only in 2002, but despite being one of the first subscription-only sites, "eBob" became an instant success.

TOM CANNAVAN

Parker is now nearing retirement age, and people close to him suggest that he is looking for a way to tactically withdraw from the daily grind, while maintaining the influence of the Robert Parker "brand". It seems that the Web, with its increasingly compelling power to spread information and build communities, is a cornerstone of his strategy.

eRobertParker, and to an extent its print alter ego *The Wine Advocate*, has gradually become the editorial work of some half-dozen part- or full-time writers, such as David Schildknecht, who specializes in Germany, Austria, and Alsace; Antonio Galloni, who focuses on Italy; and, more recently, Britain's own Neal Martin, with a special remit to cover Bordeaux and Burgundy. Parker has introduced each to the eBob community with the message that he has carefully hand-picked them and that each brings something extra to the party.

It's impossible to know how many eBob subscribers there are at US$99 per annum, but given the great man's reach and influence, it probably

TOM CANNAVAN, author of *The Good Web Guide to Wine* (Good Web Guide, 2000), has published wine-pages.com since 1995, making it one of the world's longest-established and most popular online wine magazines. He also publishes beer-pages.com and whisky-pages.com. According to Jancis Robinson MW, "wine-pages.com should be of interest to any wine lover seeking independent advice" (*Financial Times*). In Richard Ehrlich's opinion, "if all sites were this good, we'd spend more time surfing than drinking" (*The Independent on Sunday*), and Robert Parker finds wine-pages.com a "superb site. All-inclusive, friendly, easily navigated, with plenty of bells and whistles" (*The Wine Buyer's Guide*).

numbers in the thousands, adding up to a serious annual turnover. Parker is taking steps to make sure that eRobertParker is a resource that will continue even as his writing output reduces.

In the long term, this move is surely essential. But it also represents a fundamental shift in the "one man, one voice" phenomenon that built Parker. Is the brand powerful enough to survive when its founder finally hangs up his pen? Time will tell.

Uvine unplugged

I interviewed Christopher Burr for the trade magazine *Harpers Wine and Spirit Weekly* in 2000. Burr, chairman of the online wine auction site Uvine, was bullish about the potential for this revolutionary new Web-based platform for the global exchange of fine wines. He was already talking about opening offices in foreign territories and expanding the model to cover not just wine but rare whiskies and other collectables.

Throughout 2005 and 2006 there were rumblings of discontent from users of the Uvine service on the independent online discussion group ukwineforum.com. Concerns were expressed over rising charges, lack of transparency on prices, and slow delivery of wines. On 12 September 2006, one forum contributor wrote, "Has anyone sold any fine wine through a company called Uvine this year, or heard of any bad stories about Uvine? I am having extreme difficulty getting paid for wine sold in December, despite countless promises."

Just 16 days later, the news broke that Uvine had gone into administration, with evidence that scores of customers were owed substantial amounts of money. It emerged later that 55-year-old Burr

Grapevine

• **Subscription-based** wine-information sites are burgeoning. This seems especially true for those dealing with that most esoteric of wine regions, Burgundy. Clive Coates MW has given his blessing to Sarah Marsh MW, whose website theburgundybriefing.com issues an annual online report based on *en primeur* tastings, plus occasional supplements, for £25, while others swear by Allen Meadows's burghound.com, which charges US$125 for four annual updates plus access to the site's archives. Meanwhile, John Gilman asks US$120 per year for his bimonthly e-mail newsletter, available by contacting jbgilman@ix.netcom.com. Most will provide sample articles free of charge to help you decide whether or not to splash some cash.

was declared personally bankrupt in June 2006 and had resigned as chairman of Uvine on 19 September 2006.

As *Wine Report 2008* goes to press, the company is being offered for sale, and one of two bidders is Trieste Direct Investments Ltd, a company registered in the British Virgin Isles and a major shareholder in Uvine. The three remaining directors of Uvine are behind this bid, and they have stated that, if their bid is successful, they intend to repay some moneys to creditors over a number of years.

Benign virus?

"Viral marketing", the concept of exploiting the user base of the Internet to market a product at little or no cost, can be a potent technique. In the winter of 2006, a promotional coupon offering 40 per cent reductions at Thresher – supposedly intended for a small, selected audience – found its way on to various websites, blogs, and e-mail circulation lists. Within days, the coupon was making headline news, and Thresher was besieged.

Rumours circulated that this disastrous mistake could bring about the collapse of the company, and reports talked of millions of extra bottles being sold in the space of days. The truth of just how much of a "mistake" this was, as opposed to a bit of creative marketing, is difficult to ascertain. With Thresher offering a permanent "3 for 2" on all wines, the 40 per cent discount (from full-price wines only) wouldn't really hurt that much, and news of the 40 per cent coupon was deliberately spread around some influential wine websites by insiders on the deal.

Grapevine

• **The Web** has turned truly multimedia in the past couple of years, with streaming music and movies now commonplace. Wine has its own online radio station, in the shape of graperadio.com. Free to access, GrapeRadio is rather US-centric, but the quality is good and the site is easy to use. New shows are added regularly, and you can listen to over 150 broadcasts on subjects as diverse as exploiting wine myths and reports from the US Hospice du Rhône, an annual event that celebrates wines based on Rhône varieties.

• **Food and wine matching** is a perennially popular subject, and Fiona Beckett, multitasking expert in both fields, has totally revamped her website at matchingfoodandwine. com. As well as lots of freely browsable content, Fiona has launched a one-to-one expert advice service, costing £24.99 per year, which includes a free book download and a regular newsletter.

• **Blogging** might be a bit old hat by now, but wine has its fair share of wine blogs, with more springing up all the time. Try: vinography.com; http://thepour.blogs.nytimes.com; drvino.blogspot.com; brooklynguy loveswine.blogspot.com; thecaveman. blogspot.com; wineoffensive.com/blog; and weingolb.blogspot.com.

Opinion:
Talking 'bout MySpace generation

Unless you are still in your teens, you may not be fully aware of the Web phenomenon that is "social networking". Social networks have taken over from blogs as the hottest thing on the Web in the past year or two. The best known, MySpace.com, vies with the mighty Google as the single most popular website on the planet. That was enough to excite the shrewdest of moguls, Rupert Murdoch, into paying US$580 million to acquire MySpace as part of his media empire.

In these online communities, each member invites their own network of friends and associates to join the site. New members repeat the process, so the number of members and links within the network grow exponentially. Sites offer features such as an online address book, profiles with photos, and even introduction services to put like-minded individuals in touch.

Most of these networks are "youth oriented", and many revolve around a specific shared interest; MySpace itself is geared towards the independent music scene. Now there are thousands of social-networking sites trying to emulate that success, based around "lifestyle" subjects as diverse as fashion and football.

Wine got in on the social-networking act fairly late. While there are long-established online discussion groups like the UK Wine Forum section of my own wine-pages.com, the slightly anarchic, free-flowing, and multimedia style of the social networks has come to wine in the form of bottletalk.com.

Bottletalk is still in a fledgling state as *Wine Report* goes to press, but it appears to have all the stylistic bells and whistles that are prerequisite for social networks. Members can create their own profiles, including their wine interests, and they can store details of the wines they have drunk to be shared with other members.

But the commercial thinking behind Bottletalk soon becomes evident. Apart from plenty of targeted advertising, many of the wines reviewed and logged by the membership have direct links to online shops selling them, which will earn Bottletalk a commission if anyone buys.

It is too early to say whether Bottletalk's ambition is to be a genuine community of wine lovers or is something rather more commercially driven. Perhaps wine is still just too middle-aged and middle class for the MySpace generation, but it is worth checking out this site as a decent rendition of the genre and a rare nod towards yoof culture on the vinous Net.

Alexa ratings

Since the first edition of *Wine Report* I've included a snapshot of the world's 10 most popular wine websites, as suggested by Alexa.com. Partnered by Google, Alexa tracks the surfing behaviour of 10 million people, building up a picture of which websites they visit. This theoretically allows Alexa to compile popularity rankings for hundreds of thousands of websites, broken down into categories. The reliability of the statistics must be in some doubt, however. For example, Alexa lists a total of 4,215 websites in the category "wine". Apparently, the sixth most visited wine site in the world is that of Frankland Estate, a small winery in Australia. Still, some people may find this top 10 of all wine sites listed by Alexa.com useful.

Alexa's top 10 most visited wine websites

1. www.winespectator.com
2. www.novusvinum.com
3. www.erobertparker.com
4. www.foodandwine.com
5. www.localwineevents.com
6. www.franklandestate.com.au
7. www.winechina.com
8. www.wine-pages.com
9. www.winebusiness.com
10. www.decanter.com

Best Internet wine sites

[S] = paid subscription required for some/all content
[R] = no paid subscription, but registration required for some/all content
[E] = non-English-language site, but with English-language version

Editor's note: I asked Tom Cannavan not to include his own site, wine-pages.com, in any of the lists he compiled because, inevitably, he would either be accused of self-promotion or (more in line with his character) he would not rate his site highly enough. However, I would place wine-pages.com at number two under Best Wine Sites and number one under Best Wine Forums. Although I have a small corner at wine-pages.com, I receive no payment. TS

BEST WINE SITES

1. www.wine-searcher.com [S]
2. www.erobertparker.com [S]
3. www.winespectator.com [S]
4. www.cellartracker.com [S]
5. www.bbr.com
6. www.jancisrobinson.com [S]
7. www.wineloverspage.com
8. www.wineanorak.com
9. www.decanter.com [R]
10. www.burgundy-report.com

BEST WINE FORUMS

1. www.ukwineforum.com
2. www.erobertparker.com [R]
3. http://forum.auswine.com.au
4. http://groups.msn.com/bordeauxwineenthusiasts
5. www.enemyvessel.com/forum
6. www.westcoastwine.net
7. www.forums.egullet.com [R]
8. www.wldg.com
9. www.vinocellar.com/forums/categories.php
10. www.wineweb.com/fusetalk/forum/index.cfm

BEST WINE RETAILERS ON THE WEB

1. www.bbr.com (UK)
2. www.wine.com (USA)
3. www.oddbins.com (UK)
4. www.majestic.co.uk (UK)
5. www.bevmo.com (USA)
6. www.wineaccess.com (USA)
7. www.auswine.com.au (Australia)
8. www.winecommune.com (USA)
9. www.finewinelist.net (UK)
10. www.bibendumwine.co.uk (UK)

BEST SMALLER INDEPENDENTS SPECIALIZING IN REGIONS

1. www.yapp.co.uk (Rhône and Loire)
2. www.domainedirect.co.uk (Burgundy)
3. www.rogerharriswines.co.uk (Beaujolais)
4. www.nzhouseofwine.com (New Zealand)
5. www.dvino.co.uk (Italy)
6. www.frenchandlogan.com (Germany)
7. www.lsfinewines.co.uk (South of France)
8. www.australianwinesonline.co.uk (Australia)

9. www.englishwine.co.uk (England)
10. www.nickdobsonwines.co.uk (Austria, Switzerland)

BEST REGIONAL WINE SITES

Sites in national language. Those with an English-language version are marked [E].

Argentina
www.winesofargentina.org [E]
Australia
www.wineaustralia.com
www.winestate.com.au
Austria
www.austrian.wine.co.at [E]
www.weinserver.at
Belgium
www.boschberg.be [E]
Brazil
www.academiadovinho.com.br
Bulgaria
www.bulgarianwine.com/Pages/bulg.htm [E]
Canada
www.canwine.com
www.winesofcanada.com
   British Columbia
   www.bcwine.com
   Ontario
   www.winesofontario.org
Chile
www.winesofchile.org [E]
China
www.winechina.com/en/ [E]
www.wineeducation.org/chinadet.html
Croatia
www.bluedanubewine.com/croatia.html [E]
Cyprus
www.cyprus-wine.com [E]
www.wine-pages.com/guests/contrib/nncyprus.htm
Czech Republic
www.znovin.cz [E]
www.czecot.cz/?id_tema=16 [E]
Denmark
www.vinbladet.dk/uk/ [E]
www.vinavl.dk

France
www.frenchwinesfood.com [E]
www.terroir-france.com [E]
www.abrege.com/lpv

  Alsace
  www.alsacewine.com [E]
  www.alsace-route-des-vins.com [E]

  Bordeaux
  www.bordeaux.com [E]
  www.medoc.org [E]
  www.sauternes.com

  Burgundy
  www.bivb.com [E]
  www.burgundy-report.com

  Champagne
  www.champagne.fr [E]
  www.champagnemagic.com [E]

  Corsica
  www.corsicanwines.com [E]

  Jura
  www.jura-vins.com [E]

  Languedoc-Roussillon
  www.languedoc-wines.com [E]
  www.coteaux-languedoc.com [E]
  www.vinsduroussillon.com

  Loire
  www.interloire.com
  www.loirevalleywine.com [E]

  Provence
  www.provenceweb.fr/e/mag/terroir/vin [E]

  Rhône
  www.vins-rhone.com [E]

  Southwest of France
  www.vins-gaillac.com [E]

Georgia
www.gws.ge [E]

Germany
www.winepage.de [E]
www.germanwine.de/english [E]

Greece
www.allaboutgreekwine.com [E]
www.greekwinemakers.com [E]

  Macedonia
  www.macedonian-heritage.gr/Wine [E]

Hungary
www.winesofhungary.com [E]

Indonesia
www.hattenwines.com [E]

Israel
www.israelwines.co.il [E]
www.stratsplace.com/rogov/israel [E]

Italy
www.italianmade.com/wines/home.cfm [E]
www.italianwineguide.com [E]

  Piedmont
  www.piedmontwines.net [E]

  Tuscany
  www.chianticlassico.com [E]
  www.wine-toscana.com [E]

Japan
www.kizan.co.jp/eng/japanwine_e.html [E]

Latvia
www.doynabeer.com/wine [E]

Lebanon
www.chateaumusar.com.lb [E]
www.chateaukefraya.com [E]

Luxembourg
www.luxvin.lu [E]

Malta
www.marsovinwinery.com [E]

Mexico
mexicanwines.homestead.com [E]

Moldova
www.turism.md/eng/wine [E]

Morocco
www.lescelliersdemeknes.com [E]

New Zealand
www.nzwine.com
www.wineoftheweek.com

Peru
www.easy-wine.net/peru-wine.htm [E]
www.tacama.com [E]

Portugal
www.portugal-info.net/wines/general.htm [E]
www.vinhos.online.pt

  Madeira
  www.madeirawineguide.com [E]
  www.madeirawinecompany.com [E]

  Port
  www.ivp.pt [E]
  www.portwine.com [E]

Romania
www.aromawine.com/wines.htm [E]

Russia
www.russiawines.com [E]

Slovenia
www.matkurja.com/projects/wine [E]

South Africa
www.grape.co.za
www.wosa.co.za
www.wine.co.za

Spain
www.jrnet.com/vino [E]
www.verema.com/en [E]

   Ribera del Duero
   www.riberadelduero.es [E]

   Rioja
   www.riojawine.com [E]

   Sherry
   www.sherry.org [E]

Switzerland
www.wine.ch [E]

Tunisia
www.tourismtunisia.com/eatingout/
   wines.html [E]

United Kingdom
www.englishwineproducers.com
www.english-wine.com

United States
www.allamericanwineries.com

   California
   www.napavintners.com
   www.wineinstitute.org

   New York
   www.fingerlakeswinecountry.com

   Oregon
   www.oregonwine.org

   Texas
   www.texaswines.org

   Washington
   www.washingtonwine.org
   www.columbiavalleywine.com

Uruguay
www.winesofuruguay.com [E]

BEST WINE-SITE LINKS

www.winelinks.ch
www.bluewine.com
www.grape-nutz.com/links.html

BEST VINTAGE-CHART SITE

www.erobertparker.com/info/
   vintagechart1.asp

BEST TASTING-NOTES SITES

www.erobertparker.com [S]
www.finewinediary.com
www.winemega.com [E]
www.stratsplace.com/rogov
www.yakshaya.com
www.thewinedoctor.com
www.metawines.com
www.gangofpour.com

BEST WINE-EDUCATION SITES

www.rac.ac.uk/?_id=1512
www.wset.co.uk
www.wineeducation.org
www.wineeducators.com
www.wine.gurus.com

BEST VITICULTURE SITES

www.crcv.com.au
http://winegrapes.tamu.edu

BEST OENOLOGY SITE

http://en.wikipedia.org/wiki/Winemaking

BEST GRAPE-VARIETIES SITE

www.wine-lovers-page.com/wineguest/
wgg.html

BEST SITES FOR FOOD-AND-WINE PAIRING

www.matchingfoodandwine.com
www.winealchemy.com
www.forkandbottle.com

THE FAR SIDE OF WINE

www.corkjester.com
www.dibbukbox.com
www.valentinomonticello.com
www.rupissed.com
www.winespirit.org
www.winelabels.org
www.gmon.com/tech/stng.shtml
www.howstuffworks.com/question603.
htm

The 100 Most Exciting Wine Finds

A number of these wines will be available on certain markets, but many are so new, restricted in production, or downright obscure that the only way to get hold of them would be to visit the producer – if he or she has not already sold out.

The entire *raison d'être* of this section is to bring to the attention of serious wine enthusiasts the different and most surprising wines being developed in classic areas, the best wines from emerging regions, and other cutting-edge stuff. The prices are retail per bottle in the local currency of the country of origin (see About This Guide, p.5). My tasting note follows the contributor's own note, for comparison or contrast, or simply a different take.

Seigneurs de Ribeaupierre 2005
Trimbach (Alsace, €21) *Although this wine needs at least another three years to express the full range of spicy bottle aromas on the nose, the palate is already scintillating, and it possesses outstanding finesse.* Tom Stevenson

2003 by Bollinger (Champagne, €65) *A soft and sumptuous champagne, with a gloriously slow-releasing pin-cushion mousse that feels utterly satisfying in the mouth, and none of the angular oakiness that has, until now, been the consistent hallmark of this most traditional of champagne houses.* Tom Stevenson

Nicolás Catena Zapata 2002
Bodega Catena Zapata, Mendoza (Argentina, AP 320) *The quality of the 2002 really comes through in this super-premium red, arguably the best yet from Catena. It's a blend of 68 per cent Cabernet Sauvignon and 32 per cent Malbec, showing ripe, textured cassis and berry fruit with vanilla and cigar-box notes from 24 months in French oak. Supple, lingering tannins.* Tim Atkin MW
There are some floral aromas among those cigar-box notes, Tim. Very elegant, poised, and lengthy. TS

Le Grand Clos Pinot Noir 2004 Le Clos Jordanne, Ontario (Canada, C$60) *Winemaker Thomas Bachelder, with experience in Oregon and Burgundy, has made the best Pinot Noir that Canada has produced. Ruby colour; minerally, cherry nose; rich mouthfeel, a real sense of terroir here, could easily pass for a Gevrey-Chambertin; great balance with exciting tension between the fruit, alcohol, oak, and acidity; great length.* Tony Aspler
I couldn't agree more, Tony. I was so impressed when I tasted this and other

single-vineyard Pinot Noirs with Thomas Bachelder last year in the Finger Lakes (he drove down with Peter Gamble to show me their wines over dinner when I was judging at the IEWC), that I later secured a bottle to show to a Pinot Noir addict in Australia. TS

Eszencia NV Signal Hill (South Africa, R2,000) *The incredible sweetness of this 2002 blend of Furmint, Chenin, and Sauvignon makes for a fascinating nectar thanks to the nervy 16 g/l acidity. Long-lingering apricot, honey, and orange marmalade, along with raisiny notes. Unprecedented and uncertifiable in South Africa, it has been generously applauded by Tokaji winemakers (and most others allowed a few expensive sips).* Tim James
There being little point in tasting this blind, I am not ashamed to say that I consumed, rather than merely tasted, a small glass of this extraordinary wine with friends at the end of a dinner, then took the remains to my local wine bar for the guys and girls to enjoy. That 16 g/l of acidity does make it rather Eszencia-like and will hold the wine together over the next few decades. Like the real stuff, this wine will benefit from long-term ageing. TS

Shotfire Ridge Quartage 2004 Thorn-Clarke, Barossa Valley (Australia, A$23) *An affordable multi-trophy winner, this is medium-bodied, elegant, and distinctively Cabernet family, swimming against the tide of overripe, oaky, alcoholic Aussie reds. It's a blend of Cabernet Sauvignon, Merlot, Malbec, and Petit Verdot. Blackberry, blackcurrant, cedar aromas; smoothly ripe and gentle of tannin.* Huon Hooke
Unashamed, gluggy fruit that does indeed finish elegantly. TS

Moscatel de Setúbal Trilogia NV José Maria da Fonseca (Portugal, €120)

The nose is a symphony of dark, treacly, marmalade scents, intense and awe-inspiring. Mint and chocolate join on the palate, against a boiled-down orange-marmalade background. It's dark and complex, with amazing length. Charles Metcalfe
I cannot believe the finesse of this wine, Charles: it's magnificent! TS

Gran Corte VII 2004 Pulenta Estate, Alto Agrelo, Mendoza (Argentina, AP 105) *Despite the heavyweight bottle and the comparatively high (14 per cent) alcohol level, this blend of Cabernet Sauvignon, Malbec, Merlot, Tannat, and Petit Verdot is surprisingly approachable and elegant, with bright violet and red-fruit aromas, seductive tannins, and remarkable finesse and length on the palate.* Tim Atkin MW
I couldn't agree more. An exquisite wine with soft, seductive, beautiful fruit. Such a charmer, I purchased a couple of cases. TS

Croft Quinta da Roeda Vintage Port 2004 (Port & Madeira, €30) *Floral, still in its first bloom of youth, with great purity of fruit. Suave, with fine-grained tannins. By no means the biggest or most imposing of vintage ports, but a wine that is delicious now or in 10 years. Great to see this flagship estate back on form after years in the wilderness.* Richard Mayson
Modern, sleek, fruit-driven dream of a single-quinta port. TS

Ashbourne 2004 Ashbourne (South Africa, R235) *The second edition (the first was 2001) of a deeply serious cooler-climate Pinotage from the Walker Bay area. Understated, subtle yet confident, almost bordeaux-like in ripe-tannin structure, with a fresh charm to the varietal raspberries and a vein of minerality. Still very youthful.* Tim James

A mysterious wine! Quite the most delicate and fragrant Pinotage I have ever tasted, Ashbourne has the graceful balance of a beautiful Pinot Noir, but without any evidently Pinot fruit, and — yes — there is something bordeaux-like about it. Not sure if it's the tannin structure. I thought it was more in the fruit. Whatever, it certainly rings the bordeaux bell as much as it does the Pinot Noir bell in the mind. Yet it's obviously neither. A charming wine with distinctive notes of rape seed. TS

Alta Tierra Syrah 2004 Falernia, Elqui (Chile, CLP 8,500) *It's the elegance and purity of expression in Falernia's Syrah that have won it so many friends; this 2004 is full of herby, fresh meat aromas, and it has a spicy, mid-weight palate that doesn't try too hard.* Peter Richards
Lovely nose, Peter — classic Syrah. And I haven't even tasted it! Very elegant fruit with a smattering of cracked black peppercorns. So Rhône! Not big. But rich. With finesse. And length. Drink now or in five years: your choice. TS

Tradición Palo Cortado VORS Tradición (Sherry, €50) *A top-quality wine of great age, showing the complexity of a palo cortado and the colour appropriate to its age; dry without being astringent, with an elegant finish and great length.* Julian Jeffs QC
Deep, deep flavour, with the true finesse of an authentic, mature palo cortado. TS

Nebbiolo 2004 Arrivo, Adelaide Hills (Australia, A$55) *This is an excellent Neb from young vines: rich and deep, with burned sugar, leather, kola root, and dark berry flavours that are fruit-led and mouth-filling. The tannins are ample but smooth: a far cry from the* harsh, drying tannins of old-fashioned examples. Huon Hooke
A stand-out, Huon! I'm not sure that I would pick this out as Australian in a line-up of Italian Nebbiolos. TS

Manigold Vineyard Gewurztraminer 2005 Peninsula Cellars, Michigan (Atlantic Northeast, US$20) *While the majority of Gewurztraminers in the USA are sweet, simple, aromatic quaffers, the Manigold has the required floral, spicy, bitter-citrus, lychee-nut qualities, but also a ton of power, intensity, and texture on the palate — and it finishes dry. This one clocked in at 14.5 per cent alcohol!* Sandra Silfven
Although this really needs a couple of years' bottle-age (the 2003 is only just filling out), the 2006 really is another classic vintage from Bryan Ulbrich. I think he has pushed the ripeness envelope at the Manigold vineyard almost as far as it will go, although the alcohol showing on the finish now is precisely what will be needed in a few years to turbo-charge the spice. TS

Henriques & Henriques 15 Year Old Verdelho Madeira (Port & Madeira, €25 per 50-cl bottle) *Mid-amber; floral, fragrant, and wonderfully expressive aromas; lime marmalade, very pure and well poised, with fine acidity to offset the richness of age. Exquisite.* Richard Mayson
Beautifully smooth and complete. Quite sweet for Verdelho. Such finesse. Exquisite… oh, sorry, you've already said that! TS

Grüner Veltliner Stockkultur 2005 Prager, Wachau (Austria, €30) *Toni Bodenstein's "Noah's Ark" project has assembled historic and forgotten Grüner Veltliner clones in a goblet planting. This first harvest from the project shows what stunning potential*

these old grapes have in the right hands. Philipp Blom

You forgot to mention that it's sweet. Beautifully balanced sweetness, but distinctively sweet. Stunning acidity-enhanced minerality. TS

Bourgueil Mi-Pente 2005 Jacky Blot, Domaine de la Butte (Loire Valley, €15)
Wow… the oodles of fruit and spice on the nose promise no more than what comes next – massive wild fruit and ripeness underpinned by a beautifully understated backbone of oak that will melt into the wine as it matures. Lovely. Who said the Loire couldn't make world-class reds? Charles Sydney

Not me, Charles, although I do wonder what happened to the world-class Sauvignons! This sits somewhere between a garagiste St-Emilion and the New World. I want to buy it! I bought a case of Blot's Gamay last year. TS

Sparkling Zwarte Parel 2004 Genoels-Elderen (Belgium, Netherlands & Scandinavia, €16.50) *The 2004 vintage was a success in Belgium, and this sparkler has a decent, sustained yellow-straw colour, tight bubbles, a full Chardonnay nose with some fresh fruit flavours of pineapple with a touch of oak, and a clean, good, tight mouthfeel.* Fiona Morrison MW

I agree with everything you say, and more. The fruit structure and acidity are ideal for sparkling wine; the mousse displays a degree of technical expertise that is – quite frankly – exceptional; and the light hand with which the oak has been used could serve as a textbook lesson to 99 per cent of Champagne growers, who use barriques with the subtlety of an oak plank. It is evident that Belgium should be focusing on sparkling wine, very much as the best English winemakers have come to realize. TS

Warre's Bottle Matured LBV Port 1995 (Port & Madeira, €17) *Many LBVs offer little more punch than ruby, but this wine really merits the term "vintage". Deep, opaque colour, violets on the nose, a hint of dark-chocolate-like concentration, and fine, firm, black-cherry fruit. Delicious to drink now or keep. Poor man's vintage port. A bargain.* Richard Mayson

Profound richness of flavour, yet great elegance. A wonderful bargain-priced, mature LBV that definitely lists to the fruity side of port, and would age gracefully for another 10 years. TS

TMV White 2005 Tulbagh Mountain Vineyards (South Africa, R125)
Beautifully polished, yet not modern; charmingly rustic, yet not old-fashioned; this cleverly oaked, Chenin-led blend has spice, ripe mandarin orange, white peach (from a dollop of Viognier), and oxidized notes dominating the nose and palate. Slightly heady from 14 per cent alcohol. Long, with none of the sweetness associated with more heavily oaked examples, this is not for the faint-hearted, but exciting in its difference, and familiarity. Cathy van Zyl MW

Had I read your notes first, I would have been worried about the oxidized notes on nose and palate, but there was nothing to worry about in this wine. There's nothing oxidized here: I would not even say oxidative, just evolved, and it's this degree of development that has polished off the rustic edges, rendering it distinctly not old-fashioned, as you rightly observe. It's the sort of wine that could be made in the Rhône if they were allowed to grow Chenin. Aren't you glad you don't have any AOC nit-picking bureaucracy to restrain your winemakers, Cathy? TS

St-Joseph 2005 Domaine de la Côte Sainte-Epine (Rhône Valley, €11)

In a very classic style. I like the definition and purity of the fruit. Well balanced, without new oak; a very fresh wine. Olivier Poels
Spot on, Olivier! You're one of the few French wine critics I find myself agreeing with. Great value. TS

Solms Hegewisch Africana 2005
Solms-Delta (South Africa, R123) *One of very few South African dry (nearly!) reds from dried grapes (the stems twisted on the vine); its generosity and outsized proportions are beguiling, not imposing. From Shiraz; its intense cranberry aromas are lifted by fresh sage, dried fennel, touches of tobacco, and wet tea leaf; the palate refreshes with lemony acidity, agreeable tannins, and a long, lingering, sour-cherry finish. For contemplation. Cathy van Zyl MW*
Lovely, pure aromas, with extremely elegant, beautifully focused fruit on the palate. I get the sour cherries on the finish, but that will sweeten up with softer black-fruit flavours with a few years in bottle. However, stem-twisting seems unnecessarily work-intensive. I've seen the same results (cutting of the fruit from the vine's metabolism) achieved simply by cutting the fruiting canes, which are tied to the training wires, thus remaining in position. TS

Sacromonte Amontillado Seco 15 Years
Valdivia (Sherry, €30) *Perhaps 15 years is just the right age for enjoying an amontillado: it has grown into the stature of a true amontillado without the grandeur of a VORS, so it makes easy drinking. A serious wine that is also quaffable. Julian Jeffs QC*
Intriguing, beguiling nose, so seductive. True amontillado: assertively crisp, extremely dry palate. TS

Rully Les Pucelles 2005
Domaine Henri & Paul Jacqueson (Burgundy, €13) *This excellently balanced*

example is pure and full of fruit, and it will still improve. Drink from 2008. Clive Coates MW
Softer than the St-Aubin, but with equally fine acidity. Beautiful purity of fruit. No perceptible residual gas. Will age gracefully. TS

Riesling Grevenmacher Fels 2005
Château Pauqué (Luxembourg, €8) *Reminiscent of a German middle-Mosel Riesling, this has a flinty nose that only hints at what turns out to be a full-bodied wine with not unpleasant notes of sauerkraut; sweet at 40 g/l, though with only 11.5 per cent alcohol and a deep, earthy note on both palate and finish. David Furer*
Not a wine for cellaring, but its precocious petrolly aromas and honeyed sweetness on the finish make it delicious for current drinking. TS

Riesling Beerenauslese 2005
Hirtzberger, Wachau (Austria, €37) *Not every year offers the opportunity to make nobly sweet wines in the Wachau. This great Riesling is an essence of the grape and of Wachau terroir. Immensely pure and long. Philipp Blom*
Oh so young! Baked Bramley on the palate. Stunning acidity. TS

Pinot Noir 2004
Vylyan, Hungary (Eastern & Southeastern Europe, HUF 3,600) *A wine with youthful spicy aromas, with raspberries, violets, and vanilla on the nose. The cooler vintage conditions in 2004 have given real purity of fruit, elegance, and well-integrated acidity. Pinot Noir is still finding its feet in Hungary, but showing that it has great potential in the right hands. Dr Caroline Gilby MW*
Villány has always had the greatest red-wine potential in Hungary, even if it has been slow to demonstrate it, and Vylyan ranks as one of Villány's top

wo or three producers. The pure Pinot aromas on this deliciously seductive wine were so appealing that I took it to the table to accompany supper, where I was surprised to find that it matched some cheeses that I thought might overwhelm such a soft wine. TS

Paul Bosc Estate Riesling Icewine 2002 Château des Charmes, Ontario (Canada, C$60 per half-bottle) *This wine is a real charmer. Copper-gold colour; an intense bouquet of honey, dried apricot, and a hint of petrol. Unctuous and rich on the palate: spicy, burned orange and honey flavours, with balancing acidity. A voluptuous wine with great length – for erotic contemplation.* Tony Aspler
Precariously close to floor-polish aromas, but just on the right side to be outstanding! TS

Noé Pedro Ximénez VORS González Byass (Sherry, €36) *When young, Pedro Ximénez wines can be sticky and cloying, but with age they develop nuances of taste and show their age by developing an impressive, almost sharp, finish, with great length.* Julian Jeffs QC
Sensational PX, Julian. I've always thought it was an English perversion to pour wines like this over ice cream, but I see they now make this suggestion on the back label. TS

Moscato Bianco 2005 Flat Creek Estate, Texas Hill Country (Other US States, $16) *The best version yet of Texas Muscat, this bottling from Flat Creek Estate is fresher and more quaffable (assuming that's a good thing) than its late-harvest version.* Doug Frost MW
Undeniably Moscato and absolutely delightful, Doug. This is for those who appreciate the intricacies of the Moscato grape. TS

Grand Vin Castel 2004 Domaine de Castel (Israel, NIS 180) *Deep garnet towards black in colour; full-bodied, with firm tannins integrating nicely with smoky wood. On the nose and palate are raspberries, blackcurrants, vanilla, and chocolate, yielding on a long finish to hints of liquorice, tobacco, and chocolate. Generous and elegant. Best 2008–12.* Daniel Rogov
Elegance, richness, and purity of fruit, with beguiling wafts of coffee. A beautiful wine for drinking now, but with enough silky tannins to preserve the fruit for a few years, if you want to see how it ages. TS

Divino Pinot Blanc Beerenauslese Barrique Aged 2002 Winzergenossenschaft Nordheim, Franken (Germany, €29.80) *Just beginning to absorb the attractive caramel and hazelnut aromas of the barrique into a context of luscious fruit and rich texture. Still more on the fresh, rather than cloying, side of Beerenauslese.* Michael Schmidt
Definitely more Auslese sweetness than Beerenauslese, but the texture is all Beerenauslese, and this explains the relatively high alcohol (12 per cent) for the style. The aromatics need bottle age, but the rich caramelized fruit is immediately drinkable, as happens with every botrytized wine. Trying to go the Yquem route and, I have to say, succeeding! TS

Cossart Gordon Bual Colheita Madeira 1995 (Port & Madeira, €20) *Bottled in 2005. Orange/amber; pungent, candied-peel aromas, with just a hint of stewed fruit; cognac-like pungency and richness followed by bold astringency on the finish. One of the best colheita madeiras I have ever tasted.* Richard Mayson
The intense yet delicate acidity reduces the impression of sweetness to just

sweet; there is a touch of wood showing on the finish. TS

Château Belle-Vue Haut-Médoc
2003 (Bordeaux, €18) *With an amazing 27 per cent of Petit Verdot, this wine combines an exotic perfume with lovely opulent fruit, lots of volume in the mouth, and a beautifully silky finish.* David Peppercorn MW
A dash of New World opulence, yet classic Old World flavours. Absolutely perfect for drinking now. TS

Cabernet Sauvignon Yarden 2003
Golan Heights Winery (Israel, NIS 140) *Deep garnet towards royal purple; full-bodied, with generous soft tannins that coat the mouth nicely and, after 18 months in oak, a surprisingly gentle spicy and vanilla-oak influence. Opens with blackberries and black cherries, those moving to blackcurrants, hints of oriental spices, and, on the long finish, a hint of dark chocolate. Drink now–2014.* Daniel Rogov
Opulent fruit, gorgeously sweet, ripe fruit, and lovely drying tannins on the finish. TS

Vin Santo del Chianti Classico
1998 Rocca di Montegrossi, Tuscany (Central & Southern Italy, €35) *Magnificent amber-topaz-mahogany colour. Lively nose, varied and caressing, with notes of dried fruit, chestnut, caramel, marron glacé, plum, and chocolate. Full in the mouth, plenty of stuffing but nicely balanced, the aromas reminding one of those found on the nose, with an aftertaste of sweet tobacco. A wine of absolute personality and class, still very young, with great ageing potential.* Franco Ziliani
Medium-sweet to sweet, very soft and silky fruit. TS

Sauvignon Blanc 2006 Mount Riley,
Marlborough (New Zealand, NZ$15.95)

A benchmark Marlborough Sauvignon Blanc at a very realistic price. High demand has encouraged many producers to elevate their prices, but Mount Riley has held its ground. Delicate gooseberry, passion fruit, and green capsicum flavours. Bob Campbell MW
I could have written that last sentence, Bob. Definitely gooseberries (which have been sadly absent from so many Marlborough Sauvignon Blancs in recent years), just a nice hint of passion fruit in the acidity, and green capsicum without the sweaty character that some producers go mad about. TS

Riesling Tradition 2004 Schloß
Gobelsburg, Kamptal (Austria, €16) *Already a classic in its way, this Riesling flies in the face of all modern winemaking orthodoxy and is vinified as it might have been around 1900. The result has always been extremely good, but with this vintage Michael Moosbrugger has found a new dimension of purity and expressiveness.* Philipp Blom
Beautiful Riesling aroma, elegant fruit, very long. TS

Riesling 2005 Daniel & Martha
Gantenbein, Fläsch (Switzerland, SF 45) *The wine is pale, with a very aromatic nose. On the palate, there is wonderful acidity and freshness, with clear and clean aromatics. After the first sip, the complexity and length of the finish are evident.* Chandra Kurt
Has the sweetness of Auslese, but the weight of Spätlese. Elegance first: typical Chandra Kurt wine! TS

Private Bin Gewurztraminer
2006 Villa Maria Estate, East Coast (New Zealand, NZ$16.95) *Exquisite purity of flavour and defined varietal character make this inexpensive medium-dry Gewurztraminer one of*

the best buys around. Delicate Turkish-delight flavours and an ethereal texture. Bob Campbell MW

Excellent broad spice aromas, even if there is a tad of acidification, with classic Gewurz mouthfeel and more off-dry than medium-dry, I would have said. From a purist's point of view, I would have preferred no acidification whatsoever, but for an inexpensive commercial rendition of Gewurztraminer, it works brilliantly. TS

Pinot Noir 2005 Carrick, Central Otago (New Zealand, NZ$42) *The best Central Otago reds in this challenging vintage were made after a rigorous grape selection to remove any unripe berries. The hard work has paid off for Carrick, resulting in one of the region's best. Complex, fruit-driven red with layers of dark cherry and berry flavours.* Bob Campbell MW

Rich without being powerful, which should always be the essence of Pinot Noir. TS

Oloroso VOS Emilio Lustau (Sherry, €38) *Twenty years of ageing give this dry oloroso a smooth maturity. It has an interesting, complex flavour and is a perfect wine to keep the damp out in an English winter.* Julian Jeffs QC

Extraordinarily intense. TS

Ghi ke Uranos 2005 Thimiopoulos (Greece, €16) *A blend of two neighbouring single vineyards, Kaifa and Amygdalies. Perfumed crunchy fruit and wild strawberry on the nose, with spice following on the intensely rich-textured palate. Class-leading structure. Sumptuous. A real achievement from the demanding Xinomavro grape. The new benchmark.* Nico Manessis

A charming completeness for such acidity. The acidity is typically Xinomavro, but the completeness

requires a degree of finesse that is not, particularly from mid-palate to finish. Fascinating, Nico. TS

Cuvée Elena Grenache/Mourvèdre/ Syrah 2004 Syncline, Washington (Pacific Northwest, US$35) *The complexity and ripeness of this wine are immediately apparent, and carry through to a lingering finish loaded with bright, citrussy, cool-climate fruits. It's a captivating wine, with a forward and intriguing set of sauvage and tarry flavours, and very satisfying length.* Paul Gregutt

The fruit gets sweeter as you drink this wine, but there is always the rasp of leather and alcohol to keep the finish dry, although the aftertaste is really quite creamy-fruity. TS

Cotes du Crows 2005 Morgan, Monterey County (California, US$18) *Deep plum, pepper, and cranberry aroma; lush entry, with loads of superb fruit and a juicy finish.* Dan Berger

Some amylic confectionery aromas indicate a good dollop of carbonic maceration, but there is serious fruit on the mid-palate and finish. I would give this 12 months to blow away the amylic aromas, yet still retain all the freshness of its fruit. TS

Cabernet Franc 2004 Kinkead Ridge, Ohio (Atlantic Northeast, US$17) *Succulent; intensely flavoured fruit, ripe, supple tannins, and a truckload of flavours – from cherries, cassis, chocolate, and cream, to vanilla and coconut.* Sandra Silfven

This has the fruit-bush aroma without any green-fruit character on the palate. I would have preferred a tad less coconut, which could have been achieved either with less American oak or with less time in American oak, but I think this shows what promise there is in Ohio. TS

Audace Passerillé Rouge 2005

Domaine André & Mireille Tissot (Jura & Savoie, €28 per half-bottle) *An extremely bright and deep ruby colour, like a young port. Simple, smoky red fruit on the nose. The palate is fairly sweet, with some tannic structure that doesn't get in the way of the mouth-filling rich fruit. Tasting more like a low-alcohol Banyuls than a port. I thought it would be ideal with chocolate, but it turned out to be even more delicious with home-made vanilla ice cream.* Wink Lorch
Accentuated sweetness, intense sweetness, from the grape, with absolutely no fortified – port or whatever – character. All pure fruit, and intensely sweet. And, I must say, exceptionally good. I wonder how this will develop… TS

Estremadura Aurius 2003 Quinta do

Monte d'Oiro (Portugal, €40) *This really shows the wonderfully aromatic side of Touriga Nacional. The voluptuousness is beautifully restrained with the tannin corset, enlivened with flashes of acidity and an undertone of earthy Petit Verdot.* Charles Metcalfe
A substantial wine in all senses of the term, from the aromatics, which are only just beginning to evolve four years down the line, although there is a touch of VA, to the weight of fruit, which will subsume that VA one day. And the alcohol, all 14.5 per cent of it. You really should have a good cellar if you are buying this wine, and just forget about it for a few years. TS

Vin de Pays des Collines Rhodaniennes Sotanum 2004 Les

Vins de Vienne (Rhône Valley, €30) *The wine shows deep red fruit, pepper, and new oak flavours. Intense and very long, it needs three to four years' ageing to express its complexity.* Olivier Poels

Your note is right on the money as far as I'm concerned, although I think it needs just two years. Four years? Are you becoming Anglophile or am I already Francophile? TS

Vin de Pays de Vienne Sacré Blanc

2006 Jérémie Mourat (Loire Valley, €6) *A sort of blond bombshell, with primary fruit and oak jumping out of the glass in harmony. Loads of fresh, ripe pears and citrus fruit on the nose and palate. This is Chenin Blanc without complexes – lovely and clean, with a great balance of weight and fresh fruit.* Charles Sydney
I could have done without the oak, Charles, but this is a remarkably rich and tasty wine for the money. Oodles of fresh fruit. TS

Touraine Malbec Vinifera Vignes Françaises Non-greffées Vignes de

Cot 2005 Henry Marionnet (Loire Valley, €9) *A star. Enticing black-fruit aromas lead on to a really soft, intense wine with gentle, almost powdery, tannins and really ripe blackberry (but isn't it mulberry?) fruit, the whole with that touch of freshness and purity that shows off the class of the ungrafted vines.* Charles Sydney
This is the Loire pushing the envelope to such an extent that, apart from a haunting aftertaste, I would find this very difficult to pinpoint geographically under blind conditions. I can't imagine what these wines will taste like when they are 40 years plus (planted as recently as 2000), but if you've got a good cellar, I would age this jeunes vignes wine for at least five years. TS

St-Aubin Clos de la Chatenière

2005 Hubert Lamy & Fils (Burgundy, €17.50) *A wine of considerable depth, with a gently oaky base. From the best premier cru in the commune.* Clive Coates MW

Elegant, Clive. Lovely acidity, a tad of residual gas; this will age in a very toasty style. TS

Marsannay Rosé 2005 Bruno Clair (Burgundy, €12) *Well balanced, with heaps of juicy, succulent fruit. Delicious, either as an aperitif or with food.* Clive Coates MW

This wine does not hit it off with me every year, but the 2005 certainly ticks all the boxes. Very elegant fruit with a fresh-as-a-daisy finish. Lovely acids. And it does go with food. TS

Les Emirs 2003 Clos St Thomas (Lebanon, LL 12,300) *Cabernet Sauvignon, Syrah, and Grenache. Deep colour, full-bodied and full-blooded. This will delight those who like a full-on, gutsy red. Dry almonds and cherries on the nose. In the mouth, it is long, with chocolate, cherries, and a hint of liquorice, all wrapped in spices. Good length. Pound for pound the punchiest red in the St Thomas stable.* Michael Karam

The oak stands out on the nose and aftertaste, but it's not overwhelming. I'd pitch this full, firm, age-worthy wine against some good reds from southwest France, and expect it to do well. Lebanese wines are definitely stepping up to the mark! TS

Late Harvest Vignoles 2005 Stone Hill Winery, Missouri (Other US States, $30) *Unlike some of the other sweet examples from the 2005 vintage, this Vignoles finishes clean and crisp, despite the stratospheric sugars and peach/apricot jelly finish.* Doug Frost MW

Wow, Doug… stratospheric sugars, you said, and it definitely has. I prefer my Vignoles in icewine mode, with electrifying acidity, but this is indeed special, and I would expect no less from Stone Hill. TS

Kanzemer Altenberg Riesling Alte Reben 2005 Van Volxem, Saar (Germany, €28) *Firm and juicy, with a cool minerality and pronounced herbal aromas. Excellent purity of fruit, which will begin to make a greater impact in time. The wines from this estate are slow developers but promise great complexity. Maybe a little bitter in its infant stage, but it will stand it in good stead in the long term.* Michael Schmidt

Definitely one to forget for 3–4 years. TS

IGT Val di Neto Efeso 2004 Librandi, Calabria (Central & Southern Italy, €20) *Pale straw colour of brilliant lucidity. Very fresh perfumes recalling bramble, sambuca, musk, marzipan, and white peach. Intense, sappy, and mineral on the palate, with a distinct personality, long persistence, firm structure; rich, fleshy, and fruity, with a lively acidity that gives it nerve and vivacity. Full of flavour, persistent, long.* Franco Ziliani

Fresh lemongrass aromas with toasty notes, and definitely sappy, minerally fruit, yet roundness is evident. A fascinating talking point for the table. TS

Franciacorta Decennale 1996 Ca' del Bosco, Lombardy (Northern Italy, €60) *Long maturation in oak gives this Franciacorta great structure. Straw yellow in colour, very luminous. On the nose, notes of pineapple, citrus fruit, blackcurrant, and dried fruit. Creamy texture. Very rich on the palate, dry, masculine, full, creamy, with great persistence and length. Extraordinary balance.* Franco Ziliani

A beautifully complex aroma, reflected on the palate, with a perfect mousse, but this could have been even better with one or two additional grams per litre of dosage. TS

Edelzwicker 2005 Navarro, Anderson Valley (California, US$11) *Attractive combination of apple/floral and raspberry aroma from the Riesling, with a jasmine/spice note from the Gewurztraminer. Off-dry.* Dan Berger

I get more raspberry on the mid- to end palate, than nose, but maybe it was there when you tasted it and has moved on to the palate since. Nose once again more Gewurz than most non-Alsace pure Gewurztraminer. Definitely off-dry. TS

Catena Alta Chardonnay 2003 Catena Zapata, Mendoza (Argentina, AP 120) *Catena's Chardonnays have made huge qualitative strides since the development of the company's vineyards in the Uco Valley. This is fresh, crisp, and beautifully delineated, showing subtle use of French oak, a nutty, mouth-filling mid-palate, and the balance to develop for a further three to five years.* Tim Atkin MW

I absolutely agree. Beautifully integrated oak. Elegant and persistent. But the bottle weighs almost three sodding pounds! TS

Camerata Red Wine 2004 Cadence, Washington (Pacific Northwest, US$50) *This is a perfectly sculpted wine, elegant and fine, sleek and muscular. It needs time, no doubt, but it's delicious right now as well – a Zen wine.* Paul Gregutt

Sleek indeed, and oodles of oak, with sweet, ripe tannins on the finish. TS

Vino de la Tierra Castilla y León Altozano Shiraz 2005 González Byass (Spain, €4.50) *Young, purple, with great big spicy blackberries-with-black-pepper nose. On the palate there's warmth, power, extraction, and dark, dark fruit. About as subtle as a monkey's bum, true, but imagine it*

with venison casserole on a freezing winter's night, or charcoal-crusted barbecue steak on a scorching August lunchtime… John Radford

Monkey's bum, my arse! If the Aussies produced something like this, they would be raving about its Old World charm. It's a glugger, John, and I'd happily glug an entire bottle. And it's got a screwcap! TS

Vin de Pays de l'Hérault Les Pampres 2005 Clos Laval (Languedoc-Roussillon, €7.50) *Mostly Syrah and Mourvèdre, with the structure of the one and the spice of the other immediately apparent. Dark purple colour, with some translucence. Spicy nose with red fruits carrying through to the palate. Morello cherries and redcurrants. Good acidity, minerally, almost flinty, scarcely any tannins. Prunes on the finish.* Paul Strang

Delightful fruit, with echoes of smoky oak. TS

Tre Coloré 2005 McPherson Winery, Texas (Other US States, $20) *One of the first Texas reds that I've actually enjoyed, the others being more ponderous than pleasing. Composed of Syrah and Carignan with 20 per cent Viognier, this isn't great wine, but I find it balanced and friendly, poised somewhere between the pepper of Côtes du Rhône and Beaujolais-style fruitiness.* Doug Frost MW

Weird, Doug: everything I dislike about (most, not all) Viognier in a white wine is what makes this red wine so gluggy to drink. No wonder they traditionally use Viognier to soften and perfume the Syrah in the Rhône – but I am only now just wondering whether they were using enough! TS

Tempranillo 2005 Trinity Hill, Hawke's Bay (New Zealand, NZ$29.95) *After five vintages, New Zealand's only*

Tempranillo producer is getting the measure of a variety that shows plenty of promise. It's a ripe and concentrated red, with flavours that move beyond the berry-fruit spectrum to include floral/violet and spice characters. Bob Campbell MW

I detect a minor amount of carbonic maceration here, and think it would be better with a tad less. Not cut it out altogether, because it's lifting the fruit, but it should do this inconspicuously. I love the finish. Shades of top Rioja. But work in progress as a whole. TS

Riesling 2006 Peter Lehmann, Eden Valley (Australia, A$15) *If this was a Sauvignon Blanc, it would be over A$20; if a Chardonnay, over A$30. It's a classic, seamless regional Riesling scented with dried wild flowers. The finish is clean and dry, with a twist of phenolic: it's a wine that will drink well now with fish, or age well for a good six years.* Huon Hooke

So, what you're saying, Huon, is that thinking Riesling drinkers are being subsidized by it-must-be-Chardonnay drinkers. Yet another reason to emigrate Down Under, I would say! TS

Bloomsbury 2004 RidgeView (Great Britain, £17.95) *Champagne comes a very definite second best to this wine. Full, fruity, with length and elegance. Just concentrate on the balance for a bit – it's perfect.* Stephen Skelton MW

Helters Skelters, you're crazy! I've done more than my fair share to sing the praises of Mike Roberts's RidgeView sparkling wines, and it is better than some champagnes, but if you think there's nothing from Champagne that can touch it, then you've led a very sheltered life! However, I do agree that this is a very fine, extremely elegant sparkling wine. TS

Reserva Superior Syrah/Grenache/ Viognier 2005 Gracia, Cachapoal (Chile, CLP 12,000) *Smoky, meaty flavours together with crisp, dark fruit and a warming finish make this an impressive Rhône-style blend at a very reasonable price.* Peter Richards

Elegant for such an expansive wine. TS

Gala 3 2005 Luigi Bosca, Mendoza (Argentina, AP 100) *In a country where blended whites are rare, this unusual combination of 50 per cent Viognier, 40 per cent Chardonnay, and 10 per cent Riesling stands out, the acidity from the Riesling adding vivacity to the toastiness of the Chardonnay and the plump apricot flavours of the Viognier. A wine where the whole is better than the sum of its parts.* Tim Atkin MW

I would have preferred a slightly warmer fermentation (18°C [64.4°F] say, rather than 15°C [59°F]) to reduce, not get rid of, the amylic aromas, and just half the oak, but there is no denying this is a polished, appealing, modern wine. TS

Limited Release Gewurztraminer 2006 Cono Sur, Bío-Bío (Chile, CLP 1,900) *Cono Sur has made its name making bold but balanced styles of wine, and this one's no different. It has all the exotic allure typical of the variety, but the palate is fresh, persistent, and self-contained. Ludicrously good value, especially in Chile. A sign of things to come from Bío-Bío.* Peter Richards

As a dry wine, rather than a dry Gewurztraminer, this is delicious and refreshing, but it does not work as a dry Gewurztraminer because its acidification is wrong for an intrinsically low-acid variety, and it tastes as if there is a dollop of Riesling somewhere in there. Furthermore, if any of the terpenes do develop in the bottle, the spicy aromas they create will be spiky, not broad. TS

Limited Edition 2003 Carmel (Israel, NIS 155) *A full-bodied blend of 50 per cent Cabernet Sauvignon, 32 per cent Petit Verdot, 17 per cent Merlot, and 1 per cent Cabernet Franc. Deeply aromatic, with soft tannins, generous but overpowering wood in fine balance with fruits, and well-tuned acidity. On the nose and palate: blackcurrants, blackberries, spices, and sweet cedar, all leading to a remarkably long and elegant finish. Drink now–2015.* Daniel Rogov
Very rich without being too alcoholic (13.5 per cent), a touch rustic compared to the silkiness of the Grand Vin from Domaine de Castel, but that's a hard act to follow. TS

Gewurztraminer 2005 Zmor, Russian River Valley (California, US$35) *Because of the oak contact, this rose-petal-spiced wine is weightier than most, but so dry it requires well-seasoned foods.* Dan Berger
Great potential, and while the oak dominates the aromatics, it has little impact on the palate, where some of the spices destroyed on the nose are still evident. If they want to make iconic Gewurz, Dan, get them to limit the oak to 10 per cent maximum, and the oldest, most neutral oak at that, and to stop acidifying. I've never thought of the Russian River for Gewurztraminer before, but it could work. TS

Fortuna 2006 Freeman, Hilltops (Australia, A$30) *This dry white blend of five varieties is Friuli-inspired but substantially more fruit-forward and grapey than Friuli's own. It has very good depth of flavour and is more interesting than any of the grapes would be singly. It points in a healthy new direction for mono-white-varietal-obsessed Australia.* Huon Hooke

Infinitely better (at this juncture) on the palate than the nose, this is a powerful, intense, aromatic white of some serious quality in its own right. Thanks for the tip, Huon, I shall certainly follow the vintages of this seemingly special wine. TS

Coteaux du Languedoc Terrasses du Larzac Clos du Prieur Rouge 2005 Domaine de l'Hortus (Languedoc-Roussillon, €8) *Deep ruby colour, fairly translucent; woodlandish nose, brambly. Red fruits on the palate, slightly smoky. Lots of herbs and characteristic garrigue notes. Though the wine boasts 14 degrees, it tastes more like 12.5, a compliment to the winemaker. Hand-picked Syrah, Grenache, and Carignan, foot-trodden, made in tank and given 13 months in used barrels.* Paul Strang
The bottle and the wine are a darn sight more classy than the price suggests. A good little boutique red to drink now or keep a year or two. TS

Chaleur Estate Blanc 2005 DeLille, Washington (Pacific Northwest, US$33) *A blend of 79 per cent Sauvignon Blanc and 21 per cent Semillon, this rich, golden, toasty – all right, let's say it – hedonistic wine is ripe and loaded with gorgeous fruit. Sweet citrus, pineapple, grapefruit, peach, and stone fruit; it's all there, and that's just the start. As it moves through the palate, it's laced with smoke and toast, while the fruit core expands into marmalade and tupelo honey, and the wine grows unctuous and creamy.* Paul Gregutt
Not shy, is it? TS

Brunello di Montalcino 2001 Gianni Brunelli, Tuscany (Central & Southern Italy, €30) *Among the best 2001 Brunellos, this classic wine boasts a lovely ruby hue and a deep, resplendent, appetizing aroma –*

dense, warm, gently elegant, with notes of black cherry, violet, and lily, as well as Mediterranean herbs. Rich palate with well-managed tannins, firm but soft, plenty of flavour, earthy, fruity, mineral, humus, some spiciness – very expressive, with tremendous ageing potential. Franco Ziliani

Got those Mediterranean herbs straight away. It was like a breeze blowing across the Provençal scrub. And definitely a spicy finish. The mid-palate is rather austere, a bit like an old-fashioned St-Estèphe, albeit a totally different grape. You say it has tremendous ageing potential. I say it needs it! In 10 years I suspect we'll be in full agreement. TS

Bierzo Tares P3 2003 Dominio de Tares (Spain, €35) Very young, dark purple, with elegant, perfumed fruit on the nose and brambles in the background. The fruit structure comes through on the foretaste, with crisp tannins sneaking in behind to give a powerful finish: the "mean streak" of acidity that used to bedevil wines made from the Mencía has here become structure and complexity. Needs another two years. John Radford

A wine full of sense of place and sense of grape. Just one sniff tells you that you could never get a wine like this in the New World. Isn't it fascinating how it is easier to mimic a cru classé Bordeaux than it is, say, a Mencía from Bierzo? TS

Beira Interior Rogenda Reserva 2003 José Joaquim Afonso (Portugal, €5) This has all the brightness and aromatic character of top-flight Touriga Nacional from the Dão region, with the same type of granite soil. Tannins are substantial but ripe, acidity bright. Another perfect home for Touriga Nacional? Charles Metcalfe

I agree, and it's that bright, crisp acidity that lifts this wine to a different level, Charles. Unthinkable without it, delightful with it. What amazing value! TS

Tavel 2005 Prieuré de Montézargues (Rhône Valley, €10) Great fruit and good balance for this gastronomic rosé. Perfect to drink now with Mediterranean food. Olivier Poels

I'd say classic Tavel, Olivier, only classic Tavel is all too often dull and flat, whereas this is everything that an easy-drinking rosé should be: soft, fresh, and fruity. TS

Pinot Grigio 2005 Tamas Estate, California (California, US$10) White pepper, dried peach, and rose petals, with a dry, slightly austere finish. Great with poached salmon. Dan Berger

The style definitely leans more towards Italy than California. TS

Pinnacle 2003 Sumac Ridge, British Columbia (Canada, C$50) Sixty per cent Merlot, 15 per cent Cabernet Sauvignon, 15 per cent Cabernet Franc, and 10 per cent Syrah; 24 months in French and American oak. Dense ruby colour, with a smoky, tarry, blackberry nose – the Syrah sings through. Medium- to full-bodied, with a sweet and savoury palate of blackcurrant, blackberry, and dark chocolate; rich and succulent fruit, well balanced, with a thickness on the palate. California meets the Rhône Valley. Lifting the bottle is a workout. Tony Aspler

Lots of toffee-toasted, oaky blackcurrant fruit with a caramelized, crème-brûlée aftertaste. TS

Marquis des Beys 2004 Domaines des Tourelles (Lebanon, LL 30,000) From new winemaker Gerard D'Hautville, a Cabernet Sauvignon and

Syrah blend. Deep purple, medium-bodied. Not the big hitter some might expect from a flagship Lebanese wine, but pleasing nonetheless. It opens gradually to reveal cherries and mint on the nose, with peppers and berry fruits that rest nicely at the back of the mouth. Soft tannins that do not impose. Michael Karam

Clean lines of fruit, a touch of menthol on the nose, with some tarry complexity on the finish. TS

Live-a-Little Really Ravishing Red

2004 Stellar Organics, Western Cape, South Africa (Organic & Biodynamic Wines, R21) *Vegan-suitable, screwcap-sealed, Fairtrade Syrah-based red with grainy tannins offsetting really rather ravishing fruit.* Monty Waldin

Creaminess hinting of oak on nose and aftertaste; very fresh, easy-drinking fruit on the palate. Yeah, I'd knock back a bottle. TS

Gamaret 2005 Domaine du Vieux-

Clocher, Caves Leyvraz & Stevens, Switzerland (Grape Varieties, SF 15) *This slightly passerillé wine (15 per cent ABV), made using integrated production methods (lutte raisonnée), is dark red in colour, with black bigarreau-cherry reflections. Aged 18 months in oak cask, it has a fruity nose of black fruit, an ample mouthfeel, good tannins, and a long finish.* Dr François Lefort

The nose is dominated by toasted oak aromas, with hints of cappuccino, but I agree with the ample mouthfeel, good tannins, and long finish. TS

Fronton 2004 Domaine Caze

Patrimoine (Southwest France, €6) *Mid-ruby, with a bouquet of red fruits and some Cabernet grassiness. But the fruit literally bursts on the palate with typical Fronton violet, wild flowers, and liquorice, with spices from the Syrah.*

Said to have been raised in wood, but the wood must have been old because there are no oaky flavours. Ideal cassoulet wine; for me, cassoulet does not need a huge wine, just this lightish fruity wine to contrast with the goodies on the plate. Paul Strang

Not lacking in fruit or length; the grassiness and lightness make this an ideal summer lunch wine. TS

Claret 2004 Château de Val,

Bulgaria (Eastern & Southeastern Europe, BGN 16) *Lovely rich bramble nose, very pure fruit, and velvety tannins. This is a real mixture of varieties from an old family vineyard near Vidin. Not an area known for red wines, but this shows that the mould can be broken, from one of Bulgaria's new-wave boutique producers.* Dr Caroline Gilby MW

But for a touch of VA, I would be jumping up and down at the elegance of this wine. The finish and aftertaste are beautiful! TS

Bacchus Dry 2005 Camel Valley

(Great Britain, £10.95) *Fresh and fruity, with great balance, and very good length — what more could you ask of a wine?* Stephen Skelton MW

Indeed! Enticingly fresh, elderflowery aromas, with deliciously crisp, dry fruit. Reminiscent of a good Colombard from the Côtes de Gascogne. TS

Barolo Carobric 2001 Paolo Scavino,

Piemonte (Northern Italy, €45) *Ruby colour. Elegant, complex Nebbiolo notes: earth, liquorice, spices, rose, strawberry, and a hint of mushroom and tobacco. Rich, complex, intense, with solid tannins, and well balanced with fruit. Long intensity, earthy notes.* Franco Ziliani

A touch of VA, but it fits in with all the other aromas contributing to the complexity of this wine. TS

Aglianico 2003 Seghesio, Russian River Valley (California, US$39) *Surprisingly Italian in nature, with dried-fruit aromas and a tart entry that works nicely with grilled meats.* Dan Berger
Rustic, definitely not California. You're really a European at heart, Dan. TS

Creekbend Vineyard Cabernet Sauvignon 2004 Oliver Winery, Indiana (Atlantic Northeast, US$40) *Intense aromas of cassis and black cherry, followed by concentrated creamy flavours and spice, bound by ripe, supple tannins. This is from the state where corn and soya beans rule – not home-grown Cabernet Sauvignon. A shocker!* Sandra Silfven
Is it my imagination, or can I taste corn and soya beans in the creamy oakiness of this wine? TS

Vino de la Tierra Castilla y León Tempranillo 2004 Casa de la Viña (Spain, €2.90) *Still purple despite two years in the bottle, but with a lovely musky-fruit Tempranillo nose. On the palate, the fruit is prominent, with some richness, a nice balance with the tannins, and an excellent finish. All everyday Tempranillo should be like this – great value for money.* John Radford
I thought "So what?" until I saw the price (I taste blind, but with the price indicated). Water costs more than this in Spain! TS

Vin de Table Verdanel 2005 Robert & Bernard Plageoles (Southwest France, €7) *Plageoles' response to the New World. A 14.5-degree modern wine, the colour mid-yellow with greenish tints, a bouquet of russet apples, pineapples, and white chocolate. On the palate, the fruity attack is powerful with a minerality reminiscent of a Roussillon white Grenache. Long and aromatic finish.* Paul Strang

Not your average vin de table, Paul! I think I could have done without the nod to the New World and much less alcohol, but I just have to show this at the launch tasting. Definitely a food wine, which makes it, I suppose, a vin de table in the true sense. TS

Auxerrois 2005 Apostelhoeve, Netherlands (Belgium, Netherlands & Scandinavia, €9) *Pale yellow; light and spicy; quite attractive nose, floral and green, good spice, a touch of sweetness; some good, slightly green flavours, nice acidity. Well made, good length.* Ronald de Groot
Really quite perfumed. TS

Vin de Savoie Mondeuse Tradition 2004 Domaine Prieuré St-Christophe (Jura & Savoie, €15) *Youthful, yet only light depth of colour; the nose is much more powerful than the appearance. Concentrated berry fruits, with a touch of peppery spice and even leather. The palate is full-bodied, despite not being alcoholic at all by today's standards. Vibrant and concentrated redcurrant fruit is supported by a streak of acidity and medium tannins. The finish is very long indeed. Not just serious Mondeuse, but a serious red made using biodynamic methods.* Wink Lorch
I suspect that the pepperiness has developed considerably since you tasted the wine, and it's now a very dry ground white pepper. The fruit should be much riper, but it's characterful, for sure, and would nicely cut through a rustic casserole or cassoulet on a winter's night. TS

Saperavi Reserve 2005 Georgian Wines and Spirits, Georgia (Eastern & Southeastern Europe, GEL 20) *A real baby of a wine, this still needs time for the oak to settle in, but the intensity and purity of black cherry and bramble fruit are quite amazing.*

Tannins are young, too, but fine-grained and with balanced acidity – none of the leanness and austerity so typical of Saperavi. Dr Caroline Gilby MW

It is lean and austere, but I understand what you mean: it is at least approachable. And it would not be approachable without the high acidity, which focuses the fruit and cedary oak. TS

Reserve 2003 Massaya (Lebanon, LL 30,000) *Mainly Cabernet Sauvignon and Mourvèdre, with some Syrah. Hauntingly pitch-black/purple. Pleasingly autumnal and vegetal notes on the nose – burned fruit, tobacco, and damp leaves. Lovely, long, velvety balance of tannins, berries, and spices, with a hint of vanilla in the mouth.* Michael Karam

Very sappy fruit. TS

Johanniter 2006 Domaine des Bossons, Caves Leyvraz & Stevens, Switzerland (Grape Varieties, SF 9.80) *Dry white wine (12.5 per cent ABV), slightly fruity, from organic viticulture.* Dr François Lefort

Very fresh, with aromatics that are simple but appealing, like a cross between a Colombard from the Vin de Pays de Charentais and a Luxembourg Pinot Gris, but with more alcohol and, consequently, firmer body. Is there some oak? Could be interesting with food. TS

Grosskarlbacher Burgweg St Laurent Spätlese Trocken 2003 Knipser, Pfalz (Germany, €20) *The wine has developed well over the last year, integrating new wood and the full body that inevitably came with the 2003 vintage. For an underrated variety there is an amazing amount of red and dark berry fruit, with finely tuned acidity and tannins. Rather elegant for a 2003.* Michael Schmidt

While the best 2003 German Rieslings have highly evolved petrol or honeyed aromas, and are deliciously fruity, many of the 2003 barrique reds display an advanced toastiness that is beyond oakiness, and are bereft of fruit. This at least has some fruit. TS

CULT Crémant Blanc de Noirs 2004 Vinsmoselle (Luxembourg, €12) *Eighty per cent Pinot Noir and 20 per cent Pinot Blanc. The latest Crémant from Vinsmoselle is by far the best sparkling wine the cooperative has produced. Sporting medium body and acidity, fine mousse, and a defined Pinot Noir character tucked behind the slightly elevated dosage, and in flash packaging, this could help launch Crémant de Luxembourg to a wider international audience.* David Furer

Rich and full for a Crémant de Luxembourg, but it also has typically fresh acids to enliven the warm glow of Pinot fruit. TS

Arbois L'Uva Arbosiana 2005 Domaine de la Tournelle (Jura & Savoie, €5.50) *The light ruby appearance is a little dull, but the nose is the opposite, with fresh and vibrant spicy red fruits, much cleaner than most wines from the obscure Poulsard grape. On the palate, the red fruit shows through, and there is a freshness about it, with a touch of tannin. Perfect to drink with charcuterie.* Wink Lorch

This wine has to be in the Top 100 for the unusual, rather than exciting, quality that it was made without SO_2. The eradication of sulphur is on the wish list of biodynamic producers such as Olivier Humbrecht, but this wine, which is one of the better non-SO_2 wines I've encountered (most having been oxidized), does demonstrate why even non-interventionists like Humbrecht resort to the use of sulphur! TS

Index

Index compiled by Pat Carroll